TEXT AND MATERIALS
ON THE CRIMINAL JUSTICE PROCESS

TEXT AND MATERIALS
ON THE CRIMINAL
JUSTICE PROCESS

FOURTH EDITION

Nicola Padfield

BA (Oxon) Dip Crim (Cantab) DES (Aix-Marseille)
Recorder of the Crown Court

OXFORD
UNIVERSITY PRESS

OXFORD
UNIVERSITY PRESS

Great Clarendon Street, Oxford OX2 6DP

Oxford University Press is a department of the University of Oxford.
It furthers the University's objective of excellence in research, scholarship,
and education by publishing worldwide in

Oxford New York

Auckland Cape Town Dar es Salaam Hong Kong Karachi
Kuala Lumpur Madrid Melbourne Mexico City Nairobi
New Delhi Shanghai Taipei Toronto

With offices in

Argentina Austria Brazil Chile Czech Republic France Greece
Guatemala Hungary Italy Japan Poland Portugal Singapore
South Korea Switzerland Thailand Turkey Ukraine Vietnam

Oxford is a registered trade mark of Oxford University Press
in the UK and in certain other countries

Published in the United States
by Oxford University Press Inc., New York

First published 1995
This edition 2008

British Library Cataloguing in Publication Data

Data available

Library of Congress Cataloging in Publication Data

Padfield, Nicola.
    Text and materials on the criminal justice process / Nicola Padfield. — 4th ed.
      p. cm.
    Includes index.
    ISBN 978–0–19–929653–8
  1. Criminal justice, Administration of—Great Britain.   I. Title.
II. Title: Criminal justice process.
    KD7876.P33 2008
    345.41'05—dc22   2008015653

Typeset by Newgen Imaging Systems (P) Ltd, Chennai, India
Printed in Great Britain
on acid-free paper by
Ashford Colour Press Ltd, Gosport, Hampshire

ISBN 978–0–19–929653–8

10 9 8 7 6 5 4 3 2 1

PREFACE

Since the first edition of this book, the pace of change in the criminal justice system has not slowed. Nor has the quality of justice obviously improved. The seminal review of the criminal justice process at the time of the first edition was the Royal Commission on Criminal Justice (1993). In the last few years there has been a further flurry of 'official' reviews of the system. In updating this edition, I have sought to give proper space to such reports and to academic and research critiques of criminal justice: as a result, citation of statutory material as well as Government White Papers, now so easily downloaded from the Internet, have been kept to the minimum. The selection of materials remains idiosyncratic: designed to stimulate thought, as much as anything. Readers are warmly invited to let me know what they think of my selection and to suggest alternative materials (to nmp21@cam.ac.uk).

The shape of the book continues to emphasize each discrete part of the decision-making process, whereas the Government appears committed to 'team working', 'joined-up' criminal justice, and inter-agency cooperation in criminal justice. It might therefore be argued that a book divided as this one is, is out of date. I would argue that the opposite is true. The reality is that there are several very different players within the criminal justice process. We should not be seduced into thinking that they all sing from the same songbook. The working relationships between the various agencies must be explored, as must the legal framework within which they function. As 'Big Brother' tightens his grip, are there enough checks and balances within the process?

As ever, my thanks go to many colleagues for their help and advice. Perhaps I might single out in this edition Mike Atkins and Louise Cowen, two excellent students, both of whom gave considerable time and effort to reading the previous edition carefully, and to offering me a host of useful suggestions.

Nicola Padfield
February 2008

PREFACE TO THE FIRST EDITION

The criminal justice system has probably never been as much discussed as it has been in the last few years. We all have an interest in understanding the problems associated with crime in our society, whether we are politicians, journalists, students, academics, or simply curious citizens. The subject is popular with students, who seek not only to understand, but also to see a way forward out of the penal 'crisis' in which we seem constantly to find ourselves. Yet students cannot be expected to make judgments and to evaluate the process without access to much published material, and this book aims to address that need in a way that brings a touch of real life to the subject. It is hardly surprising that there are few books seeking to provide students with a window on these sources: the subject is vast, and constantly shifting.

The author of a criminal justice text faces a difficult challenge in deciding the angle from which to approach the subject. This book concentrates on a number of discrete stages within the criminal justice process. For this, it may be criticized for reinforcing the fallacy that there is a neat process, made up of self-contained stages, through which a criminal case will pass. However, it is only by looking at the diversity of powers exercised at different stages that one can come to see the unsystematic nature of the criminal justice process.

This is not a subject which should be learnt entirely from books. To maintain a toehold in reality, this book introduces a fictional but, I hope, credible case history. The case history is not pursued too rigorously, since it provides only an example, not a blueprint, of a criminal case. Wherever possible, however, students should try to create their own scenery, their own understanding of the environment, by arranging to 'shadow' police officers, solicitors, barristers, judges, magistrates, and probation officers 'on the job'. Visits to police stations, courts, and prisons, even brief visits, often open students' eyes and provoke a more critical and analytical response to the subject than can any class discussion.

I have chosen to include a wide variety of sources in order to reflect the depth and variety of ways in which the subject can be approached. Statutes are quoted to illustrate the legal structure behind the decision-making process, and the proliferation of statutes in this area is evidence of continual upheaval. Many of the governing 'rules' are non-statutory, and Prison Rules, Home Office Circulars, and National Standards are necessarily included. Increasingly, the boundaries of discretion are being decided by the courts by way of the judicial review procedure, and a number of such cases are therefore annotated in the book. Statutes and cases are perhaps more readily accessible to the student than is the ever-expanding body of academic publications and research studies. A number of these, as well as official and semi-official reports, are therefore extracted, and reference has been made to those which may stand the test of time. I have tried to include a wide selection of material from recent empirical work and academic analyses.

There are several ways of compiling a 'text and materials' book: many link the materials by a continuous commentary. The style adopted in this book is to leave the documents to speak for themselves: my text therefore stands alone at the beginning of each chapter. The text is designed to introduce the materials, highlighting key issues and questions. It is hoped that in this way students will sense that this is a subject with no clear 'right answers', and that no linear approach suffices.

Choosing material was at once a pleasure and a nightmare, perhaps comparable to the exercise of reducing one's favourite music to eight records for *Desert Island Discs*. The selection is not comprehensive. The aim is to whet the student's appetite for more, and to provide a balanced, catholic, grounding. I approach the subject from the perspective of a lawyer; it may therefore be that the book is of most interest to law students.

There are doubtless omissions which may surprise my colleagues: some will be oversights and some deliberate. Material in this edition has been gathered up to the end of November 1994. Whilst the errors in this book are certainly all my own, I am particularly grateful to Professor Andrew Ashworth and to Sir Derek Oulton, who both found time to read through substantial parts of the text within tight time constraints. Dr David Thomas and Mr Philip Brown were also always ready to give advice. Several students taking the MPhil in Criminology in Cambridge in 1994–95 also gave much encouragement and stimulating comments. I hope that the book will be sufficiently attractive to students, that I will have the opportunity to amend the book in a new edition. I would welcome suggestions on material which should be included, and on material which can be omitted.

Because students should be aware of the practical everyday pressures on decision makers, I have accordingly spent some time visiting and talking to those who actually make the kind of decisions discussed in the book. I am grateful to those who kindly tolerated my persistent questioning: in particular, Inspector Bill Giles and Sergeant Simon Cross of Cambridge Police Station; Mr Robert Martin, Area Manager of Cambridge Legal Aid Area Office; Mr Hew Heycock, Branch Crown Prosecutor, and Ms Sue Hemming, Principal Crown Prosecutor, of the Crown Prosecution Service in Huntingdon; Ms Ellen Yahuda, of Matthew, Grosse, & Bullock, Solicitors; and Mr Peter Johnson, Senior Probation Officer with West Yorkshire Probation Service.

Nicola Padfield
December 1994

ACKNOWLEDGMENTS

Grateful acknowledgement is made to all the authors and publishers of copyright material which appears in this book, and in particular to the following for permission to reprint material from the sources indicated:

Incorporated Council of Law Reporting: extracts from the *Law Reports: Appeal Cases* (AC), *Court of Appeal of England and Wales Criminal Division* (EWCA Crim), *Queen's Bench Division* (QB), and *Weekly Law Reports* (WLR)

King, Michael for extract from M. King, *The Framework of Criminal Justice* (1981)

Magistrates' Association for extract from Magistrates' Association Sentencing Guidelines (2004 edition)

Open University Press and the authors (copyright for these Open University Press titles has now reverted to the author of those titles) for extracts from S. Brown, *Magistrates at Work: Sentencing and Social Structure* (1991); M. Eaton, 'The Question of Bail' in P. Carlen and A. Worrall (eds), *Gender, Crime and Justice* (1987); and A. Worrall, 'Sisters in Law? Women Defendants and Women Magistrates' in P. Carlen and A. Worrall (eds), *Gender, Crime and Justice* (1987)

Oxford Centre for Criminological Research and the authors for extracts from A. Ashworth, E. Genders, G. Mansfield, J. Peay, and E. Player, *Sentencing in the Crown Court: Report of an Exploratory Study* (1984) Oxford Centre for Criminological Research Occasional Paper No 10; and R. Hood and S. Shute, *Parole in Transition: Evaluating the Impact and Effects of Changes in the Parole System: Phase Two* (1994) Oxford Centre for Criminological Research No 16

Oxford University Press for extracts from R. Hood, *Race and Sentencing: A Study in the Crown Court* (1992); and M. McConville, J. Hodgson, L. Bridges, and A. Pavlovic, *Standing Accused: The Organisation and Practice of Criminal Defence Lawyers* (1994)

Oxford University Press Journals for extracts from The British Journal of Criminology: C. Jones, 'Auditing Criminal Justice' (1993) 33 British Journal of Criminology 187; and R. Morgan, Review of M. Drakeford, K. Haines, B. Cotton, and M. Octigan, 'Pre-trial Services and the Future of Probation' (2002) British Journal of Criminology 224

Palgrave Macmillan for extract from T. Skryme, *The Changing Image of the Magistracy* (2nd edition, 1983)

Pearson Education for extract from A. James and J. Raine, *The New Politics of Criminal Justice* (1998)

Reed Elsevier (UK) Ltd trading as LexisNexis Butterworths for extracts from *All England Law Reports* (All ER); and extract from Simon's Tax Cases

Stanford University Press for extract from H. Packer, *The Limits of the Criminal Sanction* (1968)

Sweet and Maxwell Ltd for extracts from Archbold News: Attorney-General v Scotcher [2005] UKHL 36 (as reported at (2005) 6 Archbold News 3); R v Davis; R v Ellis, Gregory, Simms and Martin [2006] EWCA Crim 1155 (taken from (2006) 6 Archbold News); extracts from Criminal Appeal Reports (Cr App R): Attorney-General's Guidelines: Juries: The Exercise by the Crown of its right of stand by (1989) 88 Cr App R 124; R v McIllkenny and others (1992) 93 Cr App R 287; R v Mullen [1999] 2 Cr App R 143; R v Newton (1982) 77 Cr App R 13;

R v Paris, Abdullah and Miller (1993) 97 Cr App R 99; R v Webbe and Others [2002] 1 Cr App R (S) 82; extracts from Criminal Law Review (Crim LR): B. Block, C. Corbett, and J. Peay, 'Ordered and Directed Acquittals in the Crown Court: A Time of Change?' [1993] Crim LR 95; E. Cape, 'The Revised PACE Codes of Practice: A Further Step towards Inquisitorialism' [2003] Crim LR 95; P. Darbyshire, 'The Lamp that shows that Freedom Lives – is it worth the Candle?' [1991] Crim LR 740; L. Gelsthorpe and H. Giller, 'More Justice for Juveniles: Does More Mean Better?' [1990] Crim LR 153; A. Hoyano, L. Hoyano, G. David, and S. Goldie, 'A Study of the Impact of the Revised Code for Crown Prosecutors' [1997] Crim LR 556; R v Abdroikov [2008] Crim LR 134; R v Looseley (Attorney-General's Reference No 3 of 2000) [2002] Crim LR 301; R v McDonald [2007] Crim LR 737; R (Mondelly) v Commissioner of the Police of the Metropolis [2007] Crim LR; G. Richardson, 'Strict Liability for Regulatory Crime: the Empirical Research' [1987] Crim LR 295; J. Roording, 'The Punishment of Tax Fraud' [1996] Crim LR 240; P. Seago, C. Walker, and D. Wall, 'The Development of the Professional Magistracy in England and Wales' [2000] Crim LR 631; S. Uglow, A. Dart, A. Bottomley, and C. Hale, 'Cautioning Juveniles – Multi-Agency Impotence' [1992] Crim LR 632; extracts from European Human Rights Reports: Monnell and Morris v UK (1988) 10 EHRR 205; Stafford v UK (2002) 35 EHRR 32; Thynne, Wilson and Gunnell v United Kingdom (1991) 13 EHRR 666; and extracts from Law Quarterly Review (LQR): P. Devlin, 'The Conscience of the Jury' (1991) 107 LQR 398; and A. Ashworth, 'Should the Police be allowed to use Deception?' (1998) 114 LQR 108

Taylor and Francis for extracts from A.E. Bottoms and J.D. McClean, *Defendants in the Criminal Process* (1976); and M. McConville, A. Sanders, and R. Leng, *The Case for the Prosecution* (1991)

Taylor and Francis Journals for extracts from Criminal Justice Matters: C. Martin, 'The voluntary sector and New Labour: how civil is the partnership' (2007) 67 Criminal Justice Matters 4; and R. Reiner, 'Success or statistics? New Labour and crime control' (2007) 67 Criminal Justice Matters 4; and for extract from Journal of Social Welfare and Family Law: G. McKeever, 'Social security as a criminal sanction' (2004) 26 Journal of Social Welfare and Family Law 1

Wiley-Blackwell Publishing Ltd for extracts from Modern Law Review (MLR): R. Henham, *'Bargain Justice or Justice Denied? Sentence Discounts and the Criminal Process'* [1999] MLR 515; Lord Hoffmann, *'Human Rights and the House of Lords'* (1999) 62 MLR 159; L.C.H. Hoyano, *'Policing Flawed Police Investigations: Unravelling the Blanket'* (1999) 62 MLR 912; extract from Journal of Law and Society: R. Morgan, *'Magistrates: The Future According to Auld'* (2002) 29 J Law and Society 308; and extract from Howard Journal of Criminal Justice: A. Sanders, *'Class Bias in Prosecutions'* [1985] Howard Journal of Criminal Justice 176

Willan Publishing for extracts from M. Tonry, *Punishment and Politics: Evidence and emulation in the making of English crime control policy* (2004); K. Holloway and A. Grounds, 'Discretion and the Release of Mentally Disordered Offenders' in L. Gelsthorpe and N. Padfield (eds), *Exercising Discretion: Decision-making in the criminal justice system and beyond* (2003); and A. Worrall, *Punishment in the Community* (1997)

Extracts from Crown copyright material are reproduced under Class Licence Number C2006010631 with the permission of the Controller of OPSI and the Queen's Printer

Every effort has been made to trace and contact copyright holders prior to going to press but this has not been possible in every case. If notified, the publisher will undertake to rectify any errors or omissions at the earliest opportunity.

CONTENTS

ONE INTRODUCTION   1

TWO THE POLICE   64

THREE   **THE CROWN PROSECUTION SERVICE**   162

FOUR NON-POLICE INVESTIGATIONS   203

FIVE DEFENCE LAWYERS   235

SIX MAGISTRATES   260

SEVEN TRIAL JUDGES 319

TEN SENTENCE MANAGEMENT   447

TABLE OF STATUTES

Where sections of statutes are reproduced page numbers are shown in bold

TABLE OF STATUTORY INSTRUMENTS

Where parts of Statutory Instruments are reproduced page numbers are shown in bold

TABLE OF EUROPEAN LEGISLATION

Where parts of legislation are reproduced relevant page numbers are shown in bold

TABLE OF INTERNATIONAL COVENANTS AND TREATIES

TABLE OF CASES

Where cases are dealt with in detail page numbers are shown in bold

CHAPTER ONE

INTRODUCTION

(i) ABOUT THIS BOOK

Imagine walking home one evening, when you come across a young woman lying on the pavement, moaning. On closer inspection, you see that she looks a little drunk, and she is bleeding through her jacket. What do you do? You telephone the emergency services, dial 999. Do you ask for the police or an ambulance? Whatever you do, the matter will soon be safely out of your hands, and the National Health Service and/or the criminal justice system will take over. This book follows the processes that a case such as this will pass through in the criminal justice system.

In our fictional case, you contacted the police. Of course, in many circumstances, the police never hear about a crime. Probably less than half of all crimes are reported to the police. The factors which influence victims in their decision whether or not to report a crime were analysed by Clarkson et al (1994). They include victims' habituation to violence, their reluctance to have their own behaviour scrutinized, their fear of reprisals, their own criminality and hostility toward the police, and the social costs associated with reporting crime. And Walby and Allen (2004) found that high numbers of men and women do not report even the worst incidents of domestic violence they suffered to the police because they thought it was too trivial, or a family private matter, or because they did not want more humiliation, or because they feared more violence or that the situation would get worse if they involved the police. How many times have you witnessed a crime, or indeed been a victim of crime, and not reported it to the police?

Nor do the police record all incidents reported to them: they may not believe the complainant or they may not consider that the reported behaviour constitutes a criminal act. The British Crime Survey (BCS), which measures crimes against people living in private households by carrying out face-to-face interviews, has been conducted regularly since 1982, and it became an annual event in 2001. The proportion of crimes which are reported to the police and which are actually recorded by the police has grown in recent years: according to Crime in England and Wales 2005/06, 68 per cent of reported crime was recorded in the year to September 2005, up from 36 per cent in 1999. The BCS estimated that there were approximately 11.3 million crimes against adults living in private households on 2006/07, whereas there were 5.4 million crimes recorded by the police (Crime in England and Wales, 2006/07). The first document included at [1:1] of this chapter is the summary of the latest annual report which combines findings from the BCS and police recorded figures, but you should explore the whole document, available at <http://www.homeoffice.gov.uk/rds/crimeew0607.html>.

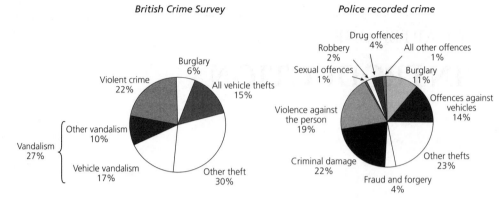

FIGURE 1.1 BCS crime and police recorded crime by type of crime, 2006/07
Source: 'Crime in England Wales 2006/07', HOSB 11/07, page 17

How useful are these broad figures? You need to read between the lines: for example, almost half of the violent crimes recorded by the BCS and half of violence against the person recorded by the police involved no injury to the victim; nor is crime evenly distributed across England and Wales: 45 per cent of recorded robbery offences in 2006/07 occurred in London (both facts taken from Crime in England and Wales, 2006/07).

Of course, the public's reporting of crime varies by type of offence. According to 'Crime in England and Wales', thefts of vehicles were most likely to be reported (94 per cent in 2005/06, 93 per cent in 2006/07), followed by burglaries in which something was stolen (81 per cent in both the most recent years). Reporting rates were relatively low for crimes such as common assault, theft from the person, and vandalism (35 per cent, 33 per cent, and 31 per cent in 2005/06; 36 per cent, 35 per cent, 32 per cent in 2006/07). Of course, it is very difficult to know how much crime there is: readers should explore <http://www.homeoffice.gov.uk/rds/index.html> for the latest statistical data. So far I have been citing the large annual Home Office Statistical Bulletin on 'Crime in England and Wales' which combines the reporting of police recorded crime and the BCS (see Nicholas, Kershaw, and Walker, 2007, extracted at **[1:1]**). At **[1:2]** is an extract from an article by Robert Reiner which considers whether or not statistical crime trends are attributable to the Government's criminal justice policy. It focuses on the inevitable unreliability of national crime data. Two reviews on national crime statistics were carried out in 2006 (one by the Statistics Commission and one by Professor Adrian Smith), but there is of course a danger in changing the counting methods: it makes long term comparisons more difficult. You might like to consider what data you think should be collected: police recorded crime figures will never paint a 'true' figure of crime; offender surveys give different results from victim surveys, but raise significant ethical and practical problems; local data may be more useful than national trends, and so on.

Despite the real challenges of measuring 'crime', what is clear is that, as we move through the process—and as we move through the chapters of this book—we are dealing with an ever-decreasing proportion of cases. Of those cases which are reported to the police, not all result in a prosecution; and not all prosecutions end in convictions—perhaps two in every hundred offences committed result in a conviction. Another useful resource of statistical data is the annual Criminal Statistics, England and Wales, a report now produced by the Office for Criminal Justice Reform which contains statistics relating to criminal court proceedings. See Figure 1.2 for example.

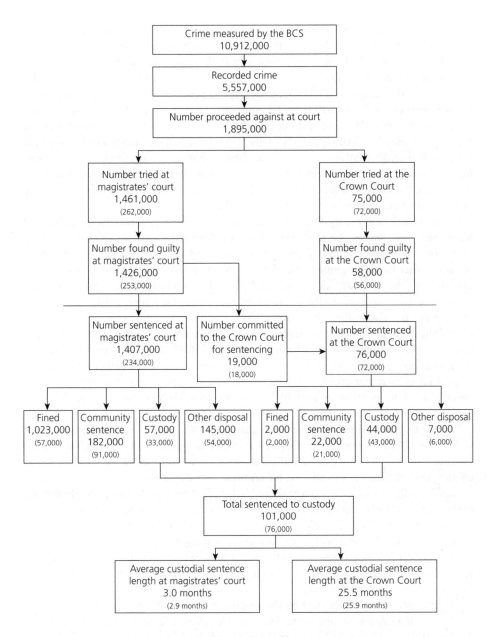

Numbers in brackets indicate figures for indictable offences.[1] Note that the average custodial sentence length for indictable offences at magistrates' courts is lower than that for all offences. The difference is small and historically these two average sentence lengths have been very close.

[1] In this publication, 'indictable offences' include 'triable-only-on-indictment' and 'triable-either-way' offences. For definitions see Chapter 6.

FIGURE 1.2 Flows through the criminal justice system, 2005

Source: Taken from Sentencing Statistics 2005, England and Wales, HOSB 03/07, page 3; also available in Criminal Statistics in England and Wales, 2005

Once an alleged offence is reported, or comes to the attention of the police in some other way, then, as we shall see in Chapter 2, the police have wide discretionary powers. They may record it or they may decide it was just an accident; they may investigate the crime further, using wide common law and statutory powers under the Police and Criminal Evidence Act 1984 (PACE); they may eventually charge an arrested person with an offence. Many criminals are never charged: they will either be summonsed to appear before a magistrates' court or be cautioned (or, in the case of young offenders, subject to a more formal reprimand and warning scheme). Increasingly Fixed Penalty Notices and Penalty Notices for Disorder are being used as an alternative to prosecution. These do not count as a conviction, yet can be imposed for offences such as behaviour likely to cause harassment, alarm, or distress to others, drunk and disorderly behaviour in a public place, destroying or damaging property up to the value of £500, and retail theft under £200.

Let us go back to our story. Our victim recovers from the attack and tells the police that her name is Rosa Bottles. She says she went to the pub with the usual group of friends, they all drank heavily, and on the way home she was involved in a fight with a man with whom she had earlier had an argument, Gerry Good. She is prepared to see the police proceed against him. The next day Gerry is arrested. What goes on in the police station between the time he is arrested and the time he is charged is perhaps the most crucial to a successful prosecution. It is also in the police station that the seeds of most miscarriages of justice are likely to be sown. In Chapter 2 we examine police powers and the safeguards for the suspect held in a police station. The Crown Prosecution Service (CPS), working in partnership with the police, may give pre-charge advice, and now make the decision whether Gerry should be charged with a minor assault or a more serious wounding offence, and are responsible for the conduct of the prosecution. We will discuss the complex relationship between the police and the CPS in Chapter 3.

But not all prosecutions are initiated by the police. Non-police and non-CPS agencies, such as the HM Revenue and Customs, the Environment Agency, and the Health and Safety Executive, deal with many criminal offences, often in very different ways. Chapter 4 thus offers a rather different perspective on the criminal justice process.

Another influence which is often neglected is that of the lawyer. The suspect's solicitor and barrister, in particular, may play a significant role in the process, since their advice about such matters as to whether a defendant should plead guilty or not guilty, whether to give evidence, and whether to appeal may have a significant impact on the way in which the case is finally proceeded with. Chapter 5, on the role of defence lawyers, will attempt to assess the appropriateness of the legal advice given to suspects at all stages in the criminal process and the very real problem of legal costs.

All criminal prosecutions start in the magistrates' court. When the alleged offender reaches the magistrates' court, more decisions are taken. The court may have to decide whether the accused should be remanded in custody or released on bail, or whether the accused should be tried on indictment by a judge and jury in the Crown Court or summarily before the magistrates. If the case remains before the magistrates, they may have to decide on sentence as well as on guilt. Since most prosecutions begin and end in the magistrates' court, they clearly merit a chapter (Chapter 6).

Our fictional case is a serious one and Gerry is charged with an indictable crime, one which can only be tried in the Crown Court by judge and jury. The roles of judge and jury at the trial stage are clearly different, and each merits separate examination (Chapters 7 and 8). If convicted, Gerry will be sentenced. The role of the judge or magistrate in sentencing (why does the jury have no role here?) will be examined in their respective chapters (see above). But the story, of course, does not end there—perhaps Gerry will appeal or seek some other review of his sentence and/or conviction, so the powers of appellate bodies must be considered (Chapter 9). In any event, the process continues beyond Gerry's conviction—he has a sentence to serve—and in Chapter 10 we look at how various criminal justice agencies exercise their wide discretionary powers in relation to sentenced offenders.

The emphasis of the book is on the decisions made by the key actors in the process, stressing the wide discretionary powers exercised. As Davis (1969) pointed out, the greatest and most frequent injustices occur where discretion is unfettered, where rules and principles provide little or no guidance. Since consistency and certainty are important objectives of the criminal justice system, it might seem that the system should be governed by clearer, pre-determined rules. Why have such wide discretionary powers been delegated to different individuals and bodies? The answer is simple: rules can be inflexible, and decisions based on purely legal criteria would be unduly rigid and harsh. The legal philosopher Ronald Dworkin famously pointed out that 'discretion, like the hole in a doughnut, does not exist except as an area left open by a surrounding belt of restriction. It is therefore a relative concept' (1977: 39). In this book, I encourage you to think about this surrounding belt of restriction, the doughnut, the socio-legal context of decision-making. For a fuller introduction to the literature on discretionary decision making, see Gelsthorpe and Padfield (eds) (2003).

If we agree that a certain degree of flexibility is necessary, has the English criminal justice system gone too far? We have moved into an age of 'multi-agency cooperation' (see in particular Chapter 10, but the other agencies described in other chapters of course cooperate closely. 'Agencies' merge, separate, and conflate to a confusing extent. Can shared decision making work in practice? The danger is that as decision making passes away from the courts, control is lost. Decisions are difficult to challenge and lines of accountability are often blurred. Much of this book is descriptive, painting a picture of decision making in the criminal process today. It does not seek to concentrate on the principles behind the process, but the student should nonetheless consider a number of preliminary issues.

(ii) IS THERE A CRIMINAL JUSTICE *SYSTEM*?

Since different parts of the criminal justice system often appear to pull in different directions, working within different (and competing) budgets, it probably should not be called a system at all. For example, the police and the Crown Prosecution Service do not necessarily have the same ambitions, and the probation service and prison service compete for a limited budget. But a system is simply, according to the *Oxford Reference Dictionary*, a 'set of connected things or parts that form a whole or work together'. Remember, too, that we are looking at a 'snapshot' of the system taken at one particular moment in time and that the different elements in the process are constantly evolving. This can help you digest some of the inconsistencies. Norrie (2001) puts English criminal law in its nineteenth-century context, and a similar historical approach to criminal procedure and evidence is also useful. No central planning at one point in history went into drawing up the skeleton of the system. Indeed, if you were inventing a criminal justice system from scratch today, how closely would it resemble our present system?

Feeney **[1:3]** explains clearly the way in which 'systems concepts' came to be applied to criminal justice. Perhaps because the different parts may clash and sometimes work against each other, we should call it a process and not a system, but even this might imply a neat 'conveyor belt' operation. Is this system really little more than a series of decisions? Each actor or agency is interdependent, as Feeney makes clear, but each is not necessarily working consistently with the others. It is one of the purposes of this book to look at the different stages of the criminal justice process in order to see the impact on the process as a whole of different decisions taken at different stages.

(iii) IDENTIFYING CHARACTERISTICS OF THE ENGLISH CRIMINAL JUSTICE PROCESS

The criminal justice system is not just a stream of unrelated decisions—there are some central themes. Two key characteristics have traditionally been singled out as running throughout the English criminal justice system. Particularly important at the trial stage in the process, they necessarily affect decision making at all stages.

(i) The system is accusatorial, or adversarial, rather than inquisitorial. Much has been made of the differences between different legal systems, but the differences can be exaggerated. The brief discussion of the differences in the Report of the Royal Commission on Criminal Justice (1993) provides a helpful summary **[1:4]**. This Royal Commission recommended no fundamental change to the accusatorial system in this country. But of course, the number of cases which end up with a 'full-blown' accusatorial trial is small. Look again at Figure 1.2.

The Royal Commission regarded the principle of the presumption of innocence as fundamental. What does this mean in practice? It certainly doesn't mean that the police actually presume that all suspects are innocent! A visit to a police station—or even to a magistrates' court where the court officials may seem to bark out 'Stand up', 'Sit down'—can give the clear impression of a presumption of guilt. Even the substantive criminal law does not always respect the presumption of innocence: strict liability offences are committed without proof of a guilty mind; and defendants are often required to prove elements of specific defences (see Ashworth and Blake (1996)). Reverse burdens of proof are not rare: the House of Lords accepted, for example, in *Sheldrake v DPP* [2004] UKHL 43 that it was proper for a person charged with being in charge of a motor vehicle having consumed excess alcohol, under section 5(1)(b) of the Road Traffic Act 1988, to have the burden of proving the defence that there was no likelihood of him driving. The presumption of innocence is a vitally important procedural safeguard: but do not misunderstand the extent to which it protects the citizen.

Attention should be paid too to the resources available to the defence in an adversarial system: the 'equality of arms' argument. After all, a heavyweight boxer is not permitted to box professionally against a puny opponent. Are the dice loaded too heavily in one direction? In an adversarial system, convictions are achieved either by proof (beyond reasonable doubt) or by an admission of guilt. There is strong pressure on defendants to plead guilty, and on the police to secure guilty pleas. If somebody admits his or her guilt, there may be little 'process' at all. Where does this leave the presumption of innocence? You should also consider the concept of 'adversarialism' in Chapter 7 where we consider the recent trend to encourage judges to 'manage' cases in a more 'hands on' manner. Clearly, a judge must be wary of too great an involvement—a difficult line to draw.

(ii) There is a strong lay element. Two chapters in this book are devoted to non-legally qualified participants in the criminal justice process: juries and magistrates. Many foreign lawyers are astonished that the powers of a judge are entrusted to lay magistrates and that lay juries are entrusted to reach verdicts without giving reasons or explanations. Increasing inter-agency cooperation at all levels also means a wider range of non-lawyer involvement. The Royal Commission on Criminal Justice (1993) **[1:4]**, in recommending the creation of a Criminal Cases Review Authority (now the Criminal Cases Review Commission (CCRC)— see Chapter 9), suggested that 'both lawyers and lay persons should be represented. We recommend that the Chairman should be chosen for his or her personal qualities rather than for any particular qualifications or background that he or she may have' (page 184). The first chairman was indeed a non-lawyer (an engineer), yet the same report concluded that more use should be made of stipendiary (legally qualified) magistrates, thus recognising the strengths of lay involvement at one point and ignoring them at another. Unfortunately the Report made no attempt to value the lay element in our criminal justice system. Lord Justice Auld's detailed *Review of the Criminal Courts* (2001) **[1:5]** recommended that the Crown Court and magistrates' courts should be replaced by a unified Criminal Court consisting of three divisions: the Crown Division, the District Division, and the Magistrates' Division. Within these three divisions lay juries and lay magistrates would have continued to play an important role. But what is the value of lay involvement, and is it worth striving to keep it? For this author, the value of trial by jury is diminished by the fact they do not give reasons for their decisions (see Chapter 8), but that is not to deny the importance of involving the ordinary citizen in important criminal justice decisions. We also see increasing use of voluntary organizations in the delivery of sentences (see Chapter 10): is this a commitment to citizen engagement, or simply a way to save money?

A third characteristic has appeared in the last three decades or so.

(iii) 'Managerialism'. The language of management and of audit punctuates the criminal justice system. Much of the Government's agenda for reform has been led by what are often called the 'three Es'—economy, efficiency, and effectiveness (see Jones **[1:6]**). In that article, written in 1993, she writes that 'the 1980s saw the "ascendancy of economy" over efficiency and effectiveness, resulting in a "managerial myopia" and a concern with short-term management innovation at the expense of a long-term focus'. The ascendancy of economy remains all too obvious: saving money is at the heart of many initiatives. But concerns with efficiency and indeed also effectiveness lie behind many recent changes. Tonry in his *Punishment and Politics: Evidence and emulation in the making of English crime control policy* (2004) **[1:7]** is deeply sceptical of the Government's commitment to effectiveness. They pay lip-service, he suggests, to what the evidence tells us, but self-interest often wins the day. For Tonry (an American professor who was Director of the Institute of Criminology in Cambridge from 1999–2004), New Labour has put on a sorry performance. If you read Government business plans, or the annual reports of key criminal justice agencies you will see key performance indicators and measures of success, which put great emphasis on financial savings. But the need to find more subtle measures of success has also been recognized. See, for example, Liebling's *Prisons and their Moral Performance* (2004) assessing the 'moral' performance of prisons.

It is worth exploring the large number of 'official' reports on criminal justice in recent years to assess their priorities: do they suffer from 'managerial myopia' or do they have a principled focus? Look at who wrote them, and at their terms of reference as well as their conclusions. A starting point might be the Royal Commission on Criminal Justice, set up in 1991 after the Court of Appeal quashed the convictions of the 'Birmingham Six', six

Irishman convicted of murder following a pub bombing in Birmingham in 1974. Its terms of reference are set out at **[1:4]** and it reported in 1993. Many critics have suggested that the Royal Commission wasted its opportunity to suggest a radical overhaul. Thus, Bridges (1994) described its report as 'a sham. It is a document that is slip-shod in its use of empirical evidence, slippery in its argumentation, and shameful in its underlying political purposes'. Is he unduly harsh? The Royal Commission was severely limited by its brief. But note too Professor Zander's dissent, which you will find quoted at greater length at **[9:1]**, where he says:

At the heart of the criminal justice system there is a fundamental principle that the process must itself have integrity. The majority suggest that the answer to prosecution wrongdoing in the investigation of crime is to deal with the wrongdoers through prosecution or disciplinary proceedings. . . . the approach is not merely insufficient, it is irrelevant to the point of principle. The more serious the case, the greater the need that the system upholds the values in the name of which it claims to act. . . . The integrity of the criminal justice system is a higher objective than the conviction of any individual.

So, you might conclude that the Royal Commission failed to take an adequate principled approach.

Another influential report—*Review of Delay in the Criminal Justice System*—was produced in 1997 by a Home Office team led by civil servant Martin Narey (later Commissioner for Correctional Services and Permanent Secretary in the Home Office), many of whose recommendations were enacted in the Crime and Disorder Act 1998. This emphasis on reducing delays became a key election pledge of the Labour Party in 1997: its manifesto, for example, committed it to halving the time from arrest to sentence for persistent young offenders. Was this emphasis misplaced? Some delays may, after all, be necessary and in the interests of justice.

A flurry of further reports appeared in 2001. There was the Government's White Paper, *Criminal Justice: The Way Ahead* (February 2001), followed by another Home Office report, *Review of the Sentencing Framework* (the Halliday Report), published in July 2001, and the much longer and fuller *Review of the Criminal Courts of England and Wales* by Lord Justice Auld (October 2001) **[1:5]**. Lord Justice Auld's terms of reference were:

A review into the practices and procedures of, and the rules of evidence applied by, the criminal courts at every level, with a view to ensuring that they deliver justice fairly, by streamlining all their processes, increasing their efficiency and strengthening the effectiveness of their relationships with others across the whole of the criminal justice system, and having regard to the interests of all parties including victims and witnesses, thereby promoting public confidence in the rule of law.

Next came the Audit Commission's *Route to Justice: Improving the pathway of offenders through the criminal justice system* (2002), and the White Paper *Justice for All* (2002) Cm 5563, which led to the very important Criminal Justice Act 2003, which made fundamental changes to the rules of criminal procedure and criminal evidence, and which will be mentioned throughout this book.

Since 2003, the pace of change has not slowed down. For example, there were two Government papers in 2006: *Delivering simple, speedy, summary justice* (from the DCA) and *Rebalancing the Criminal Justice in favour of the law abiding majority* (from the Home Office), both clearly designed to improve public confidence in the criminal justice system. And Lord Carter has been commissioned to write three influential 'market-based' reports: first, *Managing Offenders: Reducing Crime* (2003), which resulted in the creation of the National Offender Management Service (see Chapter 10, and **[10:1]**); secondly, his

Review of Legal Aid Procurement (2006) which influenced the Legal Services Act 2007 (see Chapter 5) and most recently, the *Review of Prisons: Securing the Future: Proposals for the Efficient and Sustainable use of Custody in England and Wales* (2007). Carter, who after a career in business was made a Labour peer in 2004, clearly takes a 'business-like' approach to the criminal justice system: this approach seems to be accepted unquestioningly by the Government. When reading anything (including this book!), students should keep an eye on the author (and their perspective) and on their terms of reference or aims in writing.

Running through many of these reports is the shift towards managerialism (or better management?), which can be seen in many of recent changes. Jones **[1:6]** suggests that the shift towards managerial justice has led not to more public accountability but to increased central control of criminal justice practice. For Bottoms (1994), there are four themes which lie behind many of the recent changes in criminal justice: just deserts, managerialism (he singles out its systematic, consumerist and actuarial dimensions), community, and popular punitiveness. He explains the rise of these in the context of various aspects of theories of modernity: 'the relative erosion of class and its partial replacement by interest-group and lifestyle differentiators; the decline in intermediate-level social groups and a general disembedding of social relations; and the subjective concomitants of living in a technological world'.

These themes remain relevant to the criminal justice system being 'managed' by the 'New Labour' Government since 1997. 'Tough on crime, tough on the causes of crime' was a successful election message. The Crime and Disorder Act 1998, the Youth Justice and Criminal Evidence Act 1999, the Criminal Justice and Court Services Act 2000, the Police Reform Act 2002, the Proceeds of Crime Act 2002, the Criminal Justice Act 2003, the Offender Management Act 2007, are all examples of attempts to 'tighten up' the criminal justice system. One advantage of managerialist practices might be better case management: a better ordering of the 'system'. But the greater the 'order' within the system, the greater the need for checks and balances and for accountability: the more the system appears to join-up 'against' the suspect or offender, the more vigilant we must be to ensure that the aims of the criminal justice system are not forgotten. James and Raine offer a useful reminder of the need to focus on the purpose of the criminal justice system **[1:8]**. For them it has the ancient purpose of providing security in exchange for allegiance as well as a modern purpose of protecting individual human rights. For this author, justice and fairness must lie at the heart of the process. Let us move on to evaluating the process.

(iv) EVALUATING THE CRIMINAL JUSTICE PROCESS

So, before evaluating the criminal justice system, we have to identify what the system is seeking to achieve. At one level the answer is easy: it seeks to reduce the incidence of crime in society. But it is not obvious that the criminal justice system itself is (or is even capable of) actually doing that. Perhaps it seeks merely to convict the guilty and to acquit the innocent. We should then question why, and with what justification, we punish those deemed guilty. Ashworth and Redmayne (2000), Walker and Padfield (1996), and von Hirsch and Ashworth (2005) provide some answers to these 'big' questions on crime and punishment.

A useful starting point is Packer's (1968) classic exposition of two models of the criminal process: the Due Process Model and the Crime Control Model **[1:9]**. No one would suggest today that these models are entirely satisfactory, but they do allow us to recognize the value choices that underlie the details of the criminal process. The assumptions that underlie competing policy claims have to be recognized. McConville and Baldwin (1981) suggested that the English system conforms to the Crime Control Model, pointing out, for example, the lack of due process safeguards in a system where 90 per cent of all defendants plead guilty and trial by jury is so rarely used. Their concerns are as valid today as they were then (or is the situation significantly 'worse'?).

But Packer's models are not enough. There are not just two clear-cut alternative value systems competing for priority in the criminal process. Thus, for example, the Royal Commission on Criminal Procedure[1] in its 1981 report (at page 11)—having discussed the 'two main opposing groups,... those who gave paramountcy to the principles of the presumption of innocence and the burden of proof, and those who saw the purpose of the criminal justice system as being a means to the end of bringing the guilty to justice'—went on to seek the 'fundamental balance'. How do you find this 'balance'? Bottoms and Maclean **[1:10]** identified a third model—the Liberal Bureaucratic Model—and King **[1:11]** preferred six models, three based on the perspective of the typical participants and three based on the work of social theorists. Students may well find it useful to keep these different perspectives in mind as they attempt to evaluate the different processes at work.

Other writers have sought to move away from the 'model' perspective, to identify other fundamental values and principles. Cavadino and Dignan (2007) argue that the key to what they see as a penal crisis is one of legitimacy. The penal process needs to be reconstructed around the principle of respect for human rights. Ashworth and Redmayne (2005) concentrate on the need to identify fundamental values and principles. They single out, for example, the right of an innocent person not to be convicted and the right to consistent treatment within declared policies. Ashworth's insistence on a principled approach is particularly important at a time when, as was discussed above, governments are putting increasing emphasis on managerialism and auditing, perhaps at the expense of justice (see also his *Sentencing and Criminal Justice* (2005)).

International and European standards play an increasing role in helping to identify basic principles. Thus, the European Court of Human Rights, applying the European Convention for the Protection of Human Rights and Fundamental Freedoms, is frequently asked to rule on criminal justice matters. There are frequent references in this book to judgments of the European Court of Human Rights, illustrating the way in which the court applies the Convention in practice (for example: **[2:5]**, **[7:12]**, **[9:11]**, **[10:13]**, and **[10.15]**). Since the Human Rights Act 1998 **[1:12]** incorporated the Convention into domestic law, the Convention has been used in domestic courts to challenge, for example, police surveillance techniques **[7:11]** and Parole Board decision making **[10:16]**. Here **[1:13]** we give another perhaps controversial example to illustrate ECtHR reasoning: the recent decision of the Court

---

[1] There are two Royal Commissions we will discuss in this book: the Philips Commission of 1981 (chaired by Sir Cyril Philips, a historian) which resulted in the creation of the Crown Prosecution Service (see Chapter 3) and the Runciman Commission of 1993 (chaired by Lord Runciman, a sociologist), already mentioned in this chapter. A Royal Commission is a major public inquiry set up by the Government to explore an issue of importance and controversy. Mrs Thatcher's Government did not set up any Royal Commissions: it is said she preferred action to Commissions! So the two Royal Commissions mentioned in this book were deeply significant reviews of the criminal justice process of their time, and well worth exploring. But do not confuse the two.

in *Dickson v United Kingdom* (2007) that the Government's policy on artificial insemination for prisoners fell outside any acceptable margin of appreciation, preventing a fair balance being struck between competing public and private interests and so breached Article 8 of the ECHR **[1:12]**.

Also developed under the aegis of the Council of Europe, is a set of recommended European Prison Rules, a detailed code of standards, although they are not yet mandatory. We will refer, too, in Chapter 10 to the extensive powers of inspection of the European Committee for the Prevention of Torture and Inhuman or Degrading Treatment or Punishment.

The 'other' Europe, the European Union, has only involved itself in criminal justice matters more recently. Most importantly, the Amsterdam Treaty of 1997 gave the Council of Ministers of the European Union the power to draw up a variety of legal instruments to help create an 'area of freedom, security and justice'. The most important legal instruments in this area are Framework Decisions, such as the Framework Decision on the European Arrest Warrant, which led to a degree of harmonization in the laws on extradition (see the Extradition Act 2003). Driven by concerns for security, many of the Brussels-led initiatives seem authoritarian and prosecution-minded. A lengthy consultation paper in 2003 on 'Procedural safeguards for suspects and defendants in criminal proceedings throughout the European Union' raised important issues about the difficulty of harmonizing certain aspects of criminal justice in a union made of up of many different Member States, all with different criminal laws and rules of evidence and procedure which vary enormously. Can we have enhanced police and judicial cooperation without more root-and-branch harmonization?

At an international level, the Universal Declaration of Human Rights was adopted in December 1948 by the General Assembly of the United Nations. As significant, and perhaps with potentially more impact, is the International Covenant on Civil and Political Rights (ICCPR), which came into force in 1976. The body set up by the ICCPR to monitor compliance is the Human Rights Committee. The United Kingdom has not ratified the Optional Protocol to the ICCPR, which provides for written applications to the Human Rights Committee by individuals who have been victims of violations of the Covenant's provisions. However, the United Kingdom is coming under increasing pressure to recognize a right of individual petition, which it will eventually have to do if it wishes to play a significant role in enhancing the protection of human rights around the world.

One measure of whether the system is working well is whether there is evidence of bias. Section 95 of the Criminal Justice Act 1991 **[1:14]** put the official seal of approval on the detection of discrimination. The statistics are very worrying: for example, black people are six times more likely to be stopped and searched by the police than whites; and, whereas 2 per cent of the general population of England and Wales in 2005 was estimated to be black, 12 per cent of the male prison population, and 19 per cent of the female prison population, was black **[1:15]**. At several points in this book we will review the evidence as to whether 'the system' in its many parts is biased against, for example, women or people from ethnic minorities. The difficulties in identifying bias are revealed in Home Office research findings **[1:11]** and **[1:12]**, which show that general statistics may not help us answer the question of bias (see also Fitzgerald and Sibbitt (1997), who suggest that ethnic monitoring data should be treated as 'indicators' of areas needing further scrutiny, and). Partly as a result of the Macpherson Inquiry Report (1999) into the police investigation of the killing of the black teenager, Stephen Lawrence, the Race Relations (Amendment) Act 2000 at last applied anti-discrimination law to public services, including the police. But the over-representation of black people in the criminal justice system cannot simply be explained away by racism. The evidence is far from clear, since the causes of crime are many and complex. Poverty, unemployment, poor education, environmental deprivation may all lead to a higher rate of crime **[1:13]**, **[10:8]**. Since many women and black people are poorer than the average citizen, it is difficult to identify whether any bias is the result of the criminal justice system or merely a reflection of society generally. Whilst there has been a steady trickle of equality legislation over the years (most recently the Equality Act 2006, which created the Equality and Human Rights Commission), we have yet to see significant improvements. **[10:8]** is a summary of the Corston Report, published in 2007, which suggested that this was the right time to adopt a new approach to women in the criminal justice system. By the time you read this book, you will be able to judge whether the Corston Report has just become another report, or whether the Government heeded the message that 'transformation' is required to bring gender equality to the treatment of prisoners (and compare it with the equally trenchant *Thematic Review of Women in Prison* published by the Chief HM Inspectorate of Prisons (England and Wales) in 1997).

The law seeks to impose a universal framework on diverse groups of people: but *can* there be justice in an economically unjust society? As Phillips and Bowling (2007) suggest, we need more sophisticated qualitative research, as well as quantitative measures, in order to understand changing patterns in criminal justice. Other forms of bias, defined by wealth and class (see **[4:8]**), and which may reflect either prejudice or merely statistical imbalance, are even more difficult to detect. Hood, Shute, and Seemungal **[1:19]** note an important 'cultural shift' in the treatment of ethnic minorities in the last decade but also raise important questions about perceptions of fairness.

A final word of warning: in this book we are following a relatively straightforward case study in order to understand how the system works in practice. Even if the system works quite appropriately in the case of Gerry Good, you should remain alert. Notice when the system fails—a fundamental aim of the criminal justice system must be to reduce injustice.

FURTHER READING

Ashworth, A, *Sentencing and Criminal Justice* (4th edition, 2005) Cambridge UP

Ashworth, A and Blake, M, 'The presumption of innocence in English law' [1996] Crim LR 306

Ashworth, A and Redmayne, M, *The Criminal Process* (3rd edition, 2005) Oxford UP

Bottoms, A E, 'The philosophy and politics of punishment' in Clarkson C and Morgan R, *The Politics of Sentencing* (1994) Oxford UP

Bridges, L, 'Normalising Injustice: the Royal Commission on Criminal Justice' (1994) 21 Journal of Law and Society 20

Cavadino, M and Dignan, J, *The Penal System: an Introduction* (4th edition, 2007) Sage

Clarkson, C, Cretney, A, Davis, G, and Shepherd, J, 'Assaults: the relationship between seriousness, criminalisation and punishment' [1994] Crim LR 4

Davis, K C, *Discretionary Justice: A Preliminary Inquiry* (1969) Louisiana State UP

Fitzgerald, M and Sibbitt, R, 'Ethnic Monitoring in Police Forces: a beginning' (1997) HORS No 173, HMSO

Gelsthorpe, L and Padfield, N (eds), *Discretion: Its uses in criminal justice and beyond* (2003) Willan

Hawkins, K (ed), *The Uses of Discretion* (1992) Clarendon

Hedderman, C and Gelsthorpe, L (eds), *Understanding the sentencing of women* (1997) HORS No 170, HMSO

Hedderman, C and Hough, M, *Does the criminal justice system treat men and women differently?* (1994) HORS Research Findings No 10, HMSO

Hudson, B, 'Diversity, crime and criminal justice' in Leigh, L and Zedner, L, *A Report on the administration of criminal justice in France and Germany* (1993) Royal Commission on Criminal Justice Research Study No 1, HMSO

Liebling, A, *Prisons and their Moral Performance* (2004) Oxford UP

Maguire, M, 'Crime data and statistics' in Maguire, Morgan, and Reiner (eds), *The Oxford Handbook of Criminology* (4th edition, 2007) Oxford UP

McConville, M and Baldwin, J, *Courts, Prosecution and Conviction* (1981) Oxford UP

Norrie, A, *Crime, Reason and History* (2nd edition, 2001) Cambridge UP

Phillips, C and Bowling, B, 'Ethnicities, racism, crime and criminal justice' in Maguire, Morgan, and Reiner (eds), *The Oxford Handbook of Criminology* (4th edition, 2007) Oxford UP

Shute, S, Hood, R, and Seemungal, F, *A Fair Hearing? Ethnic Minorities in the Criminal Courts* (2005) Willan

Stenson, K and Sullivan, R (eds), *Crime, Risk and Justice: the politics of crime control in liberal democracies* (2001) Willan

von Hirsch, A and Ashworth, A, *Proportionate Sentencing: Exploring the principles* (2005) Oxford UP

Walby, S and Allen J, 'Domestic Violence, sexual assault and stalking: findings from the British Crime Survey' (2004) HORS 2976, HMSO

Walker, N, *Why Punish?* (1991) Oxford Paperbacks

Walker, N and Padfield, N, *Sentencing Theory, Law and Practice* (2nd edition, 1996) Butterworths

Whittaker, C and Mackie, A, 'Managing courts effectively: the reasons for adjournments in magistrates' courts' (1997) HORS No 168, HMSO

Young J, *The Vertigo of Late Modernity* (2007) Sage

(v) A NOTE ON FREE RESOURCES

The Internet is a wonderful resource—though one which seems to result in the waste of more paper rather than less, as we all print out more and more things which we might previously have read in a library. For Government websites, good starting points are: <http://www.justice.gov.uk> and <http://www.homeoffice.gov.uk>.

It is worth looking at Parliament's website too: <http://www.parliament.uk>. Remember that whilst Parliament (the legislature) and the Government (the executive) are very different players in our political system, the notes on clauses available on Bills going through Parliament are written by Government civil servants.

Useful websites monitoring developments in the EU include <http://www.curia.europa. eu/en/transitpage.htm> and <http://www.cer.org.uk>.

Annual reports are available online (or may be bought for a hefty fee). For example, you might like to keep an eye on:

- Report of Her Majesty's Chief Inspector of Prisons for England and Wales
- Report of the Parole Board
- Report of the Prison Service
- Report of the Crown Prosecution Service
- Report of Her Majesty's Chief Inspector of Constabulary

Other documents may be available elsewhere. For example, legal aid leaflets should be available from any court or Citizens' Advice Bureau, and the Code for Crown Prosecutors is available free of charge from any Crown Prosecution Service branch office as well as on the web.

DOCUMENTS

[1:1] Nicholas, S, Kershaw, C, and Walker, A (eds), *Crime in England and Wales 2006/07*
Home Office Statistical Bulletin 11/07

This is taken from the summary:

Extent and trends (Chapter 2)

The British Crime Survey (BCS) and police recorded crime present a broadly similar picture of changes in crime since 2005/06. Overall, the BCS shows no significant change in crime (for the second year running) and police recorded crime shows a two per cent decrease. Chapter 2 provides a summary of the numbers of crimes captured by the British Crime Survey (BCS), and those crimes that are recorded by the police. It also discusses proposals for changes in the presentation of crime following the Smith and the Statistics Commission reviews of crime statistics. It calls for comments on initial steps we have made to reclassify offences and on proposals for a basket of serious crime and a weighted crime index.

- The risk of being a victim of crime as measured by the BCS, at 24 per cent, has increased by one percentage point compared to 2005/06. However, the risk of being a victim of crime is still significantly lower than the peak of 40 per cent recorded by the BCS in 1995.
- Since peaking in 1995, BCS crime has fallen by 42 per cent, representing over eight million fewer crimes, with domestic burglary and all vehicle thefts falling by over a half (59 per cent and 61 per cent respectively) and violent crime falling by 41 per cent during this period.
- Recorded crime statistics show that both domestic burglary and offences against vehicles have also fallen over the same period. Vandalism is the only BCS crime category to show a statistically significant change compared to 2005/06; increasing by 10 per cent. The amount of criminal damage recorded by the police showed no change.
- Violent crime has remained stable according to BCS interviews in 2006/07 compared with 2005/06. Recorded crime figures show a one per cent fall in violence against the person, a seven per cent fall in sexual offences and a three per cent increase in robbery for 2006/07 compared with 2005/06.

Violent and sexual crime (Chapter 3)

The number of violent crimes experienced by adults showed no statistically significant change between 2005/06 and 2006/07 BCS interviews. Police recorded violence against the person fell by one per cent between 2005/06 and 2006/07, the first fall in eight years. The BCS is considered a more reliable measure of violent crime than police recorded crime, as it is not influenced by changes in police recording, public reporting and police activity. However, the reliability of police recorded violent and sexual crime has improved in 2006/07, following several years of changes in recording practices after the introduction of the National Crime Recording Standard in April 2002.

- Violent crime as measured by the BCS has fallen by 41 per cent since a peak in 1995, representing over half a million fewer victims.
- Just under half (49 per cent) of all violent incidents reported to the BCS did not result in any injury to the victim. A similar proportion (50 per cent) of all police recorded violence against the person in 2006/07 involved no injury.
- The risk of being a victim of violent crime in the 2006/07 BCS was 3.6 per cent. Young men, aged 16 to 24, were most at risk, with 13.8 per cent experiencing a violent crime of some sort in the year prior to interview.
- Police recorded robbery increased by three per cent between 2005/06 and 2006/07. This is still 16 per cent below the 2001/02 peak in robbery.
- Recorded sexual offences fell by seven per cent between 2005/06 and 2006/07.
- The number of police recorded offences involving firearms fell by thirteen per cent between 2005/06 and 2006/07.

Property crime (Chapter 4)

The BCS and police recorded crime have both shown considerable falls in burglary and vehicle crime levels since peaks in the mid 1990s. This chapter describes the main types of high volume property crime. The majority of these are acquisitive crimes which comprise both household (burglary, vehicle-related thefts and other household thefts) and personal (theft from the person and other thefts of personal property) acquisitive crimes. In addition information on other types of property crimes such as criminal damage are presented.

- Property crime has fallen considerably since 1995. Overall household acquisitive crime, as measured by the BCS, has fallen by more than half (55 per cent) between 1995 and 2006/07 interviews, although there was no statistically significant change in acquisitive crime between 2005/06 and 2006/07. Longer-term trends show that vandalism has fallen by 11 per cent since 1995...
- Domestic burglaries and vehicle-related thefts showed no statistically significant changes between 2005/06 and 2006/07 BCS interviews. Overall, police recorded burglary fell by four per cent in 2006/07; comprising a three per cent fall in domestic burglaries and four per cent fall in non-domestic burglaries. Offences against vehicles as recorded by the police also fell by four per cent between 2005/06 and 2006/07.
- For both burglary and vehicle-related thefts, having security measures in place was strongly associated with lower levels of victimization.
- Vandalism increased by ten per cent between 2005/06 and 2006/07 as measured by the BCS. There was no change in the number of criminal damage offences recorded by the police. The number of police recorded arson offences fell by six per cent between 2005/06 and 2006/07.
- APACS (the UK Payments Association) data showed a three per cent fall in reports of plastic card fraud losses between 2005 and 2006. An estimate of the prevalence of identity fraud from the 2006/07 BCS showed that two per cent of adults had their personal details used without their permission or knowledge (at a later date) in the last 12 months.

Public perceptions (Chapter 5)

Relatively high proportions of people continue to believe crime has risen in the country as a whole and in their local area; 65 per cent of people thought there was more crime in the country as a whole; 41 per cent thought that crime in their local area had increased. As well as providing an indication of crime levels in England and Wales, the BCS also provides attitudinal measures such as public perceptions of changing crime levels; worry about crime; perceptions of anti-social behaviour; public confidence in the criminal justice system; and victim and witness satisfaction with the police. Chapter 5 presents the latest headline figures and trends for key measures.

- Worry about burglary, car crime and violent crime has remained relatively low and is unchanged since 2005/06. Worry about all three crime types has fallen by approximately one third since 1998.
- There was no statistically significant change in the proportion of people perceiving high levels of anti-social behaviour in their local area between 2005/06 and 2006/07.
- The 2006/07 BCS showed that, compared with 2005/06, public confidence in the CJS has fallen in six of the seven aspects covered. This follows general improvements from 2002/03 to 2005/06.
- Victims were satisfied with the way the police handled the matter in 58 per cent of the incidents the police came to know about. Where people had contact with the police as witnesses, 60 per cent were very or fairly satisfied with how the police handled the incident. Both of these levels have remained unchanged since 2005/06.

Geographic patterns of crime (Chapter 6)

Recorded crime data show that crime is not evenly distributed across England and Wales. Geographic patterns and concentrations of offences varied by crime type. For example, 45 per cent of recorded robbery offences occurred in London. This chapter focuses on how crime is geographically distributed across England and Wales. Patterns in crime are explored by looking at recorded crime at the geographic level of local authority. BCS data are used to look at variation in crime rates by type of area (including rural and urban areas and differing levels of deprivation).

- The 2006/07 BCS found that the risk of being a victim of crime was lower in rural areas than in urban areas. For example, two per cent of people in rural areas had been a victim of one or more violent crimes compared with four per cent of people in urban areas.
- The 2006/07 BCS also found that the risk of being a victim of crime was higher than the national average in 'hard-pressed' and 'urban prosperity' ACORN areas.
- According to the 2006/07 BCS, people living in more deprived areas were more likely to be a victim of crime than those living in less deprived areas.

[1:2] Reiner, R, 'Success or statistics? New Labour and crime control: What has happened to crime under New Labour?'
Criminal Justice Matters (2007), No 67 (at page 4)

Tony Blair's capture of the issue of law and order from the Tories with his trademark slogan tough on crime, tough on the causes of crime was one of New Labour's most surprising and characteristic political coups en route to its 1997 general election victory. During the 2005 election campaign that gave New Labour its record third win, its literature made much of a supposed triumph in the war against crime. 'When Labour came to power in 1997 we inherited a grim legacy. Crime had doubled [since the 1970s]...Overall crime is down by 30 per cent on 1997...violent crime by 26 per cent' (Labour Party, 2005). Michael Howard attacked with directly contradictory figures: 'When I was Home Secretary crime fell by 18 per cent…Under Mr Blair…Overall crime is up by 16 per cent. Violent crime is up by over 80 per cent' (Conservative Party, 2005). Neither the Labour nor the contradictory Conservative claims quoted above are based on lies: just different damned statistics. Labour s success story cites the *British Crime Survey* (BCS), the Conservative rebuttal uses the police recorded statistics. The BCS trends suggest that Tony Blair might be the greatest crime buster since Batman tamed Gotham City; the police figures give that mantle to Michael Howard. Not surprisingly the issue of the validity of these different data sets has become sharply politicised. Survey evidence suggests that the public are not buying either good news story. The BCS regularly finds that some two-thirds of the population believe crime is rising nationally. No wonder the government agonises over the reassurance gap.

So what has happened to crime under New Labour? Nobody who has studied even a few weeks of Criminology 101 will be unaware of the pitfalls of interpreting official crime statistics. Almost from their inception, the limitations of the crime figures collated nationally by the Home Office from local police records since the 1850s were well known. Because victims may not report crimes to the police and the police may not record them, and because an unknowable number of crimes occur that have no individual victims who could report them, there is a vast, incalculable dark figure of unrecorded offences. So apparent trends in the statistics may reflect changes in recording crime rather than in offending. Until quite recently not much more could be said with confidence about crime patterns although much was! The key change has been the development of victim surveys, in particular the BCS since the early 1980s. As it is not subject to the reporting and recording vicissitudes of the police data, the BCS is generally seen as a more reliable estimate of trends. It also sheds light on changes in reporting and recording patterns, making interpretation of the police recorded statistics safer.

Putting together the implications of both police recorded statistics and victim surveys suggests that there have been at least three distinct phases within what otherwise appears as a pretty unbroken story of remorseless and huge rise in the recorded rate since the mid-1950s (Reiner, 2007, ch. 3). Until the 1970s there was no other measurement of trends apart from the police statistics. But during the 1970s the General Household Survey (GHS) began to ask about burglary victimisation. Its data suggest that most of the increase in recorded burglary in that decade was due to more reporting by victims. This cannot be extrapolated necessarily to other crimes, or even for burglary to previous decades. But certainly the GHS suggests that much of the rise in the rate for this highly significant volume crime was a recording phenomenon, up to the early 1980s, and it is plausible that this applies to volume property crimes more generally.

The BCS in its first decade showed the reverse: although recorded crime rose more rapidly between 1981–1993 than BCS crime, the trends were very similar. By both measures crime rose at an explosive rate in the 1980s and early 90s. From the early 1990s, however, the police statistics and the BCS began to show different trends. The BCS continued to chart a rise until 1995, but the police data fell from 1992 to 1997. This was because the proportion of offences reported by victims and recorded by the police decreased as victimisation rose. Insurance companies made claiming more onerous, discouraging reporting by victims, and a more businesslike managerial accountability structure for policing implicitly introduced incentives to keep the recorded crime rate down. So Michael Howard's success in bringing the crime rate down was in large part a recording phenomenon.

After New Labour came to power in 1997 the two measures continued to diverge—but in the opposite direction. The BCS fell continuously from 1995 to 2005, since when it has remained roughly at the level of the first BCS conducted in 1981 before the crime boom of the 1980s. The police recorded statistics, however, began to rise again in 1998 up to 2004, since when they have begun to decline a little.

The rise in the recorded rate was due overwhelmingly to two major changes in the procedures for counting crimes used by the police: new Home Office Counting Rules in 1998, and the 2002 National Crime Recording Standard (NCRS). These two reforms clearly boosted the recorded rate substantially compared to what would have been measured previously (as shown by the alternative calculations by both methods in Walker *et al*, 2006, figure 2.6). This was a predictable consequence of the changes, because the 1998 rules made notifiable a number of offences (such as common assault and assault on a constable) that hitherto had not been included in the recorded rate, whilst the NCRS sought to make universal the *prima facie* rather than evidential criterion for recording offences, whereby police were required to record 'any notifiable offence which comes to the attention of the police' (Burrows *et al*, 2000, p. 31), even in the absence of evidence supporting the victim's report. Whatever the reasons for these reforms, keeping the crime rate down for political reasons cannot have been amongst them! This cannot be said of a further recent revision in 2006 that restores some discretion to the police not to record offences reported to them in the absence of supporting evidence. The rules as amended in 2006 specify that: 'An incident will be recorded as a crime (notifiable offence) if, on the balance of probability: (a) the circumstances as reported amount to a crime defined by law; and (b) there is no credible evidence to the contrary' (Home Office, 2006).

The BCS is free from the particular problems that make the police figures particularly unreliable as a measure of trends. However, it is not (and has never claimed to be) the authoritative index that many journalists now regularly refer to it as. It is conducted with exemplary rigour and thoughtfully reflexive scrutiny of its own methods. But as a survey of individuals to ascertain their victimisation it necessarily omits many types of offences: the supreme example of personal victimisation, homicide; crimes with individual victims who are not aware of what happened (such as successful frauds); crimes with institutional victims such as businesses, or where the victim is the public at large; consensual offences such as drug-taking, and many other serious examples. Its sampling frame excludes certain highly victimised groups such as children under 16 and the homeless. So the government's tendency to treat the BCS as the key measure is as problematic as the earlier exclusive reliance of policy-makers on the police statistics.

Nonetheless, it seems clear that overall crime and volume property crime have gone down under New Labour. This is indicated clearly by the BCS, and the contrary impression given by the police statistics is primarily due to the altered counting procedures. The omissions from the BCS, however, are arguably of increasing significance, and can only be estimated by the police statistics, or indirect measures. Murder and other serious crimes of violence have gone up, but are either not measured at all by the BCS or particularly inadequately. Drug offences are not tapped by it. Crimes against young people and the homeless are probably increasing. So the trends of the last ten years are certainly not as rosy as the BCS suggests. It is also questionable how far the reduction of overall crime is attributable to the success of New Labour criminal justice policy.

Has crime fallen because of New Labour criminal justice policy?

As far as the overall level of crime is concerned, Labour's period in office since 1997 has been a success, with victimisation returning to the levels of a quarter of a century ago. But it has got things right for the wrong reasons as Richard Garside argues (Garside, 2006). Labour captured the issue of law and order from the Conservatives in the early 1990s with the pledge to be "tough on crime, tough on the causes of crime". Over the years its rhetoric and practice have increasingly concentrated on the former, sidelining the significance of causes, especially root causes in terms of political economy (Reiner, 2007, ch. 5). In the recent panic over gun crime, it is the Conservative leader David Cameron who talks about society being badly broken (conveniently neglecting to mention that it was his party that broke it in the 1980s). Tony Blair sees the problem as having very specific causes, with policing as the main solution.

Yet as a recent comprehensive audit of Labour's criminal justice record shows, its success in boosting the resources and powers of the system bears at best little relation to the crime decline (Solomon *et al*, 2007 and see Solomon in this CJM). A review by the Prime Minister's Strategy Unit itself concluded that 80% of the crime reduction was attributable to economic factors, although it concentrates its attention almost entirely on criminal justice solutions, and this estimate is somehow omitted from the version of the report currently on the Cabinet website (Solomon *et al*, 2007, p.14).

The rise in crime up to the early 1990s, and the subsequent decline, are primarily driven by changes in political economy and culture (Reiner, 2007, ch. 4 is a detailed overview of the evidence). The decline that began in the mid-1990s was a paradoxical result of the failure of Conservative economic policy when it was driven out of the ERM, thus ending the deep recession. But as David Downes has pointed out in these pages (Downes, 2004), neither party can espouse this account. Both are locked into the law and order political auction of anything you can do, I can do tougher. So Labour s relative economic success (less long-term unemployment, less family and child poverty) has mitigated the causes of crime a little, but by stealth. And overall inequality, a major factor in generating *anomie* and crime, is something it is explicitly relaxed about.

In so far as crime control specifically has had a major impact, it is through the vastly improved security of the targets of volume property crime, especially cars and buildings. This is a great success, but has its downsides as long as the fundamental causes of crime are unabated. There is some evidence of displacement to more serious crimes such as robbery, and rising homicide is attributable in large part to economic exclusion and inequality (Dorling, 2004). Crime reduction through better physical security, desirable in itself, paradoxically feeds a sense of insecurity as its paraphernalia and routines act as constant signs of threat (Zedner, 2003). These are major factors in the reassurance gap, the failure of public opinion to recognise the declining overall levels of crime. In short, New Labour has largely delivered on its pledge to be tough on crime overall, but it needs to get tough on the economic and social causes of crime, especially more serious crimes, if it is to achieve security and a public sense of security.

References

Burrows, J, Tarling, R, Mackie, A, Lewis, R, and Taylor, G, (2000) Review of Police Forces Crime *Recording Practices*, Home Office Research Study 204. London: Home Office Research, Development and Statistics Directorate.

Conservative Party (2005) *Conservative Election Manifesto 2005*. London: Conservative Party.

Dorling, D (2004) Prime Suspect: Murder in Britain in P. Hillyard, C. Pantazis, S. Tombs and D. Gordon (eds.) *Beyond Criminology*. London: Pluto.

Downes, D (2004) New Labour and the Lost Causes of Crime , *Criminal Justice Matters*, 55: 4–5. London: CCJS.

Home Office (2006) Counting Rules for Recording *Crime, General Rule A*. www.homeoffice.gov.uk/rds/countrules.html

Garside, R (2006) *Right For the Wrong Reasons: Making Sense of Criminal Justice Failure*, London: Crime and Society Foundation.

Labour Party (2005) *Tackling Crime, Forward not Back*, March 2005, p 2. London: Labour Party.

Reiner, R (2007) *Law and Order: An Honest Citizen's Guide to Crime and Control*, Cambridge: Polity.

Solomon, E, Eades, C, Garside, R, and Rutherford, M (2007) Ten Years of Criminal Justice Under Labour: An Independent Audit. London: Centre for Crime and Justice Studies.

Walker, A, Kershaw, C, and Nicholas, S (2006) *Crime in England and Wales 2005/06*, London: Home Office.

Zedner, L (2003) 'Too Much Security?' *International Journal of the Sociology of Law* 31/1: 155–184.

[1:3] Feeney, Floyd, 'Interdependence as a working concept'
In Moxon, D (ed), *Managing Criminal Justice* (1985) HMSO (at page 8)

There may well have been a time when criminal justice was viewed as a series of separate processes connected neither with each other nor anything else. These times have long since passed, however, and today there is widespread agreement that the work of the various criminal justice agencies is closely related and that together these agencies form some kind of 'system'. There is much less agreement, however, about the nature of this system and the implications of such related concepts as interdependence of the criminal justice system.

The general idea of a system dates back at least to the ancient Greeks, who saw systems as some kind of organised whole. By the eighteenth century the system concept had already assumed great importance in branches of theoretical physics such as mechanics where it appeared in full mathematical garb. In the nineteenth century the term began to be applied to biology, and has since been extended to a wide variety of fields including engineering, physiology, international affairs, political affairs and even language. In the late 1950s and early 1960s the concept was further refined and systems analysis appeared as an 'in' method for analysing complex problems. It became common at this time to think of systems in almost every field of human and scientific endeavour. While some earlier criminal justice studies had taken something of a systems-type approach, it was not until this era that the term 'criminal justice system' first began to be used.

The application of systems concepts to criminal justice which followed these developments bore almost immediate fruit, leading to a much better understanding of the linkages among the various parts of the system and the way that the work of each agency affected the work of the other agencies involved. This knowledge proved to be very useful in thinking about criminal justice problems and 'criminal justice system' rapidly became a standard part of the criminal justice vocabulary.

The explicit application of systems concepts to criminal justice produced a number of other results as well. It exposed a great deal of divergence in the way that agencies approach particular problems and showed that the policies followed by one agency often undermined or were at cross-purposes with those followed by other agencies. It also demonstrated just how complex and interdependent the various parts of the system actually are.

Public drunkenness was an early example used to illustrate the kind of divergences that systems analysis could expose. Enforcement efforts for this crime at this time typically involved a large number of police arrests followed in America by short jail sentences and in England by fines. In both countries the offenders were rapidly back on the street, and the whole process started over again. Calculating the enormous waste of police and court effort in this revolving-door situation, systems analysts sought to devise treatment approaches that would make more productive use of the resources expended. They argued explicitly that there were benefits to be gained in overall system accomplishment by transferring resources from the police and the courts to the treatment end of the system. Experiments with detoxification programmes for street alcoholics were one result of their efforts.

Some of those who first sought to apply systems concepts to criminal justice were less impressed with the linkages among criminal justice agencies, however, than with their fragmentation. They argued that criminal justice was in reality not a system but a 'non-system'. Judged strictly by the formal definitions developed by theorists these analysts made a persuasive case.

A very broad definition, used by some general systems theorists, for example, views a system as a set of entities whose relations are specified so that deductions may be made from some relations to others or from the relations among the entities to the behaviour or history of the system. A more detailed formulation requires that the system under investigation be explicitly distinguished from its environment, the internal elements of the system be explicitly stated, the relationships between the elements of the system and between the system and its environment be explicitly stated, the use of canons of logical or mathematical reasoning in deductions relating to these relationships, and the confirmation of assertions about these relationships through scientific methods.

Even the strongest proponents of the systems approach would be hard-pressed to claim that their efforts meet the precision required by these standards. Despite this, however, most of those involved in criminal justice have come to think of it as a system. There is also considerable agreement that the system includes: the police and the prosecution; the defence; the courts; and corrections, including probation and the prisons. The medical, mental health, welfare, education and private security systems are all seen as closely related systems but not as part of the criminal justice system. As the criminal justice system receives not only clients but also political guidance, financial support, information and personnel from the larger society, it obviously is part of the general political, economic and social systems of the larger society.

One of the central features of all systems is the interdependence of the various system parts. The concept of interdependence is therefore a natural part of the systems idea. In recent years, however, interdependence has taken on special meaning in the criminal justice system, particularly in Great Britain. As this special meaning has a considerable overlap with the more general systems approach, it cannot be defined in ways that sharply distinguish the two concepts. It is perhaps best understood, however, as meaning that what one criminal justice agency does is likely to affect and be affected by other agencies and that a detailed knowledge of the kinds of interactions that are likely to take place is essential for undertaking system improvements. The idea is thus explicitly concerned with the development of improved performance in functions that cross agency lines.

In the criminal justice system interdependence occurs at many different levels—national and local; agency head and working officer; strategic, tactical and mechanical. Strategic level choices include large questions of system design or structure, and in Great Britain are generally made at the national level. Included in such choices would be issues such as whether there should be an independent prosecution service, whether probation resources should be increased in order to provide more sentencing alternatives to prison, and whether the police should receive a much larger share of the system's resources than the courts. Questions such as how the defence function is to be organised and financed and whether greater efforts should be expended on prevention as opposed to apprehension and punishment also involve strategic issues likely to be decided at the national level.

Tactical level choices generally concern use of the resources available to particular criminal justice agencies. Whilst these choices can be made at many different levels within a given organisation, they are generally made locally rather than nationally. Decisions of this kind include such things as the deployment of police forces, the hours of service provided by the courts, and how the duty solicitor rota is to function.

Perhaps the most fundamental sense in which criminal justice agencies are linked together at the tactical level lies in the process of discretionary decision-making by which cases are adjudicated and transferred from one agency to another. Cases typically begin with the discovery of a crime and the apprehension of a suspected offender by the police. After deciding whether to prosecute, the police pass the case on to the courts for adjudication. The courts in turn often secure the services of the probation service to assist in the sentencing decision, and in this decision may pass the case on either to probation or the prison service. This process is rather like an assembly line in which each agency's workload is essentially controlled by the actions of the previous agency. In most instances the decision of the transmitting agency is largely discretionary, but the receiving agency generally has little or no say in the decisions made. Probably the most important of these discretionary decisions are the decisions to arrest, to prosecute and to sentence. Obviously policies such as cautioning and non-charging by the prosecution are of major importance in this system of discretionary decision-making.

[1:4] *Report of the Royal Commission on Criminal Justice*

(1993) Cm 2263, HMSO (at page iii)

Terms of reference

To examine the effectiveness of the criminal justice system in England and Wales in securing the conviction of those guilty of criminal offences and the acquittal of those who are innocent, having regard to the efficient use of resources, and in particular to consider whether changes are needed in:

   (i) the conduct of police investigations and their supervision by senior police officers, and in particular the degree of control that is exercised by those officers over the conduct of the investigation and the gathering and preparation of evidence;

(ii) the role of the prosecutor in supervising the gathering of evidence and deciding whether to proceed with a case, and the arrangements for the disclosure of material, including unused material, to the defence;

(iii) the role of experts in criminal proceedings, their responsibilities to the court, prosecution, and defence, and the relationship between the forensic science services and the police;

(iv) the arrangement for the defence of accused persons, access to legal advice, and access to expert evidence;

(v) the opportunities available for an accused person to state his position on the matters charged and the extent to which the courts might draw proper inferences from primary facts, the conduct of the accused and any failure on his part to take advantage of an opportunity to state his position;

(vi) the powers of the court in directing proceedings, the possibility of their having an investigative role both before and during the trial, and the role of pre-trial reviews, the courts' duty in considering evidence, including uncorroborated confession evidence;

(vii) the role of the Court of Appeal in considering new evidence on appeal, including directing the investigation of allegations;

(viii) the arrangements for considering and investigating allegations of miscarriages of justice when appeal rights have been exhausted.

(At page 3:)

Adversarial or inquisitorial?

11 The criminal justice system of England and Wales, in common with other jurisdictions which have evolved with the 'Anglo-Saxon' or 'common law' tradition, is often categorised as 'adversarial'. This is in contrast to the so-called 'inquisitorial' system based on the 'Continental' or 'civil law' tradition. In this context, the term 'adversarial' is usually taken to mean the system which has the judge as an umpire who leaves the presentation of the case to the parties (prosecution and defence) on each side. These separately prepare their case and call, examine and cross-examine their witnesses. The term 'inquisitorial' describes the systems where judges may supervise the pre-trial preparation of the evidence by the police[1] and, more important, play a major part in the presentation of the evidence at trial. The judge in 'inquisitorial' systems typically calls and examines the defendant and the witnesses while the lawyers for the prosecution and the defence ask supplementary questions.

12 It is important not to overstate the differences between the two systems; all adversarial systems contain inquisitorial elements, and vice versa. But it is implicit in our terms of reference that we should consider whether a change in the direction of more inquisitorial procedures might not reduce the risks of mistaken verdicts and the need for subsequent re-examination of convictions which may be unsafe. For the reasons set out below we do not recommend the adoption of a thoroughgoing inquisitorial system. But we do recognise the force of the criticisms which can be directed at a thoroughgoing adversarial system which seems to turn a search for the truth into a contest played between opposing lawyers according to a set of rules which the jury does not necessarily accept or even understand. In some instances, such as our approach to forensic science evidence, our recommendations can fairly be interpreted as seeking to move the system in an inquisitorial direction, or at least as seeking to minimise the danger of adversarial practices being taken too far. But we have not arrived at our proposals through a theoretical assessment of the relative merits of the two legal traditions. On the contrary, we have been guided throughout by practical considerations in proposing changes which will, in our view, make our existing system more capable of serving the interests of both justice and efficiency.

13 We have sought information from a wide range of other countries' criminal jurisdictions (both adversarial and inquisitorial) in order to see whether there are lessons to be learned from them that might be applied with advantage to the criminal justice system in England and Wales. In particular, we have during two visits to Scotland looked in some depth at the Scottish system. We have not, however,

found, either in Scotland or anywhere else, a set of practices which has so clearly succeeded in resolving the problems which arise in any system of criminal justice that it furnishes the obvious model which all the others should therefore adopt. Every system is the product of a distinctive history and culture, and the more different the history and culture from our own the greater must be the danger that an attempted transplant will fail. Hardly any of those who gave evidence to the Commission suggested that the system in another jurisdiction should be adopted in England and Wales; and of those who did, not argued for it in any depth or with any supporting detail. We have, accordingly, no evidence to suggest that there is somewhere a jurisdiction in which the rights and interests of the various parties involved are so uniquely well balanced as to give the system the best of all worlds. In the relevant chapters of this report, we make occasional reference to the features of other jurisdictions by which we have been influenced in arriving at our conclusions. But we make no attempt to give them either an 'adversarial' or an 'inquisitorial' label.

14 Our reason for not recommending a change to an inquisitorial system as such is not simply fear of the consequences of an unsuccessful cultural transplant. It is also that we ourselves doubt whether the fusion of the functions of investigation and prosecution, and the direct involvement of judges in both, are more likely to serve the interests of justice than a system in which the roles of police, prosecutors, and judges are as far as possible kept separate and the judge who is responsible for the conduct of the trial is the arbiter of law but not of fact. We believe that a system in which the critical roles are kept separate offers a better protection for the innocent defendant, including protection against the risk of unnecessarily prolonged detention prior to trial. Moreover, there are 'inquisitorial' jurisdictions in which the system is moving, or being urged to move in an 'adversarial' direction. For example, Italy has sought to introduce a more adversarial approach, and in France there has been widespread criticism of the role of the *juge d'instruction*.

15 We in no way suggest, as is sometimes done, that 'Inquisitorial' systems presume suspects to be guilty until they are proved innocent. Nor do we suggest, as is also sometimes done, that 'Adversarial' systems are not concerned to unearth the facts on which the guilt or innocence of the suspect depends. Both recognise the principle of the 'burden of proof'—that is, the obligation on the prosecution to establish the defendant's guilt on the basis of evidence which the defence is entitled to contest. We regard this principle as fundamental. This, as will become apparent in later chapters, is not incompatible with changes to our system which would require the defence to disclose the outline of whatever case it intends to put forward at an earlier stage than at present, or remove from the defendant charged with an 'either way' offence the right to choose the mode of trial, or permit the judge to rule before the jury is empanelled on questions of admissibility of evidence or the production of statements of agreed facts. But defendants are always to be presumed to be innocent unless and until the prosecution has satisfied the magistrates or jury of their guilt beyond reasonable doubt.

Note

1 Although in practice this is rare. For example, in France the *juge d'instruction* plays a part in only some 10% of cases. See the Report of the French Commission Justice Penale et Droits de l'Homme, La Mise en Etat des Affairs Penales (1991) Paris.

[1:5] Auld, LJ, *Review of the Criminal Courts of England and Wales*
(2001) The Stationery Office (at pages 23–30)

Chapter 2
Summary and Recommendations

Introduction (Chapter 1—pages 7–22, rec 1)

2. The criminal law should be codified under the general oversight of a new Criminal Justice Council and by or with the support as necessary of the Law Commission. There should be codes of offences,

procedure, evidence and sentencing (paras 35–36, rec 1). See also: as to a code of criminal procedure, (Chapter 10 paras 271–280, recs 228–234); as to a code of criminal evidence, (Chapter 11, paras
76–77); and as to a sentencing code, (Chapter 11, para 198, and Chapter 12, paras 110–111).

The Criminal Justice System (Chapter 8—pages 315–336, recs 121–139)

3. A national Criminal Justice Board should replace all the existing national planning and 'operational'
bodies, including the Strategic Planning Group, and the Trial Issues Group. The new Board should be
the means by which the criminal justice departments and agencies provide over-all direction of the
criminal justice system (paras 37–66, recs 121–122). It should have an independent chairman and
include senior departmental representatives and chief executives of the main criminal justice agencies
(including the Youth Justice Board) and a small number of non-executive members (paras 67–72, recs
123–125). At local level, Local Criminal Justice Boards should be responsible for giving effect to the
national Board's directions and objectives and for management of the criminal justice system in their
areas. Both the national and local Boards should be supported by a centrally managed secretariat and
should consult regularly with the judiciary (paras 73–77, recs 126–129). The national Board should
be responsible for introducing an integrated technology system for the whole of the criminal justice
system based upon a common language and common case files, the implementation and maintenance
of which should be the task of a Criminal Case Management Agency accountable to the Board (paras
92–114, recs 137–139).

4. A Criminal Justice Council, chaired by the Lord Chief Justice or senior Justice of Appeal, should
be established to replace existing advisory and consultative bodies, including the Criminal Justice
Consultative Council and the Area Strategy Committees. It should have a statutory power and duty to
keep the criminal justice system under review, to advise the Government on all proposed reforms, to
make proposals for reform and to exercise general oversight of codification of the criminal law. The
Council should be supported by a properly resourced secretariat and research staff (paras 78–88, recs
130–135).

A unified Criminal Court (Chapter 7—pages 269–314, recs 83–120)

5. The Crown Court and magistrates' courts should be replaced by a unified Criminal Court consisting
of three Divisions: the Crown Division, constituted as the Crown Court now is, to exercise jurisdiction
over all indictable-only matters and more serious 'either-way' offences allocated to it; the District
Division, constituted by a judge, normally a District Judge or Recorder, and at least two magistrates,
to exercise jurisdiction over a mid range of 'either-way' matters of sufficient seriousness to merit up
to two years' custody; and the Magistrates' Division, constituted by a District Judge or magistrates, as
magistrates' courts now are, to exercise their present jurisdiction over all summary matters and the less
serious 'either-way' cases allocated to them (paras 2–35, recs 83–87). The courts, that is those of the
Magistrates' Division, would allocate all 'either-way' cases according to the seriousness of the alleged
offence and the circumstances of the defendant, looking at the possible outcome of the case at its
worst from the point of view of the defendant and bearing in mind the jurisdiction of each division. In
the event of a dispute as to venue, a District Judge would determine the matter after hearing representations from the prosecution and the defendant. The defendant would have no right of election to be
tried in any division (paras 36–40, recs 88–95). (In the event of the present court structure continuing,
the defendant should lose his present elective right to trial by jury in 'either-way' cases; see paragraph
10 below.)

6. Whether or not the Crown Court and magistrates' courts are replaced with a unified Criminal
Court, there should be a single centrally funded executive agency as part of the Lord Chancellor's
Department responsible for the administration of all courts, civil, criminal and family (save for the
Appellate Committee of the House of Lords), replacing the present Court Service and the Magistrates'
Courts' Committees. For the foreseeable future, circuit boundaries and administrations should remain
broadly as they are and the courts should be locally managed within the circuits and the 42 criminal
justice areas (paras 41–73, recs 96–103). Justices' clerks and legal advisers responsible to them should

continue to be responsible for the legal advice provided to the magistrates (para 74, rec 104; see also Chapter 4—Magistrates paras 50–58, recs 6–7).

Magistrates (Chapter 4—pages 94–134, recs 2–15)

7. Magistrates and District Judges should continue to exercise their established summary jurisdiction and the work should continue to be allocated between them as much as at present (paras 1–49, recs 2–5). If my recommendation for the establishment of a new unified Criminal Court with a District Division is adopted, they should also sit together in that division exercising its higher jurisdiction. I do not recommend any further extension of justices' clerks' case management jurisdiction (paras 50–58, rec 7). Steps should be taken to provide benches of magistrates that more broadly reflect the communities they serve (paras 59–86, recs 8–9). In order to strengthen the training of magistrates, the Judicial Studies Board should be made responsible, and be adequately resourced, for devising and securing the content and manner of their training (paras 91–100, recs 11–15).

Juries (Chapter 5—pages 135–225, recs 16–60)

8. Jurors should be more widely representative than they are of the national and local communities from which they are drawn. Qualification for jury service should remain the same, save that entitlement to, rather than actual, entry on an electoral role should be the criterion. Potential jurors should be identified from a combination of public registers and lists (paras 21–24, recs 17–18). While those with criminal convictions and mental disorder should continue to be disqualified from service, no one in future should be ineligible for or excusable as of right from it. Any claimed inability to serve should be a matter for discretionary deferral or excusal (paras 27–40, recs 20–24). Provision should be made to enable ethnic minority representation on juries where race is likely to be relevant to an important issue in the case (paras 52–62, rec 25).

9. The law should not be amended to permit more intrusive research than is already possible in the workings of juries, though in appropriate case trial judges and/or the Court of Appeal should be entitled to examine alleged improprieties in the jury room (paras 76–98, recs 26–29). The law should be declared, by statute if need be, that juries have no right to acquit defendants in defiance of the law or disregard of the evidence (paras 99–107, rec 30).

10. The defendant should no longer have an elective right to trial by judge and jury in 'either-way' cases. The allocation should be the responsibility of the magistrates' court alone and exercisable where there is an issue as to venue by a District Judge. The procedures of committal for trial and for sentence in 'either-way' cases should be abolished. Under my recommendation for a unified Criminal Court with three divisions, matters too serious for the Magistrates' Division would go direct either to the District or Crown Division depending on the seriousness. In the meantime 'either-way' cases for the Crown Court should be "sent" there in the same way as indictable-only cases (paras 119–172, recs 32–36). Trial by judge and jury should remain the main form of trial of the more serious offences triable on indictment, that is, those that would go to the Crown Division, subject to four exceptions. First, defendants in the Crown Court or, if my recommendations for a unified Court with three divisions is accepted, in the Crown and District Divisions, should be entitled with the court's consent to opt for trial by judge alone (paras 110–118, rec 31). Second, in serious and complex frauds the nominated trial judge should have the power to direct trial by himself and two lay members drawn from a panel established by the Lord Chancellor for the purpose (or, if the defendant requests, by himself alone) (paras 173–206, recs 37–47). Third, a youth court, constituted by a judge of an appropriate level and at least two experienced youth panel magistrates, should be given jurisdiction to hear all grave cases against young defendants unless the charges are inseparably linked to those against adults (paras 207–211, recs 48–50). Fourth, legislation should be introduced to require a judge, not a jury, to determine the issue of fitness to plead. (paras 212–213, rec 51).

The Judiciary (Chapter 6—pages 226–268, recs 61–82)

11. The current hierarchy of judges and their jurisdictions should continue, subject to my recommendations for the establishment of a District Division of a new unified Criminal Court and extension of the

powers of District Judges and magistrates when sitting in it (paras 1–18). Systems of judicial management and deployment should be strengthened and also made more flexible to enable a better match
of High Court and Circuit Judges to criminal cases, proper regard also being given to the arrangements
for civil and family justice. In particular, there should be a significant shift in heavy work from High
Court Judges to the Circuit Bench, coupled with greater flexibility in the system for allocating work
between them. Save in the case of Circuit Presiding Judges, the present rigid circuiteering pattern of
High Court Judges should be replaced by one in which they travel out to hear only the most serious
of cases (paras 19–56, recs 63–70). In implementing the recent recommendations for reforms in the
system of appointing judges, the Lord Chancellor's Department should exercise vigilance to root out
any indirect discrimination, hurry forward the substitution of assessment exercises for short interviews
and establish and publish a clear policy for the appointment of disabled persons to judicial office (paras
65–88, recs 76–78). There should be a strengthening in the training provided to judges, appropriately
enlarging the Judicial Studies Board's role for the purpose (paras 89–97, rec 79). There should be a
system of appraisal for all part-time judges, and consideration should be given to the appraisal of full-
time judges (paras 98–104 , recs 80–82).

Decriminalisation and alternatives to conventional trial (Chapter 9—pages 367–394, recs 140–151)

12. I have found little scope or justification for decriminalisation of conduct that Parliament has made
subject to penal sanctions (paras 1–6). There should, however, be greater use of a system of fixed
penalty notices subject to a right of challenge in court, for example for television licence evasion and
the existing provisions for road traffic offences (paras 7–25, recs 140–142). There is no compelling
case at present for the creation of any specialist courts, in particular, drugs or domestic violence courts
(paras 26–40). Consideration should be given to the wider use of conditional cautioning or 'caution-
plus' alongside existing and future restorative justice schemes, for which a national strategy should
be devised (paras 41–47 and 58–69, recs 143–144 and 150). Once the Financial Services Authority
has assumed full responsibility for supervision in the financial services field, consideration should be
given to transferring appropriate financial and market infringements from the criminal justice process
to the Authority's regulatory and disciplinary control. Consideration should also be given in this field
for combining parallel criminal and regulatory proceedings (paras 48–57, recs 145–149). Preparatory
work should be undertaken with a view to removal of all civil debt enforcement from courts exercising
a criminal jurisdiction (paras 70–77, rec 151).

Preparing for trial (Chapter 10—pages 395–513, recs 152–235)

13. The key to better preparation for, and efficient and effective disposal of, criminal cases is early
identification of the issues. Four essentials are: strong and independent prosecutors; efficient and
properly paid defence lawyers; ready access by defence lawyers to their clients in custody; and a modern communications system (paras 1–34, recs 152–153). All public prosecutions should take the form
of a charge, issued without reference to the courts but for which the prosecutor in all but minor,
routine or urgent cases, would have initial responsibility. It should remain the basis of the case against
a defendant regardless of the court which ultimately deals with his case, thus replacing the present mix
of charges, summonses and indictments (paras 35–63, recs 154–170). A graduated scheme of sentencing discounts should be introduced so that the earlier the plea of guilty the higher the discount for it.
This should be coupled with a system of advance indication of sentence for a defendant considering
pleading guilty (paras 91–114, recs 186–193).

14. The scheme of mutual disclosure established by the Criminal Procedure and Investigations
Act 1996 should remain, but subject to the following reforms: its expression in a single and simply
expressed instrument; a single and simple test of materiality for both stages of prosecution disclosure;
automatic prosecution disclosure of certain documents; removal from the police to the prosecutor of
such responsibility as the police have for identifying all potentially disclosable material; and encouragement, through professional conduct rules and otherwise, of the provision of adequate defence

statements (paras 115–184, recs 194–205). There should be a new statutory scheme for third party disclosure (paras 185–190, rec 206) and for instruction by the court of special independent counsel in public interest immunity cases where the court considers prosecution applications in the absence of the defendant (paras 191–197, rec 207).

15. In the preparation for trial in all criminal courts, there should be a move away from plea and directions hearings and other forms of pre-trial hearings to cooperation between the parties according to standard time-tables, wherever necessary, seeking written directions from the court. In the Crown and District Divisions and, where necessary, in the Magistrates' Division, there should then be a written or electronic 'pre-trial assessment' by the court of the parties' readiness for trial. Only if the court or the parties are unable to resolve all matters in this way should there be a pre-trial hearing before or at the stage of the pre-trial assessment. The courts should have a general power to give binding directions and rulings either in writing or at pre-trial hearings (paras 198–234, recs 208–221). In the Crown and District Divisions and, where necessary, in the Magistrates' Division, following the pre-trial assessment and in good time before hearing, the parties should prepare, for the approval of the judge and use by him, them, and the jury in the hearing, a written case and issues summary setting out in brief the substances of charge(s) and the issues to be resolved by the court (para 235; see also Chapter 11, paras 15–24, recs 235–236).

The Trial: procedures and evidence (Chapter 11—pages 514–610, recs 236–300)

16. In trials by judge and jury, the judge, by reference to the case and issues summary, copies of which should be provided to the jury, should give them fuller introduction to the case than is now conventional (paras 14–24, recs 235–236). The trial should broadly take the same form as at present, though with greater use of electronic aids in appropriate cases. The judge should sum up and direct the jury, making reference as appropriate to the case and issues summary. So far as possible, he should 'filter out' the law and fashion factual questions to the issues and the law as he knows it to be. Where he considers it appropriate, he should require the jury publicly to answer each of the questions and to declare a verdict in accordance with those answers (paras 25–55, recs 237–250).

17. In trials by judge and magistrates in the District Division, the judge should be the sole judge of law, but he and the magistrates should together be the judges of fact, each having an equal vote. The order of proceedings would be broadly the same as in the Crown Division. The judge should rule on matters of law, procedure and inadmissibility of evidence in the absence of the magistrates where it would be potentially unfair to the defendant to do so in their presence. The judge should not sum up the case to the magistrates, but should retire with them to consider the court's decision, which he would give and publicly reason as a judgment of the court. The judge should be solely responsible for sentence (paras 57–61, rec 251).

18. There should be a comprehensive review of the law of criminal evidence to identify and establish over-all and coherent principles and to make it an efficient and simple agent for securing justice. Subject to such review, I consider that the law should, in general, move away from technical rules of inadmissibility to trusting judicial and lay fact finders to give relevant evidence the weight it deserves. In particular, consideration should be given to the reform of the rules as to refreshing memory, the use of witness statements, hearsay, unfair evidence, previous misconduct of the dependant, similar fact evidence and the evidence of children (paras 76–128, recs 254–261). There should be reforms to strengthen the quality and objectivity of expert evidence and improve the manner of its presentation both from the point of view of the court and experts, following in some respects reforms made in the civil sphere by the Civil Procedure Rules (paras 129–151, recs 262–275). Urgent steps should be taken to increase the numbers and strengthen the quality of interpreters serving the criminal courts and to improve their working conditions (paras 155–162, recs 276–286). There are a number of ways in which the facilities and procedures of the courts should or could be modernised and better serve the public (paras 163–196, recs 287–295). The criminal courts should be equipped with an on-line sentencing information system (paras 200–211, recs 296–299).

Appeals (Chapter 12—pages 611–658, recs 301–328)

19. There should be the same tests for appeal against conviction and sentence respectively at all levels of appeal, namely those applicable for appeal to the Court of Appeal (paras 5–13, and 45–46, recs 300–301). There should be a single line of appeal from the Magistrates' Division (Magistrates' Courts) and above to the Court of Appeal in all criminal matters. This would involve: 1) abolition of appeal from magistrates' courts to the Crown Court by way of rehearing and its replacement by an appeal to the Crown Division (Crown Court) constituted by a judge alone; and 2) abolition of appeal from magistrates' courts and/or the Crown Court to the High Court by way of a case stated or claim for judicial review and their replacement by appeal to the Court of Appeal under its general appellate jurisdiction enlarged if and to the extent necessary (paras 14–44, recs 302–307).

20. I support the general thrust of the Law Commission's recommendations for the introduction of statutory exceptions to the double jeopardy rule, save that a prosecutor's right of appeal against acquittal should not be limited to cases of murder and allied offences, but should extend to other grave offences punishable with life or long terms of imprisonment (paras 47–65, recs 308–309). There should be provision for appeal by the defence or the prosecution against a special verdict of a jury which on its terms is perverse; see para 16 above (paras 66–67, rec 310).

21. The Court of Appeal should be reconstituted and its procedures should be improved to enable it to deal more efficiently with, on the one hand appeals involving matters of general public importance or of particular complexity and, on the other, with 'straightforward' appeals (paras 73–101, recs 311–321). The law should be amended: to widen the remit of the Sentencing Advisory Panel to include general principles of sentencing, regardless of the category of offence; and to enable the Court of Appeal to issue guidelines without having to tie them to a specific appeal before it (paras 108–111, recs 324–325).

[1:6] Jones, Carol, 'Auditing Criminal Justice'
(1993) 33 BJ of Criminology 187 (at page 199)

I have argued that the auditing process has had a profound impact upon the practice of criminal justice in Britain. Clearly, the process has a good side in so far as it has made more explicit the value preferences underlying the criminal justice system. It has also subjected criminal justice agencies to an unprecedented degree of scrutiny—the hearings of the Public Accounts Committee, which summons top civil servants and officials to answer criticisms made by the National Audit Office, have provided parliamentary accountability of a particularly robust kind.

Officials are frequently placed in 'the hot seat'. Senior law officers have been brought for the first time before a Committee of Parliament to answer criticisms, and their evidence has been published. Arguably, the National Audit Office, the Audit Commission, and the Public Accounts Committee are fulfilling the promise of 'social accounting' to render key organisations more open to public scrutiny.

At first sight, therefore, the traditional structures of accountability appear to be reinforced by the new system. The contrary view argues that auditing undermines these traditional structures. Instead of officials being responsible to ministers for their decisions, ministers are forced to rely upon the professional values of accountants and auditors. Accountants are no longer simply providers of financial information: they are in the forefront of decision-making. Policy-making thus moves outside recognised political channels.

The National Audit Office recommendation of greater liaison between all agencies of the criminal justice system (courts, police, prosecution) also weakens traditional constitutional boundaries. The pursuit of economy and effectiveness thus encourages a more intricate meshing of criminal justice agencies, whose efficiency and effectiveness are increasingly defined in terms of their 'success rate': ie convictions. The auditing process itself also enables central government to penetrate criminal justice agencies more effectively and less obtrusively. Standardisation creeps through the system via a new route. National application of the 'three Es' undercuts local distinctiveness and professional autonomy. It may also cut across national boundaries. For example, procurators fiscal in Scotland were literally 'called to account' because their practices did not accord with a set of criteria formulated in another legal system. What is marketed as a 'hands off' policy may thus actually result in a 'receding locus of power' which masks a more intricate realignment of the forces of law and order and removes existing—if imperfect—channels of accountability.

Cumulatively, there has also been a shift away from a formal commitment to rational justice and 'rule of law' to 'managerial justice'. While managerialism may pay lip-service to all the 'three Es', the 1980s saw the 'ascendancy of economy' over efficiency and effectiveness, resulting in a 'managerial myopia' and a concern with short-term managerial innovation at the expense of a long-term focus. 'Value for money' translated not only into a greater emphasis upon crime control but also into 'more crime control with fewer resources'. This produced a new definition of what the criminal justice system was for; the rights of accused persons were inefficient and uneconomic 'trappings'; due process of law was too expensive, too inefficient, and too ineffective—it 'let too many guilty persons go free'. Thus the tenets of auditing, allied to those of managerialism and devolved control, came to underpin an increasingly 'crime control'-oriented legal system.

I have argued that the construction of the consumer as a participant in the management of his or her own life served as a useful ideological strategy for stabilising this increasing focus on 'law and order' in society. This was particularly crucial at a time when the 'post—war consensus' appeared to be breaking down, where the policy was 'not to integrate the poor and underprivileged but to manage their protest'.[1] I have also argued that despite the rhetoric of consumer power there has in fact been a greater centralisation of control over criminal justice practices. This undercuts the notion of consumers being able to make strategic choices among competitors in a free market.

The increase in managerial discretion is also quite at odds with the tenets of 'rule of law' ideology, though the rhetoric of freely contracting consumers is the epitome of that bourgeois individualism found in rule of law ideology. It provides a gloss of equality where none exists. It legitimises a system of settled—or emerging—inequalities. Managerialism undercuts the distinction between formal legal rationality and technocratic rationality. It also undercuts the 'traditional apparatuses of justice' and increasingly legitimises a 'relatively naked emphasis within the criminal justice system upon criminalisation and the suppression of resistance, and a relative de-emphasising of the formal norms and values of individual justice. Typically, sociologists have predicted that a move away from formal legal rationality will result in a move towards technocratic justice. Managerialism is a hybrid form which intercepts these boundaries. It is pragmatic and instrumentalist but it is also flexible and informal, substituting discretion and 'the right of management to manage' for explicit legal rules, formal procedural norms, the principle of precedent, and due process of law. In this respect, managerialism shares what Heydebrand has termed the 'tendencies of de-juridification and de-stratification' which characterise technocratic decision-making. The 'virtue' of managerialism is that it is divorced from any substantive normative or political value. Indeed, it transforms the absence of principled policy (for example, along lines of justice and fairness) from a vice into a virtue.

Note

1 Norrie and Adelman (1989) 16(1) Journal of Law and Society 112, at page 123.

[1:7] Tonry, M, *Punishment and Politics: Evidence and emulation in the making of English crime control policy*
(2004) (at page 22)

In the Preface, Tonry 'puzzles' over why England is the only major Western country whose Government has chosen to emulate American crime-control policies and politics of the past quarter of a century, when 'many of the most notorious American innovations, including some that England has embraced and others it has considered, have been conspicuously unsuccessful, and at devastating social and economic cost'.

In Chapter 1, Tonry reviews seven features of the Criminal Justice Act 2003 (charging, community punishment orders, custody plus and minus, the Sentencing Guidelines Council, mandatory minimum sentences, preventive detention, protections against wrongful convictions) and concludes (at page 22):

The seven features of the Criminal Justice Act that I have discussed were not entirely arbitrarily chosen; others could have been selected, but they are among the most substantial and politically contentious of the Act's provisions. They demonstrate an inverse relation between the government's reliance on evidence and the political salience of a subject. In relation to the changed roles of police and prosecutors in formulating criminal charges, and the design of the new community punishment order, evidence has been considered and taken into account. These however are technical and intra-institutional issues that provoke little political or public controversy. At the spectrum's other end, in relation to defendants' procedural protections and dangerous offenders—issues about which the tabloids bray—evidence seems nether neither to have been consulted nor to have played a role.

Where there was no powerful constituency to be faced down, as with changing in the charging rules, evidence mattered. Where a powerful constituency was affronted, as with development of sentencing guidelines, the government backed down.

The Labour government's has been a sorry performance. If the principal drivers of crime-control policy proposals are evidence, ignorance and ideology or self-interest, ideology and self-interest won the day...

[1:8] James, A and Raine, J, *The New Politics of Criminal Justice*
(1998) Longmans (at page 44)

The story of the public service managerialist reforms as they affected criminal justice is one of inconsistent and piecemeal direction on the part of ministers and reluctant participation on the part of most agencies. First, in the absence of an agreed purpose for the reform of criminal justice itself (see Chapter 2), the intermediate goals of cost efficiency and service effectiveness became pre-eminent. In the absence of an agreed strategy for change, intervention by government was influenced by size of budget, ease of pickings and ministerial preference. The effort put into resisting the reforms by agencies, perhaps with only the Crown Prosecution Service as the exception, hampered any real potential for imaginative and innovative change driven by services themselves.

Second, it is arguable that the reforms could never have worked in criminal justice in any case where the three prerequisites for their success were absent. There was no market and hence no real consumer in criminal justice, and no real prospect of creating one given the special character of the key 'customer' (the offender) and difficulties for providers around market entry and exit. Without even a quasi-market in place, there was no real basis for competition between providers (Le Grand, 1990).

Together, it is argued, these two factors resulted in managerialism; that is, the introduction of a variety of methods and techniques into practice without a meaningful context. They were management tools introduced without a broad understanding, a theory or a praxis of management, and without consent to or support for the change process within agencies.

Managerialism can be, and was, heavily criticised. Its characteristically extreme rationalism in decision-making was arguably inappropriate within a complex and pluralistic setting; its simplistic conversion of service users into consumers made no sense when the service user was an offender; the use of false competition created inequality and artificiality in the contracting process which, in turn, created a paper-chase of new administrative demands.

At the same time, wrapped up in the reforms were a number of important ideas and developments which had, and have, the potential to progress criminal justice, and which can be all too easily overlooked. Among these was the impetus to needs-driven rather than provider-driven services, propelled by a formulae basis for budget calculation. Important, too, was the demand for transparency and the provision of public information in services and service performance as part of a revised approach to public accountability. There was also an emphasis on service quality which, though not necessarily realised, was to persist. Of on-going significance was the focus on service efficiency and practice effectiveness, known within criminal justice as the 'what works' debate. Above all, the identification of purchasers (or commissioners) and providers of service, though never converted into structural reform in most criminal justice settings, facilitated the realisation that public services did not necessarily need to be publicly provided. This made explicit the potential for a mixed economy of provision (public, private and voluntary).

The immediate effect of the imposition of managerial reforms on a reluctant audience was, first, to drive a deep division between government and agencies normally characterised by their conservatism. Second was the deleterious effect on staff morale, particularly among professional groups. The longer term effect is more difficult to estimate. Certainly at the end of the 1990s, variations on managerialism were embedded in criminal justice, as in the wider public service sector, in the UK and abroad, suggesting a continuing influence. At the same time, Labour's commitment to end the introduction of markets into public services, if implemented, must affect the shape of future reform. Rather than dismantling what limited markets currently exist, a more successful way forward might be to concentrate on growing the mixed economy for which the market was itself simply a tool in a transition process from a paternalistic and bureaucratic model of social welfare to a model more appropriate for the future (James, 1997). Getting beyond the market means getting beyond means to ends in criminal justice. It means actively pump-priming private and voluntary sector initiatives to generate a mixed economy; identifying the needs of offenders in addition to the needs of service providers; and, above all, agreeing an overall purpose and change strategy in criminal justice such that strategy drives behaviour and not the other way around.

(At page 116:)

In discussing the influences which have shaped criminal justice in recent years, Part I of this volume (Chapters 2–5) has argued the presence and interplay of four dynamics (politicisation, managerialism, administrative processing and public voice and participation). In thinking about criminal justice for the future, Part II has rehearsed the key features of a revised approach (Chapter 6) and a set of priorities: informing and educating public voice and participation; addressing the reality of crime as it affects the public; addressing the totality of crime, not just that small proportion which reaches the courts; and redesigning and rebalancing the organisation of criminal justice to address the requirements of an informed public rather than those of the official agencies and government departments. Finally, Chapter 7 has gone on to present a possible way forward in the interests of dialogue and discussion.

The extent to which a revised approach emerges for criminal justice depends on developments with regard to each of the four dynamics. Each has the potential to (a) contribute towards the realisation of a more effective criminal justice process and (b) address the crime problem.

The dynamic of *politicisation* is clearly important; fresh direction from political leaders is necessary to move on from the narrow preoccupation with sentencing and punishment of recent years towards a new vision for tackling crime and for relocating criminal justice firmly in its social policy context. It is also vital in the renegotiation of the 'contract' between the state and its people about a shared responsibility for crime.

The dynamic of *managerialism*—though problematic because of the tendency for management to become regarded as an end in itself rather than part of the means by which criminal justice is done better—is also important for the future. Significant weaknesses about the pre-managerial way of doing things have been highlighted and challenged. Much of the complacency and inertia of the past, particularly regarding the way the agencies have approached their responsibilities, has been driven out. The momentum for change that managerialism has created will remain an important attribute underpinning a revised approach to criminal justice. In particular, a revised approach depends on sustaining and developing those legacies of managerialism: needs-driven rather than provider-driven services, more transparency and stronger public accountability, and a focus on effectiveness and outcomes (on 'what works').

The *administrative processing* dynamic, though also in some ways associated with negative attributes of inertia and resistance to change, of organisational fragmentation, and of undue provider-orientation, is important to the revised approach. It provides the key to the translation of policy into practice. Its focus on the practitioners and on how criminal justice works in practice means that it is potentially a very important dynamic in relation to local communities being empowered to take responsibility for crime and encouraged to participate more actively in tackling the problem. The challenge is for practitioners to reorient their work and their organisational and administrative processes so that a stronger relationship with, and accountability to, local communities is achieved.

This brings us to the *public voice and participation* dynamic, which is perhaps the most important key to realisation of the revised approach. Above all, the revised approach builds upon the notion that tackling crime should begin with the reality of crime as it is experienced by the public and as it affects them. The challenge here is to find ways of capturing and engaging the full complexity of public voice and participation in appropriate ways within the criminal justice policy-making process and in its practice.

What, then, is the contemporary purpose of criminal justice? The conclusion from this volume is that first, it remains that identified in the ancient contract between the people and the state—namely, the provision of security in exchange for allegiance. Second, and relevant to the position of the UK in Europe, it is the protection of individual human rights (as presently represented in the European Convention on Human Rights, and endorsed by the Labour Government in 1997).

Recapturing that ancient purpose, and making explicit that new purpose, is the fundamental prerequisite to the rebuilding of trust in the criminal justice agencies and in government on law and order. It is also a prerequisite to public confidence in the view that crime is not, after all, out of control and that there are constructive approaches to be pursued, based on a partnership between the state and its people, which will make a difference.

[1:9] Packer, H, *The Limits of the Criminal Sanction*
(1968) Oxford UP (at page 153)

Two models of the criminal process will let us perceive the normative antinomy at the heart of the criminal law. These models are not labeled 'Is' and 'Ought', nor are they to be taken in that sense. Rather, they represent an attempt to abstract two separate value systems that compete for priority in the operation of the criminal process. Neither is presented as either corresponding to reality or representing the ideal to the exclusion of the other. The two models merely afford a convenient way to talk about the operation of a process whose day-to-day functioning involves a constant series of minute adjustments between the competing demands of two value systems and whose normative future likewise involves a series of resolutions of the tensions between competing claims.

Crime control values

(At page 158:)

The value system that underlies the Crime Control Model is based on the proposition that the repression of criminal conduct is by far the most important function to be performed by the criminal process.

The failure of law enforcement to bring criminal conduct under tight control is viewed as leading to the breakdown of public order and thence to the disappearance of an important condition of human freedom. If the laws go unenforced—which is to say, if it is perceived that there is a high percentage of failure to apprehend and convict in the criminal process—a general disregard for legal controls tends to develop. The law-abiding citizen then becomes the victim of all sorts of unjustifiable invasions of this interests. His security of person and property is sharply diminished, and, therefore, so is his liberty to function as a member of society. The claim ultimately is that the criminal process is a positive guarantor of social freedom. In order to achieve this high purpose, the Crime Control Model requires that primary attention be paid to the efficiency with which the criminal process operates to screen suspects, determine guilt, and secure appropriate dispositions of persons convicted of crime.

The model, in order to operate successfully, must produce a high rate of apprehension and conviction, and must do so in a context where the magnitudes being dealt with are very large and the resources for dealing with them are very limited. There must then be a premium on speed and finality. Speed, in turn, depends on informality and on uniformity; finality depends on minimising the occasions for challenge. The process must not be cluttered up with ceremonious rituals that do not advance the progress of a case. Facts can be established more quickly through interrogation in a police station than through the formal process of examination and cross-examination in a court. It follows that extrajudicial processes should be preferred to judicial processes, informal operations to formal ones. But informality is not enough; there must also be uniformity. Routine, stereotyped procedures are essential if large numbers are being handled. The model that will operate successfully on these presuppositions must be an administrative, almost a managerial, model. The image that comes to mind is an assembly-conveyor belt down which moves an endless stream of cases, never stopping, carrying the cases to workers who stand at fixed stations and who perform on each case as it comes by the same small but essential operation and brings it one step closer to being a finished product, or, to exchange the metaphor for the reality, a closed file. The criminal process, in this model, is seen as a screening process in which each successive stage—pre-arrest investigation, arrest, post-arrest investigation, preparation for trial, trial or entry of plea, conviction, disposition—involves a series of routinised operations whose success is gauged primarily by their tendency to pass the case alone to a successful conclusion.

What is a successful conclusion? One that throws off at an early stage those cases in which it appears unlikely that the person apprehended is an offender and then secures, as expeditiously as possible, the conviction of the rest, with a minimum of occasions for challenge, let alone post-audit. By the application of administrative expertness, primarily that of the police and prosecutors, an early determination of probable innocence or guilt emerges. Those who are probably innocent are screened out. Those who are probably guilty are passed quickly through the remaining stages of the process. The key to the operation of the model regarding those who are not screened out is what I shall call a presumption of guilt. The concept requires some explanation, since it may appear startling to assert that what appears to be the precise converse of our generally accepted ideology of a presumption of innocence can be an essential element of a model that does correspond in some respects to the actual operation of the criminal process.

The presumption of guilt is what makes it possible for the system to deal efficiently with large numbers, as the Crime Control Model demands. The supposition is that the screening processes operated by police and prosecutors are reliable indicators of probable guilt. Once a man has been arrested and investigated without being found to be probably innocent, or, to put it differently, once a determination has been made that there is enough evidence of guilt to permit holding him for further action, then all subsequent activity directed toward him is based on the view that he is probably guilty. The precise point at which this occurs will vary from case to case; in many cases it will occur as soon as the suspect is arrested, or even before, if the evidence of probable guilt that has come to the attention of the authorities is sufficiently strong. But in any case the presumption of guilt will begin to operate well before the 'suspect' becomes a 'defendant'.

The presumption of guilt is not, of course, a thing. Nor is it even a rule of law in the usual sense. It simply is the consequence of a complex of attitudes, a mood.

If there is confidence in the reliability of informal administrative fact-finding activities that take place in the early stages of the criminal process, the remaining stages of the process can be relatively perfunctory without any loss in operating efficiency. The presumption of guilt, as it operates in the Crime Control Model, is the operational expression of that confidence.

Due process values

(At page 163:)

If the Crime Control Model resembles an assembly line, the Due Process Model looks very much like an obstacle course. Each of its successive stages is designed to present formidable impediments to carrying the accused any further along in the process. Its ideology is not the converse of that underlying the Crime Control Model. It does not rest on the idea that it is not socially desirable to repress crime, although critics of its application have been known to claim so. Its ideology is composed of a complex of ideas, some of them based on judgments about the efficacy of crime control devices, others having to do with quite difference considerations. The ideology of due process is far more deeply impressed on the formal structure of the law than is the ideology of crime control; yet an accurate tracing of the strands that make it up is strangely difficult. What follows is only an attempt at an approximation.

The Due Process Model encounters its rival on the Crime Control Model's own ground in respect to the reliability of fact-finding processes. The Crime Control Model, as we have suggested, places heavy reliance on the ability of investigative and prosecutorial officers, acting in an informal setting in which their distinctive skills are given full sway, to elicit and reconstruct a tolerably accurate account of what actually took place in an alleged criminal event. The Due Process Model rejects this premise and substitutes for it a view of informal, non-adjudicative fact-finding that stresses the possibility of error. People are notoriously poor observers of disturbing events-the more emotion-arousing the context, the greater the possibility that recollection will be incorrect; confessions and admissions by persons in police custody may be induced by physical or psychological coercion so that the police end up hearing what the suspect thinks they want to hear rather than the truth; witnesses may be animated by a bias or interest that no one would trouble to discover except one specially charged with protecting the interests of the accused (as the police are not). Considerations of this kind all lead to a rejection of informal fact-finding processes as definitive of factual guilt and to an insistence on formal, adjudicative, adversary fact-finding processes in which the factual case against the accused is publicly heard by an impartial tribunal and is evaluated only after the accused has had a full opportunity to discredit the case against him. Even then, the distrust of fact-finding processes that animates the Due Process Model is not dissipated. The possibilities of human error being what they are, further scrutiny is necessary, or at least must be available, in case facts have been over-looked or suppressed in the heat of battle. How far this subsequent scrutiny must be available is a hotly controverted issue today. In the pure Due Process Model the answer would be: at least as long as there is an allegation of factual error that has not received an adjudicative hearing in a fact-finding context. The demand for finality is thus very low in the Due Process Model.

This strand of due process ideology is not enough to sustain the model. If all that were at issue between the two models was a series of questions about the reliability of fact-finding processes, we would have but one model of the criminal process, the nature of whose constituent elements would pose questions of fact not of value. Even if the discussion is confined, for the moment, to the question of reliability, it is apparent that more is at stake than simply an evaluation of what kinds of fact-finding processes, alone or in combination, are likely to produce the most nearly reliable results. The stumbling block is this: how much reliability is compatible with efficiency?

Granted that informal fact-finding will make some mistakes that can be remedied if backed up by adjudicative fact-finding, the desirability of providing this backup is not affirmed or negated by factual demonstrations or predictions that the increase in reliability will be x per cent or x plus n per cent. It still remains to ask how much weight is to be given to the competing demands of reliability (a high degree of probability in each case that factual guilt has been accurately determined) and efficiency (expeditious handling of the large numbers of cases that the process ingests). The Crime Control Model is more optimistic about the improbability of error in a significant number of cases; but it is also, though only in part therefore, more tolerant about the amount of error that it will put up with. The Due Process Model insists on the prevention and elimination of mistakes to the extent possible; the Crime Control Model accepts the probability of mistakes up to the level at which they interfere with the goal of repressing crime, either because too many guilty people are escaping or, more subtly, because general awareness of the unreliability of the process leads to a decrease in the deterrent efficacy of the criminal law. In this view, reliability and efficiency are not polar opposites but rather complementary characteristics. The system is reliable because efficient reliability becomes a matter of independent concern only when it becomes so attenuated as to impair efficiency. All of this the Due Process Model rejects. If efficiency demands short-cuts around reliability, then absolute efficiency must be rejected. The aim of the process is at least as much to protect the factually innocent as it is to convict the factually guilty. It is a little like quality control in industrial technology: tolerable deviation from standard varies with the importance of conformity to standard in the destined uses of the product. The Due Process Model resembles a factory that has to devote a substantial part of its input to quality control. This necessarily cuts down on quantitative output.

[1:10] Bottoms, A E and McClean, J D, *Defendants in the Criminal Process*

(1976) Routledge and Kegan Paul (at page 228)

The Liberal Bureaucratic Model is the model of the criminal justice process typically held by humane and enlightened clerks to the justices and Crown Court administrators in this country—as well as by many others. It differs substantially from the Crime Control Model, the model typically held by the police, since it dissents from its underlying central value-position: 'The value-system that underlies the Crime Control Model is based on the proposition that the repression of criminal conduct is by far the most important function to be performed by the criminal process' (Packer, 1969, p 158).

The Liberal Bureaucratic Model holds, rather, that the protection of individual liberty, and the need for justice to be done and to be seen to be done, must ultimately override the importance of the repression of criminal conduct. The liberal bureaucrat here joins with the advocate of Due Process in agreeing that formal adjudicative processes are very important, and moreover that—in the conventional phrase—'it is better for ten guilty men to go free than for one innocent man to be convicted'.

But the Liberal Bureaucratic Model also differs substantially from the Due Process Model. For the Due Process Model looks very much like an obstacle course. Each of its successive stages is designed to present formidable impediments to carry the accused any further along in the process...[It] resembled a factory that has to devote a substantial part of its input to quality control. *This necessarily cuts down on quantitative output* (Packer, 1969, pp 163, 165; italics added).

It is precisely this restriction on quantitative output which offends the liberal bureaucrat about the Due Process Model. The liberal bureaucrat is a practical man; he realises that things have to get done, systems have to be run. It is right that the defendant shall have substantial protections; crime control is not the overriding value of the criminal justice system. But these protections must have a limit. If it were not so, then the whole system of criminal justice, with its value to the community in the form of liberal and humane crime control, would collapse. Moreover, it is right to build in sanctions to deter those who might otherwise use their 'Due Process' rights frivolously, or to 'try it on'; an administrative system at State expense should not exist for this kind of time-wasting.

[1:11] King, M, *The Framework of Criminal Justice*

(1981) Croom Helm (at page 13)

Theoretical Models and Their Features

I Social Function	II Process Model	III Features of Court
1. Justice	Due Process Model	(a) Equality between parties (b) Rules protecting defendant against error (c) Restraint of arbitrary power (d) Presumption of innocence
2. Punishment	Crime Control Model	(a) Disregard of legal controls (b) Implicit presumption of guilt (c) High conviction rate (d) Unpleasantness of experience (e) Support for police
3. Rehabilitation	Medical Model (diagnosis, prediction and treatment selection)	(a) Information collecting procedures (b) Individualisation (c) Treatment of presumption (d) Discretion of decision-makers (e) Expertise of decision-makers or advisers (f) Relaxation of formal rules
4. Management of crime and criminals	Bureaucratic Model	(a) Independence from political considerations (b) Speed and efficiency (c) Importance of and acceptance of records (d) Minimisation of conflict (e) Minimisation of expense (f) Economical division of labour
5. Denunciation and degradation	Status Passage Model	(a) Public shaming of defendant (b) Court values reflecting community values (c) Agents' control over the process
6. Maintenance of class domination	Power Model	(a) Reinforcement of class values (b) Alienation and suppression of defendant (c) Deflection of attention from issues of class conflict (d) Differences between judges and judged (e) Paradoxes and contradictions between rhetoric and performance

[1:12] Human Rights Act 1998

Sections 1–6; 8; Schedule 1

1 The Convention Rights

(1) In this Act "the Convention rights" means the rights and fundamental freedoms set out in—

    (a) Articles 2 to 12 and 14 of the Convention,

(b) Articles 1 to 3 of the First Protocol, and

(c) Articles 1 and 2 of the Sixth Protocol,

as read with Articles 16 to 18 of the Convention.

(2) Those Articles are to have effect for the purposes of this Act subject to any designated derogation or reservation (as to which see sections 14 and 15).

(3) The Articles are set out in Schedule 1.

(4) The Lord Chancellor may by order make such amendments to this Act as he considers appropriate to reflect the effect, in relation to the United Kingdom, of a protocol.

(5) In subsection (4) "protocol" means a protocol to the Convention—

(a) which the United Kingdom has ratified; or

(b) which the United Kingdom has signed with a view to ratification.

(6) No amendment may be made by an order under subsection (4) so as to come into force before the protocol concerned is in force in relation to the United Kingdom.

2 Interpretation of Convention rights

(1) A court or tribunal determining a question which has arisen in connection with a Convention right must take into account any—

(a) judgment, decision, declaration or advisory opinion of the European Court of Human Rights,

(b) opinion of the Commission given in a report adopted under Article 31 of the Convention,

(c) decision of the Commission in connection with Article 26 or 27(2) of the Convention, or

(d) decision of the Committee of Ministers taken under Article 46 of the Convention,

whenever made or given, so far as, in the opinion of the court or tribunal, it is relevant to the proceedings in which that question has arisen.

(2) Evidence of any judgment, decision, declaration or opinion of which account may have to be taken under this section is to be given in proceedings before any court or tribunal in such manner as may be provided by rules.

(3) In this section "rules" means rules of court or, in the case of proceedings before a tribunal, rules made for the purposes of this section—

(a) by the Lord Chancellor or the Secretary of State, in relation to any proceedings outside Scotland;

(b) by the Secretary of State, in relation to proceedings in Scotland; or

(c) by a Northern Ireland department, in relation to proceedings before a tribunal in Northern Ireland—

(i) which deals with transferred matters; and

(ii) for which no rules made under paragraph (a) are in force.

Legislation

3 Interpretation of legislation

(1) So far as it is possible to do so, primary legislation and subordinate legislation must be read and given effect in a way which is compatible with the Convention rights.

(2) This section—

(a) applies to primary legislation and subordinate legislation whenever enacted;

(b) does not affect the validity, continuing operation or enforcement of any incompatible primary legislation; and

(c) does not affect the validity, continuing operation or enforcement of any incompatible subordinate legislation if (disregarding any possibility of revocation) primary legislation prevents removal of the incompatibility.

4 Declaration of incompatibility

(1) Subsection (2) applies in any proceedings in which a court determines whether a provision of primary legislation is compatible with a Convention right.

(2) If the court is satisfied that the provision is incompatible with a Convention right, it may make a declaration of that incompatibility.

(3) Subsection (4) applies in any proceedings in which a court determines whether a provision of subordinate legislation, made in the exercise of a power conferred by primary legislation, is compatible with a Convention right.

(4) If the court is satisfied—

(a) that the provision is incompatible with a Convention right, and

(b) that (disregarding any possibility of revocation) the primary legislation concerned prevents removal of the incompatibility,

it may make a declaration of that incompatibility.

(5) In this section "court" means—

(a) the House of Lords;

(b) the Judicial Committee of the Privy Council;

(c) the Courts-Martial Appeal Court;

(d) in Scotland, the High Court of Justiciary sitting otherwise than as a trial court or the Court of Session;

(e) in England and Wales or Northern Ireland, the High Court or the Court of Appeal.

(6) A declaration under this section ("a declaration of incompatibility")—

(a) does not affect the validity, continuing operation or enforcement of the provision in respect of which it is given; and

(b) is not binding on the parties to the proceedings in which it is made.

5 Right of Crown to intervene

(1) Where a court is considering whether to make a declaration of incompatibility, the Crown is entitled to notice in accordance with rules of court.

(2) In any case to which subsection (1) applies—

(a) a Minister of the Crown (or a person nominated by him),

(b) a member of the Scottish Executive,

(c) a Northern Ireland Minister,

(d) a Northern Ireland department,

is entitled, on giving notice in accordance with rules of court, to be joined as a party to the proceedings.

(3) Notice under subsection (2) may be given at any time during the proceedings.

(4) A person who has been made a party to criminal proceedings (other than in Scotland) as the result of a notice under subsection (2) may, with leave, appeal to the House of Lords against any declaration of incompatibility made in the proceedings.

(5) In subsection (4)—

"criminal proceedings" includes all proceedings before the Courts-Martial Appeal Court; and

"leave" means leave granted by the court making the declaration of incompatibility or by the House of Lords.

Public authorities

6 Acts of public authorities

(1) It is unlawful for a public authority to act in a way which is incompatible with a Convention right.

(2) Subsection (1) does not apply to an act if—

(a) as the result of one or more provisions of primary legislation, the authority could not have acted differently; or

(b) in the case of one or more provisions of, or made under, primary legislation which cannot be read or given effect in a way which is compatible with the Convention rights, the authority was acting so as to give effect to or enforce those provisions.

(3) In this section "public authority" includes—

(a) a court or tribunal, and

(b) any person certain of whose functions are functions of a public nature,

but does not include either House of Parliament or a person exercising functions in connection with proceedings in Parliament.

(4) In subsection (3) "Parliament" does not include the House of Lords in its judicial capacity.

(5) In relation to a particular act, a person is not a public authority by virtue only of subsection (3)(b) if the nature of the act is private.

(6) "An act" includes a failure to act but does not include a failure to—

(a) introduce in, or lay before, Parliament a proposal for legislation; or

(b) make any primary legislation or remedial order.

. . .

8 Judicial remedies

(1) In relation to any act (or proposed act) of a public authority which the court finds is (or would be) unlawful, it may grant such relief or remedy, or make such order, within its powers as it considers just and appropriate.

(2) But damages may be awarded only by a court which has power to award damages, or to order the payment of compensation, in civil proceedings.

(3) No award of damages is to be made unless, taking account of all the circumstances of the case, including—

(a) any other relief or remedy granted, or order made, in relation to the act in question (by that or any other court), and

(b) the consequences of any decision (of that or any other court) in respect of that act,

the court is satisfied that the award is necessary to afford just satisfaction to the person in whose favour it is made.

(4) In determining—

(a) whether to award damages, or

(b) the amount of an award,

the court must take into account the principles applied by the European Court of Human Rights in relation to the award of compensation under Article 41 of the Convention.

(5) A public authority against which damages are awarded is to be treated—

(a) in Scotland, for the purposes of section 3 of the Law Reform (Miscellaneous Provisions) (Scotland) Act 1940 as if the award were made in an action of damages in which the authority has been found liable in respect of loss or damage to the person to whom the award is made;

(b) for the purposes of the Civil Liability (Contribution) Act 1978 as liable in respect of damage suffered by the person to whom the award is made.

(6) In this section—

"court" includes a tribunal;

"damages" means damages for an unlawful act of a public authority; and

"unlawful" means unlawful under section 6(1).

SCHEDULE 1
The Articles

Section 1(3)

Part I
The Convention Rights and Freedoms

Article 2
Right to life

1 Everyone's right to life shall be protected by law. No one shall be deprived of his life intentionally save in the execution of a sentence of a court following his conviction of a crime for which this penalty is provided by law.

2 Deprivation of life shall not be regarded as inflicted in contravention of this Article when it results from the use of force which is no more than absolutely necessary:

(a) in defence of any person from unlawful violence;

(b) in order to effect a lawful arrest or to prevent the escape of a person lawfully detained;

(c) in action lawfully taken for the purpose of quelling a riot or insurrection.

Article 3
Prohibition of torture

No one shall be subjected to torture or to inhuman or degrading treatment or punishment.

Article 4
Prohibition of slavery and forced labour

1 No one shall be held in slavery or servitude.

2 No one shall be required to perform forced or compulsory labour.

3 For the purpose of this Article the term "forced or compulsory labour" shall not include:

(a) any work required to be done in the ordinary course of detention imposed according to the provisions of Article 5 of this Convention or during conditional release from such detention;

(b) any service of a military character or, in case of conscientious objectors in countries where they are recognised, service exacted instead of compulsory military service;

(c) any service exacted in case of an emergency or calamity threatening the life or well-being of the community;

(d) any work or service which forms part of normal civic obligations.

Article 5
Right to liberty and security

1 Everyone has the right to liberty and security of person. No one shall be deprived of his liberty save in the following cases and in accordance with a procedure prescribed by law:

(a) the lawful detention of a person after conviction by a competent court;

(b) the lawful arrest or detention of a person for non-compliance with the lawful order of a court or in order to secure the fulfilment of any obligation prescribed by law;

(c) the lawful arrest or detention of a person effected for the purpose of bringing him before the competent legal authority on reasonable suspicion of having committed an offence or when it is reasonably considered necessary to prevent his committing an offence or fleeing after having done so;

(d) the detention of a minor by lawful order for the purpose of educational supervision or his lawful detention for the purpose of bringing him before the competent legal authority;

(e) the lawful detention of persons for the prevention of the spreading of infectious diseases, of persons of unsound mind, alcoholics or drug addicts or vagrants;

(f) the lawful arrest or detention of a person to prevent his effecting an unauthorised entry into the country or of a person against whom action is being taken with a view to deportation or extradition.

2 Everyone who is arrested shall be informed promptly, in a language which he understands, of the reasons for his arrest and of any charge against him.

3 Everyone arrested or detained in accordance with the provisions of paragraph 1(c) of this Article shall be brought promptly before a judge or other officer authorised by law to exercise judicial power and shall be entitled to trial within a reasonable time or to release pending trial. Release may be conditioned by guarantees to appear for trial.

4 Everyone who is deprived of his liberty by arrest or detention shall be entitled to take proceedings by which the lawfulness of his detention shall be decided speedily by a court and his release ordered if the detention is not lawful.

5 Everyone who has been the victim of arrest or detention in contravention of the provisions of this Article shall have an enforceable right to compensation.

Article 6
Right to a fair trial

1 In the determination of his civil rights and obligations or of any criminal charge against him, everyone is entitled to a fair and public hearing within a reasonable time by an independent and impartial tribunal established by law. Judgment shall be pronounced publicly but the press and public may be excluded from all or part of the trial in the interest of morals, public order or national security in a democratic society, where the interests of juveniles or the protection of the private life of the parties so require, or to the extent strictly necessary in the opinion of the court in special circumstances where publicity would prejudice the interests of justice.

2 Everyone charged with a criminal offence shall be presumed innocent until proved guilty according to law.

3 Everyone charged with a criminal offence has the following minimum rights:

(a) to be informed promptly, in a language which he understands and in detail, of the nature and cause of the accusation against him;

(b) to have adequate time and facilities for the preparation of his defence;

(c) to defend himself in person or through legal assistance of his own choosing or, if he has not sufficient means to pay for legal assistance, to be given it free when the interests of justice so require;

(d) to examine or have examined witnesses against him and to obtain the attendance and examination of witnesses on his behalf under the same conditions as witnesses against him;

(e) to have the free assistance of an interpreter if he cannot understand or speak the language
used in court.

Article 7
No punishment without law

1 No one shall be held guilty of any criminal offence on account of any act or omission which did
not constitute a criminal offence under national or international law at the time when it was committed. Nor shall a heavier penalty be imposed than the one that was applicable at the time the
criminal offence was committed.

2 This Article shall not prejudice the trial and punishment of any person for any act or omission
which, at the time when it was committed, was criminal according to the general principles of law
recognised by civilised nations.

Article 8
Right to respect for private and family life

1 Everyone has the right to respect for his private and family life, his home and his correspondence.

2 There shall be no interference by a public authority with the exercise of this right except such as
is in accordance with the law and is necessary in a democratic society in the interests of national
security, public safety or the economic well-being of the country, for the prevention of disorder
or crime, for the protection of health or morals, or for the protection of the rights and freedoms
of others.

Article 9
Freedom of thought, conscience and religion

1 Everyone has the right to freedom of thought, conscience and religion; this right includes freedom
to change his religion or belief and freedom, either alone or in community with others and in
public or private, to manifest his religion or belief, in worship, teaching, practice and observance.

2 Freedom to manifest one's religion or beliefs shall be subject only to such limitations as are prescribed by law and are necessary in a democratic society in the interests of public safety, for the
protection of public order, health or morals, or for the protection of the rights and freedoms of
others.

Article 10
Freedom of expression

1 Everyone has the right to freedom of expression. This right shall include freedom to hold opinions
and to receive and impart information and ideas without interference by public authority and
regardless of frontiers. This Article shall not prevent States from requiring the licensing of broad-
casting, television or cinema enterprises.

2 The exercise of these freedoms, since it carries with it duties and responsibilities, may be subject
to such formalities, conditions, restrictions or penalties as are prescribed by law and are necessary
in a democratic society, in the interests of national security, territorial integrity or public safety, for
the prevention of disorder or crime, for the protection of health or morals, for the protection of the
reputation or rights of others, for preventing the disclosure of information received in confidence,
or for maintaining the authority and impartiality of the judiciary.

Article 11
Freedom of assembly and association

1 Everyone has the right to freedom of peaceful assembly and to freedom of association with others, including the right to form and to join trade unions for the protection of his interests.

2   No restrictions shall be placed on the exercise of these rights other than such as are prescribed by law and are necessary in a democratic society in the interests of national security or public safety, for the prevention of disorder or crime, for the protection of health or morals or for the protection of the rights and freedoms of others. This Article shall not prevent the imposition of lawful restrictions on the exercise of these rights by members of the armed forces, of the police or of the administration of the State.

Article 12
Right to marry

Men and women of marriageable age have the right to marry and to found a family, according to the national laws governing the exercise of this right.

Article 14
Prohibition of discrimination

The enjoyment of the rights and freedoms set forth in this Convention shall be secured without discrimination on any ground such as sex, race, colour, language, religion, political or other opinion, national or social origin, association with a national minority, property, birth or other status.

Article 16
Restrictions on political activity of aliens

Nothing in Articles 10, 11 and 14 shall be regarded as preventing the High Contracting Parties from imposing restrictions on the political activity of aliens.

Article 17
Prohibition of abuse of rights

Nothing in this Convention may be interpreted as implying for any State, group or person any right to engage in any activity or perform any act aimed at the destruction of any of the rights and freedoms set forth herein or at their limitation to a greater extent than is provided for in the Convention.

Article 18
Limitation on use of restrictions on rights

The restrictions permitted under this Convention to the said rights and freedoms shall not be applied for any purpose other than those for which they have been prescribed.

Part II
The First Protocol

Article 1
Protection of property

Every natural or legal person is entitled to the peaceful enjoyment of his possessions. No one shall be deprived of his possessions except in the public interest and subject to the conditions provided for by law and by the general principles of international law.

The preceding provisions shall not, however, in any way impair the right of a State to enforce such laws as it deems necessary to control the use of property in accordance with the general interest or to secure the payment of taxes or other contributions or penalties.

Article 2
Right to education

No person shall be denied the right to education. In the exercise of any functions which it assumes in relation to education and to teaching, the State shall respect the right of parents to ensure such education and teaching in conformity with their own religious and philosophical convictions.

Article 3
Right to free elections

The High Contracting Parties undertake to hold free elections at reasonable intervals by secret ballot, under conditions which will ensure the free expression of the opinion of the people in the choice of the legislature.

Part III
The Sixth Protocol

Article 1
Abolition of the death penalty

The death penalty shall be abolished. No one shall be condemned to such penalty or executed.

Article 2
Death penalty in time of war

A State may make provision in its law for the death penalty in respect of acts committed in time of war or of imminent threat of war; such penalty shall be applied only in the instances laid down in the law and in accordance with its provisions. The State shall communicate to the Secretary General of the Council of Europe the relevant provisions of that law.

[1:13] *Dickson v United Kingdom*

(2008) 46 EHRR 41

Kirk and Lorraine Dickson are British nationals who were born in 1972 and 1958, respectively. Mr Dickson is in Dovergate Prison, Uttoxeter (United Kingdom) and Mrs Dickson lives in Hull (United Kingdom). In 1994 Mr Dickson was convicted of murder and sentenced to life imprisonment with a minimum tariff of 15 years. He has no children. In 1999 he met Lorraine, via a prison pen pal network while she was also imprisoned. In 2001 they married. Mrs Dickson already had three children. The couple requested artificial insemination facilities to enable them to have a child together, arguing that it would not otherwise be possible, given Mr Dickson's earliest release date and Mrs Dickson's age. The Secretary of State refused their application. They appealed unsuccessfully in the domestic courts and then to the European Court of Human Rights.

The European Court of Human Rights (by 12 votes to 8) held that there was a breach of Art 8:

31. The European Prison Rules are recommendations of the Committee of Ministers to Member States of the Council of Europe as to the minimum standards to be applied in prisons. States are encouraged to be guided in legislation and policies by those rules and to ensure wide dissemination of the Rules to their judicial authorities as well as to prison staff and inmates.

The 1987 version of the European Prison Rules ("the 1987 Rules") notes, as its third basic principle, that:

'The purposes of the treatment of persons in custody shall be such as to sustain their health and self-respect and, so far as the length of sentence permits, to develop their sense of responsibility and encourage those attitudes and skills that will assist them to return to society with the best chance of leading law-abiding and self-supporting lives after their release.'

The latest version of those Rules adopted in 2006 ("the 2006 Rules"), replaces this above-cited principle with three principles:

"Rule 2: Persons deprived of their liberty retain all rights that are not lawfully taken away by the decision sentencing them or remanding them in custody.

...

Rule 5: Life in prison shall approximate as closely as possible the positive aspects of life in the community.

Rule 6: All detention shall be managed so as to facilitate the reintegration into free society of persons who have been deprived of their liberty."

The commentary on the 2006 Rules (prepared by the European Committee on Crime Problems—"CDPC") noted that Rule 2 emphasises that the loss of the right to liberty should not lead to an assumption that prisoners automatically lose other political, civil, social, economic and cultural rights so that restrictions should be as few as possible. Rule 5, the commentary observes, underlines the positive aspects of normalisation recognising that, while life in prison can never be the same as life in a free society, active steps should be taken to make conditions in prison as close to normal life as possible. The commentary further states that Rule 6 "recognises that prisoners, both untried and sentenced, will eventually return to the community and that prison life has to be organised with this in mind".

32. The first section of Part VII [VIII] of the 2006 Rules is entitled "the objective of the regime for sentenced prisoners" and provides, *inter alia*:

"102.1 In addition to the rules that apply to all prisoners, the regime for sentenced prisoners shall be designed to enable them to lead a responsible and crime-free life.

102.2 Imprisonment is by the deprivation of liberty a punishment in itself and therefore the regime for sentenced prisoners shall not aggravate the suffering inherent in imprisonment."

In these respects, the CDPC commentary explains that Rule 102:

"...states the objectives of the regime for prisoners in simple, positive terms. The emphasis is on measures and programmes for sentenced prisoners that will encourage and develop individual responsibility rather than focussing narrowly on the prevention of recidivism....

The new Rule is in line with the requirements of key international instruments including Article 10(3) of the [ICCPR], ...However, unlike the ICCPR, the formulation here deliberately avoids the use of the term, 'rehabilitation', which carries with it the connotation of forced treatment. Instead, it highlights the importance of providing sentenced prisoners, who often come from socially deprived backgrounds, the opportunity to develop in a way that will enable them to choose to lead law-abiding lives. In this regard Rule 102 follows the same approach as Rule 58 of the United Nations Standard Minimum Rules for the Treatment of Prisoners."

33. Rule 105.1 of the 2006 Rules provides that a systematic programme of work shall seek to contribute to meeting the objective of the prison regime. Rule 106.1 provides that a systematic programme of education, with the objective of improving prisoners' overall level of education, as well as the prospects of leading a responsible and crime-free life, shall be a key part of regimes for sentenced prisoners. Finally, Rule 107.1 requires that the release of sentenced prisoners should be accompanied by special programmes enabling them to make the transition to a law-abiding life in the community.

34. The reason for the evolution towards the 2006 Rules can be understood through two Committee of Ministers recommendations, both of which address the rehabilitative dimension of prison sentences.

(And at paragraph 68:)

...

a person retains his or her Convention rights on imprisonment, so that any restriction on those rights must be justified in each individual case. This justification can flow, *inter alia*, from the necessary and inevitable consequences of imprisonment (§ 27 of the Chamber judgment) or (as accepted by the applicants before the Grand Chamber) from an adequate link between the restriction and the circumstances of the prisoner in question. However, it cannot be based solely on what would offend public opinion.

Negative or positive obligations

69. The parties disagreed as to whether the refusal of the requested facilities constituted an interference with the applicants' existing right to beget a child (to be analysed in the context of the State's

negative obligations) or a failure by the State to grant a right which did not previously exist (an alleged positive obligation). The Chamber considered that the applicants' complaints fell to be analysed as a positive obligation.

70. The Court recalls that, although the object of Article 8 is essentially that of protecting the individual against arbitrary interference by the public authorities, it does not merely compel the State to abstain from such interference. In addition to this primarily negative undertaking, there may be positive obligations inherent in an effective respect for private and family life. These obligations may involve the adoption of measures designed to secure respect for private and family life even in the sphere of the relations of individuals between themselves. The boundaries between the State's positive and negative obligations under Article 8 do not lend themselves to precise definition. The applicable principles are nonetheless similar. In particular, in both instances regard must be had to the fair balance to be struck between the competing interests (*Odièvre c. France* [GC], n° 42326/98, § 40, CEDH 2003-III, and *Evans*, cited above, § 75).

71. The Court does not consider it necessary to decide whether it would be more appropriate to analyse the case as one concerning a positive or a negative obligation since it is of the view that the core issue in the present case (see paragraphs 77–85 below) is precisely whether a fair balance was struck between the competing public and private interests involved.

The conflicting individual and public interests

72. As to the applicants' interests, it was accepted domestically that artificial insemination remained the only realistic hope of the applicants, a couple since 1999 and married since 2001, of having a child together given the second applicant's age and the first applicant's release date. The Court considers it evident that the matter was of vital importance to the applicants.

73. The Government have cited three justifications for the Policy.

74. Before the Grand Chamber they first relied on the suggestion that losing the opportunity to beget children was an inevitable and necessary consequence of imprisonment.

Whilst the inability to beget a child might be a consequence of imprisonment, it is not an inevitable one, it not being suggested that the grant of artificial insemination facilities would involve any security issues or impose any significant administrative or financial demands on the State.

75. Secondly, before the Grand Chamber the Government appeared to maintain, although did not emphasise, another justification for the Policy namely, that public confidence in the prison system would be undermined if the punitive and deterrent elements of a sentence would be circumvented by allowing prisoners guilty of certain serious offences to conceive children.

The Court, as the Chamber, reiterates that there is no place under the Convention system, where tolerance and broadmindedness are the acknowledged hallmarks of democratic society, for automatic forfeiture of rights by prisoners based purely on what might offend public opinion (*Hirst*, cited above §70). However, the Court could accept, as did the Chamber, that the maintaining of public confidence in the penal system has a role to play in the development of penal policy. The Government also appeared to maintain that the restriction, of itself, contributed to the overall punitive objective of imprisonment. However, and while accepting that punishment remains one of the aims of imprisonment, the Court would also underline the evolution in European penal policy towards the increasing relative importance of the rehabilitative aim of imprisonment, particularly towards the end of a long prison sentence (see paragraphs 28–36 above).

76. Thirdly, the Government argued that the absence of a parent for a long period would have a negative impact on any child conceived and, consequently, on society as a whole.

The Court is prepared to accept as legitimate, for the purposes of the second paragraph of Article 8, that the authorities, when developing and applying the Policy, should concern themselves, as a matter of principle, with the welfare of any child: conception of a child was the very object of the exercise. Moreover, the State has a positive obligations to ensure the effective protection of children (*L.C.B. v. the United Kingdom*, judgment of 9 June 1998, *Reports of Judgments and Decisions* 1998-III, § 36; *Osman v. the United Kingdom*, judgment of 28 October 1998, *Reports* 1998-VIII, § 115–116; and *Z and Others v. the United Kingdom* [GC], no. 29392/95, § 73, ECHR 2001-V). However, that cannot go so far as to prevent parents who so wish from attempting to conceive a child in circumstances like those of the present case, especially as the second applicant was at liberty and could have taken care of any child conceived until such time as her husband was released.

Balancing the conflicting interests and the margin of appreciation

77. Since the national authorities make the initial assessment as to where the fair balance lies in a case before a final evaluation by this Court, a certain margin of appreciation is, in principle, accorded by this Court to those authorities as regards that assessment. The breadth of this margin varies and depends on a number of factors including the nature of the activities restricted and the aims pursued by the restrictions (*Smith and Grady v. the United Kingdom*, nos. 33985/96 and 33986/96, § 88, ECHR 1999-VI).

78. Accordingly, where a particularly important facet of an individual's existence or identity is at stake (such as the choice to become a genetic parent), the margin of appreciation accorded to a State will in general be restricted.

Where, however, there is no consensus within the Member States of the Council of Europe, either as to the relative importance of the interest at stake or as to how best to protect it, the margin will be wider. This is particularly so where the case raises complex issues and choices of social strategy: the authorities' direct knowledge of their society and its needs means that they are in principle better placed than the international judge to appreciate what is in the public interest. In such a case, the Court would generally respect the legislature's policy choice unless it is "manifestly without reasonable foundation". There will also usually be a wide margin accorded if the State is required to strike a balance between competing private and public interests or Convention rights (*Evans*, cited above, § 77).

79. Importantly, in its *Hirst* judgment , the Court commented that, while there was no European consensus on the point so that a wide margin of appreciation applied, it was not all-embracing. It found that neither the legislature nor the judiciary had sought to weigh the competing interests or assess the proportionality of the relevant restriction on prisoners. That restriction was considered to be "a blunt instrument" which indiscriminately stripped a significant category of prisoners of their Convention rights and it imposed a blanket and automatic restriction on all convicted prisoners irrespective of the length of their sentence, the nature or gravity of their offence or of their individual circumstances. The Court continued (*Hirst*, § 82):

"Such a general, automatic and indiscriminate restriction on a vitally important Convention right must be seen as falling outside any acceptable margin of appreciation, however wide that margin might be, and as being incompatible with Article 3 of Protocol No. 1."

80. In the present case, the parties disputed the breadth of the margin of appreciation to be accorded to the authorities. The applicants suggested that the margin had no role to play since the Policy had never been subjected to parliamentary scrutiny and allowed for no real proportionality examination. The Government maintained that a wide margin of appreciation applied given the positive obligation context, since the Policy was not a blanket one and since there was no European consensus on the subject.

81. The Court notes, as to the European consensus argument, that the Chamber established that more than half of the Contracting States allow for conjugal visits for prisoners (subject to a variety of different restrictions), a measure which could be seen as obviating the need for the authorities to provide additional facilities for artificial insemination. However, while the Court has expressed its approval for the evolution in several European countries towards conjugal visits, it has not yet interpreted the Convention as requiring Contracting States to make provision for such visits (see the above-cited *Aliev* judgment, at § 188). Accordingly, this is an area in which the Contracting States could enjoy a wide margin of appreciation in determining the steps to be taken to ensure compliance with the Convention with due regard to the needs and resources of the community and of individuals.

82. However, and even assuming that the judgment of the Court of Appeal in the *Mellor* case amounted to judicial consideration of the Policy under Article 8 (despite its pre-incorporation and judicial review context, see paragraphs 23–26 above), the Court considers that the Policy as structured effectively excluded any real weighing of the competing individual and public interests, and prevented the required assessment of the proportionality of a restriction, in any individual case.

In particular, and having regard to the judgment of Lord Phillips MR in the *Mellor* case and of Auld LJ in the present case, the Policy placed an inordinately high "exceptionality" burden on the applicants when requesting artificial insemination facilities (see paragraphs 13, 15–17 and 23–26 above). They had to demonstrate, in the first place, as a condition precedent to the application of the Policy, that the deprivation of artificial insemination facilities might prevent conception altogether (the "starting point"). Secondly, and of even greater significance, they had to go on to demonstrate that the circumstances of their case were "exceptional" within the meaning of the remaining criteria of the Policy ("the finishing point"). The Court considers that even if the applicants' Article 8 complaint was before the Secretary of State and the Court of Appeal, the Policy set the threshold so high against them from the outset that it did not allow a balancing of the competing individual and public interests and a proportionality test by the Secretary of State or by the domestic courts in their case, as required by the Convention (see, *mutatis mutandis*, *Smith and Grady*, cited above § 138).

83. In addition, there is no evidence that, when fixing the Policy the Secretary of State sought to weigh the relevant competing individual and public interests or assess the proportionality of the restriction. Further, since the Policy was not embodied in primary legislation, the various competing interests were never weighed, nor were issues of proportionality ever assessed, by Parliament (see the above-cited judgments in *Hirst*, § 79, and *Evans*, §§ 86–89). Indeed, the Policy was adopted, as noted in the judgment of the Court of Appeal in the *Mellor* case (see paragraph 23 above), prior to the incorporation of the Convention into domestic law.

84. The Policy may not amount to a blanket ban such as was at issue in the *Hirst* case since in principle any prisoner could apply and, as demonstrated by the statistics submitted by the Government, three couples did so successfully. Whatever the precise reason for the dearth of applications for such facilities and the refusal of the majority of the few requests maintained, the Court does not consider that the statistics provided by the Government undermine the above finding that the Policy did not permit the required proportionality assessment in an individual case. Neither was it persuasive to argue, as the Government did, that the starting point of exceptionality was reasonable since only a few persons would be affected, implying as it did the possibility of justifying the restriction of the applicants' Convention rights by the minimal number of persons adversely affected.

85. The Court therefore finds that the absence of such an assessment as regards a matter of significant importance for the applicants (see paragraph 72 above) must be seen as falling outside any acceptable margin of appreciation so that a fair balance was not struck between the competing public and private interests involved. There has, accordingly, been a violation of Article 8 of the Convention.

Compare this with the dissenting judgement of five of the judges:

As the judgment points out, a growing number of Contracting Parties have made possible conjugal visits in prisons, subject to a variety of different restrictions (paragraph 81). Nevertheless, the Court's case-law has not interpreted Articles 8 and 12 as requiring Contracting States to make provision for conjugal visits in prisons. We fail to see how it can be argued that there is no right to conjugal visits in prisons, but that there is instead a right for the provision of artificial insemination facilities in prisons (this interpretation results implicitly from paragraphs 67–68, 74, 81 and 91). Not only is this contradictory. It also plays down the wide margin of appreciation which States enjoy (and should enjoy) in this field.

The margin of appreciation of Member States is wider where there is no consensus within the States and where no core guarantees are restricted. States have direct knowledge of their society and its needs, which the Court does not have. Where they provide for an adequate legal basis, where the legal restrictions serve a legitimate aim and where there is room to balance different interests, the margin of appreciation of States should be recognized.

This is so in the instant case. The Government's Policy allowed for the balancing of interests and was not a blanket one. The British courts did balance the various interests. We fail to see how the majority of the Grand Chamber can claim that there was no weighing of the "relevant competing individual and public interests" (paragraph 83).

To the contrary, in our view the majority did not weigh several interests that ought to have deserved consideration. Thus the Court might have wished to discuss the very low chances of a positive outcome of in vitro fertilization of women aged 45 (see Bradley J. Van Voorhis, "In Vitro Fertilization", *New England Journal of Medicine* 2007 356: 4 pp. 379–386). The Court also fails to address the question whether all sorts of couples (for example, a man in prison and the woman outside, a woman in prison and the man outside, a homosexual couple with one of the partners in prison and the other outside) may request artificial insemination facilities for prisoners. We are of the opinion that in this respect too States should enjoy an important margin of appreciation.

In conclusion, in the specific circumstances of the case (the couple established a pen-pal relation while both were serving prison sentences; the couple had never lived together; there was a 14-year age difference between them; the man had a violent background; the woman was at an age where natural or artificial procreation was hardly possible and in any case risky; and any child which might be conceived would be without the presence of a father for an important part of his or her childhood years), it could not be said that the British authorities had acted arbitrarily or had neglected the welfare of the child which would be born.

[1:14] Criminal Justice Act 1991

Section 95

95 Information for financial and other purposes

(1) The Secretary of State shall in each year publish such information as he considers expedient for the purpose of—

    (a) enabling persons engaged in the administration of criminal justice to become aware of the financial implications of their decisions; or

    (b) facilitating the performance by such persons of their duty to avoid discriminating against any persons on the ground of race or sex or any other improper ground.

(2) Publication under subsection (1) above shall be effected in such manner as the Secretary of State considers appropriate for the purpose of bringing the information to the attention of the persons concerned.

[1:15] *Statistics on Race and the Criminal Justice System, 2006*

A Ministry of Justice publication under section 95 of the Criminal Justice Act 1991 (October 2007)

Executive Summary

General Findings

This report provides details of how members of the Black and Minority Ethnic (BME) community in England and Wales are represented in our Criminal Justice System. As a statistical publication, it does not aim to provide a detailed commentary on the figures. Nevertheless, analysis here shows that members of our Black communities are seven times more likely than their White counterparts to be stopped and searched, three and a half times more likely to be arrested, and six times more likely to be in prison. Many criminal justice agencies are, however, employing proportionately more people from BME communities. For example, the Prison Service has met its targets for minority ethnic representation, with the proportion of BME officers standing at 4.6% in 2005/6. The Office for Criminal Justice Reform in the Ministry of Justice is working to ensure agencies collect the data they need to enable more effective ethnic monitoring. Providing detailed statistics on the experiences of BME communities in our Criminal Justice System is an essential step towards ensuring justice for all.

TABLE A Proportion (%) of ethnic groups at different stages of the criminal justice process, England and Wales, 2005/6

	Ethnicity					
	White	Black	Asian	Other	Unknown/ not recorded	Total
General population (aged ten and over) @ 2001 census	91.3	2.8	4.7	1.2	0.0	100
Stops and searches(1)	72.2	15.4	7.9	1.6	2.9	100
Arrests(2)	83.8	9.1	5.1	1.3	0.6	100
Cautions(2)	83.5	6.3	4.5	1.4	4.4	100
Youth offences(4)	87.6	6.0	3.2	0.3	2.8	100
Tried at Crown Court(3)	76.3	12.6	7.3	3.9	-	100
Prison population(4)(5)	75.5	15.6	6.8	1.3	0.9	100

Note: Figures may not add to 100% due to rounding.

(1) Stops and searches recorded by the police under section 1 of the Police and Criminal Evidence Act 1984 and other legislation.

(2) Notifiable offences.

(3) Information on ethnicity is missing in 19% of cases; therefore, percentages are based on known ethnicity.

(4) To make the data in this row consistent with the rest of the table the proportion for Mixed has been excluded because this information is not available for stops and searches, arrests, cautions and Crown Court.

(5) Sentenced.

Specific Findings

Victims and Homicide

- The latest British Crime Survey (BCS) estimates that there were around 139,000 racially motivated incidents in 2005/06. This compares with a total of 179,000 incidents reported by the 2004/05 BCS.

- However, as with most crime, the majority of racial incidents are not reported to the police. During 2005/06 60,407 racist incidents were recorded by the police, a rise of 4% over 2004/05. There were 41,382 racially or religiously aggravated offences in 2005/06, a 12% increase from the previous year (37,028 in 2004/05). Well over half (62%) of these were offences of harassment. The clear-up rate for racially or religiously aggravated offences has improved over the last three years (34% in 2003/04, 37% in 2004/05, and 38% in 2005/06).

- The police recorded 2,327 homicides in the three-year period ending 2005/06. Ten per cent of homicides in 2005/06 were of Black people, 7% of Asian people and 4% of 'Other' minority ethnic groups. Black victims (28%) were more likely to be shot compared with Asian (10%) and White (5%) victims. Twenty-three homicides were recorded as being racially motivated over the three-year period.

Section 1 PACE: Stop and Search

- The police recorded 878,153 stop and searches under section 1 of the Police and Criminal Evidence Act 1984 and other legislation in 2005/6. This is an increase of over 3% on 2004/5, and is the highest figure since 1998/9. Of the searches carried out in 2005/6, 15% were of Black people, 8% of Asian people and 2% of people of 'Other' ethnic origin.

- Relative to the general population, Black people were seven times more likely to be stopped and searched under these powers than White people, a higher rate than 2004/5, when Black people were six times more likely to be stopped and searched than White people. Asian people were twice as likely to be stopped and searched than White people, a similar rate to the previous year. The main reason for conducting a stop and search under these powers across all ethnic groups was for drugs, as was the case in 2004/5.

- Changes in the relative proportions of Black and White people stopped and searched from 2004/5 to 2005/6 appear to be due, at least in part, to changes amongst some police forces in relation to the use of stop and search powers. Because London has the largest number of Black residents, the Metropolitan Police conduct over 75% of all stop and searches of Black people in England and Wales. Between 2004/5 and 2005/6, despite an 18% increase in the numbers of people stopped and searched in the Metropolitan Police area, disproportionality remained relatively stable; Black people were around 4.5 times more likely to be stopped and searched than White people. However, some police forces outside London significantly reduced the total number of stop and searches they conducted between 2004/5 and 2005/6. Among some of these forces, although the number of White persons stopped and searched has reduced, the numbers of Black people stopped and searched has not changed by a similar proportion. This relative difference is partly responsible for the overall increase in disproportionality.

Arrests and Cautions

- In 2005/06 1,429,785 arrests for notifiable offences took place, an increase of just under 6% on the previous year. Of these arrests, 9% were recorded as being of Black people, 5% Asian and 1% 'Other' ethnic origin. Compared with 2004/05, the number of arrests of Asian people increased by 11% and for Black people by 10%.

- Relative to the general population, Black people were 3.5 times more likely to be arrested than White people (compared with 3.4 times more likely the previous year). There were variations across forces in the proportions of individuals from different ethnic groups being arrested for specific types of offence. The police cautioned 285,116 persons for notifiable offences in 2005. Of these, 6% were recorded as Black people, 4% Asian and 1% of 'Other' ethnic origin.

- There was a lower use of cautioning for Black offenders relative to arrests (14%) compared with White offenders (20%).

Prosecutions and Sentencing

- The Crown Prosection Service (CPS) has undertaken an Equality and Diversity Impact Assessment of statutory charging covering nearly 560,000 cases in the 12 months April 2005 to March 2006, during which statutory charging was extended to all areas of England and Wales. Its main purposes are to assess the impact of statutory charging and discover if charging decisions vary with the gender, ethnicity and age of the suspect, and, when charged, the type of offence with which suspects are charged. The impact assessment revealed no variation of charging decision by the main ethnic group of the suspect except *White* suspects (25%) are slightly more likely to receive a decision to make no prosecution on evidential grounds compared to non-*White* suspects (for example, *Black, Mixed* or *Other* suspects, all lower at around 18–20%).

- Ethnicity was recorded in only 20% of the magistrates' court data supplied to the Home Office for cases in England and Wales for 2005—compared with 19% in the previous year. Combining information collected from five police force areas on magistrates' court decisions in 2005 shows that, excluding those defendants committed to the Crown Court for trial, 60% of White, 50% of Black and 42% of Asian defendants were convicted.

- In 2005 ethnicity was recorded in 81% of the Crown Court cases, up from 78% in the previous year. Combining data from the 16 police force areas with the most complete data, a greater proportion of White defendants (75%) were found guilty than Black (70%) or Asian (67%) defendants. However, custodial sentences were given to a greater proportion of Black offenders (68%) and those in the 'Other' category (73%) than White (58%) or Asian offenders (60%).

Youth Offending

- In 2005/6 there were 301,860 offences involving young offenders. Of these 85% of offenders identified themselves as White, 6% as Black, 3% as Asian, 3% as Mixed and 0.3% as Chinese or other. Of the 94,535 pre-court decisions 88% involved White people, 4% Black people, 3% Asian people, 2% Mixed and 0.3% Chinese or Other while the overall number of pre-court decisions increased by 11% from 2004/5. For pre-court disposals, people of Mixed ethnicity were more likely to attract a final warning and intervention than people of other ethnic groups. Offences committed by Black young offenders were more likely to attract a custodial sentence when compared to offences committed by other ethnic groups.

Probation

- Black offenders accounted for 6% of those commencing court orders, followed by Asian (5%), Mixed (2%), and Chinese or 'Other' offenders (1%). There is however great variation across probation areas and this reflects the ethnic composition of the resident population.

- For England and Wales in 2005 a higher proportion of members of Black and Minority Ethnic (BME) groups started pre-or post-release supervision by the National Probation Service (20%) compared with court order supervision (14%). Black and Asian offenders accounted for 9% and 6% of the total respectively.

Prisons

- In June 2006, members of BME groups accounted for 26% of the male prison population and 28% of the female population (including foreign nationals). For British Nationals, the proportion of Black prisoners relative to the population was 7.3 per 1,000 population compared to 1.3 per 1,000 for White persons. In contrast, people from 'Chinese or other' ethnic backgrounds were least likely to be in prison with a rate of 0.4 per 1,000 population. The rate for people from Asian groups was higher than for White persons but lower than that for the Mixed or Black groups i.e. 1.7 per 1,000 population.

- For adult prisoners, 59% of the Black offenders, 55% of the Chinese/Other groups, and 51% of the Asian prisoners were serving a sentence of four years or more compared with 47% for both White and Mixed group prisoners.

Complaints

- The police recorded 26,880 complaints in 2005/6; 7% of complaints made against the police were from Black people, 5% from Asian people and 1% from 'Other' minority ethnic groups.

Deaths in Police Custody

- In 2005/6, five of the 28 deaths of people who had been arrested or otherwise detained by the Police involved people from BME groups.

Practitioners in the Criminal Justice System

- In most criminal justice agencies there have been increases in the employment of people from BME groups in recent years. The Prison Service has met it's representation targets for 2005 of 4.4%.

- There was large variation amongst CJS agencies in the proportion of BME staff employed. The Serious Fraud Office and Youth Offending Teams had the highest BME representation at 22% and 17% respectively. In contrast, the lowest proportion of BME members was noted amongst members of the Judiciary which had only 3% representation from the BME community. Moreover, the majority of this group were employed at the levels of District Judge and Recorder. There are no Lord Justices of Black or other minority ethnic membership.

[1:16] Hedderman, C and Hough, M, *Does the criminal justice system treat men and women differently?*
(1994) HORS Research Findings No 10, HMSO (at page 1)

Academics, pressure groups and journalists have used a variety of criminal justice statistics to argue that the courts systematically discriminate against women. This paper shows that differences do exist in the way men and women are treated by the criminal justice system, but that these largely favour women.

The extent to which men and women offend

Criminal statistics both across time and different cultures show that an overwhelming majority of those caught, convicted and sentenced by the courts are male. Over the last ten years in England and Wales, around five males were cautioned or convicted for an indictable offence for every one female. Such statistics do not account for all crimes committed, of course. Self-report studies-not without problems of their own—ask samples about the extent to which they have committed offences; these indicate that the discrepancy between males and females is more like two males for every one female, although the sex ratio does appear to increase with offence seriousness.

Males are more likely than females to be reconvicted, according both to small-scale research and analysis of the Home Office Offenders' Index (a database which contains details of all offenders convicted of serious offences). Also, the average length of male criminal careers (3.3 years) is three times as long as that for females, although the ratio narrows when those with careers less than one year are excluded, effectively eliminating those convicted of only one offence.[1]

The types of crime men and women commit

On the basis of those convicted and cautioned, the male/female ratio in offending is at its greatest in the late teens and early 20s. This is not because females commit the same offences as males at a later age, but because they are much less likely to commit the sorts of offences committed by younger people, such as burglary, and theft from or of motor vehicles.

Although there has been a rise in the proportion of females dealt with for violence and for drug offences over the last ten years, 71% of their offences in 1992 were theft and handling—in contrast to only 43% of males.

Cautioning

Cautioning is the main disposal used for female offenders. In 1992, 61% of all females convicted or cautioned for indictable offences received a caution, compared with 36% of males. Women had higher cautioning rates across all age groups and most offences, with the exception of drugs.

A statistical exercise carried out by the Home Office examined the criminal histories of samples of those cautioned in 1985 and 1988. This showed that, whilst a majority of both sexes had no criminal history, cautioned males were twice as likely as females to have been previously convicted. They were also more likely to have been cautioned on the previous occasion.[2] The most likely explanation for this difference is the higher offending rate for males. However, without knowing more about these cases, and those in which the police took no further action or prosecuted the offender, we cannot eliminate the possibility that different standards are being applied when deciding whether to caution males and females.

Remands

A smaller proportion of female offenders are remanded in custody than males. One of the few studies to investigate the reasons[3] concluded that this was partly because women were less likely than men to fall into 'high risk' categories, defined as those who had previously failed to appear after being given court bail, or had been charged with a further offence while on bail, or were of no fixed abode. This was only part of the story, however; women falling into 'low risk' categories were still less likely to be remanded in custody than their male counterparts.

Though relevant prison statistics are incomplete, they suggest that about 30% of women who were remanded in custody are subsequently sent to prison, compared with 40% of their male counterparts. Women on bail are also less likely to receive a custodial sentence—about 5% compared with 10% of men. Taken together, these findings suggest that men and women may be treated differently both at the remand and the sentencing stage.

Sentencing

There are large overall differences in the sentencing of men and women. In particular women are far less likely than men to receive a custodial sentence for virtually all indictable offences. The only exception is for drugs, for which the proportions are roughly equal (14%).

When women do receive prison sentences, these tend to be shorter than men's: in 1992 the average length of prison sentences awarded for indictable offences at the Crown Court was 17.7 months for women aged 21 or over and 21.1 months for men. The average length was lower for females convicted of burglary, fraud and forgery, robbery, and theft and handling, but higher for criminal damage and drug offences.

According to the National Prison Survey, 38% of women serving prison sentences in 1991 were there for their first offence, but only 10% of men. Prison statistics show that a much larger proportion of the female prison population are serving custodial sentences for less serious crimes. A common statistical fallacy is to infer from these and similar statistics that the criminal justice system discriminates against women. However, nothing can be inferred about discrimination on the part of sentencers from differences between the sexes in the proportion either of first-offenders or of property offenders in prison. One has to compare the proportions sent to prison of men and women who have committed similar crimes and have similar criminal histories.

One of the reasons that women receive fewer and shorter custodial sentences than men is that they are less frequently dealt with at the Crown Court. For example, in 1992, only 14% of the females aged 17 or over who were proceeded against for an indictable offence went to the Crown Court for trial compared with 24% of males. Recent Home Office research[4] has shown that, in comparable cases, defendants who are sentenced at the Crown Court are about three times more likely to get a custodial sentence than those dealt with at magistrates' courts; such sentences also tend to be longer.

Another possible explanation for the apparently more lenient sentencing of women offenders is that, as discussed above, they are less likely to have previous convictions than men. However, analysis of an Offenders' Index sample of 21,000 offenders convicted of a serious offence in 1991 shows that women first-offenders are half as likely to be given a sentence of immediate imprisonment as male first-offenders—4% compared with 8%; and those with one, two, or three or more previous convictions were all less likely to receive custodial sentences than equivalent men. The same pattern is repeated for individual types of crime such as theft and causing actual bodily harm. Given that these two types of offence account for two-thirds of female convictions for serious offences, it is hardly surprising that such offenders constitute a large part of the female prison population.

Hood[5] reached a similar conclusion in his study of the way men and women are sentenced at Crown Court. He found that women were less likely to be sentenced to custody than men when legal and socio-demographic factors were taken into account.

Homicide

Despite recent claims to the contrary, women are at less risk of imprisonment than men even in cases of domestic homicide. An analysis of cases dealt with between 1984 and 1992 shows that 23% of females compared with only 4% of males indicted for homicide were acquitted on all charges. Of those found guilty, 80% of the women compared with 62% of the men were found guilty of the lesser charge of manslaughter; and more than two-thirds of the men convicted of manslaughter received a prison sentence compared with less than half the women. The fact remains, of course, that women are at much greater risk of domestic homicide.

Much of the controversy around recent cases has surrounded the use of the provocation defence, which is said to be less easy for women to deploy. Information on recent cases shows that 36% of the women convicted of manslaughter used this defence, and under a third (32%) of the men. By combining the percentages employing the provocation defence with the percentages of men and women convicted of manslaughter, we can infer that a defence of provocation was accepted in about 29% of cases involving female defendants compared with 20% of cases involving men.

Conclusions

This paper presents available research and statistics which call into question claims that the criminal justice system is systematically more severe towards women than men. If anything, the evidence points to more lenient treatment of women. Some caveats are needed, however. First, there is still insufficient evidence to be definitive: it could be that even when individual offence categories are examined, the statistics mask differences between men and women in the seriousness of their offending. In other words, it is possible that on the face of it, women are being treated leniently—but not as leniently as their less serious offending warrants. However, there is no statistical support for (or against) this hypothesis; and testing it would require analysis within very detailed offence categories.

Secondly, the question remains whether there is equal suitable provision for women as for men throughout the criminal justice system. There are grounds (albeit not fully researched) for believing that, in a system which deals very largely with male offenders, the needs of women offenders are not always effectively addressed. For example, an investigation by HM Inspectorate of Probation[6] found that a limited range of community penalties was available for women in some areas.

Finally, the paper has not considered whether there are disparities in treatment *within* gender. The likelihood that female offenders may overall receive more lenient treatment than males obviously does not rule out the possibility that individual women receive unusually harsh treatment.

Notes

1 Tarling, R, *Analysing Offending: data, models and interpretations* (1993) HMSO.

2 'The criminal histories of those cautioned in 1985 and 1988' (1992) Home Office Statistical Bulletin No 20/92.

3 Morgan, P and Pearce, R, 'Remand Decisions in Brighton and Bournemouth' (1989) Research and Planning Unit Paper No 53, Home Office.

4 Hedderman, C and Moxon, D, 'Magistrates' court or Crown Court? Mode of trial decisions and sentencing' (1992) Home Office Research Study No 125, HMSO.

5 Hood, R, *Race and sentencing: a study in the Crown Court* (1992) Clarendon Press.

6 HM Inspectorate of Probation, 'Report on women offenders and Probation Service provision' (1991) Home Office.

[1:17] Hedderman, C and Gelsthorpe, L (eds), *Understanding the sentencing of women*

(1997) HORS No 170, HMSO (at page vii)

Summary

A superficial examination of the criminal statistics suggests that, for virtually every type of offence, women are treated more leniently than men. This report describes the results of a two-part study of the sentencing of women. In Part I, sentencing patterns are explored in more detail using samples of men and women convicted of shoplifting, violence and drug offences in 1991. The results of this analysis, which was based on more than 13,000 cases, were then used to inform Part II of the study in which magistrates were interviewed about what they thought were the main influences on their decision-making.

Part I

Statistical tests were used, first, to examine whether an offender's sex appeared to affect the likelihood of a prison sentence once criminal and sentencing history was taken into account; and then, to model the likelihood of various other sentencing outcomes. The penalties that the model *predicted* each offender would receive were compared with the *actual* sentence men and women received.

Women shoplifters were less likely than comparable males to receive a prison sentence. They were also more likely to be sentenced to a community penalty or to be discharged. However, the results should not be interpreted as evidence of a general policy of leniency towards women shoplifters. They suggest rather that sentencers may be reluctant to fine a woman—possibly because they may be penalising her children rather than just herself. This results in many women receiving a discharge but others receiving community penalties which are rather more severe than fines.

Men and women stood an equal chance of going to prison for a first violent offence. However among repeat offenders women were less likely to receive a custodial sentence.

Women first offenders were significantly less likely than equivalent men to receive a prison sentence for a drug offence, but recidivists were equally likely to go to prison.

Among first and repeat offenders, women convicted of violence and drug offences were always more likely to be discharged and men more likely to be fined. But again, this seems to be less a consequence of a policy of leniency than a reluctance to impose one particular sentence—the fine—on women.

Part II

Nearly 200 magistrates were interviewed individually or in groups at five courts using a semi-structured questionnaire and a small sentencing exercise involving two stereotypical cases designed to bring out differences in their thinking about men and women offenders. These interviews, which were carried out between June and December 1995, took account of the findings in Part I.

Magistrates said they found it hard to compare the way they sentenced men and women because they dealt with women offenders far less frequently. However, they broadly distinguished between 'troubled' and 'troublesome' offenders, and tended to locate most women in the former category. In part this was because women tended to be first offenders, facing less serious charges than men and because they behaved more respectfully in court. In addition, magistrates tended to ascribe different motives to them. However, even when men were stealing bacon or coffee rather than alcohol or items to sell, they rarely engaged magistrates' sympathies.

Because they regarded women offenders as troubled, magistrates responded to their offending with measures (a discharge or probation) designed to assist them to lead law-abiding lives rather than punishing them. Fines were regarded as particularly unsuitable for women with children to care for and because they were seen as lacking 'independent means' for paying fines.

While magistrates stressed that 'the facts' of a case were most influential, many made references to 'common sense' or 'gut feelings' determining how they approached issues of motivation, body language or the offender's personal circumstances.

Appearance and demeanour in the courtroom were often commented on by magistrates. Although they denied that this influenced their decision-making, their comments concerning the importance of seeing the offender in court, and anecdotes about those who behaved inappropriately, suggested that these factors were influential.

(From the conclusion at page 55:)

Few people would seriously contest the notion that the criminal justice system should dispense justice fairly, regardless of sex, race, class or any other improper influence. No one is more aware of this need than the magistracy, who already spend a proportion of their training on such (human awareness) issues. But what exactly does fairness consist of in this context? In our view, it lies in consistency of approach rather than uniformity of outcome. In other words, it involves asking the same questions about factors such as employment status, family responsibilities and financial circumstances regardless of the offender's sex, rather than presuming that certain questions will only apply to males or females. From this perspective, to criticise sentencing practices on the grounds that the official statistics show different sentencing patterns would be unfair and, in any case, a futile exercise. These patterns may simply reflect the fact that the men and women who come to court differ across a wide range of factors which sentencers take into consideration when determining an appropriate sentence. In order to look at whether there is disparity in sentencing decisions, one needs therefore to look at the characteristics of those coming to court and at how sentencers say they weigh these and other factors in their decision-making. This research set out to do both these things.

In our view, neither the statistical analysis described by Dowds and Hedderman nor the interviews Gelsthorpe and Loucks carried out support the contention that differences in the way men and women are sentenced by magistrates is a consequence of anything as simple as deliberate discrimination. If that were true one would expect the statistical exercise to show women consistently receiving different sentences to men. But they do not. For example, they stood an equal chance of going to prison for a first violent offence, whereas among repeat offenders, women were less likely to go to prison. And among drug offenders, women recidivists were as likely as man to be imprisoned, but first timers were not.

In fact both parts of this study suggest that sentencing decisions are the outcome of the interactive effect of a number of factors. The most important of these is the nature of the offence. However, the offender's circumstances, the way other participants in the courtroom portray the offence and offender, the offender's appearance and behaviour in court, and how the members of each bench interact are also influential. Together these factors shape the court's perception of an offender as essentially troubled or troublesome, and this in turn determines whether help or punishment is at the heart of the court's response.

Women were more likely to be defined as troubled than men. From interviews with magistrates there seem to be a number of reasons for this. First, five out of every six of the offenders magistrates routinely deal with are male and most are under 30 years of age. Perhaps because of their sheer numbers, young men are likely to be seen as troublesome and are only very rarely viewed as troubled. As we know from the statistics, the majority of the women offenders magistrates try and sentence are charged with shoplifting. Again, from the interviews with magistrates in Part II of this study, we know that magistrates generally believe that such women steal through need rather than greed, they often have sole care of young children, and they are usually living on benefits or are dependent on a partner's income. So how are these perceptions of women translated into sentencing? The most striking consequence is that, as the analyses presented in Part I show, magistrates are reluctant to fine women. Even if this difference was found to be inspired by a desire not to financially penalise a woman's family, it carries the risk that, skipping a step on the sentencing ladder this time round, will lead to an even more severe sentence being imposed in the event of a subsequent conviction. To use probation where a fine would have been appropriate is also an ineffective use of resources (Moxon et al., 1990).

Both parts of the study show that magistrates appear to favour probation or discharges for women. The interviews carried out in Part II suggest that these measures are used with the intention of assisting rather than punishing women. Unless sending women to prison was unavoidable because of the seriousness of their offending, it was usually ruled out on the grounds that it would adversely affect their children.

We know from previous research that female offenders do indeed describe themselves as stealing through need and having responsibility for dependent children (see, for example, Carlen 1988 and Morris et al., 1995). However, neither those studies nor the current research show whether they differ from men in either respect. Examination of court records to see if male and female offenders are matched in these ways has proved difficult because records do not hold such information consistently. This is certainly an issue worth examining in future research, however, as the magistrates interviewed in Part II of this study revealed that, when considering mitigation, they were not simply responding to the fact that women and men appeared in different circumstances. Thus, for example, having family responsibilities was less central to decisions about male offenders, and being employed carried less weight when the offender was a woman. Even when a man is considered to be more troubled than troublesome, this does not necessarily have the same consequences as for a woman. On the occasions when magistrates believed that male offenders merited assistance, this tended to take the form of employment training through Community Service Orders or help with alcohol or drug addiction. These findings are strikingly similar to those reported by Farrington and Morris (1983) and Mary Eaton (1983, 1986). A key difference is that they reflect sentencing in the mid-1990s rather than the mid-1980s and occur in a period when a great deal of attention has been given to notions of fairness and justice and to race and gender issues in the delivery of justice.

Turning to the offender in the courtroom, while some magistrates recognised that body language is open to misinterpretation, most stressed the importance of seeing the offender in court, and a number were confident that they would not themselves misinterpret nonverbal cues. The research also indicated that, based on perceptions of body language and appearance, men—ethnic minority men in particular—may come across as having less respect for the court, while women are generally perceived to be inexperienced, deferential and (therefore) honest.

The internal politics of the courtroom also seem to shape magistrates' decision-making. The same information could be viewed quite differently according to which courtroom player provided it—most weight was accorded to information from prosecutors or the Clerk, who were regarded by magistrates as being impartial. Not only defence solicitors but probation officers were seen as siding with the offender.

Interaction between magistrates was also important, with experience weighing more heavily than training. Moreover, virtually all the magistrates mentioned 'common sense' or 'gut feelings' at some stage of their assessment as to who was respectful or rebellious, remorseful or rancorous; and 'common sense' was what magistrates used to explain any decision that seemed to have no other explanation or, at least, no easily expressed explanation. Yet notions of what is 'common sense' and what are reliable indicators of honesty and remorse differed among magistrates.

Taken as a whole, these findings suggest that there remains a risk that some magistrates will resort to their 'common sense' (and a gendered 'common-sense' at that) as the best arbiter of what is right, despite the fact that new magistrates receive training designed to inform them of the inherent dangers of making decisions on the basis of stereotypes and on the dangers of relying on non-verbal cues.

The difficulty to be addressed is one of finding ways to challenge stereotypical pictures of men and women, without ignoring the fact that they often (but *not* always) do have different needs and responsibilities (and these are often precisely the needs and responsibilities which fuel the stereotypes). It may also be that the time to recognise such differences is in the shape and content of particular sentences rather than in the choice between different levels of sentence, but discussion of this is beyond our remit. A number of changes may be helpful here:

- Increased emphasis on gender issues in training to counteract the fact that so many magistrates have comparatively little experience of dealing with women in the courtroom. This is probably best accomplished through the 'human awareness' element of magistrates' training which encourages them to reflect on how cultural and gender specific stereotypes inform their practices and perceptions in the courtroom in ways which could lead to unfair sentencing. Currently, such training tends to focus on race issues and it would be unfortunate if combining race and gender in this way masked the importance of either issue. it is also important to note that while 'human awareness' training is popular, it does not appear to have been subject to any large scale or systematic evaluation.

- Training on gender (and race) should be made available to *all* magistrates rather than to new magistrates alone so as to ensure that resistant or reluctant magistrates are exposed to the issues as a matter of routine.

- Where magistrates may feel that their sentencing options are constrained by a (male of female) offender's childcare responsibilities, the Probation Service should use PSRs to draw attention to the fact that suitable childcare arrangements can be made.

- Increased feedback on sentencing patterns in each court—particularly patterns relating to men and women—may also assist magistrates in the general task of achieving consistency in approach.

Finally, we would suggest that there are at least three questions which require further exploration and discussion:

- to what extent does training help to address the tendency to use gender-stereotyping in sentencing?

- to what extent do gender, race and other factors have an interactive effect on sentencing?

- are the decisions of professional sentencers subject to the same influences as those of lay magistrates?

[1:18] *Young Black People and the Criminal Justice System*
2nd Report of the Select Committee on Home Affairs, 2006–07, HC 181-I

Summary

It is important to place young black people's overrepresentation in perspective: in 84.7% of offences in 2004–05 involving young offenders aged 10–17, the young people involved classified their ethnicity as white. In 2003–04, 92% of black young people aged 10–17 were not subject to disposals in the youth justice system. However, statistics show that young black people are overrepresented at all stages of the criminal justice system. Black people constitute 2.7% of the population aged 10–17, but represent 8.5% of those of that age group arrested in England and Wales. As a group, they are more likely to be stopped and searched by the police, less likely to be given unconditional bail and more likely to be remanded in custody than white young offenders. Young black people and those of 'mixed' ethnicity are likely to receive more punitive sentences than young white people.

Data gaps prevent us from building a comprehensive picture of young black people's overrepresentation in the criminal justice system. However, the evidence we received suggests young black people are overrepresented as suspects for certain crimes such as robbery, drugs offences and—in some areas—firearms offences. Young black people are also more likely to be victims of violent crimes. There are variations in the overrepresentation of different groups within the 'black' category, and between females and males. We can say with greater certainty that the patterns of offending vary between different ethnic groups than that the level of offending varies significantly.

Some of our witnesses were concerned that the media distorts perceptions of young black people's involvement in crime. Research commissioned by this Committee contradicted this view, indicating that most members of the public reject stereotyping as regards young black people's involvement in crime.

Social exclusion is a key underlying cause of overrepresentation. Eighty per cent of Black African and Black Caribbean communities live in Neighbourhood Renewal Fund areas. Deprivation directly fuels involvement in some types of offence—such as acquisitive crime—and also has an important impact on educational achievement and the profile of the neighbourhood young people will live in. The level of school exclusions appears to be directly related to educational underachievement and both are linked to involvement in the criminal justice system.

Witnesses also emphasised factors within black communities which help exacerbate disadvantage and fuel involvement in the criminal justice system. They drew attention to a lack of father involvement and to other parenting issues. In the perceived absence of alternative routes to success, some young people also actively choose to emulate negative and violent lifestyles popularised in music and film.

Criminal justice system factors play an important role in promoting overrepresentation. There is some evidence to support allegations of direct or indirect discrimination in policing and the youth justice system. However, the perception as well as the reality of discrimination has an impact. Lack of confidence in the criminal justice system may mean some young black people take the law into their own hands or carry weapons in an attempt to distribute justice and ensure their own personal safety.

A coherent strategy to address the overrepresentation of young black people in the criminal justice system is needed to draw together departments' responses and set challenging goals to reduce overrepresentation. Within this strategy, further action is needed to address the causes of crime among young black people—entrenched poverty, educational underachievement, school exclusions, family conflict and breakdown and lack of positive role models. Some of this support will be aimed at all young black people and some should target specific at-risk groups, such as prison leavers. Finally, further action is needed to address both the realities and perceptions of criminal justice system discrimination and ensure the system meets young black peoples' needs.

[1:19] Hood, R, Shute, S, and Seemungal, F, *Ethnic Minorities in the Criminal Courts: Perceptions of Fairness and Equality of Treatment*

(2003) Lord Chancellor's Department Research Series No 2/03

Executive Summary

...

A substantial number (778) of ethnic minority and (for comparative purposes) white defendants were interviewed at the conclusion of the criminal proceedings against them. The study was conducted at both the Crown Court and magistrates' courts in three urban areas with high concentrations of ethnic minority citizens—Manchester, Birmingham, and South-East London. In addition, 150 witnesses were interviewed at the same courts, as well as 112 solicitors and barristers, 125 magistrates, 61 court staff, and 26 judges in the Crown Court. Those working in the courts were asked about their perceptions of how the courts deal with persons from ethnic minorities, and in particular whether this has changed over time. Altogether, 1,252 people were interviewed and the proceedings in more than 500 cases were observed.

Respondents were asked to classify their ethnicity according to the categories used in the national census of 2001 but, so as to make the findings comparable with official data on race and criminal justice, persons have, for most purposes, been classified as black, Asian or white.

It is important to emphasise that this is a study of how defendants and witnesses *interpreted* their experiences in the criminal courts. It is not an *objective* study of whether or not racial discrimination had actually taken place.

The Defendants' Perspective:

- Most of the defendants who were interviewed had just been convicted and sentenced, many to imprisonment, so their feelings may well have been running high. Very few had been acquitted. The sample therefore probably over-represented the kind of defendant who might be most likely to complain of unfair or racially biased treatment. The majority were interviewed by ethnic minority researchers. Defendants were given several opportunities to express any concerns about racial bias. For these reasons it is likely that the findings reflect 'a worst case scenario.'

- Leaving aside complaints which turned out *not* to be directed at the courts (i.e. mainly at the police and to a lesser extent the Crown Prosecution Service), the proportion of defendants who said their treatment had been unfair in court was *nearly a third* (31 per cent) in the Crown Court, with little difference between the ethnic minority and white defendants (33 per cent of black, 27 per cent of Asian and 29 per cent of white defendants).

- In the magistrates' courts *a quarter* of defendants (26 per cent) said they felt unfairly treated, a rather higher proportion among ethnic minority than among white defendants (26 per cent of black, 31 per cent of Asian and 19 per cent of white defendants).

- However, when ethnic minority defendants were asked whether they thought that their unfair treatment in court had *anything to do with their ethnicity*, a lower proportion said definitely 'YES': *one in five* of black defendants in the Crown Court and *one in ten* in the magistrates' courts, and *one in eight* Asian defendants in both the Crown Court and the magistrates' courts.

- Most of the defendants' complaints about racial bias concerned sentences perceived to be more severe than those they thought would have been imposed on a similarly placed white defendant. Very few perceived explicit racial bias in the conduct or attitude of judges or magistrates—only *three per cent* in the Crown Court and *one per cent* in the magistrates' courts. The majority thought the remarks made when their sentence had been imposed had been fair, and no complaints were made about racist remarks from the Bench.

- Neither age, country of birth, nor previous court appearances affected the propensity of defendants to complain of racial bias. But there were substantial variations between the court areas. These were not explained by the proportion sentenced to custody or the proportion of ethnic minority staff employed in the particular court.

The Witnesses' Perspective:

- *Sixteen per cent* of witnesses in the Crown Court complained of unfair treatment, almost the same proportion amongst black, white and Asian witnesses. But *none* of the 68 ethnic minority witnesses complained of *racial* bias. There were more complaints (mostly about inconvenience and feeling intimidated) in the magistrates' courts: one in five of white and Asian and 45 per cent of black witnesses; but *only seven per cent* of the 41 ethnic minority witnesses perceived the unfairness to have been *racially* motivated.

- *None* of the witnesses in either court complained of ill treatment by a judge or magistrate.

Issues of Confidence:

- In the Crown Court, black (38 per cent) and Asian defendants (34 per cent) were just as likely as white defendants (40 per cent) to say that they would *not* expect to be fairly treated next time they came to court. In the magistrates' courts, a higher proportion of black (39 per cent) and Asian (35 per cent) than white defendants (15%) said this.

- However, a much smaller proportion of *all* black and Asian defendants (seven per cent in the Crown Court and nine per cent in the magistrates' courts) believed they would be disadvantaged in the future *because of their ethnic origin*.

- Nevertheless, a considerably higher proportion of black (44 per cent in the Crown Court; 49 per cent in the magistrates' courts) than either Asian (33 per cent and 26 per cent) or white defendants (30 per cent and 16 per cent) believed that generally there was *not always* equal treatment of ethnic minority defendants by the courts.

The Perspective of Informed Observers—Court Officials and Lawyers:

- Most white (98 per cent) and Asian (71 per cent) clerks and ushers and white (69 per cent) and Asian (63 per cent) lawyers thought that there was nowadays *always* equal treatment of ethnic minorities by the courts. But the proportion was much lower among the black lawyers (43 per cent) and black staff (28 per cent).

- A higher proportion of black (30 per cent) and either white (13 per cent) or Asian (11 per cent) lawyers said they had personally witnessed incidents in court that they regarded as 'racist.'

The Judicial and Magisterial Perspective:

- All the judges and two-thirds of the magistrates interviewed had received training in ethnic awareness. Only two of the 26 judges and three of the 125 magistrates said that it had 'added nothing' or been 'unhelpful.' Yet only a few (2 judges and 11 magistrates) thought there was a need for *further* such training.

A Cultural Change?

- Judges mentioned that judicial attitudes and behaviour towards ethnic minority defendants had changed markedly in recent years for the better, and magistrates also reported a substantial decline in the frequency of racially inappropriate remarks. Many lawyers reported that racial bias or inappropriate language in court was becoming 'a thing of the past.'

- These positive findings, taken together with the much lower than expected proportion of defendants complaining of racial bias, may be a reflection of both general social improvements in the treatment of ethnic minorities and the specific efforts begun by the Lord Chancellor's Department in the early 1990s to heighten the awareness of all involved in the system of the need to be aware of, and guard against, racial bias.

What Still Needs to be Done?

- Although this study has revealed that the perceptions of racial bias amongst ethnic minority persons who appear before the criminal courts appear to be less widely held than in the past, the findings should not lead to complacency. The fact that one in five black and one in eight Asian defendants definitely perceived racial bias in the Crown Court, and at least one in ten in the magistrates courts, combined with the fact that black lawyers and staff were more likely to perceive racial bias than others, is sufficient cause to continue the efforts towards eliminating the vestiges of perceived unequal treatment.

- Perceptions of racial bias, more frequently held by black defendants in the Crown Court, may well arise from a belief that the disproportionately large number of black people caught up by the criminal justice and prison systems must, at least to some extent, be a reflection of racism. Every effort therefore should be made when passing sentence to demonstrate and convince defendants that no element of racial stereotyping or bias has entered into the decision.

- Among black defendants and lawyers in particular there was a belief that the authority and legitimacy of the courts, and confidence in them, would be strengthened if more personnel from ethnic minorities were seen to be playing a part in the administration of criminal justice. Indeed, in the Crown Court 31 per cent ethnic minority defendants, and in the magistrates' courts 48 per cent, said they would like more people from ethnic minorities sitting in judgment and amongst the staff of the courts. Many judges shared this view that more could be done to avoid the impression of the courts as 'white dominated institutions.'

- It should be emphasised that this research has been directed at revealing *perceptions of and beliefs about* equal treatment held by ethnic minorities who have found themselves subject to the jurisdiction of the criminal courts. It has shown that the main concern amongst the *minority* who perceived racial bias in their treatment arose from their view that the sentence imposed was more severe than a similarly placed white defendant would have received. Very few complained that they had been subjected by any court official to racist language or conduct. However, given the changing circumstances since an objective study of sentencing practices in the West Midlands in 1989 was carried out (Roger Hood, *Race and Sentencing* 1992), it is not possible to say whether that perception of differential racially biased sentencing has any basis in objective evidence.

- The findings of this study may go some way to dispelling the view that most minority ethnic defendants believe that their treatment by the courts has been racially biased. But, if it could be shown that the 'cultural change' which this study has identified has had a real impact on eliminating differential sentencing of white and ethnic minority defendants, this would further encourage the confidence of ethnic minorities in the criminal courts.

CHAPTER TWO

THE POLICE

In our case study, you rang the ambulance service to tell them that you had found an injured woman in the street. The ambulance crew radioed for the police to attend. This is a fairly typical scenario: in the majority of cases the police rely heavily on members of the public, and in particular on victims, to tell them about crimes. Between 75 per cent and 90 per cent of offences are brought to the attention of the police by victims, bystanders or other members of the public (see Phillips and Brown (1998) for a study of the arrest population in police stations). The preliminary decision of the victim to report a crime may be influenced by many factors, as was mentioned in Chapter 1.

The police officer who arrives on the scene has to make several decisions. Wide discretionary powers are exercised by those at the very lowest level in the organization: in the vast majority of cases, if a police officer chooses not to act, not to intervene, this decision will not be subject to any review. Police officers decide whether to record a crime, whether to arrest someone, whether to initiate a prosecution, whether to release a suspect on bail, whether informally to warn or formally to caution an offender. Much fieldwork has been carried out in recent years to assess 'police culture' and policing in practice. A review of some of this research, and an analysis of the efficacy of the statutory and common law limits on this discretion, will be explored later in this chapter, but it may be useful to start by looking briefly at the accountability of the police in constitutional terms.

There were 141,892 full-time equivalent police officers in England and Wales in April 2007. As well as police 'officers', the Police Reform Act 2002 introduced 'community support officers' (CSOs). In April 2007, there were 16,000 police CSOs in England and Wales and the number is rising fast (a Government commitment to 24,000 in 2008). Why? They are cheaper, of course. Their role is to provide visible re-assurance as part of 'neighbourhood policing'. Originally, the Government made it clear that CSOs would have many fewer powers than police officers, but unsurprisingly, this has now changed: section 7 of the Police and Justice Act 2006 amended the Police Reform Act to enable the Secretary of State to introduce an Order establishing a standard set of powers and duties that apply to all police CSOs. As well as these powers, CSOs may be given additional powers by their chief constables (see Statutory Instrument 2007/3202 and HO Circular 33/2007). So the differences between CSOs and police officers are beginning to shrink. Interestingly, although the number of CSOs recruited from ethnic minorities has been impressive, they are now complaining of the 'glass ceiling' which prevents their progression to full officer status.

Far more people are employed in private security firms than are employed as police officers. As Newburn and Reiner (2004) put it, 'the police, the state financed and organized body that specializes in policing, is only one aspect—and possibly a diminishing aspect—of an ensemble of policing institutions and processes' (at page 601). What used to be seen as 'public' spaces (shopping malls, courts and nightclubs, for example) are guarded by private companies. As well, private companies provide many investigative and forensic services, and of course CCTV is largely provided by private companies. Whilst the focus of this chapter is on the role of the 'classic' police officer, students should be well aware of the extent of privatization of policing in this country.

(i) POLICE ACCOUNTABILITY

The police as we know them are a modern development. Whether you conclude that they have evolved out of community-based consensus policing, or rather as agents of state control, depends on your interpretation of history. Not until the late eighteenth century did the need for a paid police force become widely accepted. The Metropolitan Police Act 1829 gave London its first police force, nicknamed 'Peelers' or 'Bobbies' after Robert Peel, the Home Secretary. In 1856 it became compulsory for every county to have a police force. Today there are still 43 separate police forces in England and Wales. Their function continually evolves: concepts such as community policing, zero-tolerance policing, intelligence-led policing, problem-oriented policing reflect changing police priorities (see Newburn and Reiner, 2004 and 2007), but our concern here is the governance of the police.

Their 'independence' has traditionally been valued as reflecting the fact that the police are not an arm of government. Strong 'security police' are a feature of dictatorships and totalitarian states; democratic government is seen to require something less centrally controlled. Yet the downside of this independence may be that the police are both inadequately powerful and inadequately accountable. Today they are governed by a curious tripartite structure—what Laws LJ called (in *R v DPP, ex p Duckenfield* [1999] 2 All ER 873) the 'interlocking roles' of three key players: chief constable, police authority, and the Home Secretary.

The Police Act 1996 **[2:1]**, much amended by the Police and Justice Act 2006, provides that a police force is under the direction and control of the chief constable. Each police area has a police authority comprising local councillors, magistrates and 'independent members'. The authority appoints the chief constable and has a duty under section 6 of the Act to 'secure the maintenance of an efficient and effective'[1] force for its area. The elected councillor element on police authorities has been reduced from two-thirds to 'a number which is greater by one' than half, reflecting the increasingly centralized control. Five members, or up to one-third of the authority, are 'independent', but appointed from a short-list prepared by the Secretary of State (for details, see Schedule 1 to the 1996 Act). The Audit Commission's 1994 **[2:2]** analysis of police accountability remains useful, but remember the increased centralization that has followed on from this.

The highly charged political atmosphere of the miners' strike in the early 1980s, along with modern policing techniques, led to the creation of such bodies as the National Criminal Intelligence Service (NCIS) and the National Crime Squad (NCS): see the Police Act 1997. Increased centralization of police powers was also recognized in sections 136–141 of the Criminal Justice and Public Order Act 1994, which extended arrangements for police officers to exercise their powers outside their home jurisdictions. More recently, the Police Reform

---

[1] A subtle change from the words 'adequate and efficient' in the Police Act 1964.

Act 2002 inserted a new section 36A into the Police Act 1996, requiring the Home Secretary to prepare a National Policing Plan and, if necessary, to issue a code of practice for the purpose of promoting the efficiency of police forces. Under section 3 he may require inspections of a police force or of the NCIS. Another major re-organization took place in 2006, following the enactment of the Serious Organised Crime and Police Act 2005, when the Serious Organised Crime Agency (SOCA) was formed from the amalgamation of NCIS, NCS, that part of HM Revenue and Customs (HMRC: see Chapter 4) dealing with drug trafficking and associated criminal finance and a part of UK Immigration dealing with organized immigration crime (UKIS). There have also been suggestions that the number of police forces would be reduced, but so far this has not happened. But there can be little doubt that the trend has been towards greater centralized control, particularly when it comes to 'serious' crime. (It is worth pondering the definition of this concept!) There have also been major changes internationally, particularly within the European Union (see Europol and Eurojust's websites). The internationalization and globalization of policing is beyond the scope of this book.

As we shall see, the police enjoy huge discretionary powers, and clearly this discretion needs to be controlled. What are the mechanisms of accountability? Political accountability is weak, given the 'interlocking roles' of chief constable, police authority and the Home Secretary. The weakness (some would argue the non-existence) of local accountability was made clear as long ago as the 1989, in the decision in *R v Secretary of State for the Home Department, ex p Northumbria Police Authority* **[2:3]**, where the Court of Appeal held that it was lawful for the Home Secretary to supply equipment to a police force without the approval of the police authority. The police authority today appears only to have as much authority as will be tolerated by the chief constable and the Home Secretary. Yet what is the best way forward? If chief constables are free from control by local or central government, to whom are they accountable? Do we want a national police force?

Another important side to police accountability is the way in which individual officers can be held to account for their decisions. This may be by the courts (criminal courts may refuse to accept evidence unlawfully obtained, for example: see **[2:17]**; or in civil courts, officers may be sued) or by internal disciplinary measures. If police priority is to catch criminals (or, to go back to Packer **[1:9]**, if they give a high priority to crime control at the expense of due process), it is vital that an internal disciplinary procedure effectively fights malpractice. The Police Act 1964 required chief officers of police to supervise all serious complaints against the police made by members of the public, and to cause them to be investigated. This procedure was widely criticized, largely for having no independent elements in the investigation process. The Police and Criminal Evidence Act 1984 (commonly known as PACE) replaced the Police Complaints Board with the Police Complaints Authority, in order that internal police investigations should be externally supervised. Nevertheless, public disquiet with a system that was both secret and not wholly independent of the police, and whereby many police officers were able to take early retirement when facing the prospect of disciplinary action, continued. The Home Affairs Select Committee Inquiry into Police Disciplinary and Complaints Procedures (1998) concluded, depressingly, that 'police complaints and disciplinary procedures are inadequate both to ensure effective management and to command public confidence'. New police discipline procedures took effect in April 1999, incorporating: the civil standard of proof; a 'fast-track' dismissal system for the most serious cases; and measures to prevent the misuse of retirements 'on medical grounds' to evade disciplinary action. This was followed by the creation, in the Police Reform Act 2002, of a new 'independent' Police Complaints Commission, which replaced the Police Complaints Authority in 2004. Any body which is 'independent' merits careful exploration: study the reports on the IPCC website. For this author, it is an encouraging trend that the number of complaints is increasing, since this may reveal greater awareness of, and trust in, the complaints process. In 2006/07 a total of 28,998 complaints were recorded across England and Wales, an increase of 10 per cent on the previous year. (Of those allegations investigated, 11 per cent were substantiated and 89 per cent were unsubstantiated: see Gleeson and Grace (2007).)

Complainants who prefer to bring civil proceedings against the police frequently find this route problematic. First, there is the problem of cost. Although (civil) legal aid may be available, this has been squeezed hugely in recent years (even more fiercely than criminal legal aid, discussed in Chapter 5). And then, although police authorities are vicariously liable for the wrongful actions of police constables, civil proceedings do nothing to reprimand the individual police officer. And even here, as *Hill v Chief Constable of West Yorkshire* **[2:4]** revealed, the courts remain reluctant to fetter police discretion in policing matters. There the House of Lords held that the police did not owe a general duty of care, under the tort of negligence, to individual members of the public to apprehend an unknown criminal. This attitude may change slowly over time: in *Osman v United Kingdom* (1998) 29 EHRR 245 the European Court of Human Rights stated that police immunity from negligence claims was only one aspect of the public interest. Note that each of the applicants was awarded £10,000 by way of compensation. Rather than extract the decision itself, the materials here **[2:5] [2:6]** reveal two very different interpretations of the European Court of Human Rights' decision. Are you convinced by Hoyano's criticisms of Lord Hoffmann's analysis? More recent decisions in the domestic courts whilst recognizing that the liability of the police is not set in stone, give little encouragement to sue. In *Brooks v Commissioner of Police of the Metropolis* [2005] **[2:7]** the House of Lords is unanimous that the police owe no duty in the law of negligence to take reasonable steps to assess whether the friend of a murder victim was a victim of crime and to accord him reasonably appropriate protection, support, assistance, and treatment if he was so assessed. Do you agree with this decision? Eventually in 2006 Mr Brooks was paid £100,000 plus costs in settlement of his other claims (of false imprisonment and under the Race Relations Acts) against the police. (See also *M v Commissioner of Police for the Metropolis* [2007] EWCA Civ 1361, where the Court of Appeal followed *Hill* and *Brooks* in deciding that a daughter could not sue the police in negligence when they failed to prosecute her step-father for indecent assault and cruelty.)

(ii) RECORDING AND ENFORCING CRIME

In theory, all laws are enforced, but in practice clearly some are enforced more than others. With limited operational resources, the police are selective in which crimes they pursue. Thus, for example, the police give a fairly low priority to enforcing laws about obscenity—but without going so far as to *refuse* to act in this area—largely because the law itself is unsatisfactory, and the police choose not to waste their resources in an area where they are particularly ineffective. In other areas, the police may choose not to enforce laws which they perceive to be outdated. In effect, this gives them a power to decriminalize. A case brought over 30 years ago is still useful in illustrating the extent of police discretion **[2:8]**. Although he lost several cases, Blackburn achieved a certain publicity for his causes by initiating judicial review proceedings, and this 'political' side-effect of judicial review may sometimes be as useful to applicants as the decision itself. A more recent example is *R v Chief Constable* *of Sussex, ex p International Trader's Ferry Ltd* [1999] 2 AC 418, in which exporters of live animals were unsuccessful in their attempts to force the police to give them greater police protection. The case was, in the words of Lord Nolan, 'an acceptance of the plain fact that there are limits to the extent to which the police can control unlawful violence in any given situation. If those limits are felt to be too narrow, the remedy lies in increasing the resources of the police. It does not lie in the imposition of further restrictions upon the discretion which the law allows to a chief constable to decide upon the best use of the resources which are in fact available to him'. Another example is provided by *R (Mondelly) v Commissioner of the Police of the Metropolis*, decided in 2006 but cited here **[2:9]** from the report in the Criminal Law Review in 2007 with Andrew Robert's commentary. Given the police guidance in 2004 on arrests for simple possession of cannabis, would you have taken the line of the dissenting judge?

To revert to the story with which this book began, PC Jane Green, the police officer called to the scene where the woman is found bleeding in the street, has to decide whether to record this as a crime. Here, she will undoubtedly record the incident. Individual police officers affect crime statistics by their decision to record an incident as an offence or not. A reported theft may be recorded as an incidence of lost property, or not recorded at all. Maybe the police officer does not believe the person who is reporting the crime, or perhaps it happened a long time ago or is considered insufficiently serious. A broken window might be an accident, but it might be recorded as criminal damage or even attempted burglary. The divergence between actual, reported, and recorded crime was noted in Chapter 1.

What guidance does the police officer have? The police have a statutory obligation to record 'notifiable offences', which broadly cover the most serious offences. The study by Farrington and Dowds **[2:10]** shows how different police practices can have astonishing results. They established that the high official crime rate in Nottingham in the 1980s resulted largely from differential police recording of crimes. Although much has been done to try to standardize the rules for the recording of crimes by the police, different practices will inevitable continue. As politicians (and funders) use the figures as measures of police performance, and to inform the distribution of resources, a certain degree of scepticism in your approach to these figures may be warranted.

Once reported and recorded, the likelihood of an offender being caught will be affected by the decision as to how much time and money is spent on an inquiry. Thus, in our case study, if resources allow, a police car will immediately drive around looking for a suspect escaping the scene of the crime. A suspect carrying a knife and wearing bloodied clothes, arrested on the day of the incident, will provide more compelling evidence than one arrested three days later!

(iii) POLICE POWERS

The statutory powers of the police in the investigation of crime were largely codified by the Police and Criminal Evidence Act 1984 (PACE) **[2:11]**, which was enacted as a result of the 1981 Report of the Royal Commission on Criminal Procedure. Whilst PACE has achieved some uniformity in police practice, widespread powers have been given to the police by subsequent Acts, such as the Public Order Act 1986, the Criminal Justice and Public Order Act (CJPOA) 1994, the Proceeds of Crime Act 2002, the Criminal Justice Act 2003, the Serious

Organised Crime Act 2005, and other statutes. Thus, PACE cannot be seen as the only code of police powers. PACE has also been amended many, many times.

PACE authorized the Secretary of State to issue codes of practice in connection with the exercise by police officers of their various statutory duties. The Criminal Justice Act 2003 abolished the necessity for revisions of the codes to be approved by an affirmative resolution of both Houses of Parliament: now they are simply laid before Parliament. Revised codes were brought into force in 1991 and 1995 to take account of new police powers contained in the CJPOA 1994. Further important revisions came into force in April 2003, 1 January 2006, 24 July 2006, 31 August 2006, 1 February 2008. There are currently eight Codes:

- Code A: on the exercise of statutory powers of stop and search, and the requirements to record public encounters.
- Code B: on searches of premises and the seizure of property found on premises and persons.
- Code C: on the detention, treatment and questioning of suspects (not related to terrorism) in police custody by police officers.
- Code D: on the identification of persons by police officers.
- Code E: on audio recording of interviews.
- Code F: on visual recording with sound of interviews with suspects. (There is no statutory requirement on police officers to visually record interviews. However, the contents of this code should be considered if an interviewing officer decides to make a visual recording with sound of an interview with a suspect).
- Code G: on the statutory power of arrest by police officers.
- Code H: on the detention, treatment and questioning of suspects related to terrorism in police custody by police officers.

By way of example, part of Code C is included at **[2:12]**. Brown **[2:13]** reviewed the research into the first ten years of life with PACE, concluding that PACE 'has not yet produced a system in balance'. Bucke and Brown **[2:14]** researched the 1995 changes: note in particular their comments on the quality of legal advice. Cape **[2:15]** explores the changing relationship between suspects and the police as a result of the 2003 changes (and see Zander (2003)).

There has been considerable debate not only about the constitutional status of these Codes, but also about the capacity of legal rules to influence police conduct. Chapter 7 includes a discussion of the trial judge's discretion to exclude evidence which was unfairly obtained. Proof of a breach of a code of practice does not necessarily lead to the exclusion of the evidence. In *Christou* **[7:10]** the Court of Appeal held that the appellants' admissions had been rightly admitted in evidence even though they had not been cautioned or informed of their rights—was the court correct in concluding that the relevant Code was 'simply not intended to apply in such a context'? Ashworth **[2:16]** seeks to test the justifications for the use of deceptive practices by the police. (His article was published before the Human Rights Act 1998 came into force in 2000.) Since then, there have been a number of important rulings applying the Human Rights Act to police practice. *R v Loosely; A-G's Reference No 3 of 2000* (2002) **[2:17]** is one such important example. It is extracted not from the full judgment but from the *Criminal Law Review* summary, which includes the brief commentary by Professor David Ormerod.

Covert and intrusive surveillance are obviously important police 'tools', and tools which must be carefully monitored. They are governed by Part III of the Police Act 1997 and by the Regulation of Investigatory Powers Act 2000, which distinguishes 'directed surveillance', 'intrusive surveillance', and the use of covert human intelligence sources. The Office of Surveillance Commissioners oversees this hugely important but largely invisible area of police activity: see Chief Surveillance Commissioner Annual Reports at <http://www.surveillancecommissioners.gov.uk>. (Particularly important to note the increasing use of surveillance powers by non-police criminal justice agencies?)

As well as Codes of Practice, Home Office circulars are used to control police discretion. These advise chief constables as to how particular policing tasks should be performed. For example, *R v Secretary of State for the Home Department, ex p Northumbria Police Authority* [2:3] concerned the lawfulness of a circular on the use of plastic bullets. Another example, is the practice of cautioning, which until 1999 was governed solely by Home Office circulars. Even today, simple cautions for adults (as opposed to 'conditional cautions': see below) are governed by a circular (HO Circular 30/2005). It is important to recognize that such circulars do not have the force of law. Nearly 20 years ago, Baldwin and Houghton (1986) painted a highly critical picture of the growth of 'government by informal decree'. If the 'informal decree' is not obeyed, no sanction for disobedience necessarily follows. Do such documents have any effect on individual police officers? 'Police culture' is not easily changed, certainly not just by a new document from the Home Office.

Let us look at some examples of police powers. Before 1984, there were a variety of laws granting powers of stop and search. Most notorious was the Vagrancy Act 1824, which gave parish constables powers to arrest vagabonds, trespassers, and loiterers. This 'sus' law was repealed in 1981, largely as a result of increasing evidence that it was being used disproportionately towards black people. The dangers of bias and prejudice within the system are clear—if police officers expect more trouble from certain individuals, the expectation can become self-fulfilling; if more attention is given to a particular section of the community, it is hardly surprising if more offences are detected amongst that group (see the data on race and criminal justice at [1:15] and [1:18]. Also, innocent people within that group will be more frequently stopped and searched. Part I of PACE [2:11] gave the police wide powers to stop and search, and to carry out road-checks, both of which are forms of detention short of arrest. Section 60 of CJPOA 1994 gave the police a wide new power to stop and search for offensive weapons in anticipation of violence—officers do not need to have grounds for suspicion against an individual before searching him under this power: a huge discretion to be exercised by junior officers out of the sight of senior officers. Now section 1 of the Criminal Justice Act 2003 has further extended the powers to stop and search by widening the definition of prohibited articles.

Many police powers are dependent upon proof of 'reasonable suspicion'. The classic definition of suspicion is that of Lord Devlin in *Hussein v Choong Fook Kam* [1970] AC 942: 'Suspicion in its ordinary meaning is a state of conjecture or surmise where proof is lacking: I suspect but I cannot prove'. The Royal Commission on Criminal Procedure (1981) concluded that it would be impracticable to formulate standards of reasonable suspicion in a statute or code of practice. It concluded (at page 29) that the requirements of notifying reasons, making records and the monitoring of such records by superior officers would be the most effective way of reducing the risk of random action. For a less complacent view, see Clayton and Tomlinson's comments on the case of *Castorina v Chief Constable of Surrey* [1980] NLJR 180: 'If the police are justified in arresting a middle-aged woman of good character on such flimsy grounds, without even questioning her as to her alibi or possible motives, then the law provides very scant protection for those suspected of crime' (at page 26).

A concept so vague as 'reasonable suspicion' is almost impossible to challenge. Constables are under a duty, imposed by section 3 of PACE, to make comprehensive records of searches, and chief constables are obliged to report annually on how many, and what kinds of, stops and searches have been carried out in their force areas. Yet these figures are not a totally accurate record of how many people are being stopped, since not all searches will have been recorded (see Code A). There is also a concern that, because the exercise of stop-and-search powers can be used as a measure of a constable's industry, the pressure on officers to stop and search poorer/disadvantaged people—rather than the more affluent, who are less likely to be out in the street—will increase.

A detailed analysis of the powers of entry, search, and seizure (Part II of PACE), the powers of arrest (Part III), the powers of detention (Part IV), and the powers of questioning and treatment of persons by the police (Part V) is beyond the scope of this book. However, let us apply the rules to our story. It seemed obvious to the ambulance crew that the victim had suffered four or five knife wounds to various parts of her upper body, arms, and chest, which necessitated many stitches and a stay in hospital. PC Green was not able to carry out a detailed interview since the ambulance crew wanted to take the woman straight to hospital, but she did establish that the woman's name is Rosa Bottles. She was drinking in the Black Bull pub with a group of friends, and at closing time there had been a fight. She mentions a few names, and says it was Gerry Good who stabbed her. PC Green goes straight to the pub, and asks the landlord, who is just going to bed, some questions. Meanwhile, two other officers in a police car are looking for Gerry Good. However, neither the landlord nor Rosa's friends seem to have witnessed the stabbing. They seem to agree that Rosa and Gerry, two regulars at the pub, had had an argument, and that Gerry had been seen following Rosa home in a fury. Rosa has a reputation as a heavy drinker, and as a 'tough cookie' capable of looking after herself.

The next day the police are able to interview Rosa at length in hospital. They also find Gerry Good, who spent the night with friends. Rather than ask him questions, they arrest him straight away and take him to the police station for questioning. For the power to arrest, see section 24 of PACE **[2:11]**, which was radically amended by section 24 of the Serious Organised Crime and Police Act 2005. The power of arrest, like the power to stop and search, is drafted in such vague terms that it is very difficult to challenge, and attempts through the courts to challenge the legality of arrests are rarely successful. The police inform Gerry that he is under arrest on suspicion of having committed a wounding. He may be searched on arrest only as authorized within section 17 of PACE **[2:11]**. If the police are still looking for the knife used in the attack, they may well wish to search Gerry's home under section 18 or 32 **[2:11]**. If so, since Gerry has not been at his home for some hours, the police officers should obtain authority from an officer of the rank of inspector or above before entering his house.

What sort of conversation will go on in the police car taking him to the police station? There has been some concern, especially since the introduction of taped interviews at police stations, about so-called 'car-seat' confessions. In Moston and Stephenson's study **[2:18]** arresting officers reported having interviewed suspects before arrival at the station in 8 per cent of cases in the sample. In addition, 31 per cent of suspects were reported to have been questioned before their arrest. They saw strong arguments in favour of the provision of portable tape recorders, and the Royal Commission (1993) recommended that a PACE code of practice should cover what is and is not permissible between the time of arrest and arrival at the police station. Brown, Ellis, and Larcombe **[2:19]** found that, although the rewording of Code of Practice C in 1991 to discourage interviews outside police stations had had some effect, such interviews still took place in 10 per cent of cases. Do you think that interviews should only happen at police stations?

As soon as Gerry is brought to the police station, the police must open a custody record. However, the reception area at the police station is a busy, sometimes chaotic, place and he may have to wait before being booked in. The custody officer, a sergeant, is responsible for the accuracy and completeness of the custody record, and all entries must be timed and signed by the maker. It is the custody officer who has the main responsibility for upholding the suspect's rights. Is it appropriate that this person should be a serving police officer? Is there a viable alternative? When Gerry eventually leaves the police station, he (or his solicitor) will be given a copy of the custody record, if he requests it.

The custody officer will inform Gerry of his rights: he has the right to consult a solicitor; the right to ask the police to notify his arrest to a relative or other named person likely to take an interest in his or her welfare; and the right to consult the PACE Codes of Practice. Sanders and Young (2007) comment that giving the police the job of 'triggering' legal advice appears to be a major obstacle to the success of the scheme: 'if suspects need protection from the police, by what logic can custody officers be expected to provide that protection?' (at page 217). The right to legal advice is, in the words of the Court of Appeal in *Samuel* [1988] QB 615, clear and unambiguous, but it is only effective if the legal profession provides the advice adequately, and we will return to this subject in Chapter 5.

The arrangements for supervising police inquiries were criticized by the Royal Commission on Criminal Justice (1993). In a research study conducted for the Royal Commission, Baldwin and Moloney **[2:20]** found that supervision as such was rare in most of the cases they studied. In the general run of cases, supervision and investigation were inextricably blurred, with supervising officers doing much of the interviewing. As Maguire and Norris (1993) comment, 'In a sense, the actual extent of malpractice, even if it is minuscule, is irrelevant…what is important is the potential for it to occur, should any officer or group of officers fail to do their job properly, and the soundness of any system designed to prevent it' (at page 3). The Royal Commission (1993) (**[1:4]** and **[2:21]**) concluded that a new approach to supervision is needed throughout the police service, with improved training in the supervision of inquiries at all levels. The need for close quality control over investigations and effective supervision remains: see Brown **[2:13]**, though even this is now sadly dated: are you surprised that there is not more empirical data in this area?

The length of time that a suspect can be held in custody without charge is strictly regulated by Part IV of PACE. For lesser offences, the period must not exceed 24 hours. A person suspected of committing a serious arrestable offence can be detained for up to 96 hours without charge, but only beyond 36 hours where a warrant is obtained from a magistrate. (The rules are controversially different for those suspected of offences of terrorism.) A review by the custody officer to check whether the criteria for detention are still satisfied must be made at regular intervals: six hours after initial detention and then at least every nine hours. In any 24-hour period a detained person must be allowed a continuous period of at least eight hours for rest, free from questioning, travel, or other interruption arising out of the investigation concerned. Police cells accommodating detainees must be adequately lit, heated, cleaned, and ventilated (see Code C: The Detention, Treatment and Questioning of Persons by Police Officers **[2:12]**). Access to toilet facilities must be provided, as well as suitable food and clothing. Despite these provisions, the student must remember that police cells and custody blocks are often dismal places.

Gerry tells the custody officer that he wants to see his solicitor, and so the custody officer rings Shaw and Co, the solicitors who have represented him in the past, and they agree to send someone. There is often no facility for private telephone calls by suspects. Ian Brown, a legally unqualified clerk from Shaw and Co, arrives soon after 1 pm. In a private interview, Gerry admits that he was in the Black Bull that night, that he had been involved in a fight, but that he hadn't used a knife and hadn't seen anyone else use one either. At 3 pm

Gerry is formally interviewed by a different police officer, since the arresting officer has now gone off duty. Ian Brown is present throughout, but says nothing. Detailed rules governing the questioning of persons held in custody are set out in Code C **[2:12]**. The suspect must be cautioned before any questions are put for the purpose of obtaining evidence. The current caution says:

You do not have to say anything, but it may harm your defence if you do not mention, when questioned, something which you later rely on in court. Anything you say may be given in evidence.

False confessions and police misconduct are two of the main causes of miscarriages of justice, and much of the Report of the Royal Commission of Criminal Justice (1993) looked at ways to improve safeguards inside the police station. A whole chapter was given over to the 'right of silence' and confession evidence. The discussion of the right to silence is reproduced at **[2:21]**. The Royal Commission concluded that, because it is the less experienced and more vulnerable suspects against whom the threat of adverse comment at trial would be likely to be more damaging, there should be no adverse comments if they do not answer police questions. In reality, few suspects exercise their right to silence, and Leng's research (1994) found no evidence that the abolition of the right to silence would lead to more convictions. Zuckerman (1994) doubted that the right to silence ever protected the weak or confused: they have always been more likely to succumb to police demands for answers despite the right. Sections 34–39 of the CJPOA 1994 **[2:22]** controversially changed the law on the right to silence, setting out the circumstances when the court or the jury may draw adverse inferences from the fact that a person did not give evidence at his trial or answer questions put to him by the police. In response to the European Court of Human Rights decision in *Murray v United Kingdom* (1996) 22 EHRR 29, section 58 of the Youth Justice and Criminal Evidence Act 1999 prevents such an inference being drawn against a silent suspect who has not yet consulted a solicitor.

An important challenge to the new rules was made in the case of the Condrons, who were convicted of drug-related offences following a direction by the trial judge stating that the jury had the option of drawing an adverse inference from silence during police interviews. Their solicitor, believing them to be suffering from heroin withdrawal symptoms, had advised them to say nothing. They were found guilty and whilst the Court of Appeal in *Condron* [1997] 1 Cr App R 185 considered the judge's direction to be flawed, it did not find the conviction to be unsafe. However, Condron complained to the European Court of Human Rights, contending that he had not received a fair trial within the meaning of Article 6(1) of the European Convention on Human Rights. The European Court of Human Rights in *Condron v United Kingdom (No 2)* (2000) 31 EHRR 1 allowed his application, stating that Condron had not received a fair trial under Article 6(1) as the jury should have been directed that, if the silence could not be attributed to Condron having no answer, or none that would stand up in cross-examination, no adverse inference should be drawn. The reason for the silence, if one is proffered, and its plausibility, should have been taken into account. However, this ruling has not prevented the domestic courts from taking a tough line: a series of cases from the Court of Appeal has confirmed that legal advice to remain silent cannot prevent an adverse inference being drawn under section 34 of the CJPOA 1994. Whilst at one level this makes sense (to have held otherwise would have given solicitors *carte blanche* to advise silence on all occasions, so undermining the change in the law), the current position can be highly problematic. In *Howell* [2003] EWCA Crim 1, [2003] Crim LR 405 the Court of Appeal confirmed that there must always be 'soundly based objective reasons' for silence, which makes the advisory role of the solicitor very difficult. As Lord Woolf put it in *Beckles*

(No 2) [2004] EWCA Crim 2766, [2005] Crim LR 560:

Where the reason put forward by a defendant for not answering questions is that he is acting on legal advice, the position is singularly delicate. On the one hand the Courts have not unreasonably wanted to avoid defendants driving a coach and horses through section 34 and by so doing defeating the statutory objective. Such an explanation is very easy for a defence to advance and difficult to investigate because of legal professional privilege. On the other hand, it is of the greatest importance that defendants should be able to be advised by their lawyer without their having to reveal the terms of that advice if they act in accordance with that advice. (at para 43)

In our case, Gerry Good is reminded of the caution, and makes admissions to the police similar to those he made earlier to the solicitor's clerk. He admits that he had an argument with Rosa Bottles earlier in the evening, when she had refused to go home with him, but continued to deny using a knife. He is very irritated at the tone of the police questioning, insisting that he is being set up. What is acceptable police practice in interviews remains unclear. There is a classic dilemma here between crime control and due process (see **[1:9]**— tactics that will often effectively uncover the truth will elicit false confessions in other cases. However many due process safeguards are imposed on the police, 'cop culture acts as a powerful crime control engine at the heart of the machinery of criminal justice' (Sanders and Young (2007) at page 63).

It has been standard practice to tape-record interviews since 1991, but the custody officer who makes the decision to charge a suspect, and with what offence, will not listen to the tape. He will rely on the version of events reported to him by the police officer who conducted the interview. At 6 pm Gerry is charged. The custody officer accepts the interviewing officer's view that there is enough evidence that it was Gerry who stabbed Rosa Bottles. A suitable charge must be made. Gerry could be charged with an offence under section 18 (grievous bodily harm with intent), section 20 (reckless grievous bodily harm), or section 47 (actual bodily harm) of the Offences Against the Person Act 1861. There may be a degree of 'over-charging': he may be charged with section 18, in the knowledge that a lower charge can be bargained in return for a guilty plea. The Code for Crown Prosecutors **[3:6]** sets out in paragraph 7 that the charges selected should reflect the seriousness of the offending; give the court adequate sentencing powers; and enable the case to be presented in a clear and simple way.

Charging standards were introduced in 1994 in order to bring more consistency to police charging practice, but it has remained a thorny issue. There has long been concern that the police selected inappropriate charges (for example, in his Annual Report for 1999–2000, HM Chief Inspector of the Crown Prosecution Service noted that in some 22 per cent of cases to which charging standards applied the police had selected inappropriate charges). In almost all cases, the inspectors agreed that the CPS had then applied the charging standards correctly, usually to downgrade the charges but sometimes to upgrade them. Auld's *Review of the Criminal Courts* **[1:5]** recommended that the CPS should assume from the police a greater responsibility for determining the charges at the outset of criminal proceedings, and this was adopted in the Criminal Justice Act 2003. We return to this subject in the next chapter, on the CPS.

Gerry is charged with an offence under section 18 of the Offences Against the Person Act 1861. Once he has been charged, the police may no longer ask him any questions relating to the offence, and will have to decide whether to grant him bail, discussed in section (v) below.

(iv) CAUTIONING

The police have a number of options when dealing with a suspect: they can take no further action (NFA); they can issue an informal warning (when no official record is made); they can give a formal or 'conditional' caution; or they can discuss a prosecution with the CPS. A number of Home Office circulars have been issued over the years seeking to achieve greater consistency in the way police forces and individual police officers decide how to proceed. Those of 1985 and 1990 encouraged greater use of cautioning, especially in relation to juveniles, noting the possible harmful effects of court appearances. The 1990 Circular introduced national standards. National figures probably still masked wide regional variations, partly reflecting the use of formal rather than informal cautioning in a given force area. Diversion from the criminal courts can have longer-term net-widening effects, in that offenders who would previously have been dealt with informally may now be formally cautioned and so may be pushed more swiftly into the criminal justice system. There is inconclusive evidence on this, since no statistics are kept on cases in which no further action is taken. However, the use of cautions attaches a stigmatizing label to the suspect, and McConville et al (1991; see also [3:10]) believe they are used on suspects where there is insufficient evidence to prosecute. Most importantly, diversion procedures may usurp the powers of the court. Nearly 20 years ago Light (1987) bemoaned the fact that drunks are now 'processed through the revolving door of the cautioning system with the prospect of any alternative facilities receding further and further into the distance'. The problems facing habitual drunks in our society are thus being effectively swept under the carpet, he argued. Due process safeguards can also disappear when vital decisions are taken 'informally'.

By 1994 the tide had turned against cautions. Home Office Circular 18/94 tightened up the guidance to the police, resulting in a decline in the number of repeat cautions. Evans and Ellis (1997) pointed to a decrease in the rate of cautioning for juveniles. Whilst the 1994 circular suggested that 'it will often be desirable for the police to liaise with local statutory and voluntary agencies', it also stressed that 'the decision to caution is in all cases one for the police, and although it is open to them to seek the advice of multi-agency panels, this should not be done as a matter of course'. It is worth noting, though, the high number of adults who continued to be cautioned. In 2001, the cautioning rate (i.e. the percentage of offenders formally cautioned as a percentage of offenders found guilty or formally cautioned) for indictable offences for men aged 21 or over was 19 per cent, and for women over 21, 32 per cent (see Criminal Statistics, 2002). By 2005, the cautioning rate was up to 25 per cent for men over 21 and an astonishing 41 per cent for women over 21 (see Criminal Statistics, 2005). This is an extraordinary feature of the English criminal justice system: most European legal systems do not entrust their police with a formal discretion not to prosecute. The latest guidance is to be found in Home Office Circular 30/2005.

The Crime and Disorder Act 1998 **[2:23]** abolished this system of cautioning for young offenders. Sections 65 and 66 of the Act introduced a system of warnings and reprimands, which result in the child or young person being referred to a Youth Offending Team (a YOT— see section 39). Whilst many welcome this welfarist approach, especially in relation to juveniles, McConville et al **[3:12]** were more sceptical. Is police dominance maintained despite the welfarist rhetoric? See Holdaway et al (2001) for an early assessment of the new system.

The next major change was the introduction of 'conditional cautions'. These originated in the Auld Report **[1:5]**, which proposed a 'discretionary power...not to prosecute, or to withdraw a prosecution, on condition (for example) that the offender submitted to some form of penalty or supervision of his conduct and/or offered some form of redress and/or submitted to medical or other treatment' (at page 381). They were introduced in Part 3 of the Criminal Justice Act 2003 (sections 22–27). The conditions to be attached to a conditional caution were originally for rehabilitative or reparative purposes (section 22(3)), but section 17 of the Police and Justice Act 2006 (not yet in force) makes financial penalties a clear part of the conditional caution. So these cautions are more like a form of 'prosecutor's sentence' than a traditional caution. This is a radical departure: prosecutors now punish? We will return to this in Chapter 3.

There are other forms of diversion, and the Government is committed to 'strengthening powers to tackle anti-social behaviour' (the name of a consultation paper published in November 2006) by 'enhancing the framework of pre-court disposals'. These include Fixed Penalty Tickets (issued by police and traffic wardens), widely accepted for traffic offences (endorsable and non-endorsable); Penalty Notices (issued by Councils); and Penalty Notices for Disorder (PNDs), introduced by sections 1–11 of Criminal Justice and Police Act 2001, and rolled out nationally in 2004. In that first year, 63,639 PNDs were issued by police forces in England and Wales, mostly for offences such as 'causing harassment, alarm or distress' (28,790 PNDs issued) and 'drunk and disorderly' (26,609 issued) (See Goffe et al, 'Penalty Notices for Disorder Statistics 2004' (HO Online Report 35/05), the only year for which statistics are so far available, but it seems obvious that the numbers will rise significantly. Is this a good thing?

(v) BAIL

Will Gerry be granted bail? His case will not be tried for many weeks. The police will have to decide whether it will be enough merely to give him a date on which he is to appear before the court. The Bail Act 1976 **[6:6]** provides a statutory presumption in favour of bail, but section 38 of PACE (as amended by CJPOA 1994, s 28) **[2:11]** sets out the grounds on which the custody officer may keep Gerry in custody. This involves him in the impossible task of predicting risk. Until section 27 of the CJPOA 1994 inserted a new section 3A in the Bail Act 1976, the custody officer could not release someone on bail subject to conditions. This section adopts the Royal Commission on Criminal Justice (1993) recommendation that the police should have the power to release a suspect on bail subject to conditions (though not a condition that they reside at a bail hostel). This power should have reduced the suspect's liability to attend court, and a person bailed by the police in this way whom it is later decided not to charge or to prosecute may thus avoid altogether a court appearance and its attendant publicity. He is also spared the unpleasant experience of a night in the cells. The disadvantage for the suspect is that he may agree to unwarranted conditions just to get away from the police station. Bucke and Brown **[2:14]** found that the power to attach conditions to police bail is being used in roughly one-fifth of cases in which suspects are bailed after charge, but that there has been little reduction in the proportion detained for court. Rather, conditions are often imposed where the suspect would formerly have been given unconditional bail. The impact of these conditions on levels of offending whilst on bail are difficult to measure. In Gerry Good's case, the police are concerned that he will go back to the Black Bull and 'have a go' at all those who have mentioned him to the police. They decide, to Gerry's fury, to keep him in the cells until the morning and take him to the magistrates' court for a remand hearing. Bail applications are discussed in Chapter 6.

The necessary paperwork must now be prepared for the court. A time-consuming task for the police is the preparation of written summaries of taped interviews. The police estimated that preparing summaries takes the equivalent of some 1,300 to 1,500 officers' full-time working hours (see the Royal Commission (1993) at page 41). Baldwin **[2:24]** questioned the accuracy of that estimate, and concluded that there is no satisfactory alternative to lawyers using the record of interview only after having played the tape itself. He suggested that some of the main benefits of tape recording interviews with suspects are being filtered away by too heavy a reliance upon the records of interviews, which are often inadequate. The Royal Commission (1993) recommended that the Home Office explore a number of options to establish the best practicable method of producing interview records for the future, but little has changed in this area.

As far as Gerry is concerned, he has now been 'set up' by the police. He does not think they have any evidence against him. What goes on in the early stages of an investigation is clearly vital to the satisfactory conviction of offenders, but also at the root of many apparently unsafe convictions. The courts have a vital role in preventing inappropriate policing: see Chapter 7, and Ashworth (1998). It was partly a recognition of the wide discretionary powers that are wielded by the police which led to the creation in 1985 of the CPS. In the next chapter, we examine the role of the CPS and the friction that has been generated between it and the police. The police are working under increasing pressure, as the demands on them outstrip any growth in resources. It is clearly essential that legal safeguards are present in the police station and not just in the courtroom: should there be greater independent scrutiny of what goes on in the police station?

FURTHER READING

Ashworth, A, 'Should the police be allowed to use deceptive practices?' (1998) 114 LQR 108

Ashworth, A and Redmayne, M, *The Criminal Process* (3rd edition, 2005) Oxford UP

Baldwin, R and Houghton, J, 'Circular arguments: the status and legitimacy of administrative rules' [1986] Public Law 239

Bucke, T, Street, R, and Brown, D, 'The Right to Silence: The Impact of the Criminal Justice and Public Order Act 1994' (2000) HORS No 199, HMSO

Chief Surveillance Commissioner Annual Reports, HMSO

Cooper, C, Anscombe, J, Aveell, J, McLean Morris, J, 'A national evaluation of Community Support Officers' (2006) HO Research Study No 297

Cotton, J and Povey, D, 'Police Complaints and Discipline, England and Wales, April 1997 to March 1998' (1998) HORS Issue 20/1998, HMSO

Gleeson, E and Grace, K, 'Police complaints: statistics for England and Wales 2006/07', IPCC Research and Statistics Series: Paper 8

Goffe, P et al, 'Penalty Notices for Disorder Statistics 2004', HO Online Report 35/05

Holdaway, S, Davidson, N, Dignan, J, Hammersley, R, Hine, J, and Marsh, P, 'New strategies to address youth offending: the national evaluation of the pilot youth offending teams' (2001) RDS Occasional Paper No 69, Home Office

Leng, R, 'The right to silence in police interrogation' (1993) RCCJ Research Study No 10, HMSO

Macpherson, W, 'The Stephen Lawrence Inquiry' (1999) Cm 4262–1, HMSO

Maguire, M and Corbett, C, *A Study of the Police Complaints System* (1991) HMSO

Maguire, M and Norris, C, 'The conduct and supervision of criminal investigations' (1993) RCCJ Research Study No 5, HMSO

Morgan, D and Stephenson, G, *Suspicion and Silence: the Right to Silence in Criminal Investigations* (1994) Blackstone

Newburn, T, *Handbook of Policing* (2003) Willan

Newburn, R and Reiner, R, 'PC Dixon to Dixon PLC: policing and policing powers since 1954' [2004] Crim LR 601

Phillips, C and Brown, D, 'Entry into the criminal justice system: a survey of police arrests and their outcomes' (1998) HORS No 185, HMSO

Report of the Royal Commission on Criminal Procedure (1981) Cmnd 8092

Rowe, M (ed), *Policing beyond Macpherson* (2007) Willan

Sanders, A, 'The limits to diversion from prosecution' (1988) 28 BJ of Criminology 513

Sanders, A and Young, R *Criminal Justice* (3rd edition, 2007) Oxford UP

Waddington, P A J, *The Strong Arm of the Law* (1991) Oxford UP

Walker, C and Starmer, K, *Justice in Error* (Chapters 1–4, 1993) Blackstone

Zander, M, 'The Revised PACE Codes' (2003) 3 Archbold News 5

Zander, M, *The Police and Criminal Evidence Act 1984* (5th edition, 2005) Sweet & Maxwell

Zuckerman, A A A, 'Trial by unfair means—the report of the Working Group on the Right to Silence' [1989] Crim LR 855

Zuckerman, A A A, 'The inevitable demise of the right to silence' (1994) 144 NLJ 1104

DOCUMENTS

[2:1] Police Act 1996 (as amended)
Sections 1–6; 6ZA–6ZC; 8A; 10–12

Part I   Organisation of Police Forces
Police areas
1 Police areas

(1) England and Wales shall be divided into police areas.

(2) The police areas referred to in subsection (1) shall be—

   (a) those listed in Schedule 1 (subject to any amendment made to that Schedule by an order under section 32 below, section 58 of the Local Government Act 1972, or section 17 of the Local Government Act 1992),

   (b) the metropolitan police district, and

   (c) the City of London police area.

(3) References in Schedule 1 to any local government area are to that area as it is for the time being, but excluding any part of it within the metropolitan police district.

Forces outside London

2 Maintenance of police forces

A police force shall be maintained for every police area for the time being listed in Schedule 1.

3 Establishment of police authorities

(1) There shall be a police authority for every police area for the time being listed in Schedule 1.

(2) A police authority established under this section for any area shall be a body corporate to be known by the name of the area with the addition of the words "Police Authority".

4 Membership of police authorities etc

(1) Subject to subsection (2), each police authority established under section 3 shall consist of seventeen members.

(2) The Secretary of State may by order provide in relation to a police authority specified in the order that the number of its members shall be a specified odd number greater than seventeen.

(3) A statutory instrument containing an order under subsection (2) shall be laid before Parliament after being made.

(4) Schedule 2 shall have effect in relation to police authorities established under section 3 and the appointment of their members.

5 Reductions in size of police authorities

(1) This section applies to any order under section 4(2) which varies or revokes an earlier order so as to reduce the number of a police authority's members.

(2) Before making an order to which this section applies, the Secretary of State shall consult—

(a) the authority, and

(b) the councils which are relevant councils in relation to the authority for the purposes of Schedule 2

(3) An order to which this section applies may include provision as to the termination of the appointment of the existing members of the authority and the making of new appointments or re-appointments.

6. General functions of police authorities

(1) Every police authority established under section 3—

(a) shall secure the maintenance of an efficient and effective police force for its area, and

(b) shall hold the chief officer of police of that force to account for the exercise of his functions and those of persons under his direction and control.

(2) In discharging its functions, every police authority established under section 3 shall have regard to—

(a) any strategic priorities determined by the Secretary of State under section 37A,

(b) any objectives determined by the authority by virtue of section 6ZB,

(c) any performance targets established by the authority, whether in compliance with a direction under section 38 or otherwise, and

(d) any plan issued by the authority by virtue of section 6ZB.

(3) In discharging any function to which a code of practice issued under section 39 relates, a police authority established under section 3 shall have regard to the code.

(5) This section shall apply in relation to the Metropolitan Police Authority as it applies in relation to a police authority established under section 3.

6ZA Power to confer particular functions on police authorities

(1) The Secretary of State may by order confer particular functions on police authorities.

(2) Without prejudice to the generality of subsection (1), an order under this section may contain provision requiring a police authority—

    (a) to monitor the performance of the police force maintained for its area in-

        (i) complying with any duty imposed on the force by or under this Act, the Human Rights Act 1998 or any other enactment;

        (ii) carrying out any plan issued by virtue of section 6ZB;

    (b) to secure that arrangements are made for that force to co-operate with other police forces whenever necessary or expedient;

    (c) to promote diversity within that force and within the authority.

(3) Before making an order under this section the Secretary of State must consult—

    (a) the Association of Police Authorities,

    (a) the Association of Chief Police Officers, and

    (a) such other persons as he thinks fit.

(4) An order under this section may make different provision for different police authorities.

(5) A statutory instrument containing an order under this section shall be subject to annulment in pursuance of a resolution of either House of Parliament.

6ZB Plans by police authorities

(1) Before the beginning of each financial year every police authority shall issue a plan (a "policing plan") setting out—

    (a) the authority's objectives ("policing objectives") for the policing of its area during that year; and

    (b) the proposed arrangements for the policing of that area for the period of three years beginning with that year.

(2) Policing objectives shall be so framed as to be consistent with any strategic priorities determined under section 37A.

(3) Before determining policing objectives, a police authority shall—

    (a) consult the relevant chief officer of police, and

    (b) consider any views obtained by the authority in accordance with arrangements made under section 96.

(4) A draft of a policing plan required to be issued by a police authority under this section shall be prepared by the relevant chief officer of police and submitted by him to the authority for it to consider.

The authority shall consult the relevant chief officer of police before issuing a policing plan which differs from the draft submitted by him under this subsection.

(5) The Secretary of State may by regulations make provision supplementing that made by this section.

(6) The regulations may make provision (further to that made by subsection (3)) as to persons who are to be consulted, and matters that are to be considered, before determining policing objectives.

(7) The regulations may contain provision as to—

    (a) matters to be dealt with in policing plans (in addition to those mentioned in subsection (1));

    (b) persons who are to be consulted, and matters that are to be considered, in preparing policing plans;

(c) modification of policing plans;

(d) persons to whom copies of policing plans are to be sent.

(8) Before making regulations under this section the Secretary of State must consult-

(a) the Association of Police Authorities,

(b) the Association of Chief Police Officers, and

(c) such other persons as he thinks fit.

(9) Regulations under this section may make different provision for different police authorities.

(10) A statutory instrument containing regulations under this section shall be subject to annulment in pursuance of a resolution of either House of Parliament.

(11) In this section "the relevant chief officer of police", in relation to a police authority, means the chief officer of police of the police force maintained by that authority.

6ZC Reports by police authorities

(1) The Secretary of State may by order require police authorities to issue reports concerning the policing of their areas.

(2) An order under this section may contain provision as to—

(a) the periods to be covered by reports, and, as regards each period, the date by which reports are to be issued;

(b) the matters to be dealt with in reports;

(c) persons to whom copies of reports are to be sent.

(3) Before making an order under this section the Secretary of State must consult—

(a) the Association of Police Authorities,

(b) the Association of Chief Police Officers, and

(c) such other persons as he thinks fit.

(4) An order under this section may make different provision for different police authorities.

(5) A statutory instrument containing an order under this section shall be subject to annulment in pursuance of a resolution of either House of Parliament.

8A Local policing summaries

(1) As soon as possible after the end of each financial year, every police authority established under section 3 shall issue a report for members of the public in the authority's area on matters relating to the policing of that area for the year.

(2) Such a report is referred to in this section as a "local policing summary".

(3) The Secretary of State may by order specify matters which are to be included in a local policing summary.

(4) A police authority shall arrange—

(a) for every local policing summary issued by it under this section to be published in such manner as appears to it to be appropriate, and

(b) for a copy of every such summary to be sent, by whatever means appear to the authority to be appropriate, to each person liable to pay any tax, precept or levy to or in respect of the authority.

(5) It shall be the duty of a police authority, in preparing and publishing a local policing summary, to have regard to any guidance given by the Secretary of State about the form and content of local policing summaries and the manner of their publication.

(6) Before making an order under subsection (3), and before giving any such guidance as is referred to in subsection (5), the Secretary of State must consult—

(a) the Association of Police Authorities;

(b) the Association of Chief Police Officers; and

(c) such other persons as he thinks fit.

(7) This section shall apply in relation to the Metropolitan Police Authority as it applies to a police authority established under section 3.

(8) A statutory instrument containing an order under subsection (3) shall be subject to annulment in pursuance of a resolution of either House of Parliament.

10 General functions of chief constables

(1) A police force maintained under section 2 shall be under the direction and control of the chief constable appointed under section 11.

(2) In discharging his functions, every chief constable shall have regard to—

(a) any arrangements involving his force that are made by virtue of section 6ZA(2)(b);

(b) the policing plan issued by the police authority for his area under section 6ZB.

11 Appointment and removal of chief constables

(1) The chief constable of a police force maintained under section 2 shall be appointed by the police authority responsible for maintaining the force, but subject to the approval of the Secretary of State and to regulations under section 50.

(2) Without prejudice to any regulations under section 50 or under the [Police Pensions Act 1976.] Police Pensions Act 1976, the police authority, acting with the approval of the Secretary of State, may call upon the chief constable to retire in the interests of efficiency or effectiveness.

(3) Before seeking the approval of the Secretary of State under subsection (2), the police authority shall give the chief constable an opportunity to make representations and shall consider any representations that he makes.

(3A) A police authority maintaining a police force under section 2, acting with the approval of the Secretary of State, may suspend from duty the chief constable of that force if—

(a) it is proposing to consider whether to exercise its power under subsection (2) to call upon the chief constable to retire or to resign and is satisfied that, in the light of the proposal, the maintenance of public confidence in that force requires the suspension; or

(b) having been notified by the Secretary of State that he is proposing to consider whether to require the police authority to exercise that power, it is satisfied that, in the light of the Secretary of State's proposal, the maintenance of public confidence in that force requires the suspension; or

(c) it has exercised that power or been sent under section 42(2A) a copy of a notice of the Secretary of State's intention to require it to exercise that power, but the retirement or resignation has not yet taken effect;

and it shall be the duty of a police authority maintaining such a force (without reference to the preceding provisions of this subsection) to suspend the chief constable of that force from duty if it is required to do so by the Secretary of State under section 42(1A).

(4) A chief constable who is called upon to retire under subsection (2) shall retire on such date as the police authority may specify or on such earlier date as may be agreed upon between him and the authority.

11A Appointment and removal of deputy chief constables

(1) Every police force maintained under section 2 shall have one or more deputy chief constables.

(2) The appointment of a person to be a deputy chief constable of a police force shall be made, in accordance with regulations under section 50, by the police authority responsible for maintaining that force.

(2A) Where the police authority responsible for maintaining a police force—

(a) proposes to increase the number of deputy chief constables that the force has, or

(b) proposes to appoint a particular person to be a deputy chief constable,

it may do so only after consultation with the chief constable and subject to the approval of the Secretary of State.

(3) Subsections (2) to (4) of section 11 shall apply in relation to a deputy chief constable as they apply in relation to a chief constable but with the omission in subsection (3A)—

(a) of paragraph (b);

(b) in paragraph (c), of the words from 'or been sent' to 'exercise that power'; and

(c) of the words after paragraph (c).

12 Assistant chief constables

(1) The ranks that may be held in a police force maintained under section 2 shall include that of assistant chief constable; and in every such police force there shall be at least one person holding that rank.

(2) Appointments and promotions to the rank of assistant chief constable shall be made, in accordance with regulations under section 50, by the police authority after consultation with the chief constable and subject to the approval of the Secretary of State.

(3) Subsections (2) to (4) of section 11 shall apply to an assistant chief constable as they apply to a chief constable but with the omission in subsection (3A)—

(a) of paragraph (b);

(b) in paragraph (c), of the words from "or been sent" to "exercise that power"; and

(c) of the words after paragraph (c).

[2:2] Audit Commission, 'Cheques and Balances: A Framework for Improving Police Accountability'

(1994) HMSO (at page 10)

Exhibit 4

Duties and powers: co-operation or conflict?

The Act seeks to balance duties and powers, but there is a degree of overlap

	Chief Constable	Police Authority	Home Office
General duty	Responsibility for the direction and control of the force	To secure the maintenance of an efficient and effective police force for its area	Must promote the efficiency and effectiveness of the police

	Chief Constable	Police Authority	Home Office
Finance	Day-to-day financial management within regulations drawn up by police authority. Prepares draft budget	Ultimate responsibility for all expenditure. Its financial regulations determine degree of delegation to chief constable. Agrees budget; issues precept	Issues guidance to encourage grant and capping level. After adverse HMIC report, may direct a police authority as to a minimum budget
Personnel	Has direction and control of police officers and civilians whom the police authority wishes to manage directly	Employs all civilians and places them under control of chief constable, except where agreed otherwise. Appoints chief constable; can call upon him to retire	Arbitrates in disputes over management of civilians. Approves appointment of chief constable and can require him to retire
Objectives and targets	Must have regard to national and local objectives and targets in discharging his functions	Must set local objectives and performance targets after consulting chief constable and obtaining the views of the community	Set national objectives and can direct police authority to establish levels of performance for these objectives. Receives a copy of the issues Plan; but does not resolve disputes over the content
Deployment of resources	Has operational control over how resources are depleted.	Local Policing Plan will specify the proposed allocation of resources. Control funding for additional resources	Can issue directions on levels of performance to aim at in relation to national objectives; this may impact upon use of resources

[2:3] *R v Secretary of State for the Home Department, ex p Northumbria Police Authority*
[1989] QB 26

The Secretary of State for the Home Department issued a circular (No 40/1986) to all chief officers of police and clerks to police authorities in England and Wales informing them that in future police requirements for plastic baton rounds and CS gas for use in the event of serious public disorder would be met from a central store to be maintained by the Secretary of State. A police authority sought to challenge the issue of the circular on the grounds that the Secretary of State had no power either by virtue of the Police Act 1964 or otherwise to maintain a central supply of such equipment, or to supply the equipment without the approval of the relevant police authority save in a situation of grave emergency. The Divisional Court dismissed the application to quash the decision of the Secretary of Sate to issue and apply the circular.

The Court of Appeal concluded that the Secretary of State had power both under the Police Act and the prerogative to supply the equipment, and the decision of the Divisional Court was affirmed.

Croom-Johnson LJ (at page 39):

It is common ground that the chief constable has complete operational control of his force. Neither the police authority nor the Secretary of State may give him any directions about that. The relationship between police forces and their appropriate local authorities was exhaustively examined by McCardie J in *Fisher v Oldham Corporation* [1930] 2 KB 364. In that case it was held that the police were not the servants of the watch committee of a borough corporation so as to make the corporation civilly liable for wrongs committed by the police. The police perform their duties as constables wholly independently of the watch committee or police authority. McCardie J gave this illustration, at pp 372–373:

> Suppose that a police officer arrested a man for a serious felony. Suppose, too, that the watch committee of the borough at once passed a resolution directing that the felon should be released. Of what value would such a resolution be? Not only would it be the plain duty of the police officer to disregard the resolution, but it would also be the duty of the chief constable to consider whether an information should not at once be laid against the members of the watch committee for a conspiracy to obstruct the course of justice.

The independence of a constable, and *a fortiori* a chief constable, from outside control, whether by a local authority or the executive, has been repeatedly upheld.

This independence of the police goes back a long way, it is not the creation of the Police Act 1964.

The financial provisions of the Act of 1964 are contained in section 8, as amended by section 25 of and Schedule 11 to the Local Government Act 1982. The effect is that all receipts of the police authority shall be paid into the police fund and all expenditure of any such police authority shall be paid out of that fund. That fund is in the exclusive control of the police authority.

Part II of the Act of 1964 is headed 'Central Supervision, Direction and Facilities.' Section 28 sets out the general duty of the Secretary of State. It reads:

> The Secretary of State shall exercise his powers under this Act in such manner and to such extent as appears to him to be best calculated to promote the efficiency of the police.

It indicates the object to be achieved by the exercise of powers conferred on him elsewhere. By section 31 he may make grants to the police authority in respect of expenses incurred for police purposes. By section 33 he has a power to make regulations, none of which are relevant for present purposes. Section 38 provides for the appointment and functions of inspectors of constabulary, who are to inspect and report to the Secretary of State on the efficiency of all police forces. They shall also carry out such other duties for the purpose of furthering police efficiency as the Secretary of State may from time to time direct.

Section 41 is important. It begins a part of the Act subheaded 'Central services'. It was under this section that the circular was sent. Section 41 says:

> The Secretary of State may provide and maintain, or may contribute towards the provisions or maintenance of, a police college, district police training centres, forensic science laboratories, wireless depots and such other organisations and services as he considers necessary or expedient for promoting the efficiency of the police.

Before the Divisional Court the police authority contended that section 41 did not give the Secretary of State power to supply equipment to the police force without the consent of the police authority. On that point the Divisional Court found in favour of the police authority. In this court the Secretary of State has argued that the Divisional Court was wrong, and that he does have the power. The Divisional Court however accepted an argument advanced by the Secretary of State that alternatively he may supply equipment, without the permission of the police authority, under the Royal prerogative. Against that finding the police authority now appeals.

It is convenient to take the section 41 point first. It is a straight matter of construction of the section, when placed in the context of the statute as a whole. It is not now contended by the Secretary of State that he can, as was stated in the circular, propose that all police requirements for plastic baton rounds and CS gas must be met from his central store. The police authority agreed that section 41 gives the Secretary of State power to maintain a central store—which it was conceded would be an 'organisation' within the meaning of that section—but it was argued that section 4(4) reserves to the authority the exclusive right to obtain equipment in discharge of its duty to secure the maintenance of an efficient police force. That the authority has financial control over the police fund was prayed in aid. The interpretation was said to be consistent with the general scheme of the statute which divides the respective functions for providing an efficient force into three: an authority to maintain, provide and equip; a chief constable to control and operate; and a Secretary of State to supervise and regulate. The authority's case was that the Police Act 1964 sets out a complete and comprehensive code which defines and limits the functions of each of those three entities. It is correct that there is a general scheme as described by the authority. The question is whether the functions are as closely limited and exclusive as is suggested.

Section 4 places a duty on the authority and gives it a discretion how the duty is to be discharged. Section 8 provides it with the funds with which to do so. But section 28 places a duty on the Secretary of State to use high powers so as to promote the efficiency of the police. Those powers include the provision of central services. It is too narrow a construction of section 41 to say, as the authority contended, that the establishments mentioned in the section are only organisations and no more, and that the central store would be another. It ignores the word 'service' in the section. If the Secretary of State gives instruction at a police college, or if a forensic science laboratory examines material sent to it by a force, he is providing services. Similarly, the supply of baton rounds or CS gas from the store is another service. It is not permissible to read into section 41 words which are not there, such as 'with the consent of the police authority'. There is no need to do so. Such services may be asked for by a chief constable in the ordinary course of carrying out his duty of efficient policing. If some payment for the service used is required, it would have to come from the police fund concerned, but if the Secretary of State is willing to make no charge there is no reason why the chief constable may not avail himself of what is available without asking the authority. To read into section 41 the words which are suggested would involve an interference by the authority in the operational discretion of the chief constable. The provisions in section 43 relating to the payment of policemen who are seconded for service under the Crown in providing the central services have no bearing on the point now at issue.

(At page 42:)

Although there has always been what is called the war prerogative, which is the Crown's right to make war and peace, Mr Keene submitted that there is no corresponding prerogative to enforce the keeping of what is popularly called the 'Queen's peace within the realm'. It does, however, contain an extensive section on 'The King as the Fountain of Justice' and courts and gaols. The argument is that if there was no prerogative power to keep the peace in 1820, at which date no organised police force existed, then all police forces exist and are controlled only by the later statutes by which they were created, and there is no residual prerogative power to draw on in cases of necessity... There were constables long before the establishment of Peel's Metropolitan Police in 1829. At all events, the assumption was early made that keeping the peace was part of the prerogative. The position of the Secretary of State is that he is one of a number of secretaries of state through whom the prerogative power is exercised. In *Harrison v Bush* (1856) 5 E & B 344 at 353, Lord Campbell CJ stated:

> In practice, to the Secretary of State for the Home Department...Belongs peculiarly the maintenance of the peace within the Kingdom, with the superintendence of the administration of justice as far as the Royal prerogative is involved in it.

By its very nature the subject of maintaining the Queen's peace and keeping law and order had over the years inevitably been dealt with by statute much more than the war prerogative has been...but I have no doubt that the Crown does have a prerogative power to keep the peace, which is bound up with its undoubted right to see that crime is prevented and justice administered. This is subject to Mr Keene's next submission, which was that any prerogative power may be lost by being overtaken by statute law...

It is clear that the Crown cannot act under the prerogative if to do so would be incompatible with statute. What was said here is that the Secretary of State's proposal under the circular would be inconsistent with the powers expressly or impliedly conferred on the police authority by section 4 of the Police Act 1964. The Divisional court rejected that submission for reasons with which I wholly agree: namely that section 4 does not expressly grant a monopoly, and that granted the possibility of an authority which declines to provide equipment required by the chief constable there is every reason not to imply a Parliamentary intent to create one.

Mr Keene's last submission was that if there is a prerogative power it can only be used in emergency and that this does not allow its use beforehand in circumstances of peace and quiet. One need only quote and adapt...passages from the speeches in *Burmah Oil Co Ltd v Lord Advocate* [1965] AC 75. That was a case concerning the war prerogative, but the same point was taken, Lord Reid said, at p 100: 'it would be very strange if the law prevented or discouraged necessary preparations until a time when it would probably be too late for them to be effective.'

The same reason must apply to the provision of equipment to the police, and to their being trained in its use, in times when there is reason to apprehend outbreaks of riot and serious civil disturbance.

Nourse LJ (at page 56):

It has not at any stage in our history been practicable to identify all the prerogative powers of the Crown. It is only by a process of piecemeal decision over a period of centuries that particular powers are seen to exist or not to exist, as the case may be. From time to time a need for more exact definition arises. The present need arises from a difference of view between the Secretary of State and a police authority over what is necessary to maintain public order, a phenomenon which has been observed only in recent times. There has probably never been a comparable occasion for investigating a prerogative of keeping the peace within the realm.

The Crown's prerogative of making war and peace, the was prerogative, has never been doubted. Its origins may not have been fully explored. Here it is important to remember that the Royal prerogative was never regarded as a collection of mere powers, to be exercised or not at the will of the sovereign. The King owed certain duties to his subjects, albeit duties of imperfect obligation whose performance could not be enforced by legal process...They include a duty to protect the lives and property of the King's subjects...

[The] scarcity of references in the books to the prerogative of keeping the peace within the realm does not disprove that it exists. Rather it may point to an unspoken assumption that it does.

[2:4] *Hill v Chief Constable of West Yorkshire*
[1988] 2 All ER 238

Between 1969 and 1980 Peter Sutcliffe (the 'Yorkshire Ripper') committed a series of 13 murders and eight attempted murders. The mother of his last murder victim sued under section 48(1) of the Police Act 1964, claiming damages against the chief constable in whose area most of the offences took place. Her claim was struck out on the ground that the police owed no duty of care to a member of the public who suffered injury through the activities of a criminal.

The House of Lords dismissed her appeal. Having held that no duty of care was owed to members of the public, Lord Keith stated (at page 243):

In my opinion there is another reason why an action for damages in negligence should not lie against the police in circumstances such as those of the present case, and that is public policy.

The general sense of public duty which motivates police forces is unlikely to be appreciably reinforced by the imposition of such liability so far as concerns their function in the investigation and suppression of crime. From time to time they make mistakes in the exercise of that function, but it is not to be doubted that they apply their best endeavours to the performance of it. In some instances the imposition of liability may lead to the exercise of a function being carried on in a detrimentally defensive frame of mind. The possibility of this happening in relation to the investigative operations of the police cannot be excluded. Further, it would be reasonable to expect that if potential liability were to be imposed it would be not uncommon for actions to be raised against police forces on the result that he went on to commit further crimes. Whilst such actions might involve allegations of a simple and straightforward types of failure, for example that a police officer negligently tripped and fell while pursuing a burglar, others would be likely to enter deeply into the general nature of a police investigation, as indeed the present action would seek to do. The manner of conduct of such an investigation must necessarily involve a variety of decisions to be made on matters of policy and discretion, for example as to which particular line of inquiry is most advantageously to be pursued and what is the most advantageous way to deploy the available resources. Many such decisions would not be regarded by the courts as appropriate to be called in question, yet elaborate investigation of the facts might be necessary to ascertain whether or not this was so. A great deal of police time, trouble and expense might be expected to have to be put into the preparation of the defence to the action and the attendance of witnesses at the trial. The result would be a significant diversion of police manpower and attention from their most important function, that of the suppression of crime. Closed investigations would require to be reopened and retraversed not with the object of bringing any criminal to justice but to ascertain whether or not they had been competently conducted. I therefore consider that Glidewell LJ, in his judgment in the Court of Appeal in the present case, was right to take the view that the police were immune from an action of this kind on grounds similar to those which in *Rondel v Worsley* were held to render a barrister immune from actions for negligence in his conduct of proceedings in court (see [1987] 1 All ER at 1183, [1988] QB 60 at 76). My Lords, for these reasons I would dismiss the appeal.

Lord Templeman (at page 244):

My Lords, the appellant, Mrs Hill, is tormented with the unshakeable belief that her daughter would be alive today if the respondent, the West Yorkshire police force, had been more efficient. That belief is entitled to respect and understanding. Damages cannot compensate for the brutal extinction of a young life and the appellant proposes that any damages awarded shall be devoted to an appropriate charity. Damages awarded by the court would not be paid by any policeman found wanting in the performance of his duty but would be paid by the public. The appellant therefore brings these proceedings with the object of obtaining an investigation into the conduct of the West Yorkshire police force so that lives shall not be lost in the future by avoidable delay in the identification and arrest of a murderer.

The question for determination in this appeal is whether an action for damages is an appropriate vehicle for investigating the efficiency of a police force. The present action will be confined to narrow albeit perplexing questions, for example whether, discounting hindsight, it should have been obvious to a senior police officer that Sutcliffe was a prime suspect, whether a senior police officer should not have been deceived by an evil hoaxer, whether an officer interviewing Sutcliffe should have been better briefed and whether a report on Sutcliffe should have been given greater attention. The court would have to consider the conduct of each police officer, to decide whether the policeman failed to attain the standard of care of a hypothetical average policeman. The court would have to decide whether an inspector is to be condemned for being as obtuse as Dr Watson. The appellant will presumably seek evidence, for what it is worth, from retired police inspectors, who would be asked whether they would have been misled by the hoaxer and whether they would have identified Sutcliffe at an earlier stage. At the end of the day the court might or might not find that there had been negligence by one or more.

It may be, and we all hope that the lessons of the Yorkshire Ripper case have been learned, that the methods of handling information and handling the press have been improved, and that co-operation between different police officers is now more highly organised. The present action would not serve any useful purpose in that regard. The present action could not consider whether the training of the West Yorkshire police force is sufficiently thorough, whether the selection of candidates for appointment or promotion is defective, whether rates of pay are sufficient to attract recruits of the required calibre, whether financial restrictions prevent the provision of modern equipment and facilities or whether the Yorkshire police force is clever enough and, if not, what can and ought to be done about it. The present action could only investigate whether an individual member of the police force conscientiously carrying out his duty was negligent when he was bemused by contradictory information or overlooked significant information or failed to draw inferences which later appeared to be obvious. That kind of investigation would not achieve the object which the appellant desires. The efficiency of a police force can only be investigated by an inquiry instituted by the national or local authorities which are responsible to the electorate for that efficiency.

Moreover, if this action lies, every citizen will be able to require the court to investigate the performance of every policeman. If the policeman concentrates on one crime, he may be accused of neglecting others. If the policeman does not arrest on suspicion a suspect with previous convictions, the police force may be held liable for subsequent crimes. The threat of litigation against a police force would not make a policeman more efficient. The necessity for defending proceedings, successfully or unsuccessfully, would distract the policeman from his duties.

This action is in my opinion misconceived and will do more harm than good. A policeman is a servant of the public and is liable to be dismissed for incompetence. A police force serves the public, and the elected representatives of the public must ensure that the public get the police force they deserve. It may be that the West Yorkshire police force was in 1980 in some respects better and in some respects worse than the public deserve. An action for damages for alleged acts of negligence by individual police officers in 1980 could not determine whether and in what respect the West Yorkshire police force can be improved in 1988. I would dismiss the appeal.

[2:5] Lord Hoffmann 'Human Rights and the House of Lords'
(1999) 62 MLR 159 (at page 162)

We have had a very recent example of a decision of the Strasbourg court giving an interpretation to the Convention which, I venture to suggest, it is inconceivable that any domestic court in this country would have adopted. I want to use this decision as an example of the potential conflict between our legal system under the new regime and the jurisprudence emanating from Strasbourg.

On 28 October 1998, judgment was given in the case of *Osman v United Kingdom*. Mrs Osman's husband had been shot and killed by an insane teacher who had formed an obsessional attachment to their young son at school. She sued the police for damages, alleging that they had been warned that the man was a danger to her family but had not taken adequate steps to protect them. The Court of Appeal struck out the action on the ground that the police could not be made liable in negligence for failing to take action in the investigation or suppression of crime. The decision was based upon the Yorkshire Ripper case, *Hill v Chief Constable of West Yorkshire*, in which the House of Lords held that the imposition of a duty of care in such circumstances would be contrary to public policy. The maintenance of police efficiency was better secured by other methods than having the question of whether they had acted reasonably in a given case expensively investigated in civil proceedings at the instance of a private litigant, with the possibility of compensation having to be paid out of the police budget.

The prospect of such an investigation and the payment of compensation might in fact be detrimental to good policing, since it might make the police defensively unwilling to take risks. Furthermore, the efficiency with which the police handled a particular investigation often depended upon the share of their resources which was devoted to that kind of investigation and questions about the allocation of resources by public authorities such as the police were not suitable for determination by judges.

Persons who suffer criminal damage have no claim to compensation solely on the ground that it could have been prevented by more efficient policing. This decision is in line with a number of recent cases on the failure of public authorities to deliver services which could have prevented loss, such as *X (Minors) v Bedford County Council* on social services, *Stovin v Wise* on highway improvements, *Capital and Counties plc v Hampshire County Council* on fire services, *O'Rourke v Camden LBC* on housing the homeless, and *Murphy v Brentwood LBC* on building inspection services. The theme which runs through these cases is that the fact that public services are provided at the public expense to confer benefits or protection on members of the public does not mean that a person who fails to receive those benefits or protection will be entitled to sue for compensation on the ground that the authority acted negligently in failing to provide them. The social justification for such a rule is that, on the one hand, the person who has failed to receive the benefit is no worse off than if it had not been provided in the first place, and on the other hand, the budgetary and efficiency grounds discussed in *Hill v Chief Constable of West Yorkshire*.

Not everyone would agree with such a rule. Some might think that it shows a somewhat niggardly attitude to people who have suffered loss because they had the misfortune not to receive some public benefit which they were reasonably entitled to expect, and that the allocation of funds for public services should budget not merely for providing the services but also for compensating those who did not receive them. It might also be said that the law is inconsistent in excluding liability in such cases but making public authorities liable when they enter into relationships which have long been recognised as giving rise to a duty of care in private law, such as between a doctor or hospital and a patient. For my part, I see no inconsistency, but I recognise that the merits of the rule are open to political debate, the question being essentially one about the obligations of the welfare state.

Mrs Osman, however, petitioned the European Court of Human Rights on the ground that the rejection of her claim was a denial of her fundamental human right under Article 6(1) of the Convention, which provides that 'in the determination of his civil rights and obligations, everyone is entitled to a hearing by a tribunal'. One might be forgiven for thinking that Mrs Osman's rights had been determined, rightly or wrongly, by a tribunal. She had been before the Court of Appeal and they had decided that even if all the allegations in her statement of claim were proved at the trial to be true, she would not be entitled under English domestic law to compensation from the police. But the Court, consisting of 17 judges including one from the United Kingdom, decided unanimously that because her action had not been allowed to proceed to trial, she had not had a hearing. What, you may ask, would be the point of a hearing which, under English law, was bound to end in the claim being dismissed? The answer, according to the European Court, was that it should not have been treated as bound to be dismissed. There should have been the possibility that on the facts alleged, Mrs Osman would win. A rule that in no circumstances should a person be able to claim compensation on the ground that the police failed to protect him from criminal injury was not proportionate to the public policy grounds advanced in its support. In other words, English domestic law failed to provide compensation out of public funds in cases in which the Strasbourg court thought it should do so.

I am not sure, on a reading of the judgment of the court and the concurring judgment of the British judge, whether they had persuaded themselves that they were really dealing with the right to a hearing rather than the merits of the substantive tort law under which the Court of Appeal had held that Mrs Osman was bound to lose. In my view, there is no disguising the fact that the case was about the latter.

I am bound to say that this decision fills me with apprehension. Under the cover of an Article which says that everyone is entitled to have his civil rights and obligations determined by a tribunal, the European Court of Human Rights is taking upon itself to decide what the content of those civil rights should be. In so doing, it is challenging the autonomy of the courts and indeed the Parliament of the United Kingdom to deal with what are essentially social welfare questions involving budgetary limits and efficient public administration. I say the Parliament of the United Kingdom because it must follow from the decision of the Strasbourg court that even if the rule in *Hill v Chief Constable of West Yorkshire* had formed part of the Police Act 1996, it would have been held to contravene the right in art. 6(1) to a hearing before a tribunal. I understand that a petition by the unsuccessful plaintiffs in *X (Minors) v Bedfordshire County Council* is already on its way and no doubt there are other cases in which the same general principle will be challenged. The whole English jurisprudence on the liability of public authorities for failure to deliver public services is open to attack on the grounds that it violates the right to a hearing before a tribunal. And although the Strasbourg court appears to contemplate the possibility that after a hearing of the facts, the court might still come to the conclusion that on grounds of public policy the claim should be dismissed, it ignores one of the principle reasons for the present doctrine, which is to avoid a trial altogether, to avoid the waste of public resources involved in a judicial investigation, usually on legal aid, as to whether the public authority should reasonably have provided the benefit or not.

It may be that the court did not understand the rather formulaic reasoning by which English courts say that no duty of care exists when they mean that the case is one in which the law does not recognise a right to compensation. It may be that they did not understand the principle by which an action is struck out without going to trial if proof of all the facts alleged would not sustain a cause of action. Either way, the case serves to reinforce the doubts I have had for a long time about the suitability, at least for this country, of having questions of human rights determined by an international tribunal made up of judges from many countries.

I would not like anyone to think that this view reflected a vulgar Euroscepticism. When it comes to questions of a common currency and a large number of other economic and social issues, the advantages and disadvantages of a common European position are matters for pragmatic decision on which one has to weigh up the evidence as best one can. I do not regard national sovereignty on every issue as either possible or desirable. But the international adjudication of questions of human rights goes much deeper because it raises an ancient question about the universality of human values. It brings into focus the conflict between the universalist philosophy of the French enlightenment, who thought that French concepts of *liberté, égalité, fraternité* were derived from our common humanity and could therefore be applied world-wide, and pluralist views such as those of that each community had its own set of values, different but not better or worse than those of other communities.

Voltaire said that morality was the same in all civilised nations. This is a half truth; of course we share a common humanity and there are some forms of behaviour such as torture which we all either reject or are unwilling to acknowledge. But even this is not inherent in civilisation: in the law of ancient Rome, the evidence of slaves was always taken under torture and none of the great Roman lawyers who developed the elaborate and sophisticated system, which forms the basis of law through so much of the world, seems to have thought this inhuman. Of course, I applaud the patient efforts of the human rights movement since the Second World War to promote the acceptance of basic human rights throughout the world. I am well aware that there are countries which deny their citizens basic human rights and which claim to be justified on grounds of cultural diversity, when the true reasons are the power and greed of their rulers. Nevertheless, I say that Voltaire's remark was only half true and that in a confident democracy such as the United Kingdom the other half is important. We do have our own hierarchy of moral values, our own culturally-determined sense of what is fair and unfair, and I think it would be wrong to submerge this under a pan-European jurisprudence of human rights.

The problem about the hierarchy of rights is not the conflict between good and evil but the conflict between good and good. Free speech is a good thing; justice is a good thing, but there are cases in which free speech and justice come into conflict with each other. For example, the law that preserves the anonymity of rape victims is an infringement of the freedom of the press, but it assists justice by encouraging women to make complaints against rapists. How then are these two desirable objectives—free speech and justice—to be reconciled with each other? There is no right answer to that question; any choice involves some degree of sacrifice. But in my view, the specific answers, the degree to which weight is given to one desirable objectives rather than another, will be culturally determined. Different communities will, through their legislatures and judges, adopt the answers which they think suit them. So the Supreme Court of the United States has ruled a State law which gave anonymity to rape victims to be unconstitutional as infringing the First Amendment right to freedom of the press, whereas such laws exist in the United Kingdom and other countries. The Supreme Court of the United States attaches what other communities may regard as an exaggerated value to the First Amendment and no doubt they think we do not respect it enough. But the difference in the answers given to the perennial conflict between goals which everyone accepts to be good shows how impractical it would be to subject the United States and the United Kingdom to a common court of human rights. If this is true of two countries so closely bound together in culture, law and history, how much more true must it be of the disparate collection of states, some old democracies, some former police states, which belong to the Council of Europe.

Of course it is true that to some extent the Strasbourg court acknowledges the fact that often there is no right answer by allowing what it calls a 'margin of appreciation' to the legislature or courts of a member State. Within limits, they are allowed to differ. And, as I have said, I accept that there is an irreducible minimum of human rights which must be universally true. But most of the jurisprudence which comes out of Strasbourg is not about the irreducible minimum. These questions tend to come into play at a point when civil society itself is called into question; they are far from the normal currency of dispute over competing values in a democracy like the United Kingdom. The *Osman* case, dealing with the substantive civil law right to financial compensation for not receiving the benefit of a social service, is as far as one can imagine from basic human rights. And I have taken it only as a very recent example: it is by no means unusual. It is often said that the tendency of every court is to increase its jurisdiction and the Strasbourg court is no exception. So far as the margin of appreciation accommodates national choices, the jurisdiction of the European court is unnecessary; so far as it does not, it is undesirable.

[2:6] Hoyano, L C H, 'Policing Flawed Police Investigations: Unravelling the Blanket'

(1999) 62 MLR 912 (at page 920)

Lord Hoffmann's critique of the intersection of tort law and the European Convention

Lord Hoffmann has stated in this journal that the *Osman* decision 'fills me with apprehension'. His Lordship contends that the ECHR, under the guise of Article 6 which says everyone is entitled to have his civil rights and obligations decided by a tribunal, has taken it upon itself to decide the content of those civil rights, which here meant the merits of the substantive tort rules governing duty of care. In so doing, His Lordship maintains, the ECHR is 'challenging the autonomy of the courts and indeed the Parliament of the United Kingdom to deal with what are essentially social welfare questions involving budgetary limits and efficient public administration'.

Is this criticism justified? Parliament, exercising its autonomy, has seen fit to require the British courts to adjudicate issues arising under the Convention, and in so doing to take into account any judgment of the ECHR. Parliament has bound neither itself nor the British courts to act on any declaration of incompatibility by the ECHR. If this amounts to an unjustifiable surrender of parliamentary autonomy, then that is a political, not a legal, issue.

The ECHR had also given due warning that while Article 6§1 does not in itself guarantee any particular content for civil rights and obligations in the substantive law of the Contracting States, and so cannot provide a vehicle for their creation by the Convention enforcement bodies, the State does not enjoy unlimited scope to remove issues of civil liability from the jurisdiction of the courts. In *Fayed v UK*, the ECHR observed:

> [It] would not be consistent with the rule of law and democratic society or with the basic principle underlying Article 6(1)—namely that civil claims must be capable of being submitted to a judge for adjudication—if, for example, a State could, without restraint or control by the Convention enforcement bodies, remove from the jurisdiction of the courts a whole range of civil claims or confer immunities from civil liability on large groups or categories of persons.

Parliament must be taken to have known of this interpretation of Article 6(1) prior to incorporating the Convention into English domestic law.

Lord Hoffmann argues that the case was really about the merits of the substantive tort law under which the Osmans were 'bound to lose', rather than about the right to a hearing; viewed from this perspective, the *Osman* case 'is as far as one can imagine from basic human rights'. However, a close examination of the Court's reasoning suggests that this criticism is less persuasive than it may initially appear.

Interestingly, at several points in his critique His Lordship treats *Hill* as conferring blanket immunity upon the police, without addressing the ECHR's crucial point that the English courts themselves had already torn some holes in that blanket, particularly through the recently resurrected 'assumption of responsibility' justification for duty of care, but then had denied the Osman plaintiffs the opportunity or prove that their case fitted within any of these exceptions or justified unravelling the blanket further.

It is of vital importance to note that the ECHR did not require English courts to rescind public policy immunity from tort liability; rather, it said that the courts must permit litigants an opportunity to contend that countervailing public policy considerations dictate that immunity should not apply to their case. This does not mean that defendants can no longer bring cost-efficient interlocutory applications to strike out pleadings on the ground that they are immune from negligence suits, as Lord Hoffmann suggests; it does mean that the court hearing such an application must approach the issue from the perspective that public policy immunity does not automatically provide a 'watertight defence'. The factors which the ECHR indicated might be relevant to an English court in deciding whether to apply the immunity rule in *Hill*—the alleged failure by an agent of the state to protect the life of a vulnerable child due to a catalogue of gravely negligent acts and omissions—brings Ahmet Osman's case much closer to 'basic human rights' as they are commonly conceptualised.

Thus it is strongly arguable that the *ratio* of *Osman* is quite narrow. Viewed in this way, the ECHR has not taken it upon itself to dictate to domestic courts the content of tort law rules but rather, in the best common law tradition, has upheld the principle that the categories of negligence are not closed, and that tort law must be allowed the flexibility to develop incrementally.

Lord Hoffmann stoutly defends the immunity conferred by *Hill* as being in line with other recent cases refusing to permit plaintiffs to sue public authorities for failure to deliver services which could have prevented their loss. But given the extensive police involvement responding to multiple complaints about the activities of Paget-Lewis over a period of 14 months, is *Osman* simply a case of nonfeasance? As the plaintiffs alleged that they, the school and the ILEA had the Osman and Perkins families, can it fairly be said in their case that 'the person who has failed to receive the benefit [of public services] is no worse off than if it had not been provided in the first place', as Lord Hoffmann asserts? Without such assurances, the Osmans might well have left the locality or made other arrangements to provide for their security; without a trial, it cannot be assumed that they did not rely upon the police to their detriment.

His Lordship contends that public authorities are currently exposed to negligence actions only when they enter into relationships which have long been recognised as giving rise to a duty of care in private law, such as between a doctor or hospital and patient. While there may be an emerging trend in that direction, such reasoning does not appear in the seminal cases delineating the applicability of negligence law to public authorities. Indeed the House of Lords expressly eschewed such a limitation in

Dorset Yacht Co Ltd v Home Office; Lord Diplock pointed out:

> To relinquish intentionally or inadvertently the custody and control of a person responsible in law for his own acts is not an act or omission which, independently of any statute, would give rise to a cause of action at common law against the custodian on the part of another person who subsequently sustained tortious damage at the hands of the person released.

It would have been impossible to establish the existence of a free-standing duty of care absent the statutory power to imprison which, at least until the recent advent of privately managed prisons, was vested solely in public authorities. *Dorset Yacht* thus cannot be explained on the basis of Lord Hoffmann's private/public distinction.

Furthermore, it is unlikely that the ECHR ruling in *Osman* will force the English courts to adjudicate policy issues involving the efficiency of public administration and the allocation of limited public resources, as Lord Hoffmann fears...

In *Osman*, there was no suggestion that the police's failure to arrest Paget-Lewis was due to a paucity of resources to dedicate to the investigation or to a policy decision not to act on the numerous complaints. While the policy/operational divide may sometimes be difficult to discern, it should have been relatively straightforward to apply here: even if the decision to arrest a suspect might conceivably fall within the realm of non-justifiable discretion, surely the inexplicable failure to implement that decision with any zeal would fall at the operational end of the spectrum.

(And at page 934:)

Conclusion

I have argued that it is possible to construe *Osman v UK* as standing for no broader proposition than that where the domestic courts have carved out some exceptions to a general rule conferring immunity upon a class of decision-makers, litigants must be afforded the opportunity to bring their cases within those exceptions or (in the case of a judge-made immunity rule) to develop new exceptions. However, some dicta in the ECHR's lead judgment point to a wider implication, that blanket immunity for any class of potential tortfeasors is likely to violate Article 6(1), as the courts must leave themselves free to examine the merits of each case and to weigh the public policy considerations for and against the existence of the duty of care in a particular case...

The Human Rights Act 1998 may signal a return to the spirit of flexibility which infused *Donoghue v Stevenson*, and to the robust view of the Court of Appeal in *Dorset Yacht* about the salutary effects of negligence law unless, that is, other English judges share the apprehension of Lord Hoffmann, and lack the confidence of Lord Nicholls in their ability to adjudicate duty of care issues on a case-by-case basis...

How much better it would be if negligence law could draw on these common law concepts to retain its original vigour and flexibility rather than forcing human rights law to do its work.

[2:7] *Brooks v Commissioner of Police of the Metropolis*
[2005] UKHL 24, [2005] 1 WLR 1495

Lord Bingham (all five judges agreed that this claim failed):

1 My Lords, Duwayne Brooks, the respondent, was present when his friend Stephen Lawrence was abused and murdered in the most notorious racist killing which our country has ever known. He also was abused and attacked. However well this crime had been investigated by the police and however sensitively he had himself been treated by the police, the respondent would inevitably have been deeply traumatised by his experience on the night of the murder and in the days and weeks which

followed. But unfortunately, as established by the public inquiry into the killing (The Stephen Lawrence Inquiry: Report of an Inquiry by Sir William Macpherson of Cluny (1999) (Cm 4262-I), the investigation was very badly conducted and the respondent himself was not treated as he should have been. He issued proceedings against the Metropolitan Police Commissioner and a number of other parties, all but one of whom were police officers....

2 ...the only issue before the House is whether, assuming the facts pleaded by the respondent to be true, the Commissioner and the officers for whom he is responsible arguably owed the respondent a common law duty sounding in damages to (1) take reasonable steps to assess whether the respondent was a victim of crime and then to accord him reasonably appropriate protection, support, assistance and treatment if he was so assessed; (2) take reasonable steps to afford the respondent the protection, assistance and support commonly afforded to a key eye-witness to a serious crime of violence; (3) afford reasonable weight to the account that the respondent gave and to act upon it accordingly.

3 ...Two considerations, however, persuade me that this appeal should be allowed and the respondent's claims in common law negligence struck out.

4 The first is that the facts of this case have been exhaustively investigated. While theoretically the facts are only to be assumed, and have not been proved, it seems most unlikely that there are factual discoveries to be made or that there will be any substantial challenge to the facts as pleaded. If the case went to trial, the judge would base his decision on essentially the same facts as are now before the House. The second consideration is that the three duties pleaded are not, in my opinion, duties which could even arguably be imposed on police officers charged in the public interest with the investigation of a very serious crime and the apprehension of those responsible. Even if it were to be thought, for reasons such as those touched on by Lord Steyn, in paras 27–29 of his opinion, that the ratio of Hill's case called for some modification, I cannot conceive that any modification would be such as would accommodate the three pleaded duties. This conclusion imports no criticism at all of the respondent's expert advisers, who have plainly pleaded the strongest duties available on the facts. But these are not duties which could be imposed on police officers without potentially undermining the officers' performance of their functions, effective performance of which serves an important public interest. That is, in my opinion, a conclusive argument in the Commissioner's favour. Fortunately, the respondent has other causes of action which he is free to pursue.

[2:8] *R v Metropolitan Police Commissioner, ex p Blackburn (No 3)*
[1973] QB 241

The applicant sought an order of *mandamus* to require the Metropolitan Police Commissioner to secure the enforcement of the law against the illegal publishing and selling of pornography. The Court of Appeal held that, although the evidence disclosed that obscene material was widely available for sale in shops, the applicant had not established that it was a case for the court to interfere with the discretion of the police in carrying out their duties.

Lord Denning MR (at page 254):

In *R v Commissioner of Police of the Metropolis, ex p Blackburn* [1968] 2 QB 118, 136, 138, 148–149, we made it clear that, in the carrying out of their duty of enforcing the law, the police have a discretion with which the courts will not interfere. There might, however, be extreme cases in which he was not carrying out his duty. And then we would. I do not think this is a case for our interference. In the past the commissioner has done what he could under the existing system and with the available manpower. The new commissioner is doing more. He is increasing the number of the Obscene Publications Squad to 18 and he is reforming it and its administration. No more can reasonably be expected.

The plain fact is, however, that the efforts of the police have hitherto been largely ineffective. Mr Blackburn amply demonstrated it by going out from this court and buying these pornographic magazines—hard and soft—at shops all over the place. I do not accede to the suggestion that the police turn a blind eye to pornography or that shops get a 'tip-off' before the police arrive. The cause of the ineffectiveness lies with the system and the framework in which the police have to operate. The Obscene Publications Act 1959 does not provide a sound foundation. It fails to provide a satisfactory test of obscenity: and it allows a defence of public good which has got out of hand. There is also considerable uncertainty as to the powers and duties of the police when they seize articles.

If the people of this country want pornography to be stamped out, the legislature must amend the Obscene Publications Act 1959 so as to make it strike unmistakably at pornography: and it must define the powers and duties of the police so as to enable them to take effective measures for the purpose. The police may well say to Parliament: 'Give us the tools and we will finish the job'. But, without efficient tools, they cannot be expected to stamp it out. Mr Blackburn has served a useful purpose in drawing the matter to our attention: but I do not think it is a case for mandamus. I would, therefore, dismiss the appeal.

[2:9] *R (Mondelly) v Commissioner of Police of the Metropolis*
[2007] Crim LR 298

M was arrested for permitting his premises to be used for the smoking of cannabis (the Misuse of Drugs Act 1971, s.8(d)). Subsequently, he was cautioned for simple possession of cannabis. He applied for the decision to caution him to be judicially reviewed in the light of the policy adopted by the Metropolitan Police in connection with the offence of simple possession. The policy relied on was that which was contained in Metropolitan Police Service Notice 3/2004, issued on the day that cannabis was reclassified as a Class C drug and entitled "Policing of Cannabis as a Class C Drug". The notice was available on the internet. The notice laid down a general policy that an officer should not arrest a person found to be in possession of cannabis for personal use unless an aggravating factor applied, but the drug should be seized. The notice stated that the policy was not intended to interfere with the discretion of a police officer. Its aim was to ensure that the least amount of time possible was spent on policing simple possession of the drug. The notice included a cross-reference to the Standard Operating Procedure as identifying the aggravating factors where an officer may consider arrest. That document (disclosed for the purposes of the case) identified various potential aggravating factors, including where the offender was a young person. None applied to M's case. M argued that, on public law principles, the police were obliged to follow the policy described in the notice unless a departure could be justified. In the absence of any of the aggravating features identified in the Standard Operating Procedure, there was no such justification.

Held, dismissing the application, that M's argument was misconceived. (1) The court considered the authorities on judicial review of decisions to caution or to prosecute (*R. v Commissioner of Police of the Metropolis Ex p. Blackburn (No.1)* [1968] Q.B. 118; *R. v Chief Constable of the Kent County Constabulary Ex p. L (A Minor)* [1993] 1 All E.R. 756; *R. v Commissioner of Police of the Metropolis Ex p. P* (1996) 8 Admin. L.R. 6; *R. v Commissioner of Police of the Metropolis Ex p. Thompson* [1997] 1 W.L.R. 1519; *R. v Adaway* [2004] EWCA Crim 2831). These authorities established (a) that generally the courts were reluctant to intervene in relation to decisions to prosecute, even in the case of juveniles; (b) that the courts were reluctant to intervene in relation to the administration of cautions; (c) the courts would refuse to intervene save where the policy which it was suggested had been breached was clear and settled; and (d) that the breach itself was established.

(2) It was wrong to extend the policy on arrest contained in the notice and apply it to the administration of cautions. M accepted that it was a necessary consequence of the submission that the arrest policy made the administration of the caution unlawful, that any prosecution of M would have been

unlawful as well. So the policy on arrest when read across to cautions, as M contended, would also become a prohibition on prosecution. That was an utterly misconceived approach to the meaning and effect of the policy. It took the policy several steps beyond its stated confines and purpose. There was nothing to suggest that the authors thought they were creating such a policy. Were there to be a police and CPS policy that no one should be prosecuted for simple possession of cannabis (unless the exceptions in the Standard Operating Procedures applied), that policy itself would be unlawful. It was not for executive prosecution policy to change the law. The implication of M's argument was that the police could suspend or dispense with part of the law.

(3) Even if it were possible to contemplate a policy having the effect for which M contended, M would have to establish that there was in fact a clear policy not to administer a caution for simple possession, departure from which must be justified. There was no such clear policy. The notice expressly provided that it was not intended to interfere with the discretion of a police officer. There was nothing in the policy that stated that it was applicable to cautioning or prosecution after arrest. The purpose of the notice was stated to be about ensuring that the least amount of police time possible was spent on simple possession of cannabis for reasons of resources and policing priorities. A person choosing to break the law by possessing cannabis could not rely on such a policy to avoid prosecution or a caution; and the policy itself was not clear (it did not state that "no further action" precluded a caution, and there was no cross-referencing between it and the guidance in the Home Office Circular 18/1994 on cautioning). There was therefore no clear and settled policy not to arrest or prosecute for simple possession.

(4) In any event, there had been no breach of the Standard Operating Procedures. M relied on a passage asserting that there should be no re-arrest for simple possession following an initial arrest for another offence. But M had not been rearrested for simple possession and there was no non-compliance with that Standard Operating Procedure. The Standard Operating Procedure said that if arrest were not appropriate, the simple possession offence should be recorded but that was not a criminal record. The Standard Operating Procedure does not deal with whether or not there should be any further prosecution or caution in express terms, although it would appear to be the expectation that that would be the end of the matter. (per Moses L.J., with whom Ouseley J. agreed, Walker J. dissenting)

. . .

Commentary (by Andrew Roberts): If the applicant suffered any procedural unfairness it did not arise from the fact that he might have been treated differently from others whom the police discovered to be in possession of cannabis. The policy concerning arrest for this offence had been widely reported in the news media. More significantly the police had published the policy in some detail. The basis of a claim of unfairness in such circumstances is that the publication of the policy creates a legitimate expectation that the applicant would be treated in a particular manner and that deviation from the policy constitutes a failure to provide the applicant with what he is due (see generally D. Galligan, *Due Process and Fair Procedures* (Oxford University Press, 1996), pp. 56–60).

The question on which the application turned was whether, in addition to creating an expectation as to arrest for possession of cannabis, the policy could also be said to have created an expectation as to the use of cautions for that offence. The basis of the application was that implicit in the policy relating to arrest was a corresponding stance in relation to the use of cautions for possession of cannabis, i.e. those individuals who would not be subject to arrest by application of the arrest policy would neither be cautioned (nor prosecuted).

Where the enforcement of substantive criminal law is subject to operational policy difficult issues of the weight that ought to be attached to the competing considerations arise. Failure on the part of the authority issuing the policy to implement it in particular cases provides the foundation of a claim of procedural unfairness described above. However, were decision-makers not permitted to deviate from the authority's policy, there is a danger of ossification of what originally constituted a "rule of thumb", offering guidance to the decision-maker, so that in effect it becomes a prescriptive rule which imposes an impermissible limitation on the scope of the substantive criminal law (see *R. v Commissioner of Police of the Metropolis Ex p. Blackburn (No.1)* [1968] Q.B. 118, per Lord Denning at p.136e–f: "Suppose a Chief Constable were to issue a directive to his men that no person should be prosecuted for stealing any goods less than £100 in value. I should have thought that the court could countermand it. He would be failing in his duty to enforce the law.")

Policies must necessarily leave scope for the exercise of discretion. While recognising that any failure to follow such policies is open to judicial review the courts have generally shown reluctance to interfere with operational decisions in which a decision-maker has declined to apply a policy. In light of this, it is unsurprising that the court in the present case disposed of the application on the grounds that one of the preconditions for judicial review was a clearly stated policy, and no such policy existed in relation to the use of cautions for possession of cannabis.

In a persuasive dissenting opinion Walker J. adopted a rather more functional approach, recognising the procedural injustice which resulted from the mistaken thinking on the part of the arresting officers. Had this not occurred the applicant would have benefited from the arrest policy, and would also have been spared a criminal record and having to surrender a sample of his DNA. It was further pointed out that administering a caution was inconsistent with the underlying purposes of the arrest policy. These included the macro-consideration of achieving consistency with an enforcement policy which takes account of the Government's reasons for reclassifying cannabis, and more specific considerations of achieving transparency and consistency in enforcement of the law between individuals.

[2:10] Farrington, D and Dowds, E, 'Why does crime decrease?'
(1984) Justice of the Peace 506 (at page 507)

We do not know why recorded crime in the whole country decreased between 1982 and 1983, but we do know why it has been decreasing in one county—Nottinghamshire. Taken at face value, the Criminal Statistics for 1981 showed that Nottinghamshire was the most criminal area in the country. For several years, Nottingham, the Metropolitan Police area and Merseyside had the three highest recorded crime rates in the country, and in 1981 Nottinghamshire regained the top position it had last held in 1977. Our research into the puzzling case of the high Nottinghamshire crime rate began in 1982. Between 1981 and 1982, whereas recorded crime in the whole country increased by 10%, in Nottinghamshire is stayed virtually unchanged, leading to a decline in Nottinghamshire's position in the 'league table' of crime rates from first to fifth. In 1983, whereas recorded crime in the whole country fell by 0.5%, the decrease in Nottinghamshire was 5%, and in the first quarter of 1984, when crime increased by 5% overall, it decreased in Nottinghamshire by 6%. These decreases will lead to a further decline in Nottinghamshire's relative standing.

The aim of our research was to compare Nottinghamshire with two other counties which were similar in many respects—Staffordshire and Leicestershire. According to the chief constables' reports, there were 87 recorded crimes per 100 population in Nottinghamshire in 1981, in comparison with 44 in Leicestershire and 40 in Staffordshire. We wanted to explain why Nottinghamshire was roughly twice as high as the other two counties.

There were basically four possible explanations:

(a) more crimes were committed (in relation to population) in Nottinghamshire;

(b) members of the public were more likely to report crimes to the police in Nottinghamshire;

(c) the police were more likely to discover crimes in Nottinghamshire; and

(d) an alleged crime which was discovered by or reported to the police was more likely to be recorded in Nottinghamshire.

In order to investigate (a) and (b), a random sample of about 1,000 adults in each county was interviewed and asked about crimes committed against them in the previous year and about whether these crimes were reported to the police. In order to investigate (c) and (d), police discovery and recording practices in the three counties were studied.

The crime survey (whose methodology was based on the British Crime Survey) indicated that the number of crimes committed in each county was far greater than the number recorded by the police: 405 per 1,000 in Nottinghamshire, in comparison with 326 in Leicestershire and 262 in Staffordshire. (These estimates include crimes against organisations and against persons under 16). The proportion of crimes reported to the police was almost exactly the same in each county, at about 40%. This led to an estimate of crimes reported to the police per 1,000 population of 162 in Nottinghamshire, 136 in Leicestershire and 102 in Staffordshire.

Comparing these figures with the recorded crime rates of 87, 44 and 40 (respectively) led to the conclusion that the ratio of recorded to reported crime was far higher in Nottinghamshire (53%) than in Leicestershire (32%) or Staffordshire (39%). If the probability of a crime known to the police being recorded had been 35% in all counties (the average of the Leicestershire and Staffordshire figures), the recorded crime rates per 1,000 population would have been 57 in Nottinghamshire, 48 in Leicestershire and 36 in Staffordshire. The police figures for Nottinghamshire were therefore about 30 crimes per 1,000 population higher than expected on the basis of the other two counties.

The study of police recording practices analysed a 1% random sample of 1981 crime reports in each county (over 1,600 in all). The main aims of this analysis were to investigate the origin of each recorded crime (eg from citizen reports or police investigatory practices) and the characteristics of each (eg the value of property stolen). The types of crimes recorded in the three counties were quite similar.

Differences—admissions

One major difference between the counties was in crimes arising from admissions, where a person apprehended for one crime admitted others which had not previously been reported to or recorded by the police. About a quarter of Nottinghamshire's crime reports originated in this way, in comparison with 4% in Leicestershire and 8% in Staffordshire. The difference between the counties in crimes arising from admissions amounted to a difference of 18–20 crimes per 1,000 population.

Differences—crime seriousness

The second major difference between the counties was in the seriousness of recorded crimes. Nearly half of the crimes of dishonesty in Nottinghamshire involved property worth £10 or less, in comparison with 29% in Leicestershire and 36% in Staffordshire. Crimes arising from admissions were especially likely to involve property worth £10 or less (72%). It seemed likely that the Nottinghamshire police were more willing to record relatively trivial crimes than the other two forces.

Adding together crimes arising from admissions and those involving property worth £10 or less, the rate in Nottinghamshire for crimes in one or both of these categories was 43 per 1,000 population, or about half the country's crime rate. The corresponding figure for the other two counties was 12 in both cases. Therefore, these two effects together accounted for a difference of 31 crimes per 1,000 population between Nottinghamshire and the other two counties—almost exactly the excess identified in the crime survey.

We therefore concluded that, of the difference in recorded crime rates between Nottinghamshire and the other two counties of about 45 offences per 1,000 population, about two-thirds reflected differences in police recording practices, while about one-third reflected real differences in crimes committed.

Since our research began, and possibly in the light of our results, the Nottinghamshire police have changed their recording practices. In particular, they decided to spend less time questioning apprehended offenders about all their crimes, and so nowadays do not record so many trivial crimes arising on admission. This is one of the major reasons why recorded crime in Nottinghamshire decreased between 1981 and 1984. Police practices in Nottinghamshire are now come comparable to those in Leicestershire and Staffordshire.

[2:11] Police and Criminal Evidence Act 1984 (as amended)

Sections 17–19; 24; 24A; 28–32; 36–38; 56; 58; 66; 76; 78

17 Entry for purpose of arrest etc

(1) Subject to the following provisions of this section, and without prejudice to any other enactment, a constable may enter and search any premises for the purpose—

    (a) of executing—

        (i) a warrant of arrest issued in connection with or arising out of criminal proceedings; or

        (ii) a warrant of commitment issued under section 76 of the Magistrates' Courts Act 1980;

    (b) of arresting a person for an arrestable offence;

    (c) of arresting a person for an offence under—

        (i) section 1 (prohibition of uniforms in connection with political objects)…of the Public Order Act 1936;

        (ii) any enactment contained in sections 6 to 8 or 10 of the Criminal Law Act 1977 (offences relating to entering and remaining on property);

        (iii) section 4 of the Public Order Act 1986 (fear or provocation of violence);

        (iiia) section 163 of the Road Traffic Act 1988 (c 52) (failure to stop when required to do so by a constable in uniform);

        (iv) section 76 of the Criminal Justice and Public Order Act 1994 (failure to comply with interim possession order);

        (v) any of sections 4,5,6(1) and (2), 7 and 8(1) and (2) of the Animal Welfare Act 2006 (offences relating to the prevention of harm to animals).

    (ca) of arresting, in pursuance of section 32(1A) of the Children and Young Persons Act 1969, any child or young person who has been remanded or committed to local authority accommodation under section 23(1) of that Act;

    (cb) of recapturing any person who is, or is deemed for any purpose to be, unlawfully at large while liable to be detained—

        (i) in a prison, remand centre, young offender institution or secure training centre, or

        (ii) in pursuance of section 92 of the Powers of Criminal Courts (Sentencing) Act 2000 (dealing with children and young persons guilty of grave crimes), in any other place;

    (d) of recapturing any person whatever who is unlawfully at large and whom he is pursuing; or

    (e) of saving life or limb or preventing serious damage to property.

(2) Except for the purpose specified in paragraph (e) of subsection (1) above, the powers of entry and search conferred by this section—

    (a) are only exercisable if the constable has reasonable grounds for believing that the person whom he is seeking is on the premises; and

    (b) are limited, in relation to premises consisting of two or more separate dwellings, to powers to enter and search—

        (i) any parts of the premises which the occupiers of any dwelling comprised in the premises use in common with the occupiers of any other such dwelling; and

        (ii) any such dwelling in which the constable has reasonable grounds for believing that the person whom he is seeking may be.

(3) The powers of entry and search conferred by this section are only exercisable for the purposes specified in subsection (1)(c)(ii) or (iv) above by a constable in uniform.

(4) The power of search conferred by this section is only a power to search to the extent that is reasonably required for the purpose for which the power of entry is exercised.

(5) Subject to subsection (6) below, all the rules of common law under which a constable has power to enter premises without a warrant are hereby abolished.

(6) Nothing in subsection (5) above affects any power of entry to deal with or prevent a breach of the peace.

18 Entry and search after arrest

(1) Subject to the following provisions of this section, a constable may enter and search any premises occupied or controlled by a person who is under arrest for an arrestable offence, if he has reasonable grounds for suspecting that there is on the premises evidence, other than items subject to legal privilege, that relates—

(a) to that offence; or

(b) to some other indictable offence which is connected with or similar to that offence.

(2) A constable may seize and retain anything for which he may search under subsection (1) above.

(3) The power to search conferred by subsection (1) above is only a power to search to the extent that is reasonably required for the purpose of discovering such evidence.

(4) Subject to subsection (5) below, the powers conferred by this section may not be exercised unless an officer of the rank of inspector or above has authorised them in writing.

(5) A constable may conduct a search under subsection (1) above—

(a) before the person is taken to a police station; and

(b) without obtaining an authorisation under subsection (4) above,

if the presence of that person at a place other than a police station is necessary for the effective investigation of the offence.

(6) If a constable conducts a search by virtue of subsection (5) above, he shall inform an officer of the rank of inspector or above that he has made the search as soon as practicable after he has made it.

(7) An officer who—

(a) authorises a search; or

(b) is informed of a search under subsection (6) above, shall make a record in writing—

(i) of the grounds for the search; and

(ii) of the nature of the evidence that was sought.

(8) If the person who was in occupation or control of the premises at the time of the search is in police detention at the time the record is to be made, the officer shall make the record as part of his custody record.

Seizure etc

19 General power of seizure etc

(1) The powers conferred by subsections (2), (3) and (4) below are exercisable by a constable who is lawfully on any premises.

(2) The constable may seize anything which is on the premises if he has reasonable grounds for believing—

(a) that it has been obtained in consequence of the commission of an offence; and

(b) that it is necessary to seize it in order to prevent it being concealed, lost, damaged, altered or destroyed.

(3) The constable may seize anything which is on the premises if he has reasonable grounds for believing—

(a) that it is evidence in relation to an offence which he is investigating or any other offence; and

(b) that it is necessary to seize it in order to prevent the evidence being concealed, lost, altered or destroyed.

(4) The constable may require any information which is stored in any electronic form and is accessible from the premises to be produced in a form in which it can be taken away and in which it is visible and legible or from which it can readily be produced in a visible and legible form if he has reasonable grounds for believing—

(a) that—

(i) it is evidence in relation to an offence which he is investigating or any other offence; or

(ii) it has been obtained in consequence of the commission of an offence; and

(b) that it is necessary to do so in order to prevent it being concealed, lost, tampered with or destroyed.

(5) The powers conferred by this section are in addition to any power otherwise conferred.

(6) No power of seizure conferred on a constable under any enactment (including an enactment contained in an Act passed after this Act) is to be taken to authorise the seizure of an item which the constable exercising the power has reasonable grounds for believing to be subject to legal privilege.

24 Arrest without warrant: constables

(1) A constable may arrest without a warrant—

(a) anyone who is about to commit an offence;

(b) anyone who is in the act of committing an offence;

(c) anyone whom he has reasonable grounds for suspecting to be about to commit an offence;

(d) anyone whom he has reasonable grounds for suspecting to be committing an offence.

(2) If a constable has reasonable grounds for suspecting that an offence has been committed, he may arrest without a warrant anyone whom he has reasonable grounds to suspect of being guilty of it.

(3) If an offence has been committed, a constable may arrest without a warrant—

(a) anyone who is guilty of the offence;

(b) anyone whom he has reasonable grounds for suspecting to be guilty of it.

(4) But the power of summary arrest conferred by subsection (1), (2) or (3) is exercisable only if the constable has reasonable grounds for believing that for any of the reasons mentioned in subsection (5) it is necessary to arrest the person in question.

(5) The reasons are—

(a) to enable the name of the person in question to be ascertained (in the case where the constable does not know, and cannot readily ascertain, the person's name, or has reasonable grounds for doubting whether a name given by the person as his name is his real name);

(b) correspondingly as regards the person's address;

(c) to prevent the person in question—

(i) causing physical injury to himself or any other person;

(ii) suffering physical injury;

(iii) causing loss of or damage to property;

(iv) committing an offence against public decency (subject to subsection (6)); or

(v) causing an unlawful obstruction of the highway;

(d) to protect a child or other vulnerable person from the person in question;

(e) to allow the prompt and effective investigation of the offence or of the conduct of the person in question;

(f) to prevent any prosecution for the offence from being hindered by the disappearance of the person in question.

(6) Subsection (5)(c)(iv) applies only where members of the public going about their normal business cannot reasonably be expected to avoid the person in question.

24A Arrest without warrant: other persons

(1) A person other than a constable may arrest without a warrant—

(a) anyone who is in the act of committing an indictable offence;

(b) anyone whom he has reasonable grounds for suspecting to be committing an indictable offence.

(2) Where an indictable offence has been committed, a person other than a constable may arrest without a warrant—

(a) anyone who is guilty of the offence;

(b) anyone whom he has reasonable grounds for suspecting to be guilty of it.

(3) But the power of summary arrest conferred by subsection (1) or (2) is exercisable only if—

(a) the person making the arrest has reasonable grounds for believing that for any of the reasons mentioned in subsection (4) it is necessary to arrest the person in question; and

(b) it appears to the person making the arrest that it is not reasonably practicable for a constable to make it instead.

(4) The reasons are to prevent the person in question—

(a) causing physical injury to himself or any other person;

(b) suffering physical injury;

(c) causing loss of or damage to property; or

(d) making off before a constable can assume responsibility for him.

(5) This section does not apply in relation to an offence under Part 3 or 3A of the Public Order Act 1986.

28 Information to be given on arrest

(1) Subject to subsection (5) below, where a person is arrested, otherwise than by being informed that he is under arrest, the arrest is not lawful unless the person arrested is informed that he is under arrest as soon as is practicable after his arrest.

(2) Where a person is arrested by a constable, subsection (1) above applies regardless of whether the fact of the arrest is obvious.

(3) Subject to subsection (5) below, no arrest is lawful unless the person arrested is informed of the ground for the arrest at the time of, or as soon as is practicable after, the arrest.

(4) Where a person is arrested by a constable, subsection (3) above applies regardless of whether the ground for the arrest is obvious.

(5) Nothing in this section is to be taken to require a person to be informed—

(a) that he is under arrest; or

(b) of the ground for the arrest,

if it was not reasonably practicable for him to be so informed by reason of his having escaped from arrest before the information could be given.

29 Voluntary attendance at police station etc

Where for the purpose of assisting with an investigation a person attends voluntarily at a police station or at any other place where a constable is present or accompanies a constable to a police station or any such other place without having been arrested—

   (a) he shall be entitled to leave at will unless he is placed under arrest;

   (b) he shall be informed at once that he is under arrest if a decision is taken by a constable to prevent him from leaving at will.

30 Arrest elsewhere than at police station

  (1) Subsection (1A) applies, where a person is at any place other than a police station

    (a) arrested by a constable for an offence; or

    (b) taken into custody by a constable after being arrested for an offence by a person other than a constable,

  (1A) The person must be taken by a constable to a police station as soon as practicable after the arrest.

  (1B) Subsection (1A) has effect subject to section 30A (release on bail) and Subsection (7) (release without trial)

  (2) Subject to subsections (3) and (5) below, the police station to which an arrested person is taken under subsection (1) above shall be a designated police station.

  (3) A constable to whom this subsection applies may take an arrested person to any police station unless it appears to the constable that it may be necessary to keep the arrested person in police detention for more than six hours.

  (4) Subsection (3) above applies—

    (a) to a constable who is working in a locality covered by a police station which is not a designated police station; and

    (b) to a constable belonging to a body of constables maintained by an authority other than a police authority.

  (5) Any constable may take an arrested person to any police station if—

    (a) either of the following conditions is satisfied—

      (i) the constable has arrested him without the assistance of any other constable and no other constable is available to assist him;

      (ii) the constable has taken him into custody from a person other than a constable without the assistance of any other constable and no other constable is available to assist him; and

    (b) it appears to the constable that he will be unable to take the arrested person to a designated police station without the arrested person injuring himself, the constable or some other person.

  (6) If the first police station to which an arrested person is taken after his arrest is not a designated police station, he shall be taken to a designated police station not more than six hours after his arrival at the first police station unless he is released previously.

  (7) A person arrested by a constable at any place other than a police station must be released without bail if the condition in subsection (7A) is satisfied.

  (7A) The condition is that, at any time before the person arrested reaches a police station, a constable is satisfied that there are no grounds of keeping him under arrest or release him on bail under section 30A.

  (8) A constable who releases a person under subsection (7) above shall record the fact that he has done so.

(9) The constable shall make the record as soon as is practicable after the release.

(10) Nothing in subsection (1A) or in Section 30A prevents a constable delaying taking a person to a police station.

(10A) The condition is that the presence of the person at a place (other than a police station) is necessary in order to carry out such investigations as it is reasonable to carry out immediately.

(11) Where there is delay in taking a person who has been arrested to a police station after his arrest, the reasons for the delay shall be recorded when he first arrives at a police station.

(12) Nothing in subsection (1) above shall be taken to affect—

(a) paragraphs 16(3) or 18(1) of Schedule 2 to the Immigration Act 1971;

(b) section 34(1) of the Criminal Justice Act 1972; or

(c) any provision of the Terrorism Act 2000.

(13) Nothing in subsection (10) above shall be taken to affect paragraph 18(3) of Schedule 2 to the Immigration Act 1971.

30A Bail elsewhere than at police station

(1) A constable may release on bail a person who is arrested or taken into custody in the circumstances mentioned in section 30(1).

(2) A person may be released on bail under subsection (1) at any time before he arrives at a police station.

(3) A person released on bail under subsection (1) must be required to attend a police station.

(3A) Where a constable releases a person on bail under subsection (1)—

(a) no recognizance for the person's surrender to custody shall be taken from the person,

(b) no security for the person's surrender to custody shall be taken from the person or from anyone else on the person's behalf,

(c) the person shall not be required to provide a surety or sureties for his surrender to custody, and

(d) no requirement to reside in a bail hostel may be imposed as a condition of bail.

(3B) Subject to subsection (3A), where a constable releases a person on bail under subsection (1) the constable may impose, as conditions of the bail, such requirements as appear to the constable to be necessary—

(a) to secure that the person surrenders to custody,

(b) to secure that the person does not commit an offence while on bail,

(c) to secure that the person does not interfere with witnesses or otherwise obstruct the course of justice, whether in relation to himself or any other person, or

(d) for the person's own protection or, if the person is under the age of 17, for the person's own welfare or in the person's own interests.

(4) Where a person is released on bail under subsection (1), a requirement may be imposed on the person as a condition of bail only under the preceding provisions of this section.

(5) The police station which the person is required to attend may be any police station.

31 Arrest for further offence

Where—

(a) a person—

(i) has been arrested for an offence; and

(ii) is at a police station in consequence of that arrest; and

(b) it appears to a constable that, if he were released from that arrest, he would be liable to arrest for some other offence,

he shall be arrested for that other offence.

32 Search upon arrest

(1) A constable may search an arrested person, in any case where the person to be searched has been arrested at a place other than a police station, if the constable has reasonable grounds for believing that the arrested person may present a danger to himself or others.

(2) Subject to subsections (3) to (5) below, a constable shall also have power in any such case—

    (a) to search the arrested person for anything—

        (i) which he might use to assist him to escape from lawful custody; or

        (ii) which might be evidence relating to an offence; and

    (b) if the offence for which he has been arrested is an indictable offence, to enter and search any premises in which he was when arrested or immediately before he was arrested for evidence relating to the offence.

(3) The power to search conferred by subsection (2) above is only a power to search to the extent that is reasonably required for the purpose of discovering any such thing or any such evidence.

(4) The powers conferred by this section to search a person are not to be construed as authorising a constable to require a person to remove any of his clothing in public other than an outer coat, jacket or gloves but they do authorise a search of a person's mouth.

(5) A constable may not search a person in the exercise of the power conferred by subsection (2)(a) above unless he has reasonable grounds for believing that the person to be searched may have concealed on him anything for which a search is permitted under that paragraph.

(6) A constable may not search premises in the exercise of the power conferred by subsection (2)(b) above unless he has reasonable grounds for believing that there is evidence for which a search is permitted under that paragraph on the premises.

(7) In so far as the power of search conferred by subsection (2)(b) above relates to premises consisting of two or more separate dwellings, it is limited to a power to search—

    (a) any dwelling in which the arrest took place or in which the person arrested was immediately before his arrest; and

    (b) any parts of the premises which the occupier of any such dwelling uses in common with the occupiers of any other dwellings comprised in the premises.

(8) A constable searching a person in the exercise of the power conferred by subsection (1) above may seize and retain anything he finds, if he has reasonable grounds for believing that the person searched might use it to cause physical injury to himself or to any other person.

(9) A constable searching a person in the exercise of the power conferred by subsection (2)(a) above may seize and retain anything he finds, other than an item subject to legal privilege, if he has reasonable grounds for believing—

    (a) that he might use it to assist him to escape from lawful custody; or

    (b) that it is evidence of an offence or has been obtained in consequence of the commission of an offence.

(10) Nothing in this section shall be taken to affect the power conferred by section 43 of the Terrorism Act 2000.

36 Custody officers at police stations

(1) One or more custody officers shall be appointed for each designated police station.

(2) A custody officer for a police station designated under section 35(1) above shall be appointed—

    (a) by the chief officer of police for the area in which the designated police station is situated; or

    (b) by such other police officer as the chief officer of police for that area may direct.

(2A) A custody officer for a police station designated under section 35(2A) above shall be appointed—

    (a) by the Chief Constable of the British Transport Police Force; or

    (b) by such other member of that Force as that Chief Constable may direct.

(3) No officer may be appointed a custody officer unless he is of at least the rank of sergeant.

(4) An officer of any rank may perform the functions of a custody officer at a designated police station if a custody officer is not readily available to perform them.

(5) Subject to the following provisions of this section and to section 39(2) below, none of the functions of a custody officer in relation to a person shall be performed by an officer who at the time when the function falls to be performed is involved in the investigation of an offence for which that person is in police detention at that time.

(6) Nothing in subsection (5) above is to be taken to prevent a custody officer—

    (a) performing any function assigned to custody officers—

        (i) by this Act; or

        (ii) by a code of practice issued under this Act;

    (b) carrying out the duty imposed on custody officers by section 39 below;

    (c) doing anything in connection with the identification of a suspect; or

    (d) doing anything under sections 7 and 8 of the Road Traffic Act 1988.

(7) Where an arrested person is taken to a police station which is not a designated police station, the functions in relation to him which at a designated police station would be the functions of a custody officer shall be performed—

    (a) by an officer who is not involved in the investigation of an offence for which he is in police detention, if such an officer is readily available; and

    (b) if no such officer is readily available, by the officer who took him to the station or any other officer.

(7A) Subject to subsection (7B), subsection (7) applies where a person attends a police station which is not a designated station to answer to bail granted under section 30A as it applies where a person is taken to such a station.

(7B) Where subsection (7) applies because of subsection (7A), the reference in subsection (7)(b) to the officer who took him to the station is to be read as a reference to the officer who granted him bail.

(8) References to a custody officer in the following provisions of this Act include references to an officer other than a custody officer who is performing the functions of a custody officer by virtue of subsection (4) or (7) above.

(9) Where by virtue of subsection (7) above an officer of a force maintained by a police authority who took an arrested person to a police station is to perform the functions of a custody officer in relation to him, the officer shall inform an officer who—

    (a) is attached to a designated police station; and

    (b) is of at least the rank of inspector,

    that he is to do so.

(10) The duty imposed by subsection (9) above shall be performed as soon as it is practicable to perform it.

37 Duties of custody officer before charge

(1) Where—

    (a) a person is arrested for an offence—

        (i) without a warrant; or

        (ii) under a warrant not endorsed for bail,...

    (b) ...

the custody officer at each police station where he is detained after his arrest shall determine whether he has before him sufficient evidence to charge that person with the offence for which he was arrested and may detain him at the police station for such period as is necessary to enable him to do so.

(2) If the custody officer determines that he does not have such evidence before him, the person arrested shall be released either on bail or without bail, unless the custody officer has reasonable grounds for believing that his detention without being charged is necessary to secure or preserve evidence relating to an offence for which he is under arrest or to obtain such evidence by questioning him.

(3) If the custody officer has reasonable grounds for so believing, he may authorise the person arrested to be kept in police detention.

(4) Where a custody officer authorises a person who has not been charged to be kept in police detention, he shall, as soon as is practicable, make a written record of the grounds for the detention.

(5) Subject to subsection (6) below, the written record shall be made in the presence of the person arrested who shall at that time be informed by the custody officer of the grounds for his detention.

(6) Subsection (5) above shall not apply where the person arrested is, at the time when the written record is made—

    (a) incapable of understanding what is said to him;

    (b) violent or likely to become violent; or

    (c) in urgent need of medical attention.

(7) Subject to section 41(7) below, if the custody officer determines that he has before him sufficient evidence to charge the person arrested with the offence for which he was arrested, the person arrested—

    (a) shall be charged; or

    (b) shall be released without charge, either on bail or without bail.

(7A) The decision as to how a person is to be dealt with under subsection (7) above shall be that of the custody officer.

(7B) Where a person is dealt with under subsection (7)(a) above, it shall be the duty of the custody officer to inform him that he is being released, or (as the case may be) detained, to enable the Director of Public Prosecutions to make a decision under section 37B below.

(8) Where—

    (a) a person is released under subsection (7)(b) above; and

    (b) at the time of his release a decision whether he should be prosecuted for the offence for which he was arrested has not been taken,

it shall be the duty of the custody officer so to inform him.

(8A) Subsection (8B) applies if the offence for which the person is arrested is one in relation to which a sample could be taken under section 63B below and the custody officer—

(a) is required in pursuance of subsection (2) above to release the person arrested and decides to release him on bail, or

(b) decides in pursuance of subsection (7)(a) or (b) above to release the person without charge and on bail.

(8B) The detention of the person may be continued to enable a sample to be taken under section 63B, but this subsection does not permit a person to be detained for a period of more than 24 hours after the relevant time.

(9) If the person arrested is not in a fit state to be dealt with under subsection (7) above, he may be kept in police detention until he is.

(10) The duty imposed on the custody officer under subsection (1) above shall be carried out by him as soon as practicable after the person arrested arrives at the police station or, in the case of a person arrested at the police station, as soon as practicable after the arrest.

(15) In this Part of this Act—

"arrested juvenile" means a person arrested with or without a warrant who appears to be under the age of 17...;

"endorsed for bail" means endorsed with a direction for bail in accordance with section 117(2) of the Magistrates' Courts Act 1980.

38 Duties of custody officer after charge

(1) Where a person arrested for an offence otherwise than under a warrant endorsed for bail is charged with an offence, the custody officer shall, subject to section 25 of the Criminal Justice and Public Order Act 1994, order his release from police detention, either on bail or without bail, unless—

(a) if the person arrested is not an arrested juvenile—

(i) his name or address cannot be ascertained or the custody officer has reasonable grounds for doubting whether a name or address furnished by him as his name or address is his real name or address;

(ii) the custody officer has reasonable grounds for believing that the person arrested will fail to appear in court to answer to bail;

(iii) in the case of a person arrested for an imprisonable offence, the custody officer has reasonable grounds for believing that the detention of the person arrested is necessary to prevent him from committing an offence;

(iiia) in the case of a person who has attained the age of 18, the custody officer has reasonable grounds for believing that the detention of the person is necessary to enable a sample to be taken from him under section 63B below;

(iv) in the case of a person arrested for an offence which is not an imprisonable offence, the custody officer has reasonable grounds for believing that the detention of the person arrested is necessary to prevent him from causing physical injury to any other person or from causing loss of or damage to property;

(v) the custody officer has reasonable grounds for believing that the detention of the person arrested is necessary to prevent him from interfering with the administration of justice or with the investigation of offences or of a particular offence; or

(vi) the custody officer has reasonable grounds for believing that the detention of the person arrested is necessary for his own protection;

(b) if he is an arrested juvenile—

(i) any of the requirements of paragraph (a) above is satisfied; or

(ii) the custody officer has reasonable grounds for believing that he ought to be detained in his own interests.

(2) If the release of a person arrested is not required by subsection (1) above, the custody officer may authorise him to be kept in police detention but may not authorise a person to be kept in police detention by virtue of subsection (1)(a)(iiia) after the end of the period of six hours beginning when he was charged with the offence.

(2A) The custody officer, in taking the decisions required by subsection (1)(a) and (b) above (except (a)(i) and (vi) and (b)(ii)), shall have regard to the same considerations as those which a court is required to have regard to in taking the corresponding decisions under paragraph 2 of Part I of Schedule I to the Bail Act 1976.

(3) Where a custody officer authorises a person who has been charged to be kept in police detention, he shall, as soon as practicable, make a written record of the grounds for the detention.

(4) Subject to subsection (5) below, the written record shall be made in the presence of the person charged who shall at that time be informed by the custody officer of the grounds for his detention.

(5) Subsection (4) above shall not apply where the person charged is, at the time when the written record is made—

(a) incapable of understanding what is said to him;

(b) violent or likely to become violent; or

(c) in urgent need of medical attention.

(6) Where a custody officer authorises an arrested juvenile to be kept in police detention under subsection (1) above, the custody officer shall, unless he certifies—

(a) that, by reason of such circumstances as are specified in the certificate, it is impracticable for him to do so; or

(b) in the case of an arrested juvenile who has attained the age of 12 years, that no secure accommodation is available and that keeping him in other local authority accommodation would not be adequate to protect the public from serious harm from him,

secure that the arrested juvenile is moved to local authority accommodation.

(6A) In this section—

"local authority accommodation" means accommodation provided by or on behalf of a local authority (within the meaning of the Children Act 1989);

"minimum age" means the age specified in section 63B(3)(b) below;

"secure accommodation" means accommodation provided for the purpose of restricting liberty;

"sexual offence" and "violent offence" have the same meanings as in the Powers of Criminal Courts (Sentencing) Act 2000;

and any reference, in relation to an arrested juvenile charged with a violent or sexual offence, to protecting the public from serious harm from him shall be construed as a reference to protecting members of the public from death or serious personal injury, whether physical or psychological, occasioned by further such offences committed by him.

(6B) Where an arrested juvenile is moved to local authority accommodation under subsection (6) above, it shall be lawful for any person acting on behalf of the authority to detain him.

(7) A certificate made under subsection (6) above in respect of an arrested juvenile shall be produced to the court before which he is first brought thereafter.

(7A) In this section "imprisonable offence" has the same meaning as in Schedule 1 to the Bail Act 1976.

(8) In this Part of this Act "local authority" has the same meaning as in the Children Act 1989.

56 Right to have someone informed when arrested

(1) Where a person has been arrested and is being held in custody in a police station or other premises, he shall be entitled, if he so requests, to have one friend or relative or other person who is known to him or who is likely to take an interest in his welfare told, as soon as is practicable except to the extent that delay is permitted by this section, that he has been arrested and is being detained there.

(2) Delay is only permitted—

    (a) in the case of a person who is in police detention for an indictable offence; and

    (b) if an officer of at least the rank of inspector authorises it.

(3) In any case the person in custody must be permitted to exercise the right conferred by subsection (1) above within 36 hours from the relevant time, as defined in section 41(2) above.

(4) An officer may give an authorisation under subsection (2) above orally or in writing but, if he gives it orally, he shall confirm it in writing as soon as is practicable.

(5) Subject to subsection (5A) below an officer may only authorise delay where he has reasonable grounds for believing that telling the named person of the arrest—

    (a) will lead to interference with or harm to evidence connected with an indictable offence or interference with or physical injury to other persons; or

    (b) will lead to the alerting of other persons suspected of having committed such an offence but not yet arrested for it; or

    (c) will hinder the recovery of any property obtained as a result of such an offence.

(5A) An officer may also authorise delay where he has reasonable grounds for believing that—

    (a) the person detained for the indictable offence has benefited from his criminal conduct, and

    (b) the recovery of the value of the property constituting the benefit will be hindered by telling the named person of the arrest.

(5B) For the purposes of subsection (5A) above the question whether a person has benefited from his criminal conduct is to be decided in accordance with Part 2 of the Proceeds of Crime Act 2002.

(6) If a delay is authorised—

    (a) the detained person shall be told the reason for it; and

    (b) the reason shall be noted on his custody record.

(7) The duties imposed by subsection (6) above shall be performed as soon as is practicable.

(8) The rights conferred by this section on a person detained at a police station or other premises are exercisable whenever he is transferred from one place to another; and this section applies to each subsequent occasion on which they are exercisable as it applies to the first such occasion.

(9) There may be no further delay in permitting the exercise of the right conferred by subsection (1) above once the reason for authorising delay ceases to subsist.

(10) Nothing in this section applies to a person arrested or detained under the terrorism provisions.

58 Access to legal advice

(1) A person arrested and held in custody in a police station or other premises shall be entitled, if he so requests, to consult a solicitor privately at any time.

(2) Subject to subsection (3) below, a request under subsection (1) above and the time at which it was made shall be recorded in the custody record.

(3) Such a request need not be recorded in the custody record of a person who makes it at a time while he is at a court after being charged with an offence.

(4) If a person makes such a request, he must be permitted to consult a solicitor as soon as is practicable except to the extent that delay is permitted by this section.

(5) In any case he must be permitted to consult a solicitor within 36 hours from the relevant time, as defined in section 41(2) above.

(6) Delay in compliance with a request is only permitted—

(a) in the case of a person who is in police detention for an indictable offence; and

(b) if an officer of at least the rank of superintendent authorises it.

(7) An officer may give an authorisation under subsection (6) above orally or in writing but, if he gives it orally, he shall confirm it in writing as soon as is practicable.

(8) Subject to subsection (8A) below an officer may only authorise delay where he has reasonable grounds for believing that the exercise of the right conferred by subsection (1) above at the time when the person detained desires to exercise it—

(a) will lead to interference with or harm to evidence connected with an indictable offence or interference with or physical injury to other persons; or

(b) will lead to the alerting of other persons suspected of having committed such an offence but not yet arrested for it; or

(c) will hinder the recovery of any property obtained as a result of such an offence.

(8A) An officer may also authorise delay where he has reasonable grounds for believing that—

(a) the person detained for the indictable offence has benefited from his criminal conduct, and

(b) the recovery of the value of the property constituting the benefit will be hindered by the exercise of the right conferred by subsection (1) above.

(8B) For the purposes of subsection (8A) above the question whether a person has benefited from his criminal conduct is to be decided in accordance with Part 2 of the Proceeds of Crime Act 2002.

(9) If delay is authorised—

(a) the detained person shall be told the reason for it; and

(b) the reason shall be noted on his custody record.

(10) The duties imposed by subsection (9) above shall be performed as soon as is practicable.

(11) There may be no further delay in permitting the exercise of the right conferred by subsection (1) above once the reason for authorising delay ceases to subsist.

(12) Nothing in this section applies to a person arrested or detained under the terrorism provisions.

66 Codes of practice

(1) The Secretary of State shall issue codes of practice in connection with—

(a) the exercise by police officers of statutory powers—
   (i) to search a person without first arresting him; or
   (ii) to search a vehicle without making an arrest; or
   (iii) to arrest a person.

(b) the detention, treatment, questioning and identification of persons by police officers;

(c) searches of premises by police officers; and

(d) the seizure of property found by police officers on persons or premises.

(2) Codes shall (in particular) include provision in connection with the exercise by police officers of powers under section 63B above.

76 Confessions

(1) In any proceedings a confession made by an accused person may be given in evidence against him in so far as it is relevant to any matter in issue in the proceedings and is not excluded by the court in pursuance of this section.

(2) If, in any proceedings where the prosecution proposes to give in evidence a confession made by an accused person, it is represented to the court that the confession was or may have been obtained—

(a) by oppression of the person who made it; or

(b) in consequence of anything said or done which was likely, in the circumstances existing at the time, to render unreliable any confession which might be made by him in consequence thereof,

the court shall not allow the confession to be given in evidence against him except in so far as the prosecution proves to the court beyond reasonable doubt that the confession (notwithstanding that it may be true) was not obtained as aforesaid.

(3) In any proceedings where the prosecution proposes to give in evidence a confession made by an accused person, the court may of its own motion require the prosecution, as a condition of allowing it to do so, to prove that the confession was not obtained as mentioned in subsection (2) above.

(4) The fact that a confession is wholly or partly excluded in pursuance of this section shall not affect the admissibility in evidence—

(a) of any facts discovered as a result of the confession; or

(b) where the confession is relevant as showing that the accused speaks, writes or expresses himself in a particular way, of so much of the confession as is necessary to show that he does so.

(5) Evidence that a fact to which this subsection applies was discovered as a result of a statement made by an accused person shall not be admissible unless evidence of how it was discovered is given by him or on his behalf.

(6) Subsection (5) above applies—

(a) to any fact discovered as a result of a confession which is wholly excluded in pursuance of this section; and

(b) to any fact discovered as a result of a confession which is partly so excluded, if the fact is discovered as a result of the excluded part of the confession.

(7) Nothing in Part VII of this Act shall prejudice the admissibility of a confession made by an accused person.

(8) In this section "oppression" includes torture, inhuman or degrading treatment, and the use or threat of violence (whether or not amounting to torture).

(9) Where the proceedings mentioned in subsection (1) above are proceedings before a magistrates' court inquiring into an offence as examining justices this section shall have effect with the omission of

(a) in subsection (1) the words "and is not excluded by the court in pursuance of this section", and

(b) subsections (2) to (6) and (8).

78 Exclusion of unfair evidence

(1) In any proceedings the court may refuse to allow evidence on which the prosecution proposes to rely to be given if it appears to the court that, having regard to all the circumstances, including the

circumstances in which the evidence was obtained, the admission of the evidence would have such an adverse effect on the fairness of the proceedings that the court ought not to admit it.

(2) Nothing in this section shall prejudice any rule of law requiring a court to exclude evidence.

(3) This section shall not apply in the case of proceedings before a magistrates' court inquiring into an offence as examining justices.

[2:12] Code of Practice C: The Detention, Treatment and Questioning of Persons by Police Officers

(2008) HMSO

1 General

1.1 All persons in custody must be dealt with expeditiously, and released as soon as the need for detention no longer applies.

1.1A A custody officer must perform the functions in this Code as soon as practicable. A custody officer will not be in breach of this Code if delay is justifiable and reasonable steps are taken to prevent unnecessary delay. The custody record shall show when a delay has occurred and the reason. See Note 1H

1.2 This Code of Practice must be readily available at all police stations for consultation by:

- police officers
- police staff
- detained persons
- members of the public.

1.3 The provisions of this Code:

- include the Annexes
- do not include the Notes for Guidance.

1.4 If an officer has any suspicion, or is told in good faith, that a person of any age may be mentally disordered or otherwise mentally vulnerable, in the absence of clear evidence to dispel that suspicion, the person shall be treated as such for the purposes of this Code. See Note 1G

1.5 If anyone appears to be under 17, they shall be treated as a juvenile for the purposes of this Code in the absence of clear evidence that they are older.

1.6 If a person appears to be blind, seriously visually impaired, deaf, unable to read or speak or has difficulty orally because of a speech impediment, they shall be treated as such for the purposes of this Code in the absence of clear evidence to the contrary.

1.7 'The appropriate adult' means, in the case of a:

(a) juvenile:

  (i) the parent, guardian or, if the juvenile is in local authority or voluntary organisation care, or is otherwise being looked after under the Children Act 1989, a person representing that authority or organisation;

  (ii) a social worker of a local authority;

  (iii) failing these, some other responsible adult aged 18 or over who is not a police officer or employed by the police.

(b) person who is mentally disordered or mentally vulnerable: See Note 1D

  (iv) a relative, guardian or other person responsible for their care or custody;

(v) someone experienced in dealing with mentally disordered or mentally vulnerable people but who is not a police officer or employed by the police;

(vi) failing these, some other responsible adult aged 18 or over who is not a police officer or employed by the police.

1.8 If this Code requires a person be given certain information, they do not have to be given it if at the time they are incapable of understanding what is said, are violent or may become violent or in urgent need of medical attention, but they must be given it as soon as practicable.

1.9 References to a custody officer include any:—

- police officer; or
- designated staff custody officer acting in the exercise or performance of the powers and duties conferred or imposed on them by their designation,
  performing the functions of a custody officer. See Note 1J.

1.9 A When this Code requires the prior authority or agreement of an officer of at least inspector or superintendent rank, that authority may be given by a sergeant or chief inspector authorised to perform the functions of the higher rank under the Police and Criminal Evidence Act 1984 (PACE), section 107.

1.10 Subject to paragraph 1.12, this Code applies to people in custody at police stations in England and Wales, whether or not they have been arrested, and to those removed to a police station as a place of safety under the Mental Health Act 1983, sections 135 and 136. Section 15 applies solely to people in police detention, e.g. those brought to a police station under arrest or arrested at a police station for an offence after going there voluntarily.

1.11 People detained under the Terrorism Act 2000, Schedule 8 and section 41 and other provisions of that Act are not subject to any part of this Code. Such persons are subject to the Code of Practice for detention, treatment and questioning of persons by police officers detained under that Act.

1.12 This Code's provisions do not apply to people in custody:

(i) arrested on warrants issued in Scotland by officers under the Criminal Justice and Public Order Act 1994, section 136(2), or arrested or detained without warrant by officers from a police force in Scotland under section 137(2). In these cases, police powers and duties and the person's rights and entitlements whilst at a police station in England or Wales are the same as those in Scotland;

(ii) arrested under the Immigration and Asylum Act 1999, section 142(3) in order to have their fingerprints taken;

(iii) whose detention is authorised by an immigration officer under the Immigration Act 1971;

(iv) who are convicted or remanded prisoners held in police cells on behalf of the Prison Service under the Imprisonment (Temporary Provisions) Act 1980;

(v) not used

(vi) detained for searches under stop and search powers except as required by Code A.

The provisions on conditions of detention and treatment in sections 8 and 9 must be considered as the minimum standards of treatment for such detainees.

1.13 In this Code:

(a) 'designated person' means a person other than a police officer, designated under the Police Reform Act 2002, Part 4 who has specified powers and duties of police officers conferred or imposed on them;

(b) reference to a police officer includes a designated person acting in the exercise or performance of the powers and duties conferred or imposed on them by their designation.

1.14 Designated persons are entitled to use reasonable force as follows:-

(a) when exercising a power conferred on them which allows a police officer exercising that power to use reasonable force, a designated person has the same entitlement to use force; and

(b) at other times when carrying out duties conferred or imposed on them that also entitle them to use reasonable force, for example:

  • when at a police station carrying out the duty to keep detainees for whom they are responsible under control and to assist any other police officer or designated person to keep any detainee under control and to prevent their escape.

  • when securing, or assisting any other police officer or designated person in securing, the detention of a person at a police station.

  • when escorting, or assisting any other police officer or designated person in escorting, a detainee within a police station.

  • for the purpose of saving life or limb; or

  • preventing serious damage to property.

1.15 Nothing in this Code prevents the custody officer, or other officer given custody of the detainee, from allowing police staff who are not designated persons to carry out individual procedures or tasks at the police station if the law allows. However, the officer remains responsible for making sure the procedures and tasks are carried out correctly in accordance with the Codes of Practice. Any such person must be:

(a) a person employed by a police authority maintaining a police force and under the control and direction of the Chief Officer of that force;

(b) employed by a person with whom a police authority has a contract for the provision of services relating to persons arrested or otherwise in custody.

1.16 Designated persons and other police staff must have regard to any relevant provisions of the Codes of Practice.

1.17 References to pocket books include any official report book issued to police officers or other police staff.

Notes for guidance

1A Although certain sections of this Code apply specifically to people in custody at police stations, those there voluntarily to assist with an investigation should be treated with no less consideration, e.g. offered refreshments at appropriate times, and enjoy an absolute right to obtain legal advice or communicate with anyone outside the police station.

1B A person, including a parent or guardian, should not be an appropriate adult if they:

  • are

    — suspected of involvement in the offence

    — the victim

    — a witness

    — involved in the investigation

  • received admissions prior to attending to act as the appropriate adult.

Note: If a juvenile's parent is estranged from the juvenile, they should not be asked to act as the appropriate adult if the juvenile expressly and specifically objects to their presence.

1C If a juvenile admits an offence to, or in the presence of, a social worker or member of a youth offending team other than during the time that person is acting as the juvenile's appropriate adult, another appropriate adult should be appointed in the interest of fairness.

1D In the case of people who are mentally disordered or otherwise mentally vulnerable, it may be more satisfactory if the appropriate adult is someone experienced or trained in their care rather than a relative lacking such qualifications. But if the detainee prefers a relative to a better qualified stranger or objects to a particular person their wishes should, if practicable, be respected.

1E A detainee should always be given an opportunity, when an appropriate adult is called to the police station, to consult privately with a solicitor in the appropriate adult's absence if they want. An appropriate adult is not subject to legal privilege.

1F A solicitor or independent custody visitor (formerly a lay visitor) present at the police station in that capacity may not be the appropriate adult.

1G 'Mentally vulnerable' applies to any detainee who, because of their mental state or capacity, may not understand the significance of what is said, of questions or of their replies. 'Mental disorder' is defined in the Mental Health Act 1983, section 1(2) as 'mental illness, arrested or incomplete development of mind, psychopathic disorder and any other disorder or disability of mind'. When the custody officer has any doubt about the mental state or capacity of a detainee, that detainee should be treated as mentally vulnerable and an appropriate adult called.

1H Paragraph 1.1A is intended to cover delays which may occur in processing detainees e.g. if:

- a large number of suspects are brought into the station simultaneously to be placed in custody;
- interview rooms are all being used;
- there are difficulties contacting an appropriate adult, solicitor or interpreter.

1I The custody officer must remind the appropriate adult and detainee about the right to legal advice and record any reasons for waiving it in accordance with section 6.

1J The designation of police staff custody officers applies only in police areas where an order commencing the provisions of the Police Reform Act 2002, section 38 and Schedule 4A, for designating police staff custody officers is in effect.

1K This Code does not affect the principle that all citizens have a duty to help police officers to prevent crime and discover offenders. This is a civic rather than a legal duty; but when a police officer is trying to discover whether, or by whom, an offence has been committed he is entitled to question any person from whom he thinks useful information can be obtained, subject to the restrictions imposed by this Code. A person's declaration that he is unwilling to reply does not alter this entitlement.

2 Custody records

2.1A When a person is brought to a police station:

- under arrest
- is arrested at the police station having attended there voluntarily or
- attends a police station to answer bail

they should be brought before the custody officer as soon as practicable after their arrival at the station or, if appropriate, following arrest after attending the police station voluntarily. This applies to designated and non-designated police stations. A person is deemed to be "at a police station" for these purposes if they are within the boundary of any building or enclosed yard which forms part of that police station.

2.1 A separate custody record must be opened as soon as practicable for each person brought to a police station under arrest or arrested at the station having gone there voluntarily or attending a police station in answer to street bail. All information recorded under this Code must be recorded as soon as practicable in the custody record unless otherwise specified. Any audio or video recording made in the custody area is not part of the custody record.

2.2 If any action requires the authority of an officer of a specified rank, subject to paragraph 2.6A, their name and rank must be noted in the custody record.

2.3 The custody officer is responsible for the custody record's accuracy and completeness and for making sure the record or copy of the record accompanies a detainee if they are transferred to another police station. The record shall show the:

- time and reason for transfer;
- time a person is released from detention.

2.4 A solicitor or appropriate adult must be permitted to consult a detainee's custody record as soon as practicable after their arrival at the station and at any other time whilst the person is detained. Arrangements for this access must be agreed with the custody officer and may not unreasonably interfere with the custody officer's duties.

2.4A When a detainee leaves police detention or is taken before a court they, their legal representative or appropriate adult shall be given, on request, a copy of the custody record as soon as practicable. This entitlement lasts for 12 months after release.

2.5 The detainee, appropriate adult or legal representative shall be permitted to inspect the original custody record after the detainee has left police detention provided they give reasonable notice of their request. Any such inspection shall be noted in the custody record.

2.6 Subject to paragraph 2.6A, all entries in custody records must be timed and signed by the maker. Records entered on computer shall be timed and contain the operator's identification.

2.6A Nothing in this Code requires the identity of officers or other police staff to be recorded or disclosed:

(a) not used;

(b) if the officer or police staff reasonably believe recording or disclosing their name might put them in danger.

In these cases, they shall use their warrant or other identification numbers and the name of their police station. See Note 2A

2.7 The fact and time of any detainee's refusal to sign a custody record, when asked in accordance with this Code, must be recorded.

Note for guidance

2A The purpose of paragraph 2.6A(b) is to protect those involved in serious organised crime investigations or arrests of particularly violent suspects when there is reliable information that those arrested or their associates may threaten or cause harm to those involved. In cases of doubt, an officer of inspector rank or above should be consulted.

3 Initial action

(a) Detained persons—normal procedure

3.1 When a person is brought to a police station under arrest or arrested at the station having gone there voluntarily, the custody officer must make sure the person is told clearly about the following continuing rights which may be exercised at any stage during the period in custody:

(i) the right to have someone informed of their arrest as in section 5;

(ii) the right to consult privately with a solicitor and that free independent legal advice is available;

(iii) the right to consult these Codes of Practice. See Note 3D

3.2 The detainee must also be given:

- a written notice setting out:
  — the above three rights;
  — the arrangements for obtaining legal advice;

— the right to a copy of the custody record as in paragraph 2.4A;

— the caution in the terms prescribed in section 10.

- an additional written notice briefly setting out their entitlements while in custody, see Notes 3A and 3B.

Note: The detainee shall be asked to sign the custody record to acknowledge receipt of these notices. Any refusal must be recorded on the custody record.

3.3 A citizen of an independent Commonwealth country or a national of a foreign country, including the Republic of Ireland, must be informed as soon as practicable about their rights of communication with their High Commission, Embassy or Consulate. See section 7

3.4 The custody officer shall:

- record the offence(s) that the detainee has been arrested for and the reason(s) for the arrest on the custody record. See paragraph 10.3 and Code G paragraphs 2.2 and 4.3.

- note on the custody record any comment the detainee makes in relation to the arresting officer's account but shall not invite comment. If the arresting officer is not physically present when the detainee is brought to a police station, the arresting officer's account must be made available to the custody officer remotely or by a third party on the arresting officer's behalf. If the custody officer authorises a person's detention the detainee must be informed of the grounds as soon as practicable and before they are questioned about any offence;

- note any comment the detainee makes in respect of the decision to detain them but shall not invite comment;

- not put specific questions to the detainee regarding their involvement in any offence, nor in respect of any comments they may make in response to the arresting officer's account or the decision to place them in detention. Such an exchange is likely to constitute an interview as in paragraph 11.1A and require the associated safeguards in section 11.

See paragraph 11.13 in respect of unsolicited comments.

3.5 The custody officer shall:

(a) ask the detainee, whether at this time, they:

   (i) would like legal advice, see paragraph 6.5;

   (ii) want someone informed of their detention, see section 5;

(b) ask the detainee to sign the custody record to confirm their decisions in respect of (a);

(c) determine whether the detainee:

   (iii) is, or might be, in need of medical treatment or attention, see section 9;

   (iv) requires:

- an appropriate adult;
- help to check documentation;
- an interpreter;

(d) record the decision in respect of (c).

3.6 When determining these needs the custody officer is responsible for initiating an assessment to consider whether the detainee is likely to present specific risks to custody staff or themselves. Such assessments should always include a check on the Police National Computer, to be carried out as soon as practicable, to identify any risks highlighted in relation to the detainee. Although such assessments are primarily the custody officer's responsibility, it may be necessary for them to consult and involve others, Codes of practice—Code C Detention, treatment and questioning of persons by police officers 11 e.g. the arresting officer or an appropriate health care professional, see paragraph 9.13. Reasons for delaying the initiation or completion of the assessment must be recorded.

3.7 Chief Officers should ensure that arrangements for proper and effective risk assessments required by paragraph 3.6 are implemented in respect of all detainees at police stations in their area.

3.8 Risk assessments must follow a structured process which clearly defines the categories of risk to be considered and the results must be incorporated in the detainee's custody record. The custody officer is responsible for making sure those responsible for the detainee's custody are appropriately briefed about the risks. If no specific risks are identified by the assessment, that should be noted in the custody record. See Note 3E and paragraph 9.14.

3.9 The custody officer is responsible for implementing the response to any specific risk assessment, e.g.:

- reducing opportunities for self harm;
- calling a health care professional;
- increasing levels of monitoring or observation.

3.10 Risk assessment is an ongoing process and assessments must always be subject to review if circumstances change.

3.11 If video cameras are installed in the custody area, notices shall be prominently displayed showing cameras are in use. Any request to have video cameras switched off shall be refused.

(b) Detained persons—special groups

3.12 If the detainee appears deaf or there is doubt about their hearing or speaking ability or ability to understand English, and the custody officer cannot establish effective communication, the custody officer must, as soon as practicable, call an interpreter for assistance in the action under paragraphs 3.1–3.5. See section 13

3.13 If the detainee is a juvenile, the custody officer must, if it is practicable, ascertain the identity of a person responsible for their welfare. That person:

- may be:
  - the parent or guardian;
  - if the juvenile is in local authority or voluntary organisation care, or is otherwise being looked after under the Children Act 1989, a person appointed by that authority or organisation to have responsibility for the juvenile's welfare;
  - any other person who has, for the time being, assumed responsibility for the juvenile's welfare.
- must be informed as soon as practicable that the juvenile has been arrested, why they have been arrested and where they are detained. This right is in addition to the juvenile's right in section 5 not to be held incommunicado. See Note 3C

3.14 If a juvenile is known to be subject to a court order under which a person or organisation is given any degree of statutory responsibility to supervise or otherwise monitor them, reasonable steps must also be taken to notify that person or organisation (the 'responsible officer'). The responsible officer will normally be a member of a Youth Offending Team, except for a curfew order which involves electronic monitoring when the contractor providing the monitoring will normally be the responsible officer.

3.15 If the detainee is a juvenile, mentally disordered or otherwise mentally vulnerable, the custody officer must, as soon as practicable:

- inform the appropriate adult, who in the case of a juvenile may or may not be a person responsible for their welfare, as in paragraph 3.13, of:
  - the grounds for their detention;
  - their whereabouts.
- ask the adult to come to the police station to see the detainee.

3.16 It is imperative that a mentally disordered or otherwise mentally vulnerable person, detained under the Mental Health Act 1983, section 136, be assessed as soon as possible. If that assessment is to take place at the police station, an approved social worker and a registered medical practitioner shall be called to the station as soon as possible in order to interview and examine the detainee. Once the detainee has been interviewed, examined and suitable arrangements made for their treatment or care, they can no longer be detained under section 136. A detainee must be immediately discharged from detention under section 136 if a registered medical practitioner, having examined them, concludes they are not mentally disordered within the meaning of the Act.

3.17 If the appropriate adult is:

- already at the police station, the provisions of paragraphs 3.1 to 3.5 must be complied with in the appropriate adult's presence;
- not at the station when these provisions are complied with, they must be complied with again in the presence of the appropriate adult when they arrive.

3.18 The detainee shall be advised that:

- the duties of the appropriate adult include giving advice and assistance;
- they can consult privately with the appropriate adult at any time.

3.19 If the detainee, or appropriate adult on the detainee's behalf, asks for a solicitor to be called to give legal advice, the provisions of section 6 apply.

3.20 If the detainee is blind, seriously visually impaired or unable to read, the custody officer shall make sure their solicitor, relative, appropriate adult or some other person likely to take an interest in them and not involved in the investigation is available to help check any documentation. When this Code requires written consent or signing the person assisting may be asked to sign instead, if the detainee prefers. This paragraph does not require an appropriate adult to be called solely to assist in checking and signing documentation for a person who is not a juvenile, or mentally disordered or otherwise mentally vulnerable (see paragraph 3.15).

(c) Persons attending a police station voluntarily

3.21 Anybody attending a police station voluntarily to assist with an investigation may leave at will unless arrested. See Note 1K. If it is decided they shall not be allowed to leave, they must be informed at once that they are under arrest and brought before the custody officer, who is responsible for making sure they are notified of their rights in the same way as other detainees. If they are not arrested but are cautioned as in section 10, the person who gives the caution must, at the same time, inform them they are not under arrest, they are not obliged to remain at the station but if they remain at the station they may obtain free and independent legal advice if they want. They shall be told the right to legal advice includes the right to speak with a solicitor on the telephone and be asked if they want to do so.

3.22 If a person attending the police station voluntarily asks about their entitlement to legal advice, they shall be given a copy of the notice explaining the arrangements for obtaining legal advice. See paragraph 3.2

(d) Documentation

3.23 The grounds for a person's detention shall be recorded, in the person's presence if practicable.

3.24 Action taken under paragraphs 3.12 to 3.20 shall be recorded.

(e) Persons answering street bail

3.25 When a person is answering street bail, the custody officer should link any documentation held in relation to arrest with the custody record. Any further action shall be recorded on the custody record in accordance with paragraphs 3.23 and 3.24 above.

Notes for guidance

3A The notice of entitlements should:

- list the entitlements in this Code, including:
  - visits and contact with outside parties, including special provisions for Commonwealth citizens and foreign nationals;
  - reasonable standards of physical comfort;
  - adequate food and drink;
  - access to toilets and washing facilities, clothing, medical attention, and exercise when practicable.
- mention the:
  - provisions relating to the conduct of interviews;
  - circumstances in which an appropriate adult should be available to assist the detainee and their statutory rights to make representation whenever the period of their detention is reviewed.

3B In addition to notices in English, translations should be available in Welsh, the main minority ethnic languages and the principal European languages, whenever they are likely to be helpful. Audio versions of the notice should also be made available.

3C If the juvenile is in local authority or voluntary organisation care but living with their parents or other adults responsible for their welfare, although there is no legal obligation to inform them, they should normally be contacted, as well as the authority or organisation unless suspected of involvement in the offence concerned. Even if the juvenile is not living with their parents, consideration should be given to informing them.

3D The right to consult the Codes of Practice does not entitle the person concerned to delay unreasonably any necessary investigative or administrative action whilst they do so. Examples of action which need not be delayed unreasonably include:

- procedures requiring the provision of breath, blood or urine specimens under the Road Traffic Act 1988 or the Transport and Works Act 1992;
- searching detainees at the police station;
- taking fingerprints, footwear impressions or non-intimate samples without consent for evidential purposes.

3E Home Office Circular 32/2000 provides more detailed guidance on risk assessments and identifies key risk areas which should always be considered.

4 Detainee's property

(a) Action

4.1 The custody officer is responsible for:

(a) ascertaining what property a detainee:
  (i) has with them when they come to the police station, whether on:
    - arrest or re-detention on answering to bail;
    - commitment to prison custody on the order or sentence of a court;
    - lodgement at the police station with a view to their production in court from prison custody;
    - transfer from detention at another station or hospital;
    - detention under the Mental Health Act 1983, section 135 or 136;
    - remand into police custody on the authority of a court

(ii) might have acquired for an unlawful or harmful purpose while in custody;

(b) the safekeeping of any property taken from a detainee which remains at the police station.

The custody officer may search the detainee or authorise their being searched to the extent they consider necessary, provided a search of intimate parts of the body or involving the removal of more than outer clothing is only made as in Annex A. A search may only be carried out by an officer of the same sex as the detainee. See Note 4A Codes of practice—Code C Detention, treatment and questioning of persons by police officers

4.2 Detainees may retain clothing and personal effects at their own risk unless the custody officer considers they may use them to cause harm to themselves or others, interfere with evidence, damage property, effect an escape or they are needed as evidence. In this event the custody officer may withhold such articles as they consider necessary and must tell the detainee why.

4.3 Personal effects are those items a detainee may lawfully need, use or refer to while in detention but do not include cash and other items of value.

(b) Documentation

4.4 It is a matter for the custody officer to determine whether a record should be made of the property a detained person has with him or had taken from him on arrest. Any record made is not required to be kept as part of the custody record but the custody record should be noted as to where such a record exists. Whenever a record is made the detainee shall be allowed to check and sign the record of property as correct. Any refusal to sign shall be recorded.

4.5 If a detainee is not allowed to keep any article of clothing or personal effects, the reason must be recorded.

Notes for guidance

4A PACE, Section 54(1) and paragraph 4.1 require a detainee to be searched when it is clear the custody officer will have continuing duties in relation to that detainee or when that detainee's behaviour or offence makes an inventory appropriate. They do not require every detainee to be searched, e.g. if it is clear a person will only be detained for a short period and is not to be placed in a cell, the custody officer may decide not to search them. In such a case the custody record will be endorsed 'not searched', paragraph 4.4 will not apply, and the detainee will be invited to sign the entry. If the detainee refuses, the custody officer will be obliged to ascertain what property they have in accordance with paragraph 4.1.

4B Paragraph 4.4 does not require the custody officer to record on the custody record property in the detainee's possession on arrest if, by virtue of its nature, quantity or size, it is not practicable to remove it to the police station.

4C Paragraph 4.4 does not require items of clothing worn by the person be recorded unless withheld by the custody officer as in paragraph 4.2.

5 Right not to be held incommunicado

(a) Action

5.1 Any person arrested and held in custody at a police station or other premises may, on request, have one person known to them or likely to take an interest in their welfare informed at public expense of their whereabouts as soon as practicable. If the person cannot be contacted the detainee may choose up to two alternatives. If they cannot be contacted, the person in charge of detention or the investigation has discretion to allow further attempts until the information has been conveyed. See Notes 5C and 5D

5.2 The exercise of the above right in respect of each person nominated may be delayed only in accordance with Annex B.

5.3 The above right may be exercised each time a detainee is taken to another police station.

5.4 The detainee may receive visits at the custody officer's discretion. See Note 5B

5.5 If a friend, relative or person with an interest in the detainee's welfare enquires about their whereabouts, this information shall be given if the suspect agrees and Annex B does not apply. See Note 5D

5.6 The detainee shall be given writing materials, on request, and allowed to telephone one person for a reasonable time, see Notes 5A and 5E. Either or both these privileges may be denied or delayed if an officer of inspector rank or above considers sending a letter or making a telephone call may result in any of the consequences in:

(a) Annex B paragraphs 1 and 2 and the person is detained in connection with an indictable offence;

(b) Not used

Nothing in this paragraph permits the restriction or denial of the rights in paragraphs 5.1 and 6.1.

5.7 Before any letter or message is sent, or telephone call made, the detainee shall be informed that what they say in any letter, call or message (other than in a communication to a solicitor) may be read or listened to and may be given in evidence. A telephone call may be terminated if it is being abused. The costs can be at public expense at the custody officer's discretion.

5.7A Any delay or denial of the rights in this section should be proportionate and should last no longer than necessary.

(b) Documentation

5.8 A record must be kept of any:

(a) request made under this section and the action taken;

(b) letters, messages or telephone calls made or received or visit received;

(c) refusal by the detainee to have information about them given to an outside enquirer. The detainee must be asked to countersign the record accordingly and any refusal recorded.

Notes for guidance

5A A person may request an interpreter to interpret a telephone call or translate a letter.

5B At the custody officer's discretion, visits should be allowed when possible, subject to having sufficient personnel to supervise a visit and any possible hindrance to the investigation.

5C If the detainee does not know anyone to contact for advice or support or cannot contact a friend or relative, the custody officer should bear in mind any local voluntary bodies or other organisations who might be able to help. Paragraph 6.1 applies if legal advice is required.

5D In some circumstances it may not be appropriate to use the telephone to disclose information under paragraphs 5.1 and 5.5.

5E The telephone call at paragraph 5.6 is in addition to any communication under paragraphs 5.1 and 6.1.

6 Right to legal advice

(a) Action

6.1 Unless Annex B applies, all detainees must be informed that they may at any time consult and communicate privately with a solicitor, whether in person, in writing or by telephone, and that free independent legal advice is available. See paragraph 3.1, Note 6B, 6B1, 6B2 and Note 6J

6.2 Not Used

6.3 A poster advertising the right to legal advice must be prominently displayed in the charging area of every police station. See Note 6H

6.4 No police officer should, at any time, do or say anything with the intention of dissuading a detainee from obtaining legal advice.

6.5 The exercise of the right of access to legal advice may be delayed only as in Annex B. Whenever legal advice is requested, and unless Annex B applies, the custody officer must act without delay to secure the provision of such advice. If, on being informed or reminded of this right, the detainee declines to speak to a solicitor in person, the officer should point out that the right includes the right to speak with a solicitor on the telephone. If the detainee continues to waive this right the officer should ask them why and any reasons should be recorded on the custody record or the interview record as appropriate. Reminders of the right to legal advice must be given as in paragraphs 3.5, 11.2, 15.4, 16.4, 2B of Annex A, 3 of Annex K and 16.5 and Code D, paragraphs 3.17(ii) and 6.3. Once it is clear a detainee does not want to speak to a solicitor in person or by telephone they should cease to be asked their reasons. See Note 6K

6.5A n the case of a juvenile, an appropriate adult should consider whether legal advice from a solicitor is required. If the juvenile indicates that they do not want legal advice, the appropriate adult has the right to ask for a solicitor to attend if this would be in the best interests of the person. However, the detained person cannot be forced to see the solicitor if he is adamant that he does not wish to do so.

6.6 A detainee who wants legal advice may not be interviewed or continue to be interviewed until they have received such advice unless:

(a) Annex B applies, when the restriction on drawing adverse inferences from silence in Annex C will apply because the detainee is not allowed an opportunity to consult a solicitor; or

(b) an officer of superintendent rank or above has reasonable grounds for believing that:

(i) the consequent delay might:
- lead to interference with, or harm to, evidence connected with an offence;
- lead to interference with, or physical harm to, other people;
- lead to serious loss of, or damage to, property;
- lead to alerting other people suspected of having committed an offence but not yet arrested for it;
- hinder the recovery of property obtained in consequence of the commission of an offence.

(ii) when a solicitor, including a duty solicitor, has been contacted and has agreed to attend, awaiting their arrival would cause unreasonable delay to the process of investigation.

Note: In these cases the restriction on drawing adverse inferences from silence in Annex C will apply because the detainee is not allowed an opportunity to consult a solicitor.

(c) the solicitor the detainee has nominated or selected from a list:

(i) cannot be contacted;

(ii) has previously indicated they do not wish to be contacted; or

(iii) having been contacted, has declined to attend; and

the detainee has been advised of the Duty Solicitor Scheme but has declined to ask for the duty solicitor.

In these circumstances the interview may be started or continued without further delay provided an officer of inspector rank or above has agreed to the interview proceeding.

Note: The restriction on drawing adverse inferences from silence in Annex C will not apply because the detainee is allowed an opportunity to consult the duty solicitor;

(d) the detainee changes their mind, about wanting legal advice.

In these circumstances the interview may be started or continued without delay provided that:

(i) the detainee agrees to do so , in writing or on the interview record made in accordance with Code E or F; and

(ii) an officer of inspector rank or above has inquired about the detainee's reasons for their change of mind and gives authority for the interview to proceed.

Confirmation of the detainee's agreement, their change of mind, the reasons for it if given and, subject to paragraph 2.6A, the name of the authorising officer shall be recorded in the written interview record or the interview record made in accordance with Code E or F. See Note 6I. Note: In these circumstances the restriction on drawing adverse inferences from silence in Annex C will not apply because the detainee is allowed an opportunity to consult a solicitor if they wish.

6.7 If paragraph 6.6(b)(i) applies, once sufficient information has been obtained to avert the risk, questioning must cease until the detainee has received legal advice unless paragraph 6.6(a), (b)(ii), (c) or (d) applies.

6.8 A detainee who has been permitted to consult a solicitor shall be entitled on request to have the solicitor present when they are interviewed unless one of the exceptions in paragraph 6.6 applies.

6.9 The solicitor may only be required to leave the interview if their conduct is such that the interviewer is unable properly to put questions to the suspect. See Notes 6D and 6E

6.10 If the interviewer considers a solicitor is acting in such a way, they will stop the interview and consult an officer not below superintendent rank, if one is readily available, and otherwise an officer not below inspector rank not connected with the investigation. After speaking to the solicitor, the officer consulted will decide if the interview should continue in the presence of that solicitor. If they decide it should not, the suspect will be given the opportunity to consult another solicitor before the interview continues and that solicitor given an opportunity to be present at the interview. See Note 6E

6.11 The removal of a solicitor from an interview is a serious step and, if it occurs, the officer of superintendent rank or above who took the decision will consider if the incident should be reported to the Law Society. If the decision to remove the solicitor has been taken by an officer below superintendent rank, the facts must be reported to an officer of superintendent rank or above who will similarly consider whether a report to the Law Society would be appropriate. When the solicitor concerned is a duty solicitor, the report should be both to the Law Society and to the Legal Services Commission.

6.12 'Solicitor' in this Code means:

- a solicitor who holds a current practising certificate
- an accredited or probationary representative included on the register of representatives maintained by the Legal Services Commission.

6.12A An accredited or probationary representative sent to provide advice by, and on behalf of, a solicitor shall be admitted to the police station for this purpose unless an officer of inspector rank or above considers such a visit will hinder the investigation and directs otherwise. Hindering the investigation does not include giving proper legal advice to a detainee as in Note 6D. Once admitted to the police station, paragraphs 6.6 to 6.10 apply.

6.13 In exercising their discretion under paragraph 6.12A, the officer should take into account in particular:

- whether:
  — the identity and status of an accredited or probationary representative have been satisfactorily established;
  — they are of suitable character to provide legal advice, e.g. a person with a criminal record is unlikely to be suitable unless the conviction was for a minor offence and not recent.
- any other matters in any written letter of authorisation provided by the solicitor on whose behalf the person is attending the police station. See Note 6F

6.14 If the inspector refuses access to an accredited or probationary representative or a decision is taken that such a person should not be permitted to remain at an interview, the inspector must notify the solicitor on whose behalf the representative was acting and give them an opportunity to make alternative arrangements. The detainee must be informed and the custody record noted.

6.15 If a solicitor arrives at the station to see a particular person, that person must, unless Annex B applies, be so informed whether or not they are being interviewed and asked if they would like to see the solicitor. This applies even if the detainee has declined legal advice or, having requested it, subsequently agreed to be interviewed without receiving advice. The solicitor's attendance and the detainee's decision must be noted in the custody record.

(b) Documentation

6.16 Any request for legal advice and the action taken shall be recorded.

6.17 A record shall be made in the interview record if a detainee asks for legal advice and an interview is begun either in the absence of a solicitor or their representative, or they have been required to leave an interview.

Notes for guidance

6A In considering if paragraph 6.6(b) applies, the officer should, if practicable, ask the solicitor for an estimate of how long it will take to come to the station and relate this to the time detention is permitted, the time of day (i.e. whether the rest period under paragraph 12.2 is imminent) and the requirements of other investigations. If the solicitor is on their way or is to set off immediately, it will not normally be appropriate to begin an interview before they arrive. If it appears necessary to begin an interview before the solicitor's arrival, they should be given an indication of how long the police would be able to wait before 6.6(b) applies so there is an opportunity to make arrangements for someone else to provide legal advice.

6B A detainee who asks for legal advice should be given an opportunity to consult a specific solicitor or another solicitor from that solicitor's firm or the duty solicitor. If advice is not available by these means, or they do not want to consult the duty solicitor, the detainee should be given an opportunity to choose a solicitor from a list of those willing to provide legal advice. If this solicitor is unavailable, they may choose up to two alternatives. If these attempts are unsuccessful, the custody officer has discretion to allow further attempts until a solicitor has been contacted and agrees to provide legal advice. Apart from carrying out these duties, an officer must not advise the suspect about any particular firm of solicitors. See Notes for Guidance 6B1 and 6B2 below.

6B1 With effect from 1 February 2008, Note for Guidance 6B above will cease to apply in the following forces areas:

Greater Manchester Police

West Midlands Police

West Yorkshire Police

and the following provisions will apply to those force areas: a detainee who asks for legal advice to be paid for by himself should be given an opportunity to consult a specific solicitor or another solicitor from that solicitor's firm. If this solicitor is unavailable by these means, they may choose up to two alternatives. If these attempts are unsuccessful, the custody officer has discretion to allow further attempts until a solicitor has been contacted and agrees to provide legal advice. Otherwise, publicly funded legal advice shall in the first instance be accessed by telephoning a call centre authorised by the Legal Services Commission (LSC) to deal with calls from the police station. The Defence Solicitor Call Centre will determine whether legal advice should be limited to telephone advice or whether a solicitor should attend. Legal advice will be by telephone if a detainee is:

- detained for a non-imprisonable offence,
- arrested on a bench warrant for failing to appear and being held for production before the court (except where the solicitor has clear documentary evidence available that would result in the client being released from custody),

- arrested on suspicion of driving with excess alcohol (failure to provide a specimen, driving whilst unfit/drunk in charge of a motor vehicle), or
- detained in relation to breach of police or court bail conditions.

An attendance by a solicitor for an offence suitable for telephone advice will depend on whether limited exceptions apply, such as:

- whether the police are going to carry out an interview or an identification parade,
- whether the detainee is eligible for assistance from an appropriate adult,
- whether the detainee is unable to communicate over the telephone,
- whether the detainee alleges serious maltreatment by the police.

Apart from carrying out these duties, an officer must not advise the suspect about any particular firm of solicitors. See Note for Guidance 6B2 below.

6B2 With effect from 21 April 2008, the contents of Notes for Guidance 6B and 6B1 above will be superseded by this paragraph in all police forces areas in England and Wales by the following. A detainee who asks for legal advice to be paid for by himself should be given an opportunity to consult a specific solicitor or another solicitor from that solicitor's firm. If this solicitor is unavailable by these means, they may choose up to two alternatives. If these attempts are unsuccessful, the custody officer has discretion to allow further attempts until a solicitor has been contacted and agrees to provide legal advice. Otherwise, publicly funded legal advice shall in the first instance be accessed by telephoning a call centre authorised by the Legal Services Commission (LSC) to deal with calls from the police station. The Defence Solicitor Call Centre will determine whether legal advice should be limited to telephone advice or whether a solicitor should attend. Legal advice will be by telephone if a detainee is:

- detained for a non-imprisonable offence,
- arrested on a bench warrant for failing to appear and being held for production before the court (except where the solicitor has clear documentary evidence available that would result in the client being released from custody),
- arrested on suspicion of driving with excess alcohol (failure to provide a specimen, driving whilst unfit/drunk in charge of a motor vehicle), or
- detained in relation to breach of police or court bail conditions.

An attendance by a solicitor for an offence suitable for telephone advice will depend on whether limited exceptions apply, such as:

- whether the police are going to carry out an interview or an identification parade,
- whether the detainee is eligible for assistance from an appropriate adult,
- whether the detainee is unable to communicate over the telephone,
- whether the detainee alleges serious maltreatment by the police.

Apart from carrying out these duties, an officer must not advise the suspect about any particular firm of solicitors.

6C Not Used

6D A detainee has a right to free legal advice and to be represented by a solicitor. Legal advice by telephone advice may be provided in respect of those offences listed in Note for Guidance 6B1 and 6B2 above. The Defence Solicitor Call Centre will determine whether attendance is required by a solicitor. The solicitor's only role in the police station is to protect and advance the legal rights of their client. On occasions this may require the solicitor to give advice which has t he effect of the client avoiding giving evidence which strengthens a prosecution case. The solicitor may intervene in order to seek clarification, challenge an improper question to their client or the manner in which it is put, advise their client not to reply to particular questions, or if they wish to give their client further legal advice.

Paragraph 6.9 only applies if the solicitor's approach or conduct prevents or unreasonably obstructs proper questions being put to the suspect or the suspect's response being recorded. Examples of unacceptable conduct include answering questions on a suspect's behalf or providing written replies for the suspect to quote.

6E An officer who takes the decision to exclude a solicitor must be in a position to satisfy the court the decision was properly made. In order to do this they may need to witness what is happening.

6F If an officer of at least inspector rank considers a particular solicitor or firm of solicitors is persistently sending probationary representatives who are unsuited to provide legal advice, they should inform an officer of at least superintendent rank, who may wish to take the matter up with the Law Society.

6G Subject to the constraints of Annex B, a solicitor may advise more than one client in an investigation if they wish. Any question of a conflict of interest is for the solicitor under their professional code of conduct. If, however, waiting for a solicitor to give advice to one client may lead to unreasonable delay to the interview with another, the provisions of paragraph 6.6(b) may apply.

6H In addition to a poster in English, a poster or posters containing translations into Welsh, the main minority ethnic languages and the principal European languages should be displayed wherever they are likely to be helpful and it is practicable to do so.

6I Paragraph 6.6(d) requires the authorisation of an officer of inspector rank or above to the continuation of an interview when a detainee who wanted legal advice changes their mind. It is permissible for such authorisation to be given over the telephone, if the authorising officer is able to satisfy themselves about the reason for the detainee's change of mind and is satisfied it is proper to continue the interview in those circumstances.

6J Whenever a detainee exercises their right to legal advice by consulting or communicating with a solicitor, they must be allowed to do so in private. This right to consult or communicate in private is fundamental. If the requirement for privacy is compromised because what is said or written by the detainee or solicitor for the purpose of giving and receiving legal advice is overheard, listened to, or read by others without the informed consent of the detainee, the right will effectively have been denied. When a detainee chooses to speak to a solicitor on the telephone, they should be allowed to do so in private unless this is impractical because of the design and layout of the custody area or the location of telephones. However, the normal expectation should be that facilities will be available, unless they are being used, at all police stations to enable detainees to speak in private to a solicitor either face to face or over the telephone.

6K A detainee is not obliged to give reasons for declining legal advice and should not be pressed to do so.

7 Citizens of independent Commonwealth countries or foreign nationals

(a) Action

7.1 Any citizen of an independent Commonwealth country or a national of a foreign country, including the Republic of Ireland, may communicate at any time with the appropriate High Commission, Embassy or Consulate. The detainee must be informed as soon as practicable of:

- this right;
- their right, upon request, to have their High Commission, Embassy or Consulate told of their whereabouts and the grounds for their detention. Such a request should be acted upon as soon as practicable.

7.2 If a detainee is a citizen of a country with which a bilateral consular convention or agreement is in force requiring notification of arrest, the appropriate High Commission, Embassy or Consulate shall be informed as soon as practicable, subject to paragraph 7.4. The countries to which this applies as at 1 April 2003 are listed in Annex F.

7.3 Consular officers may visit one of their nationals in police detention to talk to them and, if required, to arrange for legal advice. Such visits shall take place out of the hearing of a police officer.

7.4 Notwithstanding the provisions of consular conventions, if the detainee is a political refugee whether for reasons of race, nationality, political opinion or religion, or is seeking political asylum, consular officers shall not be informed of the arrest of one of their nationals or given access or information about them except at the detainee's express request.

(b) Documentation

7.5 A record shall be made when a detainee is informed of their rights under this section and of any communications with a High Commission, Embassy or Consulate.

Note for guidance

7A The exercise of the rights in this section may not be interfered with even though Annex B applies.

8 Conditions of detention

(a) Action

8.1 So far as it is practicable, not more than one detainee should be detained in each cell.

8.2 Cells in use must be adequately heated, cleaned and ventilated. They must be adequately lit, subject to such dimming as is compatible with safety and security to allow people detained overnight to sleep. No additional restraints shall be used within a locked cell unless absolutely necessary and then only restraint equipment, approved for use in that force by the Chief Officer, which is reasonable and necessary in the circumstances having regard to the detainee's demeanour and with a view to ensuring their safety and the safety of others. If a detainee is deaf, mentally disordered or otherwise mentally vulnerable, particular care must be taken when deciding whether to use any form of approved restraints.

8.3 Blankets, mattresses, pillows and other bedding supplied shall be of a reasonable standard and in a clean and sanitary condition. See Note 8A

8.4 Access to toilet and washing facilities must be provided.

8.5 If it is necessary to remove a detainee's clothes for the purposes of investigation, for hygiene, health reasons or cleaning, replacement clothing of a reasonable standard of comfort and cleanliness shall be provided. A detainee may not be interviewed unless adequate clothing has been offered.

8.6 At least two light meals and one main meal should be offered in any 24 hour period. See Note 8B. Drinks should be provided at meal times and upon reasonable request between meals. Whenever necessary, advice shall be sought from the appropriate health care professional, see Note 9A, on medical and dietary matters. As far as practicable, meals provided shall offer a varied diet and meet any specific dietary needs or religious beliefs the detainee may have. The detainee may, at the custody officer's discretion, have meals supplied by their family or friends at their expense. See Note 8A

8.7 Brief outdoor exercise shall be offered daily if practicable.

8.8 A juvenile shall not be placed in a police cell unless no other secure accommodation is available and the custody officer considers it is not practicable to supervise them if they are not placed in a cell or that a cell provides more comfortable accommodation than other secure accommodation in the station. A juvenile may not be placed in a cell with a detained adult.

(b) Documentation

8.9 A record must be kept of replacement clothing and meals offered.

8.10 If a juvenile is placed in a cell, the reason must be recorded.

8.11 The use of any restraints on a detainee whilst in a cell, the reasons for it and, if appropriate, the arrangements for enhanced supervision of the detainee whilst so restrained, shall be recorded. See paragraph 3.9

Notes for guidance

8A The provisions in paragraph 8.3 and 8.6 respectively are of particular importance in the case of a person likely to be detained for an extended period. In deciding whether to allow meals to be supplied by family or friends, the custody officer is entitled to take account of the risk of items being concealed in any food or package and the officer's duties and responsibilities under food handling legislation. 8B Meals should, so far as practicable, be offered at recognised meal times, or at other times that take account of when the detainee last had a meal.

[2:13] Brown, D, 'PACE ten years on: a review of the research'
(1997) HORS No 155, HMSO (at pages ix–xx)

The Police and Criminal Evidence Act 1984 (PACE) is the direct outcome of the Royal Commission on Criminal Procedure's (RCCP) recommendations for systematic reform in the investigative process. The provisions of the Act are designed to match up to principles of fairness (for both police and suspect), openness and workability. Overall, they are intended to strike a balance between the public interest in solving crime and the rights and liberties of suspects.

A considerable body of research on the operation of the Act now exists, and this is reviewed in this report. The main areas examined are as follows.

Stop and search: PACE introduced a general power to stop and search persons or vehicles for stolen or prohibited articles. The safeguards include the requirement to keep records and to inform the person stopped of the reasons for police action.

Entry, search and seizure: PACE provides powers to search premises for evidence, to search premises in connection with making an arrest and to seize evidence. Safeguards relate to the level of authority required to search, the keeping of records and provisions of reasons for searches.

Arrest: PACE rationalises police arrest powers. The basis for arrest is reasonable grounds for suspicion. In less serious offences, arrests may only be made where service of a summons is impracticable.

Detention: detention is only permissible where necessary to secure or preserve evidence, or obtain evidence by questioning. Custody officers, independent from the investigation, decide on the necessity of detention and look after the suspect's welfare while in custody. An upper limit of 24 hours is put on detention without charge, other than in a limited group of 'serious arrestable offences'. Officers of inspector rank or above review the need for further detention at specified intervals.

Questioning and treatment of suspects: suspects have statutory rights to legal advice and to have someone informed of their detention under PACE. They may not generally be interviewed until they have received legal advice, if requested. Accurate records of interviews must be made. Juveniles and the mentally disordered or handicapped must not be interviewed in the absence of an 'appropriate adult'. PACE defines circumstances in which interview evidence is liable to be excluded.

Accountability and supervision: PACE emphasises the need for the reviewability of police actions and the importance of internal police supervision. Custody records for each prisoner must record events occurring during detention. Certain decisions—delaying access to legal advice, for example—must be made by senior officers independent from the investigation. External accountability is enhanced through changes to the police complaints procedure, including the formation of the independent Police Complaints Authority, which supervises the investigation of serious allegations. The Act also provides for arrangements to be made to obtain the views of the community about policing.

The main findings of research are summarised below.

Stop and search

Pre-PACE research points to considerable under-recording of stops and suggests that the decision to stop was often based on hunch or stereotyping, with Afro-Caribbeans more likely to be stopped than white people. Records of stops were rarely inspected by supervisors. Only a small minority of stops led to arrest.

Frequency of stop and search has increased under PACE, although to some extent this may be an artefact of better recording. Stop/searches occur most frequently in the Metropolitan Police. Around one in eight searches lead to an arrest.

It is doubtful if stops are always made on the basis of reasonable suspicion. Where the suspect's consent is obtained, this may not always be fully informed,

Afro-Caribbeans are more likely to be stopped than white people or Asians, more likely to be repeatedly stopped, and more likely to be searched following a stop.

Entry, search and seizure

Stemming from clearer statutory powers, there has been a rise in the proportion of searches of premises authorised by the police rather than under court warrants. The most frequently used powers are those to search premises upon or after arrest. Around 15% of searches are conducted with the occupant's consent.

Around three-quarters of searches on warrant and about half of other searches lead to the seizure of property, usually stolen goods. However, it is doubtful whether all searches are conducted on the basis of reasonable suspicion.

Around half of those whose premises are searched are satisfied with the conduct of the search. Where there is dissatisfaction it is caused by officers' failures to identify themselves, provide a copy of the search warrant or state their search powers.

PACE powers to obtain access to confidential information are proving a valuable asset, although problems may arise where large volumes of material are sought or where some explanation of the material found is required.

Arrest and detention

Although PACE was intended to restrict arrest to situations in which it was strictly necessary, suspects are very rarely summonsed instead. However, there are indications of increased police professionalism and that arrests are now made on a firmer evidential basis. Fewer than before are made without independent evidence.

Black people are arrested at a higher rate than white people, but this does not appear to be because weaker evidence is used to justify their arrest.

Custody officers rarely scrutinise the necessity for a suspect's detention in any detail and almost all those arrested are detained. Similarly, reviews of detention after 6 and 15 hours are largely routinised procedures lacking any substantial enquiry.

Under PACE, those arrested for serious offences are generally held for shorter periods than before but in less serious cases several factors (such as waiting for legal advice or the arrival of appropriate adults) have pushed the length of detention up.

PACE limits on length of detention have not generally created problems for investigating officers.

There is considerable regional variation in the bailing of suspects after charge, probably reflecting different interpretations of the PACE bail criteria, particularly in relation to the risks of reoffending.

Treatment of suspects

The effectiveness of custody officers in looking after the suspect's welfare is constrained by pressure of work and lack of direct oversight of some aspects of the detention process. However, they appear able to maintain a viewpoint independent of that of investigating officers.

Detainees are generally given written and spoken information about their rights, although not always clearly. There is little evidence that rights are systematically denied.

A large and increasing proportion of suspects are aware of their basic rights although some confusions remain and the written information provided is not always found to be helpful.

Nearly 20% of detainees ask to have someone informed of their arrest and implementation of requests is rarely formally delayed. Only around 12% of detainees ask to make a telephone call, and only five receive visitors.

Doctors are called to examine prisoners in about 7% of cases (although in the Metropolitan Police this rises to 25%), usually where detainees are believed to be drunk, but also where mental disorder or mental handicap is suspected.

Legal advice

The great majority of suspects are given information about their right to legal advice. Improved information has been provided since the first revised PACE Codes of Practice were introduced, raising awareness among suspects that legal advice is free. Custody officers may exercise considerable influence over whether legal advice is sought.

Requests for legal advice have more than doubled under PACE and have increased further since. Nearly 40% of suspects now request advice, although there are large regional variations.

Over 80% of those who request legal advice eventually receive it. Cancellation of requests often occur where the chosen adviser is unavailable or where the parents of juveniles consider a lawyer unnecessary.

In around 70% of cases in which legal advice is given, the adviser attends the police station, but in the remainder advice is given solely over the telephone. A significant proportion of advice is provided by non-qualified solicitors' representatives.

Legal advisers often obtain only sketchy information about cases from the police, either because they do not ask for it or because the police withhold it. Generally, consultations with clients prior to police interviews are brief. The advice given is usually either neutral in character or to co-operate with police questions. Advice to remain silent is given in around a fifth of legal advice cases.

In most police interviews legal advisers are passive and do not always intervene to curtail oppressive or repetitive questioning or to allow suspects to present their version of events.

Access to legal advice was occasionally delayed when PACE was first introduced but this now occurs only exceptionally.

Interviews with suspects

Under PACE, interviews are rarely conducted with those who are unfit to be questioned. Suspects are also interviewed less frequently. Interviews do sometimes occur with those suffering from psychological conditions due to the difficulties in identifying such disorders.

Securing a confession remains an important aim of interviewing suspects, although this is now probably more to supplement other evidence.

Interviewing officers continue to use tactics designed to secure a confession, although unacceptable tactics (for example, exploiting police control over bail and charge decisions) are now used less often.

Some forms of questioning raise concerns about false confessions. These concerns are mitigated—although not entirely removed—by the fact that in over 90% of cases preceded with by the police independent corroborative evidence is obtained.

Between 55% and 60% of those interviewed confess—little different from pre-PACE estimates. Confessions are less likely where suspects are legally advised or the evidence is weak; they are more likely in cases involving juveniles or strong evidence.

Audio-taping of interviews has led to fewer disputes in court about what was said and has improved the flow of questioning. However, there are considerable problems with written records of taped interview prepared by police officers, with up to half suffering from the omission of salient points, prolixity or prosecution bias. Records prepared by civilians are significantly better in terms of quality and cost.

Video-taping of interviews has raised some technical problems but has proved its value as a supervisory and training tool. It also appears to offer advantages over audio-taping in a significant minority of cases—some very serious—by clarifying what was taking place in the interview room. However, few videos are presently played at court.

Little supervision or monitoring of interviewing takes place. One reason is that supervisory responsibility often rests with those who conduct interviews; another is supervisors' reluctance to risk injuring the professional pride of interviewing officers.

Some questioning of suspects occurs outside of formal police station interviews. Up to 10% of suspects are interviewed after arrest and prior to arrival at the station; up to a third of suspects who are charged may have made admissions prior to reaching the station. Once at the station, a certain amount of unregulated questioning by case officers still occurs.

Right of silence

Research has provided widely varying estimates of the use by suspects of the right of silence but it would appear that, under PACE, initially around 5% of suspects outside London and up to 9% in London refused to answer all questions, while 5% and 7% respectively refused to answer some questions of significance. This represents little change from the pre-PACE situation.

Data from recent studies (albeit pre-dating the implementation of the Criminal Justice and Public Order Act 1994) suggest that increasing numbers of suspects are staying silent and that 10% are refusing all questions and 13% some significant questions.

Suspects detained for more serious offences, those with previous convictions and those who have taken legal advice are more likely to refuse police questions. In the latter instance, this a direct result of legal advice in only a minority of cases. More often, advisers either proffer no such advice, go along with their client's wishes or urge the opposite course.

Some interviewing officers abandon interviews with silent suspects but others have various techniques—such as increasing the pressure by revealing further incriminating information—to elicit answers.

Police decisions to take no further action are largely unrelated to whether suspects have exercised their right of silence. There also appears to be no link with CPS decisions to discontinue cases.

Those who plead not guilty at court are more likely to have refused to answer police questions than those who plead guilty. However, those pleading not guilty who have exercised their right of silence are less likely to be acquitted than other defendants.

Significant minorities of defendants who plead not guilty raise defences not previously mentioned during questioning. However, few such defences genuinely amount to 'ambushes' because, for example, they relate to matters the suspect could not have raised during police interviews.

Juveniles

Up to a fifth of suspects detained by the police are aged 16 or under. In around two-thirds of cases parents or relatives act as appropriate adults but, in 20% or more, social workers fulfil this function.

Parents are often not well-equipped to act as appropriate adults because they may know little about police procedures or what is acceptable in police interviews, may be emotionally upset at their child's predicament, or may take sides with or against the police. Their role is often not explained to them by the police. They tend to play little part in police interviews.

Social workers also often lack training in the appropriate adult's role. The quality of their response is related to the organisation of juvenile justice work in social services departments and the extent to which staff specialise in this area. Like parents, they generally remain passive during police interviews.

Around 60% of juveniles' time in custody is spent waiting for an appropriate adult to attend. Demands on social services mean that waits are often longer for social worker than relatives. On average, however, juveniles are detained for shorter periods than adults.

Juveniles are given full information about their rights less often than adults and in some cases information is either not given at all or not until an adult is present. There have been recent improvements in this situation.

Juveniles are less likely than adults to request legal advice and there is far more variation between areas in request rates than for adults. There is evidence that the police sometimes delay or avoid taking forward requests by juveniles for legal advice.

There is some evidence that juveniles are more likely than adults to provide admissions, although questioning is not often oppressive. Admissions are most often provided where there is strong evidence, the juveniles has no previous convictions and the offence is less serious.

PACE and the mentally disordered and mentally handicapped

Up to 2% of detainees are treated by the police as mentally disordered or mentally handicapped. Up to one-third are brought to the police station as a place of safety rather than on suspicion of committing an offence. Identifying detainees with mental health problems presents difficulties for custody officers and substantially more detainees may in fact need an appropriate adult.

Custody officers often summon the police surgeon in the first instance and in many cases, acting on the doctor's advice, do not then call for an appropriate adult.

Ensuring that detainees with mental health problems understand their rights is problematic. Experiments with simplified versions of the notices currently provided to all suspects have had some success in raising levels of understanding.

The role of the appropriate adult raises a number of problems. Firstly, there is sometimes confusion as to whether social workers are acting in this role or making an assessment under the Mental Health Act. Secondly, custody officers may not always be right in assuming that professionals know what is expected of them as appropriate adults. Thirdly, there is a lack of clarity about the status of information confided in appropriate adults by detainees.

The interviewing of those with mental health problems raises dangers of generating false confessions and of over-ready compliance, leading to inaccurate replies. Police officers tend to over-estimate the reliability of the information provided.

Appropriate adults seldom intervene during interviews with mentally disordered or mentally handicapped suspects and may not always constitute an adequate safeguard against the production of unreliable interview evidence.

Supervision and accountability

Supervision

Detectives receive relatively little training in the supervision of investigations; in consequence, investigative errors or shortcomings may be overlooked.

Effective supervision of investigations is impeded by the low visibility of much detective work, issues of professional pride (especially in relation to interviewing skills) and an emphasis on quantity rather than quality of clear-ups.

The bulk of investigations are supervised by lower-ranking officers, who have their own caseloads to cope with, and not by senior officers. This carried the risk that malpractice or incompetence may pass unnoticed.

There is tighter supervision by senior officers in major inquiries and in special squads. In major inquiries, supervision is more directive, there are quality control procedures and teams are comprised of officers without established loyalties to each other. In special squads, there is rigorous scrutiny of the evidence before offenders are targeted and tight managerial control over dealings with informants.

Complaints

No recent research has been carried out in this area. Work carried out in 1987 suggested that, at that time, the Police Complaints Authority (PCA) was less likely to select assault cases than others for supervision. Complaints of assault tend to be particularly difficult to prove and this may have had a bearing on the PCA's decision.

PCA supervision varied from passive, active or directive, depending on how complex and how high profile cases were. Where investigations were supervised, action was more frequently taken against officers, complaints were less often withdrawn, reports were of better quality and investigation was speedier.

Most complainants were dissatisfied with the outcome of supervised cases, although they were more likely than other complainants to feel their case had been treated seriously and to receive good feedback and less likely to have experienced pressure to withdraw. Investigating officers felt that the PCA had little impact on the outcome of investigations, although its attention to the case put them on their mettle.

Informal resolution of complaints were generally not popular with officers subject to complaint since they felt that accepting it was seen as admitting guilt. Officers did not view meetings between officer and complainant as productive.

Where complaints were informally resolved, most complainants accepted this outcome as satis-factory, despite persuasion to take this course in some cases. Complainants were dissatisfied at not meeting officers subject to complaint and with lack of feedback.

A third of complainants reported attempts to dissuade them registering a complaint. Of those with-drawing and proceeding, a majority reported attempts to secure a withdrawal.

Over two-thirds of complainants were dissatisfied with the outcome of their complaint, usually due to the lack of an apology or of an explanation for decisions reached. Those whose complaints were informally resolved were the most satisfied.

Investigating officers were concerned to be seen by complainants to be taking their grievances ser-iously, although they accepted that the low chances of substantiation meant that many complainants would ultimately be dissatisfied. The thoroughness of investigations meant that they tended to be slow, and this was the subject of considerable criticism by officers subject to complaint.

Public attitude surveys show that up to two-thirds of the public know of the PCA, although rather fewer are aware that it is impartial and independent from the police. Levels of awareness are far lower among members of ethnic minority groups.

Police community consultative committees

Consultation arrangements now exist in most parts of the country. However, there have been difficul-ties recruiting members representative of local communities, particularly those from minority ethnic groups and younger people. Meetings are infrequent in some areas and, where public, have tended to be poorly attended.

Agenda are sometimes dominated by police authorities. For their part, the police have not always been willing to share information, especially where it relates to operational matters.

The effectiveness of consultative groups appears to be constrained by several factors including: lack of formal authority; absence of hard-edged information; ignorance of policing issues; pro-police orien-tation; and non-representativeness. However, some groups are notably successful in actively involving local people. Others, which contain influential coalitions of representatives from political parties, local government and statutory and voluntary agencies are effective in raising their agendas with the police.

Conclusions

Fairness, openness and workability

The review concludes that PACE has introduced a greater element of fairness into pre-charge pro-cedures, in that suspects are now more aware of their rights and given the chance to exercise them, although there remain areas in which improvement is required. There are also benefits for the police in terms of clearer and more certain powers, particularly at the station.

However, both police and suspect may suffer from the lack of clarity in relation to powers outside the station, particularly stop, search and entry powers, while, at the station, the suspect may be at a disadvantage due to the lack of clear delineation of what interview tactics are permissible.

The extent to which the exercise of police powers outside the police station can be reviewed after the event is limited where officers act with the apparent consent of the suspect. Reviewability of police action, both at the station and outside, is also constrained by dependence on official records, which may be incomplete, unreliable or unverifiable.

PACE powers are generally more workable than their predecessors, because they provide clarifi-cation and certainty, particularly in relation to detention at the station. However, the use of stop and search and entry and search powers remains problematic, and officers often prefer to operate with the subject's consent.

Legal regulation of policing

Police behaviour appears to be more strongly influenced by PACE rules inside the police station than out. The reason for this difference is probably that insufficient account was taken of the strong informal working rules which determine how the police behave on the street.

The lessons to be drawn from the experience of implementing PACE are that new legal rules can alter existing working practices provided that: they are clear; their introduction is accompanied by adequate training; there are effective sanctions and supervision; and the public are aware of their rights and of police powers.

Balance in the investigative process

The review concludes that PACE has not yet produced a system in balance, in the sense that police powers and safe guards for the suspect are generally well matched in key areas.

In relation to the exercise of stop and search and entry and search powers and the treatment of at risk groups, suspects may be at a relative disadvantage. However, at the police station suspects may be benefiting considerably from the availability of legal advice and use of the right of silence, to the detriment of the public interest in bringing criminals to account.

The picture is a shifting one, and current initiatives in the criminal justice field may go some way towards producing a balanced pre-charge process.

[2:14] Bucke, T and Brown, D, 'In police custody: police powers and suspects' rights under the revised PACE Codes of Practice'
(1997) HORS No 174, HMSO (at page 69)

The main aim of this study was to examine changes in the revised PACE Codes of Practice concerning those in police detention. It also sought to investigate other related changes arising from the CJPOA and to monitor a number of aspects in the operation of PACE. In this concluding chapter the main findings of the research are discussed along with their implications.

Appropriate adults

In line with the Codes of Practice appropriate adults were provided in the majority of cases involving juvenile and mentally disordered or handicapped detainees.[2] However, shortcomings were found in the level of guidance provided to appropriate adults. Custody officers rarely gave advice to those acting as appropriate adults about the role, and were unlikely to be asked for any. The implication of this lack of guidance is that a large proportion of those acting as appropriate adults, particular those other than social workers, probably do not know what their role actually is, and could be said to be acting as appropriate adults in name only.

The research also examined the suitability of those acting as appropriate adults for juvenile detainees. Here the reactions of family members on finding a child in police custody could undermine their ability to be an appropriate adult. Notable proportions of family members were found to be distressed or hostile to the juvenile, leading to various reactions including remoteness, antagonism and, in some cases, violence. In slightly more cases family members were described as either supportive or calm. However, such demeanours did not mean that the appropriate adult role was adequately fulfilled. As revealed by other research (see Palmer and Hart, 1996; Evans, 1993) many parents were simply passive observers, making few or no interventions and providing little advice or assistance to the juvenile. The actions of those who became involved revealed their confusion about the role, with some parents advising their children to remain silent and others encouraging them to confess. The effectiveness of parents acting as appropriate adults and providing a safeguard is an important issue. Juveniles represent around *one in five detainees* and parents act as appropriate adults in the majority of cases. The research also raised questions about the suitability of those other than family members acting as appropriate adults.

Concerns about the role of appropriate adults led the RCCJ to recommend a comprehensive review of the role, functions, qualifications, training and availability of appropriate adults. This review was instituted by the Home Office in 1994. The resulting Appropriate Adults Working Group was also asked to consider three other issues. Firstly, the changes to Code C needed to give effect to any recommendations. Secondly, whether the police required clearer guidance about the criteria to be used in considering the need for an appropriate adult. Thirdly, and following another RCCJ recommendation, whether there was a need for a rule governing the status of information passed by suspects to appropriate adults. The Working Group reported in mid-1995 and made a series of wide ranging recommendations which are currently under consideration. A future Home Office circular will provide the police with further guidance on appropriate adults, with associated changes possibly being made to the Codes of Practice.

Legal advice

Studies since the introduction of PACE have indicated rises in suspects requesting legal advice. The current study found a further increase, with four out of ten suspects now making requests. One explanation for this is the increase in requests among juvenile suspects. However, the level of legal advice actually received was only slightly higher than in previous studies, indicating a rise in the attrition rate. Reasons given by suspects for refusing legal advice were rarely recorded by custody officers; in those cases where they were, the majority of suspects simply said that the situation did not merit it.

Comparisons with previous research suggest that legal consultations have increased in duration. The changes to the right of silence mean that suspects in custody require sound legal advice on their position when being questioned by officers. As a result legal advisers need to take time to guide their clients on how to respond to police questions in the context of the inferences that may be drawn from silence. The quality of legal advice received by suspects has been the source of some criticism in the past, notably surrounding the use of unqualified legal staff. As a result the Law Society introduced a scheme whereby those passing a series of tests can become 'accredited representatives' and receive the same status as solicitors. The current study indicates that the proportion of unqualified legal staff advising at police stations has declined, due to a rise in solicitors attending and the introduction of 'accredited representatives'. Whether this development has led to any improvement in the legal advice suspects receive remains unclear.

The right of silence

The extent to which suspects used the right of silence was found to have declined compared to estimates from studies conducted before the new provisions. 'No comment' interviews were found to have fallen by just under a half, while the selective answering of questions had fallen by just under a third. Reductions in the use of silence were found to be greatest among those receiving legal advice. However, confessions by suspects during interviews remained at the same level as before the new provisions. Suspects therefore appear to be responding to police questions without making admissions of guilt any more than before. One possibility is that more suspects are providing officers with statements which, while not admissions of guilt, can be tested against other evidence. The full implications of the new provisions will depend on what happens in the prosecution and trial processes; however these will be addressed in a forthcoming report which will provide further information from this research and other work.

Disposal of juvenile suspects

One of the most pronounced developments found in the study concerned juveniles. Probably as a result of a Home Office circular advising against multiple cautions, juveniles were more likely to be charged and less likely to be cautioned. Furthermore decisions on juveniles were made much earlier in the process than in the past. Consequently, there was a decline in juveniles being bailed for inquiries or reported for summons, with disposal decisions being increasingly made at the end of detention. Finally, once charged juveniles were more likely than before to be refused bail and detained for court.

These developments have a number of consequences. First, juveniles are less likely to be diverted away from prosecution than in the past. This is linked to a decline in the role of juvenile bureaux or panels, with decisions on juvenile cases increasingly the sole responsibility of police officers. Second, changes in the disposal of juveniles together with the rise in their requests for legal advice, means that previous divisions in the treatment of juvenile and adult suspects appear much less distinct. Third, these developments mean that a greater number of juveniles will be at liberty having been charged by the police and bailed pending various court appearances. An unintended consequence of this may be a rise in the levels of offending on bail.

DNA sampling

Alterations to the Code of Practice have provided far greater scope for DNA sampling, with officers now able to take samples from a much larger range of suspects than in the past. However, the study found samples to be taken from a relatively small proportion of suspects. Clearly intimate samples were only taken in very specific cases, while non-intimate samples were also taken selectively. This may be due to ACPO and Home Office guidance advising that non-intimate samples should only be taken for certain types of crime (ie offences against the person, sexual offences and burglaries). Samples were taken for other forms of crime, although it is likely that the suspects concerned had previous links to the offences in the designated categories. The vast majority of samples were taken in order to build up the DNA database and, while the proportion of suspects sampled appears relatively small, it should be noted that approximately 1.5 million people enter police custody every year. Selective sampling therefore is likely to add a substantial number of people to the database over the forthcoming years.

Note

2 Although the level of provision was much lower for mentally disordered detainees compared to juveniles.

[2:15] Cape, E, 'The revised PACE Codes of Practice: a further step towards inquisitorialism'
[2003] Crim LR 355

The third major revision of the Codes of Practice issued by the Home Secretary under powers granted by Part VI of the Police and Criminal Evidence Act 1984 (PACE) came into force on April 1, 2003.[3] This followed a review that started in December 1999, but which was repeatedly delayed as a result of a heavy legislative programme affecting provisions in the codes, a continuing concern with police stop and search powers—particularly their disproportionate use against ethnic minorities—and finally a joint Home Office/Cabinet Office review of PACE which reported, after deliberating for only six months, in November 2002.[4]

Since the last major revision of the PACE Codes in 1995,[5] there have been a number of changes and modifications falling short of a full revision, although a revised version of Code A[6] was issued in 1999. In April 2002 Code D[7] was temporarily modified[8] so that video identification became, in effect, the preferred method of visual identification procedure. It also sought to negate some of the effects of the House of Lords decision in *R. v Forbes*[9] so that an identification procedure would not have to be held if 'it would serve no useful purpose in proving or disproving' a suspect's involvement in an offence. The following month, modifications to Codes C and D that originally applied to three police force areas[10] were extended to six other police areas.[11] These modifications added a new s.17 to Code C and a new Note for Guidance to Code D, reflecting the powers contained in s.63B PACE[12] to test for Class A drugs people charged with certain offences. The drug-testing modifications have not been incorporated into the revised Codes C and D that came into force at the beginning of April, and presumably will only be incorporated if and when it is decided to extend the drug-testing powers to the whole of England and Wales. Also in May 2002 a new Code F, *Code of Practice on visual recording with sound of interviews with suspects*, was introduced which only applies to interviews conducted in those police stations that are piloting video recording of police interviews.[13] The pilot ends in May 2003 when presumably the Home Office will decide whether to extend visual recording of police interviews to other parts of the country.

The changes to the codes are, broadly, of four types. First, there are technical and stylistic changes designed to improve the layout, and aid understanding, of code provisions. Secondly, there are a large number of changes reflecting statutory changes since the last code revisions, particularly those contained in the Youth Justice and Criminal Evidence Act 1999, the Terrorism Act 2000, the Criminal Justice and Police Act 2001, the Anti-terrorism, Crime and Security Act 2001 and the Police Reform Act 2002. Thirdly, Code A and Code C contain new provisions designed to improve the way in which the police deal with members of the public and suspects. However, the fourth category consists of provisions that were clearly wanted by the police because they enhance their powers over suspects. It should be noted that many of the provisions of the Codes, although not those in Code A, apply to civilians granted certain 'police' powers as a result of designation under Chapter 1 of Part 4 of the Police Reform Act 2002.[14]

Notes

3 PACE (Codes of Practice) (Statutory Powers of Stop and Search) Order 2002, SI 2002/3075 and PACE (Codes of Practice) (Codes B to E) (No. 2) Order 2003, SI 2003/703.

4 Home Office/Cabinet Office, *PACE Review: Report of the Joint Home Office/Cabinet Office Review of the Police and Criminal Evidence Act 1984*, November 2002 (hereafter 'PACE Review'). For a critical commentary see M. Zander, 'The Joint Review of PACE: a deplorable report' (2003) 153 N.L.J. 204.

5 See D. Wolchover and A. Heaton-Armstrong, 'Questioning and Identification: Changes under P.A.C.E. '95' [1995] Crim.L.R. 356.

6 *Code of Practice for the exercise by police officers of statutory powers of stop and search.*

7 *Code of Practice for the identification of persons by police officers.* Despite its title, much of the code is concerned with identification by non-police officers.

8 PACE, s. 67 was amended by Criminal Justice and Police Act 2001, s. 77 to enable the Secretary of State to modify a code without publishing, and consulting upon, a draft as required by PACE, s. 67(1). See PACE (Codes of Practice) (Temporary Modifications to Code D) Order 2002/615. For a review of these and other modifications see E. Cape, 'A PACE in the wrong direction' (2002) August Legal Action 24.

9 [2001] 1 All E.R. 686, [2001] Crim.L.R. 649.

10 Staffordshire, Nottinghamshire and the Metropolitan Police. See PACE (Codes of Practice) (Modification) Order 2001, SI 2001/2254.

11 See PACE (Codes of Practice) (Modifications to Code C and Code D) (Certain Police Areas) Order 2002, SI 2002/1150. Further areas were added by PACE (Codes of Practice) (Modifications to Code C and Code D) (Certain Police Areas) (Amendment) Order 2002, SI 2002/1863. They were also introduced without consultation under the powers noted in n. 6.

12 Inserted by the Criminal Justice and Court Services Act 2000, s. 57.

13 PACE (Codes of Practice) (Visual Recording of Interviews) Order 2002, SI 2002/1266, issued under PACE, s. 60A(1)(a) as inserted by the Criminal Justice and Police Act 2001, s. 76. For the police stations to which it applies, see PACE (Visual Recording of Interviews) (Certain Police Areas) Order 2002, SI 2002/1069 and PACE (Visual Recording of Interviews) (Certain Police Areas) (No. 2) Order 2002, SI 2002/2527.

14 The powers of designated persons are set out in Sch. 4 of the Police Reform Act 2002. For implementation see The Police Reform Act 2002 (Commencement No.1) Order 2002, SI 2002/2306, and The Police Reform Act 2002 (Commencement No. 3) Order 2002, SI 2002/2750.

(And at page 368:)

Conclusions

This review of the revised Codes of Practice is necessarily selective and the effect of the revisions, particularly those provisions designed to improve stop and search practice and the treatment of vulnerable suspects, will depend to a large extent on the resources the police are willing to devote to training custody and other relevant officers. Disappointingly, this issue was largely ignored in the PACE Review.[15] Although there have been efforts to simplify the language and structure of the codes, the fact is that in the past decade successive governments and courts have considerably increased the complexity of the law relating to the investigative stage of the criminal process. The PACE Review partially recognised this but its preferred solutions, to reduce the consultation requirements applying to revision of the codes,[16] and to rework the codes into a 'Three Tier' framework with the codes containing key principle and detailed guidance being moved to National Standards, is unlikely to improve matters.[17] In the recent case of *R v Howell*[18] the Court of Appeal stated that 'the police interview and the trial are to be seen as part of a continuous process in which the suspect is engaged from the beginning', describing this a 'benign continuum'. What the court failed to adequately recognise is that the police have, in recent years, been given considerable inquisitorial powers to deploy at a stage of the criminal process in which the accused is increasingly regarded as the subject of a police inquiry, but the product of which is available for use by the prosecution for adversarial purposes. The revisions of the codes of practice may only properly be understood in this context.

Notes

15 Although it did recommend that, depending on the availability of funding, best practice should be promoted 'via the National Centre for Policing Excellence to be established within Centrex and via the Police Standards Unit' and which could be 'linked to the Centrex work on Policing Knowledge Maps'!

16 To be implemented when clause 7 of the Criminal Justice Bill is enacted.

17 Of particular concern was an apparent acceptance by the Review of the police view that 'detail...can be used by solicitors to undermine cases.'

18 [2003] EWCA Crim 1, [2003] Crim LR 405.

[2:16] Ashworth, A, 'Should the police be allowed to use deception?'

(1998) 114 LQR 108 (at page 138)

There is a long line of judicial authority to the effect that a criminal court may properly exclude evidence which has been obtained by means of a trick, sometimes justified by reference to the privilege against self-incrimination. The aim of this article has been to conduct a deeper examination: rather than relying on judicial authority, and not confining the discussion to the reception of evidence by courts, it has set out to articulate and to test the justifications for the use of deceptive practices by the police and other law enforcement agencies. The conclusions, in brief, are as follows:

(i) that lying in court is absolutely wrong because it compromises the integrity of the criminal justice system, and any attempt to justify it in terms of convicting the factually guilty is constitutionally and morally unsustainable;

(ii) that at any earlier stage in the criminal process 'tricks about rights' are wrong for similar reasons, in so far as the rights are recognised in the European Convention on Human Rights, in domestic legislation or in the Codes of Practice;

(iii) that for this purpose a trick should be defined so as to include any deception, including a failure to inform a suspect when there is a duty to do so; but,

(iv) that there are distinctly fewer moral objections to the use of disguises, informers or other agents at the investigative stage, so long as this does not involve prompting or questioning a suspect in relation to an incident in a way that undermines rights that should be protected; and

(v) that there are also fewer moral objections to covert tape recording or electronic surveillance, although the moral objections to 'bugging' private premises remain strong and should only be overcome in situations where the justifications for invading privacy are powerful and properly tested.

In relation to undercover policing and the use of electronic devices, the community's interests in the prevention and detection of crime may justify a judicious use of these practices, subject to appropriate safeguards. There is a need for controls for two distinct reasons—to prevent the abuse of power by law enforcement agencies, and to ensure that any relevant rights of citizens are recognised and protected. Questions of accountability and of the criteria on which the deployment of these policing methods should be justified must be tackled more convincingly than they are in the Police Act 1997. The admissibility of evidence obtained in contravention of the principles is a separate issue, although several of the arguments discussed above are relevant.

In respect of undercover policing, operations ought to be approved at a high level of command within the police service. Customs and Excise, or whatever agency in concerned; and they should be subject to scrutiny by, for example, the Chief Inspector of Constabulary. So far as the criteria are concerned, it must be established the normal methods of gathering evidence would be 'bound to fail', and the reasons for this must be recorded; the police officer(s) involved in the undercover work must be briefed specifically about the rights of others that must be respected, particularly in terms of not trying to prompt admissions.

Turning to electronic, telephonic and other forms of surveillance, this is likely to involve interference with the privacy and/or the property rights of citizens, and it should therefore be taken far more seriously than it has been hitherto. English law is truly in a lamentable state, and requires both greater consistency and firmer principle. The lack of consistency derives not merely from the variety of separate statutory regimes that exist (eg the Interception of Communications Act 1985, the Intelligence Services Act 1994, the Security Services Act 1996, and the Police Act 1997), but also from the failure of these statutes to cover several forms of electronic surveillance and communications equipment. The lack of principle stems from the desire (at least in previous years) to keep to a minimal compliance with the European Convention. Instead, greater attention should be given to principled criteria for determining whether permission should be granted. Five points should be considered. First, the nature of the right of privacy and the reasons for it should be spelt out. Second, there must be a clear and circumscribed indication of the level of seriousness of offence necessary to justify an incursion on the right of privacy: mere references to 'crimes of violence' is much too broad, whereas a criterion of offences serious enough to attract at least three years imprisonment for an adult of good character gives a better indication of the necessary threshold. Third, it must be shown that the use of electronic devices is necessary, and that no less intrusive method would be likely to succeed. Fourth, it must be shown that the electronic device has good prospects of success. Fifth, any curtailment of the right of privacy should be kept to a minimum.

This discussion of accountability and criteria should not distract attention from the central argument that, in principle, the police should recognise a duty not to use deceptive practices in the investigation of crime. In those limited circumstances in which deceptive practices or electronic surveillance can be justified, the reasons for the general duty and the exceptions should form part of police training and re-training, with a view to implanting them in police culture. For so long as the restrictions are regarded as pointless or irritating handicaps to the pursuit of proper goals, law enforcement officers will be tempted to try to circumvent them or simply to ignore them.

[2:17] *R v Looseley; A-G's Reference (No 3 of 2000)*
[2002] Crim LR 301

House of Lords; Lord Nicholls of Birkenhead, Lord Mackay of Clashfern, Lord Hoffmann, Lord Hutton, and Lord Scott of Foscote: 25 October 2001; [2001] UKHL 53.

L was charged with supplying or being concerned in the supply of heroin to an undercover police officer known as 'Rob' who was part of an undercover operation mounted by the police in 1999 in Guildford because of their concern about the trade in Class A drugs in that area. Rob's evidence was that a man in a public house had provided him with the appellant's first name and telephone number and suggested he should telephone the appellant if he wished to obtain drugs. Rob telephoned the appellant who agreed that he could 'sort him out a couple of bags' and gave him directions to his flat. The appellant drove Rob from the flat to the supplier's home where the appellant left the car taking £30 from Rob. He returned saying he had the 'stuff'. He kept a small quantity for himself and gave the remainder to Rob. On analysis the package was found to contain 152 milligrams of heroin at 100 per cent purity. Four days later a similar transaction took place and a third transaction took place three days after that. At the trial the defence submitted, as a preliminary issue, that the indictment ought to be stayed as an abuse of the process of the court or, alternatively, that Rob's evidence should be excluded under section 78(1) of the Police and Criminal Evidence Act 1984. The judge ruled against those submissions and the appellant changed his pleas to guilty. His appeal against conviction was dismissed by the Court of Appeal on the grounds that although if a person had been incited or entrapped by a law enforcement officer into committing an offence then the officer's evidence should be excluded under section 78, where the officer, as in this case, had done no more that give the appellant the opportunity to break the law and the appellant had freely taken advantage of that opportunity in circumstances where it appeared he would have behaved in the same way if the opportunity had been offered by anyone else, there was no reason why the officer's evidence should be excluded. The Court of Appeal certified the following point of law of general public importance: 'Should the judge have refused to admit the evidence of the undercover police officer 'Rob' because the role played by 'Rob' went beyond mere observation and involved asking the appellant to supply him with heroin, a request to which, on the judge's findings, the appellant readily agreed?'

In the second case, the Attorney-General referred a point of law to the Court of Appeal after the acquittal of an accused charged with supplying or being concerned in the supply to another of a Class A drug. Undercover police officers had asked S if he wanted to buy some contraband cigarettes. S took them to the accused and after conversations about cigarettes, the police officers asked the accused if he could sort them out some 'brown'. After further conversations the police officers persuaded the accused to provide them with heroin. The accused said at one stage 'I'm not really into heroin myself'. He also said, when interviewed by the police, that the officers 'were getting me cheap fags, so as far as I was concerned a favour for a favour'. At the trial the judge ruled that the police officers went further than was permissible and in fact incited and procured this accused to commit an offence which he would not otherwise have committed. On the accused's acquittal, the Attorney-General referred the following point of law to the Court of Appeal for its opinion: 'In a case involving the commission of offences by an accused at the instigation of undercover police officers, to what extent, if any, have: (i) the judicial discretion conferred by section 78 of the Police and Criminal Evidence Act 1984; and (ii) the power to stay the proceedings as an abuse of the court been modified by Article 6 of the European Convention of the Protection of Human Rights and Fundamental Freedoms and the jurisprudence of the European Court of Human Rights?' The Court of Appeal answered the question in the negative and ruled that the trial judge had erred in staying the proceedings. The question of law was further referred to the House of Lords.

Held, that it was a fundamental principle of the rule of law that every court had an inherent power and duty to prevent abuse of its process. It was simply not acceptable that the State through its agents should lure its citizens into committing acts forbidden by the law and then seek to prosecute them for doing so. That would be entrapment and misuse of State power. The role of the courts was to stand between the State and its citizens and to make sure this did not happen. Although entrapment was not a substantive defence, English law had now developed remedies in respect of entrapment: the court might stay the relevant criminal proceedings or it might exclude evidence pursuant to section 78. The grant of a stay should normally be regarded as the appropriate response in a case of entrapment. Police conduct which brought about State-created crime was unacceptable and improper but if the police conduct preceding the commission of the offence was no more than might have been expected from others in the circumstances it was not to be regarded as inciting or instigating crime, or luring a person into committing a crime. In the latter situation the police did no more than others could be expected to do and did not create the crime artificially. In assessing the propriety of police conduct proportionality had a role to play; the greater the degree of intrusiveness, the closer the court would scrutinise the reasons for using it. Ultimately, the overall consideration was always whether the conduct of the police or other law enforcement agency was so seriously improper as to bring the administration of justice into disrepute. Accordingly, L's appeal would be dismissed since the undercover officer in that case did no more than present himself as an ordinary customer to an active drug dealer. On the Attorney-General's reference, affirming the Court of Appeal's decision in part, the court's power to exclude evidence under section 78 or to stay proceedings were unaffected by article 6. But in this case the trial judge was entitled to stay the proceedings on the ground that the police officer had instigated the drug offence by offering an inducement of a profitable trade in contraband cigarettes, an inducement which would not ordinarily be associated with the commission of that offence.

Sang (1979) 69 Cr.App.R. 282, [1980] A.C. 402, HL; *R. v. Horseferry Road Magistrates' Court, ex p. Bennett* (1994) 98 Cr.App.R. 114, [1994] 1 A.C. 42, HL; *Latif and Shahzad* [1996] 2 Cr.App.R. 92 [1996] 1 W.L.R. 104, HL, *Teixeira de Castro v. Portugal* [1998] 28 E.H.R.R. 101 and *Nottingham City Council v. Amin* [2001] 1 Cr.App.R. 426, [2000] 1 W.L.R. 1071, DC considered.

Decision of the Court of Appeal (Criminal Division) in *Looseley* affirmed.

Decision of the Court of Appeal (Criminal Division) in *Attorney-General's Reference (No. 3 of 2000)* reversed in part.

Commentary (by Professor David Ormerod): For the comment on the decision of the Court of Appeal in the *Attorney-General's Reference (No. 3 of 2000)* see [2001] Crim.L.R. 645, and for a comprehensive analysis of the House of Lords decisions and its broader implications, see A. Ashworth, 'Re-drawing the Boundaries of Entrapment' [2002] Crim.L.R. 249.

As Ashworth observes, at a general level, the decision is to be welcomed for clarifying the rationale of, and remedies available for, entrapment. The unanimous decision that although there is no defence of entrapment, nevertheless the principal remedy for entrapment is a stay for abuse of process, demonstrates how significant that doctrine has become. Although the remedy of a stay for abuse looks like a defence created through the back door, the House of Lords acknowledged that, on this point at least, *Sang* had been 'overtaken': per Lord Nicholls at paragraph 16.

On narrower issues the decision is welcome for some clarification of definitions: 'incitement' in this context is not to be construed in its technical criminal law sense. The House of Lords is also to be commended for emphasising that the predisposition of the accused is not a key factor. Indeed, Lord Hoffmann reasons that since the court's inquiry is about abuse of process and not about whether D has a defence or is blameworthy, any predisposition is 'irrelevant', otherwise than in the police forming a reasonable suspicion. This approach prevents the potential for abuse of this pro-active policing method which the decision of the Court of Appeal left open. With the central question of entrapment now clearly stated to be whether the police conduct was 'unexceptional', and the House of Lords' endorsement of a need for prior suspicion and even possibly authorisation, the decision puts the law in this area on a more acceptable foundation. Inevitably, there is still some room for clarification of the application of the principles in hard cases. Prime candidates for argument will be the relevance of the vulnerability of the accused and precisely what amounts to 'unexceptional' behaviour in organised criminal activity.

[2:18] Moston, S and Stephenson, G M, 'The Questioning and Interviewing of Suspects Outside the Police Station'
(1993) RCCJ Research Study No 22, HMSO (at page 46)

This study has shown that in a large number of cases suspects are questioned, interviewed, or have other conversations with police officers prior to their arrival at the police station. In most cases there is no record of the content of these exchanges and even when records are ostensibly kept, they are typically inadequate. Even under ideal circumstances, contemporaneous notes are not suited for encounters outside the police station and there are strong arguments in favour of the provision of portable recorders.

Encounters outside the police station are important for understanding why suspects make admissions inside the police station. Interviews inside the police station, either recorded on audio or video tape, contain only one part of the relevant exchanges between the suspect and police officers. The current legislation, by emphasising the importance of interviews inside the police station has resulted in a situation in which evidence gathered outside the station is seemingly of minimal value. It is widely assumed that the use of tape or video recording equipment inside the station gives a complete picture of the interview with a suspect. This assumption appears to be incorrect. The statement made by suspects on tape are the outcome of a series of conversations with police officers. The interview inside the police station is merely the final part of this process.

[2:19] Brown, D, Ellis, T, and Larcombe, K, 'Changing the Code: Police Detention under the Revised Codes of Practice'
(1992) HORS No 129, HMSO (at page vi)

This report examines the operation and impact of recently introduced revisions to Code C of the Police and Criminal Evidence Act. This Code contains detailed guidance to the police on the detention, treatment and questioning of suspects. Among the revisions, which came into effect on 1 April 1991, are the following:

- More information is to be given to the suspect about the right to legal advice and there is more detailed guidance about putting the right into practice.
- Suspects are to be told of their entitlements over and above their statutory rights.
- Interviews away from police stations may only be carried out in very limited circumstances. There are tighter rules on recording comments made outside of interview and on allowing interviews without a solicitor present.
- For vulnerable groups—particularly juveniles—the Code defines more closely who is suitable to act as an 'appropriate adult' to advise and assist.
- The research was conducted in six different forces in two phases, the first before the new Codes were introduced and the second afterwards. The main findings were as follows:
- The great majority of suspects were given written notices about their rights, although custody records tended to over-record that this had been done and compliance varied between stations. The police are not obliged to provide such information to 'non-PACE' prisoners (eg those held on warrant); however, in phase two these groups were given leaflets about their rights more often.

- Very high proportions of suspects were given at least some spoken information about their rights and this increased still further under the new Code. However, the extra information which is now required was not always given: although nearly three-quarters were told the important fact that legal advice was free, only around half were told it was independent and few were told a legal consultation would be in private. Furthermore, there was considerable variation between stations.

- In around a quarter of cases in phase two, rights were not given clearly, despite a stipulation in the new Code. Other features of the way rights were given may also have swayed some suspects against asking for legal advice.

- Inspectors were lax in recording in custody records whether they had reminded suspects at review times of their right to free legal advice.

- Suspects were often preoccupied at the time they were given their rights but very high proportion recalled being given some information. They were more knowledgeable in phase two about the right to legal advice, especially about the fact that it was free.

- Suspects frequently confused the right to have someone informed of their detention and their entitlement to a telephone call. The new notice of entitlements proved a useful source of information about, for example, the availability of medical attention and the conditions of custody.

- About a fifth of suspects asked to have someone informed of their detention. Contact was known to have been made in about 60% of these cases but the outcome of requests was often not recorded, despite the requirement of Code C. The power to delay informing someone was hardly ever used.

- There was a large increase in the proportion of suspects requesting legal advice, from 24% to 32%. There were considerable differences between stations in request rates for legal advice, but all showed increases in demand, particularly among those detained for offences of intermediate seriousness. This is attributed to the increase in information communicated about rights.

- Of those who did not request legal advice or who only requested it at a later stage, nearly half said they would have asked for a solicitor if one had been to hand on their arrival. It is estimated that this would have led to a request rate for legal advice of between 50% and 66%.

- Despite the increase in requests for legal advice, contact was made with a solicitor by custody officers in more cases: 87% of cases in phase two compared with 80% in phase one. However, the time taken to contact solicitors increased and more requests fell to the duty solicitor scheme.

- The proportion of suspects who spoke to a legal adviser increased: a quarter of all suspects in phase two had a legal consultation. Around two-thirds of advice was given in person. However, the situation varied considerably between stations and up to 80% of advice was given over the telephone in some stations.

- The increase in legal advice has meant that far more suspects who are interviewed have talked to a legal adviser beforehand. However, after giving advice, legal advisers are less often remaining to attend police interviews with their clients. The extent to which they attend interviews varied considerably between stations. When they attended, they seldom interrupted the interview to advise their clients.

- The proportion of cases in which police officers asked suspects questions after arrest and before arrival at the station nearly halved, to 10% in phase two. Moreover, relatively little of the questioning in phase two amounted to an interview as defined in the new Code.

- In phase one, 18% of suspects admitted the offence or made some form of damaging statement prior to arrival at the station, whether in response to police questions or volunteered; in phase two this was true of only 9% of cases.

- Social workers rather than parents are more often acting as appropriate adults in juvenile cases. And, where the suspect is mentally disordered or handicapped, specialist or psychiatric social workers are increasingly involved. Parents often appeared unsuited to the role of appropriate adult; custody officers rarely explained what was expected of them, as is required by the new Code C.

- There has been an improvement in the information juveniles are given about their rights and in their implementation, but juveniles remain at a disadvantage compared with adults. For example, rights are not always implemented when requested if an adult has not yet arrived, information about rights is not always reiterated when an adult arrives, and juveniles are often given little option about having anyone other than the appropriate adult informed of their detention.

- Requests for legal advice by juveniles increased in phase two but remained lower than for adults. There continued to be very wide variations between stations in demand for legal advice by juveniles.

- The report concluded that the new Codes have achieved some degree of success in influencing police behaviour—for example, in providing suspects with information about their rights—but there remains scope for improvement in this and other areas. Other areas for concern that are highlighted are the lack of privacy in talking to solicitors on the telephone, and variations in the amount of legal advice given in person, in the attendance of legal advisers at police interviews and in access to legal advice by juveniles.

(At page 91:)

Compliance with the revised Code

In the introductory chapter, it was noted that the regulation of policing by formal rules is by no means unproblematic. A variety of cultural and practical aspects of police work may determine levels of observance and PACE is no exception. However, previous researchers have differed in their views about the effects of PACE on police practice. On the one hand, there are those who believe that there has been radical change. On the other hand McConville et al (1991) argue that little or any significance has altered, claiming that policing is dominated by 'crime control' values, to which PACE and the Codes of Practice are subordinate. In relation to police detention they maintain that custody officers tend to co-operate with colleagues carrying out investigations in denying suspects their rights. The requirement to keep detailed records is seen as an apparent legitimisation of practice rather than ensuring that what takes place is within the spirit of the rules.

There have been both successes and failures in securing compliance with the new provisions.

Successes

If a balance sheet were to be drawn up, the following would rate as, at the least, moderate successes. Firstly, those detained are being given more information about their rights by means of written notices and spoken information. The police may even be playing safe in some cases by giving this information out where the recipient cannot understand it (to those detained as a place of safety, for example). Importantly, a substantial proportion of suspects are told legal advice is free, information which formerly had to be gleaned from a Law Society leaflet which was patchily distributed. And virtually all who are given a notice of rights are also given the notice of their entitlement while in custody; this contains information which before was only available from reading the Codes of Practice—a right few took up.

Secondly, the facility with which the suspect may exercise the right to legal advice has been enhanced. Reminders of this right are being given at the bulk of reviews and police interviews, as the revised Code requires. It also appears that reviews that would have been conducted while suspects were asleep are more often brought forward to enable them to respond to such reminders (or make other representations). Furthermore, delays of access to legal advice, which used to occur in around 1% of cases, are now hardly ever sought. This is probably not a direct consequence of new guidance in the Code; however, it is in accordance with the revised Code, which in turn reflects the substance of prior Court of Appeal decisions.

Thirdly, the frequency with which suspects are questioned outside the police station appears to have declined, reflecting compliance with new restrictions in the revised Code.

Lastly, there have been moves to ensure that the role of appropriate adult is played by persons who are genuinely appropriate. This means calls upon social workers where parents are also victims or witnesses to the crime or have received admissions.

Failures

Turning to the negative side, the following points may be singled out. Perhaps the most important is the frequent failure by custody officers to deliver information—particularly about the right to legal advice—in accordance with various stipulations in the revised Code. Hardly any suspects were told that the right to consult a solicitor involved a private consultation; only just over half were told legal advice was independent; and over a quarter were not told that it was free. Observers categorised the way information was given as unclear or too fast in over a quarter of cases. Mention of the right to consult the Codes of Practice was also omitted in a significant minority of cases. In addition, a variety of other features of the way rights were given may have tended to bias the suspect against asking for legal advice in some cases, for example, reference to difficulties involved in securing a solicitor.

Are these deficiencies part of what McConville et al (1991) would view as an attempt to evade legal controls and to deny suspects their rights? Is there, in effect, some form of implicit agreement between custody officers and colleagues investigating crime? The strong impression of observers in the present study, based on many hours' presence in custody areas in six different forces, is that it is rarely possible to construe custody officers' actions in this way. Probably closer to the mark is Dixon's (1991) view that the way rights are given reflects the routinisation of familiar tasks and performances without appreciation of the suspect's dilemma. However, what is familiar to the custody officer may not be to the suspect.

It is unlikely that Dixon's interpretation reflects the full range of different attitudes of custody officers. Some may issue rights cursorily because they believe that suspects who are clearly 'guilty' and sure to be charged will gain little advantage from them; therefore, it matters not whether they are given full information. Their hope that the suspect will not request a solicitor is not in sympathy with the investigating officer but primarily to save the work involved in contacting a solicitor and having the suspect on their hands for longer. Others may be brief where they believe suspects are already familiar with their rights. These assumptions are probably often correct, but do not excuse the omissions of information required by the Code. Furthermore, they may sometimes be wrong and this alone should justify the provisions of full information even where it seems superfluous. For example, more than one person who had been arrested before and who was interviewed by observers was under the impression that the duty solicitor was a solicitor employed by the police. Certain information may be omitted because custody officers feel it is valueless: for example, that legal advice is in private, when in fact telephone conversations usually occur within the hearing of everyone in the custody area.

Another negative point concerns juveniles. The research suggests that clarifications in the Code respecting the rights to legal advice and to have someone informed of their detention have not entirely removed the problems that may arise with the implementation of these rights. In particular, juveniles do not always have a free choice to exercise either right. Firstly, custody officers tend to treat contact with a person responsible for the juvenile's welfare (who normally then acts as appropriate adult) as notification under s 56 of PACE, despite C 3.7 which points out that these are separate rights. Secondly, juveniles are generally told of their rights to legal advice on arrival, but decisions on contacting a solicitor are still sometimes deferred until an adult arrives, new guidance notwithstanding (C 3G). This can lead to requests initially made being cancelled later. Custody officers also assume in some cases that juveniles are incapable of deciding on legal advice, when comparatively little explanation would enable them to make a decision.

The operation of the revised Code may also be called into question in certain other areas. There are some deficiencies in record-keeping and, in particular with documenting reminders of the right to legal advice at reviews. Although the research found that in a majority of cases such reminders were given, they were rarely recorded. Since this falls to inspectors, who are themselves the supervisors of custody officers and responsible for checking that their record-keeping is correct, it is an important omission.

Remaining with inspectors, there is some doubt about the value of the provision requiring their permission before an interview can be conducted with someone who has asked for legal advice but not received it. In most cases in which this was sought, observers gained the impression that this procedure had become routinised and effectively rubber-stamped decisions already made at a lower level. Similar criticisms have been made of other PACE procedures, and particularly those for authorising and reviewing detention.

Lastly, mention must be made of the confusion between the right to have someone informed and the entitlement to a telephone call. Custody officers must inform suspects of the former; the latter is contained in the new notice of entitlements. Suspects were hopelessly confused by the two and generally did not discern that they were separate. The revised Code does nothing to correct this confusion and custody officers hardly ever sought to explain the difference. The provision in the Code allowing telephone calls to be delayed or denied in arrestable offences led on a few occasions to denial of outside contact where the suspect had in fact only asked for the police to inform someone. This confusion suggests the need for more explicit guidance.

The impact of the revised Code

How successful have the new provisions been in getting the message about legal advice across? The research suggests a modest degree of success. While most suspects were aware in both phases of the study that they had the right to a solicitor, the proportion who were aware that advice was free rose substantially. Reminders at reviews and prior to interviews that this right could be exercised later also appear generally to have sunk in, although few of those who had not requested a solicitor on arrival acted upon them. However, only a minority noticed the new posters advertising free legal advice. These are positioned in the custody area and suspects may have been too concerned with events to read them. Placing such notices on cell walls might have led to an increase in suspects' awareness of their content.

More people detained by the police now request legal advice. With a request rate of 32%, the study showed that the proportion of suspects asking for a solicitor has risen by one-third since the revised Codes were introduced. It cannot be said for certain that the increase in information available to suspects is the sole cause for this rise—awareness of the right to advice may also have grown independently—but it is believed that it is an important factor. Two important issues will be raised here, which arise from this trend. Firstly, the unevenness in demand, particularly among juveniles; secondly, the capacity of the legal profession to respond.

Unevenness of demand for legal advice

Previous studies have drawn attention to the wide variation in requests for legal advice between police stations. Part of the variation has been attributed to different patterns of offending, different populations of juvenile suspects, and the type of duty solicitor scheme in operation. Much of the variation remains explained. In the present study, request rates for solicitors varied widely. It is useful, however, to consider adults and juveniles separately because the pattern of demand for solicitors differed quite substantially.

There was evidence of a reduction in the amount of variation in the demand for solicitors among adults. There was greater clustering of request rates around the mean, and, generally, stations with low rates in phase one tended to experience above average rises in demand for solicitors in phase two. This may suggest that, under present arrangements for providing advice, there is a certain threshold beyond which demand for solicitors is unlikely to rise and that, given the right conditions may amount to the kind of provision of information that is laid down in the revised Code. There was still a difference between the lowest and highest request rates of 14 percentage points. To the extent that this variation is not explained by difference in offence mix, it is likely to be accounted for by local differences in the provision of legal advice and suspects' awareness of these, and differences in the way information about rights was conveyed, which, as was shown in Chapter 2, may still be quite considerable.

The variation in requests for legal advice among juveniles remains extreme. The lower and upper limits were 4% and 42% in phase one, and 7% and 58% in phase two. The research suggests that only a limited amount of this variation is due to differences in the criminal experience of juvenile suspects. Particularly where demand is low, it is likely that this results to some extent from juveniles' choices about solicitors being constrained by the way in which rights are given. This question has been considered above. Clearly, considerations of equity dictate that juveniles at all stations should be offered equal access to the rights to which they are entitled.

The best way of achieving this is a matter of some debate. It may be argued that juveniles are sometime too young to make an informed decision about legal advice and that this should await the arrival of an adult. However, to do so entails delay. When an adult arrives, he or she may be understandably reluctant to involve the juvenile in a further wait while a solicitor is contacted. Under present rules, the correct procedure (unless the juvenile is clearly incapable of comprehending what is said) is to allow him or her a free choice about legal advice on arrival; if a solicitor is requested, effect should be given to this decision straightaway. However, this may work against the juvenile if their decision is not to request a solicitor. It may be the wrong decision in the circumstances, but if presented to the adult on their arrival as the juvenile's wishes, it may create a presumption against obtaining legal advice. Some of these difficulties might be lessened if legal advice were readily available at the police station—an issue considered below.

The section on the capacity of the legal profession to respond is to be found at extract **[5:2]**.

[2:20] Baldwin, J and Moloney, T, 'Supervision of Police Investigations in Serious Criminal Cases'
(1993) RCCJ Research Study No 4, HMSO (at page 74)

Two distinct models of supervision emerge from this analysis of the investigative process. Major inquiries led by senior officers are supervised in the sense that the officer in charge of the investigation directs operations and assumes a full managerial role in the inquiry. By contrast, in investigations involving small numbers of officers, the ethos of teamwork prevails. The formal supervisor is usually no more than a name on the case papers. The dichotomy is such that it could almost be said that in the former case investigations are supervised, whilst in the latter they are not.

Our abiding impression is that too great a responsibility is being placed on the shoulders of junior officers. The cases included in this study were very serious in nature, and, as a detective constable in Birmingham observed of a section 18 assault case we had been discussing, 'If you try to equate the weight or value of that particular job with something in industry, you wouldn't have someone on such a low echelon in a company dealing with that thing because it would be too big a responsibility.' The question that is raised in this research is therefore whether it is appropriate for officers of constable rank to be expected to investigate and supervise offences of this gravity.

We have noted that the detective constables we interviewed were confident about their own abilities to cope with running such investigations, but it is revealing that three-quarters of them voiced reservations about the laxity of supervision in serious investigations within the police service as a whole. Almost all officers to whom we spoke could easily recount horror stories of working with others whose supervision was not highly regarded, and there are of course enough well-publicised instances of miscarriages of justice to indicate that there has been on occasions in the past a total breakdown in standards of supervision.

It is interesting that the criticisms of standards of supervision that were made by the officers who were interviewed were not directed at immediate colleagues but instead at senior officers. The latter were often seen as being out of touch from the hurly-burly of investigations and so in a weak position to comment upon the way they were being conducted, still less to supervise them. However, it is likely that such attitudes reveal more about the prevailing police culture (a basic tenet of which is that officers have confidence in their immediate colleagues) than about how well these officers might have conducted inquiries.

It seems to us that improvements in standards of supervision might best be effected through an enhancement of the role of sergeant. At present the rank of sergeant within the police service tends to be viewed as an incremental promotion from the rank of constable, and, while they are formally senior to constables, this formality belies an everyday reality where, particularly in the CID, sergeants tend often to be treated as equals by junior colleagues.

The sergeant is, then, very much the *primus inter pares* within the CID, and there are powerful structural imperatives within the police service which produce the relative impotence of the rank. Two factors in particular are significant in this context. First, the difference in pay between constables and sergeants is not great (not nearly as substantial as between sergeants and inspectors, for example), and this affects the way that sergeants are viewed and how in turn they view themselves. Second, and more important, the daily realities of police work tend to prevent sergeants from distancing themselves from their colleagues. The workload of the CID as a rule ensures that sergeants are required to become as immersed in the investigation of offences as detective constables. As one inspector put it in interview, 'Detective sergeants become little more than detective constables because it's a question of all shoulders to the wheel.' In such circumstances, sergeants' authority and capacity to supervise are greatly reduced.

Making the rank of sergeant more substantial would provide a viable alternative to the present 'open-door' policy of senior officers to which we have already referred. The sergeant is in a much better position than officers of higher rank to be acquainted with the strengths and shortcomings of investigating officers and is also better placed to find out about any problems which may develop during the course of an inquiry carried out by a junior officer. By increasing the sergeant's authority and opportunities for supervision, effective intervention in the routine inquiry would be greatly facilitated. Needless to say, increasing the responsibility and authority of the sergeant rank would have resource implications. It would entail enhanced training and remuneration, and would therefore be costly to implement.

Seeking to strengthen supervision at ground level by this means seems to us more likely to be effective than alternatives based upon interposing, as has often been suggested, a senior prosecutorial or quasi-judicial figure at the head of major inquiries. The involvement of outside figures in criminal investigations is a feature of certain inquisitorial systems, but such notions fit uneasily within the adversarial processes which have traditionally operated in this country. Such proposals do nonetheless enjoy certain appeal as mechanisms for countering what are seen by many as unhealthy police tendencies to pursue single-mindedly the conviction of suspects. The problem of police officers becoming psychologically committed to a certain line of inquiry and unwilling to test alternative theories has been recognised in this country for many years, and, when we put to the officers we interviewed the idea that some outside official might be involved in major investigations, we were surprised that it was favourably received by many of them. Some officers have no strong opinion on the subject but it is interesting to note that, of the remainder, as many favoured the idea as resisted it.

Although there would seem to be little advantage in having Crown Prosecutors as supervisors of inquiries, considerable benefit might nonetheless be derived from seeking to involve them early on in the investigative process. Crown Prosecutors already participate at an early stage in some inquiries, and there is in our view much to be gained from extending this practice. One main benefit is that they could examine whatever evidence the police have collected at that stage and more effectively direct that further inquiries be made along lines they seemed appropriate. Earlier involvement of the Crown Prosecution Service would serve in this way to enhance confidence in the integrity of investigations. If all materials collected by the police in the course of an investigation were handed over to Crown

Prosecutors, then they would be in a much stronger position than at present to provide some real direction of inquiries.

Although criticisms have been made in this report about aspects of the police investigations we have examined, it is appropriate that we convey the admirable qualities that were evident to us when we spoke to the officers concerned—their enthusiasm, espirit de corps, commitment, sense of fair play, loyalty and the like. We did not conclude that these were officers who were thrusting remorselessly for conviction; nor did we find that they were often uncaring or slipshod about the way that the people with whom they dealt were treated. But the conclusion we draw, after having spoken at some length with officers, is that the procedures that presently operate, as far as supervision of investigations is concerned, contain the potential for laxity, if not abuse. They allow too great a latitude to officers of constable rank in the way that they conduct inquiries, while at the same time imposing heavy responsibilities upon them. As we have noted in this report, supervision is often regarded by officers as an abstract and artificial concept, almost as a figment of the academic imagination. It is time that the idea of supervision, based upon real responsibility and authority and grounded on rank, was resurrected.

[2:21] Royal Commission on Criminal Justice

(1993) Cm 2263, HMSO (at page 52)

(iii) Arguments for retaining the right of silence

13 Those opposed to any weakening of the right of silence in response to police questioning include the Bar Council, Law Society and the Criminal Bar Association, who do not accept that it could be right to allow suspects to be threatened with the possibility of adverse comment simply because they refused to answer police questions. They say that not only are the circumstances of police interrogation disorientating and intimidating in themselves, but there can be justification for requiring a suspect to answer questions when he or she may be unclear both about the nature of the offence which he or she is alleged to have committed and about the legal definitions of intent, dishonesty and so forth on which an indictment may turn. Innocent suspects' reasons for remaining silent may include, for example, the protection of family or friends, a sense of bewilderment, embarrassment or outrage, or a reasoned decision to wait until the allegation against them has been set out in detail and they have had the benefit of considered legal advice. Members of ethnic or other minority groups may have particular reasons of their own for fearing that any answers they give will be unfairly used against them. There is the risk that, if the police were allowed to warn suspects who declined to answer their questions that they faced the prospect of adverse comment at trial, such a power would sometimes be abused. It is now well established that certain people, including some who are not mentally ill or handicapped, will confess to offences they did not commit whether or not there has been impropriety on the part of the police. The threat of adverse comment at trial may increase the risk of confused or vulnerable suspects making false confessions.

14 Those who take this view argue that it would, for all these reasons, be against the interests of justice to weaken the protection afforded to the innocent suspect by the right of silence. They do not agree that the present safeguard against adverse comment necessarily encourages the police to press too hard for confessions. It may indeed be the case that the police do sometimes try too hard and too exclusively to obtain a formal confession; but they maintain that, if silence is not of itself acceptable evidence, the police should thereby be encouraged to look for other evidence by which the prosecution case can be strengthened. If the right not to answer police questions were removed, adverse comment at the trial would enable a prosecution case which was otherwise too weak to secure a conviction to be strengthened in the minds of the jury by the implication that the defendant's silence automatically supported it.

...

(v) Our conclusions

20 In the light of all the evidence put before us, we have had to weigh against each other two conflicting considerations. One is the prospect, if adverse comment at trial were to be permissible, of an increase in the number of convictions of guilty defendants who have refused to answer police questions. The other is the risk of an increase in the number of innocent defendants who are convicted because they have made admissions prejudicial to themselves through the fear of adverse comment at trial or whose silence has been taken by the jury to add sufficient weight to the prosecution case to turn a not guilty verdict into one of guilty.

21 Two of us take the view that it would be right for adverse comment (as suggested in paragraph 11 above) to be permitted at the trial and for a consequential amendment (on the lines of the example in paragraph 10 above) to be made to the wording of the caution. In the appropriate case the jury could thus be invited to draw its own conclusions as to whether the silence in the case in question supported the evidence pointing to guilt. The two of us who take this view believe that it is amply justified by the arguments set out in paragraphs 6 to 12 above. They accept that the majority of us are reluctant to take this step for, among other reasons, fear of weakening the safeguards that exist for the vulnerable suspect. The minority would, however, strengthen those safeguards in other ways and in any case believe that the right of silence offers little or no protection to the vulnerable. There is some evidence, as well as the experience of the police service, which in their view implies that it is not the vulnerable but the experienced criminal who shelters behind the right of silence.

22 The majority of us, however, believe that the possibility of an increase in the conviction of the guilty is outweighed by the risk that the extra pressure on suspects to talk in the police station and the adverse inferences invited if they do not may result in more convictions of the innocent. They recommend retaining the present caution and trial direction unamended. In taking this view, the majority acknowledge the frustration which many police officers feel when confronted with suspects who refuse to offer any explanation whatever of strong prima facie evidence that they have committed an offence. But they doubt whether the possibility of adverse comment at trial would make the difference which the police suppose. The experienced professional criminals who wish to remain silent are likely to continue to do so and will justify their silence by stating at trial that their solicitors have advised them to say nothing at least until the allegations against them have been fully disclosed. It may be that more defendants would be convicted whose refusal to answer police questions had been the subject of adverse comment; but the majority believe that their number would not be nearly as great as it popularly imagined.

23 It is the less experienced and more vulnerable suspects against whom the threat of adverse comment would be likely to be more damaging. There are too many cases of improper pressures being brought to bear on suspects in police custody, even where the safeguards of PACE and the codes of practice have been supposedly in force, for the majority to regard this with equanimity. As far as silence at the police station is concerned, therefore, the majority find themselves taking the same stance as the majority of the Royal Commission on Criminal Procedure (RCCP) which said, at paragraph 4.50 on its Report that, if adverse inferences could be drawn from silence, 'It might put strong (and additional) psychological pressure upon some suspects to answer questions without knowing precisely what was the substance of and evidence for the accusations against them ... This in our view might well increase the risk of innocent people, particularly those under suspicion for the first time, making damaging statements ... On the other hand, the guilty person who knew the system would be inclined to sit it out ... If the police had sufficient evidence to mount a case without a statement from him, it would still be to the guilty suspect's advantage to keep to himself as long as possible a false defence which was capable of being shown to be such by investigation. It might just be believed by the jury despite the fact that the prosecution and the judge would be able to comment.'

24 In the majority's view, therefore, in accordance with the recommendations which are argued more fully in chapter six, it is when, but only when, the prosecution case has been fully disclosed that defendants should be required to offer an answer to the charges made against them at the risk of adverse comment at trial on any new defence they then disclose, or on any departure from the defence

which they previously disclosed. They may still choose to run the risk of such comment, or indeed to remain silent throughout their trial. But if they do, it will be in the knowledge that their hope of an acquittal rests on the ability of defending counsel either to convince the jury that there is a reasonable explanation for the departure or, where silence is maintained throughout, to discredit the prosecution evidence in the jury's eyes. As argued below, it should be open to the judge, as now in serious fraud cases, to comment on any new defence or any departure from an earlier line of defence.

25 In reaching this view the majority have considered whether there may be a special category of case where a different approach is needed. This is where a crime may have been committed, more than one person is present, and it is impossible to say who has committed the offence. This typically happens when one of two parents is suspected of injuring or murdering a child but it is impossible to say which one. It must not, however, be supposed that removing the right of silence would be the solution in such cases. It would not enable the prosecution to establish which of them had committed the offence if both nevertheless insisted on remaining silent. Nor would the possibility of adverse comment at the trial enable a court or a jury to determine in respect of which of them the silence should be taken as corroboration. We have every sympathy with the public concern over such cases but it seems to us that they need approaching in a different way, perhaps, where children are the victims, by extending the concept of absolute liability for a child's safety.

[2:22] Criminal Justice and Public Order Act 1994 (as amended)
Sections 34–38

34 Effect of accused's failure to mention facts when questioned or charged

(1) Where, in any proceedings against a person for an offence, evidence is given that the accused—

   (a) at any time before he was charged with the offence, on being questioned under caution by a constable trying to discover whether or by whom the offence had been committed, failed to mention any fact relied on in his defence in those proceedings; or

   (b) on being charged with the offence or officially informed that he might be prosecuted for it, failed to mention any such fact,

   being a fact which in the circumstances existing at the time the accused could reasonably have been expected to mention when so questioned, charged or informed, as the case may be, subsection (2) below applies.

(2) Where this subsection applies—

   (a) a magistrates' court inquiring into the offence as examining justices;

   (b) a judge, in deciding whether to grant an application made by the accused under Paragraph 2 of Schedule 3 to the Crime and Disorder act 1998;

   (c) the court, in determining whether there is a case to answer; and

   (d) the court or jury, in determining whether the accused is guilty of the offence charged,

   may draw such inferences from the failure as appear proper.

(2A) Where the accused was at an authorised place of detention at the time of the failure, subsections (1) and (2) above do not apply if he had not been allowed an opportunity to consult a solicitor prior to being questioned, charged or informed as mentioned in subsection (1) above.

(3) Subject to any directions by the court, evidence tending to establish the failure may be given before or after evidence tending to establish the fact which the accused is alleged to have failed to mention.

(4) This section applies in relation to questioning by persons (other than constables) charged with the duty of investigating offences or charging offenders as it applies in relation to questioning

by constables; and in subsection (1) above "officially informed" means informed by a constable or any such person.

(5) This section does not—

(a) prejudice the admissibility in evidence of the silence or other reaction of the accused in the face of anything said in his presence relating to the conduct in respect of which he is charged, in so far as evidence thereof would be admissible apart from this section; or

(b) preclude the drawing of any inference from any such silence or other reaction of the accused which could properly be drawn apart from this section.

(6) This section does not apply in relation to a failure to mention a fact if the failure occurred before the commencement of this section.

35 Effect of accused's silence at trial

(1) At the trial of any person...for an offence, subsections (2) and (3) below apply unless—

(a) the accused's guilt is not in issue; or

(b) it appears to the court that the physical or mental condition of the accused makes it undesirable for him to give evidence;

but subsection (2) below does not apply if, at the conclusion of the evidence for the prosecution, his legal representative informs the court that the accused will give evidence or, where he is unrepresented, the court ascertains from him that he will give evidence.

(2) Where this subsection applies, the court shall, at the conclusion of the evidence for the prosecution, satisfy itself (in the case of proceedings on indictment, in the presence of the jury) that the accused is aware that the stage has been reached at which evidence can be given for the defence and that he can, if he wishes, give evidence and that, if he chooses not to give evidence, or having been sworn, without good cause refuses to answer any question, it will be permissible for the court or jury to draw such inferences as appear proper from his failure to give evidence or his refusal, without good cause, to answer any question.

(3) Where this subsection applies, the court or jury, in determining whether the accused is guilty of the offence charged, may draw such inferences as appear proper from the failure of the accused to give evidence or his refusal, without good cause, to answer any question.

(4) This section does not render the accused compellable to give evidence on his own behalf, and he shall accordingly not be guilty of contempt of court by reason of a failure to do so.

(5) For the purposes of this section a person who, having been sworn, refuses to answer any question shall be taken to do so without good cause unless—

(a) he is entitled to refuse to answer the question by virtue of any enactment, whenever passed or made, or on the ground of privilege; or

(b) the court in the exercise of its general discretion excuses him from answering it.

(7) This section applies—

(a) in relation to proceedings on indictment for an offence, only if the person charged with the offence is arraigned on or after the commencement of this section;

(b) in relation to proceedings in a magistrates' court, only if the time when the court begins to receive evidence in the proceedings falls after the commencement of this section.

36 Effect of accused's failure or refusal to account for objects, substances or marks

(1) Where—

(a) a person is arrested by a constable, and there is—

(i) on his person; or

(ii) in or on his clothing or footwear; or

(iii) otherwise in his possession; or

(iv) in any place in which he is at the time of his arrest,

any object, substance or mark, or there is any mark on any such object; and

(b) that or another constable investigating the case reasonably believes that the presence of the object, substance or mark may be attributable to the participation of the person arrested in the commission of an offence specified by the constable; and

(c) the constable informs the person arrested that he so believes, and requests him to account for the presence of the object, substance or mark; and

(d) the person fails or refuses to do so,

then if, in any proceedings against the person for the offence so specified, evidence of those matters is given, subsection (2) below applies.

(2) Where this subsection applies—

(a) a magistrates' court inquiring into the offence as examining justices;

(b) a judge, in deciding whether to grant an application made by the accused under Paragraph 2 of Schedule 3 to the Crime and Disorder Act 1998;

(c) the court, in determining whether there is a case to answer; and

(d) the court or jury, in determining whether the accused is guilty of the offence charged,

may draw such inferences from the failure or refusal as appear proper.

(3) Subsections (1) and (2) above apply to the condition of clothing or footwear as they apply to a substance or mark thereon.

(4) Subsections (1) and (2) above do not apply unless the accused was told in ordinary language by the constable when making the request mentioned in subsection (1)(c) above what the effect of this section would be if he failed or refused to comply with the request.

(4A) Where the accused was at an authorised place of detention at the time of the failure or refusal, subsections (1) and (2) above do not apply if he had not been allowed an opportunity to consult a solicitor prior to the request being made.

(5) This section applies in relation to officers of customs and excise as it applies in relation to constables.

(6) This section does not preclude the drawing of any inference from a failure or refusal of the accused to account for the presence of an object, substance or mark or from the condition of clothing or footwear which could properly be drawn apart from this section.

(7) This section does not apply in relation to a failure or refusal which occurred before the commencement of this section.

37 Effect of accused's failure or refusal to account for presence at a particular place

(1) Where—

(a) a person arrested by a constable was found by him at a place at or about the time the offence for which he was arrested is alleged to have been committed; and

(b) that or another constable investigating the offence reasonably believes that the presence of the person at that place and at that time may be attributable to his participation in the commission of the offence; and

(c) the constable informs the person that he so believes, and requests him to account for that presence; and

(d) the person fails or refuses to do so,

then if, in any proceedings against the person for the offence, evidence of those matters is given, subsection (2) below applies.

(2) Where this subsection applies—

    (a) a magistrates' court inquiring into the offence as examining justices;

    (b) a judge, in deciding whether to grant an application made by the accused under Paragraph 2 of Schedule 3 to the Crime and Disorder Act 1998;

    (c) the court, in determining whether there is a case to answer; and

    (d) the court or jury, in determining whether the accused is guilty of the offence charged,

may draw such inferences from the failure or refusal as appear proper.

(3) Subsections (1) and (2) do not apply unless the accused was told in ordinary language by the constable when making the request mentioned in subsection (1)(c) above what the effect of this section would be if he failed or refused to comply with the request.

(3A) Where the accused was at an authorised place of detention at the time of the failure or refusal, subsections (1) and (2) do not apply if he had not been allowed an opportunity to consult a solicitor prior to the request being made.

(4) This section applies in relation to officers of customs and excise as it applies in relation to constables.

(5) This section does not preclude the drawing of any inference from a failure or refusal of the accused to account for his presence at a place which could properly be drawn apart from this section.

(6) This section does not apply in relation to a failure or refusal which occurred before the commencement of this section.

38 Interpretation and savings for sections 34, 35, 36 and 37

(1) In sections 34, 35, 36 and 37 of this Act—

"legal representative" means an authorised advocate or authorised litigator, as defined by section 119(1) of the Courts and Legal Services Act 1990; and

"place" includes any building or part of a building, any vehicle, vessel, aircraft or hovercraft and any other place whatsoever.

(2) In sections 34(2), 35(3), 36(2) and 37(2), references to an offence charged include references to any other offence of which the accused could lawfully be convicted on that charge.

(2A) In each of sections 34(2A), 36(4A) and 37(3A) "authorised place of detention" means—

    (a) a police station; or

    (b) any other place prescribed for the purposes of that provision by order made by the Secretary of State;

and the power to make an order under this subsection shall be exercisable by statutory instrument which shall be subject to annulment in pursuance of a resolution of either House of Parliament.

(3) A person shall not have the proceedings against him transferred to the Crown Court for trial, have a case to answer or be convicted of an offence solely on an inference drawn from such a failure or refusal as is mentioned in section 34(2), 35(3), 36(2) or 37(2).

(4) A judge shall not refuse to grant such an application as is mentioned in section 34(2)(b), 36(2)(b) and 37(2)(b) solely on an inference drawn from such a failure as is mentioned in section 34(2), 36(2) or 37(2).

(5) Nothing in sections 34, 35, 36 or 37 prejudices the operation of a provision of any enactment which provides (in whatever words) that any answer or evidence given by a person in specified circumstances shall not be admissible in evidence against him or some other person in any proceedings or class of proceedings (however described, and whether civil or criminal).

In this subsection, the reference to giving evidence is a reference to giving evidence in any manner, whether by furnishing information, making discovery, producing documents or otherwise.

(6) Nothing in sections 34, 35, 36 or 37 prejudices any power of a court, in any proceedings, to exclude evidence (whether by preventing questions being put or otherwise) at its discretion.

[2:23] Crime and Disorder Act 1998
Sections 65–66

65 Reprimands and warnings

(1) Subsections (2) to (5) below apply where—

    (a) a constable has evidence that a child or young person ("the offender") has committed an offence;

    (b) the constable considers that the evidence is such that, if the offender were prosecuted for the offence, there would be a realistic prospect of his being convicted;

    (c) the offender admits to the constable that he committed the offence;

    (d) the offender has not previously been convicted of an offence; and

    (e) the constable is satisfied that it would not be in the public interest for the offender to be prosecuted.

(2) Subject to subsection (4) below, the constable may reprimand the offender if the offender has not previously been reprimanded or warned.

(3) The constable may warn the offender if—

    (a) the offender has not previously been warned; or

    (b) where the offender has previously been warned, the offence was committed more than two years after the date of the previous warning and the constable considers the offence to be not so serious as to require a charge to be brought;

but no person may be warned under paragraph (b) above more than once.

(4) Where the offender has not been previously reprimanded, the constable shall warn rather than reprimand the offender if he considers the offence to be so serious as to require a warning.

(5) The constable shall—

    (a) where the offender is under the age of 17, give any reprimand or warning in the presence of an appropriate adult; and

    (b) explain to the offender and, where he is under that age, the appropriate adult in ordinary language—

        (i) in the case of a reprimand, the effect of subsection (5)(a) of section 66 below;

        (ii) in the case of a warning, the effect of subsections (1), (2), (4) and (5)(b) and (c) of that section, and any guidance issued under subsection (3) of that section.

(6) The Secretary of State shall publish, in such manner as he considers appropriate, guidance as to—

    (a) the circumstances in which it is appropriate to give reprimands or warnings, including criteria for determining—

        (i) for the purposes of subsection (3)(b) above, whether an offence is not so serious as to require a charge to be brought; and

      (ii) for the purposes of subsection (4) above, whether an offence is so serious as to require a warning;

(aa) the places where reprimands and warnings may be given;

  (b) the category of constable by whom reprimands and warnings may be given; and

  (c) the form which reprimands and warnings are to take and the manner in which they are to be given and recorded.

(7) In this section "appropriate adult", in relation to a child or young person, means—

  (a) his parent or guardian or, if he is in the care of a local authority or voluntary organisation, a person representing that authority or organisation;

  (b) a social worker of a local authority;

  (c) if no person falling within paragraph (a) or (b) above is available, any responsible person aged 18 or over who is not a police officer or a person employed by the police.

(8) No caution shall be given to a child or young person after the commencement of this section.

(9) Any reference (however expressed) in any enactment passed before or in the same Session as this Act to a person being cautioned shall be construed, in relation to any time after that commencement, as including a reference to a child or young person being reprimanded or warned.

66 Effect of reprimands and warnings

(1) Where a constable warns a person under section 65 above, he shall as soon as practicable refer the person to a youth offending team.

(2) A youth offending team—

  (a) shall assess any person referred to them under subsection (1) above; and

  (b) unless they consider it inappropriate to do so, shall arrange for him to participate in a rehabilitation programme.

(3) The Secretary of State shall publish, in such manner as he considers appropriate, guidance as to—

  (a) what should be included in a rehabilitation programme arranged for a person under subsection (2) above;

  (b) the manner in which any failure by a person to participate in such a programme is to be recorded; and

  (c) the persons to whom any such failure is to be notified.

(4) Where a person who has been warned under section 65 above is convicted of an offence committed within two years of the warning, the court by or before which he is so convicted—

  (a) shall not make an order under subsection (1)(b) (conditional discharge) of section 12 of the Powers of Criminal Courts (Sentencing) Act 2000 in respect of the offence unless it is of the opinion that there are exceptional circumstances relating to the offence or the offender which justify its doing so; and

  (b) where it does so, shall state in open court that it is of that opinion and why it is.

(5) The following, namely—

  (a) any reprimand of a person under section 65 above;

  (b) any warning of a person under that section; and

  (c) any report on a failure by a person to participate in a rehabilitation programme arranged for him under subsection (2) above,

may be cited in criminal proceedings in the same circumstances as a conviction of the person may be cited.

(6) In this section "rehabilitation programme" means a programme the purpose of which is to rehabilitate participants and to prevent them from re-offending.

[2:24] Baldwin, J, 'Preparing Records of Taped Interviews'
(1993) RCCJ Research Study No 2, HMSO (at page 21)

The picture that has emerged from this study is bleak. Even the most progressive forces in the country are failing to produce good quality records of interview in a sufficiently high proportion of cases. Furthermore, the guidance from the Home Office on the subject appears to be unpromising. In tackling the difficulties of compiling balanced records of interview, there is no easy solution and, after years of endeavour, one must surely now be pessimistic about the ability of the police service consistently to prepare records of interview up to the standard required.

The results of this study, which closely parallel those of the author's earlier study in the West Midlands, indicate that there is about a 50% chance that any record of interview will be faulty or misleading—a proportion that increases with the length of interviews. In this study, assessments of the quality of records of interview have been made with a certain charity, and this means that, if anything, it presents the summaries in an unduly favourable light. Yet even when imaginative approaches are examined, records of interview remain dangerously flawed in a high percentage of cases. There seem to be fundamental and inherent difficulties that undermine the usefulness of the records of interview prepared by police officers.

There are, however, some crumbs of comfort. If police officers are to continue to be required to produce the records of interview, then one might derive some consolation from the fact that the approaches adopted both in Bitterne and in Northamptonshire probably indicate the best ways of going about it. If the deficiencies noted in this report that arise in these areas were remedied, then standards could be significantly raised. It is easy to see how improvements could be made if greater care were taken in identifying relevant passages for transcription and if the records of interview did not focus on narrowly defined parts of an interview. Even so, it must be recognised that the main attractions of both approaches—that they will produce savings in police manpower—tend to encourage this kind of corner cutting.

There is unlikely to be any final solution to the problems that have been identified in compiling balanced and fair records of interview. Police officers' summaries are for a variety of reasons almost inevitably flawed in a substantial proportion of cases. It seems unrealistic to expect that police officers, who possess a wide range of literary abilities, will be able to produce the type of balanced and succinct summary that is needed. It is too tall an order for any group, and it is clear that police officers are not well suited to it. It became increasingly evident in carrying out the present study that police officers, because of their temperament, aptitude, educational background, tradition and training, are unlikely to be predisposed to summarise complex materials in a way that can safely be relied upon by other parties. The solution seems not to lie in more police training, and it is unlikely that Circulars from the Home Office, however carefully drafted, can do much to improve matters.

The inherent difficulties of preparing an accurate précis are compounded by the need to exercise sound judgment about what can be left out without distortion, and, the more summaries that one examines, the more convinced one becomes that police officers suffer from an understandable, and probably ineradicable, tendency to view matters through a prosecution prism. The compilation of summaries is not a neutral fact-gathering exercise but one that depends on intuitive judgment. In consequence the scope for conscious and unconscious bias (not to mention more subtle attempts at distortion) is infinite.

While the task remains the responsibility of the police service, it seems inevitable that such problems will arise. Where the interview forms an important part of the prosecution case—and in many cases it is the crux—it is surely unprofessional for lawyers (particularly defence lawyers) to take police officers' summaries on trust. It is not simply that officers may not have the aptitude or the ability to prepare such documents adequately or that they may seek to slant them in favour of the prosecution: it is rather a matter of lawyers in an adversarial system performing their own roles professionally. It is surely incumbent upon defence lawyers, particularly where they have not themselves been in attendance at the police station, to play the tape.

There is in the author's view no effective substitute for the lawyers involved in criminal cases taking the time to do this in a much higher proportion of cases than happens at present. As noted earlier in this report, most interviews are relatively short, and the tapes provide the best picture available of what has taken place in the interview room. It has to be recognised that such a move would have important resource implications, and it is extremely doubtful whether an overstretched Crown Prosecution Service would be able to cope with the added burden of playing tapes without an increase in manpower. Yet, if Crown Prosecutors are to carry out their most critical function effectively—that of case review in order to decide on the appropriate cause of action—then playing the tape must be regarded as a central and unavoidable part of that function.

The compromise of involving civilians in the process, as happens in Bitterne and Northamptonshire, indicates a possible direction for progress, although this solution is unlikely to be one that appeals to all police forces. Even when adopted, more determined efforts will need to be made in the future to ensure that the civilians concerned are themselves adequately trained, and, no less important, that they have fully absorbed the legal significance of what is required in these documents. An ability in the art of précis is a necessary, but not a sufficient, qualification for this work. And it is important to remember that, whether civilians or police officers carry out the work, active supervision and monitoring need to be provided within the police service.

The message of this report is clear: there is no satisfactory alternative to lawyers using the record of interview only after having played the tape itself. This should not be looked on as a purist's solution or as impractical and prohibitively expensive: it is rather the only sure way of avoiding the high risk strategy of taking the records of interview on trust—and the odds at present are greatly inferior to those that apply in Russian roulette. If this conclusion is justified in the four police forces which have made the greatest effort to overcome the problems, then it surely applies even more strongly elsewhere. The expenditure of lawyers' time will mean that records of interview can return to being genuine summaries rather than transcripts, and there will be substantial savings of police officers' time as a result. More important, the lawyers can then be confident—in a way that is certainly not possible at present—that their decision making is soundly based.

CHAPTER THREE

THE CROWN PROSECUTION SERVICE

The police now think they have enough evidence to charge Gerry Good with 'causing grievous bodily harm with intent', contrary to section 18 of the Offences Against the Person Act 1861 (an offence triable on indictment only—i.e. before a judge and jury in the Crown Court). But he will still not necessarily be prosecuted. The Crown Prosecution Service (CPS) has responsibility under the Prosecution of Offences Act 1985 **[3:1]** for the conduct of all criminal proceedings. The CPS has in effect a veto over prosecution. They also advise the police on cases for possible prosecution, review cases submitted by the police, and, where the decision is to prosecute, they determine the charge in all but minor cases. They prepare cases for court, thereby having a significant influence on the distribution of cases between the Crown Courts and magistrates' courts, and in indictable crimes will be involved in the transfer of the case to the Crown Court. In other cases, the CPS may be involved in responding to bail applications and in appeals against decisions by magistrates to grant bail. Increasingly, CPS staff also present cases at court, rather than relying on members of the independent Bar. In others, they prepare the case for trial, and brief counsel (a barrister) to prosecute. They prepare the documents for the Crown in the event of an appeal. Now a key player, the CPS were only invented in 1985.

(i) BACKGROUND

Until 1986, the police were responsible for initiating criminal prosecutions, and bringing cases to court. Of the 43 police forces, 31 had their own prosecution departments, and the rest used private firms of solicitors to carry out prosecutions. The Director of Public Prosecutions Department in London dealt with all murder prosecutions and certain other cases, such as those involving national security or public figures. A Royal Commission on Criminal Procedure (chaired by Sir Cyril Philips), set up in 1977 and reporting in 1981, concluded that the traditional police role in investigating crime was incompatible with the objectivity required in prosecution. The police were not in a position to take a sufficiently broad view when applying public interest criteria to prosecution decisions. They criticized the inconsistent policies pursued by different police forces, especially in relation to the decision whether or not to prosecute, and concluded that too many weak cases were being pursued, resulting in a high percentage of trials in which the judge directed a verdict of not guilty at the close of the prosecution case. They therefore recommended a new prosecution service. In 1983 the Home Office published a White Paper, *The Investigation and Prosecution of Criminal Offences in England and Wales*, which favoured a national organization with strong local features.

The Prosecution of Offences Act 1985 **[3:1]**, which was brought into force in 1986, still lays down the framework for prosecutions. The CPS is headed by the Director of Public Prosecutions (DPP), under the Attorney-General, and has its headquarters in London. It has two main functions: to provide an objective assessment of the results of police investigation; and to prosecute those cases which pass the tests laid down in the Code for Crown Prosecutors. The CPS ran into serious problems at birth. Many of its initial problems were financial: in 1987–98, the CPS cost £134 million, almost double the estimated £70 million. Moreover, the managerial structure proved unworkable and had to be reorganized in September 1989 and again in 1993. Until 1993 the CPS was organized into 31 areas covering England and Wales, usually aligned with one, or sometimes two, police force areas, but in that year the 31 areas were reduced to 13 in order to rationalize area administration and to delegate more responsibility to the areas. The financial problems were exacerbated by the difficulty of recruiting enough well-qualified staff, which meant that the service had to use numerous agency lawyers, who were both expensive and, since they worked only occasional days, unable to see cases through consistently.

The problems did not disappear: in 1998 Sir Iain Glidewell was asked to review the CPS and he produced a detailed report in June 1998 **[3:2]**. He found that the 1993 reorganization had been a mistake, and that the CPS should be divided into 42 areas, coterminous with police areas. This reorganization took place in 1999, and each area is now headed by a Chief Crown Prosecutor, and is subdivided into two or more branches. There is, in effect a 43rd area now: CPS Direct, which gives out-of-hours charging advice.

(ii) THE ROLE AND LEGAL STATUS OF THE CROWN PROSECUTION SERVICE

It is important to remember that the CPS was a totally new creature to the English legal system in 1986. Its relationship with the police continues to evolve. Until recently, the police took the decision to charge a suspect and then passed a file to the CPS. However, now the police must consult the CPS much earlier in the process: the precise rules are complex (see section 28 of and Schedule 2 to the Criminal Justice Act (CJA) 2003), but in reality the relationship between the police and CPS is now governed by the DPP's Guidance on Charging (the current version available at <http://www.cps.gov.uk> is the 3rd edition, February 2007). Thus:

where it appears likely that a charge will be determined by Crown Prosecutors, Custody Officers must direct investigating officers to consult a Duty Prosecutor as soon as is practicable after a person is taken into custody. This will enable early agreement to be reached as to the Report and evidential requirements and, where appropriate, for any period of bail to be determined to permit submission of the Report to the Crown Prosecutor for a Charging Decision.

We saw in Chapter 2, that the police may decide to caution a suspect rather than initiate a prosecution. This they may do without CPS involvement. The picture has become much more complicated since the introduction of 'conditional cautions' in the CJA 2003. A conditional caution is in fact a caution with conditions, and can only be given where the prosecutor thinks that it is appropriate to do so. There is as yet no published research on how the CJA 2003 changes are working, but it is worth heeding these words of warning:

> The Government are taking our judicial system down a route that could lead to the widespread use of administrative punishment instead of the impartial hearing that is given in a magistrates' court. Fair trial safeguards and the involvement of the independent court in the delivery of punishment are in the wider public interest and in the interest of the victims of crime. (Baroness Anelay, HL, 1 November, 2006)

Despite this, Parliament voted in section 17 of the Police and Justice Act 2006 to allow financial penalties of up to £250 as a condition of a conditional caution: a prosecutor's fine. This has not been implemented at the time of writing.

How does the citizen challenge decisions taken by the CPS? The first case in which a court had to decide whether CPS decisions were subject to judicial review was *R v Chief Constable of Kent, ex p L* [3:3], in which the Divisional Court explored the legal relationship between the police and the CPS. Whilst the court held that the police decision (to charge) was not reviewable, in respect of juveniles, the discretion of the CPS to continue or discontinue criminal proceedings may be reviewable in limited circumstances. Watkins LJ was fearful of 'opening too wide the door of review of the discretion', but are the dangers of not opening that door not equally manifest? Despite his warning, there has been no shortage of applications for judicial review of CPS decision making. Uglow et al [3:4], in their review of the implications of this case, were concerned not so much about the dangers of administrative and non-reviewable decision making, but that the courts' concentration on formal criminal justice agencies ignores the increasingly important informal approaches. A more recent case which illustrates Uglow et al's concern is *R (F) v CPS* [2003] EWHC 3266, (2004) 168 JP 93. A 14-year-old had been a passenger in a car taken by two other boys. He refused to admit an offence of aggravated vehicle taking and so was not eligible for a reprimand or warning under the Crime and Disorder Act 1998, section 65(1)(c). When he appeared in court, his solicitor indicated that the boy might be prepared to admit the offence and so the case was adjourned. However, the police said they were unable to re-interview the boy once he had been charged (see PACE Code C paragraph 16.5 [2:12]) and so when the case returned to court the CPS stuck to their decision to prosecute. The boy applied for judicial review of the CPS's decision that it would not exercise its power to discontinue criminal proceedings against him. The High Court refused this application, holding that the police had been acting lawfully in declining to re-interview the boy and that it would be wrong for the court to interfere with this decision. The court makes clear that not only were the police acting perfectly properly not re-interviewing, given the wording of paragraph 16.5, but that it would be 'quite wrong to interfere with operational decisions of the police'. Further, 'save in exceptional circumstances, it is quite inappropriate for this court to step into the shoes of the Crown Prosecutor and to retake decisions which Parliament has entrusted to the Crown Prosecutor under the Prosecution of Offences Act 1985' (Jackson J, paragraph 77).

Whilst the decision to prosecute is very difficult to challenge, it may be slightly easier to challenge a decision not to prosecute. In *R v DPP, ex p C* [1995] 1 Cr App R 136, the Divisional Court allowed an application by a wife for judicial review of a decision by the DPP not to prosecute her husband for buggery, contrary to section 12 of the Sexual Offences Act 1956. The court held that the prosecutor had not followed the Code for Crown Prosecutors, and remitted the case to the DPP for further consideration. The case was cited in the famous decision of the House of Lords (supported by the European Court of Human Rights) in *R (on the application of Pretty) v DPP* [2002] 1 AC 800, upholding the DPP's refusal to undertake not to prosecute Mrs Pretty's husband if he helped her to die. She suffered from motor neurone disease, and was physically unable to end her own life. Her husband was prepared to help her die provided he had an undertaking that he would not be prosecuted. The House of Lords was unanimous that Mrs Pretty could not establish any breach of any Convention right. Beyond that, although the DPP can make statements about prosecuting policy, he had no power to give a 'proleptic grant of immunity from prosecution.... The power to dispense with and suspend laws and the execution of laws without the consent of Parliament was denied to the crown and its servants by the Bill of Rights 1688' (per Lord Bingham at paragraph 39).

Even if the courts are reluctant to interfere with the discretionary powers of the CPS, they may discharge or stay a case because of 'abuse of process'. *R v Croydon Justices, ex p Dean* **[3:5]** reveals a trial judge's control over the actions of the CPS by their power to discharge a case for abuse of process (and see also *Townsend, Dearsley and Bretscher* [1998] Crim LR 126). *Ex p Dean* is an important authority discussed by the House of Lords in their decision in *Jones v Whalley* **[4:11]** on the right to bring a private prosecution. It was also cited in the high profile case of *Hamza (Abu)* [2007] 2 WLR 226. Abu Hamza unsuccessfully appealed against his convictions for 'soliciting to murder' (contrary to the Offences against the Person Act 1861, section 4), using threatening, abusive, or insulting words or behaviour with intent to stir up racial hatred, possessing threatening, abusive, or insulting sound recordings with intent to stir up racial hatred, and possessing a document or record containing information of a kind likely to be useful to a person committing or preparing to commit an act of terrorism. Most of the counts related to speeches given by him between 1997 and 2000; the sound recordings were cassettes of these speeches and the documents were ten volumes of the *Afghani Jihad Encyclopaedia*. The cassettes and Encyclopaedia had been seized by police in 1999, following his arrest on suspicion of involvement in a terrorist incident in the Yemen, but had been returned to him later in 1999 and he had been informed that no further action would be taken. The Court of Appeal, led by the Lord Chief Justice, rejected the argument that there had been an abuse of process because the returning of his materials gave him a legitimate expectation that he would not later be prosecuted for possession of them. The court concluded that:

It is not likely to constitute an abuse of process to proceed with a prosecution unless (i) there has been an unequivocal representation by those with the conduct of the investigation or prosecution of a case that the defendant will not be prosecuted and (ii) that the defendant has acted on that representation to his detriment. Even then, if facts come to light which were not known when the representation was made, these may justify proceeding with the prosecution despite the representation (paragraph 54).

This case, the Court of Appeal said, fell a long way short of satisfying these criteria. The fact that the police did not prosecute the appellant in 1999 could not be taken as an assurance, let alone an unequivocal assurance, that they would not do so in the future. Nor could the Home Secretary's decision to deprive the appellant of his British citizenship in 2003 be taken as an implicit assurance that the appellant would not be prosecuted.

The House of Lords decided in *R v Manchester Crown Court, ex p DPP* [1993] 2 All ER 663 that the decision of a Crown Court judge (see Chapter 7) to stay an indictment as an abuse of process was not open to judicial review. This decision may prevent delays, but it also meant that the CPS had no power until recently to challenge a decision to stay which it believed to be wrong. The Criminal Justice Act 2003, section 58 gave the prosecution the right to appeal against a 'terminating ruling' (see Chapter 9).

(iii) THE CODE FOR CROWN PROSECUTORS

When determining charges, Crown Prosecutors and custody officers must apply the principles contained in the latest edition of the Code for Crown Prosecutors **[3:6]** i.e. there must be enough evidence to provide a realistic prospect of conviction and it must be in the public interest to proceed. The CPS has a duty to keep the evidence continually under review. Thus, in our case, a Crown Prosecutor should have been consulted by the police before Gerry was charged. At this stage, he can be remanded in custody as long as a 'threshold' test has been passed: this only requires 'reasonable suspicion' that the suspect committed the offence. Someone from the CPS (probably a Designated Caseworker) will attend the magistrates' court for the bail hearing the morning after Gerry was charged, and the file will come back to the CPS branch office at the end of the day. Any decision to discontinue proceedings can only be taken by a Crown Prosecutor. The basic guidance of the Code for Crown Prosecutors **[3:6]** is amplified by the CPS policy manual, which is not published, but the CPS's website is full of useful documents. The DPP has a duty under the Prosecution of Offences Act 1985, section 10 **[3:1]** to issue the code, but this does not mean that the Code amounts to delegated legislation. The DPP's guidance must cover three areas: the decision to prosecute; the selection of the appropriate charges; and the representations to be made to magistrates about where the defendant should face trial in either-way offences. The current version of the Code, the fifth since 1985, was published in 2004. By simplifying the language, the CPS hoped that it was also clarifying the Code. Is it now so simple and lacking in detail that it says very little? Hoyano et al **[3:7]** interviewed CPS personnel even before this latest simplification and concluded that the impact of the Code had had a very limited effect on actual case decisions. The reality is that CPS staff followed more sophisticated guidance.

In deciding whether to continue a prosecution, the Crown Prosecutor or designated caseworker considers two questions. First is the question of the sufficiency of the evidence. The evidential threshold is a 'realistic prospect of conviction'. This is an objective test: is it more likely than not that the defendant will be convicted? The evidence must be admissible and reliable. We will see in Chapter 7 that there are no clear rules on admissibility of evidence—the judge has a wide discretion under the Police and Criminal Evidence Act 1984 (PACE) to decide what should be admitted. This element, therefore, is very difficult to predict. It may be even more difficult to predict how the jury or magistrates will decide questions of fact. They will have the benefit of hearing both the prosecution and defence cases before they make their decision. Ashworth and Redmayne (2005) question whether this predictive test is more appropriate than a test of 'intrinsic merits' of the evidence, and Sanders (1994) was clear that he believed a better test would be whether a particular jury or bench ought to convict. The CPS does not review the case only once, but must keep the decision to carry on with a case continually under review—should a single test of 'a realistic prospect of conviction' be applied at whatever stage in the criminal process?

The second task for the Crown Prosecutor is to apply the 'public interest' criterion. The Code **[3:6]** was revised to list more clearly the factors which tend in favour of, and those which tend against, a prosecution. Could the required balancing act be more clearly expressed? Ashworth and Fionda (1994), commenting on the subtle relationship between the Code and the Home Office circular on the cautioning of offenders, concluded that '[i]t is desirable that all parts of the system should have a coherent policy, but who should call the tune?' (at page 903). Narey's answer was that the police should—he concluded that 'the scope to discontinue cases in the public interest on the grounds that the offence is not serious or the likely penalty is trivial should be removed' in order that the decision on what type of offending behaviour is suitable for prosecution would be once again one for the police (1997, at page 14). However, Glidewell **[3:2]** advised that this was too sweeping a reform. The tension between the respective roles of police and prosecutor lives on: the police may issue a formal caution, but, as we shall see, the CPS decide on conditional cautions.

The CPS relies on the police for its information. This is a particular problem where the defendant intends to plead guilty. The file may be very small and the CPS have little information on which to assess the factors relevant to the public interest criterion. The file may also exaggerate the police construction of the case against the suspect—for example, the extent to which the suspect confessed. One way to alleviate this problem is to provide the CPS with material from other sources. In the early 1990s, the Probation Service (see Chapter 10) introduced Public Interest Case Assessment (PICA) units in a number of areas. These units provided information for the CPS in cases where there might be personal or other circumstances that might justify the discontinuance of a prosecution on the public interest factors in the Code for Crown Prosecutors. Whilst Crisp, Whittaker, and Harris (1995) suggested that such schemes were very useful in providing the CPS with verified and relevant information about a defendant's version of events, their research also revealed the difficulty in assessing cost-effectiveness in criminal justice initiatives. In his review of an interesting book by Drakeford, Haines, Cotton, and Octigan, Morgan **[3:8]** uses the decline of PICA units to show how funding issues in a 'non-joined-up' criminal justice system lead to misguided decision making. The problems are doubtless compounded by the privatization of bail hostels: in 2007 ClearSprings won a national contract to provide (see Probation Circular 33/2007 for further details) bail accommodation and support, but at the time of writing it is not clear how suspects (and their lawyers) will be able to access these easily.

The CPS has a duty to disclose to the defence unused material. What happens if it doesn't wish to do so? The Criminal Procedure and Investigations Act 1996 introduced a statutory scheme whereby the prosecution must make primary disclosure of all previously undisclosed material which, in the prosecution's view(!), might undermine the case for the prosecution. The defendant must then give a defence statement to the prosecution and the court, setting out in general terms the nature of the defence and the matters on which the defence take issue with the prosecution. The prosecution must then make a 'secondary' disclosure of 'all previously undisclosed material which might reasonably be expected to assist the accused's defence as disclosed by the defence statement'. This still applies to all investigations started before 4 April 2005, but Part 5 of the CJA 2003 made important changes: first, there is now a single, continuing, test for the disclosure of unused prosecution material. More importantly, in the case of trial on indictment, the defence now have a general duty to give the prosecution notice of the witnesses they propose to call (see Chapter 5).

Clearly, any failure to disclose relevant evidence undermines the right to a fair trial, and it can be argued that if relevant evidence has to be excluded in the public interest, then the prosecution should not be sustained (see also Lord Justice Scott's report into the Matrix Churchill ('arms to Iraq') trial, which collapsed for this reason (HCP 1995–96 115) and *Rowe and Davis v United Kingdom* (2000) 30 EHRR 1; *Edwards and Lewis v United Kingdom* [2003] Crim LR 890). Where the trial judge rules that the defendant cannot have a fair trial without disclosure, the prosecution have the stark choice: disclosure, or drop the prosecution.

Thus, in Gerry Good's case, the Crown Prosecutor must keep the evidence under review. She believes that the witness statements and Gerry's own unsatisfactory statements to the police are sufficient evidence against him, though she does ask the police to continue their investigations, particularly looking for the knife or evidence of blood stains. Applying the factors in the Code **[3:6]**, the CPS decides that the public interest suggests that the prosecu-tion should proceed. Paragraph 6.4 states that 'a prosecution is likely to be needed' where a weapon is used or if the defendant's previous convictions are relevant to the present offence. What does this mean? Gerry has previous convictions: in what way might they be relevant? In Gerry's case, none of the common public interest factors against prosecution is relevant, and so the case will proceed to trial.

The Crown Prosecutor must also decide what is the right offence with which to charge Gerry. In this case, they may well be uncertain whether to charge under section 18 or section 20 of the Offences Against the Persons Act (OAPA) 1861: section 18, wounding or grievous bodily harm with intent, maximum sentence life imprisonment; section 20, reckless griev-ous bodily harm, maximum sentence 5 years. The distinction is one of intent: the CPS will look for evidence of what Gerry intended when he allegedly hit Rosa. Note that the Code specifically warns against proceeding with a more serious charge simply to encourage the defendant to plead guilty to a lesser charge, an issue we will return to in Chapter 5 when discussing plea bargaining. Let us decide they decide the evidence supports a charge of an offence under section 18. You will see the indictment at the start of Chapter 7.

In our story, Gerry was granted bail by the magistrates. The Crime and Disorder Act 1998, section 51, provides that indictable cases will be 'sent' automatically for trial at the Crown Court, and Gerry Good will not have to return to the magistrates' court for com-mittal proceedings, although he will be able to apply to have the case dismissed. Before the case is listed for trial, there will be a 'plea and case management hearing' hearing (PCMH) in the Crown Court, within three or four weeks of the transfer. Its purpose is to ensure that all necessary steps have been taken in preparation for trial and sufficient information has been provided for a trial date to be arranged. Not long ago it was right to say that whilst Crown Prosecutors and Designated Case Workers frequently conducted proceedings in the magistrates' court, they did not generally have 'rights of audience' in the Crown Court and so had to brief counsel (instruct an independent barrister). This was been a longstanding sore with the CPS, which has maintained that both recruitment and performance standards would improve if it could conduct its own cases. The tide started to turn in its favour in 1993, when the Lord Chancellor's Advisory Committee on Legal Education and Conduct approved part of the Law Society's application for rights of audience by extending them to suitably qualified solicitors in private practice, but employed barristers and solicitors still did not have the right to appear in the higher courts. The argument against granting the CPS rights of audience is based on the view that the Bar needs to be composed of those who prosecute and those who defend. To give rights of audience to the CPS would fundamentally change the 'independent' Bar. Block, Corbett, and Peay **[3:10]** were critical of counsel's per-formance in many of their cases, and certainly the current system of last-minute briefing of counsel does suggest that the CPS should have greater responsibility at the trial stage. Block et al recommended that counsel should be obliged in the Bar Code of Practice to give advice to the CPS on receipt of the brief, and that Crown Prosecutors of a certain specified degree of seniority should have rights of audience in the Crown Court and the right of judicial appointment. Narey (1997) concluded that pre-trial hearings would become more effect-ive if conducted by Crown Prosecutors, who should therefore be given rights of audience. Now employed solicitors with Higher Rights qualifications present some cases in the Crown Court. Employed barristers have also been granted limited higher court rights of audience. This has challenged the role of the independent Bar: we return to the subject of the proper role of the CPS in the final section of this chapter.

(iv) THE ATTORNEY-GENERAL AND THE DIRECTOR OF PUBLIC PROSECUTIONS

As the Prosecution of Offences Act 1985 makes clear **[3:1]**, the DPP is appointed by the Attorney-General (AG) (section 2) and discharges his functions under the superintendence of the AG (section 3). The AG at the time of writing is Baroness Scotland. The Attorney-General and her deputy, the Solicitor General, are the Government's chief legal advisers, advising on domestic and international law. The Attorney-General is also a Government Minister. They have, as well, important 'public interest' roles in relation to criminal cases, superintending the work of the Crown Prosecution Service, the Serious Fraud Office, and the Director of Public Prosecutions. More specifically, the AG's consent is required to prosecute certain offences, and the Attorney-General may terminate criminal proceedings on indictment before a judge and jury by the entry of a *nolle prosequi*. This puts an end to the prosecution, rather like a stay on proceedings. Prosecutors can discontinue, withdraw or offer no evidence in their cases, but only the Attorney-General may enter a *nolle*. The Attorney-General's discretion is extremely wide and cannot be questioned by the courts; it is used where there is no other way of ending proceedings (the AG's website states that the most common reason is the ill health of a defendant). All appeals against unduly lenient sentences (see **[7:18]** and **[9:13]**) are done in the name of the AG, and it is the AG who, under section 36 of the Criminal Justice Act 1972, may seek the opinion of the Court of Appeal on a point of law which has arisen in the case when someone who has been tried on indictment has been acquitted. **[3:9]** is merely a Government consultation paper but it reflects what appears to be a genuine consultation. There may be significant change in the role of the AG in the near future.

The DPP's post, on the other hand, is less overtly political and controversial. Perhaps the Attorney-General should simply 'lose' her criminal justice roles to the DPP who would be answerable to Parliament and to the courts.

(v) EVALUATION

For Lord Justice Auld **[1:5]** an essential in preparing for trial is 'a strong, independent, and adequately resourced prosecutor in control of the case at least from the point of charge'. How can we measure whether Crown Prosecutors live up to this? Initially, we could consider whether the CPS is inclined to pursue weak cases, or whether it drops too many cases that should have been pursued. Whilst there can be no cut-and-dried measure of success, we can try to measure it in a number of different ways (see Ashworth and Redmayne (2005) for a more detailed analysis). First, the acquittal rate: perhaps those who are acquitted should not have been prosecuted.

TABLE 3.1 Crown Court acquittals

	Acquittals of those who plead not guilty	Acquittals by the jury after trial
1993	58%	42%
1997	60%	40%
2001	66%	43%
2005	65%	Not published separately

Source: Criminal Statistics 1997, 2001 (paragraphs 6.32 and 6.34), Criminal Statistics 2005 (Table 2.10)

But as we saw in section (i) above, it is difficult to predict the outcome of cases, especially without a clear knowledge of the defence case. These figures do not necessarily mean that all those acquitted by a jury after a trial should not have been tried in the first place. We will attempt to evaluate jury decision making in Chapter 8. The CPS itself prefers to advertise the conviction rate (which according to their Annual Report 2006–07, page 6) rose from 78.6 per cent during 2003–04 to 80.4 per cent in 2004–05, 82.3 per cent in 2005–06, and 83.7 per cent in 2006–07. This of course reflects the increasing proportion of defendants who plead guilty: jury trial is relatively rare: see Chapter 8.

Secondly, we can look at the discontinuance rate. Crisp and Moxon (1994) found a termination rate of between 10 per cent and 20 per cent. Glidewell **[3:2]**, pointing out a discontinuation rate of 12 per cent of cases, states that there is evidence that the discontinuance rate varies greatly with types of offence, with (worryingly) the highest discontinuance rates for charges of violence against the person and criminal damage. Since then the discontinuance rate has continued to fall slightly, but the CPS now put more emphasis on 'unsuccessful outcomes', which represent all outcomes other than a conviction, i.e. discontinuances and withdrawals, discharged committals, dismissals and acquittals, and what they call 'administrative finalizations'.

TABLE 3.2 Unsuccessful outcomes as a % of all outcome

2003/04	21.4%
2004/05	19.6%
2005/06	17.7%
2006/07	16.3%

Source: CPS Annual Report 2006/07, page 6

It is not clear whether these 'unsuccessful outcomes' are 'successes' or 'failures'—is the CPS successfully weeding out weak cases or should they have been weeded out sooner? Since the public interest factors specified for police cautioning are similar to those in the Code for Crown Prosecutors **[3:6]**, it is curious that so many cases remain in the system to be able to be discontinued by the CPS. Whether the CPS adequately manages the discontinuance process is another question—Cretney and Davis (1996), for example, found evidence of a tendency to blame women who withdraw their complaints against their violent partners, concluding that there is a serious dislocation between the interests of domestic assault victims and the goals pursued by the CPS. Clearly closer working between police and CPS is designed to reduce the discontinuance rate.

A third measure of success (or failure) is the number of judge-directed acquittals in the Crown Court. Here we must distinguish between directed acquittals (where the judge rules that the prosecution has not established a case to answer) and ordered acquittals (where the prosecution offers no evidence). As Block, Corbett, and Peay (1993) **[3:10]** made clear, neither measure is straightforward. However, they were able to conclude that three-quarters of directed acquittals were definitely or possibly foreseeable, and some criticism of the CPS was clearly merited. According to the Judicial and Court Statistics 2006, during 2006, 59 per cent (16,982) of the defendants who pleaded not guilty (28,821) in the Crown Court were acquitted, representing 21 per cent of the total 80,947 dealt with who recorded a plea. Of those 16,982, 58 per cent were discharged by the judge, 10 per cent were acquitted on the direction of the judge, 1 per cent were otherwise acquitted and 30 per cent were acquitted by a jury. It would be very useful to have more research on the reasons why so many juries were discharged by the judge.

The relationship of the CPS with the police remains problematic. At exactly what point does the CPS take over? Under the Prosecution of Offences Act 1985, section 3(2)(e) **[3:1]** it is the duty of the DPP to give advice to police forces on matters relating to criminal offences. However, the police seem reluctant to seek advice in specific cases. Moxon and Crisp (quoted in the Royal Commission on Criminal Justice (1993) at page 72) suggested that the police asked for prior advice in only 4 per cent of cases. The Royal Commission concluded that guidelines should be formulated to ensure that advice is sought consistently in more complex or serious cases.

Is it feasible to involve the CPS at the beginning of investigations? Should the CPS have greater control over the provision of information? Should they be able to compel further investigations? The Royal Commission on Criminal Justice (1993) **[1:4]**, with one dissent, fudged the issue by deciding that better and more formal consultation, and earlier liaison with the police, would resolve the problems. The Glidewell Report **[3:2]** recommended a single integrated unit, a 'Criminal Justice Unit'—a CPS unit with some police staff—so that the CPS could assume responsibility for 'the prosecution process immediately following charge'. Yet Auld **[1:5]** recommended that the CPS should determine charge in all but minor, routine offences. Putting the CPS back into the police station may lead to a more effective system, but it raises other concerns. For example, since the police remain in control of the information that reaches the CPS, will the CPS lose much of the 'independence' which is also crucial? More importantly, to what extent does the CPS working closely with the police limit their role as 'independent' reviewers of police decision making?

This discussion has concerned the early involvement of the CPS in investigations. It is also interesting to consider its involvement in the later stages of a prosecution. We have seen that the CPS (largely as an economy measure but also in order to create better job satisfaction for good lawyers) is increasingly presenting cases in the Crown Court. Then there is the question of the prosecution's involvement in the sentencing process. We will see in Chapter 7 that the prosecution currently plays a very small role at the sentencing stage. But this is changing: see the sentencing manual which now appears on the CPS website. Currently the prosecutor is likely to remind the judge of the facts of the case, check that he or she has the latest version of the defendant's previous convictions, the pre-sentence report, and is aware of relevant law. But the prosecution does not call for a particular sentence. If they did, the defence would be able to respond with a more focused plea in mitigation. Would the effect be an increase or a decrease in sentencing levels? Defence lawyers tend to fear that prosecutors would 'talk' up sentencing levels, but it might well be that they would be conscious of the costs of imprisonment and lengths of imprisonment might come down. We return to sentencing issues in Chapter 7.

In Chapter 2 we mentioned the police involvement in juvenile liaison bodies and multi-agency panels. Gelsthorpe and Giller **[3:11]** questioned the relationship of the CPS with multi-agency panels, arguing that it should move 'from operational philosophy to professional ideology'—it needed an articulated set of objectives that could be measured and monitored. The first step towards this was taken in 1993 when the CPS issued its Statement of Purpose and Values. Since then many initiatives have been taken to strengthen its profile in the criminal justice system. There is no doubting that the CPS is now a key player. Yet the CPS cannot breach police control unless it has real powers. As McConville et al **[3:12]** argued, the CPS is a 'police-dependent body'. Sanders (1987) commented on the difficulties of grafting an inquisitorial element onto an adversarial system. Today, as the police and CPS work ever more closely together, you should consider whether the balance of power is weighted to heavily in favour of prosecutors. We look at this in Chapter 5, when considering the role of defence lawyers.

Meanwhile, in Chapter 4 we look at those prosecutions that are not initiated by the police. This raises the question whether greater consistency would be achieved if prosecutions initiated by such bodies as the Environment Agency were brought under the CPS umbrella.

FURTHER READING

Annual Reports of the Crown Prosecution Service, and of HM Inspectorate of the Crown Prosecution Service

Ashworth, A and Fionda, J, 'The New Code for Crown Prosecutors: Prosecution, Accountability and the Public Interest' [1994] Crim LR 894

Ashworth, A and Redmayne, M, *The Criminal Justice Process: an evaluative study* (3rd edition, 2005) Oxford UP

Block, B, Corbett, C, and Peay, J, 'Ordered and Directed Acquittals in the Crown Court' (1993) RCCJ Research Study No 15, HMSO

Cretney, A and Davis, G, 'Prosecuting "Domestic" Assault' [1996] Crim LR 162

Crisp, D and Moxon, D, 'Case screening by the CPS: how and why are cases terminated' (1994) HORS No 137, HMSO

Crisp, D, Whittaker, C, and Harris, J, 'Public Interest Case Assessment Schemes' (1995) HORS No 138, HMSO

Hall Williams, J E, *The Role of the Prosecutor* (1988) Avebury

Hilsom, C, 'Discretion to Prosecute and Judicial Review' [1993] Crim LR 739

Home Office, 'An Independent Prosecution Service for England and Wales' (1983) Cmnd 9074, HMSO.

Mansfield, G and Peay, J, *The Director of Public Prosecutions: Principles and Practices for the Crown Prosecutor* (1987) Tavistock

Mills, B, 'The Code for Crown Prosecutors' (1994) 144 NLJ 899

Sanders, A, 'Constructing the Case for the Prosecution' (1987) 14 Journal of Law & Society 229

Sanders, A, 'The Silent Code' (1994) 144 NLJ 946

DOCUMENTS

[3:1] Prosecution of Offences Act 1985 (as amended)
Sections 1–3; 10; 16

1 The Crown Prosecution Service

(1) There shall be a prosecuting service for England and Wales (to be known as the "Crown Prosecution Service") consisting of—

    (a) the Director of Public Prosecutions, who shall be head of the Service;

    (b) the Chief Crown Prosecutors, designated under subsection (4) below, each of whom shall be the member of the Service responsible to the Director for supervising the operation of the Service in his area; and

    (c) the other staff appointed by the Director under this section.

(2) The Director shall appoint such staff for the Service as, with the approval of the Treasury as to numbers, remuneration and other terms and conditions of service, he considers necessary for the discharge of his functions.

(3) The Director may designate any member of the Service who has a general qualification (within the meaning of section 71 of the Courts and Legal Services Act 1990) for the purposes of this subsection, and any person so designated shall be known as a Crown Prosecutor.

(4) The Director shall divide England and Wales into areas and, for each of those areas, designate a Crown Prosecutor for the purposes of this subsection and any person so designated shall be known as a Chief Crown Prosecutor.

(5) The Director may, from time to time, vary the division of England and Wales made for the purposes of subsection (4) above.

(6) Without prejudice to any functions which may have been assigned to him in his capacity as a member of the Service, every Crown Prosecutor shall have all the powers of the Director as to the institution and conduct of proceedings but shall exercise those powers under the direction of the Director.

(7) Where any enactment (whenever passed)—

    (a) prevents any step from being taken without the consent of the Director or without his consent or the consent of another; or

    (b) requires any step to be taken by or in relation to the Director;

    any consent given by or, as the case may be, step taken by or in relation to, a Crown Prosecutor shall be treated, for the purposes of that enactment, as given by or, as the case may be, taken by or in relation to the Director.

2 The Director of Public Prosecutions

(1) The Director of Public Prosecutions shall be appointed by the Attorney General.

(2) The Director must be a person who has a 10 year general qualification, within the meaning of section 71 of the Courts and Legal Services Act 1990.

(3) There shall be paid to the Director such remuneration as the Attorney General may, with the approval of the Treasury, determine.

3 Functions of the Director

(1) The Director shall discharge his functions under this or any other enactment under the superintendence of the Attorney General.

(2) It shall be the duty of the Director, subject to any provisions contained in the Criminal Justice Act 1987—

  (a) to take over the conduct of all criminal proceedings, other than specified proceedings, instituted on behalf of a police force (whether by a member of that force or by any other person);

  (aa) to take over the conduct of any criminal proceedings instituted by an immigration officer (as defined for the purposes of the Immigration Act 1971) acting in his capacity as such an officer;

  (b) to institute and have the conduct of criminal proceedings in any case where it appears to him that—
  (i) the importance or difficulty of the case makes it appropriate that proceedings should be instituted by him; or
  (ii) it is otherwise appropriate for proceedings to be instituted by him;

  (ba) to institute and have the conduct of any criminal proceedings in any case where the proceedings relate to the subject-matter of a report a copy of which has been sent to him under paragraph 23 or 24 of Schedule 3 to the Police Reform Act 2002 (c. 30) (reports on investigations into conduct of persons serving with the police);

  (c) to take over the conduct of all binding over proceedings instituted on behalf of a police force (whether by a member of that force or by any other person);

  (d) to take over the conduct of all proceedings begun by summons issued under section 3 of the Obscene Publications Act 1959 (forfeiture of obscene articles);

  (e) to give, to such extent as he considers appropriate, advice to police forces on all matters relating to criminal offences;

  (ea) to have the conduct of any extradition proceedings;

  (eb) to give, to such extent as he considers appropriate, and to such persons as he considers appropriate, advice on any matters relating to extradition proceedings or proposed extradition proceedings;

  (ec) to give, to such extent as he considers appropriate, advice to immigration officers on matters relating to criminal offences;

  (f) to appear for the prosecution, when directed by the court to do so, on any appeal under—
  (i) section 1 of the Administration of Justice Act 1960 (appeal from the High Court in criminal cases);
  (ii) Part I or Part II of the Criminal Appeal Act 1968 (appeals from the Crown Court to the criminal division of the Court of Appeal and thence to the House of Lords); or
  (iii) section 108 of the Magistrates' Courts Act 1980 (right of appeal to Crown Court) as it applies, by virtue of subsection (5) of section 12 of the Contempt of Court Act 1981, to orders made under section 12 (contempt of magistrates' courts); and

  (fa) to have the conduct of applications for orders under section 1C of the Crime and Disorder Act 1998 (orders made on conviction of certain offences) and section 14A of the Football Spectators Act 1989 (banning orders made on conviction of certain offences);

  (faa) where it appears to him appropriate to do so, to have the conduct of applications made by him for orders under section 14B of the Football Spectators Act 1989 (banning orders made on complaint);

  (fb) where it appears to him appropriate to do so, to have the conduct of applications under section 1CA(3) of the Crime and Disorder Act 1998 for the variation or discharge of orders made under section 1C of that Act;

  (fc) where it appears to him appropriate to do so, to appear on any application under section 1CA of that Act made by a person subject to an order under section 1C of that Act for the variation or discharge of the order.

(ff) to discharge such duties as are conferred on him by, or in relation to, Part 5 or 8 of the Proceeds of Crime Act 2002 (c. 29) (civil recovery of the proceeds etc. of unlawful conduct, civil recovery investigations and disclosure orders in relation to confiscation investigations);

(g) to discharge such other functions as may from time to time be assigned to him by the Attorney General in pursuance of this paragraph.

(3) In this section—

"the court" means—

(a) in the case of an appeal to or from the criminal division of the Court of Appeal, that division;

(b) in the case of an appeal from a Divisional Court of the Queen's Bench Division, the Divisional Court; and

(c) in the case of an appeal against an order of a magistrates' court, the Crown Court;

"police force" means any police force maintained by a police authority under the Police Act 1996, the National Crime Squad and any other body of constables for the time being specified by order made by the Secretary of State for the purposes of this section; and

"specified proceedings" means proceedings which fall within any category for the time being specified by order made by the Attorney General for the purposes of this section.

(4) The power to make orders under subsection (3) above shall be exercisable by statutory instrument subject to annulment in pursuance of a resolution of either House of Parliament.

. . .

10 Guidelines for Crown Prosecutors

(1) The Director shall issue a Code for Crown Prosecutors giving guidance on general principles to be applied by them—

(a) in determining, in any case—

(i) whether proceedings for an offence should be instituted or, where proceedings have been instituted, whether they should be discontinued; or

(ii) what charges should be preferred; and

(b) in considering, in any case, representations to be made by them to any magistrates' court about the mode of trial suitable for that case.

(2) The Director may from time to time make alterations in the Code.

(3) The provisions of the Code shall be set out in the Director's report under section 9 of this Act for the year in which the Code is issued; and any alteration in the Code shall be set out in his report under that section for the year in which the alteration is made.

16 Defence costs

(1) Where—

(a) an information laid before a justice of the peace for any area, charging any person with an offence, is not proceeded with;

(b) a magistrates' court inquiring into an indictable offence as examining justices determines not to commit the accused for trial;

(c) a magistrates' court dealing summarily with an offence dismisses the information;

that court or, in a case falling within paragraph (a) above, a magistrates' court for that area, may make an order in favour of the accused for a payment to be made out of central funds in respect of his costs (a "defendant's costs order").

(2) Where—

    (a) any person is not tried for an offence for which he has been indicted or committed for trial; or

    (aa) a notice of transfer is given under a relevant transfer provision but a person in relation to whose case it is given is not tried on a charge to which it relates; or

    (b) any person is tried on indictment and acquitted on any count in the indictment;

the Crown Court may make a defendant's costs order in favour of the accused.

(3) Where a person convicted of an offence by a magistrates' court appeals to the Crown Court under section 108 of the Magistrates' Courts Act 1980 (right of appeal against conviction or sentence) and, in consequence of the decision on appeal—

    (a) his conviction is set aside; or

    (b) a less severe punishment is awarded;

the Crown Court may make a defendant's costs order in favour of the accused.

(4) Where the Court of Appeal—

    (a) allows an appeal under Part I of the Criminal Appeal Act 1968 against—

        (i) conviction;

        (ii) a verdict of not guilty by reason of insanity; or

        (iii) a finding under the Criminal Procedure (Insanity) Act 1964 that the appellant is under a disability, or that he did the act or made the omission charged against him;

    (aa) directs under section 8(1B) of the Criminal Appeal Act 1968 the entry of a judgment and verdict of acquittal;

    (b) on an appeal under that Part against conviction—

        (i) substitutes a verdict of guilty of another offence;

        (ii) in a case where a special verdict has been found, orders a different conclusion on the effect of that verdict to be recorded; or

        (iii) is of the opinion that the case falls within paragraph (a) or (b) of section 6(1) of that Act (cases where the court substitutes a finding of insanity or unfitness to plead); or

    (c) on an appeal under that Part against sentence, exercises its powers under section 11(3) of that Act (powers where the court considers that the appellant should be sentenced differently for an offence for which he was dealt with by the court below);

    (d) allows, to any extent, an appeal under s 16A of that Act (appeal against order made in cases of insanity or unfitness to plead)

the court may make a defendant's costs order in favour of the accused.

(4A) The court may also make a defendant's costs order in favour of the accused on an appeal under section 9(11) of the Criminal Justice Act 1987 (appeals against orders or rulings at preparatory hearings).

(5) Where—

    (a) any proceedings in a criminal cause or matter are determined before a Divisional Court of the Queen's Bench Division;

    (b) the House of Lords determines an appeal, or application for leave to appeal, from such a Divisional Court in a criminal cause or matter;

    (c) the Court of Appeal determines an application for leave to appeal to the House of Lords under Part II of the Criminal Appeal Act 1968; or

    (d) the House of Lords determines an appeal, or application for leave to appeal, under Part II of that Act;

the court may make a defendant's costs order in favour of the accused.

(6) A defendant's costs order shall, subject to the following provisions of this section, be for the payment out of central funds, to the person in whose favour the order is made, of such amount as the court considers reasonably sufficient to compensate him for any expenses properly incurred by him in the proceedings.

(7) Where a court makes a defendant's costs order but is of the opinion that there are circumstances which make it inappropriate that the person in whose favour the order is made should recover the full amount mentioned in subsection (6) above, the court shall—

(a) assess what amount would, in its opinion, be just and reasonable; and

(b) specify that amount in the order.

(9) Subject to subsection (7) above, the amount to be paid out of central funds in pursuance of a defendant's costs order shall—

(c) be specified in the order, in any case where the court considers it appropriate for the amount to be so specified and the person in whose favour the order is made agrees the amount; and

(d) in any other case, be determined in accordance with regulations made by the Lord Chancellor for the purposes of this section.

(10) Subsection (6) above shall have effect, in relation to any case falling within subsection (1)(a) or (2)(a) above, as if for the words "in the proceedings" there were substituted the words "in or about the defence".

(11) Where a person ordered to be retried is acquitted at his retrial, the costs which may be ordered to be paid out of central funds under this section shall include—

(a) any costs which, at the original trial, could have been ordered to be so paid under this section if he had been acquitted; and

(b) if no order was made under this section in respect of his expenses on appeal, any sums for the payment of which such an order could have been made.

(12) In subsection (2)(aa) "relevant transfer provision" means—

(a) section 4 of the Criminal Justice Act 1987, or

(b) section 53 of the Criminal Justice Act 1991.

[3:2] Review of the Crown Prosecution Service
(1998) Chaired by Sir Iain Glidewell (at page 4 of the summary)

How the prosecution process works at present

13 In order to present the case for the prosecution in court the CPS needs to have a file containing the evidence and other relevant information, including any criminal record the defendant may have. While it is for the police to obtain the evidence as part of the process of investigation, in our view the assembly of the file is part of the conduct of the proceedings for which the CPS is, or should be, responsible. Until now, however, the police have continued to compile prosecution files in a special unit often called an Administrative Support Unit (ASU). The most critical point in the flow of case papers between the investigating officer and the CPS prosecutor in court is at the interface between the ASU and the CPS Branch office.

14 Another cause of discord between the police and the CPS stems from the power of the CPS to discontinue a prosecution. One of a CPS lawyer's most important tasks is to review the evidence in the file in order to decide whether it justifies the charge laid by the police, applying criteria set out in the 'Code for Crown Prosecutors'. If the evidence is not sufficient, the lawyer may either substitute a lesser

charge ('downgrading') or discontinue the prosecution altogether. The exercise of this power, which was newly-given in 1986, was resented at that time by some police officers, but most now recognise and accept that it is a valuable provision which should ensure that only those prosecutions proceed to court in which there is an appropriate chance of a conviction in accordance with the Code. This is a safeguard not only for defendants who should not have been charged but also for the public purse.

How the CPS has performed

15 Our Terms of Reference require us to 'assess whether the CPS has contributed to the falling number of convictions for recorded crime'. One thing is clear: the CPS is not concerned with the vast majority of recorded crime. The CPS is responsible for the conduct of all criminal proceedings after there has been a charge by the police or a summons. In 1996, of the crimes recorded by the police (nearly 5 million), only one in every nine (576,000) resulted in a charge or summons. Recorded crimes do not include the large number of motoring offences, so the CPS is concerned with only one out of nine recorded crimes.

16 From there onwards our task becomes more difficult. To carry out such an assessment we have had to examine the available statistics, which has not proved an easy matter. The Home Office, the Court Service and the CPS each produce statistics relating to criminal prosecutions and often the figures within apparently similar parameters are inconsistent with each other. It was to be expected that when the CPS came into existence convictions would fall as a proportion of total cases simply as a result of the CPS properly exercising their new power to discontinue some cases. However, figures produced by the CPS have shown that in recent years the proportion of cases in the Crown Court resulting in conviction has increased, but this trend differs from that shown by the figures published in the Judicial Statistics produced by the Court Service, which show a decline in convictions over the period 1985 to 1996. We have tried but failed to find an explanation for the disparity in the two sets of statistics. We cannot therefore say that the CPS figures are wrong. We have recommended that attempts are made to agree one set of figures.

17 Overall the CPS discontinues prosecutions in, on average, 12% of cases where the police have charged. The CPS Inspectorate have found, in their consideration of Branch performance, few decisions to discontinue which they considered wrong. However, there is some evidence that the average rate of discontinuance varies greatly between types of offence, with the highest discontinuance rates being for charges of violence against the person and criminal damage, and the lowest for motoring offences. This is clearly a matter for concern, the reasons for which must be investigated.

18 We have been specifically asked to comment on the proposal in the Narey Report that the CPS should no longer have the power to discontinue cases on certain public interest grounds, namely that the court is likely to impose a nominal penalty or that the loss involved is small. We have recommended that the proposal should not be adopted but that the incidence of discontinuance on these grounds should be rare. To that end we have also recommended a small amendment to the Code for Crown Prosecutors.

19 Charges are sometimes downgraded and such few statistics as are available seem to show that this happens most frequently with those which relate to serious crime, public order offences and road traffic accidents causing death. We have no evidence which proves that downgrading happens when it should not. Nonetheless, we suspect that inappropriate downgrading does occur and have recommended that cases of downgrading are specifically examined by the Inspectorate during visits to CPS Units. Both the police and the CPS are helped by the existence of guidance in the form of Charging Standards and whilst we approve their existence we have raised questions about the content of some of the standards. More information is needed about the reasons why charges are downgraded. We have recommended research to consider both this matter and discontinuance.

20 The CPS figures show that the proportion of those pleading Not Guilty in the Crown Court who were convicted increased between 1991–92 and 1996–97 to about 40%. We have, however, given particular consideration to the statistics relating to acquittals in the Crown Court. Both the CPS statistics and Judicial Statistics agree that in 1996 less than half of these were acquittals by a jury. In

other words, more than half of all acquittals in the Crown Court resulted from an order or direction of the judge. There are often good reasons why such an order or direction should be made—a vital witness may not appear to give evidence or may prove unreliable in the witness box—but nevertheless the statistic is a cause for concern. In our view, when the CPS has decided to proceed with a case after review, it is reasonable to expect that, unless a major witness is absent, the case will be strong enough to be put before a jury. We conclude that the performance of some parts of the CPS in this respect is not as good as it should be, and improvement is needed.

21 The overall conclusion from this study of the available statistics is that in various respects there has been the improvement in the effectiveness and efficiency of the prosecution process which was expected to result from the setting up of the CPS in 1986. Where the statistics show a recent improvement, that is often a recovery from a deterioration which took place in the years immediately after 1986. We do not place responsibility for this situation wholly on the CPS; in large part it stems from the failure of the police, the CPS and the courts to set overall objectives and agree the role and the responsibility of each in achieving those objectives.

22 Also under the heading 'How the CPS has performed' the Report contains a chapter describing the present state of the relationships between the CPS and the other agencies with whom it works and to whom it relates in the criminal justice system. The tensions between the police and the CPS which existed in the early years have been greatly eased, but in some places have not disappeared. There is still a tendency for each to blame the other if a prosecution file is incomplete or some other essential document missing, and, as a result, a case has to be adjourned. In order to establish their independence from the police after 1986, many in the CPS became isolationist, creating a rift in communication. In addition, many police ASUs are not functioning as effectively as they did when they were first created. As a result the CPS finds that it has to duplicate some of the work the ASU staff have done, in order to prepare a satisfactory prosecution file. It is important to seek a remedy for both problems.

23 There are frequent complaints by both magistrates and judges of inefficiency in case preparation or delay on the part of the CPS. Often the CPS is not the cause of the delay, but sometimes it properly has to accept the blame. Part of the problem lies with court listing practices, into which the CPS at present has no input. Timeliness is a most important aspect of the fair and effective prosecution of crime, but at present the magistrates' courts and the CPS have different, and often inconsistent, performance indicators for timeliness.

24 In the Crown Court, all cases are at present prosecuted by members of the Bar. Both judges and the Bar raised several issues on which action, either by the CPS or by government departments, is needed. They include a considerable disparity between the higher fees paid to defence counsel under the Legal Aid Scheme and those paid to prosecuting counsel briefed by the CPS; the issue of briefs being returned by counsel; problems arising from a shortage of CPS staff in the Crown Court, and a difficulty in Counsel obtaining fresh instructions while in court. These are all matters we address.

25 Finally in this part of the Report we consider the proper role of the CPS in relation to victims and witnesses, particularly its obligations arising out of the Victim's Charter.

26 Our assessment of the CPS is that it has the potential to become a lively, successful and esteemed part of the criminal justice system, but that, sadly, none of these adjectives applies to the Service as a whole at present. If the Service—by which we mean all the members of its staff—is to achieve its potential, it faces three challenges. Firstly, there must be a change in the priority given to the various levels of casework; the 'centre of gravity' must move from the bulk of relatively minor cases in the magistrates' court in order to concentrate on more serious crime, particularly the gravest types, in the Crown Court. Secondly, the overall organisation, the structure and the style of management of the CPS will have to change. Government has started this process by deciding that the CPS should in future be divided into 42 Areas, each headed by a Chief Crown Prosecutor. Each of these CCPs should be given as much freedom as possible to run his area in his own way, and he should suggest his staff to enable them to get on with the core job of prosecuting. Thirdly, the CPS must establish more clearly its position as an integral part of the criminal justice process. It is no longer the 'new kid on the block'.

The future of the CPS in the criminal justice system

27 The role of the CPS within the criminal justice system has not until now been spelt out and put into the context of its key objectives and related performance indicators. Nor have the relationships with the police and the courts been properly defined. At present neither the police nor the CPS have overall responsibility for the preparation of the case file. We have therefore recommended that the CPS should take responsibility for:

- the prosecution process immediately following charge;
- arranging the initial hearing in the Magistrates' Court;
- witness availability, witness warning and witness care.

...

The future organisation of the CPS

36 On coming into office in 1997 the Government announced that the CPS was to be reorganised into a structure of 42 Areas, each to be coterminous with a police force. Our Terms of Reference include that reorganisation as the basis for our work. It would be possible to make a change to a 42 Area structure with minimal disturbance to the current Branch and Headquarters organisation. However, this would not achieve the devolution which we believe is essential. Our view is that the reorganisation should be taken as an opportunity for a genuinely new start, building on the achievements of the past 12 years but creating a form of management at both national and local levels which is different in both structure and style.

37 The objectives of the changes that we propose are to:

- set up a 'decentralised national service' through the genuine devolution of as much responsibility and accountability as possible to the CCPs in the new Areas;
- redefine the role of the Headquarters organisation;
- ensure that all but the most senior lawyers in the CPS, including CCPs, spend much more of their time prosecuting;
- improve the career structure for all staff;
- give each CCP responsibility for managing the administrative support and services in his Area, subject only to the constraints of nationally based accounting and data processing systems;
- reduce the bureaucracy by prioritising the information flows and limiting the Headquarters' support functions to a few key advisory services.

...

63 In the past two years the CPS has established an Inspectorate, which publishes reports both on standards of casework in Areas or Branches, and on specific themes. We are impressed by the quality of these reports, but we believe and recommend that the Inspectorate should be made more independent by having a lay Chairman appointed by the Attorney-General and a number of lay members, and that its remit should be widened. We make proposals to achieve these aims.

[3:3] *R v Chief Constable of Kent County Constabulary, ex p L; R v DPP, ex p B*
[1993] 1 All ER 756

Two separate cases were decided together. The applicant L was a 16-year-old boy who was charged with assault occasioning actual bodily harm. Although the criteria for cautioning were made out in his case, it was decided that the circumstances of the case were too serious for a caution to be appropriate. The applicant B was a 12-year-old girl who was charged with theft. She had not been cautioned as she had not admitted the offence. Both applicants unsuccessfully sought judicial review of the decision to prosecute them.

Watkins LJ (at page 767):

The point has not previously arisen for determination. That probably is because the CPS are comparatively new to the prosecution process. They have unquestionably the sole power to decide whether a prosecution should proceed. They are entirely dominant in that very important respect and all the erstwhile corresponding power of the police has been stripped away. The CPS are the prosecutor and the police are the initiators of criminal proceedings which may, or may not, dependent upon the decision of the CPS, be disposed of by the courts. The power of the CPS includes that of referring a case back to the police for a caution to be substituted for the continuance of proceedings.

I have come to the conclusion that if judicial review lies in relation to current criminal proceedings, in contrast to a failure to take any action against a person suspected of a criminal offence, it lies against the body which has the last and decisive word, the CPS.

A refusal to prosecute or even possibly to caution by the police is another matter. In that event the police may be vulnerable to judicial review, but only upon a basis which, as the cases show, is rather severely circumscribed.

The extent of that basis appears in the well-known judgments of Lord Denning MR, Salmon and Edmund Davies LJJ in *R v Metropolitan Police Comr, ex p Blackburn* [1968] 1 All ER 763, [1968] 2 QB 118. In a later case, *R v Metropolitan Police Comr, ex p Blackburn (No 3)* [1973] 1 All ER 324 at 331, [1973] QB 241 at 254, Lord Denning MR, referring to a failure to enforce the law, stated: '... the police have a discretion with which the courts will not interfere. There might, however, be extreme cases in which he [the commissioner] was not carrying out his duty. And then we would'.

In *R v General Council of the Bar, ex p Percival* [1990] 3 All ER 137 at 152, [1991] 1 QB 212 at 234, in giving the judgment of the court, I stated having quoted from, inter alia, *ex p Blackburn* [1968] 1 All ER 763, [1968] 2 QB 118:

> Reference was also made by counsel...to a passage in de Smith's Judicial Review of Administrative Action 94th edn, 1980 pp 549–550, to the effect that the discretion of a prosecuting authority though broad is not unreviewable. In our view such discretion is plainly reviewable but the question is whether the limits of review should be as strict as those contended for by the Bar Council. Much will depend, we think, on the powers of the body subject to review, the procedures which it is required to follow and on the way in which a particular proceeding has been conducted; there is potentially an almost infinite variety of circumstances. We do not think it right that strict defined limits should be set to the judicial review of a body which can broadly be described as a prosecuting authority. Each case must be considered with due regard to the powers, functions and procedures of the body concerned and the manner in which it has dealt (or not dealt) with the particular complaint or application.

That was obviously not intended to indicate a lesser limitation for judicial review of the police than appears in *ex p Blackburn*. The statement relates to other bodies with very different responsibilities and discretions to which perhaps a less rigorous approach to judicial review might apply.

In the present cases it is not inaction by the police which is complained of but the positive action of charging the two applicants and thus commencing criminal proceedings instead of in L's case cautioning him and in the case of B taking no action against her whatsoever, as well, of course, as the failure of the CPS to discontinue proceedings in both cases.

It seems to me that a decision to discontinue proceedings by the CPS can be equated with a decision by the police not to prosecute and is, therefore, open to judicial review only upon the restricted basis available to someone, assuming he has locus standi, seeking to challenge a decision by the police. Accordingly, that situation does not require further to be addressed in this judgment.

I have come to the conclusion that, in respect of juveniles, the discretion of the CPS to continue or to discontinue criminal proceedings is reviewable by this court but only where it can be demonstrated that the decision was made regardless of or clearly contrary to a settled policy of the Director of Public Prosecutions evolved in the public interest, for example the policy of cautioning juveniles, a policy which the CPS are bound to apply, where appropriate, to the exercise of their discretion to continue or discontinue criminal proceedings. But I envisage that it will be only rarely that a defendant could succeed in showing that a decision was fatally flawed in such a manner as that.

The policy of cautioning, instead of prosecuting, has for some time now been well settled and plays a prominent part in the process of decision-making both by the police and by the CPS when consideration has properly to be given to whether, in any individual case, there should be (a) no action taken or (b) a caution delivered or (c) a prosecution and thereafter (d) a continuance or discontinuance of criminal proceedings.

That policy applied, obviously, to the case of L. It did not apply to the case of B because cautioning was not for her an option. The policy, which can, I think, rightly be so called, which is applicable to her is another. It is that which is far more generally expressed, that is to say that a prosecution should not occur unless it is required in the public interest, regard being given to the stigma of a conviction which can cause irreparable harm to the future prospects of a young person and to his previous character, parental attitude and the likelihood of the offence being repeated: see the Attorney-General's 1983 guidelines.

I find it very difficult to envisage, with regard to that policy, a circumstance, fraud or dishonesty apart possible, which would allow of a challenge to a decision to prosecute or to continue proceedings unless it could be demonstrated, in the case of a juvenile, that there had been either a total disregard of the policy or, contrary to it, a lack of inquiry into the circumstances and background of that person, previous offences and general character and so on, by the prosecutor and later by the CPS. But here too I envisage the possibility of showing that such disregard had happened as unlikely. Therefore, although the CPS decision may in principle be reviewed, in practice it is rarely likely to be successfully reviewed.

I have confined my views as to the availability of judicial review of a CPS decision not to discontinue a prosecution to the position of juveniles because, of course, the present cases involve only juveniles. My view as to the position of adults, on the other hand, in this respect is that judicial review of a decision not to discontinue a prosecution is unlikely to be available. the danger of opening too wide the door of review of the discretion to continue a prosecution is manifest and such review, if it exists, must, therefore, be confined to very narrow limits. Juveniles and the policy with regard to them are, in my view, in a special position.

[3:4] Uglow, S, Dart, A, Bottomley, A, and Hale, C, 'Cautioning Juveniles—Multi-Agency Impotence'
[1992] Crim LR 632 (at page 640)

This article discusses the role of the less formal parts of the criminal justice system, here Kent's local multi-agency Juvenile Offender Liaison Team (JOLT), in the light of the decision in *R v Chief Constable of Kent, ex parte L* [see **[3:2]**].

For those interested in juvenile justice, this case could be significant for a different set of reasons. The Home Office guidelines on cautioning can be seen as combining legal criteria, such as an admission of guilt, sufficiency of evidence and the seriousness of the offence, with concerns about the welfare of the offender and presumptions against the prosecution of juveniles and the likely consequences should they be convicted. The Home Office guidelines encourage consultation with agencies such as JOLT largely to enable the police better to evaluate the issues about the welfare of the offender. What is interesting about this case is the extent to which those issues went largely unmentioned. The arguments presented in court as well as Watkins LJ's judgment concentrated on the legal relationship between the decision making agencies (who has 'the last and decisive word?') and the reasonableness of the interpretation of one of the criteria, namely the seriousness of the offence.

The presumption against prosecution provided the background to the applicant's ability to challenge the decision to prosecute. However, the decision itself was defended by the police and the CPS arguing that the procedures followed allowed for separate decision making processes and a full examination of the criteria laid down in the Home Office guidelines. This concentration on the processes used to come to the decision rather than on the consequences of the decision (which is symptomatic of judicial review in general) can be seen as making the welfare of the juvenile secondary to the considerations of due process. It is interesting to note that the one agency most directly concerned with welfare and least involved with legal process, namely JOLT, was considered by the court only insofar as its actions affected those of the police and the CPS. The decision and power to prosecute was left in the hands of those agencies most closely associated with criminal justice than juvenile welfare.

This situation should not be surprising. The role of the CPS in the prosecution process is governed by statute and the police have a well-established duty to protect the public against crime. JOLT and similar agencies across the country have no statutory basis and owe their existence to the co-operation of many agencies involved with juveniles and juvenile offenders at a local level. Thus their basis cannot be derived from the social services; or education departments' concern for the welfare of minors, the police concern with crime prevention or the probation service's concern for the rehabilitation of offenders. Rather multi-agency groups work within the spaces between and within the overlapping interests of the agencies involved with juveniles, playing a vital co-ordinating role. However, the indeterminacy of their position could be seen as a contributory factor in marginalising their role in the eyes of the law. It would appear that depending on circumstances, multi-agency teams are seen as appendages of the agencies with more clearly defined roles or with a statutory basis. In this case JOLT was seen merely as a part of the police and the CPS decision-making process, notwithstanding the high congruence rates between JOLT recommendations and subsequent police decisions. This concentration on the more formal criminal justice agencies could be in need of revision as informal approaches to criminal justice become increasingly common; for adults as well as for juveniles in reparation and mediation as well as simple diversion.

[3:5] *R v Croydon Justices, ex p Dean*
[1993] 3 All ER 129

The applicant and two others were arrested on suspicion of murdering a man who had been stabbed and killed in woodland. The applicant did not take part in the actual killing, but after it had taken place, he went to the scene of the crime with the others and helped them destroy the victim's car. He was interviewed by the police, agreed to be a prosecution witness and was released without charge. He was subsequently interviewed again and was told that he was a prosecution witness and had the protection of the police. After a conference with the police, the CPS decided that he should be charged under section 4 of the Criminal Law Act 1967 with assisting in the destruction of the victim's car, knowing it was evidence, with intent to impede the apprehension of the other defendants. He was charged and committed for trial, and then applied for judicial review to quash his committal to the Crown Court.

The Divisional Court held that, whereas ordinarily an application to quash a committal ought to be made to the Crown Court before the start of a trial, exceptionally a committal to stand trial which took place in breach of a promise that the defendant would not be prosecuted could be quashed where there was, as in this case, an abuse of process.

Staughton LJ (at page 135):

It is submitted on behalf of the Crown Prosecution Service that they alone are entitled, and bound, to decide who shall be prosecuted, at any rate in this category of case; and that the police had no authority and no right to tell Dean that he would not be prosecuted for any offence in connection with the murder; see the Prosecution of Offences Act 1985, s 3(2). I can readily accept that. I also accept that the point is one of constitutional importance. But I cannot accept the submission of Mr Collins that, in consequence, no such conduct by the police can ever give rise to an abuse of process. The effect on George Dean, or for that matter on his father, of an undertaking or promise or representation by the police was likely to have been the same in this case whether it was or was not authorised by the Crown Prosecution Service. It is true that they might have asked their solicitor whether an undertaking, promise or representation by the police was binding; and he might have asked the Crown Prosecution Service whether it was made with their authority. But it seems unreasonable to expect that in this case. If the Crown Prosecution Service find that their powers are being usurped by the police, the remedy must surely be a greater degree of liaison at an early stage.

[3:6] Code for Crown Prosecutors
(5th edition, 2004)

1 Introduction

1.1 The decision to prosecute an individual is a serious step. Fair and effective prosecution is essential to the maintenance of law and order. Even in a small case a prosecution has serious implications for all involved—victims, witnesses and defendants. The Crown Prosecution Service applies the Code for Crown Prosecutors so that it can make fair and consistent decisions about prosecutions.

1.2 The Code helps the Crown Prosecution Service to play its part in making sure that justice is done. It contains information that is important to police officers and others who work in the criminal justice system and to the general public. Police officers should take account of the Code when they are deciding whether to charge a person with an offence.

1.3 The Code is also designed to make sure that everyone knows the principles that the Crown Prosecution Service applies when carrying out its work. By applying the same principles, everyone involved in the system is helping to treat victims fairly and to prosecute fairly but effectively.

2 General Principles

2.1 Each case is unique and must be considered on its own facts and merits. However, there are general principles that apply to the way in which Crown Prosecutors must approach every case.

2.2 Crown Prosecutors must be fair, independent and objective. They must not let any personal views about ethnic or national origin, sex, religious beliefs, political views or the sexual orientation of the suspect, victim or witness influence their decisions. They must not be affected by improper or undue pressure from any source.

2.3 It is the duty of Crown Prosecutors to make sure that the right person is prosecuted for the right offence. In doing so, Crown Prosecutors must always act in the interests of justice and not solely for the purpose of obtaining a conviction.

2.4 Crown Prosecutors should provide guidance and advice to investigators throughout the investigative and prosecuting process. This may include lines of inquiry, evidential requirements and assistance in any pre-charge procedures. Crown Prosecutors will be proactive in identifying and, where possible, rectifying evidential deficiencies and in bringing to an early conclusion those cases that cannot be strengthened by further investigation.

2.5 It is the duty of Crown Prosecutors to review, advise on and prosecute cases, ensuring that the law is properly applied, that all relevant evidence is put before the court and that obligations of disclosure are complied with, in accordance with the principles set out in this Code.

2.6 The CPS is a public authority for the purposes of the Human Rights Act 1998. Crown Prosecutors must apply the principles of the European Convention on Human Rights in accordance with the Act.

3 The Decision to Prosecute

3.1 In most cases, Crown Prosecutors are responsible for deciding whether a person should be charged with a criminal offence, and if so, what that offence should be. Crown Prosecutors make these decisions in accordance with this Code and the Director's Guidance on Charging. In those cases where the police determine the charge, which are usually more minor and routine cases, they apply the same provisions.

3.2 Crown Prosecutors make charging decisions in accordance with the Full Code Test (see section 5 below), other than in those limited circumstances where the Threshold Test applies (see section 6 below).

3.3 The Threshold Test applies where the case is one in which it is proposed to keep the suspect in custody after charge, but the evidence required to apply the Full Code Test is not yet available.

3.4 Where a Crown Prosecutor makes a charging decision in accordance with the Threshold Test, the case must be reviewed in accordance with the Full Code Test as soon as reasonably practicable, taking into account the progress of the investigation.

4 Review

4.1 Each case that the Crown Prosecution Service receives from the police is reviewed to make sure that it is right to proceed with a prosecution. Unless the Threshold Test applies, the Crown Prosecution Service will only start or continue with a prosecution when the case has passed both stages of the Full Code Test.

4.2 Review is a continuing process and Crown Prosecutors must take account of any change in circumstances. Wherever possible, they should talk to the police first if they are thinking about changing the charges or stopping the case. Crown Prosecutors should also tell the police if they believe that some additional evidence may strengthen the case. This gives the police the chance to provide more information that may affect the decision.

4.3 The Crown Prosecution Service and the police work closely together, but the final responsibility for the decision whether or not a charge or a case should go ahead rests with the Crown Prosecution Service.

5 The Full Code Test

5.1 The Full Code Test has two stages. The first stage is consideration of the evidence. If the case does not pass the evidential stage it must not go ahead no matter how important or serious it may be. If the case does pass the evidential stage, Crown Prosecutors must proceed to the second stage and decide if a prosecution is needed in the public interest. The evidential and public interest stages are explained below.

The Evidential Stage

5.2 Crown Prosecutors must be satisfied that there is enough evidence to provide a 'realistic prospect of conviction' against each defendant on each charge. They must consider what the defence case may be, and how that is likely to affect the prosecution case.

5.3 A realistic prospect of conviction is an objective test. It means that a jury or bench of magistrates, properly directed in accordance with the law, is more likely than not to convict the defendant of the charge alleged. This is a separate test from the one that the criminal courts themselves must apply. A court should only convict if satisfied so that it is sure of a defendant's guilt.

5.3 When deciding whether there is enough evidence to prosecute, Crown Prosecutors must consider whether the evidence can be used and is reliable. There will be many cases in which the evidence does not give any cause for concern. But there will also be cases in which the evidence may not be as strong as it first appears. Crown Prosecutors must ask themselves the following questions:

Can the evidence be used in court?

a   Is it likely that the evidence will be excluded by the court? There are certain legal rules which might mean that evidence which seems relevant cannot be given at a trial. For example, is it likely that the evidence will be excluded because of the way in which it was gathered or because of the rule against using hearsay as evidence? If so, is there enough other evidence for a realistic prospect of conviction?

Is the evidence reliable?

b   Is there evidence which might support or detract from the reliability of a confession? Is the reliability affected by factors such as the defendant's age, intelligence or level of understanding?

c   What explanation has the defendant given? Is a court likely to find it credible in the light of the evidence as a whole? Does it support an innocent explanation?

d   If the identity of the defendant is likely to be questioned, is the evidence about this strong enough?

e   Is the witness's background likely to weaken the prosecution case? For example, does the witness have any motive that may affect his or her attitude to the case, or a relevant previous conviction?

f   Are there concerns over the accuracy or credibility of a witness? Are these concerns based on evidence or simply information with nothing to support it? Is there further evidence which the police should be asked to seek out which may support or detract from the account of the witness?

5.5 Crown Prosecutors should not ignore evidence because they are not sure that it can be used or is reliable. But they should look closely at it when deciding if there is a realistic prospect of conviction.

The Public Interest Stage

5.6 In 1951, Lord Shawcross, who was Attorney General, made the classic statement on public interest, which has been supported by Attorneys General ever since: 'It has never been the rule in this country—I hope it never will be—that suspected criminal offences must automatically be the subject of prosecution'. (House of Commons Debates, volume 483, column 681, 29 January 1951.)

5.7 The public interest must be considered in each case where there is enough evidence to provide a realistic prospect of conviction. Although there may be public interest factors against prosecution in a particular case, often the prosecution should go ahead and those factors should be put to the court for consideration when sentence is being passed. A prosecution will usually take place unless there are public interest factors tending against prosecution which clearly outweigh those tending in favour, or it appears more appropriate in all the circumstances of the case to divert the person from prosecution (see section 8 below).

5.8 Crown Prosecutors must balance factors for and against prosecution carefully and fairly. Public interest factors that can affect the decision to prosecute usually depend on the seriousness of the offence or the circumstances of the suspect. Some factors may increase the need to prosecute but others may suggest that another course of action would be better.

The following lists of some common public interest factors, both for and against prosecution, are not exhaustive. The factors that apply will depend on the facts in each case.

Some common public interest factors in favour of prosecution

5.9 The more serious the offence, the more likely it is that a prosecution will be needed in the public interest. A prosecution is likely to be needed if:

a a conviction is likely to result in a significant sentence;

b a conviction is likely to result in a confiscation or any other order;

c a weapon was used or violence was threatened during the commission of the offence;

d the offence was committed against a person serving the public (for example, a police or prison officer, or a nurse);

e the defendant was in a position of authority or trust;

f the evidence shows that the defendant was a ringleader or an organiser of the offence;

g there is evidence that the offence was premeditated;

h there is evidence that the offence was carried out by a group;

i the victim of the offence was vulnerable, has been put in considerable fear, or suffered personal attack, damage or disturbance;

j the offence was committed in the presence of, or in close proximity to, a child;

k the offence was motivated by any form of discrimination against the victim's ethnic or national origin, disability, sex, religious beliefs, political views or sexual orientation, or the suspect demonstrated hostility towards the victim based on any of those characteristics;

l there is a marked difference between the actual or mental ages of the defendant and the victim, or if there is any element of corruption;

m the defendant's previous convictions or cautions are relevant to the present offence;

n the defendant is alleged to have committed the offence while under an order of the court;

o there are grounds for believing that the offence is likely to be continued or repeated , for example, by a history of recurring conduct;

p the offence, although not serious in itself, is widespread in the area where it was committed; or

q a prosecution would have a significant positive impact on maintaining community confidence.

Some common public interest factors against prosecution

5.10 A prosecution is less likely to be needed if:

a the court is likely to impose a nominal penalty;

b the defendant has already been made the subject of a sentence and any further conviction would be unlikely to result in the imposition of an additional sentence or order, unless the nature of the particular offence requires a prosecution or the defendant withdraws consent to have an offence taken into consideration during sentencing;

c the offence was committed as a result of a genuine mistake or misunderstanding (these factors must be balanced against the seriousness of the offence);

d the loss or harm can be described as minor and was the result of a single incident, particularly if it was caused by a misjudgement;

e there has been a long delay between the offence taking place and the date of the trial, unless:

- the offence is serious;
- the delay has been caused in part by the defendant;
- the offence has only recently come to light; or
- the complexity of the offence has meant that there has been a long investigation;

f a prosecution is likely to have a bad effect on the victim's physical or mental health, always bearing in mind the seriousness of the offence;

g the defendant is elderly or is, or was at the time of the offence, suffering from significant mental or physical ill health, unless the offence is serious or there is a real possibility that it may be repeated. The Crown Prosecution Service, where necessary, applies Home Office guidelines about how to deal with mentally disordered offenders. Crown Prosecutors must balance the desirability of diverting a defendant who is suffering from significant mental or physical ill health with the need to safeguard the general public;

h the defendant has put right the loss or harm that was caused (but defendants must not avoid prosecution solely because they pay compensation); or

i details may be made public that could harm sources of information, international relations or national security.

5.11 Deciding on the public interest is not simply a matter of adding up the number of factors on each side. Crown Prosecutors must decide how important each factor is in the circumstances of each case and go on to make an overall assessment.

The relationship between the victim and the public interest

5.12 The Crown Prosecution Service does not act for victims or the families of victims in the same way as solicitors act for their clients. Crown Prosecutors act on behalf of the public and not just in the interests of any particular individual. However, when considering the public interest, Crown Prosecutors should always take into account the consequences for the victim of whether or not to prosecute, and any views expressed by the victim or the victim's family.

5.13 It is important that a victim is told about a decision which makes a significant difference to the case in which they are involved. Crown Prosecutors should ensure that they follow any agreed procedures.

6 The Threshold Test

6.1 The Threshold Test requires Crown Prosecutors to decide whether there is at least a reasonable suspicion that the suspect has committed an offence, and if there is, whether it is in the public interest to charge that suspect.

6.2 The Threshold Test is applied to those cases in which it would not be appropriate to release a suspect on bail after charge, but the evidence to apply the Full Code Test is not yet available.

6.3 There are statutory limits that restrict the time a suspect may remain in police custody before a decision has to be made whether to charge or release the suspect. There will be cases where the suspect in custody presents a substantial bail risk if released, but much of the evidence may not be available at the time the charging decision has to be made. Crown Prosecutors will apply the Threshold Test to such cases for a limited period.

6.4 The evidential decision in each case will require consideration of a number of factors including:

- the evidence available at the time;
- the likelihood and nature of further evidence being obtained;
- the reasonableness for believing that evidence will become available;
- the time it will take to gather that evidence and the steps being taken to do so;
- the impact the expected evidence will have on the case;
- the charges that the evidence will support.

6.5 The public interest means the same as under the Full Code Test, but will be based on the information available at the time of charge which will often be limited.

6.6 A decision to charge and withhold bail must be kept under review. The evidence gathered must be regularly assessed to ensure the charge is still appropriate and that continued objection to bail is justified. The Full Code Test must be applied as soon as reasonably practicable.

7 Selection of Charges

7.1 Crown Prosecutors should select charges which:

a   reflect the seriousness of the offending;

b   give the court adequate sentencing powers; and

c   enable the case to be presented in a clear and simple way.

This means that Crown Prosecutors may not always continue with the most serious charge where there is a choice. Further, Crown Prosecutors should not continue with more charges than are necessary.

7.2 Crown Prosecutors should never go ahead with more charges than are necessary just to encourage a defendant to plead guilty to a few. In the same way, they should never go ahead with a more serious charge just to encourage a defendant to plead guilty to a less serious one.

7.3 Crown Prosecutors should not change the charge simply because of the decision made by the court or the defendant about where the case will be heard.

8 Diversion from Prosecution

Adults

8.1 When deciding whether a case should be prosecuted in the courts, Crown Prosecutors should consider the alternatives to prosecution. Where appropriate, the availability of suitable rehabilitative, reparative or restorative justice processes can be considered.

8.2 Alternatives to prosecution for adult suspects include a simple caution and a conditional caution.

Simple caution

8.3 A simple caution should only be given if the public interest justifies it and in accordance with Home Office guidelines. Where it is felt that such a caution is appropriate, Crown Prosecutors must inform the police so they can caution the suspect. If the caution is not administered, because the suspect refuses to accept it, a Crown Prosecutor may review the case again.

Conditional caution

8.4 A conditional caution may be appropriate where a Crown Prosecutor considers that while the public interest justifies a prosecution, the interests of the suspect, victim and community may be better served by the suspect complying with suitable conditions aimed at rehabilitation or reparation. These may include restorative processes.

8.5 Crown Prosecutors must be satisfied that there is sufficient evidence for a realistic prospect of conviction and that the public interest would justify a prosecution should the offer of a conditional caution be refused or the offender fail to comply with the agreed conditions of the caution.

8.6 In reaching their decision, Crown Prosecutors should follow the Conditional Cautions Code of Practice and any guidance on conditional cautioning issued or approved by the Director of Public Prosecutions.

8.7 Where Crown Prosecutors consider a conditional caution to be appropriate, they must inform the police, or other authority responsible for administering the conditional caution, as well as providing an indication of the appropriate conditions so that the conditional caution can be administered.

Youths

8.8 Crown Prosecutors must consider the interests of a youth when deciding whether it is in the public interest to prosecute. However Crown Prosecutors should not avoid prosecuting simply because of the defendant's age. The seriousness of the offence or the youth's past behaviour is very important.

8.9 Cases involving youths are usually only referred to the Crown Prosecution Service for prosecution if the youth has already received a reprimand and final warning, unless the offence is so serious that neither of these were appropriate or the youth does not admit committing the offence.

Reprimands and final warnings are intended to prevent re-offending and the fact that a further offence has occurred indicates that attempts to divert the youth from the court system have not been effective. So the public interest will usually require a prosecution in such cases, unless there are clear public interest factors against prosecution.

9 Mode of Trial

9.1 The Crown Prosecution Service applies the current guidelines for magistrates who have to decide whether cases should be tried in the Crown Court when the offence gives the option and the defendant does not indicate a guilty plea. Crown Prosecutors should recommend Crown Court trial when they are satisfied that the guidelines require them to do so.

9.2 Speed must never be the only reason for asking for a case to stay in the magistrates' courts. But Crown Prosecutors should consider the effect of any likely delay if they send a case to the Crown Court, and any possible stress on victims and witnesses if the case is delayed.

10 Accepting Guilty Pleas

10.1 Defendants may want to plead guilty to some, but not all, of the charges. Alternatively, they may want to plead guilty to a different, possibly less serious, charge because they are admitting only part of the crime. Crown Prosecutors should only accept the defendant's plea if they think the court is able to pass a sentence that matches the seriousness of the offending, particularly where there are aggravating features. Crown Prosecutors must never accept a guilty plea just because it is convenient.

10.2 In considering whether the pleas offered are acceptable, Crown Prosecutors should ensure that the interests of the victim and, where possible, any views expressed by the victim or victim's family, are taken into account when deciding whether it is in the public interest to accept the plea. However, the decision rests with the Crown Prosecutor.

10.3 It must be made clear to the court on what basis any plea is advanced and accepted. In cases where a defendant pleads guilty to the charges but on the basis of facts that are different from the prosecution case, and where this may significantly affect sentence, the court should be invited to hear evidence to determine what happened, and then sentence on that basis.

10.4 Where a defendant has previously indicated that he or she will ask the court to take an offence into consideration when sentencing, but then declines to admit that offence at court, Crown Prosecutors will consider whether a prosecution is required for that offence. Crown Prosecutors should explain to the defence advocate and the court that the prosecution of that offence may be subject to further review.

10.5 Particular care must be taken when considering pleas which would enable the defendant to avoid the imposition of a mandatory minimum sentence. When pleas are offered, Crown Prosecutors must bear in mind the fact that ancillary orders can be made with some offences but not with others.

11 Prosecutors' Role in Sentencing

11.1 Crown Prosecutors should draw the court's attention to:

- any aggravating or mitigating factors disclosed by the prosecution case;
- any victim personal statement;
- where appropriate, evidence of the impact of the offending on a community;
- any statutory provisions or sentencing guidelines which may assist;
- any relevant statutory provisions relating to ancillary orders (such as anti-social behaviour orders).

11.2 The Crown Prosecutor should challenge any assertion made by the defence in mitigation that is inaccurate, misleading or derogatory. If the defence persist in the assertion, and it appears relevant to the sentence, the court should be invited to hear evidence to determine the facts and sentence accordingly.

12 Re-starting a Prosecution

12.1 People should be able to rely on decisions taken by the Crown Prosecution Service. Normally, if the Crown Prosecution Service tells a suspect or defendant that there will not be a prosecution, or that the prosecution has been stopped, that is the end of the matter and the case will not start again. But occasionally there are special reasons why the Crown Prosecution Service will re-start the prosecution, particularly if the case is serious.

12.2 These reasons include:

a rare cases where a new look at the original decision shows that it was clearly wrong and should not be allowed to stand;

b cases which are stopped so that more evidence which is likely to become available in the fairly near future can be collected and prepared. In these cases, the Crown Prosecutor will tell the defendant that the prosecution may well start again; and

c cases which are stopped because of a lack of evidence but where more significant evidence is discovered later.

12.3 There may also be exceptional cases in which, following an acquittal of a serious offence, the Crown Prosecutor may, with the written consent of the Director of Public Prosecutions, apply to the Court of Appeal for an order quashing the acquittal and requiring the defendant to be retried, in accordance with Part 10 of the Criminal Justice Act 2003.

[3:7] Hoyano, A, Hoyano, L, David, G, and Goldie, S, 'A Study of the Impact of the Revised Code for Crown Prosecutors'
[1997] Crim LR 556 (at page 557)

In a detailed critique of the revised Code, published in tandem with a response from the CPS, Andrew Ashworth and Julia Fionda generally welcomed the revisions to the Code, but also expressed a number of concerns. For example, they suggested that there had been a change of emphasis in the direction of a greater propensity to prosecute, particularly in relation to young defendants, and they questioned whether the independence of the CPS may not have been compromised by apparent submission to politically inspired changes of policy.

The CPS commissioned two research studies to gauge the impact of the revised Code. The first of these was conducted 'in-house' and examined police views of the revised Code in terms of its clarity, accessibility, and relevance to their work. Secondly, the CPS commissioned us to ascertain whether the evidential and public interest tests were being implemented in line with the guidance contained in the revised Code, and to discover what impact, if any, the revision had had upon prosecutors' case decisions. The terms of reference provided that the research was to be completed in a six-month period beginning September 1995 and that it was to be conducted by way of 80 interviews with CPS personnel in four CPS areas. Four branch offices were selected from within each area. The interview sample included all grades of personnel, from caseworkers to Branch Crown Prosecutors. The interviews, which were tape-recorded, included discussion of specific case scenarios.

Is the revised Code an improvement?

One aim of the revisions was to make the Code more easily understood outside the CPS. Almost all the prosecutors whom we interviewed considered that the Code had been rendered more accessible to the police and to members of the public. That still of course leaves the question of whether a simplified document is of assistance to prosecutors themselves.

(At page 564:)

The role of the CPS as a filter for evidentially weak cases and for cases which it would not be in the public interest to pursue is important and demanding in equal measure. Our impression from meeting prosecutors is that it is a responsibility which they take very seriously; but equally many of them feel that factors limiting their discretion are not understood by the public, and that they are often unfairly criticised as a result.

It is our overall impression, based on this survey, that prosecutors in the four areas which we examined adopt a common approach in terms of the way they view cases and the factors which they consider. There was no discernible variation in response by area to any of the issues and questions which we raised in our interviews. This of course cannot be taken as proof that *case decisions* are consistent on a national basis; that is beyond the scope of a study based on interviews with CPS staff, but such interviews do at least provide an indicator. At the same time one must acknowledge that the Code itself guides decision-making only at a very basic level. It is a signpost rather than a map, indicating a general direction rather than providing a detailed route.

According to the Attorney-General, the review of the Code was designed:

(1) to make it more easily understood by the police and members of the public;

(2) to clarify the evidential criterion and the requirement that there be a realistic prospect of conviction; and

(3) to bring out more clearly the public interest factors in favour of a prosecution.

Our interviewees were almost unanimous in their view that the first aim has been achieved. However it is apparent that the revised Code has not been so successful in achieving the other two objectives. Prosecutors appeared uncertain as to whether the revisions were intended to send a strong signal that they should be prosecuting more cases, whether in fact any change of direction was desired, or whether there was perceived to be some inconsistency in prosecutorial decision-making which needed to be corrected. In particular it would seem that the CPS has not adequately explained to its own prosecutors why the phrase 'more likely than not' was inserted into the evidential criterion in the revised version of the Code.

Whatever the purpose of the changes to the Code, the impact upon prosecutors' decisions seems to have been fairly marginal. This is mainly because the Code tests are not susceptible to precise gradations and so prosecutors rely to a large extent on experience, both their own and that of their colleagues. The clarifications and guidance in the revised Code did not represent, for most prosecutors, a strong enough distinction to override this. Detailed policy directives relating to specific offences and problems *do* however make a difference. If changes in decision-making are required, it is clear that specific directives are more effective than altering the language of the Code in ways which do not convey—or at least, do not convey in forthright terms—a specific change of direction. This does not derogate from the value of the Code as a tool for training prosecutors who have recently joined the CPS.

[3:8] Morgan, R, Review of Drakeford, M, Haines, K, Cotton, B, and Octigan, M, *Pre-trial Services and the Future of Probation*
(2002) BJ of Criminology 224

Given the pace of contemporary events, there is seldom an ideal time to write and publish a policy-focused book. Do it before a major structural change and the published analysis is, or appears to be, out of date. Wait to start writing until the new structure is in place and one risks missing the priority-setting tide. Drakeford and his co-authors must have faced this dilemma. They presumably collected most of their data (though their research methodological note is somewhat opaque on chronology) at about the time it became apparent that there was to be a National Probation Service, in place since April 2001 as a result of the Criminal Justice and Court Services Act 2000. But they pressed ahead with their text without waiting to see what form the national service was to take. In retrospect it seems a less than happy choice. One cannot but feel that their core fieldwork material—an account of pre-trial services in three probation areas—and their relatively timeless policy objective—furthering the expansion of probation-led pre-trial services—would have been better served had they waited until they could formulate recommendations welded to the current realities of governance. As it is, we are presented in Chapter 5 with reportage of largely irrelevant outdated opinion as to whether there *should* be a national service, and the reader is offered no guidance as to how the authors' project might best be pursued within the new tripartite framework comprising a National Probation Directorate, and 42 local Probation Boards and Chief Officers. This is a pity. A well-timed and linked article or two would have done the job better. The authors' data and argument are nevertheless worthy of close attention.

Pre-trial probation-led services largely comprise bail information and support (including accommodation) schemes. That is, ways of collecting information about accused persons' community ties, and where a remand in custody might be justified, putting in place arrangements which might satisfy the interests of justice and public protection without resort to custody or excessive restriction. There is a powerful case for linking these efforts with information and support for victims—something Drakeford and his colleagues do not discuss—because, as a good deal of evidence makes clear, victims, particularly victims of violence, are often very concerned as to where 'their' offender is during the pre-trial phase of criminal proceedings.

The authors briefly trace the legal framework for the granting and withholding of bail and describe the expanding remand population and the haphazard history of bail information and support schemes in England and Wales from the 1970s onwards. In the first half of the 1990s bail information schemes were extended to most magistrates' courts and some remand prisons by means of a hypothecated Home Office grant which was withdrawn in 1995. Thereafter the funding of pre-trial services was transferred to mainstream probation budgets, which coincidentally were substantially cut back. It is a feature of an unjoined-up criminal justice system that the principal financial beneficiaries of bail information and support services are the CPS and the courts (who are thereby better able to make informed and speedy decisions) and the Prison Service (who are required to accommodate fewer or more short-term remand prisoners), whereas the bail service provider, the Probation Service, incurs increased costs and pressures. It was no surprise, therefore, that when put under budgetary pressure after 1995, bail information and support services declined in number and in some probation areas disappeared altogether.

Are bail information and support services effective? Drakeford and his colleagues suggest that this question can be answered in a variety of ways. Are accused persons who would otherwise have likely been remanded in custody given conditional or unconditional bail, or accused persons who would otherwise have been granted conditional bail subject to no or fewer bail conditions? If so, do these defendants (a) attend court as required and/or (b) not commit further offences or commit fewer or less serious offences and/or (c) retain their employment or maintain their family and other responsibilities and/or (d) address the criminogenic factors underlying their offending behaviour so as to reduce their offending in the future? The authors' review of the research literature suggests that the answer to the effectiveness question is generally positive and that bail services are cost-effective. Remands in custody are reduced as a result of both court and prison based bail information schemes and reoffending rates among the additional bailees appear to be no higher than among bailees generally. The picture regarding the expensive use of probation hostels for bailees is more equivocal because the evidence suggests that a significant proportion would probably not have been remanded in custody.

The authors' survey of pre-trial services in three probation areas indicates that it is currently very variable in character. It is usually the bottom-up product of enthusiastic local managers, often dependent on partnerships with voluntary agencies and, because focused on unconvicted suspects, reminiscent of 'old' as opposed to 'new' probation—that is, a client-centred focus on individuals' social problems—though there are examples of a more top-down emphasis on targets, crime reduction and cost effectiveness.

The big question, however, is how to take matters forward in the new world of a single minister for probation and prisons, a joint probation and prisons Correctional Services Strategy Board (which the minister chairs), a National Probation Directorate and 42 Probation Boards empowered by s.5 of the CJCSA to ensure that there is sufficient provision (including contracted-out provision) locally to protect the public and reduce offending, including 'giving assistance to persons remanded on bail' and 'providing accommodation in approved premises for persons who have any time been charged with an offence'. The fact that this brave new world does not figure in a book entitled *The Future of Probation* should prompt someone, perhaps the author, to pick up the baton in a mainstream journal article.

[3:9] Ministry of Justice, *The Governance of Britain: A Consultation on the Role of the Attorney General* (2007) Cm 7192

The first section is on the history and role of the law officers. The paper then continues:

2. The Current Role of the Attorney General—Fit For the 21st century?

2.1 The Attorney General's role comprises a complex mixture of common law and statutory functions acquired over the centuries, some of which are exercised in a Governmental capacity and some in an independent public interest capacity.

   2.2 Successive holders of the office have made a major contribution to upholding the rule of law and the administration of justice, helping to ensure that the Government acts in accordance with the law and with the highest standards of legal propriety, and enhancing the role of the prosecuting authorities at the heart of the criminal justice system. However it is right now to consider, as part of the programme of constitutional reform set out in The Governance of Britain, how best the role of Attorney General should be configured to meet Britain's needs in the 21st century.

   2.3 Reform of the Attorney General's role is proposed in the Government's paper on *The Governance of Britain*...That consultation paper specifically includes a proposal to seek to surrender or limit the powers to direct prosecutors in individual criminal cases, "which [the Government] considers, should not, in a modern democracy, be exercised exclusively by the executive". This is discussed further below. But the wider implications of proposals in this Green Paper for the Attorney General's role should also be considered. For example:

- Does the proposal to put prerogative executive powers on a statutory basis, subject to Parliamentary scrutiny and control, mean that Parliament should have access to the Attorney General's advice on these issues, or to some other source of legal advice?

- Do new ways need to be found of ensuring that, when Parliament exercises such powers, it does so in accordance with the rule of law?

2.4 In addition, one of the themes of The Governance of Britain is greater involvement of Parliament, and there may be implications for the way in which the Attorney General is accountable to Parliament— for example the use of new mechanisms to provide greater accountability for cases involving sensitive intelligence and security issues (see paragraph 1.36 above).

   2.5 The current multi-faceted nature of the Attorney's role has given rise to a debate which has focussed mainly on the tension between the Attorney's political status as a Government Minister and the functions as:

- The Government's chief legal adviser. The question arises how the Attorney General can give independent legal advice to Government when he or she is part of Government. The Attorney would fall with the Government and can be dismissed by the Prime Minister like any other minister. This question was raised particularly in relation to the advice on the legality of military action against Iraq in 2003.

- The independent guardian of the public interest. For example, in the Gouriet case the then Attorney General refused consent to the bringing of proceedings to enforce the law against the Union of

Post Office Workers, whose members had refused to handle mail between England & Wales and South Africa, in a protest against apartheid. That decision was taken in the Attorney General's independent public interest capacity, though the Government of the day also clearly had a legitimate policy against apartheid. In the area of sensitive prosecutions, the Al-Yamamah arms contract with Saudi Arabia is the most recent example. Some have questioned how the Attorney General can be seen to be impartial in weighing up or advising on the public interest on matters in which the Government may itself have a strong policy interest (for example in the protection of jobs).

Attorney General as Government Minister and legal adviser

2.6 The first area of tension arises between the Attorney General's position as a Government Minister, and the role as the provider of independent and impartial legal advice to Government. Attorneys General have worked on the clear basis that their duty is to give wholly independent and impartial legal advice, and they are bound by professional codes of conduct to that effect.

2.7 However, some believe that the Attorney General cannot truly be (or be seen to be) independent from the Government (or party), with the result that the Attorney General's advice lacks at least the appearance of complete impartiality, or even that the Attorney may come under pressure to slant the advice in a particular way to support the Government or political party in Government.

2.8 On the other hand it has been argued that the advice of the Attorney General is more likely to be accepted by Ministers because it comes from one of their number, who understands the wider political and policy context, rather than being provided externally. Thus it is the Attorney General's membership of the Government that gives the advice to Ministerial colleagues its credibility and authority with them.

2.9 Furthermore, it is argued, the Attorney General's advice, as well as needing of course to be honest and authoritative, is advice to a particular client (the Government) on how its policies may lawfully be achieved, including advice on the legal risks attached, the prospects of successful challenge and so on. It is, like other legal advice, subject to legal professional privilege and is not generally published. In this way, the Attorney General operates like an in-house lawyer. It is generally accepted that in-house lawyers (including those in business or the Government Legal Service) are entirely capable of providing independent legal advice to the highest professional standards.

2.10 However, some commentators have suggested that the Attorney General's advice to Government should not (or not always) be treated in the same way as legal advice given to a private organisation. The Government is not a business and the relationship of the Attorney General to the Government is arguably of a different order to that of other in-house lawyers. This raises the question of whether, at least for some purposes, "the public" (or Parliament), rather than the Government, should be treated as the Attorney General's client. Lord Bingham has said:

> "There seems to me to be room to question whether the ordinary rules of client privilege, appropriate enough in other circumstances, should apply to a law officer's opinion on the lawfulness of war; it is not unrealistic in my view to regard the public, those who are to fight and perhaps die, rather than the government, as the client."

2.11 Concern has similarly been expressed that the legal advice which the Government receives from the Attorney General is not generally disclosed to Parliament or to the public, even where the advice relates to very significant decisions, for example the decision to take military action against Iraq in 2003 . . .

Exercise of public interest functions

2.12 The second area of perceived tension arises between the Attorney General's position as a Government Minister and politician and the post's public interest functions. This has given rise to the suggestion or perception that the Attorney General might come under pressure to exercise those public interest functions in a way which reflects the political or policy interests of the Government or party to which he or she belongs, rather than wholly independently and in the public interest.

(i) Functions in relation to individual prosecutions

2.13 Particular concerns have been expressed about the Attorney General's role in relation to decisions about individual criminal cases, including the granting or withholding of consents to prosecute and in relation to those cases where the Attorney General is consulted by the prosecuting authorities as part of the superintendence role, and where there is perceived to be a risk of conflict of interest. In its recent report the Constitutional Affairs Select Committee commented: "The Attorney General's responsibility for prosecutions has emerged as one of the most problematic aspects of his or her role." ... To address such concerns, other common law jurisdictions have moved to separate the ministerial role from individual prosecution decisions (Annex B sets out some examples).

2.14 The Attorney General's role in relation to consents to prosecution has been considered by the Law Commission. The Law Commission concluded that the existing functions of the Attorney General to give consent to prosecutions should (if not abolished altogether) be transferred to the DPP except where the offence involved national security or had some international element....

2.15 However, some commentators, including some who gave evidence to the Constitutional Affairs Select Committee, have taken the view that, for all its tensions, the advantages of the current system outweigh the disadvantages.

(ii) Other public interest functions

Much of the comment about potential conflict between the Attorney General's Governmental and public interest functions, as discussed above, relates to the role in relation to individual criminal prosecutions. However the Attorney General has a range of other public interest functions which, similarly, have to be exercised independently of Government. These include:

- The bringing of proceedings for contempt of court
- Intervening in certain family and charity cases to protect the public interest
- Bringing proceedings to restrain vexatious litigants
- Appointment of advocates to the court (neutral advisers to the court) and special advocates (to represent the interests of parties in cases involving sensitive national security issues).

2.17 On occasion, the contempt role can be controversial and (as in relation to prosecutions) give rise to accusations that the Attorney General has (for example) acted to restrain a publication for political motives. Any alternative model for exercising this role would still involve striking a balance between the interests of justice and the freedom of the press, often in the most sensitive of cases, and could therefore sometimes be controversial.

2.18 For the most part the Attorney General's other public interest functions have not attracted controversy or criticism and there is seldom any suggestion that they have been exercised for any political or other improper motive.

The paper then concludes with a section on options for change.

[3:10] Block, B, Corbett, C, and Peay, J, 'Ordered and Directed Acquittals in the Crown Court: A Time of Change?'

[1993] Crim LR 95 (at page 100)

Foreseeability and avoidability: how accountable are the CPS?

Of the sample of 100 non-jury acquittals, there were 71 ordered acquittals, 28 directed acquittals and one mixed acquittal, where there were two indictments and one was acquitted by order and one by direction. Although fewer than half of ordered acquittals were considered definitely or possibly foreseeable, three-quarters of directed acquittals were so classified. This supports our view, derived from the study, that directed acquittals result largely from weak cases that should have been discontinued, whereas ordered acquittals often result from unforeseeable circumstances. This may be considered to challenge Zander's assertion that ordered acquittals represent an even weaker category of case than where the judge directs an acquittal.[1] Our study shows that in fact there are at least two categories of ordered acquittals: those weak cases that are spotted by the CPS immediately after committal, and others—seemingly good cases—which weaken unpredictably before committal or trial. Of all ordered acquittals in our sample (71), 14 were listed for mention (the former category) and 37 weakened nearer or on the day of trial (the latter category).

Use of the term 'weak cases' implies criticism of the CPS, but this is misleading. The real basis for criticism is the distinction between predictably weak cases which the CPS fail to spot and unpredictably weak cases. Of fundamentally weak cases, the CPS may be held responsible for those resulting in ordered acquittals that should have been spotted even before committal, and for those ending in directed acquittals due to weaknesses not spotted at all. Any analysis of the national statistics which is used as a basis for assessing the performance of the CPS needs to take account of these distinctions.

Accordingly, the increase in the proportion of ordered to directed acquittals could be interpreted as reflecting the increasing ability of the CPS to identify weak cases, which then result in ordered rather than directed acquittals. Consistent with this would be the numbers of ordered acquittals due to witnesses or victims not turning up at trial—a feature of the unforeseeably weak ordered acquittal group—possibly being due to police not chasing up witnesses rather than CPS inaction. The results of this study, however, equally suggest that many weak cases could have been identified and discontinued before committal. Such action would have prevented the inclusion of these cases in the national statistics of non-jury acquittals completely. These avoidable non-jury acquittals constitute between 15% and 43% of this sample of cases—the 15% figure representing the lowest level of prosecutorial inefficiency (those cases foreseeably weak pre-committal) and 43% the highest (including all those possibly foreseeable cases which might have been identified at or immediately after committal). Moreover, it is surprising that some weak cases, where the weakness was foreseeable (and agreed as such by the CPS assessor), were allowed to proceed to directed acquittals. Although small in number (five), it is an indictment of the CPS that these cases were not converted into ordered acquittals by earlier CPS action, or prevented from becoming acquittals at all by even earlier discontinuance.

Note

1 This includes those acquitted by the judge where no evidence is offered (for example, because of the refusal of a witness to testify). Zander, M 'What the Annual Statistics Tell Us about Pleas and Acquittals' (1991) Crim LR 252.

(At page 105:)

The results of this inquiry show that of a sample of 100 non-jury acquittals, although 45 were unavoidable due to entirely unforeseen and unforeseeable circumstances, the remainder could or might have been avoided, and in 22 cases even the CPS assessor said that the acquittal was foreseeable and arguably therefore ought to have been avoided. In a minimum of 15%, where it was assessed that a directed or ordered acquittal could have been foreseen prior to committal, the case should have been terminated or manifest deficiencies in the evidence rectified. These acquittals were clearly the responsibility of the CPS in the first instance. Once the case had been committed, blame could more properly be laid with counsel, who did not always advise the CPS that a case was weak or that certain evidence was lacking. Other acquittals too were not attributable to the CPS but stemmed from the intervention of the trial judges, or lack of intervention by counsel.

In view of the limited sample size, it would be unwise to make too many claims on the basis of the findings of the present study. However, as there is no reason to believe that the sample was in any way typical of non-jury acquittals some limited observations and recommendations for change will be advanced. It is suggested that, if implemented, the following modifications to the system could reduce substantially the proportion of non-jury acquittals.

First, the powers of the CPS need enhancing. It is all too easy for a case to seem watertight at committal yet to become manifestly unsafe between committal and trial. A further review of the evidence may reveal it to be not so strong as previously believed, or counsel can point out deficiencies that were missed. Where this occurs, all that the CPS can do at present is to list the case for mention; they cannot discontinue. At the beginning of the trial counsel can offer no evidence and the judge can order an acquittal. Since Grafton, however, the judge cannot interfere with counsel's decision not to offer any further evidence and must direct an acquittal. It is anomalous that the CPS cannot discontinue before trial when they have full discretion to offer no further evidence at the trial up to the end of the prosecution case. Clearly, ordered acquittals of this type could be eliminated if section 23 of the Prosecution of Offences Act 1985 were amended so that the CPS were able to discontinue at any time up to the beginning of Crown Court trial.

[3:11] Gelsthorpe, L and Giller, H, 'More Justice for Juveniles: Does More Mean Better?'

[1990] Crim LR 153 (at page 161)

Dissent and independence

The Crown Prosecution Service was set up as an 'independent' service to 'promote consistency and fairness' and to 'reduce the proportion of cases pursued despite lack of sufficient evidence' amongst other things. Indeed, one of the underlying themes in the setting up of the Service was that it should be an important counterbalance to the increased police powers provided by the Police and Criminal Evidence Act 1984.

Despite this, the Crown Prosecution Service remains dependent upon the police for information. Since the raison d'être of the police is to detect and prevent crime we might reasonably expect a presumption in favour of prosecution with respect to those cases they refer to the Crown Prosecution Service. Andrew Sanders has shown how information from the police is constructed in such a way as to suggest that prosecution is both expedient and desirable. He refers to the potential for discounting evidence, to the fact that the police do not actively seek information that could establish innocence and to the fact that the police do not see their role extending to checking the defence story if doing so would be difficult, even when, for example, following up the story is beyond the resources of the defence. Sanders establishes that cases are not simply about sets of objective facts which can be ascertained once and for all. The police try to construct strong cases by eliminating ambiguity and removing features which undermine cases. Those cases which they present to the Crown Prosecution Service are generally only those cases which they want to prosecute. The Crown Prosecution Service has inquisitorial power to vet cases, to screen them and to halt those which are evidentially insufficient, but it has more sources to explore the cases in depth. The Crown Prosecution Service remains dependent upon the police for the carefully constructed accounts it receives. Indeed, many Crown Prosecutors we interviewed resisted the idea of receiving information from any source other than the police, or at least, resisted the idea of unlimited information.

What is of interest here in the context of juvenile cases, is that we found the police used the same set of conceptual categories as Crown Prosecutors in their decisions to divert or refer cases to court. For those recommended for prosecution the police 'construction' of the cases provides the basis for Crown Prosecution Service assessment and review. The Crown Prosecutors depend on the police for a core of information which could be quickly and routinely checked. Information on offenders and their offences is transmitted to the Crown Prosecution Service with the tacit understanding that these are all cases which deserve to go to court. There was a commonality in their approach and use of their conceptual categories. But the question remains, if the police and Crown Prosecutors use similar conceptual categories in their approach to decision-making, why is it that disagreements occur? A superficial analysis here might be to suggest that the police and Crown Prosecutors have different tolerance levels of 'trouble', different standards or different policies. This is not the case. Rather, it is that perceptions of 'trouble' need to be redefined by the Crown Prosecution Service in the context of its own organisational goals. Thus despite Crown Prosecutors' reliance on police constructions of cases, they do assess cases in the light of the exigencies of everyday organisational practice and it is these which shape their 'operational philosophy'.

At its simplest an organisational priority of the Crown Prosecution Service is to effect a smooth-functioning of the prosecution process. The chief 'problem relevance' in pursuing this is the limitation on available time and human resources. The 'operational philosophy' adopted is one which tests out whether the case as presented by the police is 'routine' or 'potentially problematic'. This is done by assessing the case for the factors we have identified. This assessment is a two-fold process: first the case is assessed by reference to technical considerations—evidential sufficiency, previous referrals, procedural soundness, seriousness of the offence. Where potential problems arise in this assessment reference is made to secondary considerations—agency intervention, personal circumstances, tariff-guessing and the ability to bide one's time.

In the majority of cases the police provide sufficient technical information and there is little (if any) reference to secondary material. In routine cases there is little in the way of 'character assessment'. The more problematic the information to substantiate the first-order technical considerations, however, the more pressure there is to rebut the presumption in favour of prosecution. The presence of problematic technical considerations in a case potentially threatens the smooth-functioning of the prosecution process. In these circumstances, prosecutors examine the information around the secondary considerations to determine whether a potentially problematic prosecution should be given an organisational priority. 'Independence', therefore, emerges not from some Olympian platform of values nor from some discrete professional ideology but from the organisational context—from what we have termed the 'operational philosophy'.

From operational philosophy to professional ideology

Interestingly, the recent Crown Prosecution Service report on Juvenile Proceedings (1989) envisages change in the organisational context of prosecution decisions. One of the main recommendations states that:

'The Crown Prosecution Service should be seen to be promoting multi-agency panels. If properly constituted they offer the best method of achieving the correct decision in individual cases (paragraph 6.4)'.

The Report notes the following points in their favour:

(i) they provide a structures forum where all agencies can make their views known;

(ii) a better decision should be reached if all interested parties are involved;

(iii) the Crown Prosecution Service should only receive cases where a prosecution is deemed to be necessary;

(iv) the Crown Prosecution Service should not be open to the accusation that it was simply rubber stamping a police decision to prosecute. (paragraph 6.1).

The recommendation begs a number of questions: why does the Crown Prosecution Service want information from other agencies? What information is required? Would this information be filtered through to the Crown Prosecution Service independently of the Police? How would the information be used? Does more information necessarily mean better decisions?

Clearly, more information from agencies is expected to lead to 'better' decision-making and to the enhancement of the independent status of the Crown Prosecution Service. But this does not address the fact that organisational priorities and constraints currently 'drive' practice considerations. On the one hand the Crown Prosecution Service appears to function on the basis of an 'operational philosophy'—the smooth functioning of the prosecution process—on the other, it appears resistant to the development of a 'professional ideology' which would, above all other things, mark its independent status.

The development of a 'professional ideology' would involve an explicit declaration of beliefs, principles and objectives. Secondly, strategies would have to be adopted to achieve the objectives. Thirdly, the objectives would have to be translated into measurable criteria and targets set. Fourthly, monitoring would have to be carried out to assess whether or not targets had been met. Lastly, policies and practices would have to be evaluated in the light of data derived from monitoring processes.

Such a development would bring both advantages and difficulties. Positively, such an approach would reinforce the central position of the Crown Prosecution Service in the criminal justice system. But areas of difficulty include the issue of accountability and the problem of the lack of coherence and consistency. To whom would the Crown Prosecution Service be accountable, central government or local government? What if the Crown Prosecution Service were to develop objectives based on a percentage usage of custodial sentences per court and local government declared itself a 'custody-free zone'? With regard to the issue of coherency and consistency it is not at all clear how objectives would be set. Given that there is presently a wide variation in views amongst juvenile specialists in the Crown Prosecution Service, who would determine the values and principles to be used? While the current Code for Crown Prosecutors does provide a general statement of intent with respect to the diversion of juveniles from court, it does not provide specific objectives. Sanders makes much the same point in his discussion of the 'public interest'.[2]

> '[There is an] absence of any clearly stated view of the public interest…Even the existence, let alone the content, of one universal 'public interest' is far from self-evident. If any concept of public interest is to have legitimacy, it must be based on specific, clearly articulated and publicly debated values'.

The analogy is clear: an articulated set of objectives which can be measured and monitored would enable the Crown Prosecution Service to develop a professional ideology and with it a pivotal position in the criminal justice system. The current practice of an 'operational philosophy' does not achieve this.

Note

2   Sanders, A 'Incorporating the 'Public Interest' in the Decision to Prosecute', in Hall Williams (ed) *The Role of the Crown Prosecutor* (1988).

[3:12] McConville, M, Sanders, A, and Leng, R, *The Case for the Prosecution*

(1991) Routledge (at page 124)

All cases which are either charged or reported for summons are subject to review both within the police and by the Crown Prosecution Service. Since the CPS was superimposed upon the pre-existing policy system rather than replacing any part of it, there is considerable duplication and overlap of functions. For both organisations the grounds of review are the same and involve consideration of whether the public interest is best served by prosecution or some other disposal, whether the evidence establishes a realistic prospect of conviction and whether the proposed charge is appropriate in law. Although the CPS, like the police reviewer, is isolated from operational policing, the prosecutor may seek to influence the investigation process by requesting that specific further inquiries be made. However, certain functions are exclusively the preserve of one or other organisation. The police have total control over which cases enter the system and only the police caution or informally warn an offender. In juvenile cases it is the job of the police to solicit the views of other agencies with responsibility for the welfare of children. On the other hand, the CPS has responsibility for the conduct of the case in court, may drop or amend charges and has ultimate veto of prosecution.

All forces have instituted special procedures to enable agencies with responsibility for the welfare of children to take part in the juvenile decision-making process. The official purpose of these juvenile liaison procedures is to ensure that public interest factors including the welfare of the child are considered on an individual basis. The police are under a statutory duty to notify Social Services if they are going to prosecute a juvenile (s 5(8) Children and Young Persons Act 1969). The systems in operation vary considerably ranging from permanent multi-agency bureaux as pioneered by Northampton to less elaborate systems in which the views of the other agencies are solicited by post or telephone. In the forces which we researched, one force relied upon home visits conducted by specialist police officers to obtain information about the circumstances of juvenile suspects, with the views of the other agencies obtained by post or telephone. One force considered juvenile cases at a regular juvenile liaison meeting convened by the police and attended by representatives of Social Services and the Probation Service. In the third force a specialist juvenile liaison officer collected information and views from the other agencies, with the option of convening a 'panel' in the event of persistent disagreement about a particular case.

Conventional explanations for the development of the CPS and juvenile liaison procedures can be traced to the argument of the objectivity required in prosecution and the need to take a broader view when applying public policy criteria to prosecution decisions. Under this view, CPS and juvenile liaison provide effective scrutiny of earlier police decisions because the individuals involved are independent of the police and operate according to the skills and values of their own professions.

Another interpretation is that such agencies and procedures are simply doing the state's job for it more efficiently than previously, albeit in a 'welfare disguise'—whether by 'winning by appearing to lose' in the case of the CPS or by adopting a 'corporatist approach' in the case of juvenile liaison. Corporatism refers, in Pratt's words, to the tendencies found in advanced welfare societies whereby the capacity for conflict and disruption is reduced by means of the centralisation of police, increased government intervention, and the co-option of various professional and interest groups into a collective whole with homogenous aims and objectives. (Pratt, 1989,[3] citing Unger, 1976).

Under corporatism, the legal process takes on the form of bureaucratic-administrative law, blurring the boundary between the public and private realms, and increasingly concerned to develop routinised criteria in order to enable dispositions to be effected according to an extra-judicial tariff in the most efficient manner. We shall argue, especially in relation to juvenile liaison bureaux, that this corporatist tendency is apparent in the dominant position occupied by the police in all decisions, in the co-option of other professionals into police ideologies and in the routinisation of extra-judicial decision making.

As we described in earlier chapters, constructing the case is not simply an exercise in collecting together and marshalling all relevant information. Rather the selection, creation and presentation of the evidence is geared towards the objective which the police seek to achieve, and effectively dominates later review procedures. Because the police expect case review and understand the ground rules which govern it, they can anticipate it. Thus, the 'seriousness' of an offence may be manipulated by description: an attack may be 'vicious', 'unprovoked', or premeditated; a shop theft may be 'motivated by pure greed'; a suspected shoplifter may have 'looked round furtively'; emphasis on the suspect's own words may be used to convey the officer's view of the case, as by stressing that a shoplifter said 'it just seemed easy' thereby perhaps negating a doubt the reviewer might have about the offence being rooted in forgetfulness, illness or stress. Construction by omission is equally significant. Thus in one case a store detective had suggested to a suspect that she had forgotten to pay. This was criticised by the CPS reviewer who requested the police to advise the store detective not to make such suggestions when questioning shoplifters in future. Case construction may also be a means of co-opting non-police reviewers into police ideology and values or may convey a more general message about local policing imperatives. Thus, the offence in question may be 'rife' in that part of town, the suspect may be described as a 'football hooligan'. ˙

The rhetoric of prosecution decision making emphasises objectivity, impartiality and individualisation. Police influence over a case is said to be confined to the investigation and case preparation stages with ultimate decision making by the prosecutor applying rigorous tests of public interest and evidential sufficiency. The reality is a system of routinised decision-making embodying an overwhelming propensity to prosecute, bolstered by the presumption that earlier decisions were properly made and should not be overturned. The system is dominated throughout it stages by the interests and values of the police, with the CPS playing an essentially subordinate and reactive role.

Note

3 Pratt, J 'Corporatism: the third model of juvenile justice', 29 BJ of Criminology 236.

(At page 147:)

In the welfarist rhetoric of the criminal justice process, no individual is charged until after the case has been thoroughly reviewed, not only within the police but also ultimately by an independent and impartial prosecuting agency divorced from the investigatory functions of the police. This review process, it is claimed operates to overcome the danger that 'case commitment' by arresting and case officers may lead to unjustified charging, and, generally, to ensure that individuals are brought to court only where there is a realistic prospect of conviction on the basis of the evidence and where it is also in the public interest to deal with the matter by way of prosecution. The special position of juveniles has led to the creation of juvenile liaison bodies where representatives of the caring agencies can give further impetus to non-prosecution by bringing to the forefront non-police values and ideologies.

In reality, the system of review is corporatist in nature: marked by continued police dominance of decision making, a propensity to prosecute, extra-judicial tariffs, routinisation rather than individualised judgment and the broad rejection of public interest criteria. Police dominance is primarily secured by their control over how cases are constructed, a function which enables them to anticipate and thus control review. Although the police have been required to involve other agencies in decision-making, this has been done within police structures (juvenile liaison bureaux) and on police terms but surrounded by a welfarist rhetoric which masks a structure whose objectives appear to be the opposite of its rubric. The CPS, far from being an independent agency, is a police-dependent body, confining review to evidence-sufficiency questions, eschewing public interest criteria, utilising the contradictory and malleable nature of the principles in the codes to further narrowly conceived objectives and, at its worst, adopting an uncritical support-the-police mandate.

CHAPTER FOUR

NON-POLICE INVESTIGATIONS

Although defendants are most likely to be introduced to the criminal justice system by the victim and a police investigation, there are other, contrasting, routes to prosecution that merit a separate chapter, since different prosecuting authorities have very different policies and priorities. As much as a quarter of all prosecutions of adults for non-motoring offences are not initiated by the police. Every year people are prosecuted for tax and customs offences, for social security frauds, for failing to purchase a TV licence, or for failing to hold a valid motor vehicle excise licence (tax disc).

Companies as well as individuals are prosecuted by non-police organizations. Every year many people die at work, and many more are severely injured. Disasters such as the sinking of a ferry, a train crash, or a fire in a public place often reveal corporate incompetence and criminality. They are likely to be investigated by the Health and Safety Executive (HSE) (and sometimes by the police as well). Then there is corporate fraud. The amount of tax evaded by companies and individuals every year is huge. Fifteen years ago, Levi (1993) estimated that one particular case being investigated by the Serious Fraud Office involved a sum equal to the total annual losses from vehicle-related crime. Today the Government appears to have woken up to the problem of serious fraud. A *Fraud Review* was published in 2006, and the Government has announced the setting up of a National Fraud Strategic Authority. Identifying the extent of the problem is a good start: the police estimate that *reported fraud alone* costs the economy and society at least £13.9 billion a year (Levi et al, 2007). Fraud is therefore unsurprisingly a focus of this chapter.

Non-police prosecutions are even more important if we look at the number of offences rather than the number of offenders. In fact, the scale of crimes committed other than by 'ordinary people' on the street is so vast that we often find it easier to ignore it! Lidstone et al [4:1] carried out a wide-scale study for the 1981 Royal Commission on Criminal Procedure. Although now more than 25 years old, it is a useful starting point, highlighting the wide range of factors which at that time influenced the number of prosecutions an agency undertook. The ten most common types of non-police prosecutions in that study were (in descending order of their use by the courts): the Post Office (including TV licence cases); the British Transport Police; the Department of the Environment (vehicle excise licences); local authorities; retail stores; the Department of Health and Social Security (as it then was); London Transport; Customs and Excise; private individuals; and Regional Traffic Commissioners. It is difficult to discover a list of the key 'agencies' involved today: the list would surely include those discussed below.

A consideration of each 'agency' raises some common concerns. One is the fine line which exists today between criminal and civil enforcement. Roording [4:2] is clearly shocked at what he learns of England when he arrives to research the Inland Revenue in the 1990s: the blurring of civil and criminal penalties, and the failure of academics to take the subject seriously. Add to this the fact that many criminal offences in this area, often unhelpfully known as 'regulatory offences' do not require the prosecution to prove fault. The relevance of this strict liability to enforcement practices is discussed by Richardson [4:3]. Although this article is quite old, the concerns raised are just as relevant today. She raises the problem of the usurpation of the criminal trial by administrative discretion.

Another concern is the difficulty in challenging decisions to prosecute. The supermarket chain Tesco failed in its attempt to challenge the decision of a local authority to prosecute only large, nationally recognized stores in respect of Sunday trading contrary to the Shops Act 1950: *see R v Kirklees Metropolitan Borough Council, ex p Tesco Stores Ltd* (1993) Times, 26 October. And the (then) Inland Revenue's policy of selective enforcement was unsuccessfully challenged in *R v IRC, ex p Mead and Cook* [4:4] (see also *R v IRC, ex p Allen* [1997] STC 1141, where Allen had offered to settle allegations of tax evasion by paying £1 million but was nonetheless prosecuted: his application to challenge the decision to prosecute him by way of judicial review was unsuccessful). The court appears to accept without difficulty a policy that leaves the discretion to prosecute challengeable only when it is proved to be 'irrational'.

(i) REVENUE AND CUSTOMS FRAUDS

HM Revenue and Customs (HMRC) was formed in April 2005 (see Commissioners for Revenue and Customs Act 2005), following the merger of Inland Revenue and HM Customs and Excise (HMCE) Departments. This followed on from the recommendations of Gus O'Donnell's Review of the Revenue Departments, published in 2004. Whilst this document discussed the need to ensure 'resources are allocated effectively so as to minimize tax losses to the Exchequer and so ensure public services are well financed' (page 12), it had little to say on enforcement and prosecution policy. More guidance can be found in HM Revenue and Customs Recovery Manual, (available at <http://www.hmrc.gov.uk/manuals/recmanual/index.htm>).

The function of prosecuting HMRC's criminal casework is undertaken by the Revenue and Customs Prosecution Office (RCPO), an 'independent' prosecuting authority reporting to the Attorney-General. This resulted from two reviews of a series of spectacular failures in prosecutions: first, the Gower Hammond Review (2000) into the failure of two major drugs prosecutions conducted by Customs in the late 1990s, which urged greater independence of prosecutors from investigators, and secondly, the Butterfield Report (2003) into the mistakes in both investigation and prosecution in the London City Bond cases, which went further, urging 'a complete separation of the prosecuting function for HM Customs and Excise's criminal cases from the organisation itself, through the creation of a separate prosecuting authority'. This Report explored the collapse of a high profile investigation and prosecution of 15 defendants on charges of conspiracy to cheat the public revenue of duty on beer and spirits. The trial judge had ordered not guilty verdicts on day 35 of the trial, expressing particular concern on issues of non-disclosure. Mr Justice Butterfield made a number of recommendations on law enforcement (that HMCE should remain as an independent investigating force, but better procedures for handling human sources were urgently necessary), on prosecution (greater independence), and on the criminal justice system (on disclosure, case management, and the retention of intercepted materials within the Regulation of Investigatory Powers Act 2000 regime).

A recurring theme of this book is the need to question the reality and value of 'independence' in this context. What exactly does RCPO do, and to what extent is it truly independent? Some useful material is to be gathered from its annual reports. Thus, we learn that it is divided in to five divisions, A–E:

Division A: Direct Tax Fraud Including income tax, corporation tax and organized tax credit fraud based on identity theft.

Division B: Commercial Fraud including large-scale VAT fraud and more complex Missing Trader Intra-Community Fraud (MTIC). Also known as 'carousel fraud', this is seen as a key priority. Here is an example, from the Annual Report 2005/06:

R v Jones and Woolley Daniel Jones and Jeffrey Woolley organized an MTIC fraud that involved buying mobile phones from fictitious UK companies and selling them to other mobile phone brokers, with the proceeds going to a company in Ireland. Over a period of nearly a year, Woolley bought the phones from two missing or hijacked traders, sold them on to other UK traders and sent the VAT to the Irish company. Jones ran a number of companies, which received VAT from firms involved in buying and selling mobile phones. The mobile phones were simply there to perpetrate the fraud by using false receipts to charge VAT on the transactions. The men were convicted of cheating the Revenue of £58 million following an HMRC investigation lasting over three years. Jones was sentenced to 6 years imprisonment and Woolley was sentenced to 2 years imprisonment. (RCPO Annual Report 2005/06, page 22)

Division C: Border Detections including drug smuggling through ports and airports, export controls and sanctions violations.

Division D: Duty and Excise including alcohol, tobacco and hydrocarbon oils duty fraud.

Division E: Serious Organised Crime. This covers large-scale drug importation and associated money laundering. It is also responsible for the enforcement of confiscation orders made in foreign courts against assets located in the UK.

We already noted in Chapter 2, on the police, the creation of the Serious Organised Crime Agency (SOCA). It is difficult to imagine the extent of the confusions which must arise between the various bodies investigating crime. We are told in the RCPO's Annual Report 2005/06 (at page 12) that it has adapted a 'dual prosecutor model', whereby RCPO prosecutes large-scale drug importation and associated money laundering activity. Clearly RCPO work closely with the Crown Prosecution Service (CPS), but the territorial divides between the various organizations seem fraught with difficulties. Add to this the fact that legal advice will be crucial throughout the obviously lengthy investigations and intelligence work necessitated by drug and fraud conspiracies, and one has to question the meaning and value of independence in this context. Note that the overlapping roles will lead to successful appeals: the Divisional Court in *R v Stafford Justices, ex p Customs and Excise Commissioners* [1991] 2 QB 339 unsurprisingly rejected an argument that once a custody officer in a police station had charged the applicant with an offence under the Drug Trafficking Offences Act 1986, the (then) Customs and Excise Commissioners were no longer entitled to prosecute her. The charging process is neutral in this context: proceedings are only instituted on behalf of a police force when it is the police who have investigated, arrested, and brought the arrested person to the custody officer. And in *R (Hunt) v Criminal Case Review Commission* [2001]

QB 1108 the Administrative Court confirmed that the Inland Revenue could pursue pros-ecutions in the Crown Court and did not need the consent of the Attorney-General to do so. Two interesting cases where the Court of Appeal applied the PACE Code of Practice C: *The Detention, Treatment and Questioning of Persons by the Police* [2:12] to the behaviour of Customs officers questioning suspects at Heathrow Airport are *R v Okafor* [1994] 3 All ER 741 and *R v Owusu* [2007] EWCA Crim 340 (where, having found a breach of Code C, the conviction was quashed because the evidence of some answers to questions should have been excluded: but a retrial was ordered).

Note carefully HMRC's Criminal Investigation policy [4:5]. It is HMRC's policy to deal with fraud by the use of 'cost effective' Civil Investigation of Fraud (CIF) procedures, where appropriate. Following the report of the Keith Committee *Report on the Enforcement Powers of the Revenue Departments* (1983) Cmnd 8822, the range of sanctions available to the Revenue Departments was extended. Compounding, which enables them to force com-pliance as well as a financial penalty, is today widely used as an alternative to taking legal proceedings. Other 'non-judicial penalties' include seizure of goods, vehicles, or equipment used in smuggling or revenue offences. Civil fraud procedures were introduced for VAT by the Finance Act 1986 and were extended to excise duty frauds and customs duties frauds by sections 7–14 of and Schedule 4 and 5 to the Finance Act 1994. This is part of a process of decriminalization of many (often strict liability) offences, in stark contrast to the crim-inilization of much other anti-social behaviour. Dee Cook's work has been important in highlighting the different approaches taken in benefit frauds. In her (2006) book, *Criminal and Social Justice* she asks (at page 46) 'when it comes to fiddling the state, is there one law for the (relatively) rich and another for the poor in contemporary Britain?' She points out how the taxpayer has historically been valued as a law-abiding and productive citizen and a giver of revenue for State services. She notes a plummeting of the number of Inland Revenue prosecutions and a dramatic reduction in yields from investigation work from the early 1990s to the early 2000s. She argues that the current prosecution policy seems to work well—for the fraudster (see page 52).

The emphasis of this section has been on the prosecution policy of the taxation authorities, which is so much more selective than that of the police. However, McBarnet (1992) went fur-ther, pointing out that social control through law is challenged not just by those who abuse the law but also by those who use it. She stresses the manipulability of the law in this area and the scope for bending it to specific interests so that 'economic elites with the resources to buy legal creativity can also buy immunity from the law' (at page 266). Dee Cook goes so far as to argue that traditional hatred of personal taxation has led to 'agency investigation and prosecution policies and broader political priorities designed to appeal to middle England' (2006, page 60). But remember that Roording's (1996) (Dutch) perspective also criticizes the 'huge and institutionalised pressure' on taxpayers to confess and to cooperate (see [4:2]). Should the system be less informal?

(ii) BENEFIT FRAUDS

The Department of Work and Pensions (DWP) (and its agency JobCentrePlus) uses a Fraud Investigation Service to investigate benefit theft (estimated at around £900 million in 2004/05; £700 million in 2006/07). The current sanctions policy of the DWP is included at

[4:6]. The Department's solicitors are bound by the Code for Crown Prosecutors (see paragraph 4.4.3). Would the next logical step be to bring these prosecutions under the CPS? We return to this question in the final section of this chapter.

Dee Cook in her books of 1989 and 2006 analysed the different responses to tax and social security frauds. She found that in 1986/87, when 457 tax evaders were prosecuted, 8,000 people were prosecuted for falsely claiming Supplementary Benefit (the predecessor of Income Support). As we have noted above, Cook develops these arguments further in another book in 2006 which uses data from the 1990s and early 2000s to suggest that the picture has not improved. She suggests that the differences can be explained in terms of the different histories of taxation and welfare and, subsequently, the ideological construction of taxpayers as 'givers' to, and benefit claimants as 'takers' from, the State. McKeever **[4:7]** reviews a recent change in the law which shows the dangers which arise from draconian legislation. She argues that making the receipt of social security conditional upon compliance with a community sentence is counterproductive. Readers will also find her 1999 article useful, where she highlights the possibility of fraud arising from claimant confusion rather than dishonesty (see Further reading). The stark difference in the way that benefit fraud is dealt with is also illustrated by the numbers of prosecutions: as the Sentencing Advisory Panel (2007) point out, there has been 'a decrease in the number of offenders sentenced for offences against HM Revenue and Customs (from 1,212 in 1999 to 362 in 2005), of whom around 85 per cent are men, and an increase in the number sentenced for certain benefit fraud offences (from 710 in 1999 to 3,530 in 2005), of whom approximately 55 per cent are women'. Are current policies exaggerating the 'one law for the rich and another for the poor' approach, identified by Dee Cook? The increasing ratio of women offenders which results from current policies should also raise questions in your mind.

(iii) HEALTH AND SAFETY EXECUTIVE

The Report of the Health and Safety Offences and Penalties 2004/05 tells us that in 2004/05, the HSE brought 712 prosecutions—78 per cent of that in 2002/03 (908 prosecutions), and 74 per cent of that in 2003/04 (963 prosecutions). As the website (<http://www.hse.gov.uk/enforce/off0405/>) explains:

We don't take enforcement action lightly. Visits from our inspectors give duty holders the opportunity to get expert advice face to face. A proportionate approach is taken to any breaches, so in less serious cases, the inspector will explain how the duty holder is not complying with the law and advise them how to put the problem right. The inspector will explain legal requirements and good practice, as well as confirming the advice in writing if asked. However, failure to follow the advice from our inspectors is often taken into account by courts if that failure results in harm.

Where the breach of the law is more serious, the inspector may serve a notice on the duty holder. The inspector can serve:

- an improvement notice, which requires duty holders to take remedial action on specific breaches of the law within a specified time limit;

- a prohibition notice, which is issued in cases where the inspector believes that a work activity involves, or will involve, a risk of serious personal injury. Prohibition notices can take two forms:
  - immediate prohibition notices, which stop a work activity immediately until a risk is dealt with; and
  - deferred prohibition notices, which stop a work activity within a specified time limit.

When an inspector issues a notice, it is an opportunity for the duty holder to put things right and prevent future incidents. If the duty holder fails to comply with the notice, prosecution is likely to follow.

The policies that lie behind health and safety prosecutions can therefore provide useful comparisons to police decision-making: the HSE do not 'take enforcement lightly'. Should there be greater flexibility in police enforcement policies? Or should there be more attempts to monitor this flexible (and potentially unfair) HSE approach?

(iv) THE ENVIRONMENT AGENCY

The Environment Agency has four 'key principles' of good enforcement: proportionality, consistency, transparency, targeting (see <http://www.environment-agency.gov.uk>, which includes the Agency's enforcement and prosecution policy and its 'functional guidelines' for staff).

TABLE 4.1 Prosecutions, fines, and enforcement notices served by the Environment Agency, 2005/06 (2004/05 figures in brackets)

Permit	Successful prosecutions	Fines awarded (£)	Enforcement notices
Water quality discharge consents	39 (11)	189,650 (88,800)	1 (4)
IPC or IPPC authorizations	6 (4)	149,000 (92,000)	47 (16)
Waste regulation licences	6 (19)	118,000 (211,500)	248 (0)
Radioactive substances licences	1 (0)	16,000 (-)	2 (3)
Water resources abstraction licences	4 (6)	13,250 (315,700)	0 (5)

What do these figures tell us? Perhaps not a great deal. Let us look briefly at how the system works. A person or company needs consent to discharge any trade or sewage effluent into rivers, lakes, or coastal waters. Discharge consents usually specify the volume, nature, and composition of the discharge. Most consents are for sewage treatment plants and the sewerage network, but the remaining consents are for 'traders' such as power stations, mineral works, and factories. Normally the local water company issues consents for discharges to the sewerage system itself. Operators of Integrated Pollution Prevention and Control (IPPC) processes need an authorization for their particular process. The Environment Agency grants authorizations for the potentially most polluting industrial processes (Part A processes). Local authorities grant the authorizations for the smaller, less polluting processes (Part B processes). Authorizations specify certain operation and discharge conditions that operators must show they meet. But only exceptionally it appears will the Agency prosecute. As its published enforcement and prosecution policy tells us: 'We believe that prevention is better than cure'. You will find its 119-page Guidance for the enforcement and prosecution policy on its website (at the time of going to press, it was the 17th published version, issued in December 2007).

Hutter's fascinating analysis of the work of Environmental Health Officers in *The Reasonable Arm of the Law?* (1988) explored how the criminal law was then used to regulate business activities. She suggested that where the offender was seen as basically 'good and respectable' the enforcement agency concerned tended to adopt what is often described as an accommodative approach, seeking compliance through negotiation. Only where the alleged offender was seen as 'bad' did the agency need to enforce compliance. Compliance is also necessary since, if the regulator does not have the cooperation of the offender, they will often not discover offending until 'accidents' happen. The aim of this compliance strategy is prevention, not punishment. The enforcer will negotiate with the firms against whom they are enforcing the law, in a way that cannot happen between the police and a small-time crook, who has no bargaining counters with which to negotiate (echoes here of Cook's arguments summarized above). Richardson et al (1982), though clearly very dated, is still useful in encouraging you to ask the big questions: Why do governments intervene in the affairs of business? Is the use of the criminal sanction an appropriate means of persuading industry to comply with governmental controls? Sanders **[4:8]** shows how this approach of selective enforcement and selective charging leads to class bias.

Are these regulatory bodies right to give priority to compliance over prosecution? For the sake of consistency, should all prosecutions be brought under the CPS umbrella? But is there a difference in principle between these offences and police cases that explains why they should be treated differently?

(v) SERIOUS FRAUD OFFICE

The Serious Fraud Office (SFO) was established by the Criminal Justice Act (CJA) 1987, following the report of the Roskill Committee on Fraud Trials (1986). The Committee's most controversial recommendation—that in some complex fraud cases the trial should take place not before a judge and jury but before a 'fraud trials tribunal' comprising a judge and two members with financial expertise—was rejected by the Government (though we will see in Chapter 8 how this has, in some measure, been adopted). However, many of its other proposals on fraud trials were acted upon in the CJA 1987.

The SFO investigates and prosecutes the most serious frauds in England, Wales, and Northern Ireland, but the numbers are small (for example, it was responsible for eight trials in 2001/02, involving 13 defendants: 10 were convicted and three acquitted; in 2006/07, 11 trials were completed, involving 21 defendants: 15 were convicted and six acquitted). It is accountable through its director to the Attorney-General and so to Parliament. Investigations are conducted by interdisciplinary teams of lawyers, police officers and accountants. Most of the police officers are members of the Metropolitan Police or the City of London police.

Thus, the investigatory and prosecution roles were combined in one office, just after they had been separated in the case of 'standard' criminal offences, by the creation of the CPS in 1985. Does the special and complex nature of some frauds make continuity of investigation and prosecution desirable—is fraud necessarily more difficult than other crime? It is not clear exactly where the line between serious fraud and other fraud is drawn, and many serious frauds continue to be dealt with by the CPS. Another difficult line to draw is that which separates the work of the SFO from that of the Financial Services Authority, created by the Financial Services Act 1986. It has now, following the Financial Services and Markets Act 2000, taken over responsibility for the 'detection, investigation and prosecution' of some financial crime. The key criterion we use when deciding whether to accept a case is that the suspected fraud appears to be so serious or complex that its investigation should be carried out by those responsible for its prosecution. The SFO's website explains that:

SFO resources must be focused on major and complicated fraud. Factors considered: does the value of the alleged fraud exceed £1 million? is there a significant international dimension? is the case likely to be of widespread public concern? does the case require highly specialised knowledge, e.g. of financial markets? is there a need to use the SFO's special powers, such as Section 2 of the Criminal Justice Act?

Note the CJA Act 1987, section 2 **[4:9]**: the SFO has wide powers of investigation as well as of prosecution. Its powers to compel a suspect to answer questions or otherwise to furnish information, and to require the production of documents, were examined by the House of Lords in *R v Director of Serious Fraud, ex p Smith* **[4:10]**. The European Court of Human Rights in *Saunders v United Kingdom* (1996) 23 EHRR 313 held that the admission in evidence at the applicant's trial of transcripts of interviews with Department of Trade and Industry inspectors violated Article 6(1) of the European Convention on Human Rights (see **[1:12]**). Article 6(1) presupposes that the prosecution must prove its case without resort to evidence obtained through methods of coercion. As a result of this decision, section 59 (together with Schedule 3) of the Youth Justice and Criminal Evidence Act 1999 now restricts the use that can be made of answers obtained under compulsory powers of questioning in legislation such as the Companies Act 2006. Are there implications here for the provisions of the Criminal Justice and Public Order Act (CJPOA) 1994 restricting the right to silence?

We saw in Chapter 3 how the CPS is handicapped in providing an independent review of police decisions by not having its own powers of investigation. Since the SFO has its own investigators, it should perhaps have a high record of success. However, as Levi (1993) made clear, measuring the success or otherwise of the SFO is not easy. It is impossible to tell whether non-prosecutions are due to political or other extra-legal factors, and prosecution policies can undergo significant shifts if large funds are made available—this happened, for example, with the special Treasury 'votes' for the Bank of Credit and Commerce International investigation. Levi argued that many prosecutions go ahead despite foreseeable weaknesses in the case, and proposes greater judicial involvement before the trial. On the other hand, he fears that prosecution decisions in cases of white-collar crime will become driven almost entirely by cost considerations, a risk exacerbated by the media and the political tendency to look at the huge costs of the individual trial, ignoring the huge dimensions of the misconduct to which they relate (at page 196). If the prosecution of serious frauds proves so difficult, and so expensive, perhaps there is an argument for leaving these cases to the civil law or to administrative regulation. But would this be letting the affluent, white-collar criminal off too lightly? What price are we prepared to pay?

How far have things moved on since 1993? There is no doubt that there is significant public and Governmental concern about the extent of fraud, and its effects on the economy and wider society. An interesting perspective on why people choose to commit white-collar crime is offered by Shover and Hochstetler (2006). They distinguish 'ordinary' and 'upper-world' white-collar crime, and present reasons theoretically for believing that both have increased substantially in recent decades (including the growing supply of white-collar lure and non-credible oversight). It seems that the criminal law can play only a small part in dealing with this problem. The Government hopes that the Fraud Act 2006, which repealed the earlier law of fraud creating new broad substantive offences, will secure more convictions. But the Government's own interdepartmental review into the detection, investigation, and prosecution of fraud (2006) recognizes that there are many institutional and practical hurdles which go far beyond the law itself if we want to reduce fraud.

(vi) PRIVATE PROSECUTIONS

Many of the prosecutions mentioned in this chapter might be considered 'private prosecutions'. For example, the Royal Society for the Prevention of Cruelty to Animals (RSPCA) has its own prosecution department, and when it prosecutes uses private lawyers.

Lord Wilberforce in *Gouriet v Union of Post Office Workers* [1978] AC 435 described the right of the individual to institute a private prosecution 'as a valuable constitutional safe-guard against inertia or partiality on the part of authority' (at page 477). But the value of this right should not be exaggerated. Legal aid is not available to a private prosecutor, and in any case the right is in effect controlled by the Attorney-General (see Chapter 3), who may take over the prosecution and, if he thinks fit, enter a plea of *nolle prosequi* ('we do not wish to prosecute'). It is not unusual for the Attorney-General to make clear that if a private prosecution were to be launched, he would stop it. This happened in the case of a priest who threatened to prosecute the doctors who, having sought authority from the House of Lords in *Airedale NHS Trust v Bland* [1993] AC 789, 'killed' Tony Bland, a patient in a persistent vegetative state. Thus the Attorney-General in effect has a veto on law enforcement. In *Jones v Whalley* **[4:11]**, Lord Bingham described the right to prosecute privately as:

a somewhat anomalous historical survival . . . A crime is an offence against the good order of the state. It is for the state by its appropriate agencies to investigate alleged crimes and decide whether offenders should be prosecuted. In times past, with no public prosecution service and ill-organised means of enforcing the law, the prosecution of offenders necessarily depended on the involvement of private individuals, but that is no longer so. The surviving right of private prosecution is of questionable value, and can be exercised in a way damaging to the public interest. (paragraphs 15–16)

Lord Mance in that case quotes the Law Commission's *Report on Consents to Prosecution* (1988, LC 255):

We . . . do not believe that it is appropriate to consider abolishing the right of private prosecution without specific consideration which has neither been sought nor given in this project. The issues raised on the question of retention of the right of private prosecution are complex and they are not capable of being resolved within the scope of this report (paragraph 5.13). They mention three important issues:

(1) There is always a risk that an individual Crown prosecutor will either misapply the code or—more likely, given the width of the code tests—apply a personal interpretation to the tests which, although not wrong, might differ from that of other prosecutors.

(2) The code itself may, in the eyes of some, fail to achieve a proper balance between the rights of the defendant and the interests of the community.

(3) It should not be assumed that if it is wrong to bring a public prosecution then it is also wrong to bring a private prosecution. If, for example, a case is turned down by the [Crown Prosecution Service] because it fails the evidential sufficiency test, but only just; if the private prosecutor knows that the defendant is guilty (because, say, he or she was the victim and can identify the offender); and if the case is a serious one, then a private prosecution might be thought desirable.

So the right lives on in a half-hearted manner. Private prosecutions, and prosecutions by non-police agencies, raise many questions: whether getting people to agree not to break the law (compliance) is sometimes a better strategy than prosecution; whether these bodies have too many discretionary powers. It is important to remember that a case like Gerry Good's enters the criminal justice system through the 'normal', police, route, but it is certainly not the only route.

FURTHER READING

Attorney-General *Fraud Review* (2006) <http://www.attorneygeneral.gov.uk/the_fraud_review_page.html>

Butterfield, Mr Justice, *Review of criminal investigations and prosecutions conducted by HM Customs and Excise* (2003) <http://www.hm-treasury.gov.uk>

Cook, D, *Rich Law, Poor Law* (1989) Open UP

Cook, D, *Criminal and Social Justice* (2006) Sage

Croall, H, *Understanding White Collar Crime* (2001) Open UP

Gower, J and Hammond, A, *Report on Customs and Excise prosecutions* (2000)

Hawkins, K, *Environment and Enforcement* (1984) Oxford UP

Hawkins, K and Thomas J M (eds), *Enforcing Regulation* (1984) Kluwer-Nijhoff

Hutter, B, *The Reasonable Arm of the Law?* (1988) Oxford UP

Jones, K, *Law and Economy: the legal regulation of corporate capital* (1982) Academic Press

Kirk, D N and Woodcock, A J J, *Serious Fraud: Investigation and Trial* (1992) Butterworths

Levi, M, *The Phantom Capitalists* (2008) Ashgate

Levi, M, *The Investigation, Prosecution and Trial of Serious Fraud* (1993) RCCJ Research Study No 14, HMSO

Levi, M, Burrows, J, Fleming, M, and Hopkins, M, *The Nature, Extent and Economic Impact of Fraud in the UK* (2007) ACPO

McBarnet, D, *Crime, Compliance and Control* (2004) Ashgate

McKeever, G, 'Detecting, Prosecuting and Punishing Benefit Fraud: The Social Security Administration (Fraud) Act 1997' (1999) 62 MLR 261

McKeever, G, 'Tackling Benefit Fraud' (2003) 32 Industrial Law Journal 326

Nelken, D, 'White-Collar Crime' in Maguire, Morgan, and Reiner (eds), *The Oxford Handbook of Criminology* (3rd edition, 2002)

Richardson, G, Ogus, A, and Burrows, P, *Policing Pollution* (1982) Clarendon Press

Sentencing Advisory Panel, Consultation Paper on *Sentencing for Fraud Offences* (2007)

Shover, N and Hochstetler, A, *Choosing White Collar Crime* (2006) Cambridge UP

DOCUMENTS

[4:1] Lidstone, K W, Hogg, R, and Sutcliffe, F, *Prosecutions by Private Individuals and Non-Police Agencies*

(1980) HMSO (at page 180)

The prosecuting policies and statistics of nine agencies were considered in some detail—these were the DHSS, The Post Office, the NTVLRO (television licence evasion), the DVLC (vehicle excise licence cases), the Inland Revenue, Customs and Excise, and Health and Safety Executive, the Department of Trade and the Ministry of Agriculture Fisheries and Food. These agencies were selected on the basis of several considerations: we sought to include those agencies which have a large prosecutorial work-load as well as those other agencies which, although prosecuting infrequently, fulfil important public functions within which the investigation and/or prosecution of criminal offences plays a significant part. It was found that there were considerable differences in policy between (and sometimes within) agencies. For example, among the revenue-collecting agencies, NTVLRO and DVLC prosecuted far more readily than did the Inland Revenue; within the DHSS, non-compliance with national insurance payments was treated a great deal more lightly than social security fraud; within the Department of Trade there were important differences in policies and types of arrangements for investigation and prosecution in respect of company registration cases, companies investigations, bankruptcy cases and company frauds. A further marked feature of this study of major agencies was the vast potential for further prosecution clearly available in many instances. This was most obvious in agencies which saw their primary task as securing compliance with legislation through persuasion and education (such as the Health and Safety Executive) or through negotiated settlements and penalties short of prosecution (such as the Inland Revenue). Even agencies which prosecuted relatively frequently, such as NTVLRO and DVLC, had considerable further potential for prosecution. Further investigation showed that in nearly all cases the role and extent of prosecution was related to the perceived primary task of the agency. Only the DHSS (in social security cases) and the Post Office tended to see infractions as unambiguously 'criminal', to be pursued through the deterrent and retributive mechanisms of the criminal law; in the case of the DHSS this policy presented the agency with a problem in reconciling this stance with its primary role as a dispenser of welfare benefits.

In Chapter 4 some of the minor agencies were considered, and a group of particular interest here were the 'voluntary agencies' such as the RSPCA, the RSPB and Friends of the Earth. In general they tended to be reluctant prosecutors, deploring the relative inactivity of the police and other law enforcement agencies concerning their special area of interest; lacking resources themselves to prosecute to any great extent and therefore largely dependent on the police (though here the RSPCA was something of an exception); and only mounting their own prosecutions where the police were unwilling to act.

The court study had given a picture of prosecutorial activity by non-police bodies in 12 courts. The bulk of these were agency prosecutions, rather than prosecutions by private individuals, firms or voluntary bodies. (Some of the latter, such as retail stores and the RSPCA, were in any case reluctant prosecutors.) Among the agencies, however, further investigation revealed vast differences in the numbers of prosecutions, and in prosecution policy. It may be helpful finally to set out in schematic form some of the factors (not all previously mentioned in this summary) which may influence the number of prosecutions an agency undertakes:

(a) The population at risk of offending. Some agencies (like DVLC, NTVLRO and the Inland Revenue) potentially affect nearly every household in the country; others (like to Law Society and the General Nursing Council) will because of their restricted populations at risk never be major prosecutors. But not all 'large risk' agencies prosecute widely; the Inland Revenue is a notable example.

(b) The availability of alternative measures short of prosecution. Some agencies have such methods as formal alternatives, and tend to use them extensively: examples are Inland Revenue, Customs and Excise, and Health and Safety Executive; and the methods include compounding, seizure of goods, enforcement notices and cautions.

(c) The resources available to investigate offences. Several agencies have to restrict their investigative activities because of lack of resources (for example DVLC, Department of Trade and some local authorities). When one metropolitan Passenger Transport Executive set up a squad of plain clothes inspectors to police fare evasion, it was so successful in discovering evaders that a second squad and set up, and the numbers prosecuted soared on each occasion.

(d) The difficulty of proof. Agencies such as the Inland Revenue and the Department of Trade face severe tests of proof in large-scale fraud cases. The subject matter of the charges is often complex, and the prosecutor has to prove intention or at least recklessness. The defendants are often sophisticated and well advised. If a guilty plea is unlikely then prosecution may well be discouraged, especially if, as in the case of Inland Revenue, other courses are open to the agency. This does not apply to offences of strict liability such as using a motor vehicle without a vehicle excise licence, but even here there is often great difficulty in identifying the user of the vehicle.

(e) Political pressure. Both DHSS (markedly) and the Wages Inspectorate (marginally) have increased their prosecutorial work in recent years, in response to different kinds of direct political pressure.

(f) The perception of the primary task of the agency. Agencies which perceive their primary task as educative and persuasive have particularly low prosecution rates in relation to known offences (for example Health and Safety, local authorities). Even quite extensive prosecutors, like NTVLRO and DVLC, will be found not to prosecute in a sizeable proportion of cases if compliance can be secured through other means: for them, revenue collection, not prosecution, remains the primary goal. Conversely, agencies like the larger special police forces tend to see their activity as primarily law enforcement, and therefore use prosecution as a first rather than last resort.

(g) The perception of the offence. A widespread view in many agencies was that the offences involved were not really crime in the proper sense, and therefore not appropriate for automatic prosecution; such a view obviously encourages the use of other methods to secure compliance. A view of this kind may be challenged by outsiders (as it is, for example, by critics of the minimal prosecution policies of the Inland Revenue and the Health and Safety Executive), but this still may not affect the agency's perception. Varying perceptions of different offences may produce markedly different enforcement policies within a single agency, for example social security fraud as against non-compliance cases within the DHSS.

(h) Police reluctance to be involved. Retail stores and electricity boards in London would not themselves prosecute at all if the police would do so; the voluntary agencies also tend to prosecute only because of the perceived reluctance or of inaction by other law enforcement agencies, especially the police. The DHSS may in future be forced to seek wider investigative powers for its officers, and perhaps take on some cases currently prosecuted by the police, if a projected reduction in police co-operation occurs.

[4:2] Roording, J, 'The Punishment of Tax Fraud'

[1996] Crim LR 240 (at page 240)

In this article I intend to explore the field of punishment of tax fraud in the United Kingdom. I will make use of information I gathered with the Inland Revenue, inter alia through discussions with certain officials. As a Dutch lawyer I will necessarily take a continental view, and I shall introduce a perspective which has gained some popularity in the Netherlands recently. In this perspective the criminal law is seen as a system of punishment (a sanctions system) which, together with other such systems (especially the administrative sanctions system), is part of a wider field of law which could be called the law of sanctions. It is thought that these sanctions systems have much in common (ie the same purposes), and that all are governed by the same basic principles (for which reference is often made to Article 6 of the European Convention for the Protection of Human Rights and Fundamental Freedoms (ECHR)), so that a more integrated approach is advisable. This perspective provides a framework which makes possible a critical assessment of law enforcement practices of regulatory agencies from the point of view of the rights of suspects and offenders. At the same time it also focuses on alternative ways of punishment which could relieve the overburdened criminal justice system.

The sanctions systems in the field of tax

This sketch of the sanctions systems in the field of tax is limited to the procedures of the Inland Revenue (IR), which is responsible for the administration of direct taxes, such as income tax and corporation tax, in the United Kingdom. (I do not propose to deal with Customs and Excise, who are responsible for the administration of customs, excise and VAT and to that end have separate enforcement powers at their disposal; Customs and Excise have a fundamentally different approach from that of the Inland Revenue.) Two ways of punishment are open to the Inland Revenue: imposition of a civil penalty, and prosecution. Penalties (see Chapter X of the Taxes Management Act (TMA) 1970) are usually imposed by an officer of the Board of Inland Revenue, but in certain cases by an independent body called the (General or Special) Commissioners and in certain cases by the court. Statute either sets the maximum penalty at a fixed amount (for example in case of a simple failure to deliver a return; TMA 1970, s 93(1)(a): maximum penalty 300) or at 100 per cent of the tax due (in case of a more serious offence, where there is fraud or negligence; see for example s 95 (incorrect return or account)). From a determination of a penalty by an officer of the Board appeal lies, first, to the Commissioners (s 100B(2)) and then to the High Court (s 100B(3)).

Besides imposing a civil penalty the Inland Revenue can also choose to initiate criminal proceedings. Usually the IR will not leave this to the police and the Crown Prosecution Service but bring a prosecution itself. Several charges are available: offences under the general criminal law, such as false accounting (s 17 of the Theft Act 1968), or cheating the public revenue, an offence under the common law. In contrast with Customs and Excise the Inland Revenue has no power to compound criminal proceedings. Theoretically the IR can impose a civil penalty and at the same time institute a prosecution for the same offence. It is however settled practice not to impose a penalty for an offence which has already been dealt with by the criminal court.

(At page 248:)

In my view the way tax fraud is punished in the United Kingdom is not satisfactory. My main criticism concerns the huge and institutionalised pressure which is exerted on taxpayers to make them confess and co-operate. It is true that there will be pressure in any system in which the criminal law operates as an alternative to another, less 'heavy' sanctions system (heavy both in terms of sanctions and in terms of procedures). However, in the English system of punishment of tax fraud the pressure is extra strong, because the Inland Revenue seeks to keep the case in the informal sphere as long as possible. There the IR can dictate its own rules, and the formal procedures become a 'big stick'. By contrast, taxpayers have more protection in the Netherlands. There the tax department must choose between prosecution and the imposition of an administrative penalty. There is no third, informal way. In addition, the criminal and administrative spheres seem to be more clearly demarcated with respect to one another. This will be even more so when a current Bill is enacted which goes so far as to determine that once a prosecution or a penalty procedure has reached a certain point, there is no return; the other way is closed then. Further safeguards, which apply in penalty procedures, are a right of access to court, the right to be informed about the grounds of the accusation, and a duty on the Revenue to prove the mental element of the offence (fraud or negligence). The new Bill mentioned above even acknowledges the right to silence with regard to administrative penalty procedures.

The root of the problem seems to me that in the English legal system, systems of punishment outside the criminal law hardly get any attention, whether from the courts or from academics.[1] It is not yet recognised that these sanctions systems show big similarities to the criminal law: in practice they operate as a very important alternative to the criminal sanctions system, with the same purpose, ie to enforce the law) and with the same means (eg fines). Unless and until this is recognised, grey areas such as that of the settlement of tax fraud will continue to exist and they will be governed by practical rules rather than legal principles.

[4:3] Richardson, G, 'Strict Liability for Regulatory Crime: the Empirical Research'
[1987] Crim LR 295 (at page 303)

In an article chiefly concerned with the debate surrounding the use of strict liability in the regulatory context, Richardson raises the thorny issue of the usurpation of the criminal trial by administrative discretion.

To an extent the empirical data, by emphasising the practical relevance of the offender's intent, might suggest that the concern over the propriety of strict liability is irrelevant. Such a conclusion is not inevitable, however. In the first place, although the data indicate that 'blameless innocents' are rarely prosecuted, the traditionalist is unlikely to be satisfied since the determination of 'blame' is made privately by an administrative agent rather than publicly with the full procedural protection of a criminal trial. Secondly, there is still the argument, referred to briefly above, that the use of strict liability serves both to detract from the significance of regulatory offences and to distinguish them from the main body of the criminal law. The introduction of strict liability into early factory legislation, for example, is thought to have placed a part in the marginalisation of early factory crime. In this sense, strict liability can be said to further the interests of the regulated by reducing the significance of non-compliance.

To some extent the first problem, the usurpation of the criminal trial by administrative discretion, can be met by the introduction of civil penalties in place of strict criminal liability. The device is common in the United States where crimes of strict liability are rare. But the mere removal of the criminal label provides no real solution to the problem of administrative discretion and must serve further to marginalise the prohibited activity. Arguably, the question of liability for corporate offences is not a 'problem' to be tackled in isolation but must be seen as merely one element of the regulatory scheme.

Whether or not regulatory offences constitute 'real' crime, the majority can be readily distinguished from the mass of traditional street crime as currently regarded. The distinction does not, however, rely on the narrow argument that regulatory crime is different because it is less serious and therefore strict liability is acceptable because penalties are low. It springs instead from the nature of the regulatory objective.

Legislative schemes regulating corporate conduct are primarily designed to prevent particular harms and are certainly seen in that light by those responsible for their enforcement. In large part, therefore, the overall legitimacy of any regulatory scheme and of the separate elements within it will flow from their combined ability to prevent harm. Each element will both contribute to and reflect the legitimacy of the whole.

In the first place protective regulation must provide for the proper definition of the prohibited event and the closer the relationship between the event and the harm, the more justifiable will be the prohibition. In addition, the research suggests that the more evidently justifiable or rational the prohibition the more assiduous will be the enforcement. In such a context, if the prohibition event is potentially harmful irrespective of the offender's mental state as classified by current criminal law principles, then there can be little instrumental justification for demanding the presence of fault as defined by those principles. Further, the corporate actor typically behaves in a particular way, installs a certain plant, for example, or markets a given drug, because of the anticipated benefits. To place 'properly' defined restrictions on such 'voluntary' behaviour and to penalise non-compliance is not to persecute the innocent even in the absence of any legally recognised degree of fault.

Secondly, if as is claimed here, the primary justification for regulatory prohibition rests on the need to prevent harm, then arguably the sanctions imposed on non-compliance should be designed with that end in view. This question inevitably raises highly contentious issues within the field of penal theory which go far beyond the scope of this article. Nonetheless, the proper role of the penal sanctions cannot be ignored in any consideration of regulatory crime.

With regard to traditional offences the prevention of future harm as the justification for criminal punishment has been severely challenged. In relation to regulatory offences, however, the argument may carry less weight. In the first place corporate offending is often regarded as less intractable than traditional criminality: the application of criminal sanctions might successfully deter, incapacitate, or even rehabilitate. Secondly, with regard to the problem of inequality of treatment, which is often linked to the preventative use of criminal sanctions, Braithwaite has argued that complete equality for regulatory offenders is beyond the scope of any criminal justice system and that the need to prevent serious harm, Thalidomide or Bhopal for example, should take priority over strict equality of treatment. Finally the rearrangement of a company's practices and procedures in order to ensure that it operates without causing harm is not open to the same moral considerations as the coerced rearranging of a psyche. In the light of these considerations most commentators identify harm prevention constrained by the principles of retribution as the primary rationale for the punishment of corporate offences in general and regulatory offences in particular.

It would appear, therefore, that the sanction has considerable potential to further the objectives of the regulatory scheme, and indeed in the United States a variety of sanctioning options have been tried or considered including: equity fines, adverse publicity, redress facilitation through plea bargaining, the integration of civil and criminal claims, community service orders and corporate probation. However, in the United Kingdom, despite widespread doubts as to its efficacy, the fine remains the most common sanction. Arguably, more effort is required to devise alternatives which effectively exploit the supposed susceptibility of corporate offenders to deterrence, incapacitation and rehabilitation.

In sum, the routine enforcement of regulatory offences typically exposes strict liability as merely one element within a regulatory scheme, the overall thrust of which is preventative. The extent to which the use of strict liability in particular is justified, it is claimed, will depend on the acceptability of the whole scheme which will itself be derived from the outcome of a number of policy choices. The principles of traditional criminal law and penology should not be applied automatically to the regulatory context.

[4:4] *R v IRC, ex p Mead and Cook*
[1992] STC 482

In November 1990, the Commissioners of Inland Revenue ordered the prosecution of the applicants for criminal offences in connection with tax evasion, and in March 1991, summonses were served on them. The prosecution had arisen out of the Revenue's investigation of the tax affairs of an accountant who had acted as the accountant to the applicants and to other taxpayers. The applicants sought judicial review of the decision to prosecute them, claiming that a comparison of the applicants' cases should have been made with those of the other taxpayers and only if there were distinguishing features which made the applicants' cases more serious than the others was the decision to prosecute them justified.

The application was dismissed.

Stuart-Smith LJ (at page 492):

The crucial factor in the present case is that the Revenue operate a selective policy of prosecution. They do so for three main reasons: first their primary objective is the collection of revenue and not the punishment of offenders; second they have inadequate resources to prosecute everyone who dishonestly evades payment of taxes; and third and perhaps most importantly they consider it necessary to prosecute in some cases because of the deterrent effect that this has on the general body of taxpayers, since they know that they behave dishonestly they may be prosecuted. It is inherent in such a policy that there may be inconsistency and unfairness as between one dishonest taxpayer and another who is guilty of a very similar offence. Nevertheless while not challenging the validity of the policy Mr Beloff submits that there must be grafted on to it requirement to treat all dishonest taxpayers guilty of similar offences for two reasons. First it is inconsistent with the policy and cannot be operated consistently with it, you cannot be both selective and treat every case alike. Second it seems to be quite impracticable. How are the Revenue to decide what cases are like? What is to be the basis of the group of cases that has to be considered? Over what period of time are the group to be considered? Are all cases involving forgery to be in one group? Or those involving forgery and false accounting? Are those who make a full disclosure to be in the same group as those who deny that they have acted dishonestly, although the Revenue consider that there is evidence that they have? These questions only have to be posed to demonstrate that it is quite impossible to answer them; and certainly in my judgment Mr Beloff was quite unable to proffer any convincing answer. What he did say was that there is an identifiable group of taxpayers here who were all clients of Mr Scannell. That appears to me to be a wholly adventitious and irrelevant consideration. It does not affect the nature or gravity of the offence; it only arises because in the course of investigation Mr Scannell's tax affairs the Revenue have uncovered alleged dishonest tax evasion on the part of a number of his clients, he is simply the common source from which the inquiry springs and the information flows.

There may be other dishonest taxpayers who have been advised by dishonest accountants and who have embarked on similar schemes; why should they not be part of the group? Does the group consist only of the six other taxpayers referred to in Mr Bunker's affidavit or the much larger number who are still being investigated and may turn out to have indulged in similar practices?

In my judgment the requirement of fairness and consistency in the light of the Revenue's selective policy of prosecution is that each case is considered on its merits fairly and dispassionately to see whether the criteria for prosecution was satisfied; there is no dispute that the applicants' cases were so considered. The decision to prosecute must then be taken in good faith for the purpose of fulfilling the Revenue's objectives of collecting taxes and not for some ulterior, extraneous or improper purpose, such as the pursuit of some racialist bias, political vendetta or corrupt motive. This again is not in dispute.

The principle that a public body must not frustrate a citizen's legitimate expectation takes the case no further. The only legitimate expectation that a dishonest taxpayer can have is that he may be selected for prosecution in accordance with the Revenue's stated policy; and that in considering whether to do so the decision-maker will act fairly in the sense that I have just defined.

Only if that policy could be attacked on the grounds of irrationality could the applicants succeed. They do not attempt to do so. It was a policy that was approved by the Keith Committee and it seems to me, for the three reasons that I have given earlier, not only a rational policy but very probably the only workable policy.

For these reasons, in my judgment, this application must be dismissed.

[4:5] HMRC Criminal Investigation Policy

At <http://www.hmrc.gov.uk/prosecutions/crim-inv-policy.htm>

Criminal investigation powers and safeguards

HMRC's aim is to secure the highest level of compliance with the law and regulations governing direct and indirect taxes and other regimes for which they are responsible. Criminal investigation, with a view to prosecution by the Revenue and Customs Prosecutions Office (RCPO) in England and Wales—or the appropriate prosecuting authority in Scotland and Northern Ireland, is an important part of HMRC's overall enforcement strategy.

It is HMRC's policy to deal with fraud by use of the cost effective Civil Investigation of Fraud (CIF) procedures, wherever appropriate. Criminal Investigation will be reserved for cases where HMRC needs to send a strong deterrent message or where the conduct involved is such that only a criminal sanction is appropriate.

However, HMRC reserves complete discretion to conduct a criminal investigation in any case and to carry out these investigations across a range of offences and in all the areas for which the Commissioners of HMRC have responsibility.

Examples of the kind of circumstances in which HMRC will generally consider commencing a criminal, rather than civil investigations are:

- In cases of organised criminal gangs attacking the tax system or systematic frauds where losses represents a serious threat to the tax base, including conspiracy;
- Where an individual holds a position of trust or responsibility;
- Where materially false statements are made or materially false documents are provided in the course of a civil investigation;
- Where, pursuing an avoidance scheme, reliance is placed on a false or altered document or such reliance or material facts are misrepresented to enhance the credibility of a scheme;
- Where deliberate concealment, deception, conspiracy or corruption is suspected;
- In cases involving the use of false or forged documents;
- In cases involving importation or exportation breaching prohibitions and restrictions;
- In cases involving money laundering with particular focus on advisors, accountants, solicitors and others acting in a 'professional' capacity who provide the means to put tainted money out of reach of law enforcement;
- Where the perpetrator has committed previous offences / there is a repeated course of unlawful conduct or previous civil action;
- In cases involving theft, or the misuse or un lawful destruction of HMRC documents;
- Where there is evidence of assault on, threats to, or the impersonation of HMRC officials;
- Where there is a link to suspected wider criminality, whether domestic or international, involving offences not under the administration of HMRC.

When considering whether a case should be investigated under the Civil Investigation of Fraud procedures or is the subject of a criminal investigation, one factor will be whether the taxpayer(s) has made a complete and unprompted disclosure of the offences committed.

However, there are certain fiscal offences where HMRC will not usually adopt the Civil Investigation of Fraud approach. Examples of these are:

- VAT Missing Trader Intra-Community (MTIC) Fraud
- Vat 'Bogus' registration repayment fraud
- Organised Tax Credit fraud

[4:6] Sanction Policy of the Department for Work and Pensions

(Version 2, May 2006. This extract is not quite the complete document)

1. Sanction Policy of the Department for Work and Pensions

1.1 This document sets out the policy of the Department for Work and Pensions (DWP) towards sanctions, including criminal prosecutions, for offences relating to 'National' benefit fraud.

1.2 'Local' benefits (Housing Benefit and Council Tax Benefit) are administered by Local Authorities as part of their statutory local government functions. The sanctions policy in each Local Authority is therefore a matter for its members. However in practice Local Authority sanction policy broadly follows the approach of the DWP.

2. General Principles

2.1 The Department for Work and Pensions is committed to the prevention, detection, correction, investigation and, where appropriate, prosecution of fraudulent benefit claims.

2.2 The aim is to prevent criminal offences occurring by making it clear to our customers that they have a responsibility to provide accurate and timely information about their claims; to punish wrongdoing; and to deter offending.

2.3 This policy supports the Department's Public Service Agreement (PSA 10) to reduce losses from fraud and error for people in working age, on Income Support and Jobseeker's Allowance, with a 50% reduction by March 2006 and in Housing Benefit, with a 25% reduction by March 2006. A new PSA 10 target will commence in April 2006 to reduce losses from fraud and error in Income Support and Jobseeker's Allowance for people of working age by 15% by 2010, measured against a new baseline set in 2005/2006. It also provides a full response to the need to be effective against fraud in the full range of welfare benefits.

2.4 Each potential fraud referral is assessed against national criteria. This assessment will result either in cases being investigated further under criminal investigation standards as set out within the remainder of this document or referred for customer compliance action. Customer compliance action usually comprises a robust interview with the customer where they are questioned about any allegations. Further action depends upon the outcome of the interview but they will be reminded of their responsibilities and may be advised about future conduct and required to rectify or withdraw their claim.

2.5 Each case that is subject to criminal investigation is considered on its own merits, having regard to all of the facts, before an appropriate sanction is administered.

3. Organisation

3.1 Criminal investigations are undertaken by the Department's Fraud Investigation Service (FIS) in accordance with:

- the Police and Criminal Evidence Act 1984 (PACE) and its codes of practice
- the Criminal Procedure and Investigations Act 1996 (CPIA) and its codes of practice
- all other relevant legislative and common-law rules
- Departmental policy
- advice from the Department's Solicitors Branch.

3.2 Fraud Investigation Service investigators receive Professionalism in Security (PINS) training which is accredited by Portsmouth University. Additional guidance is provided by the Fraud Procedures and Instructions Manual which is regularly updated to ensure that:

- investigations are conducted in a legal and professional manner
- policy and legislation is correctly applied, and
- approved working methods are applied.

3.3 In England and Wales the Department's Solicitors are a prosecuting authority in their own right. There are five Area Legal Offices who advise on whether a case is suitable for prosecution and then take the case forward. Most cases are seen before a Magistrates Court, although the more serious cases are usually referred to Crown Court.

3.4 Departmental Prosecuting Solicitors provide advice and guidance to investigators throughout the investigative and prosecuting process. They do not conduct any part of the investigation but advise on the investigator's obligations, evidential requirements and any appropriate charges. Departmental Solicitors are also responsible for identifying those cases which are not suitable for criminal prosecution for evidential and/or public interest reasons.

3.5 The Department's Technical Support provides guidance to investigators on policy and technical matters.

3.6 In Northern Ireland the practice is to refer cases suitable for prosecution to the Director of Public Prosecutions, whilst in Scotland cases thought suitable for prosecution go to the Procurator Fiscal.

3.7 The Department also works closely with Local Authorities operating under similar prosecution practices and has a Partnership Agreement with them to support joint working activity such as joint Interviews under Caution and joint investigations, to aid in the tackling of Housing Benefit and Council Tax Benefit fraud.

4. Sanction Process

4.1 Where an offence has been committed the Department can consider administering a caution, offering an administrative penalty, or instigating a prosecution. The choice will depend on the factors below.

4.2 Cautions:

4.2.1 A formal caution is an administrative sanction that the Department in England and Wales is able to offer as an alternative to a prosecution as long as specific criteria are met, and the case is one the Department could take to court if the caution was refused.

4.2.2 Cautions are usually aimed at the less serious benefit frauds and those where the overpayment is under £2,000. It also provides an additional tool for the Fraud Investigation Service to use in those cases where the deterrent effect is considered a sufficient and suitable alternative to prosecution or an administrative penalty.

4.2.3 The offender must admit to the offence in an Interview Under Caution and provide informed consent to being cautioned. To be able to offer a caution requires the same standard of criminal evidence as for a prosecution and should only be offered if the Department could prosecute should the caution be refused.

4.2.4 If the customer is subsequently prosecuted for another benefit offence the formal caution may be cited in court.

4.2.5 In Scotland a caution is known as an administrative caution which cannot be cited in court, but may be referred to in a report submitted to the procurator fiscal for consideration of prosecution of any subsequent offence.

4.3 Administrative penalties:

4.3.1 An administrative penalty is the offer to the customer to agree to pay a financial penalty where the customer has caused benefit to be overpaid to them, by either an act or omission. The amount of the penalty is currently stipulated at 30 per cent of the amount of the gross overpayment.

4.3.2 It is current DWP policy to offer these penalties where the case is deemed to be not so serious and the offer of an administrative penalty is considered a suitable alternative to prosecution, and where the gross overpayment has been adjudicated to be under £2,000. Unlike cautions no admission of guilt is required from the customer before offering an administrative penalty, although there is a statutory requirement for investigators to ensure that there are grounds for instituting criminal proceedings for an offence relating to the overpayment.

4.4 Prosecutions:

4.4.1 If there is sufficient evidence the Department will refer the case to the Departmental Solicitors for consideration of criminal prosecution where one or more of the following criteria are met:

- The gross adjudicated overpayment (including Housing and Council Tax Benefit) is £2,000 or over
- False identities or other personal details have been used
- False or forged documents have been used
- Official documents have been altered or falsified
- The person concerned occupied a position of trust
- The person concerned assisted or encouraged others to commit offences
- There is evidence of premeditation or organised fraud
- The person concerned has relevant previous convictions
- The customer had previously been convicted of benefit fraud
- The amount of the adjudicated overpayment is under £2,000 and the offer of an administrative penalty or formal caution is not accepted.

4.4.2 In all cases, including those which do not fall within any of the above criteria, the Departmental Solicitors retain discretion as to whether criminal proceedings are started. All cases referred to Departmental Solicitors may be prosecuted under any of the 'Relevant Legislation' listed in Annex 1

4.4.3 The Department's Solicitors are bound by the Code for Crown Prosecutors. A copy of the Code can be obtained either on the CPS website www.CPS.gov.uk . . .

[4:7] McKeever, G, 'Social security as a criminal sanction'

(2004) 26(1) Journal of Social Welfare and Family Law 1

Introduction

The social security system concerns itself with poverty and need, the criminal justice system with punishment and deterrence. There has always been some commonality between the two systems and this overlap is now becoming more prominent. Today we see criminal law being used as a sanction in social security, perhaps most obviously in the punishment of social security fraud—a criminal offence which punishes fraudulent declarations of eligibility for social security benefits. It may be that such reliance on the criminal justice system is an appropriate means of meeting an objective of the social security system, although arguably it ignores the reality of individual benefit fraud and reacts disproportionately to 'suspect' claimants (McKeever, 1999). However, there have been other controversial developments in this grey area of overlap which, while purporting to complement and bolster the policy objectives of the social security and criminal justice systems, are more likely to undermine them. Of particular concern is the Child Support, Pensions and Social Security Act 2000, which provides that social security benefits can be withheld from convicted criminal offenders who breach the terms of their community sentences. As a result, key aspects of social security regulation have now become a criminal sanction. This specific illustration is merely an example of a more general problem of overlap between criminal justice and social security, but one which will highlight the nature of the difficulty for claimants and offenders as citizens within an increasingly authoritarian climate of social control. This paper examines the rationale for the introduction of the sanctions as a punishment and the concept of compliance with a community sentence as a condition of benefit receipt, analysing the terms of the social contract which now exist between citizen and state. It explores the difficulties which arise as a result of the legislation and assesses how it will meet the Government's stated objective of ensuring compliance with community sentences.

Conclusion

It is clear that social security is increasingly being used as a means of social control and a criminal punishment and ss 62 and 63 of the CSP&SSA are indicative of this. The general problems with this trend are illustrated by the specific problems with the sanctions. The purpose of the sanctions is two-fold. First, they are intended to advance criminal justice policy by making community sentences more effective and ensuring that convicted criminals abide by the terms of their sentence. Second, they are intended to act as a reminder to claimants that their entitlement to benefit is conditional and that failure to comply will result in benefit being withdrawn. The short-term impact of the sanction could arguably achieve both objectives. Breach by offenders will no longer go unnoticed or unpunished. Similarly, a claimant who loses their benefit as a result of failing to comply with the conditions set out in CSP&SSA will be clear that they are not automatically entitled to benefit and that their benefit can be withdrawn if all the entitlement conditions are not met.

However, the problem with sections 62 and 63 is that their long-term impact renders their short term success pointless. The sanctions will clearly cause difficulties for offenders, which will ultimately undermine both criminal justice and social security policy. The overriding objective of the criminal justice system is to prevent offenders from re-offending. However, denying offenders access to legitimate income and adding to their social and behavioural problems will inevitably perpetuate the cycle of offending. It therefore provides a punishment which creates a bigger problem than the relatively minor one it solves. Similarly, the central objective of the social security system is to relieve poverty and deprivation. Instead, ss 62 and 63 undermine the rights of claimants to a basic entitlement and push claimants into greater poverty. This goes beyond the difficulties with the concept of responsibilization or contract welfare and runs contrary to attempts to address social exclusion, inequality and deprivation that the Government has committed itself to (Department for Work and Pensions, 2001). The problems which will almost certainly manifest themselves as a result of the sanctions mean that ss 62 and 63 are counterproductive. The Government is clearly frustrated with the elusive concept of crime control, but it needs to address its short term objectives in a more strategic manner. Its current response does not change the dynamics or reality of the problem. Even on the assumption that the original sentence was justly imposed, and that some sanction is required for the breach, these provisions are not justifiable. Most offenders will not understand their new obligations under the redefined social contract and their awareness will come at an extortionate cost to them. The price for this is paid not just by the offender but by a society which continues to alienate, exclude and marginalize such individuals. For offenders, claimants and the rest of society this is too high a price to pay.

[4:8] Sanders, A, 'Class Bias in Prosecutions'
[1985] Howard Journal of Criminal Justice 176 (at page 194)

This article has sought to demonstrate first, that prosecution patterns exhibit class bias. Second that bias is a product of the divergent policies and procedures of different law enforcement agencies. Third, that these divergent practices and contrasting outcomes cannot be justified by conventional explanations. To explain these processes would involve considerations of political economy that are beyond the scope of this article. However, some tentative lines of future enquiry can be suggested...this, as is common in this field, begs the question of why one class of people who commit crime is not seen as criminal whereas another class of people is.

A different starting point would be to compare the roles of the police and non-police agencies (in this instance the HMFI). Let us take seriously the idea that HMFI practice is aimed at enforcing, rather than mystifying, the law. Since higher standards of health and safety, and this a broad compliance with the law, is the aim of the HMFI the methods used would obviously be those that effect the most satisfactory compromise between (i) doing that job most effectively; (ii) using HMFI resources effectively and (iii) not disrupting normal business activity. HMFI policy can be seen to balance (i) against (ii) and (iii). This is not surprising. All that is contestable under current social arrangements is the weight given to either (i) or to (ii) and (iii).

The police are in a quite different position, as indeed is the DHSS Inspectorate. If they do their job effectively—that is, suppress crime—they will not disrupt normal business activity. Their offenders' economic activities are either non-existent or easily done by others. Resources are a potential consideration, but the use of arrest and detection rates to measure police officers' effectiveness actually pushes police activity away from concern to use resources in a cost effective manner.

Moreover, crime suppression can be seen simply as an extension of the police's primary role. Historically, order maintenance was their primary role, and the prosecution of offenders constituted one way of maintaining order. As we have seen, public order charges are a resource for the police officer, but only if those charges can be translated easily into prosecutions. Prosecution then, is an essential weapon in the armoury of the police. For a government wishing to spend less on social security, prosecution has a similar function in relation to possible DHSS offenders. Arrest and charge procedures evolved to process public order offences speedily. Most police prosecutions—primarily but not wholly working class—now also get processed by these procedures, which do not facilitate non-prosecution dispositions. Middle class offenders rarely get caught in these processes since middle class persons rarely disrupt middle class order.

The police and HMFI are not directed in the ways described. Having decided to take some action against a suspect, their decisions are not determined by structural or instrumental imperatives. They will be guided, however, by numerous considerations that flow from these structural conditions. For the HMFI the disruption to business caused by prosecution will indeed be a consideration, the welfare of the workers often being a part of this. Another consideration will be Levi's positive stereotype of the businessman. The historical background to the HMFI's relationship with industry is one of conflict avoidance, and there is also a cultural and class affinity between professionals—in this case factory inspectors and businessmen. This all contributes to prosecution avoidance. Between the police and large sections of the working class there is a history of conflict, no cultural and class affinity, and a negative stereotype. Indeed, the police are said to see themselves as stopping society slipping into chaos. These different sets of conditions create propensities. Whether a particular prosecution decision will conform to a particular propensity will still be dependent, in part, upon the law enforcer's decision how best to enforce the law.

Prosecution can be seen as an ultimate sanction: the end result if the suspect and law enforcer cannot strike a bargain. What, in other words, will the suspect give in exchange for a caution? Factory managers can offer better behaviour, plus jobs and a concrete economic activity; enforcement notices represent a way of holding them to that bargain. But working class and unemployed people have little to offer. Racketeers are an exception for they have money to offer and have made some very advantageous bargains in the past. The promise of good future behaviour is all that most offenders apprehended by the police can offer. Here again stereotyping and cultural and class affinity plays its part. Accepting this promise entails assessment of the suspect's creditability, his moral character. the HMFI, as we have seen, also has to assess this. The plausibility of the suspect's future intentions, in the structural context outlined, as assessed by particular law enforcement agencies, is on trial. Shoplifting sales managers and negligent production managers are bound to be more credible in this context than most suspects whom the police encounter.

It could be argued that this is irrelevant, as if the HMFI prosecuted a high percentage of cases they would be in court so much that their work would grind to a halt. The HMFI therefore adapts its law enforcement practice to its level of resources. The pattern of resource allocation does clearly show government to be, predictably, more concerned about 'normal' crime than about factory crime. But institutions are not totally passive in these matters...If the HMFI wish to draw attention to its under-resourcing by government, tying itself up in court through prosecution would be a very effective strategy. The important question is not 'why don't the HMFI prosecute more?', but 'why don't the HMFI seek more resources which could enable them to prosecute more?'

I hope that this demonstrates that law enforcement activity can be related to socio-economic structure without resorting to conspiracy theory. I have also sought to show that bias need not be explained
by police dishonesty, rule breaking, or prejudice. As all the victim surveys show, crime abounds in
modern Britain, making selective crime processing necessary. The criminal law allows almost absolute
discretion in prosecutions. Thus patterned class bias is produced by the police operating a legally proper
positive propensity to prosecute, whilst agencies dealing with the middle classes operate an equally
legally proper propensity to not prosecute. Whilst this is the mechanism through which bias occurs, its
source lies in the economic and social differences between different types of 'crime' and 'criminal'. To
understand prosecution patterns the micro-processes of law enforcement need to be situated in their
concrete socio-economic and legal context.

[4:9] Criminal Justice Act 1987 (as amended)
Sections 1–3

1 The Serious Fraud Office

(1) A Serious Fraud Office shall be constituted for England and Wales and Northern Ireland.

(2) The Attorney General shall appoint a person to be the Director of the Serious Fraud Office
(referred to in this Part of this Act as "the Director"), and he shall discharge his functions under
the superintendence of the Attorney General.

(3) The Director may investigate any suspected offence which appears to him on reasonable grounds
to involve serious or complex fraud.

(4) The Director may, if he thinks fit, conduct any such investigation in conjunction either with the
police or with any other person who is, in the opinion of the Director, a proper person to be
concerned in it.

(5) The Director may—

   (a) institute and have the conduct of any criminal proceedings which appear to him to relate to
   such fraud; and

   (b) take over the conduct of any such proceedings at any stage.

(6) The Director shall discharge such other functions in relation to fraud as may from time to time be
assigned to him by the Attorney General.

(6A) The Director has the functions conferred on him by, or in relation to, Part 5 or 8 of the Proceeds
of Crime Act 2002, (c. 29) (civil recovery of the proceeds etc. of unlawful conduct, civil recovery
investigations and disclosure orders in relation to confiscation investigations).

(7) The Director may designate for the purposes of subsection (5) above any member of the Serious
Fraud Office who is—

   (a) a barrister in England and Wales or Northern Ireland;

   (b) a solicitor of the Supreme Court; or

   (c) a solicitor of the Supreme Court of Judicature of Northern Ireland.

(8) Any member so designated shall, without prejudice to any functions which may have been
assigned to him in his capacity as a member of that Office, have all the powers of the Director as
to the institution and conduct of proceedings but shall exercise those powers under the direction
of the Director.

(9) Any member so designated who is a barrister in Northern Ireland or a solicitor of the Supreme
Court of Judicature of Northern Ireland shall have—

(a) in any court the rights of audience enjoyed by solicitors of the Supreme Court of Judicature of Northern Ireland, and in the Crown Court in Northern Ireland, such additional rights of audience as may be given by virtue of subsection (11) below; and

(b) in the Crown Court in Northern Ireland, the rights of audience enjoyed by barristers employed by the Director of Public Prosecutions for Northern Ireland.

(10) Subject to subsection (11) below, the reference in subsection (9)(a) above to rights of audience enjoyed by solicitors of the Supreme Court of Judicature of Northern Ireland is a reference to such rights enjoyed in the Crown Court in Northern Ireland as restricted by any direction given by the Lord Chief Justice of Northern Ireland under section 50 of the Judicature (Northern Ireland) Act 1978.

(11) For the purpose of giving any member so designated who is a barrister in Northern Ireland or a solicitor of the Supreme Court of Judicature of Northern Ireland additional rights of audience in the Crown Court in Northern Ireland, the Lord Chief Justice of Northern Ireland may direct that any direction given by him under the said section 50 shall not apply to such members.

(12) Schedule 1 to this Act shall have effect.

(13) For the purposes of this section (including that Schedule) references to the conduct of any proceedings include references to the proceedings being discontinued and to the taking of any steps (including the bringing of appeals and making of representations in respect of applications for bail) which may be taken in relation to them.

(14) In the application of this section (including that Schedule) to Northern Ireland references to the Attorney General are to be construed as references to him in his capacity as Attorney General for Northern Ireland.

2 Director's investigation powers

(1) The powers of the Director under this section shall be exercisable, but only for the purposes of an investigation under section 1 above, or, on a request made by an authority entitled to make such a request, in any case in which it appears to him that there is good reason to do so for the purpose of investigating the affairs, or any aspect of the affairs, of any person.

(1A) The authorities entitled to request the Director to exercise his powers under this section are—

(a) the Attorney-General of the Isle of Man, Jersey or Guernsey, acting under legislation corresponding to section 1 of this Act and having effect in the Island whose Attorney-General makes the request; and

(b) the Secretary of State acting under section 4(2A) of the Criminal Justice (International Co-operation) Act 1990, in response to a request received by him from an overseas court, tribunal or authority (an "overseas authority").

(1B) The Director shall not exercise his powers on a request from the Secretary of State acting in response to a request received from an overseas authority within subsection (1A)(b) above unless it appears to the Director on reasonable grounds that the offence in respect of which he has been requested to obtain evidence involves serious or complex fraud.

(2) The Director may by notice in writing require the person whose affairs are to be investigated ("the person under investigation") or any other person whom he has reason to believe has relevant information to answer questions or otherwise furnish information with respect to any matter relevant to the investigation at a specified place and either at a specified time or forthwith.

(3) The Director may by notice in writing require the person under investigation or any other person to produce at such place as may be specified in the notice and either forthwith or at such time as may be so specified any specified documents which appear to the Director to relate to any

matter relevant to the investigation or any documents of a specified description which appear to him so to relate; and—

  (a) if any such documents are produced, the Director may—
   (i) take copies or extracts from them;
   (ii) require the person producing them to provide an explanation of any of them;

  (b) if any such documents are not produced, the Director may require the person who was required to produce them to state, to the best of his knowledge and belief, where they are.

(4) Where, on information on oath laid by a member of the Serious Fraud Office, a justice of the peace is satisfied, in relation to any documents, that there are reasonable grounds for believing—

  (a) that—
   (i) a person has failed to comply with an obligation under this section to produce them;
   (ii) it is not practicable to serve a notice under subsection (3) above in relation to them; or
   (iii) the service of such a notice in relation to them might seriously prejudice the investigation; and

  (b) that they are on premises specified in the information,

he may issue such a warrant as is mentioned in subsection (5) below.

(5) The warrant referred to above is a warrant authorising any constable—

  (a) to enter (using such force as is reasonably necessary for the purpose) and search the premises, and

  (b) to take possession of any documents appearing to be documents of the description specified in the information or to take in relation to any documents so appearing any other steps which may appear to be necessary for preserving them and preventing interference with them.

(6) Unless it is not practicable in the circumstances, a constable executing a warrant issued under subsection (4) above shall be accompanied by an appropriate person.

(7) In subsection (6) above "appropriate person" means—

  (a) a member of the Serious Fraud Office; or

  (b) some person who is not a member of that Office but whom the Director has authorised to accompany the constable.

(8) A statement by a person in response to a requirement imposed by virtue of this section may only be used in evidence against him—

  (a) on a prosecution for an offence under subsection (14) below; or

  (b) on a prosecution for some other offence where in giving evidence he makes a statement inconsistent with it.

(8AA) However, the statement may not be used against that person by virtue of paragraph (b) of subsection (8) unless evidence relating to it is adduced, or a question relating to it is asked, by or on behalf of that person in the proceedings arising out of the prosecution.

(8A) Any evidence obtained by the Director for use by an overseas authority shall be furnished by him to the Secretary of State for transmission to the overseas authority which requested it.

(8B) If in order to comply with the request of the overseas authority it is necessary for any evidence obtained by the Director to be accompanied by any certificate, affidavit or other verifying document, the Director shall also furnish for transmission such document of that nature as may be specified by the Secretary of State when asking the Director to obtain the evidence.

(8C) Where any evidence obtained by the Director for use by an overseas authority consists of a document the original or a copy shall be transmitted, and where it consists of any other article the article itself or a description, photograph or other representation of it shall be transmitted, as may be necessary in order to comply with the request of the overseas authority.

(8D) The references in subsections (8A) to (8C) above to evidence obtained by the Director include references to evidence obtained by him by virtue of the exercise by a constable, in the course of a search authorised by a warrant issued under subsection (4) above, of powers conferred by section 50 of the Criminal Justice and Police Act 2001.

 (9) A person shall not under this section be required to disclose any information or produce any document which he would be entitled to refuse to disclose or produce on grounds of legal professional privilege in proceedings in the High Court, except that a lawyer may be required to furnish the name and address of his client.

(10) A person shall not under this section be required to disclose information or produce a document in respect of which he owes an obligation of confidence by virtue of carrying on any banking business unless—

(a) the person to whom the obligation of confidence is owed consents to the disclosure or pro-duction; or

(b) the Director has authorised the making of the requirement or, if it is impracticable for him to act personally, a member of the Serious Fraud Office designated by him for the purposes of this subsection has done so.

(11) Without prejudice to the power of the Director to assign functions to members of the Serious Fraud Office, the Director may authorise any competent investigator (other than a constable) who is not a member of that Office to exercise on his behalf all or any of the powers conferred by this section, but no such authority shall be granted except for the purpose of investigating the affairs, or any aspect of the affairs, of a person specified in the authority.

(12) No person shall be bound to comply with any requirement imposed by a person exercising pow-ers by virtue of any authority granted under subsection (11) above unless he has, if required to do so, produced evidence of his authority.

(13) Any person who without reasonable excuse fails to comply with a requirement imposed on him under this section shall be guilty of an offence and liable on summary conviction to imprisonment for a term not exceeding six months or to a fine not exceeding level 5 on the standard scale or to both.

(14) A person who, in purported compliance with a requirement under this section—

(a) makes a statement which he knows to be false or misleading in a material particular; or

(b) recklessly makes a statement which is false or misleading in a material particular,

shall be guilty of an offence.

(15) A person guilty of an offence under subsection (14) above shall—

(a) on conviction on indictment, be liable to imprisonment for a term not exceeding two years or to a fine or to both; and

(b) on summary conviction, be liable to imprisonment for a term not exceeding six months or to a fine not exceeding the statutory maximum, or to both.

(16) Where any person—

(a) knows or suspects that an investigation by the police or the Serious Fraud Office into serious or complex fraud is being or is likely to be carried out; and

(b) falsifies, conceals, destroys or otherwise disposes of, or causes or permits the falsification, concealment, destruction or disposal of documents which he knows or suspects are or would be relevant to such an investigation, he shall be guilty of an offence unless he proves that he had no intention of concealing the facts disclosed by the documents from persons carrying out such an investigation.

(17) A person guilty of an offence under subsection (16) above shall—

(a) on conviction on indictment, be liable to imprisonment for a term not exceeding 7 years or to a fine or to both; and

(b) on summary conviction, be liable to imprisonment for a term not exceeding 6 months or to a fine not exceeding the statutory maximum or to both.

(18) In this section, "documents" includes information recorded in any form and, in relation to information recorded otherwise than in legible form, references to its production include references to producing a copy of the information in legible form; and "evidence" (in relation to subsections (1A)(b), (8A), (8B) and (8C) above) includes documents and other articles.

(19) In the application of this section to Scotland, the reference to a justice of the peace is to be construed as a reference to the sheriff; and in the application of this section to Northern Ireland, subsection (4) above shall have effect as if for the references to information there were substituted references to a complaint.

3 Disclosure of information

(1) Where any information subject to an obligation of secrecy under the Taxes Management Act 1970 has been disclosed by the Commissioners of Inland Revenue or an officer of those Commissioners to any member of the Serious Fraud Office for the purposes of any prosecution of an offence relating to inland revenue, that information may be disclosed by any member of the Serious Fraud Office—

(a) for the purposes of any prosecution of which that Office has the conduct;

(b) to any member of the Crown Prosecution Service for the purposes of any prosecution of an offence relating to inland revenue; and

(c) to the Director of Public Prosecutions for Northern Ireland for the purposes of any prosecution of an offence relating to inland revenue,

but not otherwise.

(2) Where the Serious Fraud Office has the conduct of any prosecution of an offence which does not relate to inland revenue, the court may not prevent the prosecution from relying on any evidence under section 78 of the Police and Criminal Evidence Act 1984 (discretion to exclude unfair evidence) by reason only of the fact that the information concerned was disclosed by the Commissioners of Inland Revenue or an officer of those Commissioners for the purposes of any prosecution of an offence relating to inland revenue.

(3) Where any information is subject to an obligation of secrecy imposed by or under any enactment other than an enactment contained in the Taxes Management Act 1970, the obligation shall not have effect to prohibit the disclosure of that information to any person in his capacity as a member of the Serious Fraud Office but any information disclosed by virtue of this subsection may only be disclosed by a member of the Serious Fraud Office for the purposes of any prosecution in England and Wales, Northern Ireland or elsewhere and may only be disclosed by such a member if he is designated by the Director for the purposes of this subsection.

(4) Without prejudice to his power to enter into agreements apart from this subsection, the Director may enter into a written agreement for the supply of information to or by him subject, in either case, to an obligation not to disclose the information concerned otherwise than for a specified purpose.

(5) Subject to subsections (1) and (3) above and to any provision of an agreement for the supply of information which restricts the disclosure of the information supplied, information obtained by any person in his capacity as a member of the Serious Fraud Office may be disclosed by any member of that Office designated by the Director for the purposes of this subsection—

(a) to any government department or Northern Ireland department or other authority or body discharging its functions on behalf of the Crown (including the Crown in right of Her Majesty's Government in Northern Ireland);

(b) to any competent authority;

(c) for the purposes of any prosecution in England and Wales, Northern Ireland or elsewhere; and

(d) for the purposes of assisting any public or other authority for the time being designated for the purposes of this paragraph by an order made by the Secretary of State to discharge any functions which are specified in the order.

(6) The following are competent authorities for the purposes of subsection (5) above—

(a) an inspector appointed under Part XIV of the Companies Act 1985 or Part XV of the Companies (Northern Ireland) Order 1986;

(b) an Official Receiver;

(c) the Accountant in Bankruptcy;

(d) the Official Receiver for Northern Ireland;

(e) a person appointed under—
   (i) section 167 of the Financial Services and Markets Act 2000 (general investigations),
   (ii) section 168 of that Act (investigations in particular cases),
   (iii) section 169(1)(b) of that Act (investigation in support of overseas regulator),
   (iv) section 284 of that Act (investigations into affairs of certain collective investment schemes), or
   (v) regulations made as a result of section 262(2)(k) of that Act (investigations into open-ended investment companies),
   to conduct an investigation;

(f) a body corporate established in accordance with section 212(1) of the Financial Services and Markets Act 2000 (compensation scheme manager);

(l) any body having supervisory, regulatory or disciplinary functions in relation to any profession or any area of commercial activity; and

(m) any person or body having, under the law of any country or territory outside the United Kingdom, functions corresponding to any of the functions of any person or body mentioned in any of the foregoing paragraphs.

(n) any person or body having, under the Treaty on European Union or any other treaty to which the United Kingdom is a party, the function of receiving information of the kind in question; and

(o) any person or body having, under the law of any country or territory outside the United Kingdom, the function of receiving information relating to the proceeds of crime.

(7) An order under subsection (5)(d) above may impose conditions subject to which, and otherwise restrict the circumstances in which, information may be disclosed under that paragraph.

(8) In subsections (1) and (2) "former Inland Revenue matter" means a matter listed in Schedule 1 to the Commissioners for Revenue and Customs Act 2005 except for paragraphs 2, 10, 13, 14, 15, 17, 19, 28, 29 and 30.

[4:10] *R v Director of Serious Fraud Office, ex p Smith*
[1993] AC 1

The applicant had been charged with an offence under the Companies Act 1985. Subsequently he was served with a notice to attend the SFO to answer questions. He sought judicial review of the Director's decision to enforce compliance with the requirements of the notice.

The House of Lords held that although there was a strong presumption against interpreting a statute as taking away the right to silence, it was the plain intention of the Criminal Justice Act 1987 that the powers of the Director of the SFO should not come to an end when the person under investigation had been charged.

Lord Mustill (at page 44):

In conclusion I wish to emphasise that if this appeal is allowed the House will not thereby have chosen to re-establish in relation to a limited class of offence an inquisitorial method of ascertaining the truth in criminal cases which English law has long since repudiated in favour of an adversarial process. We were much pressed in argument with submissions that, although fraudulent conduct has become a serious social evil, there are other evils just as grave, or even graver, which have not attracted any special powers; that if the reason for giving exceptional powers to the Serious Fraud Office is that many frauds involve complicated transactions which are difficult to unravel, then the same could be said of the long and complex trials (for instance arising from charges of affray, or of the importation and supply of prohibited drugs) to which no such powers have been applied; and that, moreover, the powers of the Office are made available even where the transactions in question are not complicated, since the Act applies to 'serious or complex fraud'—not 'serious and complex fraud.'

Now these and similar comments would require careful scrutiny if the thrust of the argument were to the effect that Parliament could not have intended to establish an inquisitorial regime of this kind in relation to serious or complex fraud alone. But in fact no such argument is or could be made, for it is indisputable and undisputed that this is just what Parliament set out to do, and has effectively done. In truth the adverse comments are criticisms, not of the Director's contention that the powers created by the Act apply in the situation now under review, but of the policy and scope of the Act itself. These we may not entertain. As Windeyer J said in *Rees v Kratzmann* (1965) 114 CLR 63, 80:

> 'If the legislature thinks that in this field the public interest overcomes some of the common law's traditional considerations for the individual, then effect must be given to the statute which embodies this policy.'

In the present case the only issue is whether there is something in the language of the Act or by necessary implication, to show that the policy embodied in the Act should not be given effect as regards the questioning of a suspect who has been charged. Being of the opinion that there is not. I would allow this appeal.

[4:11] *Jones v Whalley*
[2006] UKHL 41, [2006] 3 WLR 179

Whalley admitted having assaulted Jones and had accepted a written police caution in respect of an offence of assault occasioning actual bodily harm. The caution form stated that acceptance of the caution meant that he would not have to go before a criminal court. But Jones subsequently decided to bring a private prosecution against him. When the matter came before the magistrates, they stayed the proceedings as an abuse of process, but the Divisional Court lifted the stay. Whalley submitted that since he had agreed to be cautioned on an express assurance by the police that he would not have to go before a criminal court in connection with the matter, it would be an abuse of process for J to bring a private prosecution against him. J submitted that the right of private prosecution was expressly preserved by the Prosecution of Offences Act 1985 s. 6 and that he should not be deprived of his right by a misstatement in a police form.

The House of Lords unanimously allowed the appeal. Save where the DPP was under a duty to take over the conduct of proceedings or, not being under a duty, chose to do so, Part I of the 1985 Act did not preclude the bringing of a private prosecution. To that extent the right of private prosecution survived. But allowing private prosecutions to proceed, despite an assurance that the offender would not have to go to court, would tend to undermine not only the nonstatutory system of cautions, but also the schemes for cautioning young offenders and adult offenders that Parliament had endorsed in the Crime and Disorder Act 1998 and the Criminal Justice Act 2003. A court was entitled to ensure that its process was not misused in that way. There were five speeches in the House but here are extracts from only two of them:

Lord Bingham:

...

15 The broad lines of the argument may be summarised in this way. The practice of cautioning, originally developed by the police as a pragmatic response to a certain class of case, has grown into something much more sophisticated and specific, as evidenced by the statutory regimes established by the 1998 and 2003 Acts and a series of Home Office Circulars. While there are obvious differences between the young offender, conditional cautioning and simple cautioning regimes, they have shared objectives of seeking to keep people out of the criminal courts and preventing further offending. Underlying a decision to reprimand, warn, caution conditionally or caution simpliciter, and fundamental to each, is a judgment made by a responsible official that prosecution would not be in the public interest, or at least that the public interest would be better served by not prosecuting. Such a judgment, like a decision not to prosecute, is not immune from challenge. If shown to be unlawful on any of the familiar grounds relied on to seek judicial review, it may be quashed and set aside. But so long as the decision stands the judgment should be respected, and it would be wrong in principle to allow it to be circumvented at the behest of a private prosecutor whose motives may have little or nothing to do with the public interest. The right to prosecute privately is a factor of little weight in the balance, since it is a somewhat anomalous historical survival; it cannot outweigh an extant decision of a responsible official on what will best serve the public interest. On this argument, paradoxically, the statement made in the form given to Mr Whalley, in its reference to going before a criminal court, was accurate, and the statement in the Hayter forms was inaccurate.

16 I see very considerable force in this argument. A crime is an offence against the good order of the state. It is for the state by its appropriate agencies to investigate alleged crimes and decide whether offenders should be prosecuted. In times past, with no public prosecution service and ill-organised means of enforcing the law, the prosecution of offenders necessarily depended on the involvement of private individuals, but that is no longer so. The surviving right of private prosecution is of questionable value, and can be exercised in a way damaging to the public interest. I would not, therefore, reject this argument. But nor do I think the House should in this appeal accept it, for reasons which I find, cumulatively, to be compelling. It was not advanced in the Divisional Court, so we lack the benefit of its judgment on it. It was scarcely foreshadowed in Mr Whalley's written case, and there was no hint that the correctness of Hayter was to be challenged. Thus Mr Swift had little opportunity to prepare an argument in reply. The question is one of some importance, and should not be resolved in the absence of representation of the Crown or any police force, both of whom might be expected to have views on how the issue should be decided. The question is one which might well benefit from legislative attention. It is not necessary to resolve this question to decide the present appeal.

17 For these reasons and those given by my noble and learned friend Lord Rodger of Earlsferry with which I agree, I would therefore allow the appeal on the narrower ground, set aside the decision of the

Divisional Court, uphold the decision of the Justices and dismiss the proceedings. I would invite written submissions on costs within 14 days.

Lord Rodger of Earlsferry:

...

21 When the police officer cautioned Mr Whalley, he was not acting under a statutory scheme. But nor was he off on a frolic of his own, or on a frolic of the Greater Manchester Police. On the contrary, he was acting in accordance with an officially recognised policy which was intended to be followed by police forces throughout the country in accordance with guidance issued by the Home Office. The current guidance was to be found in Home Office Circular 18/1994, to which was annexed a revised version of the National Standards for Cautioning. Paragraph 1 of the Standards describes the purposes of a formal caution as being to deal quickly and simply with less serious offenders, "to divert them from unnecessary appearance in the criminal courts," and to reduce the chances of their re-offending. All worthwhile policy objectives. Before the police can contemplate administering a caution, there must be sufficient evidence of the offender's guilt and he must admit the offence. Provided these requirements are met, "consideration should be given to whether a caution is in the public interest": para 3. The police are told that they should take into account the public interest principles described in the Code for Crown Prosecutors. In their turn, Crown Prosecutors are told in para 8.3 of the current Code for Crown Prosecutors that a simple caution should only be given if the public interest justifies it and in accordance with Home Office guidelines.

22 What is clear from the National Standards is that a police officer should not decide to administer a caution, rather than to prosecute, unless he is satisfied that cautioning rather than prosecution is in the public interest. Presumably, the officer in this case was so satisfied. If that view was untenable, his decision to caution rather than to prosecute could be set aside on judicial review. But Mr Jones has not challenged the officer's decision. The assumption must be that the police officer was entitled to decide that it was in the public interest for Mr Whalley to be given a caution and so avoid an "unnecessary appearance in the criminal courts". On that basis the officer represented to Mr Whalley that he would not have to go before a criminal court for the offence.

23 In these circumstances, where such an assurance had been given to Mr Whalley, any subsequent decision by the Crown Prosecutor to prosecute him would have been capable of being regarded as an abuse of process: R v Croydon Justices, Ex p Dean [1993] QB 769, 778F–G per Staughton LJ. What happened in this case, however, was that Mr Jones, a private individual, unconnected with the police or prosecuting authorities, initiated the prosecution, despite the assurance given to Mr Whalley. Whether or not Mr Jones was consulted before the police officer took the decision to caution rather than to prosecute and to give that assurance, he was certainly not a party to it. So there is no question of Mr Jones being estopped from initiating the prosecution. Nor did he do anything to give Mr Whalley any legitimate expectation that he would not be prosecuted. The question is, rather, whether the magistrates were entitled to stay the proceedings because it offended their sense of justice and propriety to be asked to try the accused in these circumstances: R v Horseferry Road Magistrates' Court, Ex p Bennett [1994] 1 AC 42, 74G–H per Lord Lowry.

24 Nowadays public prosecutions are the rule. So, usually, the court will be concerned to prevent its process being misused by a public prosecutor. But, in times gone by, when private prosecutions were the rule, the court must have had the power to guard against the corresponding danger of its process being misused by a private prosecutor. So, in this case the justices had the same power to stay for abuse of process as they would have had in the case of a public prosecution. Having duly considered the matter, the justices came to the view that it would be an abuse of their process to allow Mr Jones to continue with the prosecution of Mr Whalley, after the police had given him an assurance that he would not have to go to court in respect of the offence. Clearly, they considered that it offended their sense of justice and propriety to be asked to try the accused in the face of that assurance, irrespective

of the fact that the prosecution was initiated by a private individual rather than by a public official. Not only was that a view which was open to the justices, but it is one which I share.

25 Looking at the matter from a slightly different angle, it seems to me that allowing private prosecutions to proceed, despite an assurance that the offender would not have to go to court, would tend to undermine not only the non-statutory system of cautions, but also the schemes for cautioning young offenders and adult offenders which Parliament has endorsed in the Crime and Disorder Act 1998 and the Criminal Justice Act 2003. A court is entitled to ensure that its process is not misused in this way.

26 In the course of the hearing, the House was referred to the decision of the Divisional Court in Hayter v L [1998] 1 WLR 854. In that case the defendants had assaulted and injured a young man. The police cautioned them, but the terms of the caution indicated that it did not preclude the bringing of proceedings by an aggrieved party. The victim's father then initiated a prosecution of the defendants. They contended that the proceedings should be stayed as an abuse of process. The justices dismissed the informations, but the Divisional Court allowed the prosecutor's appeal.

27 The qualification in a caution of that type means that the decision in Hayter is distinguishable from the present case and, for that reason, the House did not hear full submissions on it. I accordingly agree with my noble and learned friend, Lord Bingham of Cornhill, that it would not be appropriate to express a concluded view about the broader argument relating to it. Accordingly, I make only one tentative observation.

28 Plainly, the Hayter type of qualification to the caution would alert the offender to the lingering possibility of a private prosecution. So the reaction of a court to being asked to try the case in such circumstances might well be different from its reaction in a case where the caution was not qualified in that way—although, in Hayter's case, the qualification does not actually seem to have weighed with the justices. The point which concerns me, however, is not the effect of such a qualified caution on the court's sense of propriety and justice, but, rather, whether it is proper for a police officer to insert the qualification in the caution and, if so, in what circumstances.

29 The National Standards indicate that a police officer should not administer a caution unless he concludes that it is in the public interest to divert the offender from an unnecessary appearance in the criminal courts. Prima facie, this would seem to suggest that the officer should have concluded that it is unnecessary for the offender to appear in the criminal courts, whether at the instance of a public or a private prosecutor. Some support for that view might perhaps be found in para 7 of the Home Office circular which contemplates the police giving the victim details of the offender in order to institute civil, but not criminal, proceedings. On that assumption, however, it would be difficult to see how the officer could administer a caution but simultaneously contemplate—by including the Hayter qualification—that it could be in the public interest for the offender to be prosecuted by the victim. The inclusion of the qualification suggests, however, that the officer has concluded that, while it would not be in the public interest for a public prosecution to be mounted, it would none the less be legitimate, and not contrary to the public interest, for the victim to prosecute, if so advised. Your Lordships heard no submissions on whether it is appropriate for a police officer to issue a caution, with the various consequences for the offender, on that basis. Nor was counsel in a position to explain whether there is an established practice of issuing such qualified cautions in certain kinds of cases. So I simply draw attention to the point but express no view on it.

30 For these reasons, as well as for those given by Lord Bingham, I would allow the appeal and make the order which he proposes.

CHAPTER FIVE

DEFENCE LAWYERS

The pivotal role of lawyers in the criminal justice system is often overlooked. In an adversarial system, those who assess the criminal justice system too often concentrate on the system weighed against the defendant. Yet the most effective due process safeguard is a strong defence team. Lord Justice Auld **[1:5]** identified two essentials to balance the prosecution: 'an experienced, motivated defence lawyer or lawyers who are adequately paid for pre-trial preparation' and 'ready access by defence lawyers to clients in custody'. And there is a significant European Court of Human Rights jurisprudence on the right to free and confidential legal advice under Article 6 (see **[1:12]**: see for example, *Brennan v United Kingdom* (2002) 34 EHRR 18). In England most defendants tried for the more serious offences are legally represented, often at taxpayers' expense. We should therefore examine the impact and quality of this legal advice.

The legal profession is still divided into two branches. Solicitors are the first port of call for legal advice, while a barrister may advise on legal problems, usually when briefed by a solicitor, and normally represent defendants at trial in the Crown Court. Of course, many of those who work in solicitors' offices are not legally qualified or may hold other qualifications, such as those of the Institute of Legal Executives (ILEX). The Courts and Legal Services Act 1990 granted to the Lord Chancellor's Advisory Committee on Legal Education and Conduct (ACLEC) the right to make new rules to allow solicitors rights of audience in the higher courts. The Access to Justice Act 1999 replaced ACLEC by a 'smaller and less expensive' committee, the Legal Services Consultative Panel, with the aim of reducing the barriers between the different branches of the profession; and section 36 of the Act specifically grants rights of audience to every barrister and solicitor in relation to all proceedings (subject to the rules of conduct of the professional bodies and their training requirements). The Lord Chancellor (now the Minister of Justice) was given vast powers to change professional rules and to appoint the members of the Consultative Panel. A discussion of whether or not the public is best served by a divided legal profession is beyond the scope of this book, but Kerridge and Davis (1999) caution against 'the drift towards unification'. The Legal Services Act 2007 may well lead to more blurring of the traditional distinctions. It makes three important changes: it creates a Legal Services Board to regulate the legal professions, as well as a new Office of Legal Complaints. Most originally, it seeks to encourage 'alternative business structures' (ASBs) allowing different types of lawyers and non-lawyers to work together, but ASBs are unlikely to be fully implemented until 2011. For the moment, it remains usual for solicitors, who may well present their own cases in the magistrates' courts, to brief counsel to represent their clients in the Crown Court or on appeal.

The extract **[5:1]** from McConville et al's hard-hitting analysis of solicitors' firms in England and Wales in the early 1990s reveals the importance of due process safeguards in an adversarial legal system. The deficiencies highlighted by this research led the authors to question the effectiveness of various reforms, with their emphasis on managerialism and cost-effectiveness. The authors proposed what they called 'a cultural transformation' in criminal defence work and a reassertion of defendants' rights within an adversarial system. The extracts included here reflect the research conclusions rather than the reality which lay ahead. The reality is that the picture has not improved and that things do not always go as they should in the police station. This is transparently clear from the case law as well as the research evidence. For example, *R v Grant* [2005] EWCA Crim 1089, [2006] QB 60 was one of three cases in which the Lincolnshire police placed secret listening devices in the exercise yard of a police station. In each case privileged communications between detained suspects, later defendants, and their legal advisers were recorded. This caused the judges in two of the cases to stay the proceedings as an abuse of process. The Court of Appeal in *Grant*, the third case, allowed the appeal. Laws LJ said:

We are in no doubt but that in general unlawful acts of the kind done in this case, amounting to a deliberate violation of a suspected person's right to legal professional privilege, are so great an affront to the integrity of the justice system, and therefore the rule of law, that the associated prosecution is rendered abusive and ought not to be countenanced by the court. (at paragraph 54)

It is not unknown for the police to break the rules, and suspects deserve competent well paid legal representatives.

(i) LEGAL AID

Recent years have seen a decrease in the number of solicitors' firms accepting criminal work. The decline is revealed in the Legal Services Commission's annual reports: in 2001/02, the number of firms offering criminal defence services declined from 3,500 to 2,909 firms in a year; by 2006/07 it had slipped down to 2,510. Whilst bigger firms may be more efficient, quality assurance and value for money have driven many firms away. An extra chapter in this book could usefully have studied the decision making in the Legal Services Commission (LSC) and the Ministry of Justice: more important than the structure of the legal profession is the provision of adequate funds to enable good lawyers to work in the field of criminal justice. In 2001 the Criminal Defence Service (CDS), administered by the LSC, took over from the Legal Aid Board the provision of public funding for criminal defence work (see the Access to Justice Act 1999). The CDS was created 'for the purpose of securing that individuals involved in criminal investigations or criminal proceedings have access to such advice, assistance and representation as the interests of justice require' (section 12(1)). The most radical innovations have been, first, the Public Defender Service, established in 2001, where salaried lawyers provide legal representation, employed directly by the LSC. This service has been launched in only in a few pilot sites, some of which have already closed and others are being monitored: see <http://www.legalservices.gov.uk/aboutus/how/strategic_publications.asp>. The second innovation is CDS Direct, a telephone helpline that provides non-means-tested legal advice direct to suspects detained in a police station, launched in 2005. This service seems set to expand: and needs careful monitoring. It may well be cheaper and quicker to provide advice: but will it be as good (and indeed confidential)?

The vast majority of legal services continue to be provided by private practitioners. Private firms must hold a General Criminal Contract to carry out publicly funded criminal defence work. Funding issues predominate: not only the level of fees but their structure too. 'Standard fees' for magistrates' court work were introduced in 1993, despite strong opposition from the solicitors' profession. The danger of paying solicitors a standard, or fixed, fee is that they may either cut corners or turn away difficult cases. Auld **[1:5]** argued that the current fee structure was 'fundamentally flawed' in that it does not provide an adequate reward or incentive for preparatory work. The fee structure should instead encourage efficient preparation of cases. Lord Carter was asked by the Government in 2005 to carry out a review of legal procurement, and his report was published in July 2006. This was followed by a consultation paper *Legal Aid: a sustainable future*, published jointly by the Ministry of Justice and the Legal Services Commission and then the White Paper *Legal Aid Reform: The Way Ahead* (Cm 6993, 2006). The Government seems committed to what they call a market-based system, which will include: fixed fees for legal aid work in police stations; revised fees for magistrates' courts in urban areas; a revised Crown Court graduated fees scheme for advocates; a new litigators' Crown Court graduated fees scheme; and a new panel of providers authorized to provide services in Very High Cost Cases (VHCC). As we go to print, there is still great controversy surrounding these changes, and **[5:2]** is the summary of the conclusions of the Constitutional Affairs Committee of the House of Commons in 2007. The vital importance of providing good quality independent and confidential advice in our legal system must not be underestimated. At the same time the Government has a bigger agenda than simply the provision of legal advice at taxpayers' expense: the Legal Services Act 2007 creates an ambitious new framework for the regulation of both privately and publicly funded lawyers.

Who pays for legal aid? The taxpayer, of course. But also suspects, who often have to dig into their own pockets. With effect from October 2006, a defendant's right to receive legal aid for a case before a magistrates' court became subject not only to a merits test, but also to a means test. Means testing had been abolished in 1999, but disappointingly it has now been re-introduced. The Government says that this is 'on target to save £35 million a year': i.e. the suspect and the lawyer may be paying the price! There is an eligibility calculator at <http://www.legalservices.gov.uk/criminal/getting_legal_aid/eligibility_calculator.asp>.

(ii) LEGAL ADVICE AT POLICE STATIONS

In our scenario, Gerry Good was arrested by the police and taken to the police station. As we saw in Chapter 2, the police have a duty to inform him of his right, under section 58 of PACE, to obtain legal advice at the police station free of charge regardless of his means. The decision of the Court of Appeal in *Samuel* [1988] QB 615 shows how seriously the courts take this right, though there are other cases, such as *Alladice* (1988) 87 Cr App R 380, where the conviction has been upheld despite a breach of section 58. We saw in Chapter 2 that, in response to the European Court of Human Rights decision in *Murray* (1996) 22 EHRR 29, section 58 of the Youth Justice and Criminal Evidence Act 1999 prevents any inference being drawn from a suspect's silence prior to consulting a solicitor. Yet, perhaps surprisingly, this right to free legal advice is not exercised by many suspects. Sanders et al's (1989) study showed that about a quarter of all arrested people asked for a solicitor. Brown, Ellis, and Larcombe **[5:3]** suggest that the 1991 revision of PACE Code C (on the detention, treatment, and questioning of suspects) led to a small increase in the proportion of suspects receiving legal advice. They concluded that, in the early 1990s, three-quarters of suspects were being informed of the right, and of the fact that the legal advice was free, and just over half were told that the legal advice was independent, but very few were told that the consultation would be in private. They suggested a scheme under which legally qualified personnel are present at main police stations on a round-the-clock basis to avoid the problem of local variations in the provision of legal advice. The cost implications of this, however, suggest that it is highly unlikely: the way forward, as we have seen, seems to be telephone advice.

At present, where suspects do not choose their 'own' solicitor, they may choose from a list of local solicitors, which the police will provide (or by ringing a centralized telephone number). When a duty solicitor is requested under the '24-hour scheme', a telephone referral service is contacted. The telephone call system to duty solicitors required at police stations has been contracted out since 1994 (the Automobile Association won the first contract!). The current system has been much criticized, not least because the police have to answer the phones, and because confidential facilities are often not available.

Gerry Good was arrested in the morning and might have found someone from his solicitors less willing to come if he had been arrested at night. As we saw in Chapter 2, he rang the firm of solicitors who had represented him before. It was, as is often the case, an employee with no legal qualifications who came to the police station to represent him. The need for good quality legal advice is vital. The most striking point to emerge from Baldwin's recordings of police interviews [5:4] was the general passivity of legal representatives at the interviews. There are even striking examples in the case law, such as *Miller, Paris and Abdullahi* [5:5] where judges expressed strong and well-deserved criticism of legal advisers. That case may be 15 years old, but it should still serve as a 'wake-up' call for sloppy legal advisers.

McConville and Hodgson [5:6], too, considered that many advisers lacked adequate legal knowledge and confidence, and that sometimes they seemed to identify more with the police than with the suspect. Their conclusions are all the more striking in view of the removal of the unqualified right to remain silent under police questioning and at trial (by the Criminal Justice and Public Order Act (CJPOA) 1994 [2:22], discussed in Chapter 2). Good quality legal advice is essential. For example, McConville and Hodgson [5:6] found that many legal advisers left the police station before the formal interview took place, and others only gave advice by telephone. The Law Society introduced regulations in 1995 preventing solicitors' representatives who have not passed an accredited examination in police station skills from giving advice in police stations. It would be interesting to know whether courses such as ILEX's six-week home study Police Station Representatives Accreditation Scheme (now see the Criminal Litigation Accreditation Scheme Police Station Qualification) have led to improvements in the standard of advice offered.

(iii) ROLE OF DEFENCE LAWYERS BEFORE AND AT TRIAL

Let us return to Gerry's case. Ian Brown, an employee of the firm, was present at his interview. Once Gerry had been charged by the police, he was refused bail. The next morning he was represented by Mary Chapman, a solicitor with the firm, at his successful bail application in the magistrates' court. Whilst there he filled in the necessary forms to apply for legal representation, and his application was processed by court staff. In Gerry's case, there is no question that he qualifies for legal aid—he is facing a charge of wounding, his liberty is at stake, and so he falls within the 'interests of justice' criteria. Means testing, which was abolished in 1999, was re-introduced in October 2006: Gerry will have to complete the very complex questionnaire to see if he qualifies: see <http://www.legalservices.gov.uk/criminal/getting_legal_aid/eligibility_calculator.asp>. As well, at the end of a trial a judge may order defendants, depending on their means, to contribute to the costs of the case.

How do solicitors decide what work is necessary in preparing a defence? Clearly, solicitors have an enormous influence on the outcome of a case. Their decisions about interviewing alibi witnesses, checking police summaries or commissioning independent medical or forensic experts can make all the difference to the strength of a defendant's case. But whether defence solicitors take such actions may well depend on whether their pay structure rewards such work (hence the vital importance of a good funding scheme). Although Gerry's solicitor represented him at the bail application, she decides to brief counsel to represent him at his trial. Gerry's first meeting with his barrister may well be at the Crown Court shortly before the trial is due to begin. Zander and Henderson (1993) found that 44 per cent of defence barristers said that the brief had previously been returned by someone else. No fewer than 25 per cent of defence barristers in contested cases had received the brief later than 4 pm on the day before the trial. Perhaps this is not so surprising: barristers, being self-employed, are likely to hold onto a brief until the last minute in case their present case finishes earlier than expected. The Royal Commission on Criminal Justice (1993) commented (at page 118) on the need to reconstruct the scale of fees to encourage counsel to give adequate priority to pre-trial preparation. This is the message reinforced by Auld **[1:5]**. Current legal aid reforms are seeking to tackle the continuing problem of 'returned briefs': this is a problem affecting the prosecution, the Crown Prosecution Service, as much as the defence.

An accused person has to make two vital decisions pre-trial: first, whether to plead guilty or not guilty; and, secondly, with offences triable either way, whether to opt for trial by jury in the Crown Court. The two will often be considered together (though the Government proposed abolishing a defendant's right to choose trial by jury) and the advice given first by solicitors and later by barristers may be decisive. Hedderman and Moxon **[5:7]** studied the reasons for the decisions leading to Crown Court trial. Most of those who chose to be tried at the Crown Court were influenced by the prospect of acquittal, although 82 per cent ended up pleading guilty. Again, more than half of those who elected trial by jury said that the possibility of a lighter sentence at the Crown Court influenced their decision, even though judges were three times more likely to impose a custodial sentence and the sentences that they imposed were much longer. Riley and Vennard **[6:5]** suggest that one reason for defendants opting for the Crown Court is that they themselves have greater confidence at a hearing in that court. The fact that 82 per cent ended up pleading guilty, despite having opted for jury trial because of its higher rate of acquittal, is not really surprising: in many cases, the prosecution agrees to accept a guilty plea to a lesser charge only at the last minute. It may well be that it is only when they meet their barrister at the door of the court that defendants finally realize that an acquittal may be unlikely. Note that HM Inspector of Court Administration stated, very worryingly, in his Annual Report (2006/07) that 'in many courthouses the privacy of defendants' conversations with their legal representative could not be guaranteed' (at page 18).

Zander and Henderson (1993) found that 26 per cent of defendants changed their plea to guilty at a late stage, thus causing trials to 'crack'. Is this because people who want to plead not guilty are persuaded to change their minds, or because people who really always planned to plead guilty 'play the system'? If the defendant is confident that ultimately he will be sent to prison, he may seek to delay the fateful day as long as possible. Narey (1997) commented that 'a substantial proportion of elections are little more than an expensive manipulation of the criminal justice system and are not concerned with any wish to establish innocence in front of a jury' (at page 2).

The substantial sentence discount given for guilty pleas must have a strong influence on many defendants. As we will see in Chapter 7, defendants who plead guilty at the first possible opportunity will usually receive a third 'discount' on the usual sentence. Bargains as to plea are often distinguished from bargains as to sentence: sentence bargains necessarily involve the judge, and will therefore be examined in Chapter 7, although the questions concerning the legitimacy of such bargains are the same as those discussed here. The Royal Commission's reasons for recommending that judges should be able to indicate sentence are included at **[7:6]**.

Should there be such pressure on people to plead guilty? Zander and Henderson's Crown Court study for the Royal Commission (1993) controversially led some to argue that perhaps 1,400 innocent people plead guilty every year. Yet the Royal Commission concluded that as long as people were adequately advised and that they were in fact guilty, there was nothing wrong with a system of inducements to encourage them to plead guilty. Following this, the CJPOA 1994 put the discount for guilty pleas on a statutory footing, and this discount is now governed by section 144 of the Criminal Justice Act 2003 and by the definitive guideline of the Sentencing Guidelines Council (see Chapter 7). Sanders and Young (2007), in a chapter which they call 'the mass production of guilty pleas', are highly critical, arguing that a system of plea bargaining undermines the rule of law by allowing the State to secure convictions based on vague and unsubstantiated allegations. Defence lawyers spend more time negotiating away defendants' rights than they do in upholding them. This encouragement of guilty pleas is hard to reconcile with adversarial principles.

In Gerry's case, a bargain as to plea might involve an agreement that, in return for his pleading guilty to the less serious charge of section 20 (maximum sentence = 5 years' imprisonment), the prosecution will drop the more serious charge under section 18 (maximum sentence = life imprisonment). This can be done without any involvement on the part of the judge, although it is possible for the judge or magistrates to insist that the prosecution proceeds with the more serious charge. Thus, in the trial of Peter Sutcliffe (the 'Yorkshire Ripper') in 1981 the judge insisted that the charges of murder were proceeded with, even though the Attorney-General was willing to accept a plea of guilty to manslaughter by reason of diminished responsibility. Gerry maintains with his solicitor that he will plead not guilty and so she does not attempt to negotiate a pre-trial plea bargain. On the morning of the trial, there is some informal negotiation in the robing room between counsel for both sides, but the prosecution decide to continue with the charge under section 18, largely because of the evidence that Rosa Bottles was pursued for half a mile from the pub, which they argue suggests that Gerry intended to wound her. His criminal record may also influence their decision.

Defence counsel's role at the trial itself is, of course, vital. In conjunction with the solicitor, many tactical decisions have to be made: which witnesses to call, whether the defendant should give evidence, exactly what questions to ask, and whether to cross-examine or re-examine. In Gerry's case, the barrister, Tim Moffat, is a fiery young man with whom Gerry feels little sympathy when he meets him briefly in court before the trial, but he seems to know his job. He may or may not have been the barrister who represented him (briefly) at the Plea and Case Management Hearing (PCMH). The personal performance of counsel is likely to have an impact on the jury. Lawyers may have a split loyalty: should they argue fully every point in their client's case or should they think of the public interest in, for example, a brief trial? Their own career prospects may lead them at times to leave some aspects of their client's case unexplored, especially if they think that the judge is unsympathetic. If a solicitor or barrister considers the client to be undeserving, they may provide a poorer service. The eloquence of counsel inevitably affects the verdict: a persuasive barrister will be more effective than a poor one. The Royal Commission on Criminal Justice (1993) recommended limiting the length of opening and closing speeches to 15 and 30 minutes, respectively. Would this be appropriate? In the event of conviction, defence counsel has the stage again, making a speech in mitigation on behalf of the offender, to give to the court the defendant's explanation of the offence and any other matters going in the defendant's favour.

What happens if lawyers are incompetent? Paying clients may vote with their feet and change solicitors, but when the taxpayer is footing the bill, it is more difficult to keep adequate control over incompetence, and the Government continues, as we have seen, to work on ways of monitoring performance. Poor performance by barristers should mean that solicitors do not brief them again, but is this adequate quality control, since solicitors themselves will rarely be in court to carry out effective monitoring (often sending less senior members of staff instead)? In *Ensor* **[5:8]** the Court of Appeal confirmed an earlier ruling to the effect that a mistaken or unwise decision by counsel could not normally be regarded as a proper ground of appeal. The Royal Commission (1993) was critical of this narrow test: 'It cannot possibly be right that there should be defendants serving prison sentences for no other reason than that their lawyers made a decision which later turns out to have been mistaken'. Malleson **[5:9]**, in her review of grounds for appeal, found that in 9 out of 300 cases, lawyers' errors were cited as grounds of appeal. Not surprisingly, all these defendants were either unrepresented or had changed legal advisers, and none were granted leave to appeal. The Royal Commission concluded that vast improvements were needed in the provision of advice: 'We recommend that both branches of the profession take all necessary steps to ensure that practitioners not only perform their duty to see the client at the end of the case, as most do, but also give preliminary advice both orally and in writing'.

The European Court of Human Rights ruling in *Boner v United Kingdom, Maxwell v United Kingdom* (1994), that the refusal of legal aid for an appeal was a breach of a prisoner's rights under Article 6(3) of the European Convention on Human Rights **[1:12]**, may have encouraged the authorities to be more ready to grant legal representation. But Plotnikoff and Woolfson's **[5:10]** conclusions on the quality of legal advice confirm the view that, within an adversarial system, good quality representation is essential. The fallacy in the argument that, since defendants are frequently legally represented, there is now less of a need to keep due process safeguards within the system, is obvious. Low pay deters good lawyers moving into publicly funded legal work.

Cape (2004) reviews the rise (and fall?) of the defence lawyer in the English legal system over the last 50 years. Noting that Government spending on criminal legal aid is almost certainly proportionately greater than in any other jurisdiction, he chides not only the Government (for reducing spending on criminal legal aid, without heeding the clear warning from the LSC that Government policies and new laws are a major contributor to increasing costs) but also the legal profession (who must take seriously its responsibilities for ensuring the development of a competent body of lawyers skilled in an adversarial role).

FURTHER READING

Abel, R L, *The Legal Profession in England and Wales* (1988) Basil Blackwell

Ashworth, A and Blake, M, 'Some ethical issues in prosecuting and defending criminal cases' [1998] Criminal Law Review 16

Boon, A and Levin J, *The Ethics and Conduct of Lawyers in England and Wales* (1999) Hart

Cape, E, 'Incompetent police station advice and the exclusion of evidence' [2002] Crim LR 471

Cape, E, 'The rise (and fall?) of a criminal defence profession' [2004] Crim LR 401

Cape, E, 'Rebalancing the criminal justice process: ethical challenges for criminal defence lawyers' (2006) 9 Legal Ethics 56

Carter, P, *Review of the Procurement of Criminal Defence Services: Market-Based Reform* (2006) DCA

Kerridge, R and Davis, G, 'Reform of the Legal Profession: Alternative Way Ahead' (1999) 62 MLR 807

HMIC, *Modernising the Police Service: Role, Management and Deployment of Police Staff in the Police Service of England and Wales* (2004) HMIC

IPCC, Deaths during or following police contact: Statistics for England and Wales 2006/07 (2007)

IPCC, Police Complaints: Statistics for England and Wales 2006/07 (2007)

McConville, M and Mirsky, C, 'Looking through the Guilty Plea Glass: The Structural Framework of English and American State Courts' [1993] 2 Social and Legal Studies 173

Morrison, J and Leith, P, *The Barrister's World and the Nature of Law* (1992) Open UP

Pannick, D, *Advocates* (1993) Oxford Paperbacks

Sanders, A, Bridges, L, Mulvaney, A, and Crozier, G, *Advice and Assistance at Police Stations and the 24-Hour Duty Solicitor Scheme* (1989) Lord Chancellor's Department

Young, R and Wilcox, R, 'The merits of legal aid in the magistrates' courts revisited' [2007] Crim LR 109

Zander, M and Henderson, P, *Crown Court Study* (1993) RCCJ Research Study No 19, HMSO

DOCUMENTS

[5:1] McConville, M, Hodgson, J, Bridges, L, and Pavlovic, A, *Standing Accused: The Organization and Practice of Criminal Defence Lawyers*

(1994) Clarendon Press (from Chapter 5: Advisers at Interrogation, at page 126)

Until recently, routine police interrogation methods were well-hidden from courts, solicitors and researchers. Interrogations were essentially police–citizen encounters with outsiders barred from access, accounts of which were police constructions. The accounts attested to the probity of police character, their honesty of purpose, and the reasonableness of their questioning. Clients' accounts, by contrast, were presumptively illegitimate and the official (police) accounts undermined what little credibility suspects might otherwise have enjoyed. The legal profession accepted an element of wrong-doing by the police and misconduct was sometimes established at court but, by and large, the products of interrogation were under police control and collectively they portrayed a system which operated with correctness, restraint and regularity.

Following PACE, the police are presented with a new problem in that they no longer have exclusive control over accounts of interrogations. This has caused a seismic change in the nature of those accounts, with contemporaneous records bearing practically no relation to the world created by the police in their pre-PACE evidence. Whilst this in itself ought to be a matter of concern, it is clear that police goals remain unchanged, although their capacity to instantiate those goals is now imperfect. None the less, the police continue to try to enhance their own credibility and undermine that of the suspect. In this process, rules relating to admissibility are not of central concern to them and they are prepared to bring to bear dubious methods of inquiry.

Although the police are now more frequently than before forced to carry out interrogations in the presence of defence advisers, this has not proved a major restraint. Despite gaining access, the legal profession has no thought out strategy of how to use that access. In part, this is because they have been socialised into accepting as legitimate methods which are objectionable or dubious. In part, they have such a narrow definition of what they *can* do, that they end up by making no objections to police practices. And in part, there has been such insufficient thought given to interrogation, that they do not know what is or is not proper.

It is not simply a question of know-how and technical competence, however, but rather a question of attitude and values. Looked at as a whole, advisers who attend police stations accept uncritically the propriety and legitimacy of police action, even where what they witness themselves, what they hear from clients, and what they suspect goes on, leaves them convinced that the police break the rules and in other ways are beyond the law. The reason for this is that many advisers, like the police, instinctively believe, without requiring substantiation through evidence, that there is a case to answer, and that it is the client who must give the answer. This in turn springs from a working assumption that the client is probably factually guilty. In line with these ideologies, advisers permit the police free rein in interrogations and thereby legitimate dubious police methodologies.

(From Chapter 8: The Solicitor at Court: Plea and Mitigation, at page 210:)

The routine nature of work in most solicitors' offices is more than matched by the routinisation of their plea settlement and mitigation practices. For the most part, solicitors do not see magistrates' courts as trial venues but as places where defendants can be processed through guilty pleas without, in general, any risk of severe sanction. The idea that the prosecution should be 'put to the proof'—required to establish a case against the defendant—is not accepted as 'valid' or 'realistic' by defence solicitors. Whilst it would be misleading and unfair to argue that solicitors do not care about their client, so strong is their presumption of guilt and their faith in the prosecution's case, that they fail to see their own role in the production of pleas, and their implication in ambiguous or inconsistent pleas of guilt. But it is not right to argue that solicitors are socialised, through court and prosecutorial inspired disciplinary mechanisms, into non-adversarial practices: they join hands with prosecutors not out of fear of sanction but because they share similar social and crime control values. Whether they like it or not, solicitors, by routinising pleas and mitigation, invite the state to see them as delivering standard services.

(From Chapter 10: Solicitors, Barristers and the Crown Court, at page 267:)

In organisational terms, Crown Court cases occupy a regraded position in the structure of the typical firm of solicitors. One or two firms were exceptional in employing competent and experienced clerks and legal executives. Here, the case was prepared well in advance and a real effort made to engage in proactive defence work. Witnesses were sought and pursued until contacted; enquiry agents were sent to draw up plans of the scene of the crime; and forensic experts were employed in response to the client's assertion of inaccurate or fabricated evidence. However, these individuals were quite exceptional even within the firms in which they were employed. In the majority of practices much preparatory work is undertaken by non-qualified staff, and solicitors themselves have little contact with routine Crown Court cases. Lack of care in the preparation of these cases may be partially remedied if there is a case conference with counsel in advance of the court hearing, but reliance on this risks loss of witnesses and other information, and routinely results in the collection of evidence whose value is reduced by its staleness. In an unacceptably high number of cases, evidence is still being gathered long after the time when it was first available, sometimes during the trial itself.

In these cases, solicitors view the tasks of their staff, particularly in attending court, as undemanding and insignificant. The role definition applied to staff, leads solicitors to employ junior, casual or part-time individuals who are not otherwise involved in the case at all. The fact that the rates of remuneration are so low shows that it is not just solicitors who undervalue these tasks but the state itself.

The confidence that solicitors have in the system for handling of Crown Court cases is not based upon a rigorous evaluation of the process. With occasional outstanding exceptions, the average solicitor has little involvement in preparing these cases, and what work is done is often too little and too late. Whilst case conferences can make good some of the earlier shortcomings, these do not occur in most cases. At best, conferences can stimulate clerks to set in train investigative tasks that should have taken place much earlier with the increased risk of loss of information or a reduction in its value. In addition to this, cases are routinely vulnerable to changes of counsel and the late delivery of briefs, in several instances being put into the hands of barristers on the day of the hearing itself. With only inexperienced or casual staff from firms in attendance and without a record of what took place at conferences, solicitors themselves are in no position to evaluate the performance of counsel or any subsequent complaint from the client. Given this context, the trust the solicitors repose in counsel can be based only in images they have of barristers as experts possessing recipe knowledge revealed to 'insiders' as part of the process of Crown Court decision-making.

Whilst our observations confirmed that some barristers are strongly committed to cases, understanding of the need for a sympathetic approach, and careful to test the underlying basis of a guilty plea, counsel in general do not exhibit these positive characteristics. Strikingly, on the hearing day at court, but also in conferences in chambers, barristers evince little interest in scrutinising the evidence or in attempting to convince the defendant of its weight and probative value. Rather, conferences are treated as 'disclosure interviews', the purpose of which is to extract a plea of guilty from the client. In this process, what the prosecution alleges, what witnesses may say, and what the client wishes to say, are not discussed. In place of forensic testing, 'the evidence' is reified, set up as a totality, and invested with a force which irresistibly points to guilt. In place of evidence, a whole gamut of persuasive tactics is deployed against clients enabling barristers to take control of cases and to prevent most clients from becoming, in any real sense, defendants.

If the logic of this process is towards a guilty plea, the precise details of the final arrangements are high contingent. In some cases, barristers act to restrain complaint individuals from pleading to any and all charges, but in other cases the client's will is given free and unsupervised rein. A small proportion of defendants may resist pressure to capitulate but, deprived of support from solicitors' representatives, few can successfully hold out for long. Compliance is made more likely by the 'offers' which percolate through following prosecution counsel's review of the worth of the prosecution. Whilst the result of this prosecution review is usually a scaling down of the charges in predictable ways, it sometimes appears to have nothing to do with a rational assessment of the evidence but instead is an attempt to get a plea to *something*. When barristers introduce into discussions sentencing and charge propensities of particular judges and dark suggestions of backstairs' dealings, the contingent nature of the outcome is beyond measurement and can only be stated.

[5:2] Constitutional Affairs Committee of the House of Commons, Implementation of the Carter Review of Legal Aid
(3rd Report of 2006/07)

Summary

This report examines the Government's proposals for radical reform of the Legal Aid system. The Government plans to change the basis on which Legal Aid is to be procured by introducing a transitional system of fixed and graduated fees for cases (rather than payment on an hourly basis as is the practice now in many areas of legal aid work) as a way of preparing for full competitive tendering for Legal Aid contracts by solicitors.

The Government is rightly concerned about the considerable increase in the Legal Aid budget in recent years. The purpose of these reforms is to find a way of halting these increases and easing the pressure on civil legal aid. To do this, it suggests a wholesale reform of the Legal Aid system, even though the two main areas in which expenditure has risen unsustainably are Crown Court defence work and public law children cases—other areas of expenditure are either stable or, in real terms, declining. Despite the rise in Legal Aid expenditure, in recent years there has been considerable financial pressure on solicitors providing Legal Aid services. Many have stopped doing Legal Aid work.

Legal Aid practitioners and others have criticised the plans for imposing fixed and graduated fees in the transitional period. They are seen as over-complex, rigid and likely to impose unsustainable cuts in the fee income of solicitors' firms. The plans have not been based on adequate data. The most vulnerable clients—those most in need of Legal Aid assistance—are likely to suffer. The plans for a transitional scheme should not proceed.

The Government's goal is to introduce a market-based approach by way of Best Value Tendering. No detailed plans for how this will work have been made public. The Legal Services Commission has not yet thought through how it intends to implement this reform. There is a complete lack of reliable research into the potential effects of competitive tendering on legal aid suppliers and clients. These proposals need to be tried out in a geographically limited area before any general scheme is introduced.

The drive to limit the cost of provision of Legal Aid by ensuring price competitiveness raises questions about the continuing quality of the advice provided by Legal Aid solicitors, especially in areas of specialist expertise. A system of peer review is proposed to ensure the maintenance of high quality. There are concerns about peer review's effectiveness, particularly under a system of competitive tendering.

The Government's plan is to involve fewer but larger solicitors' firms in the Legal Aid system in order to achieve administrative savings. We doubt whether the potential savings resulting from such a move would justify the risks inherent in this change. There is no evidence to suggest that larger providers would necessarily be more efficient and deliver legal aid work at a higher quality than smaller providers.

The impact of the reforms on black and minority ethnic (BME) firms and their clients is one of our main areas of concern. Such firms will be disproportionately disadvantaged by these proposals. The question has been raised whether they would constitute a breach of Race Equality legislation.

The clear breakdown in the relationship between the Legal Services Commission and suppliers has been a disquieting aspect of the inquiry. This has recently come to a crisis point. Before any successful reform can be implemented, the two sides must rebuild a sense of trust in each other.

Overall, while we support the fundamental aims of the reforms and recognise that there is an urgent necessity to limit Legal Aid expenditure, we believe that the Government has introduced these plans too quickly, in too rigid a way and with insufficient evidence.

[5:3] Brown, D, Ellis, T, and Larcombe, K, *Changing the Code: Police Detention under the Revised Codes of Practice*
(1992) HO Research Study No 129, HMSO (at page 96)

The right to legal advice is only an effective right if the legal profession are able to deliver that advice adequately. The increase in demand for their services among suspects inevitably places additional strain on the profession. This comes at a time when there is already considerable debate among solicitors about the system of remunerating them for attendance at the police station. At one station in the present study, duty solicitors went on strike during phase two of the observational study (although this did not cause any obvious difficulties securing the attendance of solicitors).

There is clear evidence from the research that the coverage of advisory work at the police station by the legal profession is variable in the extreme and that this has suffered in some respects, almost certainly on account of rising demand. While more suspects are consulting legal advisers and they are attending the station more often, they are remaining for interviews between police and suspect far less frequently. Furthermore, a suspect's prospects of seeing a legal adviser at the police station and of having one present at interview vary considerably. Someone arrested at Peterborough or Wednesfield, for example, could virtually depend on seeing a legal adviser at the police station; however, someone taken to Weston Favell or Wellingborough would be fortunate to receive anything other than advice over the telephone. At the latter two stations, suspects would be even luckier to have a legal adviser present at a police interview: they attended only 11% and 20% of interviews at these stations in cases in which advice was requested. At Peterborough and Wednesfield, on the other hand, legal advisers were present at nearly two-thirds and 84% of such interviews. There is some evidence to suggest, too, that suspects' decisions about legal advice may be affected by its availability. It is probably no coincidence that, at Peterborough, the proportion of suspects requesting solicitors was high and at Wellingborough low.

This variation in the provision of advice probably owes much to different local arrangements for providing advice: for example, the strength of the duty solicitor scheme, the proximity of firms to police stations, the number of firms prepared to carry out advisory work there and whether representatives are widely employed to provide such advice. Whatever the reason for the variation, it raises, as with juveniles, issues about equitable treatment of criminal suspects and equality of access to legal advice. The revised Code has gone a considerable way towards ensuring that suspects (adults in particular) are treated equally in the provision of information about rights and providing the facility to request those rights. It is unable to ensure that the right to legal advice is implemented equitably. How this could be achieved is beyond the scope of the report. The answer may rest with some form of scheme under which legally qualified personnel are present at main police stations on a round-the-clock basis. As reported in Chapter 3, this might overcome the reservations of many about requesting a solicitor, as long as those who staffed the scheme did not become too closely identified with the police. It would also ensure that those who did want advice could depend on it being delivered without delay and in person, with the option of requesting attendance at police interviews if desired. It would also ensure that appropriate adults in cases involving juveniles would not be confronted with further delay after they arrived if they did opt for legal advice.

The giving of legal advice at the police station through the consistent presence of a solicitor would also eradicate a major difficulty with present arrangements, namely the provision of much advice by telephone and in conditions of considerable lack of privacy. Sanders et al (1989)[1] have pointed out that suspects tend to find telephone advice of lesser utility than advice at the station. Stations also do not generally possess dedicated facilities for private telephone consultations. Ad hoc arrangements were sometimes made, but conversations between solicitor and client were usually conducted in the custody area within the hearing of anyone in the vicinity, including investigating officers. The level of noise sometimes made such consultations extremely difficult, and police present often tended to make little effort to minimise the disruption. Bearing in mind that nearly one-third of all legal advice is given over the telephone, this is clearly an unsatisfactory state of affairs and detracts heavily from the value of this right.

Note

1 See Further reading section.

[5:4] Baldwin, J, *The Role of Legal Representatives at the Police Station*
(1992) RCCJ Research Study No 3, HMSO (at page 52)

As noted earlier in this report, a critical question is whether lawyers should be acting more forcefully on their clients' behalf at the police station. There is a good deal of scope for them to do so, and there were only a few lawyers on the video tapes who demonstrated that they could wield much authority in the interview room if the need arose. Some lawyers were more tolerant than were others of police officers who adopted harrying tactics, who persisted doggedly with certain lines of questioning or who made crude assumptions of guilt. Searching questions need to be asked, therefore, about how far legal representatives—who are in most instances unqualified legal personnel—can be said to be providing adequate protection to their clients in the police station.

The lawyers' view of their role at the police interviews reflects the way that their attitudes have been moulded by the history of their relations with the police. The interview takes place on police territory and it is police officers who are in charge of it. Officers often describe it as 'their' interview, and the lawyers contacted in this study did not commonly see it in other terms. Although police attitudes towards the presence of solicitors have shifted in the course of the past decade—reflecting to a considerable extent the changes brought in by the PACE legislation—lawyers continue to be treated with circumspection and suspicion. While they are no longer regarded as gatecrashers at interviews, they are nonetheless only tolerated at police stations if they behave appropriately. Advising clients not to answer questions or intervening at interviews are not seen by police as reasonable forms of behaviour. It is only if they toe the line that lawyers are regarded as acceptable participants at police interviews.

Passivity and compliance on the part of lawyers are therefore the normal, the expected, almost the required responses at the police station. Solicitors are conditioned by their history, their experience, even their own professional training and guidance, to be passive in the police interview room, and the existing rules reinforce this by giving police officers the upper hand. The lawyers' role in the interview room remains a precarious one, and it is no real surprise to note that the junior staff who mainly turn up to police stations are more inclined to facilitate police questioning than they are to challenge it.

[5:5] *R v Paris, Abdullahi and Miller*
(1993) 97 Cr App 99

The three appellants were convicted of the murder of a Cardiff prostitute. There was no forensic evidence against them. Against Miller, the prosecution case rested on the evidence of two discredited witnesses, Miller's own admissions, and admissions he made to two visitors when in prison. After hearing part of the confession evidence on tape, the trial judge ruled it admissible. On appeal, it was contended that Miller's confession was unreliable, having been obtained by oppression.

The Court of Appeal, in quashing the convictions, held that it was undoubtedly oppressive within the meaning of section 76(2) of PACE to shout at a suspect what they wanted him to say after he had denied involvement over 300 times, particularly since the person in question was on the borderline of mental handicap. The Lord Chief Justice was critical of both the police and the suspect's solicitor.

Lord Taylor CJ (at page 109):

Before parting with this case, we should comment on the apparent failure of the provisions in the Police and Criminal Evidence Act 1984, to prevent evidence obtained by oppression and impropriety from being admitted. In our judgment, the circumstances of this case do not indicate flaws in those provisions. They do indicate a combination of human errors.

First, the police officers adopted techniques of interrogation which were wholly contrary to the spirit and in many instances the letter of the codes laid down under the Act. In our view, those responsible for police training and discipline must take all necessary steps to see the guidelines are followed.

Secondly, although we did not hear what his instructions were, the solicitor who sat in on the interviews, seems to have done that and little else. Guidelines for solicitors on 'advising a suspect in the police station' were first published by the Law Society in 1985 with second and third editions in 1988 and 1991. The current edition provides under paragraph 6 as follows, inter alia:

'6.3.2 you may need to intervene if the questions are:...(c) oppressive, threatening or insulting;

6.3.3 you should intervene if the officer is not asking questions but only making his/her own comments...

6.4.1 if questions are improper or improperly put, you should intervene and be prepared to explain your objections...

6.4.2 if improprieties remain uncorrected or continue, advise the suspect of his/her right to remain silent.'

It is of the first importance that a solicitor fulfilling the exacting duty of assisting a suspect during interviews should follow the guidelines and discharge his function responsibly and courageously. Otherwise, his presence may actually render disservice. We can only assume that in the present case the officers took the view that unless and until the solicitor intervened, they could not be criticised for going too far. If that is so, they were wholly wrong.

Finally, it is most regrettable that the worst example of the police excesses (tape 7) was not played in full to the learned judge before he ruled on admissibility.

Despite this combination of errors, it must be pointed out that the record of timings and the tape recordings of the interviews required by the Act, have enabled this Court to review what took place and, albeit belatedly, to allow these appeals. At the conclusion, we now direct the learned Registrar to send copies of tape 7 to the Chief Inspector of Constabulary, to the Director of Public Prosecutions and to the Chairman of the Royal Commission on Criminal Justice.

[5:6] McConville, M and Hodgson, J, *Custodial Legal Advice and the Right to Silence*
(1993) RCCJ Research Study No 16, HMSO (at page 16)

2.2 All the firms that we examined had established their own in-house system for responding to requests for advice at any time of day or night. To service demand, firms had established rota systems, to which most members of staff were allocated. In addition, some firms regularly contracted out work to individuals on a piece-work basis or used the services of outside agencies to handle night and week-end calls or, in some cases, any and all calls which came to the firm. A very prominent pattern in high volume criminal defence firms was the employment of former police officers to discharge police station advice work as well as to undertake other tasks such as the interviewing of witnesses. In the present study, which replicates the findings of the long-term study in which the authors have been engaged for the past three and a half years, some 47% of firms employed former police officers for police station work. In addition to this, outside agencies, staffed by former police officers, had grown up to service the needs of several firms in respect of own solicitor requests, and two of the firms of solicitors studied (as well as others in the same localities) regularly contracted out work to such agencies.

Who attends police stations to give legal advice

2.3 Whilst earlier research cited above has indicated recourse to representatives in 'own solicitor' cases at a rate exceeding 40%, the findings of our study show that the true rate is much higher. Our study suggests that the rate of recourse to representatives may well be as high as three-quarters as Table 2.1 shows.

TABLE 2.1 The status of advisers attending police stations in response to requests from suspects

Status of Adviser	n	%
Admitted solicitor	44	24.4
Articled clerk	28	15.6
Clerk on staff	56	31.1
Former police officer	38	21.1
Non-staff clerk	8	4.4
Outside agency	6	3.3
Totals	180	99.9

The figures disclosed in Table 2.1 if anything overstate the frequency with which solicitors acting on their own account respond to requests for advice since on some of the occasions where solicitors went to the police station they did so in their capacity as duty solicitors. Moreover, where a solicitor attended with a non-qualified member of staff (n=6) we classified the status of the adviser as 'solicitor' even though, in such cases, it was usual after the initial client consultation, for the solicitor to leave the non-qualified member of staff to handle alone the interrogation and any subsequent advice sessions.

The overall figures hide some differences between firms: whilst, as we have seen, many firms used the services of former police officers, a majority did not, some expressing themselves to be shocked at the practices of their colleagues; and, in a few firms, it was clear, not only from the cases we observed but also from our conversations with firms' personnel, that solicitors made strenuous efforts to attend police stations.

(At page 199:)

It has become increasingly evident that the low level of personnel utilised in the provision of legal advice at police stations and the resultant poor quality of that advice is unlikely to be amenable to immediate reform. Rather, it is a product of the overall structure of the private solicitors' profession, its ideologies, and the way in which it is currently organised to provide criminal defence services as a whole. This is not simply a function, as spokespersons for the profession often claim, of the financial restrictions imposed under legal aid, although it is likely that the problem of poor quality advice will be exacerbated if the proposed introduction of standard fees (instead of hourly rates of payment) for magistrates' court criminal defence work goes ahead. However, there are no plans to alter the current hourly basis for payment under legal aid for police station advice, and the rates for which such payments are made are already among the highest available to the profession for any form of legal aid work. As a result, the overall income derived by solicitors for this one aspect of their criminal defence work now amounts to over £50m per annum, or the equivalent of more than a quarter of the total amount they receive for representation of defendants in all stages of magistrates' court proceedings. In the light of this and the political context of even greater government pressure to control growth in legal aid expenditure, there is likely to be very little scope for improving rates of payment for police station advice work.

Nor is there any evidence that higher rates of payment would, in themselves, bring about any real improvements in the quality of advice, or of advisers, at police stations. For example, duty solicitors already receive enhanced payments, one-third higher than those paid to other solicitors, for attending police stations during unsocial hours. Yet research (Sanders et al, 1989) has shown that, despite this extra financial incentive, duty solicitors consistently provide telephone advice to suspects in police stations, rather than attending on them personally, far more frequently than do 'own' solicitors for equivalent types of case. Nor have recent rule changes to the official duty solicitor arrangements, designed to encourage more attendance at police stations, had any visible effect in reducing rates of telephone advice by duty solicitors.

By contrast, the greater frequency with which other solicitors do ensure that an adviser attends personally on suspects at police stations is without doubt related to the wider licence they have, compared with duty solicitors, to employ unqualified staff to undertake this work. Our research indicates that the rate of use of non-qualified staff by 'own' solicitors may in fact be considerably higher than shown in previous studies. And, again, the fact that this practice is of doubtful legality under the formal rules governing payments out of legal aid funds, certainly where firms routinely use outside agents to carry out police station visits on their behalf, does not seem to deter them in any way. Nor should this be surprising, given the lack of any systematic means of monitoring solicitors' behaviour in this respect, and of enforcing the rules on non-delegation to outside agents and, even more so, the fact that the downgrading of police station advice work is now deeply ingrained in the general organisation of solicitors' criminal defence practices.

Indeed, the reality of these practices is that criminal defence solicitors have come increasingly to rely on their firms being able to undertake ever larger volumes of routine representation in magistrates' courts (solicitors being excluded, at least at present, from most forms of advocacy in the higher criminal courts). The central organising principle of solicitors' criminal defence practices, therefore, is to ensure the maximum deployment of qualified staff on in-court advocacy, with the result that most out-of-court and non-advocacy services are delegated to other staff. In this context, it may be important to solicitors, for the purposes of customer satisfaction and retention, to ensure that established clients at least receive an attendance at the police station by some personal 'representative' of the firm, even though the status of the person is often deliberately left vague so far as the police and especially clients are concerned. On the other hand, as solicitors currently perceive the organisational imperatives of criminal defence work, it is considered not viable, both in financial and social/personal terms, for qualified staff to be deployed routinely on police station work and thereby diverted, directly or indirectly (because of the out-of-hours work it entails), from regular magistrates' court advocacy.

The result is that police station advice, far from being given the central role in an adversarial process that both the law and sociological analysis would assign to it, has been effectively redefined by solicitors in essentially non-adversarial terms, as at best carrying out an administrative 'watching brief' over police interrogations and hardly involving advocacy on behalf of the client at all. Altering this situation would require a major re-focusing of solicitors' criminal defence practices as a whole, with much greater importance being attached to the less visible, out-of-court aspects of the work. Such a restructuring may be impossible within the present organisation of the profession and of legal aid, and it is certainly difficult to see how it could be achieved in the face of even tighter budgetary restrictions on legal aid expenditure as a whole.

'Ideological drift' and law reform

11.17 The logic of our findings is that the right to silence should be strengthened rather than further weakened or attenuated. The collective effect of 'reforms' in this area has been to adversely change the position of the accused in the criminal justice process without any empirical grounding or proper philosophical justification. In fact, the criminal justice process has been reshaped without attention being paid to its foundational principle, namely, that it has grown out of the duty upon the state to demonstrate its right to punish those believed to be involved in criminal activity. It is this principle which ultimately imposes strict standards of proof upon the Crown and prevents it from compelling the suspect to co-operate in the investigation or to testify. Whilst the Crown may, in seeking to discharge its burden of proof, utilise information voluntarily provided by the suspect, those who rely upon silence do no more than ask the state to discharge the burden imposed on it by law.

In this context, the integrity, autonomy and right to self-respect of individuals arrested by the police, so vigorously defended by the Royal Commission on Criminal Procedure (1981) is already at risk in the practice and ideology of criminal justice today. The police have moved historically from a position in which they had no access to detain persons to one today in which they have unmediated access. Alongside this, citizens have moved from a position in which they were asked if they had *anything* to say, to one in which they may be held in detention until the police are satisfied that they have *nothing* left to say (Code C, para 16.1). Nothing could better symbolise the primacy given in policing to arrest over information-gathering, and the subversion of a 'right' to silence into a legal requirement to remain in police detention and interrogation until the police decide that no more can be wrung out of the arrestee.

[5:7] Hedderman, C and Moxon, D, *Magistrates' Court or Crown Court? Mode of Trial Decisions and Sentencing*
(1992) HORS No 125, HMSO (from the Summary, at page vi)

In recent years there has been a large increase in the proportion of triable-either-way cases which have been committed to the Crown Court for trial. This has contributed to an increase in the remand population and the sentenced prison population. It also has substantial resource implications for the Crown Prosecution Service, the courts and the legal aid fund.

There is only very limited information as to why magistrates and defendants take the mode of trial decisions they do. Apart from the extra burdens which Crown Court trials impose on the criminal justice system, comparisons of published statistics suggest that Crown Court trials are much more likely to lead to custodial sentences being imposed. However, there has not hitherto been a study comparing severity of sentence at the two venues while controlling the main case factors. The present study sought to remedy this omission and confirms that those dealt with at the Crown Court are at much greater risk of custody, even after allowing for differences in case characteristics. The study was concerned with the way in which convicted offenders were dealt with at the two venues, and the reasons for the decisions leading to Crown Court trial, not with the trial process itself. Acquitted defendants were not, therefore, included.

The main findings are:

- Almost 60% of cases dealt with in the Crown Court were sent there because magistrates declined jurisdiction. Yet magistrates' sentencing powers would have been sufficient to deal with a majority of these cases.

- Nearly three quarters of those denied a choice of venue would have chosen to be dealt with at a magistrates' court (mostly in the expectation of a lighter sentence and/or a quicker trial).

- Most of those who chose to be dealt with at the Crown Court were influenced by the prospect of acquittal; yet the majority (82%) ended up pleading guilty to all charges on which they were convicted.

- There was little evidence that the considerable variation in sentencing practice between individual courts has any systematic influence on defendants' decisions as to venue.

- More than half of those who elected Crown Court trial said that the possibility of a lighter sentence at the Crown Court influenced their decision. Yet the Crown Court made far more use of custody than magistrates' courts, irrespective of the area. This remained true when courts were matched on a number of factors. This analysis showed that judges were three times as likely to impose immediate custody, and sentences were on average two and a half times as long. Overall, therefore, they imposed more than seven times as much custody in comparable cases.

- One third of defendants who elected trial would, in retrospect, have preferred to have been dealt with at a magistrates' court.

- 70% of those who elected Crown Court trial had done so on the advice of a barrister or solicitor. Only five per cent had been advised to opt for summary trial.

- A substantial number of defendants, including some who intended to plead guilty from the outset, chose to be dealt with at the Crown Court because they did not trust magistrates to give due weight to their case, often feeling that they would be biased in favour of the police; in almost one quarter of cases where solicitors advised their client to plead guilty from the outset they nevertheless favoured Crown Court trial.

- Late changes of plea were often associated with late changes in the offences charged, and it is possible that if charges could have been agreed prior to the mode of trial decision more defendants would have been content to accept summary trial.

- Even where magistrates declined jurisdiction, well over half the defendants received sentences that could have been imposed by magistrates.

- For all types of offence, victims were much more likely to receive compensation if the case was dealt with by a magistrates' court. This remained true even after allowing for the greater use of custody (which usually precludes a compensation order) at the Crown Court.

- Social inquiry reports appeared most influential in diverting offenders away from fines and towards probation-based disposals; there was no evidence that they had a significant influence on courts' use of custody.

(From Discussion and Conclusions, at page 38:)

The decision of magistrates or defendants in relation to mode of trial has a particularly strong and wide-ranging influence on other agencies, with very substantial cost implications. For example, in 1988–89 the cost of a contested case in a magistrates' court was £295 as compared with £3,100 at the Crown Court; average prosecution costs were £50 at magistrates' courts compared with £460 at the Crown Court. And defendants dealt within the Crown Court are much more likely to have a social inquiry report prepared on them, at a cost (in 1988–89 of £210). Legal aid costs too, were several times higher though comparative figures are currently not available.

Differences in the costs of the various disposals, however, make the biggest overall difference to the cost of trials at the two venues. The high cost of imprisonment makes the largest contribution to this, but community service orders (£25 per week with an average duration of 35 weeks) also contribute to the difference, albeit with some offsetting benefits for the community. By contrast fines, which were used far more by magistrates' courts than the Crown Court, were estimated in 1989 to have yielded an average of £77 per either way case, after allowing for collection costs (see Magistrates' Courts' Scrutiny, 1989). Magistrates' courts were also much more likely to compensate victims.

High standards of justice and public confidence in the criminal justice system are, of course, of fundamental importance. Such considerations have ensured the survival of jury trial in a very wide range of cases, and the freedom to have offences tried at the Crown Court is increasingly exercised. So what is achieved by having such a large number of cases dealt with in the Crown Court?

Whilst the extra financial costs of Crown Court trial are clear enough, the benefits are less easily measured. No one can say with confidence which venue is more successful at convicting the guilty and acquitting the innocent, but since the Crown Court acquits more defendants than do magistrates' courts some defendants clearly benefit from a Crown Court trial. The benefits for those convicted are harder to discern. Some feel that they have had 'a fairer trial', and this perceived benefit cannot be lightly dismissed. Nevertheless, for many defendants the decision to take their case to the Crown Court has meant time in prison—whether on remand or under sentence—which might otherwise have been reduced or avoided altogether. Subjective feelings about fairness are seemingly at odds with the practical consequences of the mode of trial decision which are often simply that the defendant received a more severe penalty.

The defendants' choice

Those who *choose* to be tried at the Crown Court do so for two main reasons, often based on misconceptions. First, Crown Court trial is seen as offering a better prospect of acquittal, second, as securing a lighter sentence (often through negotiations over charges). Although the chances of acquittal are better at the Crown Court, for many this is nullified by their eventual guilty plea. The Justices' Clerks' Society commented:

> 'Defendants will elect and lawyers will advise clients to elect jury trial in cases where there exists no credible defence in the hope there will be returned a perverse verdict.'

The finding that a majority of those interviewed who elected did eventually admit their guilt, usually on legal advice (presumably as hopes of a perverse verdict fade) makes it difficult to refute the substance of this claim—namely that guilty defendants with weak cases frequently opt for the Crown Court.

The finding that so many people believe that they will receive a lighter sentence at the Crown Court is puzzling, though expectations of lesser charges and the greater likelihood of a social inquiry report may influence this view. Whilst there are no doubt instances where the Crown Court imposes a less severe sentence than a magistrates' court would have, the study provides overwhelming evidence that as a general rule the decision to go to the Crown Court carries with it a far greater risk of a custodial sentence and of a much longer sentence when custody is imposed.

If there were stronger incentives for resolving decisions relating to charge and plea *before* the mode of trial decision is taken, this could play a part in redistributing cases to the magistrates' courts. From the point of view of those sentenced, venue is likely to be much more important than plea or, in most cases, charge, in terms of the eventual penalty. This point perhaps needs to be taken more fully into account when defendants are advised about mode of trial.

It was perhaps disappointing to find that so many defendants (and solicitors) gave as a reason for electing Crown Court trial that they would learn more about the prosecution case. When advance disclosure was introduced it had been hoped that it would lead to more cases being dealt with at magistrates' courts since it would no longer be necessary to opt for Crown Court trial in order to secure details of the prosecution case. However, it would seem that the information available to the defence, which may be only a brief summary, is often felt to be insufficient.

Directed committals

From interviews with prosecutors, justices' clerks and magistrates it was clear that elections for trial were widely regarded as the major reason why so many cases were committed to the Crown Court. It is therefore important to bear in mind that magistrates themselves were responsible for sending three-fifths of the cases in the study to the Crown Court—a proportion that has grown in recent years, and continues to do so. (However, it should be borne in mind that some interviewees said that in committing for trial magistrates were sometimes anticipating the known preference of the accused. It is not known how often this occurs.)

Under the Magistrates' Courts Act 1980 magistrates should, when considering whether or not to decline jurisdiction, 'have regard to whether the circumstances make the offence one of serious character, whether the punishment they have the power to inflict would be adequate and...any other circumstances which appear to the court to make it more suitable for the offence to be tried one way rather than the other'. At first sight, it is not clear how 'serious character' can be considered separately from consideration of whether sentencing powers are adequate. However, a relatively serious offence may sometimes attract a sentence which a lower court could have imposed, for reasons which have no bearing on the mode of trial decision. There may, for example, be exceptional mitigating factors such as severe stress; or the offender may have made restitution to the victim since the committal decision was taken.

In some respects the 1990 national mode of trial guidelines seek to strengthen the presumption in favour of summary trial. For example, many courts have a threshold of £2,000 for property offences and this has been raised to £4,000. Also, although many domestic burglaries will continue to be seen as unsuitable for summary trial, the guidelines make it clear that this should not be automatic.

The guidelines list aggravating factors that may be associated with particular offences, such as 'professional hallmarks' in a burglary or handling case, or 'use of a weapon of a kind likely to cause serious injury' in an ABH or GBH case. It is stated that cases should be tried summarily unless one or more of the listed features is present and that its sentencing powers are insufficient. However, general observations are made, which include: 'the defendant's antecedents and personal mitigating circumstances are irrelevant for the purpose of deciding mode of trial'. Given the influence of such factors in the sentencing process it is difficult to see how courts can divorce consideration of whether their sentencing powers are sufficient from consideration of factors relating to the offender. It would seem that factors which in the abstract are regarded as serious do not always lead to more severe sentences being imposed. As an example, the Home Office study of Crown Court sentencing (Moxon[2]) found that theft involving breach of trust attracted unsuspended custody rather less often than the 'other theft' category.

Given that some of the factors affecting sentence are regarded as irrelevant to the mode of trial decision, it is inevitable that Crown Court sentences will sometimes be less severe than those available to magistrates. But the scale on which this occurs does raise a number of questions. For example, are magistrates being asked to take decisions without sufficient information, and therefore forming an exaggerated view of the seriousness of the case? Are magistrates too often being asked to take mode of trial decisions on the basis of charges which have not been finalised?

One consequence of the Criminal Justice Act 1991 will be to remove antecedents as a factor to be considered when committing a defendant for sentence. Magistrates will therefore be able to commit any defendant for sentence, which should make it easier for them to try borderline cases as they will no longer run the risk of having to pass sentence on a first offender when the case turns out to be much more serious than they had anticipated.

In conclusion, the high cost of Crown Court trial, both in terms of direct costs and the indirect costs of more severe sentences and a higher remand population, seems to offer few tangible benefits, least of all for defendants. The fact that magistrates' courts in some areas manage to deal with a much higher proportion of either way cases than others, with no obvious difficulties, suggests that the scope for the CPS and magistrates to agree on summary trial in many more cases is very considerable. This view is supported, too, by the fact that far more either way cases were dealt by way of summary trial in the past. And the fact that magistrates rarely find it necessary to use their sentencing powers to the full—only one in ten defendants received custodial sentences, with an average duration of only 2.8 months—also suggests that they could take a more robust view of the suitability of cases for summary trial. Defendants and their legal advisers, for their part, should be in no doubt that if they do not have the evidence to sustain a not guilty plea they would, in many instances, be well advised to opt for summary trial.

If the recent trend could be reversed, the rewards would be considerable. Pressure on the Crown Court, the Crown Prosecution Service, the legal aid fund and prisons could be eased, and many defendants would avoid custody or receive shorter terms of imprisonment.

Note

1 Moxon, D, *Sentencing Practice in the Crown Court* (1988) 103 HORS, HMSO.

[5:8] *R v Ensor*

[1989] 1 WLR 497

The appellant was tried on two counts of rape, each of a different woman. He wanted an application for severance to be made. Counsel concluded that an application would fail, and that some advantage would accrue from having the counts tried together and no application for severance was made. The appellant was convicted on both counts. The Court of Appeal dismissed the appeal.

Lord Lane CJ (at pages 501):

We must look a little more closely at the extent to which this court will concern itself with what passes between an accused person and his legal representatives.

Mr Escott Cox contends that in a criminal trial defending counsel is only obliged to seek specific instructions from his client in relation to two matters: first, as to plea; and, secondly, as to whether the client himself wishes to give evidence. All other decisions are for counsel, and it is for him to decide, as a matter of discretion, which matters, if any, needed to be discussed with the accused. The discretion is one, he submits, which this court will not attempt directly to review, although it might, for example, in a wholly exceptional case be prepared to consider whether compelling evidence which was available but which defence counsel for no good reason refused to lead renders the conviction unsafe and unsatisfactory.

Mr Jeffreys relied heavily on *R v Irwin* [1987] 1 WLR 902, decided by another division of this court on 19 February 1987. That was a case in which at a retrial counsel for the defence decided not to call alibi witnesses who had given evidence at the earlier trial which had ended in a disagreement. On appeal it was said, at p 905g, that the question was not whether counsel was right in thinking that the witnesses should not be called but whether he was entitled to bind his client. The court held that he was not entitled to do so, asserting at p 906h, that on this topic there is no authority to be found in any criminal case.

It seems that the court in *R v Irwin* [1987] 1 WLR 902 was not referred to the decision of this court in *R v Novac* (1976) 65 Cr App Rep 107. There the court was concerned with the topic we have to consider in the present case, namely, the question of severance. A number of defendants each faced a conspiracy count and counts alleging specific offences, and one defendant, Raywood, applied for the specific offence count against him to be severed from the conspiracy count. The application was refused but his appeal succeeded on the basis that the application ought to have been allowed, and Bridge LJ giving the judgment of the court, continued at p 112:

> 'It is surprising that no application similar to that made on behalf of Raywood should have been made on behalf of Novac or Andrew-Cohen to sever the specific offence counts against them. [Counsel] for Novac told us that he thought it pointless to make such an application after the application on behalf of Raywood had been refused. But we can see no basis which would have justified him in assuming that the one application must necessarily be determined in the same way as the other. It was for him to make an application to sever on his own client's behalf if thought appropriate. *No such application having been made there can be no basis for complaint in this court that the conspiracy and related counts were heard together in Novac's case with the specific offence counts.*' (Our emphasis).

In *Novac* the court does not seem to have considered it necessary to inquire whether counsel in refraining from making an application to sever acted with or without the express authority of his client, no doubt because generally speaking this court will always proceed upon the basis that what counsel does is done with the authority of the client who has instructed counsel to conduct his case.

In *R v Gaultam*, (1987) Times, 4 March, which was decided by this court on 27 February 1987, a few days after the appeal in *R v Irwin* had been heard, Taylor J said:

> 'It should be clearly understood that if defending counsel in the course of his conduct of the case makes a decision, or takes a course which later appears to have been mistaken or unwise, that generally speaking has never been regarded as a proper ground for an appeal.'

That was a shoplifting case in which counsel, for what were patently good reasons, had declined to lead medical evidence at the trial until after the jury had returned a verdict.

On 12 March 1987 another division of this court heard the appeal of Alan John Swain who contended, with apparent justification, that his counsel, by incompetent cross-examination, had introduced evidence which was prejudicial to his case, which was then amplified by the witness in answer to a question put to him by the judge. In an attempt to circumvent the difficulties which he faced arising out of what was said in *R v Gaultam*, counsel at the hearing of the appeal sought to rely mainly on the intervention of the judge, but the court found that what was said in answer to the judge added nothing to what had already been said by the witness to counsel. Various other points were considered with which we need not now be concerned, but O'Connor LJ, giving the judgment of the court, said that, if the court had any lurking doubt that the appellant might have suffered some injustice as a result of flagrantly incompetent advocacy by his advocate, then it would quash the convictions, but in that particular case it had no such doubts.

We consider the correct approach to be that which was indicated by this court in *R v Gaultam* subject only to the qualification to which O'Connor LJ referred in *R v Swain* (unreported). We consider further that the decision in *R v Irwin* [1987] 1 WLR 902, even if it can be reconciled with *R v Novac*—which we doubt—should be regarded as being confined to its own facts. This ground of appeal accordingly fails, because counsel's carefully considered decision not to apply to sever the charges, even if erroneous, cannot possibly be described as incompetent, let alone flagrantly incompetent, advocacy.

[5:9] Malleson, K *Review of the Appeal Process*
(1993) RCCJ Research Study No 17, HMSO (at page 38)

Taken together the findings from these two comparative studies indicate that when compared with legally assisted applications unassisted applications are:

(i) Poorly presented and ill-informed.

(ii) More frequently based on substantive issues concerning the justice of their conviction rather than technical or legal grounds.

(iii) More commonly based on the alleged errors of counsel as grounds for appeal despite the fact that the Court will very rarely hear such an appeal.

(iv) Dealt with in very brief judgments by the single judge and the full Court.

(v) Very unlikely to be granted leave to appeal.

The findings of this research lend support to the concern that unassisted applications are at a disadvantage in the appeal system so that there may be cases with merit which are not identified. Without a detailed study of a large number of individual unassisted cases it is difficult to estimate how many cases with merit are wrongly weeded out by the present 'two tier' system and how best they could in future be identified.

In addition to concern about the nature and treatment of unassisted applications which enter the system, this research highlights the danger that there may be meritorious cases without legal support which do not enter the system in the first place. An unknown number of unassisted convicted persons whose cases have merit may be deterred from appealing because they are aware that unassisted applications are very rarely successful and because they believe that they will serve a longer sentence if their application fails despite the fact that the single judge and the full Court very rarely apply the time loss rules.

Recommendations

Appellants should have a right to legal assistance in presenting an application for leave to appeal for consideration by the single judge and renewing a refused application to the full court.

The findings of the research are such that consideration should be given as to whether the present 'two tier' system needs to be reformed. It is accepted as a basic principle of justice that persons accused of serious offences with limited resources should have legal assistance to defend themselves however weak that defence may be in the view of their legal advisers. We do not expect counsel to decline to present a person's defence in Court because he has determined that it is unlikely to succeed. On this principle we should expect that each convicted person has a similar right to assistance in preparing and presenting an appeal. Just as an accused person instructs his or her solicitor on a defence or provides information for mitigation in a guilty plea so a convicted person should, if he or she wishes, after receiving legal advice, instruct a solicitor in the preparation of an appeal. Counsel may advise that the grounds will be unlikely to succeed, but that decision should be for the single judge alone.

Under the present system an appellant with a meritorious case but without legal assistance must have substantial financial, intellectual, and psychological resources if their appeal is to succeed. If they are in custody, they are particularly reliant on the support and goodwill of others outside. This means that people with limited abilities and resources, such as mentally disordered or handicapped people, young people, or those whose spoken or written English is poor are most disadvantaged. These are also the people who, as miscarriages of justice cases over the years have highlighted, are most likely to be the victims of injustice in the legal system and thus may have most need of the appeal system. The right to legal assistance on appeal would particularly help these vulnerable groups.

If the single judge was retained, this change would not amount to the introduction of a right to appeal, but rather a right to legal assistance in preparing an application for leave to appeal. If all applications were drafted by counsel and submitted by solicitors we could be confident that they would be judged equally on their merits alone.

This reform should not add any great cost to the legal aid bill because the overall numbers affected would be relatively small. Under the present system counsel must advise on appeal, and will draft grounds of appeal in many cases. The change would only affect those few cases where counsel has not provided advice on appeal or advises against appealing where the convicted person still wishes to appeal and requests that grounds be drafted on his or her behalf. While the cost of this change would be small, the potential benefit would be great in that the appeal system would be seen to be more open, accessible and fair at a time when its public credibility is at a particularly low point.

[See also extract at **[9:5]**.]

[5:10] Plotnikoff, J and Woolfson, R, *Information and Advice for Prisoners about Grounds for Appeal and the Appeal Process*
(1993) RCCJ Research Study No 18, HMSO (at page 115)

This chapter discusses the results of the research and proposes some changes at improving the quality of advice and information provided to potential appellants in custody. The objective of these is to specify the commitment on the part of the legal profession and the prisons to providing a defined level of service to inmates and to ensure that the nature of the service is made known to all.

With one exception, none of the recommendations made lends itself to a simple costing exercise and this has not been attempted.

The legal profession

The nature and extent of the service provided to clients by lawyers in the 28 days following conviction or sentence are very variable. There is widespread ignorance both of some aspects of the law on appeal and of the guidelines to good practice on the responsibilities of legal advisers during this period. The first findings and recommendations relate to the guidelines themselves.

The Bar GGP[3], Law Society GGP[4] and CACD Guide[5] are inconsistent and contain a number of omissions. Specific areas where inconsistencies occur are the length of time that counsel should take to provide written grounds to the solicitor and the powers that exist to order loss of time in the case of frivolous appeals. None of the guidance documents currently reflects both the legal position relating to loss of time and the actual practice in recent years. The Law Society GGP wrongly states that the maximum that can be forfeited is 90 days and omits to mention that the single judge as well as the full Court has the power to issue such an order. None of the documents reflects the infrequency of time loss awards or that the maximum lost in recent years is 28 days.

Over half the solicitors who responded were unaware that the CACD cannot impose a sentence of greater severity than that awarded by the Crown Court. The legal position is not mentioned in any of the guides.

The CACD Guide stipulates that immediately after the conclusion of the case a client should be given a written note of counsel's view, even if this is only provisional, on the advisability of an appeal. Such a note does not constitute written advice but it does provide the client with a record of counsel's view, however provisional, on the advisability of an appeal. This is not mentioned in either the Bar GGP or the Law Society GGP. Responses to the questionnaires sent out during the study revealed that 89% of solicitors and 99% of counsel never hand over anything written at this meeting. No-one did so as a matter of course.

The Law Society GGP makes no mention of including in the brief to counsel a request to furnish written advice on appeal in the event of a conviction. When solicitors were asked whether counsel provide signed grounds without being specifically asked to do so, only 22% said they always did so. Eight per cent said this never happens.

The duty of solicitors to provide advice and keep clients and their families informed is interpreted in differing ways. One quarter of prisoners said they received no appeals advice from their lawyers at any point during the 28 days following conviction or sentence. Only 39% of inmates claimed to have received appeals advice from a lawyer since coming to prison. This situation may be due, at least in part, to confusion over exactly what costs can reasonably be claimed under the trial legal aid order, an issue not covered in any of the guideline documents. Twenty per cent of solicitors said that they do not charge at all for work done in this period and over a third who do charge said that they had had payments refused or reduced.

Recommendation 1: The appeals sections in The Law Society and Bar Guides to Good Practice produced by the Standing Commission on Efficiency and the Guide to Proceedings in the Court of Appeal Criminal Division need to be revised. The revision process should be co-ordinated to ensure that the recommendations in these documents are harmonised.

The following specific areas need to be addressed during this exercise:

(i) whether it is realistic to expect the solicitor to be present at call visits at court following conclusion of the case and, if not, the consequences that flow from delegation of this duty to a representative

(ii) the completion and handing over at the end of the case of the form at Appendix 1 in the CACD Guide, indicating counsel's view on the advisability of appeal

(iii) the time limit within which counsel should provide the professional client with written advice on the advisability of an appeal and, where appropriate, signed grounds

(iv) the time limit within a copy of counsel's opinion should be forwarded to the client

(v) the rules and practice relating to loss of time orders

(vi) the activities and costs, including prison visits, relating to advice and assistance on appeals that it is reasonable to fund under the trial legal aid order.

None of the guides contains any provision for the specific problems of clients who do not speak English. Thirty-nine per cent of solicitors and 23% of barristers indicated in their responses that they did not feel able to provide an adequate service to such clients. The following recommendation is a first step towards improving the situation.

Recommendation 2: All forms and written guidance relating to the appeals process should be translated into other languages. The solicitor should include in the brief to counsel a copy of the check-off from Appendix 1 both in English and in the first language of the client where this is different. Counsel should complete both forms at the conclusion of the case. This practice should be included in the guidance documents.

Although many clients are visited in the cells at court immediately following the case, there is no absolute right to such a visit. Both lawyers and prisoners complained of the consultation being cut short by prison or police authorities keen to transport the convicted person to prison. The defendant is often confused and in a state of shock or distress at this time, it may be the last meeting between lawyer and client and time must be made available to allow a written note on counsel's view of an appeal to be handed over and explained.

Recommendation 3: Convicted or sentenced defendants who are legally represented should have a right to a 15 minute meeting with their lawyers at Crown Court following the end of the case for the purpose of discussing counsel's opinion of prospects for an appeal.

Revision of policy documents can only play a limited part in rectifying practices that deny convicted defendants full access to the appeals process. Only through a process of education can there be any real expectation that best practice will become standard practice. For many criminal practitioners, proceeding with an appeal is a relatively infrequent occurrence. Nevertheless, initial procedures relating to provision of advice on appeals apply to all cases that result in a conviction and should form part of the continuing education for lawyers in criminal practice.

Recommendation 4: The Law Society and the Bar Council should take steps to ensure that the guidance they provide on good practice is reflected in the programmes of continuing education for legal practitioners and their representatives working on criminal cases.

Notes

1 *The Crown Court Guide—A Guide to Good Practice* General Council of the Bar.

2 *The Crown Court Guide—A Guide to Good Practice*, The Law Society.

3 *A Guide to Proceedings in the Court of Appeal Criminal Division*, pronounced by the Criminal Appeals Office.

CHAPTER SIX

MAGISTRATES

One of the most surprising aspects of the English criminal justice system is the vast role given to lay magistrates. Questions of both guilt and sentence in about 98 per cent of all criminal prosecutions are decided by magistrates.

TABLE 6.1 Number of offenders sentenced in the magistrates' courts

1993	1,357,800
1997	1,860,000
2001	1,280,000
2005	1,426,000
2006	1,362,900

Source: Criminal Statistics 1993, 1997, 2001 (paragraph 7.18, Cm 5696), 2005 (Table 2.4, HO Statistical Bulletin 19/06), 2006, Table 2.8

The bulk of these prosecutions were for purely summary offences, which can only be tried in a magistrates' court, and include many minor motoring offences (though not the most minor, which are dealt with by fixed penalty notices issued by the police). The remainder (perhaps 20 per cent) are offences triable either way, which may be tried either in a magistrates' court or in the Crown Court. Even in a case such as Gerry Good's, where he will eventually be tried before a jury, some key decisions are taken in the magistrates' court. Magistrates' justice is cheap and relatively fast—but is amateur justice fair? This question is all the more important given the general shift towards transferring more serious cases down to the magistrates' courts (and the less serious from the courts altogether). It is also important to note the increasing use of lawyer stipendiary magistrates, now known as district judges (magistrates' courts), who sit alone. Is this fairer than a tribunal of lay magistrates? How can we tell?

(i) ROLE OF THE LAY MAGISTRACY

The almost 29,000 lay magistrates in England and Wales sit in magistrates' courts. Until 1992 the Home Office controlled the organization of magistrates' courts, whilst the Lord Chancellor appointed and dismissed magistrates. This inconsistency led to the transfer of the management of magistrates' courts to the Lord Chancellor's Department. Meanwhile, new funding arrangements were introduced, putting cash limits on all courts, in effect penalizing those that failed to process cases speedily enough. The reorganization of Magistrates' Courts Committees (MCCs) proposed in the White Paper *A New Framework for Local Justice* was achieved in the Police and Magistrates' Courts Act 1994. Section 69 gave the Lord Chancellor the power to replace two or more MCCs with a single MCC. Thus until recently, local MCCs, with a Justices' Chief Executive as chief administrative officer, managed the courts. Then the Access to Justice Act 1999 added more flexibility to the rules, allowing alteration of the various territorial units that make up the magistrates' courts service and allowing summary cases to be heard outside the commission area in which they arose. Lord Justice Auld **[1:5]** recognized the importance of local justice and indeed suggested (at page 272) that 'all members of the judiciary, whether lay or professional, should be brought within the responsibility of the local Resident Judge and the judicial hierarchy of which he is part'. He pointed out the difficulty of identifying what precisely it is that is to be valued in 'local justice': he distinguishes geographical locality from the locality of those dispensing justice. These issues are explored in depth by Seago et al **[6:1]** in their research into the expanded use of district judges. Morgan **[6:2]** argues for greater use of lay magistrates in the criminal justice process, a view which this author strongly supports.

Now the Courts Act 2003 has fundamentally changed the organization of magistrates' courts. It imposed on the Lord Chancellor a duty to ensure 'an efficient and effective' system to support the courts. The Act created Courts Boards (Court Administration Councils, in the original Bill) and local justice areas which replaced the old commission areas and petty session areas. The reality is more centralization, with local consultation: now the Lord Chancellor not only appoints and dismisses magistrates, but he also gives directions as to the places at which magistrates' courts may sit and as to the distribution of court business. He may specify local justice areas and make orders altering them.

Will the Court Boards create regional bureaucracies, too large to be adequately responsive to local needs? You might like to look at the HM Inspectorate of Court Administration reports (<http://www.hmica.gov.uk>) as well as the HM Courts Service's website: do 'managerialist' (see **[1:6]**) and cost-cutting priorities mean that justice and due process are becoming poor relations to economy? Does it matter if the magistracy is becoming less of a 'local' body?

Lay magistrates are appointed by the Lord Chancellor (Minister of Justice) from names submitted by local advisory committees. Until 1992 the names of those on the committees were usually kept secret, but now they are published. Most are senior or recently retired magistrates, themselves appointed by the Lord Chancellor. Following the recommendations of the Home Affairs Select Committee on Judicial Appointments (1996), the Lord Chancellor revised the appointment procedures. The changes, in the form of a Direction to Advisory Committees in 1998, should have resulted in a more standardized approach to the appointment of magistrates. Magistrates have to retire at 70. They may be dismissed by the Lord Chancellor, who, controversially, does not have to give reasons for a dismissal. In 1986 Kathleen Cripps, a Derbyshire magistrate, unsuccessfully sought judicial review of the

Lord Chancellor's decision to dismiss her after she had demonstrated on behalf of CND (the Campaign for Nuclear Disarmament) outside her courthouse.

The key characteristics of the lay magistracy are that they are unpaid and non-lawyers. Nowadays, they receive expenses, but the possibility of lost earnings inevitably deters many potential applicants. A magistrate is expected to sit for 26 days a year. For the self-employed this is a hefty commitment, and for those in employment, job and promotion prospects, as well as pay, may suffer. It is not surprising that the social balance of the bench is often criticized. A classic account of the merits of the lay magistracy is provided by Skyrme [6:3]. It is worth comparing his analysis with, for example, the more critical approach of Gifford (1986), who recommended a much more proactive search for magistrates, and suggested that magistrates should only serve limited terms of office in order that they should not become case-hardened. Unfortunately he did not attempt to evaluate the financial implications of his recommendations. Darbyshire (1997) is critical of the class, political, ethnicity, and age profile of the magistracy. Have things changed? The table below provides data on the number of appointments made in recent years, the proportion of those who were women, and the proportion that classified themselves as from a Black or Minority Ethnic (BME) background.

TABLE 6.2   Appointments to the magistracy

Year	1998	1998/ 99	1999/ 2000	2000/ 2001	2001/ 2002	2002/ 2003	2003/ 2004	2004/ 2005	2005/ 2006
Men	816	654	692	703	763	714	777	909	1132
Women	793	624	731	633	711	696	701	857	1080
Total	1609	1278	1423	1366	1474	1410	1478	1766	2212
% Women	49.2%	48.8%	51.3%	46.3%	48.2%	49.3%	47.4%	48.5%	51.1%
% BME	6.5%	7.6%	8.6%	9.3%	8.5%	8.2%	8.5%	8.09%	10.17%

Source: Eighth Judicial Appointments Report—1 October 2005 to 31 March 2006 (DCA, 2007)

Women have been well represented for years on the lay magistracy: the typical magistrate for several decades may have been the middle class woman returning to work after her children went to school and wanting useful, but not necessarily paid, part-time employment. The number of magistrates from ethnic minorities is also increasing, but here the problem, seems more one of retention. It may be that neither women nor people from ethnic minorities are under-represented: but it is the socio-economic or class profile of the magistracy which needs to change to make it more representative of society as a whole. Explore the web to see whether you think that the search for magistrates is as you would want it to be. Recommend the role to your friends!

Since 1966 magistrates have had to attend compulsory training courses on law and procedure, and on how to act judicially, but these courses are necessarily brief. During their time as magistrates they will also attend sentencing conferences and undergo continuing training of 12 hours every three years. But to criticize them because they are not trained is to miss the point: they are chosen as lay people, and advised on the law by a professional clerk. Since they normally sit in benches of three, junior magistrates have plenty of time to learn from their senior colleagues.

Most of the magistrates' work is done in open court, though they may sign arrest and search warrants and emergency protection orders at home. They also have a role in family law, sitting in the Family Proceedings Court, dealing with maintenance, residence, and contact orders, as well as questions concerning children in need of care. Criminal cases involving children (under 14) and young persons (14–17 inclusive) are normally dealt with in the Youth Court, where hearings are in private and should be more informal than those before the adult court. There must be at least one magistrate of each sex sitting on the panel of three in the Youth Court. They exercise very different sentencing powers from those available in the adult court.

Riley and Vennard [6:5] suggested that defendants have less faith in the magistrates' courts than they do in jury trials. Even the supposed cost advantages need to be properly evaluated. Of course, minor offences should be processed quickly, cheaply, and uniformly. Thus, few object to fixed penalties for minor motoring offences. However, more serious offences such as assault occasioning actual bodily harm and criminal damage up to a value of £5,000 are now triable only by magistrates. Is the line between summary jurisdiction and trials on indictment drawn in the right place? Do you think that Auld's recommendation [1:5] of a third, intermediate, tier (a judge and two lay magistrates) should have been explored further?

(ii) DISTRICT JUDGES

A significant recent development has been the increasing number of district judges (or stipendiary magistrates as they were until 1999). DJs, or 'stipes', as they are still sometimes colloquially known, are qualified lawyers, who must have a seven-year general qualification (i.e. have held rights of audience in relation to any class of proceedings for at least seven years).

TABLE 6.3 Numbers of district judges (magistrates' courts) and stipendiary magistrates

1990	64 stipendiaries (48 of them in London)
1994	78 full-time stipendiaries (supported by 90 acting stipendiaries)
1998	78 full-time stipendiaries (supported by 90 acting stipendiaries)
2003	105 DJ (MC) and 150 Deputies (part-time)
2006	134 (full-time) and 169 Deputies

Source: Judicial Statistics

District judges sit alone. Although in theory they share the workload with lay magistrates, in practice they will hear the cases that are likely to last more than one day or which involve difficult points of law. Both Metropolitan district judges, sitting in London, and provincial district judges, who may preside in courts over a wide area, are likely to wield a strong influence in their courts. This was encouraged in both the Royal Commission (1993; [1:4])—which suggested (at page 142) a 'more systematic approach' to the role of stipendiary magistrates, and their deployment on a slightly wider scale—and in the Police and Magistrates' Courts

Act 1994, which provides in section 72 that 'the chief Metropolitan stipendiary magistrate shall by virtue of his office be the chairman of any magistrates' courts committee for an area which consists of or includes the whole of the inner London area'. As Rozenburg (1994) pointed out, 'Elsewhere in our criminal justice system the initial finding of guilt or innocence is made by ordinary people—juries or magistrates. But a stipendiary magistrate decides the facts as well as the law: he or she is given less pay than a circuit judge for more responsibility. Any move towards the greater use of stipendiaries should be resisted' (at page 341).

District judges are also more likely to become case-hardened and judicially 'burnt out' than lay magistrates. The Lord Chancellor set up a working party in 1994 to produce guidelines identifying more clearly the respective roles of district judges and the lay bench. Narey (1997), whilst noting that stipendiaries were 'vastly more effective' in managing the parties in any given case, rejected the possibility of a substantial increase in the number or proportion of DJs. The most recent detailed research on magistrates is Morgan and Russell's 2000 report **[6:4]**, commissioned on behalf of the Lord Chancellor's Department and Home Office to explore the relationship between law and professional magistrates. Do you agree with their emphasis on the importance of 'active citizens in an active community'? This report clearly influenced Auld **[1:5]** in his recommendation that magistrates and district judges should continue to exercise their established summary jurisdiction. The student of the magistrates' courts should, however, watch closely the evolving relationship between professional and lay magistrates.

(iii) THE JUSTICES' CLERK

The justices' clerk, a barrister or solicitor of not less than five years standing, also has a somewhat ambiguous role in the magistrates' court. A creature of statute (see the Justices of the Peace Act 1968, and now the Courts Act 2003, sections 27 and 28) their role is to provide legal advice to lay magistrates, to deliver certain judicial functions and to supervise those appointed beneath them. Their position in the new Court Service has been deeply disputed, in part because of the problems of bringing together what were very different practices in the various Magistrates Courts' Committees under one national organization, but also due to underlying tensions surrounding the 'management' of the courts (see the consultation on the 'model' for the provision of justices' clerks in England and Wales of 2006, and the report of 2007 which followed the consultation, both on the Ministry of Justice's website). The post of justices' chief executive was introduced in 1994 and every MCC appointed one to manage its area. The Access to Justice Act 1999 removed the requirement for justice's chief executives to be qualified lawyers, and transferred responsibility for certain administrative functions from justices' clerks to justices' chief executives. But this division has gone with the introduction of the new Court Service. The justices' clerk leads the legal team in each area: under him or her will be the legal advisers to individual magistrates' courts.

Thus, in reality, the clerk in court will be a legal adviser, who may be a qualified barrister or solicitor or who may have recognized Court Clerk qualifications. Since the line between advice and instruction is a thin one, it is difficult to measure whether clerks overstep their purely advisory role. Clerks should, for example, advise on the admissibility of evidence (a question of law) but not on the credibility of a witness (a question of fact). They should advise on appropriate sentences but not on the actual sentence. In recent years, they have also been granted more administrative powers: Narey (1997) went so far as to suggest that the presumption should be that cases should not be put before magistrates until they are ready to proceed. There are concerns that legal advisers and their legal manager, the justice's clerk, might start to usurp the proper role of the magistrates. In their management role, the clerks already have a great influence, since they control the listing of cases. Under the Justices Clerks Rules 2005 and the Justices' Clerks Regulations 2006, justices' clerks may perform tasks which are authorized to be done by, to, or before a single magistrate (allowing agreed adjournments and giving directions for trials). The justice's clerk may delegate these powers to legal advisers. All parties are bound by the Criminal Procedure Rules: see **[7:2]**. Darbyshire (1999) casts a critical eye over the role of the justices' clerk arguing strongly that judicial responsibility should not be delegated to court clerks.

(iv) LEGAL AID DECISIONS

We saw in Chapter 2 how all suspects in a police station are entitled to free legal advice. The same is not true in the magistrates' courts. Duty solicitor schemes in magistrates' courts exist, but within tight constraints, funded under either the Advice and Assistance or the Advocacy Assistance rules of the Criminal Defence Service. A duty solicitor may not give advice on a not guilty plea: this is provided instead under the legal representation scheme. Nor is the duty solicitor scheme applicable in most non-imprisonable offences, i.e. minor offences. The legal framework for the public funding of legal representation in the courts is the Access to Justice Act 1999 and the Criminal Defence Service Act 2006 (see Chapter 5).

Thus, in our case, Gerry Good will have to complete a series of complex forms and he or his solicitor will submit them to his local magistrates' court. What criteria do court staff apply in deciding whether an applicant requires financial assistance in meeting the costs of his case? There are two tests. First, the merits test, or 'interests of justice' test, which is still based on the so-called 'Widgery criteria' laid down by a committee chaired by the then Lord Chief Justice, Lord Widgery in 1966. These criteria are complex and imprecise. Factors to be taken into account in deciding 'the interests of justice' include: the likelihood of a custodial sentence; the legal difficulty of the case; the defendant's ability to understand the proceedings; and the nature of the defence case. Extraordinarily, while the Criminal Defence Service Act 2006 transferred the authority to carry out the 'Interests of Justice' test from the court to the Legal Services Commission, they have delegated the task back to HM Court Service! If these criteria are adequate, do staff take them seriously in considering applications? We need some empirical research. The second test is a means test: although in 2006/07, 502,578 representation orders were made in the magistrates' court, the number will shrink as new funding agreements bite: see Chapter 5. And remember that national statistics may mask significant local and regional variations.

(v) BAIL DECISIONS

Since the accused is presumed innocent until proved guilty, it is hardly surprising that under the provisions of the Bail Act 1976 **[6:6]** there is a general right to bail. As Raifeartaigh (1997) put it, 'the presumption of innocence forbids liberty depriving measures which are premised on the view that the accused is guilty of a crime unless he has been duly convicted by a court of that offence' (at page 18). Does the Bail Act 1976 pass this test? Look at Schedule 1, which provides three grounds for refusing bail—where the court has substantial grounds for believing that if a defendant were remanded on bail, they would: (i) fail to surrender to custody; (ii) commit an offence while on bail; or (iii) interfere with witnesses or otherwise obstruct the course of justice. All turn on questions of predicting risk.

The Criminal Justice and Public Order Act 1994 curtailed the right to bail by introducing two exceptions. Under section 25, a person charged with, or convicted of, murder or attempted murder, rape or attempted rape, or manslaughter, was to be automatically remanded in custody if they had previous convictions for any of those offences. Similarly, under section 26, those accused or convicted of an indictable offence, or one triable either way which appeared to have been committed when the defendant was on bail, 'need not' be granted bail. Imprisonment without trial sits uncomfortably alongside the presumption of innocence, and the European Court of Human Rights found in *Caballero v United Kingdom* (2000) 30 EHRR 643 (followed in *SBC v United Kingdom* (2001) 34 EHRR 619) that the automatic denial of bail was an infringement of the European Convention on Human Rights, Article 5 [1:12]. Meanwhile, the Government had already anticipated this finding: section 25 was amended by the Crime and Disorder Act 1998, section 56, and again more significant amendments were made by the Criminal Justice Act 2003.

However, the reality is that many suspects are indeed existing offenders and cannot responsibly be left in the community pending their trial. The right of the public to protection and the rights of the suspect thus clash dramatically.

TABLE 6.4 Numbers of remand prisoners

	Average remand population in prisons
1992	10,100
1998	12,600 (higher than ever before)
2000	11,270
November 2007	12,879

Source: Prison Statistics 1998, 2001; Population in Custody (monthly figures), Ministry of Justice

Conditions in remand prisons are some of the worst in British prisons, and some 15-year-olds may find themselves in Prison Service custody because of the shortage of local authority secure accommodation. The thematic review of conditions for unsentenced prisoners, carried out by HM Chief Inspector of Prisons [6:7], makes uncomfortable reading. The extract here covers only the strategic issues and recommendations, but the whole report is worth reading. It reminds readers of the miserable conditions for many remand prisoners, of the enormous social and economic dislocation caused by a period of imprisonment. For example, 41 per cent of unsentenced women are held more than 50 miles from home. This figure rises to 44 per cent for young women. Before custody, one-third of men and one-quarter of women had been in employment, but only 18 per cent of men and 11 per cent of women expected to have a job to go to on release.

As a group, remand prisoners tend to be anxious, socially isolated, victimized and disturbed. Shockingly, of the 92 self-inflicted deaths in English and Welsh prisons in 2007, 41 were prisoners on remand. It is obviously a particularly difficult time for prisoners. The HM Chief Inspectors' Report quoted at **[6:7]** also reports the results of two surveys: one sent to the governors/directors of the 53 prisons holding unsentenced prisoners, the other the results of questionnaires completed by 711 prisoners. There was a clear mismatch between the facilities that governors believed they were providing and what prisoners claimed to be their actual experience. For example, according to the governors' survey, outside exercise was available in most prisons (81 per cent) for a period of about an hour every day. However, the prisoner survey showed that over one-third of young prisoners and 17 per cent of adults had no outside exercise at all, and only just over one-third had anything approaching the figure that was quoted in the governors' survey. Governors of all but one prison were confident that a set of legal reference books was available for the use of remand prisoners, but only 11 per cent of men and 12 per cent of women prisoners said they had such access. Fewer than half of the 63 per cent of prisoners who wanted to see a bail information or legal services officer, had in fact been able to do so.

Could more of these people have been safely left in the community? Two contrasting figures should be looked at: offending rates by those on bail; and the acquittal rate of those who have been remanded in custody. Morgan (1992) showed the difficulties involved in assessing the rates of offending while on bail, though the proportion of defendants convicted of offences committed whilst on bail is about 10–12 per cent. The acquittal rate of those who have been remanded in custody has been remarkably constant over the last few years: 23 per cent for men and 21 per cent women (this figure includes those whose cases are not proceeded with); another one-fifth receive community sentences, and a further one-fifth of men and one-third of women remand prisoners receive a fine, discharge, or other non-custodial sentence. In 2005, if we look at the number of cases which get to trial, 50 per cent of those remanded in custody were sentenced to immediate custody, 16 per cent to community sentences, and 18 per cent were acquitted (Criminal Statistics 2005, paragraph 4.11).

Let us apply the test to Gerry Good. How can we know if he will turn up for trial, or whether he will commit an offence while on bail? He has a criminal record, but he is meant to be presumed innocent of his present offence until proved guilty. Are magistrates adequately equipped to evaluate the risks he presents? We noted in Chapter 3 the lack of information available to the courts in deciding bail applications. In the early 1990s, there were significant efforts to improve the quality of this information. In 1992 Lloyd **[6:8]** analysed the impact of various bail information schemes and tried to assess whether such information is best presented to the court direct, or via the CPS or defence solicitors. Morgan and Henderson **[6.9]** reported on the Bail Process Project, set up in 1992 in five court areas to improve the quality of information available to magistrates. Their conclusion that reducing waiting times for trials would reduce the rate of offending on bail can have come as no surprise! Yet, as we saw in **[3:8]**, funding cuts have meant that much less is being done to provide bail accommodation. To try and reduce the population of unconvicted prisoners, the Government has awarded a national contract to ClearSprings Ltd in 2007 to provide privately run bail hostels (see Probation Circular 33/2007 and Chapter 10). It will be interesting to learn in due course whether this has a significant effect on the remand population in prison.

A key question is whether it is just to remand someone in custody because of a statistical risk that they will re-offend. Eaton **[6:10]** usefully pointed out the added hurdle faced by women who are not tied into typical family models: they are less likely to be granted bail. Her conclusion was stark: 'In applications for bail, we have more than a description of an acceptable model of the family and its associated gender roles: we have an acknowledge-ment that such a family structure may offer a form of control comparable to that offered by the prison system'. Worrall **[6:11]** developed this analysis of women as 'socially constructed within the discourses of domesticity, sexuality and pathology' when she contrasted the atti-tudes of women magistrates to women defendants with the attitudes of their male colleagues on the bench. With regard to magistrates' treatment of defendants from different ethnic groups, Brown and Hullin (1993) studied contested bail applications in Leeds in 1989 and did not uncover any significant differences in treatment. There is clearly a need for much more current research to test whether the situation has changed.

In Gerry Good's case, the bail application lasts less than 20 minutes. The magistrates grant him bail subject to two conditions: one that he does not go within 500 yards of the Black Bull public house, and the second that he reports to the police station three times a week. They lecture him on the need to avoid his victim, and their decision is clearly influenced by the fact that they are convinced by his solicitor, Mary Chapman, that he has a permanent home. Where the magistrates are doubtful about releasing a defendant on bail, they may attach conditions, or require security or sureties. Hucklesby (1994) explored the inconsistent use of conditional bail by magistrates. Security involves the deposit of a thing of value, normally a passport, to stop someone leaving the country. Sureties are people who know the defend-ant and are prepared to put up a sum of money, a recognizance, against the risk that the defendant will fail to appear. Doubts whether it is just to put this pressure on families and friends to act as informal janitors means that sureties are asked for rarely in English courts, and they do not pay the money over in advance (however, this did not stop the Government making parents liable for their children's fines in the Criminal Justice Act 1991). Motivated by a desire to reduce the number of adjournments in criminal proceedings, the Government introduced three measures in the Crime and Disorder Act 1998, which may have resulted in the increased use of sureties (but data is hard to find):

(1) section 54(1) enabled the police and the courts to require a surety in any case where it is believed that the deposit of a security will 'increase the likelihood of a bailed defend-ant appearing in court when required'. Thus, the court may take the view that an up-front payment, in the form of a surety, will be more effective in securing the defendant's attendance than the availability of a surety with the means to enter into a recognizance for a more substantial sum;

(2) section 54(2) introduced a new power to require a defendant, as a condition of bail, to seek an interview with a legal representative. This addressed the concern that many adjourn-ments are granted simply for the purpose of sorting out legal representation; and

(3) section 55 strengthened existing procedures for the forfeiture of recognizances in bail cases to encourage sureties to make greater efforts to ensure that the defendant appears in court.

More important has been the increased use of electronic tagging for adults granted bail (since September 2005). According to the *Criminal Statistics 2005*, 'data reported by the electronic monitoring suppliers indicates that the number of adult defendants tagged on bail increased from 157 on 31 August 2005 to 492 on 31 December 2005' (at paragraph 54.6). And in 2006, 'Data reported by the electronic monitoring suppliers show that 6,356 adult defendants were tagged on bail in 2006 and the end month caseload increased from 492 on 31 December 2005 to 1,685 on 31 December 2006' (at paragraph 4.6). But it is not clear that electronic tagging is reducing the remand population: is it instead being used where otherwise offenders might have received unconditional bail? Again, we need more research (but see Cassidy et al (2005)).

What rights of appeal exist from the bail decisions taken by magistrates? It is perhaps surprising that it was not until the Bail (Amendment) Act 1993 **[6:12]** that the prosecution first gained a right of appeal where a court granted bail to someone charged with a serious offence. The Criminal Justice and Public Order Act (CJPOA) 1994, section 30 also strengthened the courts' powers to reconsider a bail decision at any time in indictable cases if information comes to light that was not available to the police or the court when the original bail decision was taken. The 1993 Act has been amended many times: the version we publish here is the most recent: major changes were introduced in both the Criminal Justice Act 2003 and the Police and Justice Act 2006 to simplify appeal procedures.

Under the Magistrates' Courts Act 1980, section 128, a magistrates' court has power to remand a defendant in custody for up to eight days in the first instance, but thereafter may remand them for up to 28 days, provided that the defendant is present in court and has previously been remanded for the same offence. He may be remanded in custody in his absence if he consents. On conviction but pending appeal, the offender may apply for bail. Part 68 of the Criminal Procedure Rules (see **[7:2]**) deals with Bail Pending Appeal. Whether a person should be kept in custody pending an appeal against conviction, or indeed between conviction and the time sentence is passed, raises similar questions to those discussed above.

(vi) MODE OF TRIAL

All crimes are either indictable, summary, or 'triable either way'. Indictable offences are tried by judge and jury in the Crown Court (see the next two chapters); summary offences in the magistrates' court. For the last 20 years, in cases involving either-way offences, the venue for trial has been determined following a procedure laid down by the Magistrates' Courts Act 1980, sections 19, 20. If the magistrates decided that the case was suitable to be dealt with summarily, they informed the defendant that they might either consent to be tried in the magistrates' court or elect to be tried before a jury. The list of offences which are triable either way is hardly logical. For example, defendants can elect jury trial if they are found with a small amount of cannabis, or are charged with minor shoplifting (if charged: remember that many such offenders will nowadays be cautioned or receive a Fixed Penalty Notice: see Chapter 2), whereas the more serious offence of assaulting a police officer can only be tried summarily. The categorization of offences makes sense only if one looks at the nineteenth-century origins of much of the criminal law, and the piecemeal way in which some offences have been re-classified downwards in recent years in order to avoid the costs of trial by jury. National Mode of Trial Guidelines, designed to help magistrates decide whether to commit a case for trial, were issued in 1990 by the Lord Chief Justice, and have been revised by the Criminal Justice Consultative Council. The Home Office consultation paper *Determining Mode of Trial in Either-Way Cases* (1998), laid the ground for the Home Secretary's announcement in 1999 that magistrates, rather than defendants, should decide whether an either-way case should go to jury trial. The Government introduced in the House of Lords the Criminal Justice (Mode of Trial) Bill 1999, which sought to remove defendants' rights to choose trial by jury, but this was defeated. The Government, undeterred, reintroduced the Bill in the House of Commons but was met by a similar revolt. Consideration of whether the Government's offensive on the defendant's right to elect jury trial is well placed must wait until Chapter 8!

Clearly the cost arguments weigh heavily in favour of trial in a magistrates' court. Hedderman and Moxon's research **[5:7]** showed that magistrates sent for trial a large number of cases that they could have tried themselves, and that defendants often opt for trial by jury on the basis that they are going to plead not guilty, but then end up pleading guilty. Riley and Vennard **[6:5]** stressed the need to examine magistrates' reasons for declining to hear a case. At the time of that research, magistrates had no knowledge of defendants' circumstances or previous convictions in making their decision. Riley and Vennard found that magistrates only disagreed with the prosecutor's proposal that the case was suitable for summary trial in 23 out of 663 cases. The Royal Commission on Criminal Justice (1993) looked at the position in Scotland, where the mode of trial decision rests with the prosecuting authority, but concluded that this would not be acceptable in England, at least for the time being. It recommended that, if the prosecution and defence could reach agreement on the mode of trial, that should be legally binding. If they are unable to agree, the decision should remain with the court. It proposed that a defendant's right to elect trial by jury should be abolished: in effect, a dramatic way of making more offences triable only by magistrates. Narey (1997) agreed, concluding that magistrates would be well able to distinguish those defendants who, because of potential loss of reputation or for other reasons, were justified in seeking a Crown Court hearing. Auld's *Review of the Criminal Courts (2001)* **[1:5]** considered that it might be more appropriate for district judges to make the allocation decision. Part 6 of the Criminal Justice Act 2003 (sections 41–42, with Schedule 3) provides for the sending to the Crown Court of those cases which need to go there, giving effect to a number of Auld's recommendations including making magistrates aware, when they determine allocation, of any previous convictions of the defendant; removing the option of committal for sentence in cases which the magistrates decide to hear; allowing defendants in cases where summary trial is considered appropriate to seek a broad indication of the sentence they would face if they were to plead guilty at that point; and replacing committal proceedings and transfers in serious fraud and child witness cases with a common system for sending cases to the Crown Court, based on the present arrangements for indictable-only cases. It seemed initially that these provisions would be swiftly brought into force, and the Sentencing Guidelines Council consulted on a draft *National Allocation Guidelines 2006*, anticipating that the new system would be introduced in the autumn of 2006. However that (and the provisions increasing the sentencing powers of magistrates) seems to be on indefinite hold.

(vii) PRE-TRIAL HEARINGS

It is important that weak cases be filtered out. Until 1967, all cases to be tried by jury went through a preliminary hearing in the magistrates' court (committal proceedings) where the magistrates took oral evidence to decide whether the prosecution had made out a *prima facie* case. From 1967 the vast majority of cases were dealt with as 'paper committals'. Where an accused person was legally represented, magistrates' courts could, with defendants' agreement, commit for trial to the Crown Court without any consideration of the evidence. In other cases, the court examined the strength of the evidence and decided whether it warranted committal for trial. However, the CJPOA 1994 sought to abolish committal proceedings: the prosecution was now simply to give a notice of transfer to the defendant and to the court, and unless the defendant applied to have the case dismissed, the notice of transfer would take effect automatically. These provisions, which were hastily added to the Bill, proved unworkable and were never brought into force. Narey (1997) concluded that indictable-only cases should start their life in the Crown Court rather than staring in the magistrates' courts, and this was enacted in the Crime and Disorder Act 1998, section 51 [2:23]. Offenders charged with indictable offences are simply 'sent' to the Crown Court for trial. How are weak cases to be filtered out? Defendants may apply for the dismissal of any charge at any time before they are arraigned (see Schedule 3 to the Act).

Meanwhile, the Criminal Procedure and Investigations Act 1996 introduced a new 'plea before venue' system, which meant that defendants who intend to plead guilty to either-way offences are automatically dealt with summarily. Since sentences imposed by magistrates are significantly less severe (see [5:7]), this must seem unproblematic for those who wish to take the benefit of this, and of the discount for guilty pleas. But it puts further pressure to plead guilty on those who genuinely wish to contest their guilt, and who have not yet seen or heard the prosecution case against them. It also resulted in an extraordinary increase in the number of people committed by magistrates for sentence in the Crown Court: from 7,303 in 1997 to 19,192 in one year (1998/99), a figure which has remained fairly constant (19,245 in 2005/06; all data from *Sentencing Statistics, 2006* (HOSB 03/07), Table 1.1). These people have pleaded guilty, but the magistrates decide that the appropriate sentence may well be greater than they have the power to impose (six months' imprisonment or a fine of £5,000), and so the defendant finds his case sent to the Crown Court for sentencing.

An important function of committal proceedings used to be that it gave the defendant a preview of the case against him. The Magistrates' Courts (Advance Information) Rules 1985 (SI 1985/601) required the prosecution to disclose a summary of the case in either-way cases. Because these summaries were often inadequate, or even misleading, in the 1990s it became standard practice to disclose all witness statements. The position was revolutionized by the Criminal Procedure and Investigations Act 1996. The police then had a 'primary' duty to disclose to the defence only such prosecution material which 'in the prosecutor's opinion might undermine the case for the prosecution'. The defence then has a duty to disclose a statement of the defence, including the reasons why the defence takes issue with the prosecution case. Secondary prosecution disclosure should then reveal material 'which might be reasonably expected to assist the accused's defence'. There is clearly a huge danger where the primary duty of the prosecution is so subjective, and where adverse inferences may be drawn at trial where the defence fails to disclose a line of defence or changes tack at trial. The Criminal Justice Act 2003 in Part 5 seeks to make the test for primary disclosure an objective one, and also requires more to be included in defence statements. The issue of advance disclosure in our adversarial system inevitably remains a thorny and difficult area of law.

(viii) TRIAL AND SENTENCING

In summary trials, if the defendant appears, the court clerk will read out the charge(s) and ask the defendant whether he pleads guilty or not guilty. If the defendant pleads guilty, the court may convict him without hearing the evidence.

TABLE 6.5 Proportion of defendants in magistrates' courts pleading guilty

	Either-way offences	Summary non-motoring offences	Summary motoring offences
1985	65%	70%	76%
1992	48%	52%	61%
1997	50%	47%	57%
1998	54%	45%	59%
2000	54%	42%	54%
2004	55%	39%	54%
2006	58%	37%	57%

Source: Criminal Statistics 1997, 2001, Table 6.4; 2006, Table 2.9

In the early 1990s, as more defendants made use of their right to plead not guilty, so greater pressures were put on them to plead guilty, thus further undermining due process safeguards. Thus, discounts for guilty pleas were introduced in section 48 of the CJPOA 1994, and are now governed by section144 of the Criminal Justice Act (CJA) 2003 and the Sentencing Guidelines Council's Guideline on Reduction in Sentence for a *Guilty Plea* **[7:4]**. We deal with this in Chapter 7, simply because the one-third discount has a bigger (and therefore more controversial) effect in sentencing decisions made in the Crown Court.

If a defendant pleads not guilty, the magistrates will hear the evidence from both parties, and either convict the defendant or dismiss the case. Many researchers have suggested that magistrates are 'prosecution-minded' and 'conviction-minded'. Thus, Parker, Sumner, and Jarvis (1985) concluded that magistrates reinterpret legislation and court reports in order to make a moral assessment of each offender; and that local sentencing traditions are maintained by local training, by the apprenticeship model—whereby a magistrate spends several years as a 'winger' before taking the chair in court—and by the local selection process. Brown **[6:14]** interviewed many magistrates in six different courts, carrying out a 'sociological study in the construction of knowledge in organisational life', leading her to conclude that magistrates deal with cases according to depersonalized routines, which takes away the individuality of defendants.

If the accused fails to appear, the court may, on proof of service of summons, proceed in their absence, or they may adjourn the hearing. The Magistrates' Courts Act 1980, section 12 allows defendants to plead guilty by post for certain minor offences. Where they are convicted, the court may proceed to sentence immediately, or it may adjourn the case if further information is required before sentencing. If magistrates decide that their sentencing powers are inadequate they may commit the convicted offender to the Crown Court for sentence. As a result of the plea before venue introduced in 1997 (see above), there has been a significant increase in the number of cases being committed for sentence. Cases committed to the Crown Court for sentence are heard by a judge sitting with between two and four magistrates. The Access to Justice Act 1999, section 79 removed the requirement for magistrates to sit on committals for sentence. Whilst this change might have been economical, it removed a useful mechanism for developing consistency in magistrates' sentencing practice. In fact, it was not brought into force and was repealed in 2004. In 2006 the number of committals for sentence received at the Crown Court was 35,768.

Governments seem to enjoy changing the law on sentencing! Let us start the story simply with the Powers of Criminal Courts (Sentencing) Act 2000 (PCC(S)A 2000), which was a welcome attempt to codify sentencing law. It built on the Criminal Justice Act 1991, which had introduced a new framework for sentencing. The underlying message of the 1991 Act was that the sentence should be in proportion to the seriousness of the offence of which the offender was convicted. At the time, it was not clear what effect the Act would have on sentencers: at one level, it appeared to reproduce in a convoluted and complicated way much of what sentencers were already doing. However, it was not long before the government panicked and 'toughened up' the message—by means of the Criminal Justice Act 1993—in what Ashworth and Gibson (1994) called 'one of the most remarkable volte-faces in the history of penal policy in England and Wales' (at page 101). Whilst the original Act had provided that a sentencer—in deciding whether a case was so serious that only a custodial sentence could be justified, or whether a case was serious enough to warrant a community sentence—could look at only one other associated offence, now the court may look at 'one or more' associated offences.

Another example of 'toughening up' was the replacement of the original section 29, which required the court to ignore previous convictions unless they demonstrated aggravating features of the offence for which sentence was being passed. This section made little sense, but probably only meant that a bad record should not lead to a disproportionate sentence. However, the Home Secretary feared that the section might be being interpreted as meaning that courts were no longer allowed to take notice of previous convictions. The replacement section (section 151 of the PCC(S)A 2000) allowed courts to take into account previous convictions and 'failure to respond to previous sentences' in considering seriousness, and made it compulsory for courts to treat offending while on bail as an aggravating feature (the current version is section 143(2) of the CJA 2003).

Many, many Acts of Parliament have tinkered with the sentencing framework since 2000: but the Criminal Justice Act 2003 introduced the most radical changes. Part 12 of this Act concerns sentencing. It starts with general provisions including a section which specifies the 'purposes of sentencing'. Thus, section 142 provides that:

(1) Any court dealing with an offender in respect of his offence must have regard to the following purposes of sentencing—

   (a) the punishment of offenders,

   (b) the reduction of crime (including its reduction by deterrence),

   (c) the reform and rehabilitation of offenders,

   (d) the protection of the public, and

   (e) the making of reparation by offenders to persons affected by their offences.

The Act also sets out principles for determining the seriousness of an offence (section 143), for reductions in sentences for early guilty pleas (section 144), and aggravating factors where the offence was motivated by the offender's race, religion, disability, or sexual orientation (sections 145–146). Sections 147 to 151 set out general restrictions on imposing community sentences and sections 152 to 153 perform a similar function in relation to custodial sentences. Sections 154 to 155 amend the existing limits on magistrates' court's powers to impose custodial sentences. Sections 156 to 160 set out the procedural requirements for imposing community and custodial sentences. They deal, in particular, with pre-sentence reports and other requirements in the case of mentally disordered offenders. Section 161 provides for pre-sentence drug testing when the court is considering imposing a community sentence or a suspended sentence in order to help the court to decide whether drug treatment and testing is necessary. Sections 162 to 165 deal with the court's powers to impose and remit fines.

Chapter 2 of Part 12 of the 2003 Act provides for community orders for offenders aged 16 or over. For offences committed before the implementation of the Act there were a number of different community orders: community rehabilitation orders (until 2000 known as probation orders); community punishment orders (previously community service orders); community punishment and rehabilitation orders (previously combination orders); curfew orders; and drug treatment and testing orders, drug abstinence orders, and exclusion orders. This Act creates a single generic community sentence, which combines requirements currently available under different community sentences. The requirements available with a generic community sentence will be:

- compulsory (unpaid) work;
- participation in any specified activities;
- programmes aimed at changing offending behaviour;
- prohibition from certain activities;
- curfew;
- exclusion from certain areas;
- residence requirement;
- mental health treatment (with consent of the offender);
- drug treatment and testing (with consent of the offender);
- alcohol treatment (with consent of the offender);
- supervision;
- attendance centre requirements (for those under 25).

Chapter 3 of Part 12 of the CJA 2003 introduced new rules on prison sentences of less than 12 months. Sections 181 and 182 make provision for the new sentence (described informally as 'custody plus') that was to replace all short prison sentences of under 12 months (with the exception of intermittent custody). It would have been made up of a short period in custody of up to three months followed by a longer period under supervision in the community of a minimum of six months. When sentencing, the court was to specify the lengths of the two parts and attach specific requirements, based upon those available under the generic community sentence, to the supervision part of the sentence so as to address the rehabilitative needs of the offender. However, it appears that custody plus will not now be introduced: financial considerations mean that the resources have not been found to supervise these offenders in the community.

The Act also introduced intermittent custody (see sections 183 to 186), but following pilot tests, this too has been shelved. Where an intermittent custody order was made, the 'custodial periods' were served a few days at a time, while the licence period ran between the blocks of custody. It was designed to enable offenders to maintain jobs, family ties, or education, but it proved difficult to find appropriate offenders, and was inappropriately expensive to manage. Intermittent custody has therefore also disappeared off the horizon (though it is not lamented, unlike 'custody plus' which had been widely welcomed).

Magistrates also have the power to send offenders to prison for up to six months for one offence, or up to 12 months in total. (The CJA 2003 extends this to 12 months, but neither this nor custody plus have been introduced.) Because of the short sentences that they serve, those sentenced by magistrates' courts account for only about 10 per cent of the prison population, but it is a strikingly high figure, accounting for nearly half of those sent to prison in any one year.

TABLE 6.6 Numbers of people ('first receptions') received into prison

	Total	Sentenced by magistrates' courts
1992	69,832	36,962
1998	91,282	48,910
2000	129,700	50,380
2005	132,058	57,250

Source: Prison Statistics 1992, 1998, 2000, paragraphs 1.20–1.21; 2005 data: Offender management Caseload Statistics 2006, Table 7.1, and Sentencing Statistics 2005

Suspended sentences came back into fashion in the CJA 2003. They were first introduced in 1967, but the 1991 Criminal Justice Act, with its emphasis on desert and commensurate sentences, had specified that they could only be imposed in 'exceptional circumstances'. Now (see sections 189–195) a court can suspend a short custodial sentence (as described in section 181) for between six months and two years on condition that the offender undertakes activities in the community. These activities are chosen by the court from the list available under the generic community sentence. If the offender breaches the terms of the suspension the suspended sentence is activated. The commission of a further offence during the period of suspension also counts as a breach, and the offender's existing suspended sentence is normally activated when the court sentences him for the new offence. The sentencing court has the power to review the progress of an offender under the new suspended sentence. This power of review already existed for Drug Treatment and Testing Orders: it may be seen as an important shift in the function of sentencing judges in England and Wales. However, the Criminal Justice and Immigration Bill 2007 will remove the power of magistrates to suspend a sentence of imprisonment: for summary offences the use of suspended sentences has increased dramatically since April 2005 and the Government's concern is that many people may now be receiving suspended sentences who would previously have received community penalties (see Mair et al (2007)). However, the effect of this change may of course be to increase the number of immediate sentences of imprisonment. This is a good example of the need for detailed empirical research into magistrates' sentencing decision making, research evidence which is sadly lacking.

The most common penalty in the magistrates' court is a fine. How should these be fixed? Unit fines were introduced in 1992 (by the CJA 1991), designed to enable the court to deprive offenders of a proportion of their disposable weekly income for a number of weeks, and so to be fairer between offenders of different wealth. They were abolished after less than a year, largely because the individual units had been inappropriately valued and because defendants were reluctant to fill in the means form. No attempt was made to improve the unit fines system: it was abruptly dumped. Magistrates now simply follow the advice of the

Magistrates' Association (a voluntary association to which most magistrates belong): 'if imposing a fine, remember to increase or decrease the amount according to the financial circumstances of the offender'. Surprisingly, the Association encourages courts to build on the many different local means forms currently in existence as a way of acquiring adequate information about the offender. A guideline means form might be more useful. The current statutory maximum fine in the magistrates' court is £5,000. Flood-Page and Mackie (1998), in their study of sentencing practice in magistrates' courts in 1994/95, found a wide range of methods used to calculate the size of a fine. They also found a decline in the use of fines (and compensation orders), concluding that 'if some probation schemes require greater resources but achieve more, as some evidence suggests, then there may be a case for reversing the decline in the use of fines partly in order to release resources for more effective intervention with fewer offenders' (at page 129). The Sentencing Advisory Panel commissioned research in 2007 (see Raine et al (2007)) which concluded that the detailed approach and working practices continues to vary between different courts and indeed different sentencers.

The Sentencing Guidelines Council, which was created in the CJA 2003, issues guidelines for magistrates as well as judges. Indeed, as we go to press, they are consulting on revised magistrates' courts sentencing guidelines. Such guidelines have been available for a number of years. As long ago as 1966, the Magistrates' Association produced 'Suggestions for Road Traffic Penalties', and in 1989 a 'Sentencing Guide for Criminal Offences (other than Road Traffic)', together with a table of suggested compensation levels. The guidelines are set out in a clear diagrammatic form. Reproduced at **[6:15]** are the most recent version of the guidelines for three common offences. They give an 'entry point' for each offence, as a guide for an offence of average seriousness, based on a first-time offender pleading not guilty. Some of these are surprisingly high: for example, custody is the entry point for possessing an offensive weapon. In the next chapter (7) we discuss the Sentencing Guidelines Council's guidance on discounts for guilty pleas **[7:4]**.

The role of the higher courts in laying down sentencing guidelines for magistrates is minimal, since most appeals are heard by the Crown Court, whose decisions receive little publicity. It is unsurprising therefore that magistrates' sentencing has long been criticized for its inconsistencies and local variations However, the truth is that we know very little about this important area: there is a huge need for empirical studies of sentencing practices.

Magistrates have the power to correct their errors within 28 days, under the Magistrates' Courts Act 1980, section 142. Until 1990, magistrates, although indemnified out of public funds, were personally liable for acting in excess of jurisdiction. Fear that too many claims would lead to defensive judging, which is not in the public interest, led to the amendment of the Justices of the Peace Act 1979, sections 44 and 45 by the Courts and Legal Services Act 1990, section 108. This put magistrates on the same footing as judges, and they are now only liable where they act in bad faith, even when acting outside their jurisdiction.

A final but important discretionary power of magistrates relates to costs, under the Prosecution of Offences Act 1985, section 16 **[3:1]**. If a defendant is acquitted, they are not automatically entitled to costs from the prosecution, and even if an order as to costs is made, it may be for a lesser sum than the amount that was actually spent.

A conclusion—read again **[6:2]** and **[6:3]**. This author believes that there is an important role for lay magistrates in the criminal justice process. Do you?

FURTHER READING

Ashworth, A, *Sentencing and Criminal Justice* (4th edition, 2005) Cambridge UP

Ashworth, A and Gibson, B, 'The Criminal Justice Act 1993: Altering the Sentencing Framework' [1994] Crim LR 101

Brown, I and Hullin, R, 'Contested Bail Applications: the treatment of ethnic minority and white offenders' [1993] Crim LR 107

Carlen, P, *Magistrates' Justice* (1976) Martin Robertson

Cassidy, D, Harper G, and Brown, S, *Understanding Electronic Monitoring of Juveniles on Bail or Remand to Local Authority Accommodation* (2005) Home Office Online Report 21/05

Gifford, T, *Where's the Justice?* (1986) Fontana

Darbyshire, P, 'An Essay on the Importance and Neglect of the Magistracy' [1997] Crim LR 627

Darbyshire, P, 'For the New Lord Chancellor—Some Causes for Concern about Magistrates' [1997] Crim LR 861

Darbyshire, P, 'A Comment on the powers of magistrates' clerks' [1999] Crim LR 377

Easton, M and Piper, C, *Sentencing and Punishment: The Quest for Justice* (2005) Oxford UP

Flood-Page, C and Mackie, A, *Sentencing Practice: an examination of decisions in magistrates' courts and the Crown Court in the mid-1990s* (1998) HORS No 180, HMSO

Grove, T, *A Magistrate's Tale: A Front Line Report from a new JP* (2003) Bloomsbury

Hucklesby, A, 'Bail in Criminal Cases' in McConville, M and Wilson, G (eds), *The Handbook of the Criminal Justice Process* (2002) Oxford UP

King, M and May, C, *Black Magistrates* (1985) Cobden Trust

Mair, G, Cross, N, and Taylor, S, *The use and impact of the community order and the suspended sentence order* (2007) CCJS

Morgan, P M, *Offending While on Bail: A Survey of Recent Studies* (1992) HORPU Paper No 65, HMSO

Morgan, R and Jones, S, 'Bail or Jail?' in Stockdale, E and Casale, S (eds), *Criminal Justice under Stress* (1992) Blackstone

Morgan, R and Russell, N, *The judiciary in the magistrates' courts* (2000) Home Office

Parker, H, Sumner, M, and Jarvis, G, *Unmasking the Magistrates* (1989) Open UP

Raifeartaigh, U N, 'Reconciling bail law with the presumption of innocence' (1997) 17 OJLS 1

Raine, J, et al, *Methods of calculating fines in magistrates' courts* (2007) Sentencing Advisory Panel

Rozenburg, J, *The Search for Justice* (1994) Hodder & Staughton

Walker, N and Padfield, N, *Sentencing: Theory, Law and Practice* (2nd edition, 1996) Butterworths

Plus the websites mentioned in Chapter 1 (pages 13–14)

DOCUMENTS

[6:1] Seago, P, Walker, C, and Wall, D, 'The Development of the Professional Magistracy in England and Wales'

[2000] Crim LR 631 (at page 648)

Stipendiary magistrates as out-of-towners

Judicial independence might be compromised in a third, primarily geographical, sense if power is centralised through the expansion of stipendiaries. On this ground, there is the fear that local justice will erode as the links with local communities, as reflected through the backgrounds, experience and outlooks of lay justices, are diluted. Public confidence in the judiciary, in part generated by the judiciary being identifiable with the society which it judges, might then be dented. According to the Home Affairs Committee Report, the Lord Chancellor's Department makes a clear distinction between lay and professional magistrates in terms of how far they should represent the community, but it accepts that in order to ensure confidence, the public should see people like themselves on the bench.[1]

One might begin to explore this allegation in the same way as the previous allegation, in other words, to consider whether stipendiaries should be viewed as unreflective of local interests and then to consider the ways in which the lay magistracy might avoid this charge. However, the furtherance of local justice may, unlike the previous sites for debate, be itself a contested value, the justifiability of which must also be explored.

The localism of lay and professional magistrates

The concept of geographically sensitive justice is troublingly vague, but such a lay 'bench ethos' can be constructed from what Carlen calls a 'mass of situationally evolved knowledge'.[2] Lay magistrates do seem to view themselves as the 'custodians of the community', representing and understanding the locality and its customs and values, so that a 'threat to the community becomes a threat to the magistracy and vice versa.'[3] In addition, the rules of appointment expressly state that magistrates must live within 15 miles of the boundary of the commission area.[4] By contrast, as already described, stipendiary magistrates will have a nation-wide commission throughout England and Wales under section 78(1) of the Access to Justice Act 1999, as opposed to their present appointment to a commission area, although they will still be allocated to a base court. The expectation is that they will become more mobile, which could provide some support for the supposition that stipendiary magistrates are less socially reflexive than lay magistrates.

A counter-argument to the claims of lay localism is that localism is itself much diluted in contemporary times. There are, for example, far fewer magistrates' courts sites than in the past, so that any local attachments will be less strong for all justices, whether lay or professional. This trend was given a boost by a Home Office Consultation Paper on *The Size of Benches*[5] which pressed for both the abolition of benches with fewer than 12 magistrates and also a reduction in the number of petty sessional areas. Consequently, the number of benches has been reduced from nearly 650 to under 400 as a result. The administrative squeeze has also been backed by cash limits from 1992 onwards, all of which prompted the closure of smaller court-houses in favour of larger inner-city court buildings. This combination of changes could be said to remove the physical and symbolic link between localities and magisterial justice,[6] though one might argue that the socio-geographical bounds of 'localities' are now considerably wider, so that the alteration of the court boundaries is in correspondence with the expansion of, for example, manageable drives to work, shops or entertainment. The logical next step would be to rationalise further in terms of the provision of judicial administration. In this way, as justice becomes less localised, why should magistrates' courts buildings be distinct from Crown Court buildings? Why should there be a separation of the staff working within them? And most controversial of all, in the absence of any practical need for, as opposed to abstract ideology of, localism, why is there a need for lay justices to reflect local connections?[7]

Local justice as a desirable justice

Even if local justice is a characteristic of lay magistrates more so than stipendiary magistrates, is it consistent with good quality justice?[8] The arguments for it seem to revolve around concepts such as trial by one's peers, as well as the benefits of local knowledge and sensitivity to local needs. More generally, all recent major studies have supported the continuance of a fundamentally lay and local system as a democratic and educative 'bridge' between the public and the courts.[9]

Yet criticism arises whenever local differences do markedly emerge, on the grounds that localism infringes concepts of justice in the sense of treatment as an equal.[10] For example, the pressure group Liberty complained in their report, *Unequal Before the Law*, in 1992[11] that like cases were not being treated alike in terms of magisterial custodial sentencing differentials. Disproportionate legal aid grants/refusals are also treated as problematic.[12] The Lord Chancellor adverted to the dilemma in a speech in 1999:

> 'Local diversity is your unique strength—the factor which can take into account the idiosyncrasies of local culture and behaviour. But society can be hard in its judgment on what it perceives as inconsistency. The public, and the media, look critically at the decisions of bench against bench. They can interpret differences as proof that the magistrates are uncertain amongst themselves, and that nature of justice that you get depends on where you live.'[13]

Conversely, a professional, non-local background may actually assist independence by ensuring greater standardisation which will engender consumer confidence in judicial standards. One response has been the introduction of training for lay justices since 1966,[14] which might be said to blur the lay/professional boundary.

Conclusion: judicial independence and local accountabilities

Salaried judges predominate in the summary criminal courts of many other common law jurisdictions—including Scotland, Northern Ireland and the Republic of Ireland, as well as Australia, Canada, New Zealand and the USA.[15] However, the wholesale replacement of the lay magistracy is not, and never has been, government policy for England and Wales. The exclusive employment of stipendiary magistrates would be more expensive, and the fundamental principles of citizenship, democracy and the protection of individual rights call for representative, and therefore predominantly lay and local, involvement at all levels of justice whether achieved by a jury or lay magistrates.[16] Though the Criminal Courts Review being conducted by Lord Justice Auld[17] has the authority to reconsider this balance between lay and professional, there are few signs that the demise of the laity in justice, even if recommended, would be politically acceptable.

Equally, the extinction of stipendiary magistrates seems highly impracticable and improbable. In the first place, a significant number of Benches find it difficult to appoint sufficient lay justices, and our calculations suggest that it would probably require thousands of extra volunteers completely to replace the stipendiary magistrates, which would also mean unwieldy Benches of over 700 in the larger City courts. So, the consensus seems to be a compromise between legality and local laity. A strong rhetorical emphasis at the summary level rests upon 'community', as articulated through lay involvement: lay magistrates are 'a bridge between the public and a court system which might otherwise seem remote'.[18] But the lay judiciary must work within a framework of legal formality and have training and professional assistance through clerks—and so they are turned into, what Burney calls, 'half-baked professionals'.[19] One might then depict the stipendiary as a further form of complementary compromise to community involvement—dealing with cases or case-loads which lay justices find too hot or too heavy to handle. In order to achieve this supportive role, there seems to be broad support for an 'integrationalist' approach whereby there is a greater presence of stipendiaries, but their function is 'to support rather than supersede lay magistrates'.[20] Consistent with this approach, the increase in the number of stipendiaries has been significant but remains very modest and not enough to ensure continuous national coverage in areas without a permanent stipendiary by 'semi-attached' stipendiaries.[21] Nor has the work of stipendiaries been clearly differentiated from that of the lay bench, despite suggestions along these lines by the *Venne Report*[22] and the *Narey Report*.[23]

Alongside independence, another important agenda for the future is accountability with regard to the magistracy, though the tensions between judicial independence and judicial accountability are here evident. One would expect accountability in a system which vaunts its localism, but in what senses, if any, do local judges make themselves accountable for their judicial work? First, there is legal accountability, such as through the giving of reasons (more by stipendiaries than lay justices),[24] through public access to court-rooms, through appeals to the Crown Court or by legal review in the Divisional Court. But legal decisions are not discussed in advance or endorsed after delivery by the general local public. One might argue that judicial independence would be compromised if they were, but these arguments have been faced down in regard to constabulary independence, in respect of which periodic local liaison committee meetings allow for consultation, report and complaint, though not direction or censure, by the public.[25] So, if handled correctly, 'accountability can in fact enhance the public's respect for independence.'[26] Secondly, there is still little obvious accountability in political terms, from individual clerks to the MCCs and from the MCCs to the 'paying authority'.[27]

Why are these major issues of accountability not addressed in any of the policy papers we have discussed? One might conclude that the genuine motivation for the growth of the professional magistracy is driven by the bureaucratic objectives of the New Public Managerialism, which pictures the public, including local offenders, as consumers of services rather than active citizens. The opposition, from lay magistrates, has been pitched at an ideological level, but it is equally an ideology in which the relationship with the community is one way and paternalistic rather than reflexive. Nevertheless, the insertion of a professional magistracy does call into question the justifiability and working of local justice and may, along with other changes expose at the same time the strength of the ideology as well as the weaknesses of its application. If mechanisms of accountability were to be instituted, then the position of the stipendiary in local justice might actually become less anomalous, for there would be a link between professionals and community not currently provided for. Thus, all justices, both lay and professional, would be able to claim that they represented community wishes, and the harmony of judge and judged could be achieved by a more objective conduit than a feeling in the bones of the magistrate.

Notes

1 *Home Affairs Committee Report*, para. 11; *Hansard*, H. L. Debs, Vol. 573, col. 1122, June 27, 1998, Lord Irvine.

2 P. Carlen, *Magistrates' Justice* (Martin Robertson, London, 1976), p. 75.

3 S. Brown, *Magistrates at Work* (Open University Press, Buckingham, 1991), pp. 111–112.

4 Justices of the Peace Act 1997, s. 6. The Lord Chancellor requires that candidates should have a reasonable degree of knowledge of the area to which they wish to be appointed and generally expects them to have lived in that area for a minimum of 12 months.

5 (1986). See J. W. Raine and M. J. Wilson, *Managing Criminal Justice* (Harvester Wheatsheaf, Hemel Hempstead, 1993), p. 106.

6 Concern on this ground is expressed by the *Home Affairs Committee Report*, para. 198.

7 J. W. Raine and M. J. Wilson, *Managing Criminal Justice* (Harvester Wheatsheaf, Hemel Hempstead, 1993), p. 116.

8 See Z. K. Bankowski, N. R. Hutton and J. J. McManus, *Lay Justice?* (T & T Clark, Edinburgh, 1987).

9   *Home Affairs Committee Report*, para. 198.

10 C. Alugo, J. Richards, G. Wise and J. Raine, 'The magistrates' court and the community' (1996) 160 J.P. 329.

11 Custodial sentences made up 4.96 per cent of the total in 1990, but individual petty sessional divisions varied from 17.44 per cent to 0 per cent. See also: R. Hood, *Sentencing in Magistrates' Courts* (Stevens, London, 1962); R. Tarling, *Sentencing Practice in Magistrates' Courts* (Home Office Research Study 56, London, 1979); D. Acres, 'Consistency and sentencing' (1987) 151 J.P. 343, H. Parker, M Sumner and G. Jarvis, *Unmasking the Magistrate* (Open University Press, Milton Keynes, 1989), p. 16.

12 See R. Young and D. Wall, *Access to Criminal Justice* (Blackstone Press, London, 1996), Chap. 7.

13 Speech to the Council of the Magistrates' Association (http://www.open.gov.uk/lcd/speeches/1999/25-3-99.htm; 1999).

14 See *The Training of Justices of the Peace in England and Wales* (Cmnd. 2856, HMSO, London, 1965).

15 See Sir T. Skyrme, *History of the Justices of the Peace* (Barry Rose, Chichester, 1991) Vol. 3.

16 See *Hansard*, H. L. Debs. Vol. 582, cols 1066, October 29, 1997, Lord Irvine.

17 http://www.criminal-courts-review.org.uk/.

18 *Home Affairs Committee Report*, para. 198.

19 E. Burney, J.P: *Magistrate, Court, and Community* (Hutchinson, London, 1979), p. 216.

20 *Home Affairs Committee Report*, para. 196.

21 See *Venne Report*, paras 8.4, 8.6.

22 *Venne Report*, para. 5.3.

23 *Narey Report*, para. 14.

24 *R. V. Harrow Crown Court, ex p. Dawe* (1994) 158 J.P. 250.

25 See the Police and Criminal Evidence Act 1984, s. 106.

26 M. L. Friedland, *A Place Apart* (Canada Communications Group, Ottowa, 1995), p. xiii.

27 In relation to a MCC, the 'paying authority' means any responsible local authority whose area comprises all or part of the area to which the MCC relates. The paying authority provides 20% of MCC funding, with the Lord Chancellor's Department responsible for 80%, subject to a cash limit. See the Justices of the Peace Act 1997, ss. 55, 57.

[6:2] Morgan, R, 'Magistrates: The Future According to Auld'
(2002) 29 J of Law and Society 308 (at page 314)

The problem with Auld's dismissive stance [to public opinion] is that it assumes that the judges, and the politicians they advise, are the best and sole arbiters of what system is fair and efficient and suggests that the public must then be persuaded that what what the judges have decided is ideal. I consider that position mistaken.

Of course it might be argued that since Auld has endorsed the jurisdiction and role of the lay magistracy, what is the fuss about? There are threee ripostes to this. First, Auld's dismissal of public opinion also underpins some of his more radical proposals (regarding access to jury trial, for example). Secondly, it is not clear to me that Auld has endorsed the position of the lay magistracy. Thirdly, Auld has chosen to ignore what the public, were they aware of the fact, would almost certainly find objectionable about the operation of the magistrates' courts as currently constituted, shortcomings which will be exacerbated if Auld's proposals are implemented. I will consider the latter points in reverse order.

1. An aspect of post-code justice ignored?

It is currently a matter of chance whether a defendant in magistrates' court proceedings has his or her case dealt with by lay magistrates or a district judge. It will depend on the court in which the defendant appears (some courts have a full-time district judge, most do not) and the luck of the draw if the defendant appears in a court in which a full-time district judge does sit. There are no allocational rules. There are only general allocational practices, and they vary. Does it matter whether a defendant appears before a district judge sitting alone or lay magistrates sitting as a panel of two or three? The answer, as we have seen, is yes. We do not know if the chances of acquittal are different: the number of trials in our survey were too small to test the proposition. But it makes a substantial difference when it comes to the likelihood of being remanded in custody or sentenced to immediate imprisonment. In cases where there is a possibility of that outcome our defendant is roughly twice as likely to end up in custody if he or she appears before a district judge.

What has Auld to say on this? Very little, save to say that if there is sentencing disparity between lay magistrates and district judges then the district judges are more likely to have got their decisions right:

'I believe that District Judges are more likely to follow national practice and sentencing policy guide-lines in this respect than magistrates, with their individual traditions and training, and history of disparate sentencing.'

He fails to point out that disparity may be just as much a feature of sentencing by the professional judiciary, something which the professional judiciary, supported by the Lord Chancellor's Department, has taken care to ensure is not investigated. Further, to ensure that lay magistrates are brought into sentencing line Auld proposes that in future their training be organized by the Judicial Studies Board. But he offers no other remedy. He makes no suggestion that lay magistrates and district judges should do other than continue to sit separately in his proposed Magistrates' Division and, as we have noted, he recommends that lay magistrates be excluded from sentencing decisions in his proposed District Division.

The present situation represents the very opposite of what most people think justice demands should be the case. Provision for panel decision making in more serious cases where issues of liberty are at stake is a safeguard for which there appears to be widespread support. It is significant that since the Auld Report has been published a minister has described the present arrangement as 'odd' and 'arbitrary'.

2. Endorsement of the role of lay magistrates?

Between and on the lines of the Auld Report are several reasons for doubting that the lay magistracy should feel that their role is to be safeguarded.

First, there is Auld's recommendation that in future 'the Lord Chancellor should be more ready to take the initiative to assign a District Judge to an area where, having consulted as appropriate, he is of the view that local justice in the area requires it.' That is, the initiative should not be left to the localities but seized by the centre. Auld's intervention on this issue was prompted by evidence of local benches successfully delaying the appointment of a district judge where the Magistrates' Courts Inspectorate (MCSI) and the Lord Chancellor's Department thought it desirable:

'such parochialism demeans the otherwise worthy contribution magistrates make to the running of the criminal justice system, and it should no longer hold sway.'

It seems certain that he had in mind the case of Bristol where the recent appointment of a district judge resulted not from a recommendation from the local Lord Chancellor's Advisory Committee but from the MCSI. Senior lay magistrates locally resented the proposition, and following his appointment, the professional incumbent, an experienced stipendiary who had previously worked in London was reputedly given cases to deal with which his lay colleagues considered to be undemanding and probably beneath his dignity—vehicle parking infractions and the like. That is, the lay magistrates delivered a studied insult and asserted their determination not to relinquish to the judge those more serious cases which we must assume they saw his arrival as intending to cream off.

Whatever the rights and wrongs of the Bristol case, it seems likely that Auld's recommendation will be seized on and additional district judges appointed, particularly in areas where there is evidence of delay, where the lay magistrates prove to be less flexible and where there are difficulties recruiting suitable lay magistrates: these conditions are most likely to arise in the metropolitan centres.

Secondly, though Auld says that he sees no case for altering the present balance of lay magistrates and district judges he also says that 'the position may be different' if his recommendation that there be a unified court with an intermediate tier is adopted. There would then be only a compelling case for retaining 'a sizeable lay magistracy'—how sizeable, Auld does not say, though he notes that having many more district judges would 'require a major programme of change' and would take time. It is significant that the relevant Home Office minister has already stated that:

> 'if the District Division becomes a reality, it will be necessary for District Judges to be available throughout the country (which, of course, they are not at the moment). If this happens, there may be a case for looking again at the distribution of work within the Magistrates' Division.'

I think it is also clear that, in order to pave the way for his District Division, Auld favours substantially increasing the number of district judges who he observes often sit also as recorders and that appointment as a district judge is 'emerging as the first step on a judicial rung that may lead to a permanent appointment as a Circuit Judge and, possibly, beyond'. The vertical integration of the criminal courts implies the further development of judicial careers, both of which I expect to be encouraged. All these developments would have significant implications for the role of the lay magistracy.

Thirdly, it is for above reasons that I doubt lay magistrates should feel greatly reassured by Auld's recommendation that there be no extension of justice's clerks' case management jurisdiction. What is being safeguarded is less the prerogative of lay magistrates and more the developing role of the professional judiciary. Note, for example, that Auld concludes that district judges have no need of a legally qualified clerk to sit with them in court—an anomalous provision to which we drew attention—and that it will be for district judges, not lay magistrates or justices' clerks, to determine the appropriate venue for the hearing of either-way cases in the event of the defence and prosecution disagreeing.

Fourthly, Auld's report has one or two telling comments to make about costs. Auld has practically nothing to say on costs, which makes it all the more striking that he is prepared to suggest that our attempt to estimate the cost implications of employing more district judges in place of lay magistrates is at best incomplete and at worst flawed. We found that:

- estimates of the direct costs to the LCD alone of using two types of magistrate show, not surprisingly, that lay magistrates are far cheaper. A lay justice: we estimated costs £495 per annum compared to £90,000 for a stipendiary, which translates to £3.59 compared to £20.96 per case;

- however, when overheads are loaded into the equation, the difference is far smaller—£52.10 compared to £61.78 per appearance; and

- if opportunity costs are added—a controversial issue in which fairly courageous assumptions have to be made—we estimated that lay magistrates are more expensive—£70.80 compared to £61.78 per court appearance;

- further, if the cost consequences of current differential decision-making, are added, the calculations pull in different directions. Employing more district judges will lead to fewer court appearances as a result of their more robust examination of applications: this would save money. However, district judges' greater use of custody would significantly increase costs for the Prison Service.

Auld thinks, contrary to the Magistrates' Association, that we were correct to include an estimation of opportunity as well as direct costs, but he judged that our calculations were 'necessarily somewhat theoretical and speculative and...open to criticism in a number of respects'. Of our conclusion that more district judges would likely add to the number of custodial decisions and thus costs, he says:

> 'Save as a cynical measure of expediency, it would be wrong to consider whether to change the present sharing of summary jurisdiction on the basis that District Judges are too hard or that magistrates are too soft in their decisions as to custody.'

In fact at no stage did we suggest that policy should be decided on the basis of costs: we simply attempted to estimate the likely cost consequences of different policy scenarios. Nevertheless, as we have seen, by saying that if there are sentencing disparities between judges and lay magistrates the district judges are correct, Auld is implicitly arguing that these are extra costs the criminal justice system *should* bear. By contrast the savings accruing from district judges granted fewer adjournments—which might as easily be challenged—Auld is content to accept. Indeed it is apparently not cynical for him to suggest that in our own research we almost certainly underestimated the savings likely to result under this head. He correctly points out, for example, that we failed to estimate—we do not do so because, as we acknowledged, we could find no firm basis on which to do it—the reduced knock-on costs of having fewer court appearances for the police, the legal aid budget, the CPS, and so on. It seems likely that the fact that savings may arise from making greater use of district judges will inevitably encourage their greater use. Indeed, as we argued in our report, if tougher sentencing is set aside (and that might be addressed in training for district judges), the greater the increase in the number of district judges and the greater the displacement of lay magistrates, the more likely it becomes that step savings (resulting from need for fewer courtrooms and a reduced supporting infrastructure, and possibly fewer courthouses) can be achieved.

The above ingredients in Auld suggest less commitment to the current balance of lay magistrates and district judges in the Magistrates' Division than at first appears. If I am correct, and the proportion of appearances in the magistrates' courts is increased, it will have implications for the relationship between two groups. In our survey of lay and stipendiary magistrates we found, not surprisingly, that whereas the stipendiaries could overwhelmingly think of several reasons for having more stipendiaries—faster, more efficient, better able to deal with legally complicated cases, and so on—the majority of lay magistrates could cite no reasons at all. Conversely whereas one or two stipendiaries conceded that there were arguments against having more stipendiaries—that it is unfair to have one person sitting in judgment, for example, the majority of lay magistrates subscribed to several negative arguments. The two groups do not see eye to eye on the possible futures of their respective contribution and since one group comprises unpaid volunteers, this is a factor to be heeded: lay magistrates might widely withdraw their unpaid labour were they to see their own status being diminished and their role reduced. In coming to the conclusion that the business in the magistrates' courts should be allocated as at present, Auld is endorsing the Venne Report which recommended a 'presumption' in favour of stipendiary magistrates, when available, undertaking 'heavier' work. The corollary of additional district judges doing this, if they sit alone, is that lay magistrates are relegated to dealing with the less interesting and challenging work, of having their lists intellectually asset-stripped. This is what the lay magistracy fears and dislikes. There is a real tension here. If lay magistrates perceive their role to be marginalized, it is doubtful whether their continued and widened recruitment can be assured.

The role of magistrates in the proposed district division

One of Auld's answers to the difficulties in recruiting and retaining the services of a socially representative magistracy is the 'attraction' of the 'opportunity to hear more serious and interesting trials' in his proposed District Division. In answer to the practical difficulty of finding lay magistrates with the time to hear such cases, Auld suggests that the proposals he has for the introduction of more flexible magistrates' sitting patterns, combined with evidence of lay magistrates' current availability, make this problem soluble—an opinion with which the Magistrates' Association apparently agrees:

There are many magistrates who, for one reason or another, are not restricted by their employment or other commitments to sitting for half a day a week and who might well relish the opportunity to sit on longer and more substantial cases.

Setting on one side the major arguments which can be made against Auld's proposals for a District Division—arguments which mostly hinge on the great reduction in access to and consequent number of jury trials involved—how practical and logical is the scheme he proposes in terms of lay magistrates' participation?

The first point to make is that Auld's idea of a mixed (lay and professional judges) tribunal conforms broadly to what in our own survey of other jurisdictions we described as the Germano-Scandinavian model, though the arrangement is found in several jurisdictions outside that European region. Mixed tribunals were commended to auld by Sanders. There is one important difference, however. Whereas mixed tribunals in other jurisdictions, and as proposed by Sanders, collectively determine issues of both fact (though generally not law) and sentence, Auld proposes an arrangement [in which] lay magistrates play no part in sentencing. Auld offers two reasons:

- lay magistrates would, he contends, lack the necessary competence and experience: sentencing at this level of seriousness would be very different from sentencing in the summary court and would become more complicated still were the recommendations of the Halliday Report (which proposes sentence review hearings) implemented;
- it would not be practical to involve lay magistrates: following trial most cases would have to be adjourned for sentence and 'it would often be difficult to reconstitute the same panel for the purpose of passing sentence'.

Auld's objections to lay magistrates' involvement in sentencing do not seem to me to be well grounded. If it is possible to find lay magistrates willing and able to sit on trials for several days, it should hardly be difficult to get them to return for a sentencing hearing. As for the suggestion that they lack the necessary competence and experience to do the task, this is likely to be regarded as insulting by lay magistrates and scarcely squares with Auld's earlier argument that in deciding matters of fact the magistrates would not have to be given directions by the judge because of their competence and experience in structured decision making.

Indeed so disingenuous is Auld's argument for excluding magistrates from sentencing that one wonders whether it is a smokescreen for a more serious consideration, namely, that to concede panel sentencing in the proposed District Division would throw into stark relief and call into question lone sentencing in the Magistrates' and Crown Divisions, something which, as we have seen, our surveys of the public and of lay magistrates is widely considered objectionable (though I should emphasize that we canvassed opinion on this point only with regard to serious decisions in the magistrates' courts). As regards lone sentencing by judges in the Crown Court, Auld maintains that he received no proposals for change, which is odd because the case for panel decision making in the Crown Court is clearly set out in one submission from a commentator extensively cited by him. Moreover, during the course of undertaking successive research projects I have repeatedly heard barristers argue the shortcomings of lone decision making by Crown Court judges. As for lone decision making by district judges in the magistrates' courts Auld, as we have seen, repeatedly had the objections drawn to his attention, but chose to ignore them. What is clear is that if some lay magistrates have the time to sit on lengthy trials in the District Division, they would clearly have time to sit alongside district judges in the Magistrates Division. There is a gap in Auld's logic here.

Other questions remain, however. Were lay magistrates to sit with district judges in the District Division, which lay magistrates would likely do it? And how would they do it?

I have no doubt that some lay magistrates will welcome the opportunity to try contested cases alongside district judges in the District Division and will find time to do it. Our study showed that a minority of lay magistrates are able and do devote much more of their time to the task than the minimum number of twenty-six sittings a year stipulated by the Lord Chancellor. More than one-fifth of lay magistrates already sit more than once a week—that is more than twice the minimum number of sittings—in addition to attendance at meetings, training sessions, and so on. That so many are able and willing to devote so much unpaid time to the task, generally without claiming loss of earnings (86 per cent) and often without claiming expenses either (23 per cent), reflects that fact that the magistracy is overwhelmingly middle-class, two-fifths of whom are retired. We did not analyse our data to consider the socio-economic characteristics of the frequent-sitters, but it would be surprising were they not even more disproportionately from the retired and professional/managerial ranks.

There is a dilemma to be faced, therefore. If lay magistrates are to sit with professional judges in any division they must have the training, experience, and self-confidence to act as equals to challenge the professional judges. For otherwise they may be no more than what one observer has suggested the lay judiciary are generally considered in Germany, 'decorative flower pots'. Auld recognized the objection to mixed panels that they may be dominated by the professional judges. It is an issue on which there is a great deal of anecdotal but virtually no hard evidence both with regard to practice in the Crown Court (where mixed panels hear appeals from magistrates' courts decisions) and the former Quarter Sessions (where magistrates used often to sit with professional judges). The evidence from other jurisdictions is mixed. But, having reviewed that evidence, Doran and Glenn argue that 'the very presence of the lay members may in itself influence the stance adopted by the professional'. Auld is almost certainly correct, however, to doubt that foreign examples are good indicators of the likely pattern here. English and Welsh magistrates are much more highly trained and experienced than their Scandinavian and German counterparts. They sit frequently and separately from professional judges—which their Continental equivalents do not. It is unlikely that they would defer excessively to their professional colleagues.

But the outcome would be different were the sittings of lay magistrates greatly to change. If Sanders's proposal that lay magistrates sit much less frequently were adopted, for example, them mixed tribunals would probably become participative fig-leafs. By the same token, Auld's suggestion that lay magistrates sit in more flexible patterns and possibly less often so as to broaden their recruitment and social representativeness would likely turn out to be something of a sham were magistrates, once appointed, able freely to choose how often and in what court they sat. The bench might *appear* more socially representative, but it would likely be the case that most sittings, and certainly those involving the more serious cases, would involve magistrates more socially unrepresentative than benches are now. Furthermore, at which point does the frequency of sitting engender a case-hardened approach? Auld observed that the practical distinction between lay magistrates and district judges had diminished. At what point do lay magistrates cease to be lay?

There are no easy answers to this dilemma. The essence of the magistracy is that it should be lay and socially representative. But not so lay that it cannot act with justice and self-confidently challenge the professional judges when sitting with them. My own view is that it is objectionable that serious cases should be tried and sentenced by lone judges in the present magistrates' courts. Further, the question raised by Auld's proposed District Court is whether any serious case should be sentenced by a lone decision maker. Finally, I doubt that participation in serious proceedings should be left to the personal decision of individual magistrates. It is desirable that the social composition of the magistracy be broadened. For the same reason it is equally desirable that all magistrates be involved in the trial and sentencing of serious cases.

[6:3] Skyrme, T, *The Changing Image of the Magistracy*
(2nd edition, 1983) Macmillan (at page 6)

At first sight the system seems not only anomalous but indefensible and, having regard to their powers and vast field of responsibility, it is astonishing that the justices have not only survived but have flourished in an age when established institutions have been subject to ever-increasing denigration, when the amateur has been steadily replaced by the professional and when voluntary service is anachronistic in the prevailing climate of totalitarianism. The Justice of the Peace is the kind of historical legacy that one would have expected to be the first to founder in the revolutionary flood of the post-war years. It could not have survived had it not been acceptable to successive governments and to the public at large. The explanation of its acceptability, despite certain latent defects, is probably threefold: first, the depth of the roots of the lay magistracy in the British social system and the inclination of the people to honour tradition and to preserve ancient institutions; second, the ability of the justices, as evidenced in their previous history, to adjust to changing conditions; and third, the intrinsic merits of the system itself which, if exploited and developed, give it a peculiar attraction not shared by any other form of judicial machinery.

The principal defects usually attributed to lay justices are that they are too ready to accept police evidence and that they rely too much on the advice of the clerk. In some degree both criticisms are still valid, though far less so than they were 30 years and more ago, and neither defect is altogether incurable. As against these disadvantages the justices have certain unique qualities on the credit side. From the point of view of the government they have two advantages; they are cheap and they are flexible. As they received no pay they are more cost-effective than a salaried stipendiary, though the difference is not as great as is sometimes assumed because justices work more slowly than stipendiaries and if they have to sit in two or more courts to dispose of the same amount of work there will be the additional cost of extra staff and accommodation; in addition, although not remunerated, justices are entitled to allowances which can amount to a not inconsiderable sum when several of them are sitting. Nevertheless, justices are on the whole cheaper than any other effective method of administering justice than has so far been devised. In 1965, Lord Gardiner caused inquiries to be made in 20 countries to find out in each case the numbers of whole-time judges and the cost of judicial administration. The cost (excluding police and prisons) expressed as a percentage of the annual national budget ranged from 1.46 at the top of the scale to 0.16 in the case of England, Scotland and Wales, who were at the bottom. As regards the number of judges, several counties had more than 200 per million of population while Scotland with 15 and England and Wales with 8 were again at the bottom. As was to be expected, most Common Law countries were in the lowest bracket because of their single-judge systems; thus the United States had 34 judges per million population; Australia 29 and New Zealand 24. These figures should be treated with reserve as some were based on estimates, but the position of England and Wales at the bottom of the league was generally attributed to the much larger proportion of court work disposed of by their unpaid, part-time lay magistrates compared with other countries.

Justices also appeal to the government because their system is flexible; sudden fluctuations in the volume of work can be handled by calling upon justices to sit more or less often in more or fewer courts as the need arises, whereas a whole-time judge or stipendiary has little scope to expand his output if work increases, and if it diminishes he may be left partially unemployed at public expense.

These are not the only inherent merits of a properly constituted lay justice system. Two, or preferably three, heads are better than one and they are better still if they combine intimate knowledge, experience and understanding of the problems facing different sections of the local community, which can often enable them to deal with cases more justly and efficaciously than the professional courts. The collective views of a cross-section of the population, representing different shades of opinion, can be more effective in dispensing justice acceptable to the public than the decision of a single individual necessarily drawn from a fairly narrow social class and whose experience of local problems may be limited. Justices also act as a check on one another and provide a balanced conclusion, whereas there is nothing to curb the general idiosyncrasy or the spasmodic whim or irritability of a single magistrate. Furthermore, as justices attend court at intervals they approach their task with a freshness and objectivity that is lacking in a professional judge who is wholly engaged in adjudicating day after day.

The system of lay justices reflects, through citizens participation, the traditional English involvement of the layman in the administration of justice. It enables the citizen to see that the law is his law, administered by men and women like himself, and that it is not the esoteric preserve of the lawyers. Lord Hailsham, in a speech made when he was Lord Chancellor, stressed the value of the lay magistracy as a unifying factor in society as a whole, and he described their potential influence, not only on the bench but also out of court, as 'one of the characteristic institutions holding our society together'.

The identification of the ordinary citizen with the administration of justice should therefore have a popular appeal, yet when it comes to the test the average citizen seems to prefer to be tried by a professional magistrate. This is most noticeable where there is a clear choice of tribunal, as in family and adoption proceedings, and where preference is normally shown for the professionalism of the county court rather than the lay justices' court. This may be due at least in part to the erroneous view which much of the population hold of the justices today: that they are prejudiced, prosecution-minded, middle-class bigots, motivated by lust for power and totally lacking in any feeling for those who appear before them. This description might not have been far wrong a century ago, when it could have been directed with equal justification at other institutions, but the vast changes that have occurred since then are not generally realised. The detritus of the past has been washed away and the justices of today are able to exhibit some of the latent advantages of the system which were not revealed under their predecessors. A lay justice cannot equal the professional skill of a stipendiary, but the function of magistrates is largely to decide questions of fact and for this purpose to exercise common sense and sound judgment against a background of knowledge and experience of the world at large. By this criterion the quality of the average lay justice is no less than that of the professional stipendiary.

Provided that justices are carefully chosen in the light of their ability, integrity and understanding, and can be seen to be well qualified for their work, and provided also that they are given adequate training and opportunities to enable them to become and remain proficient in the performance of their duties, then it is possible for the layman, who combines experience as a magistrate with experience in other walks of like, to offer advantages which are not to be found in the professional systems; not least of these advantages being the ability to exercise a stabilising influence within the community in which he lives to an extent not open to the professional judge. It is to this end that the reforms of the past 40 years have been largely directed.

(At page 67:)

The controversy over the social composition of the magistracy usually turns upon whether benches are predominantly upper-class to the exclusion of the rest of the population. The Lord Chancellor does not seek to strike a numerical balance between representatives of each social group; there seems to be no good reason why he should do so and it would be impossible to achieve this result because of the movement of individuals from one group to another. The declared policy of each Lord Chancellor since 1945 has been to make sure that each bench is a microcosm of the local community within which it operates, and this amounts to seeing that in every petty sessional division there are at least some justices from each of the principal social and political groups in the area and that the bench is not dominated by any one group. I would claim that we have gone a long way towards attaining this object.

[6:4] Morgan, R and Russell, N, *The Judiciary in the Magistrates' Courts*
(2000) HO RDS Occasional Paper No 66, Home Office (from the summary, at page vii)

This research was jointly commissioned by the Lord Chancellor's Department and the Home Office. The study was undertaken during the first nine months of 2000 by a research team comprising the University of Bristol and two commercial companies, RSGB (a division of Taylor Nelson Sofres plc) and CRG, Cardiff, specialists in market research and cost benefit analysis respectively.

Methodology
The research comprised seven types of data collection:

- baseline information on the budgets, buildings, court staff and magistrates' characteristics. Data were gathered both nationally and locally, and included information on ten magistrates' courts in London and the provinces, with and without stipendiaries
- 2,019 self-completed magistrates' diaries, spanning three-week sessions, covering activities, timings etc. from the ten courts
- 1,120 self-completed magistrates' questionnaires addressing issues of sitting arrangements, their views on balance between lay and stipendiaries etc. from the ten courts
- observations of 535 court sessions at the ten courts
- 400 telephone interviews with regular court users from the ten courts
- public opinion survey: conducted with a nationally representative sample of 1,753 members of public
- 23 responses to a letter to representatives of the Council of Europe member states.

Composition and working practices of the magistracy

Composition
At the time of the research the magistracy comprised:

- approximately 30,400 lay magistrates
- 96 full-time stipendiaries
- 146 part-time stipendiaries.

The lay magistracy:

- is gender balanced
- is ethnically representative of the population at a national level
- is overwhelmingly drawn from professional and managerial ranks
- comprises a high proportion (two-fifths) who have retired from full-time employment.

In comparison, stipendiaries:

- are mostly male and white
- tend to be younger.

Sitting patterns
Lay magistrates:

- sit in court an average 41.4 occasions annually (although many sit a good deal more frequently)
- devote (taking holidays into account) an extended morning or afternoon to the post once a week
- additionally spend the equivalent, on average, of a full working week on training and other duties.

The contracts of full-time stipendiaries require them to perform judicial duties five days a week, 44 weeks of the year. However there is some ambiguity as to what this means in terms of court sittings. Provincial stipendiaries sit more often than their colleagues do in London, but both groups sit in court closer to four days per week.

Lay magistrates usually sit in panels of three, but sometimes of two (16% of observed panels). Stipendiaries nearly always sit alone but on rare occasions sit together with lay magistrates.

Caseload allocation

While stipendiaries take on more or less the full range of cases and appearances, they tend to be allocated more complex, prolonged and sensitive cases. Unlike lay magistrates, their time is concentrated on triable-either-way rather than summary cases.

Working methods and decision-making

Speed

Stipendiary magistrates deal with all categories of cases and appearances more quickly than their lay colleagues because they retire from court sessions less often and more briefly (0.2 compared to 1.2 occasions per session, for only 3 compared to 16 minutes). They also deal with cases more quickly on average (9 minutes compared to 10 minutes). This means:

- stipendiaries hear 22 per cent more appearances than lay magistrates per standardised court session (12.2 compared to 10)
- if stipendiaries were allocated an identical caseload to lay magistrates, it is estimated that they would deal with 30 per cent more appearances.

The greater speed of stipendiaries is not achieved at the expense of inquisition and challenge; on the contrary, hearings before stipendiaries typically involve more questions being asked and more challenges being made.

Manner of working: adjournments and bail

Both lay and stipendiary magistrates are invariably judged to meet high standards in dealing with court business (attentiveness, clarity of pronouncements, courtesy, and so on). However, stipendiaries are considered to perform better in relation to those criteria that suggest greater confidence—showing command over the proceedings and challenging parties responsible for delay.

Fewer appearances before stipendiaries lead to adjournments (45% compared to 52%). This is partly because fewer applications are made to stipendiaries but also because they are more likely to resist applications for adjournments (97% compared to 93%). It is therefore likely that the employment of additional stipendiaries would lead to fewer court appearances overall.

Lay magistrates are less likely to:

- refuse defendants bail in cases where to prosecution seeks custody and the defence applies for bail (19% compared to 37%)
- make use of immediate custody as a sentence (12% of triable-either-way cases compared to 25%).

The employment of additional stipendiaries might therefore significantly increase the prison population.

Stipendiaries tend to run their courts themselves and rely very little on their court legal advisors when it comes to making and explaining decisions and announcements. This calls into question whether they need legally qualified court advisors.

The views of regular court practitioners

A sample of 400 court practitioners (court advisors, solicitors, CPS personnel, probation officers) were surveyed by telephone.

Very few court users expressed 'no' or only 'a little' confidence in either type of magistrate, but stipendiaries were more likely to inspire a 'great deal' or a 'lot' of confidence. Users found it harder to generalise about lay magistrates, indicating a greater range in their performance.

The court users expressed very similar views to the court observers when asked to rate dimensions of behaviour. Stipendiaries were widely seen as:

- more efficient, more consistent and more confident in their decision-making
- questioning defence lawyers appropriately
- giving clear reasons for decisions
- showing command over proceedings.

Lay magistrates were more often judged better at:

- showing courtesy to defendants and other court members
- using simple language
- showing concern to distressed victims.

But the majority of respondents did not think lay and stipendiary magistrates differed on these criteria.

Regular court practitioners, particularly lawyers and CPS personnel, said that they and their colleagues behave differently when appearing before lay and stipendiary magistrates. They:

- prepare better for stipendiaries
- try to be more precise and concise in their statements to them
- anticipate that they will be questioned and challenged more.

Court legal advisors on the other hand said that they prepare more for lay magistrates, because they anticipate the need to give legal advice to them.

Public opinions of the magistracy

A nationally representative sample of 1,753 members of the public were interviewed regarding their views on, and knowledge of the magistracy.

Whereas the overwhelming majority of the public is aware of the terms 'magistrate' and 'magistrates' court', only a minority have heard of 'lay' as opposed to 'stipendiary' magistrates.

When the difference between them is explained, almost three-quarters (73%) say that they were not aware of this difference.

Only a bare majority of respondents correctly identify that most criminal cases are dealt with in the magistrates' courts, and that juries do not make decisions there. Knowledge about the qualifications and sitting practices of lay magistrates is even less accurate. Respondents who are more knowledgeable about the system tend to have greater confidence in it.

Having had the differences explained to them, most of the public thinks that:

- lay magistrates represent the views of the community better than stipendiaries (63% compared to 9%—the remaining 28% see no difference or don't know)
- lay magistrates are more likely to be sympathetic to defendants' circumstances (41% compared to 12%)
- stipendiaries are better at making correct judgements of guilt or innocence (36% compared to 11%) and managing court business effectively (48% compared to 9%)
- there is no difference between lay and stipendiaries in awareness of the effect of crimes on victims and approaching each case afresh.

In addition, when comparing single magistrates with panels:

- a small majority of respondents (53%) consider that motoring offences are suitable to be heard by a single magistrate
- a large majority think that the more serious decisions of guilty/not guilty (74%) and sending to prison (76%) should be decided by panels of magistrates.

Most respondents think that the work of the magistrates' courts should be divided equally between the two types of magistrates, or that the type of magistrate does not matter.

The direct and indirect costs of lay and stipendiary magistrates

If only directly attributable costs (salaries, expenses, training) are considered, lay magistrates are much cheaper because they are not paid directly and many do not claim loss of earnings. A sizeable minority does not even claim their allowable travelling expenses. A lay magistrate costs on average £495 per annum compared to the £90,000 per annum total employments costs of a stipendiary. These translate into a cost per appearance before lay and stipendiary magistrates of £3.59 and £20.96 respectively (Table 1). When indirect costs (premises, administration staff, etc.) are brought into the equation the gap between the two groups narrows, to £52.10 and £61.78.

TABLE 1 The cost of appearing before lay and stipendiary magistrates (per appearance)

	Lay Magistrates	Stipendiary Magistrates
	£	£
Direct costs (salary, expenses, training)	3.59	20.96
Indirect costs (premises, administration staff etc.)	48.51	40.82
Direct & indirect costs	52.10	61.78

The effect upon costs of substituting stipendiary for lay magistrates

There would have to be a significant increase in the use of the more productive stipendiaries to enable administrative staff and courtroom reductions to be made on any scale.

If blocks of work currently undertaken by lay magistrates were transferred to stipendiaries:

- one stipendiary would be needed for every 30 magistrates, if all lay tribunals comprised three justices
- one for every 28, if the present proportion of tribunals comprising only two lay justices were to continue.

Stipendiaries' greater tendency to resist adjournments and their greater use of custody at the pre-trial and sentencing stages means that if the number of stipendiaries were doubled (assuming present patterns were retained):

- there would be a reduction of 10,270 appearances in connection with indictable offences, giving an additional cost of £0.88 million per annum (a net increase because the reduced rates of adjournments do not overcome the higher attributable costs of stipendiaries).
- the number of remands in custody would increase by 6,200 per annum. Assuming an average remand period of 46 days, this has an associated cost of around £24 million (essentially falling on the Prison Service)

- the number of custodial sentences would increase by 2,760 per annum, costing £13.6 million. Set against this is the cost of the type of sentence that the offender would have received in the place of a prison sentence. If this is taken as some form of community penalty then the overall additional cost of this increase in custodial sentences would be around £8.5 million.

The effect upon costs of substituting lay for stipendiary magistrates

Alternatively if there were no stipendiaries, then there would be an increase in the number of appearances of 10,270, the number of remands in custody would decrease by 6,200, and the number of custodial sentences would decrease by 2,760—with each of the consequent cost savings.

Other jurisdictions

Drawing on the 23 responses from the Council of Europe member states and enquiries to other (mostly Common Law) jurisdictions, it can be seen that there are three principal models of adjudication:

- the *professional*
- the *lay*
- the *hybrid* (mixed lay and professional).

Each of these can be refined in terms of whether decision-making is by single persons or panels, and the number of tiers into which criminal cases and courts are divided.

However there is no straightforward relationship between the degree to which democracy is embedded and lay involvement in judicial decision-making. Many longstanding democracies involve lay persons while other do not. The re-establishment of democracy in a country does not necessarily stimulate the introduction of lay involvement in judicial decision-making, sometimes the reverse occurs, depending on the cultural and political tradition.

The most common arrangements for lay involvement comprise lay persons making decisions in the lowest tier, or sitting alongside professional judges in the middle or higher tiers. However, it is also common that their decisions are restricted to minor non-imprisonable offences. More serious decisions are invariably made by professionals or hybrid panels.

England and Wales is the only jurisdiction identified in this research where such a high proportion of criminal cases, including serious cases, are decided by lay persons. In addition, the allocation of cases to either lay or stipendiary magistrates by chance, rather than by policy, is unique to this jurisdiction.

Conclusion

Though the research does not point in a particular policy direction, the findings do indicate how the public and court users are likely to react to certain proposals for change.

Although the public do not have strong feelings about the precise role of magistrates, they think that summary offences, particularly if not contested, can be dealt with by a single magistrate but that panels should make the more serious judicial decisions. Cost considerations suggest that this could only be achieved (in the short-term at least) by continuing to make extensive use of lay magistrates.

Criminal justice practitioners, while appreciative of the quality of service given by lay magistrates, have greater confidence in professional judges (stipendiaries). Furthermore governmental pressure to make the criminal courts more efficient, and to reduce the time that cases take to complete, will also tend to favour the greater efficiency of stipendiary magistrates. However, this has to be balanced against the potential increase in cost to the Prison Service.

The nature and balance of contributions made by lay and stipendiary magistrates could be altered to better satisfy these wider considerations, but should not prejudice the integrity and support of a system founded on strong traditions. Not only is the office of Justice of the Peace ancient and in an important tradition of voluntary public service, it is also a direct manifestation of government policy which encourages *active citizens* in an *active community*. In no other jurisdiction does the criminal court system depend so heavily on such voluntary unpaid effort. At no stage during the study was it suggested that in most respects the magistrates' courts do not work well or fail to command general confidence. It is our view, therefore, that eliminating or greatly diminishing the role of lay magistrates would not be widely understood or supported.

[6:5] Riley, D and Vennard, J, *Triable-either-way Offences: Crown Court or Magistrates' Court?*
(1988) HORS No 98, HMSO (at page 21)

The present survey lends support to the belief that a significant proportion of either-way cases which are tried at the Crown Court are committed at the discretion of the magistrates. Such cases amounted to 40% of those dealt with at the Crown Court. There was, in addition, considerable variation among the survey courts—by a factor of three—in the rate at which magistrates declined jurisdiction, reaching as high as 63% of committals to one of the four courts. The differences between the areas was evident within offence categories, suggesting that there were systematic variations in how magistrates exercised their discretion over mode of trial.

The finding that magistrates' decisions agreed with prosecution representations concerning mode of trial in 93% of cases is open to varying interpretations. The information upon which magistrates are expected to form their view concerning mode of trial is largely confined to that presented by the prosecution at the mode of trial hearing; defence solicitors in the present survey more often than not made no representations on this matter. This, coupled with the similar criteria adopted by magistrates and prosecution, seems likely to produce agreement about where the case should be tried. On the other hand, the present results suggest that while there was consistency between prosecutors' and magistrates' views about mode of trial within areas, in similar cases courts in one CPS area more often declined jurisdiction than courts in the other area.

It is recognised that, under the present rules, not all either-way cases committed at the discretion of the magistrates would be suitable for summary trial. Quite apart from considerations of offence seriousness, section 19 of the Magistrates' Courts Act 1980 requires that, in determining which mode of trial appears more suitable, the bench has regard to 'whether the punishment which a magistrates' court would have the power to inflict' for the offence 'would be adequate'. The present study did not investigate magistrates' reasons for their mode of trial decisions, therefore the impact of this consideration is unknown. Home Office statistics indicate that more than half (55%) of those convicted at the Crown Court in either-way cases receive a sentence within the sentencing powers of magistrates' courts (*Criminal Statistics* 1986, Table 7.1), but this may simply reflect the fact that some defendants are committed by magistrates for reasons other than the seriousness of the offence or their powers of punishment—such as the practice of declining to try a defendant whose co-accused has elected trial at the Crown Court. The sentence imposed by the judge will also take into account mitigating factors not known to the magistrates when deciding mode of trial.

That said, the level of sentencing in either-way cases committed to the Crown Court, together with the variation between benches in their propensity to decline jurisdiction, indicate some scope for reducing the volume of either-way cases committed at the discretion of the bench. Questions remain, however, concerning the reasons for area variation and the influence on bench policy of guidance provided by Crown Court judges.

The effect on Crown Court workload and on the remand and sentenced prisoner populations of any change in magistrates' venue decisions or in their powers to commit, would largely depend on defendants' willingness to consent to summary trial when offered a choice of venue. Among cases in the present sample committed to the Crown Court at the initiative of the bench, there was an indication from interviews with defence solicitors that about two-fifths (24) of defendants (whose venue preferences were known) would have consented to summary trial if they had been given the option.

In either-way cases considered suitable for summary trial, defendants' venue and pleas decisions largely reflected the perceived advantages and disadvantages of trial at the different venues and the strength of the prosecution case. In most cases, mode of trial decisions and pleas were consistent with defendants' intentions before being advised on these matters by defence solicitors. There was little evidence from the survey that advance disclosure or other exchanges between prosecution and defence were substantially related to defendants' choice of venue or the pleas entered at court. Confirming the results of earlier research, defendants who wanted to plead not guilty tended to see Crown Court trial as offering the better prospect of acquittal and were apparently not deterred by longer waiting times or the chance of a more severe sentence if convicted. Differences in the prospects of acquittal between the Crown Court and magistrates' courts are presumably well known to defendants and their solicitors and this may have weighed more heavily in their choice of venue than sentence considerations. Among defendants who pleaded not guilty to all charges in the present sample, 66% tried at the Crown Court were acquitted compared with 45% at summary trial. These figures do not take into account the relative strength of the prosecution and defence evidence in cases tried at the two venues, but there is some research evidence that defendants are more likely to be acquitted in the Crown Court even having accounted for differences in the nature and strength of the evidence adduced.

For defendants who admit their guilt, there are on the face of it few advantages in Crown Court trial: cases are likely to take longer to come to court and the upper limit on Crown Court sentences exceeds that in the magistrates' court. It has been argued that the additional delay at the Crown Court represents an attraction for some defendants anxious, for example, to enhance mitigating factors (such as a stable personal relationship or employment record) or to maximise time spent remanded in custody to offset a prospective custodial sentence. The present survey provides some support for this view, but according to their solicitors, most defendants who elected intending to plead guilty were motivated by factors other than delay. The reasons most frequently cited to explain this choice of venue were the defendants' previous experience with the courts, the greater confidence in a hearing at the Crown Court than before magistrates. This is consistent with the findings that some three-fifths of those who elected and eventually pleaded guilty were, at the time mode of trial was decided, actively considering contesting their cases. The decision to plead guilty often appeared to have been taken at a later stage.

The knowledge that the Crown Court can inflict a heavier sentence than the magistrates' court would seem to be a strong disincentive to electing. Criminal Statistics 1986, (Tables S1.1(A), S2.1(A)) show that the proportionate use of custody is far higher in the Crown Court for all offence groups. For example, in 1986 58% of male defendants sentenced in the Crown Court on theft or handling charges were given custodial penalties compared with 12% of those sentenced in the magistrates' court. The advice on venue offered by defence solicitors might be expected to reflect their experience of sentencing practices at the two modes of trial. On the other hand, since the Crown Court deals by and large with the more serious either-way cases, it is to be expected that the proportionate use of imprisonment is higher there than in the lower courts. In like cases it may be that judges at some courts pass more lenient sentences than magistrates, or are no more stringent. This would explain why, according to their solicitors, some defendants in the present sample elected believing they would receive a lighter sentence than if convicted by magistrates. For others, the prospect of a fairer hearing and better chance of acquittal evidently outweighed any fears about the sentence the judge might impose on conviction.

The long-standing concern to find ways of containing the number of triable-either-way cases committed for trial at the Crown Court is likely to remain a key issue if, as seems likely on the basis of past evidence, the workload at the Crown Court and the size of the remand and sentenced prisoner populations continue to grow. The present research confirms that, for defendants wishing to contest their case and for some who intend to plead guilty, the incentives to acceptance of summary trial are few. A more promising approach may, therefore, be to encourage magistrates to accept jurisdiction in a higher proportion of either-way cases. Since, however, uncertainty remains as to magistrates' reasons for declining jurisdiction, further research might usefully examine the link between bench practices and the representations made by prosecutors, having regard to the influence on local policies of guidance handed down by liaison judges.

[6:6] Bail Act 1976 (as amended)
Section 4; Schedule 1

4 General right to bail of accused persons and others

(1) A person to whom this section applies shall be granted bail except as provided in Schedule 1 to this Act.

(2) This section applies to a person who is accused of an offence when—

(a) he appears or is brought before a magistrates' court or the Crown Court in the course of or in connection with proceedings for the offence, or

(b) he applies to a court for bail or for a variation of the conditions of bail in connection with the proceedings.

This subsection does not apply as respects proceedings on or after a person's conviction of the offence or proceedings against a fugitive offender for the offence.

(3) This section also applies to a person who, having been convicted of an offence, appears or is brought before a magistrates' court to be dealt with under Part II of Schedule 3 to the Powers of Criminal Courts (Sentencing) Act 2000 (breach of certain community orders).

(4) This section also applies to a person who has been convicted of an offence and whose case is adjourned by the court for the purpose of enabling inquiries or a report to be made to assist the court in dealing with him for the offence.

(5) Schedule 1 to this Act also has effect as respects conditions of bail for a person to whom this section applies.

(6) In Schedule 1 to this Act "the defendant" means a person to whom this section applies and any reference to a defendant whose case is adjourned for inquiries or a report is a reference to a person to whom this section applies by virtue of subsection (4) above.

(7) This section is subject to section 41 of the Magistrates' Courts Act 1980 (restriction of bail by magistrates court in cases of treason).

(8) This section is subject to section 25 of the Criminal Justice and Public Order Act 1994 (exclusion of bail in cases of homicide and rape).

(9) In taking any decisions required by Part I or II of Schedule 1 to this Act, the considerations to which the court is to have regard include, so far as relevant, any misuse of controlled drugs by the defendant ("controlled drugs" and "misuse" having the same meanings as in the Misuse of Drugs Act 1971).

...

SCHEDULE 1   Persons Entitled to Bail: Supplementary Provisions

Part I
Defendants Accused or Convicted of Imprisonable Offences
Defendants to whom Part I applies

1 The following provisions of this Part of this Schedule apply to the defendant if—

(a) the offence or one of the offences of which he is accused or convicted in the proceedings is punishable with imprisonment, or

(b) his extradition is sought in respect of an offence.

Exceptions to right to bail

2(1) The defendant need not be granted bail if the court is satisfied that there are substantial grounds for believing that the defendant, if released on bail (whether subject to conditions or not) would—

(a) fail to surrender to custody, or

(b) commit an offence while on bail, or

(c) interfere with witnesses or otherwise obstruct the course of justice, whether in relation to himself or any other person.

(2) Where the defendant falls within one or more of paragraphs 2A, 6 and 6B of this Part of this Schedule, this paragraph shall not apply unless—

(a) where the defendant falls within paragraph 2A, the court is satisfied as mentioned in subparagraph (1) of that paragraph;

(b) where the defendant falls within paragraph 6, the court is satisfied as mentioned in subparagraph (1) of that paragraph;

(c) where the defendant falls within paragraph 6B, the court is satisfied as mentioned in paragraph 6A of this Part of this Schedule or paragraph 6A does not apply by virtue of paragraph 6C of this Part of this Schedule.

2A The defendant need not be granted bail if—

(a) the offence is an indictable offence or an offence triable either way; and

(b) it appears to the court that he was on bail in criminal proceedings on the date of the offence.

3 The defendant need not be granted bail if the court is satisfied that the defendant should be kept in custody for his own protection or, if he is a child or young person, for his own welfare.

4 The defendant need not be granted bail if he is in custody in pursuance of the sentence of a court or of any authority acting under any of the Services Acts.

5 The defendant need not be granted bail where the court is satisfied that it has not been practicable to obtain sufficient information for the purpose of taking the decisions required by this Part of this Schedule for want of time since the institution of the proceedings against him.

6(1) If the defendant falls within this paragraph, he may not be granted bail unless the court is satisfied that there is no significant risk that, if released on bail (whether subject to conditions or not), he would fail to surrender to custody.

(2) Subject to sub-paragraph (3) below, the defendant falls within this paragraph if—

(a) he is aged 18 or over, and

(b) it appears to the court that, having been released on bail in or in connection with the proceedings for the offence, he failed to surrender to custody.

(3) Where it appears to the court that the defendant had reasonable cause for his failure to surrender to custody, he does not fall within this paragraph unless it also appears to the court that he failed to surrender to custody at the appointed place as soon as reasonably practicable after the appointed time.

(4) For the purposes of sub-paragraph (3) above, a failure to give to the defendant a copy of the record of the decision to grant him bail shall not constitute a reasonable cause for his failure to surrender to custody.

Exception applicable to drug users in certain areas

(6A) Subject to paragraph 6C below, a defendant who falls within paragraph 6B below may not be granted bail unless the court is satisfied that there is no significant risk of his committing an offence while on bail (whether subject to conditions or not).

6B(1) A defendant falls within this paragraph if—

    (a) he is aged 18 or over;

    (b) a sample taken—

        (i) under section 63B of the Police and Criminal Evidence Act 1984 (testing for presence of Class A drugs) in connection with the offence; or

        (ii) under section 161 of the Criminal Justice Act 2003 (drug testing after conviction of an offence but before sentence),

has revealed the presence in his body of a specified Class A drug;

    (c) either the offence is one under section 5(2) or (3) of the Misuse of Drugs Act 1971 and relates to a specified Class A drug, or the court is satisfied that there are substantial grounds for believing—

        (i) that misuse by him of any specified Class A drug caused or contributed to the offence; or

        (ii) (even if it did not) that the offence was motivated wholly or partly by his intended misuse of such a drug; and

    (d) the condition set out in sub-paragraph (2) below is satisfied or (if the court is considering on a second or subsequent occasion whether or not to grant bail) has been, and continues to be, satisfied.

  (2) The condition referred to is that after the taking and analysis of the sample—

    (a) a relevant assessment has been offered to the defendant but he does not agree to undergo it; or

    (b) he has undergone a relevant assessment, and relevant follow-up has been proposed to him, but he does not agree to participate in it.

  (3) In this paragraph and paragraph 6C below—

    (a) "Class A drug" and "misuse" have the same meaning as in the Misuse of Drugs Act 1971;

    (b) "relevant assessment" and "relevant follow-up" have the meaning given by section 3(6E) of this Act;

    (c) "specified" (in relation to a Class A drug) has the same meaning as in Part 3 of the Criminal Justice and Court Services Act 2000.

6C Paragraph 6A above does not apply unless—

    (a) the court has been notified by the Secretary of State that arrangements for conducting a relevant assessment or, as the case may be, providing relevant follow-up have been made for the local justice area in which it appears to the court that the defendant would reside if granted bail; and

    (b) the notice has not been withdrawn.

Exception applicable only to defendant whose case is adjourned for inquiries or a report

7 Where his case is adjourned for inquiries or a report, the defendant need not be granted bail if it appears to the court that it would be impracticable to complete the inquiries or make the report without keeping the defendant in custody.

Restriction of conditions of bail

  8(1) Subject to sub-paragraph (3) below, where the defendant is granted bail, no conditions shall be imposed under subsections (4) to (7) (except subsection (6)(d) or (e)) of section 3 of this Act unless it appears to the court that it is necessary to do so for the purpose of preventing the occurrence of any of the events mentioned in paragraph 2 of this Part of this Schedule ...

(1A) No condition shall be imposed under section 3(6)(d) of this Act unless it appears to be necessary to do so for the purpose of enabling inquiries or a report to be made.

(2) Sub-paragraphs (1) and (1A) above also apply on any application to the court to vary the conditions of bail or to impose conditions in respect of bail which has been granted unconditionally.

(3) The restriction imposed by sub-paragraph (1A) above shall not apply to the conditions required to be imposed under section 3(6A) of this Act or operate to override the direction in section 11(3) of the Powers of Criminal Courts (Sentencing) Act 2000 to a magistrates' court to impose conditions of bail under section 3(6)(d) of this Act of the description specified in the said section 11(3) in the circumstances so specified.

Decisions under paragraph 2

9 In taking the decisions required by paragraph 2(1) or, in deciding whether it is satisfied as mentioned in paragraph 2A(1), 6(1) or 6A, of this Part of this Schedule, the court shall have regard to such of the following considerations as appear to it to be relevant, that is to say—

(a) the nature and seriousness of the offence or default (and the probable method of dealing with the defendant for it),

(b) the character, antecedents, associations and community ties of the defendant,

(c) the defendant's record as respects the fulfilment of his obligations under previous grants of bail in criminal proceedings,

(d) except in the case of a defendant whose case is adjourned for inquiries or a report, the strength of the evidence of his having committed the offence or having defaulted,

as well as to any others which appear to be relevant.

9A

9AA (1) This paragraph applies if—

(a) the defendant is under the age of 18, and

(b) it appears to the court that he was on bail in criminal proceedings on the date of the offence.

(2) In deciding for the purposes of paragraph 2(1) of this Part of this Schedule whether it is satisfied that there are substantial grounds for believing that the defendant, if released on bail (whether subject to conditions or not), would commit an offence while on bail, the court shall give particular weight to the fact that the defendant was on bail in criminal proceedings on the date of the offence.

9AB (1) Subject to sub-paragraph (2) below, this paragraph applies if—

(a) the defendant is under the age of 18, and

(b) it appears to the court that, having been released on bail in or in connection with the proceedings for the offence, he failed to surrender to custody.

(2) Where it appears to the court that the defendant had reasonable cause for his failure to surrender to custody, this paragraph does not apply unless it also appears to the court that he failed to surrender to custody at the appointed place as soon as reasonably practicable after the appointed time.

(3) In deciding for the purposes of paragraph 2(1) of this Part of this Schedule whether it is satisfied that there are substantial grounds for believing that the defendant, if released on bail (whether subject to conditions or not), would fail to surrender to custody, the court shall give particular weight to—

(a) where the defendant did not have reasonable cause for his failure to surrender to custody, the fact that he failed to surrender to custody, or

(b) where he did have reasonable cause for his failure to surrender to custody, the fact that he failed to surrender to custody at the appointed place as soon as reasonably practicable after the appointed time.

(4) For the purposes of this paragraph, a failure to give to the defendant a copy of the record of the decision to grant him bail shall not constitute a reasonable cause for his failure to surrender to custody.

Part II
Defendants Accused or Convicted of Non-Imprisonable Offences

Defendants to whom Part II applies

1 Where the offence or every offence of which the defendant is accused or convicted in the proceedings is one which is not punishable with imprisonment the following provisions of this Part of this Schedule apply.

Exceptions to right to bail

2 The defendant need not be granted bail if—

(a) it appears to the court that, having been previously granted bail in criminal proceedings, he has failed to surrender to custody in accordance with his obligations under the grant of bail; and

(b) the court believes, in view of that failure, that the defendant, if released on bail (whether subject to conditions or not) would fail to surrender to custody.

3 The defendant need not be granted bail if the court is satisfied that the defendant should be kept in custody for his own protection or, if he is a child or young person, for his own welfare.

4 The defendant need not be granted bail if he is in custody in pursuance of the sentence of a court or of any authority acting under any of the Services Acts.

5 The defendant need not be granted bail if—

(a) having been released on bail in or in connection with the proceedings for the offence, he has been arrested in pursuance of section 7 of this Act; and

(b) the court is satisfied that there are substantial grounds for believing that the defendant, if released on bail (whether subject to conditions or not) would fail to surrender to custody, commit an offence on bail or interfere with witnesses or otherwise obstruct the course of justice (whether in relation to himself or any other person).

Part IIA
Decisions where Bail Refused on Previous Hearing

1 If the court decides not to grant the defendant bail, it is the court's duty to consider, at each subsequent hearing while the defendant is a person to whom section 4 above applies and remains in custody, whether he ought to be granted bail.

2 At the first hearing after that at which the court decided not to grant the defendant bail he may support an application for bail with any argument as to fact or law that he desires (whether or not he has advanced that argument previously).

3 At subsequent hearings the court need not hear arguments as to fact or law which it has heard previously.

Part III
Interpretation

1 For the purposes of this Schedule the question whether an offence is one which is punishable with imprisonment shall be determined without regard to any enactment prohibiting or restricting the imprisonment of young offenders or first offenders.

2 References in this Schedule to previous grants of bail include—

    (a) bail granted before the coming into force of this Act;

    (b) as respects the reference in paragraph 2A of Part 1 of this Schedule (as substituted by section 14(1) of the Criminal Justice Act 2003), bail granted before the coming into force of that paragraph;

    (c) as respects the references in paragraph 6 of Part 1 of this Schedule (as substituted by section 15(1) of the Criminal Justice Act 2003), bail granted before the coming into force of that paragraph;

    (d) as respects the references in paragraph 9AA of Part 1 of this Schedule, bail granted before the coming into force of that paragraph;

    (e) as respects the references in paragraph 9AB of Part 1 of this Schedule, bail granted before the coming into force of that paragraph;

    (f) as respects the reference in paragraph 5 of Part 2 of this Schedule (as substituted by section 13(4) of the Criminal Justice Act 2003), bail granted before the coming into force of that paragraph.

3 References in this Schedule to a defendant's being kept in custody or being in custody include (where the defendant is a child or young person) references to his being kept or being in the care of a local authority in pursuance of a warrant of commitment under section 23(1) of the Children and Young Persons Act 1969.

4 In this Schedule—

"court", in the expression "sentence of a court" includes a service court as defined in section 12(1) of the Visiting Forces Act 1952 and "sentence", in that expression, shall be construed in accordance with that definition;

"default", in relation to the defendant, means the default for which he is to be dealt with under Part II of Schedule 3 to the Powers of Criminal Courts (Sentencing) Act 2000;

"the Services Acts" means the Army Act 1955, the Air Force Act 1955 and the Naval Discipline Act 1957.

[6:7] HM Chief Inspector of Prisons, *Unjust Deserts: A Thematic Review of the Treatment and Conditions for Unsentenced Prisoners in England and Wales*
(2000) (at page 123)

Strategic Issues and Recommendations for the Management of Establishments Holding Unsentenced Prisoners

12.01 This review has revealed a startling gap between what the public might reasonably expect to be in place for unsentenced prisoners and what is actually in place. More worryingly however, it also identifies a gap between the official understanding of what is being delivered as described in the replies from the *Governors' survey* and the actual experience of unsentenced prisoners; a gap largely supported by our own observations from fieldwork and inspections.

12.02 The following factors seem to be relevant to this state of affairs:

- Local prisons are overcrowded. The Prison Service has endeavoured, quite rightly, to keep the rising numbers of prisoners sent to them by the courts as close as possible to where they are to appear for trial. Also, for entirely understandable and sensible reasons the Prison Service has chosen to protect training prisons from overcrowding by concentrating this pressure on local prisons.

This has resulted in the latter holding a rising number of sentenced prisoners, both short term, who increasingly serve their whole sentences in local prisons, and longer term, who can wait for extended periods to be transferred to training prisons. The sheer pressure of numbers has therefore thwarted the development of proper regimes for unsentenced prisoners.

- Prisoners in local prisons are generally compliant. Most prisoners prefer to be held in local prisons where they are closer to their homes, friends and families than in more distant training prisons. Indeed this has been such a priority for most prisoners that they have been prepared to put up with poor conditions in order to take advantage of being able to stay in their local area. The rate of turnover in the population is also such that most prisoners tolerate their conditions on the basis that they will not have to do so for a long time. Apart from the riots of the early nineties, unsentenced prisoners have not posed serious control problems. Complaints from unsentenced prisoners themselves have not therefore provided a stimulus for change.

- The diversity of prisoner needs presents difficult challenges for staff. All offenders entering the prison system do so through local prisons. Any of these establishments might hold remands awaiting trial, convicted unsentenced and sentenced prisoners, debtors, civil prisoners, deportees or immigration detainees and those on over-crowding drafts from other local prisons. Sentenced prisoners may be short or longer sentenced and include life sentence prisoners both newly sentenced, recalled from training prisons or licence revoked. Among this mixture of prisoners will be those with violent tendencies, those who are vulnerable to attack from others, those who are mentally unwell, those who are drug misusers, those who are drug dealers, those who are depressed and suicidal and, of course those who are subsequently found not guilty. Although some may be familiar to staff from previous periods in custody, many will be unknown and the uncertainty and risk inherent in this mix creates one of the biggest challenges for managers and staff.

- Local prisons have inadequate physical facilities. Many of the old local prisons were constructed for the penal policies of a different age and lack the facilities that are required to support healthy prison regimes. Until some twenty years ago when finances for the maintenance of prison buildings became more readily available, all were in a wretched condition. Improvements have been made, notably in the abolition of 'slopping out', but most are still in need of large capital investment to make them fit for their purpose. For example, in many of the cells designed for one person but used to accommodate two, there is no suitable screen between the toilet and the living space. The Director General and his colleagues are aware of these deficiencies and are as keen as anyone else to rectify them, but do not have the necessary finance to carry out the work.

- Local prisons have a culture of disengagement with prisoners. For many decades the unspoken but unmistakable message to staff from senior Prison Service managers has been that their job is to serve the courts by taking as many prisoners as necessary, and to avoid escapes and disturbances. Given the risks associated with these tasks and the limited resources to manage them, a culture of disengagement with prisoners and risk avoidance has become established.

- Local prisons are able to resist change. The staff of local prisons become the culture carriers as they are longer serving than either the prisoners or their managers. The former pass through on short periods of remand, short sentences or on to training prisons, and the latter pass through on relatively short tours of duty as they build their careers. In these circumstances staff become disproportionately influential and without training, management and leadership for their role in a modern Prison Service, their prime motivation becomes one of making life as comfortable as possible for themselves and their colleagues, and their allegiance and commitment to the Prison Service's Statement of Purpose becomes hard to find. In such prisons there is an absence of justice and fairness in dealing with legitimate requests and complaints from prisoners, Governors appear powerless to introduce even the simplest of changes without disputes, and progress becomes impossible without a clear mandate for change from Ministers and the Prisons Board.

The Way Forward

12.03 At any time there are well over thirty thousand people held in fifty-three local prisons and remand centres in England and Wales. Some of the establishments in which they are held treat unsentenced prisoners with humanity and try to meet their individual needs; the five contracted out local prisons, for example, and most local prisons for women. Few of the suggestions for improvement in this review are entirely original in that many reflect examples of good, indeed outstanding current practice in both directly managed and contracted out establishments. One such example is the recommendation to replace the policy of separating unconvicted from convicted prisoners with an integrated approach that is based on safety and respect which has been tried and tested by at least one former Governor of a local directly managed prison. What is missing, however, is a clear unifying vision for unsentenced prisoners which details how they should be treated and the conditions in which they should be held, and a management system which ensures consistent delivery in all local prisons and remand centres.

12.04 The senior management of the Prison Service has tended to believe that the answer lies in finding capable Governors to take command of these prisons. It is true that without strong leadership nothing will change, but far more than the personal qualities of individual governors are needed if lasting change is to be achieved. I must emphasise that responsibility for this state of affairs does not lie with the current Prisons Board. Indeed, I believe that it is because of the leadership already demonstrated by the Director General that there is now a real opportunity to tackle the culture of those establishments that have been producing poor, and in some cases, unacceptable treatment and conditions for prisoners, including those held on remand, for too many years. There is every reason to be optimistic that staff in the Prison Service will respond positively to the challenge of providing a healthy and needs based regime for unsentenced prisoners as they have done successfully in other parts of the prison estate, notably high security prisons. However, they will need re-training as well as strong leadership if they are to operate in a radically different way. Many, for example, will need help to understand the needs and rights of unsentenced prisoners and the proper role of local prisons within a joined up Criminal Justice System. They will also need to understand the complex mental health problems of unsentenced prisoners and the importance of ensuring that they have access to due process.

Recommendations

12.05 I have detailed throughout this review a number of areas where change needs to be made, and a number of recommendations are included in the text. However, I have two over-riding strategic recommendations which I detail here. Firstly, in view of the physical inadequacy of the facilities and buildings within which many unsentenced prisoners are held.

I recommend that the cost of the work required to ensure that all local prisons and remand centres have the necessary facilities to hold prisoners in decent conditions should be published and that the finance to carry it out should be provided within a five year programme.

12.06 In view of the enormity of the challenge which faces the Prison Service in bringing about cultural change in many of the establishments holding unsentenced prisoners.

I recommend that a strategy is introduced by the Prisons Board, with the full support of Ministers, for a two year programme of change to identify and deliver agreed prisoner focused outcomes as detailed in this review, for all unsentenced prisoners in local prisons and remand centres. This strategy should contain a clear sense of direction for local prisons and remand centres, detail the elements of work which they should undertake and include costed service delivery agreements. The strategy should include the introduction of a mandatory and comprehensive initial and ongoing training programme for new staff and an immediate programme to re-educate current staff. There should also be a remedial element to the strategy to identify those prisons needing to achieve fundamental change in the way that unsentenced prisoners are treated. This information can be readily gathered from inspection reports over recent years. Such identified prisons should be set clear targets, based on the delivery of agreed outcomes for unsentenced prisoners. They should also be given suitable senior managers to carry out this work, which might include nominated 'change managers' with a clear briefing and training for what is to be achieved, and time in post to carry through the required changes. Such senior management teams should also be given both practical and personal support from senior functional managers in Prison Service Headquarters, and opportunities for the regular exchange of experiences through meetings with colleagues in other similar establishments.

12.07 I intend to carry out a follow up to this review in two years time, and will continue to monitor the treatment and conditions of unsentenced prisoners within my ongoing inspection programme. I look forward to witnessing the improvements which I am confident that the Prison Service can deliver, with the full backing of Ministers.

[6:8] Lloyd, C, *Bail Information Schemes: Practice and Effect*
(1992) HO RPU Paper No 69, HMSO (at page 65)

How is bail information most effective?

One of the most interesting findings of this research has been the differences in the way in which bail information has its effect in the three courts studied. While the Blackpool scheme seemed to have influenced the remand decision primarily through strengthening the defence's case for bail, at the other extreme, the Manchester scheme's effectiveness relies almost entirely on its influence on the CPS. Both these findings from the data could have been predicted from the interviews with solicitors and probation officers in the field. The Manchester CPS were universally described as an independent agency, keen to make their own decisions rather than act at the bidding of the police. Interviews with prosecutors verified this opinion: they spoke positively of bail information and, for the most part, saw it as a useful adjunct to their decision-making. By contrast the CPS at Blackpool—and to a lesser extent at Hull—were more critical of the local scheme and saw bail information primarily as an aid to the defence.

Which *modus operandi* is the most effective? Taking account of the numbers interviewed, it was the Hull scheme that seemed to divert the highest proportion of interviewed defendants from a remand in custody. It would therefore appear that bail information is most effective when used fully by the CPS and the defence.

Another possible way of influencing the remand decision would be to provide information directly to the court. Jones and Goldkamp (1991)[28] have recently criticised the bail information initiative in the UK for not involving magistrates sufficiently in the development and use of bail information. The possibility of providing bail information directly to magistrates was raised in interviews with court clerks, solicitors and probation staff and received a mixed reception. Interestingly, it was a number of defence and CPS solicitors who were in favour of the provision of information direct to the court, suggesting that information would be more effective if presented in this way. However, various criticisms of this approach was made. First, it was thought possible that some magistrates might confuse bail information sheets with social inquiry reports and assume that the sheets represented probation recommendations for bail. Second, it was pointed out that if magistrates expected bail information sheets to be presented for each defendant, if a sheet was not presented for a defendant they might automatically assume that there was nothing positive to be said, although the reason for the absence of a bail information sheet might simply be that the BIO ran out of time. As long as magistrates were adequately prepared for such a scheme's introduction, the first argument would seem to carry little weight. The second argument is more persuasive. A scheme would have to ensure complete coverage of cases where the police were objecting to bail in order to prevent this process occurring. Nevertheless it seems surprising that there has been no experimentation with a scheme that provides copies of the bail information sheet to the CPS, the defence and the court. There is a sense in which information read out in court by the prosecutor or defending solicitor lacks objectivity. While defence solicitors can refer to the fact that the information was verified by a probation officer or ancillary, the context of the presentation of this information is within the defence's argument for bail, and this may detract from the perceived 'independence' of the information.

(At page 70:)

Conclusions

The study reported here has added further support to the growing body of research and monitoring evidence which shows bail information schemes to be successful in diverting defendants from remands in custody. The importance of such work cannot be understated. Remand centres and local prisons remain the most crowded sector of the prison system, with Spartan regimes and high rates of suicide. The avoidance of a potential remand in custody is therefore saving the defendant from a period of imprisonment on remand in overcrowded conditions, and may also contribute to the likelihood of a non-custodial sentence. Moreover, the cost-effectiveness analysis presented here suggests that bail information schemes are also saving the criminal justice system a considerable amount of money.

Perhaps the most interesting part of the research has been the exploration of the different ways in which bail information has its effect in three courts. Unfortunately this issue could not be addressed adequately at Lincoln Prison because of the lack of information about CPS and defence applications. While national policy and previous research have tended to focus on the influence of bail information on the CPS, it is clear from the evidence presented here that bail information can also have a significant effect through influencing the number and strength of defence applications. While the sample of three court-based schemes is admittedly small, it is nevertheless interesting to note that the scheme which had the largest relative effect on remand decision was the one which exploited both paths of influence to the full.

However, it should be emphasised that the probation service and its BIOs have only limited powers in influencing the way in which other agencies utilise bail information: good working relationships can be forged between BIOs and prosecutors and defence solicitors, and senior probation managers can liaise with their counterparts in the other organisations. Nevertheless, perhaps the most important determinant of the way in which bail information works is the particular subculture or dynamics of the local magistrates' court, and in particular, the ethos of the local CPS branch. Bail information will be most effective in a court with a high rate of remanding in custody; a local CPS which is prepared to reconsider police requests and use bail information as a means to achieve more independent decision making; and defence solicitors who are prepared to make a bail application at first appearance.

Note

28 Jones, P R and Goldkamp, J S 'Judicial Guidelines for Pre-trial Release' (1991) 30 Howard Journal 140.

[6:9] Morgan, P M and Henderson, P, *Remand Decisions and Offending on Bail: Evaluation of the Bail Process Project*
(1998) HORS No 184 (at pages vii–x)

The aim of the Bail Process Project was to improve the quality, accuracy and timeliness of the information available to remand decision-makers so that they were better able to assess the risk of offending on bail.

Inter-agency working groups were set up in five court areas in 1992. Each group, chaired by the Justices' Clerk, studied the remand process in its own area, and identified problems that affected the information available to the police custody officers, CPS prosecutors and magistrates when they made a pre-trial decision or recommendation on bail or custody. The groups then set in hand the changes that were possible to solve these problems.

The problems that were identified are described by Burrows et al (1994) and are summarised in Appendix A of this report. The main changes that were introduced by the courts were as follows.

- In most areas, the early *availability of the defendant's criminal record* was a problem. One area was able to extend the hours of direct access to its local records from eight to twenty-four hours a day.

Another negotiated access to the more detailed record held by the National Identification Service (as compared with the brief record held on the police national computer). A third area was able to establish a mechanism whereby the court was informed if the defendant was already on bail from a different police station or court within the same police force area.

- All five areas carried out some *training of magistrates in risk assessment*, and ways of improving magistrates' awareness of bail hostel facilities in the area were explored. Three areas set up *training courses for police custody officers* on the same topic to ensure greater uniformity of practice.

- Three areas amended the *wording of bail conditions of residence or curfew*, to oblige the defendant to present himself or herself in person to police officers monitoring his/her compliance. Three areas distributed *simplified bail notices* to make the terms of bail clearer to defendants, that is, the date of the next court appearance and any conditions attached. These were issued to defendants granted unconditional bail as well as those granted bail with conditions.

- In two areas, court clerks started to keep *a record of representations made in remand decisions* so that future benches would know the reasons why earlier decisions had been made.

- Two areas made changes in court listing times to allow more *time for pre-court discussion between the agencies* and, in one area, new arrangements allowed Saturday courts to have access to the probation service.

- In two areas, local steering mechanisms were established under the Court User group to ensure *better liaison between two bail information schemes in the same area*, and to ensure general understanding of how negative information (that which might work against the granting of bail) was handled by the probation service (see Appendix D).

- In single areas, the following changes were made: a *new prison-based bail information scheme* and a *trial bail support scheme* for 18- to 25-year-olds were established; a scheme was set up to provide *volunteers to act as 'appropriate adults'* during police interviews with under-17-year-olds; and arrangements were made for a *review panel for mentally disordered offenders*.

Case tracking data were collected on cases involving bail/custody decisions in the five areas over a period of three months in 1993 and three months in 1994 (before and after the improvements suggested above). Defendants released on bail in the two samples of cases were followed up at the criminal records office to find details of any offences that were committed while they were on bail.

Analyses showed that the *proportion of defendants granted court bail who were convicted of an offence committed while they were on bail* was reduced in two of the court areas, and changed only slightly or not at all in the other three. The clear decreases were in the Horseferry Road court area (from 18% in 1993 to 11% in 1994), and in the Leicester court area (from 20% in 1993 to 12% in 1994). The proportion of persons *charged with offences committed on court bail* showed similar decreases: in Horseferry Road area from 22% to 16%, and in Leicester, from 24% to 16%.

The analyses suggest that offending on bail decreased in the Horseferry Road area because more persons were remanded in custody (the custody rates increased by six percentage points between 1993 and 1994). Leicester showed a different picture in that the custody rates went down by about five percentage points. This suggests that the reduction in offending on bail in Leicester may have been caused by some of the improvements made, such as better access to defendant's bail history, or an increased emphasis on the training of magistrates in the assessment of risk.

The analyses also showed that the rates of offending while on police bail after charge (as measured by convictions) showed a small decrease overall from 9% to 8%. There were small decreases in three areas, between two and three percentage points, no change in Newport and a small increase in Bournemouth. Bournemouth and Salford showed the lowest rates for offending on police bail (between 5% and 8%): for Salford this is probably explained by the fact that this area was found to have a much higher rate of police custody after charge (see Chapter 4).

The rates of offending on police bail as measured by charges showed a similar pattern with slightly higher figures. Over all areas, the rates changed from 12% in 1993 to 11% in 1994.

An exercise was carried out with bail decision-makers in Leicester to explore their approach to assessing risk. This established a set of factors which were held to be important, and explored how these were seen to be related to the assessment of the risk of the defendant failing to appear at court and the risk of offending while on bail (see Tables 3.1 and 3.2).

The case tracking data were analysed to explore which categories of defendant were associated with higher and lower than average rates of offending on court bail. Those with higher rates included defendants:

- with no fixed abode (42% offended on bail)
- charged with car theft or burglary (32%, 29% respectively offended on bail)
- who waited more than six months before trial (32% or more than three months (24%)
- aged 17 and under (29%)
- who had served a previous custodial sentence (28%)
- who had a previous record of breaching bail (27%)
- who were unemployed (21%).

Those with lower rates were those:

- who waited less than a month before trial (4%)
- who were in employment (7%)
- who were charged with assault (7%) or fraud (8%)
- who were 21 or over (13%).

(Rates for combinations of these factors are shown in Table 5.3.)

The Bail Process Project arose from concern about the extent of offending on bail. In 1992, there was a great deal of public discussion of the issue when three police forces published a range of figures from surveys carried out in their own areas, and the Home Office published results from its internal research. The then Home Secretary gave an undertaking to Parliament to tackle this issue by setting up pilot projects in selected local areas. The intention was to improve the quality of the information available to the courts to assist them in identifying these defendants who were most likely to offend on bail.

This commitment led to a steering committee being set up which included representatives from all the relevant criminal justice agencies, ie the police, the Crown Prosecution Service (CPS), the magistrates' courts, the probation service and the Law Society. The committee was to tackle two main tasks:

- to investigate what information was required by remand decision-makers, and in what ways the information available was judged to be deficient
- to explore ways of remedying these deficiencies and, where possible, to put these remedies into effect.

Background: who makes pre-trial decisions

In England and Wales, the majority of decisions about the granting of bail before trial arise at three points: when a suspect has been arrested by the police but the evidence available is not sufficient for charges to be brought; when a suspect has been arrested and charged with an offence; and when the court has decided to adjourn the hearing of a case to another date. The first two of these decisions are made by the police: the third is made by magistrates.

(At page 60:)

To avoid unnecessary remands in custody, and to reduce offending on bail, magistrates must target the two out of three (in the highest risk group) and the one in 16 in the lowest risk group. Such targeting might be based on information over and above the broader categories described: perhaps more detail of the current offence and how it relates to the criminal record to indicate a pattern of offending, an indication of the attitude of the defendant, and any circumstances or influences which may have a positive affect on future behaviour. However, even if such information were available, there is no guarantee that accurate predictions of offending would be possible. Another relevant factor is the waiting time before trial: the research has shown that longer waiting times are related to higher offending on bail. This suggests that, if changes in procedure or practice can be devised to reduce the waiting times for defendants on bail, there should be a corresponding reduction in offending on bail. Broad estimates suggest that a reduction in waiting times of around one month should correspond to a decrease of three per cent in offending on bail.

[6:10] Eaton, M, 'The Question of Bail'

In Carlen, P and Worrall, A (eds), *Gender, Crime and Justice* (1987) Open UP (at page 106)

Throughout the process of summary justice a model of the family is employed when dealing with both men and women defendants. This model, with a male breadwinner and a dependant woman, responsible for child-care and domestic labour, is used in pleas of mitigation and social inquiry reports. The same model also underlies current legislation on taxation and benefits and traditional policies in providing for and responding to the family. It is a model based on a sexual division of labour which has consequences for women in both waged and domestic labour. For many women it means deprivation and isolation.

In the labour market, men may expect to earn a 'family wage' since it is assumed that their earnings provide for others. Women find that the jobs available to them do not offer the same earnings. In 1982 the average full time wage for a woman was 72% of a man's wage. Women in part-time work, who constitute two-fifths of the female labour force were even worse off; their hourly rate in 1982 was, on average, 57% of the hourly rate paid to men in full-time work. As part-time workers these women have fewer rights to sick pay, holiday pay or pensions. While many married women work to keep the family above the poverty line, they are usually unable to claim for dependants if they become unemployed. Domestic responsibilities bring long hours of work for most women. One survey revealed that women with young children worked an average of seventy-seven hours a week—nearly twice as long as an industrial working week of forty hours. Child-care and housework are still assumed to be the woman's work even if she has paid employment outside the home. The choice facing many women is the 'double shift' of paid employment and domestic labour, or the isolation and lower income of full-time housework.

Isolation is not just the result of the social organisation of housework. It is also a consequence of the traditions of privacy which surround the family. The same attitude is manifest in police reluctance to respond to instances of wife assault. Those relegated to the domestic sphere are most vulnerable to the abuse of power within that sphere. Even where women do not suffer physical abuse, mental illness may be a response to the conflicting demands placed on them. Depression is more likely among women involved full-time in housework than it is among unmarried women and married women with jobs outside the home.

Within the family women are vulnerable to violence, depression and poverty and for these reasons it has been the subject of much feminist critique. Only by questioning the position of women within this structure is there any challenge to the continual subordination of women—a subordination learned and reconstituted daily within the family. Of course courts do not question the gender roles of women within the family—these are accepted as normal and natural. They are implicit in the model of family which underlies pleas of mitigation and social inquiry reports, as they are in applications for bail. But applications for bail go further than other examples of courtroom rhetoric. In applications for bail we have more than a description of an acceptable model of the family and its associated gender roles: we have an acknowledgement that such a family structure may offer a form of control comparable to that offered by the prison system.

[6:11] Worrall, A, 'Sisters in Law? Women Defendants and Women Magistrates'

In Carlen, P and Worrall, A (eds), *Gender, Crime and Justice* (1987) Open UP (at page 122)

This chapter has attempted to demonstrate that the relationship between magistrates and defendants is constructed within a discourse of common sense which, despite its inherent paradoxes and discontinuities, is represented as a consistent and coherent unity. Although magisterial common sense may appear to challenge and transgress 'expert' discourse, it is in fact a competing discourse of 'expertise'. In relation to women defendants, it is characterised by a threefold myth:

1 That magistrates can never claim to know anything about women defendants because knowledge accrues through experience and women defendants are always already invisible and inaccessible to the senses.

2 That magistrates can never generalise about women defendants *qua* women, because the law is blind to differences of gender (as of class, age, race etc.).

3 That magistrates can always reach a consensus about women defendants both because of and despite social, economic, political or, specifically, gender differences, these differences being hailed (at the point of recruitment to the Bench) and denied (at the point of judgement) in the interests of justice.

These judicial myths have been challenged, and it has been argued that magistrates construct the woman defendant within specific conditions:

1 They act 'as though' they have knowledge of women defendants, that knowledge emanating from cultural stereotypes of appropriate female behaviour and being reinforced by their own socially and discursively privileged personal life experience.

2 They invoke the ostensibly gender-neutral moral concept of *merit* to justify treating women defendants *qua* women differently from male defendants, since meritorious conduct in men and women is differentially defined.

It has been argued, additionally, that women magistrates suppress their empathetic understanding of women's positions in society (an empathy based on shared biological experience) because, having entered the masculine world of the criminal justice system by virtue of their womanhood, their ability to sustain their authority and credibility within it is dependent on their denial of that womanhood.

Nevertheless, in this chapter I have sought to demonstrate that there may exist the potential for a greater understanding of women defendants by the magistracy, if women magistrates felt more confident—and were allowed—to express their genuinely differing perspectives and opinions. The structure for such a richness and variety of contribution exists; what is lacking is the will to experience the discomfort of conflict, especially when the mechanism for achieving an apparent consensus—the appeal to, and of, common sense—is so readily available. Women magistrates, like women defendants, are socially constructed within the discourses of domesticity, sexuality and pathology. The evidence of this chapter suggests that they may indeed be 'sisters in law', subject to a common oppression but not yet able to fully recognise each other.

[6:12] Bail (Amendment) Act 1993 (as amended)

Section 1

1 Prosecution right of appeal

(1) Where a magistrates' court grants bail to a person who is charged with or convicted of an offence punishable by imprisonment the prosecution may appeal to a judge of the Crown Court against the granting of bail.

(1A) Where a magistrates' court grants bail to a person in connection with extradition proceedings, the prosecution may appeal to [the High Court] 1 against the granting of bail.

(2) Subsection (1) above applies only where the prosecution is conducted—

(a) by or on behalf of the Director of Public Prosecutions; or

(b) by a person who falls within such class or description of person as may be prescribed for the purposes of this section by order made by the Secretary of State.

(3) Such an appeal under subsection (1) or (1A) may be made only if—

(a) the prosecution made representations that bail should not be granted; and

(b) the representations were made before it was granted.

(4) In the event of the prosecution wishing to exercise the right of appeal set out in subsection (1) or (1A) above, oral notice of appeal shall be given to the magistrates' court at the conclusion of the proceedings in which such bail has been granted and before the release from custody of the person concerned.

(5) Written notice of appeal shall thereafter be served on the magistrates' court and the person concerned within two hours of the conclusion of such proceedings.

(6) Upon receipt from the prosecution of oral notice of appeal from its decision to grant bail the magistrates' court shall remand in custody the person concerned, until the appeal is determined or otherwise disposed of.

(7) Where the prosecution fails, within the period of two hours mentioned in subsection (5) above, to serve one or both of the notices required by that subsection, the appeal shall be deemed to have been disposed of.

(8) The hearing of an appeal under subsection (1) above against a decision of the magistrates' court to grant bail shall be commenced within forty-eight hours, excluding weekends and any public holiday (that is to say, Christmas Day, Good Friday or a bank holiday), from the date on which oral notice of appeal is given.

(9) At the hearing of any appeal by the prosecution under this section, such appeal shall be by way of re-hearing, and the judge hearing any such appeal may remand the person concerned in custody or may grant bail subject to such conditions (if any) as he thinks fit.

(10) In relation to a child or young person (within the meaning of the Children and Young Persons Act 1969)—

(a) the reference in subsection (1) above to an offence punishable by a term of imprisonment is to be read as a reference to an offence which would be so punishable in the case of an adult; and

(b) the reference in subsection (5) above to remand in custody is to be read subject to the provisions of section 23 of the Act of 1969 (remands to local authority accommodation).

(11) The power to make an order under subsection (2) above shall be exercisable by statutory instrument and any instrument shall be subject to annulment in pursuance of a resolution of either House of Parliament.

(12) In this section—

"extradition proceedings" means proceedings under the Extradition Act 2003;

"magistrates' court" and "court" in relation to extradition proceedings means a District Judge (Magistrates' Courts) designated in accordance with section 67 or section 139 of the Extradition Act 2003;

"prosecution" in relation to extradition proceedings means the person acting on behalf of the territory to which extradition is sought.

[6:13] *Practice Direction: Crown Court: Bail Pending Appeal*
[1983] 1 WLR 1292

1 The procedure is described in the *Guide to Proceedings in the Court of Appeal Criminal Division*. This is available at Crown Courts and is to be found at (1983) 77 Cr App Rep 138 and [1983] Crim LR 415.

2 The procedure is also set out in outline on Criminal Appeal Office Forms C (Crown Court Judge's Certificate of fitness for appeal) and BC (Crown Court Judge's Order granting bail), copies of which are held by the Crown Court. The court clerk will ensure that these forms are always available when a judge hears an application under these provisions.

3 The judge may well think it right: (a) to hear the application in chambers with a shorthand-writer present; (b) to invite the defendant's counsel to submit before the hearing of the application a draft of the grounds which he will ask the judge to certify on Form C.
  Counsel for the Crown will be better able to assist the judge at the hearing if the draft ground is sent beforehand to him also.

4 The first question is whether there exists a particular, and cogent, ground of appeal. If there is no such ground there can be no certificate, and if there is no certificate there can be no bail. A judge should not grant a certificate with regard to sentence merely in the light of mitigation to which he has, in his opinion, given due weight, nor in regard to conviction on a ground where he considers the chance of a successful appeal is not substantial. The judge should bear in mind that, where a certificate is refused, application may be made to the Court of Appeal for leave to appeal and for bail.

5 The length of the period which might elapse before the hearing of the appeal is *not* a ground of appeal appropriate to the judge's certificate.

6 That period, if there is otherwise good ground for a certificate, may be one factor in the decision whether or not to grant bail; but a judge who is minded to take this factor into account may find it advisable to have the court clerk contact the Criminal Appeal Office Listing Co-ordinator in order that he may have an accurate and up-to-date assessment of the likely waiting time. The Co-ordinator will require a general account of the weight and urgency of the case.

7 Where the defendant's representative considers the bail should be applied for as a matter of urgency the application should normally be made, in the first instance, to the trial judge, and the Court of Appeal may decline to treat such an application as urgent if there is no good reason why it has not been made to the trial judge.

[6:14] Brown, S, *Magistrates at Work: Sentencing and Social Structure*
(1991) Open UP (at page 81)

The processes of classification and translation themselves both help to create and sustain a rendering of reality in which the individual case may be diagnosed, a pathology created, a 'solution' proposed, and which in its very individuality indicates a relationship with the overall corpus of unruly youth. This offender is situated in relation to that offender; this one is not a lost cause, that one is a hardened offender. Similarly one penalty implies the whole hierarchy of penalties. Through the whole business of processing juveniles, very little attention is paid by participating actors to the *validity* of the social background representations invoked.

No desire is shown to understand the meaning of the offence from the child's point of view; rather the child must account for it in the court's terms (Why did you do it? Did you know it was wrong?). Little interest is shown in whether locking children up in detention centres actually has an effect on behaviour, few questions are asked as to whether or not the whole package of an escalating penalty may not successively reinforce the likelihood of the juvenile's being re-introduced into the 'system'.

The emphasis is on describability. The individual is transposed into a set of knowledge representations which are comprehensible not with reference to the actual lived experience and actions of the individual but rather with reference to the instrumentality of those representations: what it is that they enable, and what it is that they preclude. In this sense, Shaun, and Ian, and Nicola, and Michelle themselves, are irrelevant to the juvenile court; 'social information' does not refer to them as people but to the project of the juvenile court in reconstructing them as information objects, entities amenable to processing. Social information simplifies individuals and reduces them to docile figures on sheets of paper.

Thus classification takes away the actual individuality of defendant and the circumstances of his or her life and replaces it with a spurious individuality consisting of a series of attributes capable of judgment; Law's 'docile figures'. The potentially most unruly of the resources is the juvenile her or himself, hence their particular insertion into the business of sentencing. The simultaneous enrolment and silencing of the child is both an expression of, and necessary to, the effective deployment of power.

(At page 104:)

Magistrates control a diffuse and potentially all inclusive discourse through the operation of the socialised tariff. They exercise a real power which is based on their ability to invoke social information categories in support of decisions which in the end rest upon their powers of judgment:

> It's just a question of judgment, really, you learn by experience.
> I think a lot of lady magistrates . . . you do things by your intuition.
> We're not social workers. We have to use our common sense.
> It all comes down to . . . judgment really in the end.

The control over imprecise concepts which the use of social information involves ensures that any challenge to that judgment is particularly difficult. The structure of the bifurcatory tariff is a distinct advantage in the successful exercise of discretionary power, because it creates a facility of categories—a continuum of salvability to incorrigibility—which justifies the use of social data. In providing the heuristic mechanism by which magistrates allocate offenders on that always already existing bifurcatory slope, control indicators are techniques of power.

(Ir)rationality and the problem of decision making in the juvenile court

Ultimately, however, the techniques of power of the socialised tariff are enabled by the fundamental irrationality which characterises the most liberal of juvenile courts. The vagueness of the decision concepts with which justices have to work (good/bad home backgrounds etc) are symptomatic of the lack of substantive rationality in the decision environment within which they work. Strictly speaking, substantive rationality ends the moment when it ceases to be possible to make a computation of the type 'if x, then y' (March and Simon 1970). Even allowing that this is an ideal type rather than something which can be fully realised in most decision situations, it is clear that the magisterial task could never remotely approximate rationality. Rationality demands that goals can be clearly defined, that the means to achieve desired goals can be spelt out and that the means to achieve the desired goals are available to the decision maker.

Magistrates are faced with a highly complex decision environment since ostensibly their goal is to alter the behaviour of human beings. The goal of 'trying to prevent re-offending', 'to protect the public' or 'to help pull him back from the edge' are so diffuse as to create a good deal of uncertainty. This is without even beginning to think about the complexities of not just stopping offending behaviour but reforming a person. Such goals defy clear definition, (What is a 'useful citizen'? What is 'normal'?) let alone the formulation of sensible means to achieve them. There is no possibility of magistrates achieving the kind of global behavioural control which is connoted by such aspirations; there is certainly no 'cure' for juvenile offending which can be achieved through magisterial powers.

[6:15] *Magistrates' Association Sentencing Guide for Criminal Offences*
(2004 edition)

Criminal Damage Act 1971 s.1 Triable either way or summarily only. Consult legal adviser Penalty: Either way – Level 5 and/or 6 months Summarily – Level 4 and/or 3 months	**Criminal damage**

CONSIDER THE SERIOUSNESS OF THE OFFENCE
(INCLUDING THE IMPACT ON THE VICTIM)

GUIDELINE: → **IS DISCHARGE OR FINE APPROPRIATE?**

IS IT SERIOUS ENOUGH FOR A COMMUNITY PENALTY?

IS IT SO SERIOUS THAT ONLY CUSTODY IS APPROPRIATE?

ARE YOUR SENTENCING POWERS SUFFICIENT?

THIS IS A GUIDELINE FOR A FIRST-TIME OFFENDER PLEADING NOT GUILTY

GUIDELINE FINE – STARTING POINT C

 ## CONSIDER AGGRAVATING AND MITIGATING FACTORS AND THE WEIGHT TO ATTACH TO EACH

for example	for example
Deliberate Group offence Serious damage Targeting Vulnerable victim *This list is not exhaustive*	Impulsive action Minor damage Provocation *This list is not exhaustive*

If offender is on bail, this offence is more serious
If offender has previous convictions, their relevance and any failure to respond to previous sentences should be considered – they may increase the seriousness. The court should make it clear, when passing sentence, that this was the approach adopted.

TAKE A PRELIMINARY VIEW OF SERIOUSNESS, THEN CONSIDER OFFENDER MITIGATION

for example
Age, health (physical or mental)
Co-operation with police
Evidence of genuine remorse
Voluntary compensation

CONSIDER YOUR SENTENCE

Compare it with the suggested guideline level of sentence and reconsider your reasons carefully if you have chosen a sentence at a different level. Consider a reduction for a timely guilty plea.

DECIDE YOUR SENTENCE
NB. COMPENSATION – Give reasons if not awarding compensation

Theft	Theft Act 1968 s.1 Triable either way – see Mode of Trial Guidelines Penalty: Level 5 and/or 6 months May disqualify where committed with reference to the theft or taking of a vehicle

CONSIDER THE SERIOUSNESS OF THE OFFENCE
(INCLUDING THE IMPACT ON THE VICTIM)

IS DISCHARGE OR FINE APPROPRIATE?

GUIDELINE: ➔   *IS IT SERIOUS ENOUGH FOR A COMMUNITY PENALTY?*

IS IT SO SERIOUS THAT ONLY CUSTODY IS APPROPRIATE?

ARE YOUR SENTENCING POWERS SUFFICIENT?

THIS IS A GUIDELINE FOR A FIRST-TIME OFFENDER PLEADING NOT GUILTY

 CONSIDER AGGRAVATING AND MITIGATING FACTORS AND THE WEIGHT TO ATTACH TO EACH

for example

> High value
> Planned
> Sophisticated
> Adult involving children
> Organised team
> Related damage
> Vulnerable victim
> *This list is not exhaustive*

for example

> Impulsive action
> Low value
> *This list is not exhaustive*

If racially or religiously aggravated, or offender is on bail, this offence is more serious
If offender has previous convictions, their relevance and any failure to respond to previous
sentences should be considered – they may increase the seriousness. The court should make
it clear, when passing sentence, that this was the approach adopted.

TAKE A PRELIMINARY VIEW OF SERIOUSNESS, THEN CONSIDER OFFENDER MITIGATION

for example
> Age, health (physical or mental)
> Co-operation with police
> Evidence of genuine remorse
> Voluntary compensation

CONSIDER YOUR SENTENCE

Compare it with the suggested guideline level of sentence and reconsider
your reasons carefully if you have chosen a sentence at a different level.
Consider a reduction for a timely guilty plea.

DECIDE YOUR SENTENCE
NB. COMPENSATION – Give reasons if not awarding compensation

Wounding – grievous bodily harm	Offences Against the Person Act 1861 s. 20 Triable either way – see Mode of Trial Guidelines Penalty: Level 5 and/or 6 months

CONSIDER THE SERIOUSNESS OF THE OFFENCE
(INCLUDING THE IMPACT ON THE VICTIM)

IS DISCHARGE OR FINE APPROPRIATE?

IS IT SERIOUS ENOUGH FOR A COMMUNITY PENALTY?

IS IT SO SERIOUS THAT ONLY CUSTODY IS APPROPRIATE?

GUIDELINE: → **ARE YOUR SENTENCING POWERS SUFFICIENT?**

THIS IS A GUIDELINE FOR A FIRST-TIME OFFENDER PLEADING NOT GUILTY

 ## CONSIDER AGGRAVATING AND MITIGATING FACTORS AND THE WEIGHT TO ATTACH TO EACH

for example	for example
Abuse of trust (domestic setting)	Minor wound
Deliberate kicking/biting	Provocation
Extensive injuries	*This list is not exhaustive*
Group action	
Offender in position of authority	
On hospital/medical or school premises	
Premeditated	
Prolonged assault	
Victim particularly vulnerable	
Victim serving the public	
Weapon	
This list is not exhaustive	

If offender is on bail, this offence is more serious

If offender has previous convictions, their relevance and any failure to respond to previous sentences should be considered – they may increase the seriousness. The court should make it clear, when passing sentence, that this was the approach adopted.

TAKE A PRELIMINARY VIEW OF SERIOUSNESS, THEN CONSIDER WHETHER THE CASE SHOULD BE COMMITTED FOR SENTENCE, THEN CONSIDER OFFENDER MITIGATION

for example

Age, health (physical or mental)

Co-operation with police

Evidence of genuine remorse

Voluntary compensation

CONSIDER COMMITTAL OR YOUR SENTENCE

Compare it with the suggested guideline level of sentence and reconsider your reasons carefully if you have chosen a sentence at a different level. Consider a reduction for a timely guilty plea.

DECIDE YOUR SENTENCE

NB. COMPENSATION – Give reasons if not awarding compensation

[6:16] Henham, R, 'Bargain Justice or Justice Denied? Sentence Discounts and the Criminal Process'

[1999] MLR 515 (at page 524)

Conclusions and implications

It was assumed from the outset that in order to fully understand the operation of sentence discounts in the Crown Court the following (apparently) straightforward questions needed to be answered:

(1) did the guilty plea produce a sentence discount?

(2) what explanation was given for the sentence discount by the judge?

(3) how was the sentence discount actually reflected in the sentence?

As explained in the opening section, numerous studies (including most recently Flood-Page and Mackie) have dealt with the third question but no previous attempt has been made to monitor the operation and effectiveness of section 48 of the Criminal Justice and Public Order Act 1994 on the criminal process. In addition to its overtly crime control function of reducing the number of 'cracked trials', the section should have provided greater transparency to a process with fundamental due process and human rights implications, through improving our understanding of how the judiciary deal with the first two questions stated above in the actual sentence decision-making process. However, as we have seen, it appears a substantial minority of judges are not only failing to provide an explanation of the basis of the discount, they are not stating it at all.

There are also two areas of particular difficulty concerning the ambit of section 48 which need to be addressed. The first is that section 48 imposes no obligation on the sentencer to state the fact of a guilty plea or explain further the implications of this for any sentence discount. The second problem is that no obligation lies on the sentencer under section 48 to declare that *no* sentence discount has been given or to explain further the basis upon which such a decision has been reached. The consequences are that in these two situations in particular, we may have no idea of the sentencer's rationale in each case, unless he or she chooses to elaborate this further. It will be recalled that for the purposes of this research, it was suggested that failure to elaborate on the reasons for allowing a sentence discount when the sentencer had taken the positive step of stating that credit would be given for a guilty plea (but going no further) should be regarded as a breach of section 48(2). These ambiguities and anomalies and the convoluted language of the section are exacerbated by what appear as logical flaws in its conception relating to the sentence decision-making process. For example, the reference in section 48(1)(b) to 'the circumstances in which' the plea indication was given is specifically related to the timing of the plea in section 48(1)(a) rather than with wider concerns which may together be instrumental in deciding on the extent of any sentence discount allowed. The study found that other mitigating factors were present in 51 per cent of cases where circumstances other than the timing of the plea were referred to.

One approach to dealing with the difficulties referred to is to recast the wording of the section in its entirety as follows:

48. Reduction in sentences for guilty pleas

(1) In determining what sentence to pass on an offender who has pleaded guilty to an offence in proceedings before that or another court a court shall take into account:

   (a) the fact that the defendant has pleaded guilty

   (b) the stage in the proceedings when the offender indicated his intention to plead guilty

   (c) the extent to which the offender has shown remorse for the offence

   (d) the extent to which the offender co-operated with the Police and (or) the Crown Prosecution Service before he indicated his intention to plead guilty

(e) the extent to which the guilty plea has avoided the time and expense of a trial

(f) the extent to which the victim(s) and (or) witness(es) have been spared the ordeal of a trial

(2) If factors other than those referred to in subsection (1) above are taken into account by the court they shall be stated in open court.

(3)(a) If, as a result of taking into account any matter referred to in subsections (1) and (2) above, the court imposes a punishment which is less severe than the punishment it would otherwise have imposed, it shall state in open court that it has does so and explain its effect to the offender in ordinary language.

(b) If, having taken into account any matter referred to in subsections (1) and (2) above, the court decides not to impose a sentence which is less severe than that which it otherwise considers appropriate, it shall state this fact in open court and explain its effect to the offender in ordinary language.

It is apparent from the re-wording that the objective in section 48(1) and (2) is to ensure that the sentencer is forced to articulate the rationale for the sentence discount from a wider range of potentially relevant factors than exist under the present section, including where the discount has been given simply on the basis of the plea itself. Moreover, by virtue of the re-cast section 48(3)(b) the sentencer would be forced to state and explain why no sentence discount had been given at all.

There are, however, other areas where more specific guidance from the Court of Appeal is required. Firstly, the position regarding offences taken into consideration ('tics') and sentence discounts remains unclear, and secondly, and more importantly, it is unclear whether courts are consistently following the Court's advice in *Fearon* that a plea discount should be given irrespective of the strength of the prosecution case or continuing to apply the fifth exception in *Costen* regardless. Such guidance could, of course, follow a recommendation from the newly constituted Sentencing Advisory Panel established by section 81 of the Crime and Disorder Act 1998, but any initiative to clarify the courts approach to the application of section 48 should preferably emanate from the Court of Appeal itself which must, in any event, also have regard (inter alia) to the need to promote consistency in sentencing and the need to promote public confidence in the criminal justice system. It was, in fact, following the Government decision *not* to implement Chapter 1 of Part II of the Crime (Sentences) Act 1997 that the Lord Chief Justice issued a Practice Direction requiring sentencers to explain fully the effect of custodial sentences as part of a campaign to restore public confidence in sentencing. I would submit that the need for greater transparency in the operation of sentence discounts highlighted by this research could be adequately met by a similar practice direction from the Lord Chief Justice directed towards ensuring that sentencers not only make it clear that a sentence discount has been given, but that they also explain fully the reasons for it and state the precise effect of the discount on the sentence.

Nevertheless, Ashworth has convincingly argued that more fundamental reform of the system of sentence discounts is necessary principally on the basis that it openly contravenes a number of fundamental rights and freedoms enshrined in the European Convention of Human Rights; namely, the presumption of innocence, the privilege against self-incrimination, the right to equality of treatment and the right to a fair and public hearing. Ashworth also supports a reappraisal of the whole system of guilty pleas and suggests that either complete abolition or major changes in criminal procedure could produce a fairer system for both victims and witnesses. It is certainly true, as Fenwick points out, that victims currently have no right to participate in decisions to accept a guilty plea in return for a sentence discount or to accept a plea to a lesser charge. Hence, the victim's likely desire that the trial should proceed without the offer of a sentence discount may be ignored. Such a result may be regarded as detrimental since victims (actual and potential) clearly have an interest in seeing a true offender convicted. Further, some victims may prefer the ordeal of a court appearance to seeing the defendant receive a light sentence as a result of a sentence discount, whether graduated or not. Past support for plea discounts and the crime control ideology, with its emphasis on financial constraint, speed and finality of conviction, has been on the basis that it is broadly in the interests of victims because it spares victims the ordeal of giving evidence whilst recognising that due process rights such as the right to a fair and public hearing may be infringed and some innocent defendants may be induced to plead guilty. Fenwick is surely correct in suggesting that the perceptions of victims towards this process are actually more complex and that there is a case for establishing rights of consultation and participation in those decisions, at least for victims of serious offences.

Although cogent arguments for reform of the guilty plea system undoubtedly exist, in the short-term this research has highlighted the pressing need for increased guidance to Crown Court judges and the need for more information to be made available to defendants on the implications of the choices they make, and to victims, witnesses and the public at large, on the real consequences of the guilty plea. The research has indicated that, although the strategic policy goals of sentence discounts are being achieved, the rationale and extent of discount decisions (via section 48) are not being articulated consistently by the courts. This failure is compounded by the fact that there appear to exist unjustifiable differences between sentence discounts for different offences, differences in regional and judicial practice and cogent reasons to support a gradual reduction in the amount of the discount itself. I submit that there is consequently an urgent need for section 48 of the Criminal Justice and Public Order Act 1994 to be amended along the lines suggested to correct its manifest weaknesses; for the Lord Chief Justice to issue a practice direction on the correct approach to the use of sentence discounts by the Crown Court; for additional judicial training to reinforce the need for consistency of approach and transparency in decision-making, and for increased Court of Appeal guidance on sentence discounts (following consideration of the issue by the Sentencing Advisory Panel) to rationalise their effect as between different offences.

CHAPTER SEVEN

TRIAL JUDGES

An English judge controls a criminal trial in the Crown Court in some ways as a referee supervises a boxing match. The two sides battle it out, and he (or she, of course) stands by to check that neither side breaks the rules. But this simplistic comparison hides the fact that the judge is a powerful referee, whose decisions may often affect the outcome of the trial. It also misses the point that the two sides are not well balanced as they might be in a boxing match: the defence have fewer powers of investigation, but a great deal at stake. In our case, Gerry Good is charged with an offence under the Offences Against the Person Act 1861 (OAPA 1861), section 18. He is to be tried before a judge and jury. The role of the judge is clearly crucial to the conduct and outcome of the proceedings.

Gerry Good has been on bail. Before the case comes on for trial there will have been a plea and case management hearing (PCMH) at the Crown Court. The indictment was put to him by the clerk, and he lodged a plea of not guilty. The prosecution and defence (very likely not the lawyers who will appear at trial), though the Legal Services Commission are trying to improve continuity through funding arrangements) will have helped the judge identify key issues in the case and agreed time limits for the disclosure of documents. The case will then have been listed for trial.

On the day the trial is listed to start, Gerry Good arrives at court at 9 am in order to meet his barrister, Tim Moffat. Perhaps the judge has to deal with other matters first (a sentencing case adjourned for a pre-sentence report after a trial a few weeks previously, or perhaps another PCMH at 10 am), so Gerry's case may not come on until 11 am. Between 10 am and 11 am the lawyers involved may try unsuccessfully to bargain a guilty plea (see Chapter 5: even a late guilty plea wins some discount in sentence). The CPS applies to add an alternative count to the indictment:

Count One
Statement of Offence
Wounding with intent, contrary to section 18 of the Offences Against the Person Act 1861.

Particulars of Offence
Gerry Good on or about the 13th day of June 2007 unlawfully and maliciously wounded Rosa Bottles with intent to do her grievous bodily harm.

Count Two
Statement of Offence
Unlawful wounding, contrary to section 20 of the Offences Against the Person Act 1861.

Particulars of Offence

Gerry Good on or about the 13th day of June 2007 unlawfully and maliciously wounded Rosa Bottles.

Sometimes the defence ask the judge for an advance indication of likely sentence (if a defendant is assured, for example, that he won't go to prison if he pleads guilty, then he might change his plea even at this late stage: see (ii) below), but in our case Gerry maintains his not guilty plea. The jury is sworn (see Chapter 8). The judge takes a low profile throughout the trial. Counsel for the prosecution outlines his case to the jury and calls his witnesses: Rosa Bottles, the pub landlord, and two police officers. Witnesses will be examined by prosecution counsel, cross-examined by Gerry's counsel, and re-examined by prosecution counsel. The judge may interrupt to repeat a question or to ask the witness to go slower. She may intervene to stop inappropriate lines of questioning, but from Gerry Good's point of view, the judge seems unimportant until she makes her summing up to the jury. When she imposes the sentence, she moves to centre stage. However, in reality, she is highly influential on all the actors throughout the courtroom drama.

(i) WHO ARE THE TRIAL JUDGES?

The Crown Court sits at around 90 centres throughout England and Wales. For trial purposes in the Crown Court, offences are divided into four classes of seriousness. Although all those charged with indictable crimes are tried in the Crown Court, the more serious charges will be tried before a High Court judge, the least serious before a circuit judge or recorder (part-time judges, usually practising barristers or solicitors, who usually sit as a judge for between three and six weeks a year). The Circuit Bench was created by the Courts Act 1971 as part of a major reorganization of the criminal courts. Most judges were previously practising barristers, although since 1971 it has been possible for solicitors to sit as judges in the Crown Court. A barrister or solicitor of ten years' standing, or a Recorder who has held office for at least three years, can be appointed as a circuit judge. Thus, a solicitor may become a circuit judge after serving time as a Recorder. The Courts and Legal Services Act 1990 enabled suitably qualified solicitors to become High Court judges, and the first was appointed in 1993.

Until recently the appointment of judges was in the hands of the Government, but there have been significant changes in recent years to the selection process. Perhaps a turning point came in 1990 when the Lord Chancellor's Department issued a document explaining the system for the appointment of judges, reflecting an opening up of the recruitment process and indeed a commitment to seeking out a wider pool of applicants. Sir Leonard Peach's *Independent Scrutiny of the Appointment Processes of Judges and QCs* (1999) concluded that the process was thorough and competent, but recommended the creation of a Commissioner for Judicial Appointments with the duties of performing audits of procedures as well as carrying out the role of ombudsman for both judicial and Queen's Counsel appointments, and this was accepted. The Commissioner's post existed from 2001 until 2006, but in 2006 we saw more radical change. Uncertainty about the system of appointment had been reinforced by the Scottish High Court of Justiciary's decision in *Starrs v Procurator Fiscal* [2000] HRLR 191, where it was held that the use of temporary sheriffs, who conducted as many as 25 per cent of Scotland's criminal cases, contravened the European

Convention on Human Rights, Article 6 **[1:12]**. The court held that the appointment system failed to uphold judicial independence because temporary sheriffs' contracts were for only a year. They were hired and fired by the Lord Advocate, who, apart from being a member of the Scottish Government responsible for the legal system, is also head of the Scottish prosecution service. Lord Reed said that that did 'not square with the appearance of independence'. In 2000, the Lord Chancellor announced that 'no useful purpose' was served by having separate offices of recorder and assistant recorder. And in 2003 the Government announced that it would create a new Judicial Appointment Commission (JAC), recognizing that it was no longer acceptable for judicial appointments to be in the hands of a Government Minister. This was effected by the Constitutional Reform Act 2005, which heralded a new era in judicial appointments. The JAC started work in April 2006. It is too early to measure whether it will be effective in widening the 'range' of people appointed as judges: they have certainly devised a much more complicated and seemingly objective competition process: see <http://www.judicialappointments.gov.uk>.

TABLE 7.1 Numbers of judges

	Circuit judges	Recorders	Assistant recorders
1994	487 (28 women)	795 (42 women)	496 (51 women)
2000	561 (39 women)	907 (84 women)	446 (72 women)
2003	621 (50 women)	1,356 (50 women)	—
2007	639 (73 women)	1,201 (179 women)	—

In 2006, there were nine (1.4 per cent) circuit judges of ethnic minority origin, up from five (0.9 per cent) in 2003, and 54 (4.4 per cent) Recorders from ethnic minorities, up from 33 in 2003. Although the appointment system has been much criticized, it is only partly responsible for the narrow social and educational background of English judges, analysed most famously by Griffiths (1991) (see also Pannick (1987)). The conservatism of judges is also partly explained by the conservatism of many of those who choose to become lawyers in the first place.

The holder of the office of part-time judge or circuit judge has no special constitutional protection. Whilst the most senior judges—Law Lords, Lords Justices of Appeal, and High Court judges—can only be removed by the Queen after an address from both Houses of Parliament, other judges can be removed by the Lord Chief Justice for incapacity or misbehaviour. This is very rare, and in the case of a full-time serving judge needing to be removed, has happened just once, in 1983, when a circuit judge was removed from office after pleading guilty to several charges of smuggling. Recorders are usually appointed for at least five years, and they may not have their contracts renewed on the following grounds: misbehaviour; incapacity; persistent failure to comply with sitting requirements (without good reason); failure to comply with training requirements; sustained failure to observe the standards reasonably expected from a holder of such office; part of a reduction in numbers because of changes in operational requirements; and part of a structural change to enable recruitment of new appointees.

Defendants have little protection against an incompetent or unfair judge. Since 2006 they have been able to complain to the Judicial Appointments and Conduct Ombudsman if they believe a judge has acted unjudicially. It remains virtually impossible to sue a judge. Section

2(5) of the Crown Proceedings Act 1947 provides that the Crown cannot be sued for the tortious conduct of any person 'while discharging or purporting to discharge any responsibilities of a judicial nature vested in him'. Lord Denning's statements in *Sirros v Moore* **[7:1]** illustrate the extent of the judge's immunity from suit. The right of appeal against an incorrect decision is not always an adequate remedy, especially since justice is thereby both delayed and often costly. In *FM (a child) v Singer* [2004] EWHC 793 an 11-year-old child tried to sue a High Court judge for acting so as to 'harass, threaten or intimidate' him (in the context of a custody dispute between his parents) but the High Court struck out his claim following *Sirros v Moore*. There was no question of bad faith, and the judge was absolutely protected from being sued.

(ii) CASE MANAGEMENT AND SENTENCE BARGAINS

Judges today have an increasingly important 'case management' role. What does this mean in practice? See Rule 3 of the Criminal Procedure Rules 2005 (as amended) **[7:2]**. The Court of Appeal has also given stern advice to trial judges to try and get them to control proceedings effectively: see this attract from *R v Jisl* [2004] EWCA Crim 696 **[7:3]**. How does this fit in with traditional thoughts about the adversarial process (see **[1:4]**)?

One good example of the way the judge's role is changing is in plea bargaining. Plea and charge bargaining between the parties, prosecution, and defence was examined in Chapter 5. It can be seen as a form of sentence bargaining: if Gerry Good, or rather his solicitor or counsel, had persuaded the prosecution to drop the charge under section 18, he could have been fairly confident that, on a guilty plea to a charge under section 20, he would have received a lighter sentence than if he continued to fight the case. But here we are concerned with where the bargaining process goes one stage further, and the judge himself becomes involved in the discussions.

For many years, defendants pleading guilty have been regarded as entitled to a sentence discount of some 20–30 per cent, although the precise amount varied from judge to judge and from case to case (see *Buffrey* (1993) 14 Cr App R (S) 511); or *Claydon* (1993) 15 Cr App R (S) 526 where the Court of Appeal went so far as to say that where an offender voluntarily surrenders and confesses, a sentence discount of 50 per cent was appropriate. Then Parliament made a discount a statutory requirement: section 48 of the Criminal Justice and Public Order Act 1994 required all courts, when passing sentence, to take account of the timing and other circumstances of a plea of guilty. The current formula is found in section 144 of the Criminal Justice Act 2003. It was this Act too which created the Sentencing Guidelines Council (SGC) (see (v) below) and one of the first Guidelines issued by the SGC concerned the discount for guilty pleas. The issue remains controversial, and the SGC was asked to revise its guideline in 2007. **[7:4]** is an extract from the revised guideline.

Why is the discount controversial? As **[7:4]** makes clear, the discount is given not to reflect remorse (the defendant may get yet more discount for remorse) but as administrative convenience: the system could not cope if all defendants pleaded not guilty. Is there a danger that this discount may lead those who are not guilty to plead guilty? Zander and Henderson **[7:5]** present their findings without comment or evaluation, yet their question to the legally qualified participants in the trials they studied—on whether innocent people were pleading guilty—led some commentators to argue that perhaps 1,400 innocent people plead guilty in the Crown Court every year. However, the Royal Commission (1993) **[7:6]** believed that there was 'little if any' evidence that innocent people had pleaded guilty because of the sentence discount. But the important question is whether those who believe themselves to be innocent should be penalized for pleading not guilty.

Sentence bargains are particularly important where the defendant stands on the cusp of prison. Often he wants to know if he can be sure that, if he pleads guilty, he will avoid prison. This might well be so in the case of Gerry Good. He has several, relatively minor, previous convictions, and is now to be tried for intentional wounding (contrary to OAPA 1861, section 18). If he pleads guilty to malicious wounding (section 20), will he escape prison? For many years the Court of Appeal made it abundantly clear that there should not be informal discussions with judges on this subject: see *Turner* [1970] 2 QB 321 or *Dosseter* [1999] 2 Cr App R (S) 248 for clear examples of how the Court of Appeal discouraged unnecessary visits to the judge's room. Yet because of the cost, in terms of time and money, of cracked trials (those trials where the case is listed for trial before a jury, but on the day of the trial the defendant pleads guilty), the Royal Commission (1993) **[7:6]** recommended the partial reversal of *Turner*. It suggested that, at the request of defence counsel on instructions from the defendant, judges should be able to indicate the highest sentence that they would impose at that point, on the basis of the facts put to them. A request for such an indication might be made at a preparatory hearing called especially for this purpose, or at the trial itself. Lord Justice Auld **[1:5]** also concluded his analysis of this issue with a complex recommendation for a system of 'advance indication of sentence' for those considering pleading guilty, which should be fully recorded. The Court of Appeal took up this proposal themselves in what might be seen as the 'revolutionary' decision in *Goodyear* in 2005 **[7:7]**. What do you make of this decision? Does it reflect the 'systems' crime control mentality (re-read Packer at **[1:9]**)? The decision in *Goodyear* has been much criticized: an obvious danger with this approach is that the judge is being asked to speak with inadequate information, particularly when a pre-sentence report has not yet been prepared. *R v McDonald* **[7:8]** may lead to greater caution as the dangers of advance indications become more obvious. Perhaps the only way to relieve the pressure on the innocent to plead guilty would be to abolish the sentence discount for guilty pleas altogether. A 30 per cent discount for a plea is, after all, the equivalent of a 50 per cent increase in sentence for unsuccessfully maintaining a plea of not guilty. But for cost reasons, if no other, this proposal is highly improbable!

Another problem with both formal and informal systems of sentence discounting is that it is likely to be applied unevenly. The Royal Commission supported the policy recommended by Hood **[7:9]** of ethnic monitoring of all court outcomes. Hood provided evidence that the system of sentence discounts, combined with the tendency of Afro-Caribbean defendants to plead not guilty, put them at risk of being sentenced to longer sentences than their white peers. There is little reason to think that things are different today (see **[1:15]**).

(iii) THE JUDGE'S DISCRETION TO EXCLUDE EVIDENCE

Most evidence in court is given orally, although agreed written statements are increasingly admitted. This section only discusses the wide discretionary power of the trial judge to exclude evidence, but it should be noted that the law of evidence is deeply complex, even

more so since the reforms of the Criminal Justice Act 2003. Auld **[1:5]** called for the codification of the law of evidence. But, sadly, all that is offered in the Criminal Justice Act 2003 was
a number of hugely complex amendments to the existing law.

Judges rarely call witnesses themselves: Zander and Henderson's Crown Court study
(see **[7:5]**) found that in 19 per cent of cases judges reported that they knew of one or more
important witnesses who had not been called by either side. It is a reflection on the adversarial system (see **[1:4]**) that they do not see it as their function to call even a useful witness.
Perhaps, also, too much weight is given to the performance of individual witnesses, who
themselves are dependent on the questions of counsel for the answers they can give.

Decisions to exclude evidence may be taken at a pre-trial hearing to avoid the waste of
time and money which occurs when the jury have to be sent out during the trial for a *voire
dire* ('trial within a trial'), but usually the question is not dealt with until the trial itself. The
common law position (before the Police and Criminal Evidence Act 1984 (PACE)) on the
exclusion of evidence was summed up by Lord Goddard CJ in the Privy Council decision
Kuruma v R [1955] AC 197, at page 204:

In their Lordships' opinion, the test to be applied in considering whether evidence is admissible is
whether it is relevant to the matters in issue. If it is, it is admissible and the court is not concerned
with how the evidence was obtained...The judge always has a discretion to exclude evidence if the
strict rules of admissibility would operate unfairly against an accused...If, for instance, some piece of
evidence, e.g., a document, had been obtained from a defendant by a trick, no doubt the judge might
properly rule it out.

In that case, the Privy Council upheld the conviction of a man who had been sentenced to
death for the unlawful possession of two rounds of ammunition, after having been unlawfully searched by police officers below the authorized rank. Pre-PACE, the courts usually
left the disciplining of police officers to be performed through actions for damages, formal
complaints procedures, or by the occasional prosecution. We saw the inadequacies of these
mechanisms of accountability in Chapter 2.

Nowadays the courts are more likely to exclude evidence which has been obtained
improperly or illegally. The present law on the exclusion of evidence is to be found in sections 76(2) and 78 of PACE **[2:11]**. Read the sections carefully: at first sight, these sections
appear to be contradictory, one being mandatory, and the other discretionary. Examples of
excluded unfairly obtained evidence were given earlier in this book in *Loosely* **[2:17]** and in
Paris, Abdullahi and Miller **[5:5]**. The courts are involved in a difficult balancing act: supporting the police in the investigation of crime, yet upholding the integrity of the criminal
justice system. In *Christou* **[7:10]** the evidence gained by the police officers in an undercover
operation was acceptable and in *Bryce* **[7:11]** it was not. Can the cases be distinguished? The
law reports contain many other striking examples: in *Khan* **[7:12]** the House of Lords upheld
the trial judge's decision to admit evidence, despite the fact that the police were guilty of
a civil trespass and may have infringed the defendant's right to privacy by using an electronic listening device (a decision upheld by the European Court of Human Rights in *Khan
v United Kingdom* (2001) 31 EHRR 1016). See also *Chalkley and Jeffries* **[9:6]**). The other
example **[7:13]** we give here is the Court of Appeal's decision in *R v Davis; R v Ellis, Gregory,
Simms and Martin* [2006] EWCA Crim 1155 (taken from (2006) 6 Archbold News 3) on the
acceptability of using anonymous witnesses at a murder trial. Think hard about how you
would decide this case.

The Royal Commission on Criminal Justice (1993) was satisfied with the way that the
law was working, though Professor Zander's powerful dissent **[9:1]** is worth noting here.
The majority of the Royal Commission thought that the Court of Appeal's power to quash

convictions after breaches of PACE should be limited to cases where the jury's verdict was unsafe. But Zander stressed that the role of the Court of Appeal in promoting the observation of the crucial and complex network of the PACE rules is of the greatest importance. He believes that 'the majority would in effect be encouraging the Court of Appeal to undercut a part of [section 78]'s moral force by saying that the issue of "unfairness" can be ignored where there is sufficient evidence to show that the defendant is actually guilty' (at page 235). In Chapter 9 we return to the changes made to the powers of the Court of Appeal by the Criminal Appeal Act 1995 and the current debates.

The Royal Commission was unanimous in recommending the introduction of a rule similar to Rule 403 of the United States Federal Rules of Evidence, which empowers the judge to exclude evidence if 'although relevant, its probative value is substantially outweighed by the danger of unfair prejudice, confusion of the issues, or misleading the jury, or by considerations of undue delay, waste of time, or needless presentation of cumulative evidence'. The Commission believed that the introduction of such a rule would allow judges to be more 'robust' in preventing juries from having to sit through evidence that adds little or nothing to what is already before them. Thus, the power of the judge to control the issues that would go before the jury would be increased. Auld [1:5] on the other hand urged not only a codification of the law of evidence but also a simplification of the rules for excluding evidence on the grounds of its unfairness. What has happened since Auld is the codification not of the rues of evidence but of the secondary rules of criminal procedure (see the Criminal Procedure Rules at [7:2]). But we are still a long way from a general code of criminal procedure: a mass of different statutes apply.

(iv) THE SUMMING UP

After the evidence has been presented, and after the prosecution and defence have made their closing speeches, the judge sums up the case in order to help the jury in their task of reaching a verdict (the Judicial Studies Board's model directions to help judges to craft their summing ups are freely available at <http://www.jsboard.co.uk>: a useful student exercise is to have a go writing a summing up!).

Thus, the judge in Gerry Good's case, for example, will explain to the jury the burden and standard of proof and the respective roles of judge and jury. She will state that they may only convict if they are sure, or satisfied beyond reasonable doubt, of Gerry's guilt. She will then summarize the facts on which their decision is required, and give directions on relevant points of law. She will have to define to the jury the legal meaning of 'intent' in OAPA 1861, section 18 and explain the effect of Gerry's intoxication (if indeed he was intoxicated) on his 'intent'. She has to describe the relationship of section 18 with section 20 and explain the circumstances when the jury may bring in an alternative verdict. None of these factors are straightforward in English law: indeed, there has been a loud lobby for many years calling for a codification of the substantive criminal law (as well as of procedure and evidence), but this does not catch the politicians' imagination. Even in this simple case, the summing up is likely to last at least an hour. Should the jury be given a written copy? Judge Madge (2006) argues that written directions would help juries understand their task: it is difficult to disagree.

Should the judge be allowed to refer to the facts of the case? Even in a short case like Gerry Good's, the facts are rarely straightforward. Here, Gerry's account of his police interviews does not accord with that of the police. The jury have heard both sides of the case: can the judge present a balanced perspective to the jury? In the United States, where the summing up is known as the 'jury charge', the judge only gives the jury an explanation of the law, without reference to the facts. In England, the extent to which the judge comments on the facts is left to the discretion of the individual judge. In Gerry's case, the jury retire for a little over two hours, and return a verdict of not guilty to the section 18 offence, but guilty to the section 20 offence. Had they taken much longer, the judge would have had a discretion to allow a majority verdict (see Chapter 8).

(v) SENTENCING

After a jury brings in a verdict of guilty, the question of sentence is entirely decided by the judge. Where the defendant has pleaded not guilty, the facts will have been explored fully before the jury, before they reached their verdict. More difficult may be the case where the defendant has pleaded guilty, but where there is a wide divergence between the prosecution and defence on the facts. This is dramatically illustrated by the facts of *Newton* **[7:14]**, where the Lord Chief Justice explained the proper approach to be taken by a trial judge when dealing with the task of sentencing such a defendant. The facts of *Newton* will not arise again since consensual buggery is not a crime, but the issue is important. The trial judge may feel a pressure to accept the defendant's view of the facts, in order to save the added costs and delays of a 'trial within a trial' to establish contested facts. This can lead to a defendant being substantially under-sentenced. The guidance in *Newton* was 'updated' in *Underwood* **[7:15]**, in 2004, in which the Court if Appeal dealt with four different cases.

The statutory maximum for the offence in question is normally laid down in the statute creating the offence. Gerry was charged with an offence under section 18, but convicted of an offence under section 20, of the OAPA 1861. The Act originally laid down punishments of penal servitude, but it has been amended such that the maximum penalty for wounding with intent (contrary to section 18) is life imprisonment and the maximum penalty for wounding (contrary to section 20) is five years' imprisonment. Despite this wide theoretical difference, in practice, the normal sentencing bracket even for a section 18 offence is only three to eight years' imprisonment. Of course, when Parliament, as it sometimes does, increases the statutory maximum penalty for an offence (for example, the Criminal Justice Act 1993 raised the maximum penalty for causing death by dangerous driving from five to ten years; the Criminal Justice Act 2003 raised it further to 14 years), it may affect the normal sentencing bracket.

The statutory framework of judges' sentencing powers is similar to that discussed in the previous chapter on magistrates' powers—consolidated in the Powers of Criminal Courts (Sentencing) Act (PCC(S)A) 2000) but massively changed by the Criminal Justice Act (CJA) 2003. We noted there the role of the Sentencing Guidelines Council. The SGC arose out of a proposal of the *Halliday Report* (2001), which recommended a statutory guideline-setting body that would produce 'structured' and 'accessible' guidelines across the whole range of English sentencing law. It is chaired by the Lord Chief Justice and is made up of seven further judicial members and four non-judicial members. In addition, the Home Secretary (now the Minister of Justice) can appoint others to bring to the Council experience of sentencing policy and the administration of sentences. It has produced a wealth of sentencing guidelines for all criminal courts: courts when sentencing have a duty to have regard to them (section 172 of the CJA 2003; *Oosthuizen* [2005] EWCA Crim 1978, [2005] Crim LR 979). Browse the website (<http://www.sentencing-guidelines.gov.uk>) for definitive guidelines and the current consultations (to which you should respond!). Lord Carter was asked to investigate the long-term supply and demand for prison places and his Report (2007) recommended that a working group be set up to investigate further a 'structured sentencing framework and a permanent Sentencing Commission' (for a critical summary of this Report, see Padfield, 2007). The Minister of Justice has established this working group, under the chairmanship of Lord Justice Gage, and it will report later in 2008.

Perhaps the most controversial changes of the 2003 Act concerned the sentencing of 'dangerous' offenders. First, the Act lays down controversial provisions which establish a new scheme (at long last!) under which the court, rather than the Home Secretary determines the minimum term to be served in prison by a person convicted of murder in order to comply with the judgment of the European Court of Human Rights in *Stafford v United Kingdom* (2002) 35 EHRR 32, and the judgment of the House of Lords in *Anderson* [2003] 1 AC 837. But the Home Secretary seemed determined to have the last word: the length of this minimum term is determined by reference to the framework set out in Schedule 21. When setting a minimum term, the court must take into account three categories of starting point: a whole life order, 30 years, and 15 years. Those aged between 18 and 21 years may only be subject to the 30- and 15-year starting points. Juveniles may only be subject to a 12-year starting point. Once an offender has been allocated a starting point, the court must then consider aggravating and mitigating factors to arrive at a minimum term. The offender must serve the entirety of this minimum term before being considered for release by the Parole Board. This has greatly increased the length of time that murderers will serve. It also increases the disparity between the lengths of sentences served by murderers and those convicted of offences, such as attempted murder, who will be considered for release at the half-way point in their fixed length sentence. Once the minimum term has expired, the Parole Board will consider the person's suitability for release, and if appropriate, direct his release (see Chapter 10).

Even more controversial than the sentence for murder is the scheme of sentences for offenders who have been assessed as dangerous and have committed a specified sexual or violent offence. Where there is 'a significant risk' of 'serious harm' from future 'specified offences' likely to be committed by the offender the court now has only the choice between imposing a life sentence or imprisonment for public protection (see section 225). Imprisonment for public protection (IPP) is available even where the defendant has no previous convictions (section 229(2)). If the defendant has a previous conviction for a 'relevant offence' (most sexual or violent offences) then the court 'must assume' that there is a significant risk of future serious harm, unless the court considers that it would be 'unreasonable' to conclude that there is such a risk. This has led to a large increase in the number of people serving indeterminate sentences, and the Criminal Justice and Immigration Bill 2007 (being debated in Parliament as we go to press) will give judges more discretion to avoid the current statutory 'assumption'. The 2003 Act also introduced a new form of extended sentence: 'dangerous' offenders who have been convicted of a trigger sexual or violent offence (listed in Schedule 15) for which the maximum penalty is between two and ten years are given an extended sentence. This sentence is a determinate sentence served in custody to the half way point, with release during the whole of the second half of the sentence being on the recommendation of the Parole Board. In addition extended supervision periods of up to five years for violent offenders and eight years for sexual offenders must be added to the sentence.

So, in sentencing an offender, the judge will take account of the facts of the offence, the circumstances of the offender, and the plea in mitigation. In Gerry Good's case, the judge decides to adjourn the case for the preparation of a pre-sentence report (PSR). The judge must now decide whether or not to remand Gerry in custody pending sentence (see Chapter 6 for a discussion of bail). In the event, defence counsel having stressed the fact that Gerry has respected the terms of his conditional bail over the past few months, the judge continues his bail but warns him that although he is seeking a PSR, Gerry should anticipate a custodial sentence.

At the resumed hearing, counsel for the prosecution may call a police officer (the 'antecedents officer') to give details of Gerry Good's previous convictions, and he will ensure that the judge has a copy of the PSR. The role of defence counsel in presenting a plea in mitigation, and in deciding whether to call witnesses in support of the defendant's good character, was raised in Chapter 5. A court duty probation officer will be in court to speak, if necessary, to the pre-sentence report. The report on Gerry Good is included in Chapter 10. The judge gives Gerry Good a brief lecture on why she finds it impossible in this case to do other than impose an immediate custodial sentence. Stockdale (1967) questioned the value of such homilies: it is doubtful whether they have any general or particular deterrent effect—'a far more likely effect is a general and particular resentment, and sometimes a contempt for the court' (at page 34). But the judge does have a duty to explain the sentence, and to give reasons to explain his or her decision-making process. The task is no easy one: the audience is the public, the victim, the media, as well as the defendant. The Judicial Studies Board publishes model 'forms of words', which are available at <http://www.jsboard.co.uk/criminal_law/index.htm>.

This book is not a textbook on sentencing: several such are mentioned in the Further reading. But readers should be well aware of the complexity of the law. Gerry Good is eventually sentenced to two years in prison. Will he appeal? The Court of Appeal will only vary the sentence imposed at trial where it is 'manifestly excessive or wrong in principle' (Criminal Appeal Act 1968, section 2 **[9:4]**), and so the judge's discretion is rarely interfered with.

TABLE 7.2 Appeals against sentence

	Offenders sentenced in the Crown Court	Applications for leave to appeal against sentence	Successful appeals against sentence
1993	69,500	4,848	1,309
1998	80,400	6,550	1,589
2001	72,100	5,497	1,101
2006	77,000	5,082	1,391

Source: Judicial Statistics 2001; Table 1.8; Criminal Statistics 2001, Chapter 7; Sentencing Statistics 2006, Chapter 1; Judicial Statistics 2006, page 13

Two recent sentencing judgments of the Court of Appeal (Criminal Division) are included (**[7:13]** and **[7:14]**) to illustrate the sort of guidance available to the trial judge. Students should browse through electronic databases, or, even better, hard copies of the Criminal Appeal Reports (Sentencing). These serve as a useful reminder of the conditions in which many offenders live, and the very repetition of these sad and often tragic pictures of life is a challenge for those who study the criminal justice system: this 'system' is dealing with very real individuals (see also **[1:15]**–**[1:19]**). Judges develop different reputations as sentencers, and doubtless the reputation of the individual judge has an important influence on the decision of the defendant whether to plead guilty. In 1980 Ashworth et al **[7:19]** carried out a 'pilot study' into sentencing policy and practices in the Crown Court. The Lord Chief Justice then refused permission for the work to proceed any further. Although much has changed in the intervening years, the discussion extracted remains a useful summary of the case for academic research in this area. Hood's more recent study **[7:9]** was the first large-scale statistical attempt to try to assess whether defendants of different ethnic origin were treated equally when sentenced in the Crown Courts. Much more research should be carried out into how, in practice, judges actually reach decisions. Currently the Institute of Criminology at the University of Cambridge is carrying out a huge research project, based on court records—but access has been difficult, and court files do not always record all the reasons for a sentence.

Until 1988, only the defence had the right to appeal, but since the enactment of the Criminal Justice Act 1988, section 36 the Attorney-General may refer 'unduly lenient' sentences to the Court of Appeal. Chapter 9 raises arguments in support of a wider prosecution right of appeal, to encourage a more thorough review of sentencing decisions. Another attempt to limit discretion in this field was been the creation of the Sentencing Advisory Panel (SAP) by the Crime and Disorder Act 1998, the predecessor to the Sentencing Guidelines Council. It started work in 1999, originally providing advice to the Court of Appeal (see Chapter 9), but now its advice is given to the SGC. As we have noted, a working party headed by Gage LJ is currently reviewing the role of the SAP and SGC. Sentencing law and practice remains very much on the political agenda.

FURTHER READING

Alschuler, A W, 'An Exchange of Concessions' [1992] 142 NLJ 937

Ashworth, A, *Sentencing and Criminal Justice* (4th edition, 2005) Weidenfeld & Nicolson

Carter, P, *Securing the Future: proposals for the efficient and sustainable use of custody in England and Wales* (2007) Ministry of Justice

Devlin, P, *The Judge* (1979) Oxford UP

Griffith, J A G, *The Politics of the Judiciary* (5th edition, 1997) Fontana

Halliday, J, *Making Punishments work: a review of the sentencing framework for England and Wales* (2001) Home Office

Home Office, *Statistics on Race and the Criminal Justice System* (annual)

Madge, N, 'Summing up—a judge's perspective' [2006] Crim LR 817

Padfield, N, 'Securing the Future? Lord Carter's narrow approach' (2007) 50 JP 876

Pannick, D, *Judges* (1987) Oxford UP

Pattenden, R, *Judicial Discretion and Criminal Litigation* (1990) Oxford UP

Rock, P, *The Social World of the English Crown Court* (1993) Clarendon Press

Spencer, J R, 'Orality and the Evidence of Absence Witnesses' [1994] Crim LR 628

Stevens, R, *The Independence of the Judiciary* (1993) Oxford UP

Stevens, R, 'Unpacking the Judges' (1993) Current Legal Problems 1

Stockdale, E, *The Court and the Offender* (1967) Gollanz

Thomas, D A, *Current Sentencing Practice* (constantly updated) Sweet & Maxwell

Thomas D A, 'Criminal Justice Act 2003: Custodial sentences' [2004] Crim LR 702

Walker, N and Padfield, N, *Sentencing: Theory, Law and Practice* (2nd edition, 1996) Butterworths

DOCUMENTS

[7:1] *Sirros v Moore*

[1975] QB 118

A judge in the Crown Court heard an appeal against the decision of magistrates to recommend to the Home Secretary that the appellant be deported. The magistrates had directed that he should not be detained pending the Home Secretary's decision. Having dismissed the appeal, the judge then ordered that the appellant be held in custody. The Court of Appeal held that because the judge had not adopted the right procedure, the order on which the appellant was taken into custody was invalid and he had rightly been released on habeas corpus. However, the judge was immune from liability in a civil action for damages.

Lord Denning MR (at page 136):

(iii) The modern courts

In the old days, as I have said, there was a sharp distinction between the inferior courts and the superior courts. Whatever may have been the reason for this distinction, it is no longer valid.

There has been no case on the subject for the last one hundred years at least. And during this time our judicial system has changed out of all knowledge. So great is this change that it is now appropriate for us to reconsider the principles which should be applied to judicial acts. In this new age I would take my stand on this: as a matter of principle the judges of superior courts have no greater claim to immunity than the judges of the lower courts. Every judge of the courts of this land—from the highest to the lowest—should be protected to the same degree, and liable to the same degree. If the reason underlying this immunity is to ensure 'that they may be free in thought and independent in judgment,' it applies to every judge, whatever his rank. Each should be protected from liability to damages when he is acting judicially. Each should be able to do his work in complete independence and free from fear. He should not have to turn the pages of his books with trembling fingers, asking himself: 'If I do this, shall I be liable in damages?' So long as he does his work in the honest belief that it is within his jurisdiction, then he is not liable to an action. He may be mistaken in the fact. He may be ignorant of the law. What he does may be outside his jurisdiction—in fact or in law—but so long as he honestly believes it to be within his jurisdiction, he should not be liable. Once he honestly entertains this belief, nothing else will make him liable. He is not to be plagued with allegations of malice or ill-will or bias or anything of the kind. Actions based on such allegations have been struck out and will continue to be struck out. Nothing will make him liable except it be shown that he was not acting judicially, knowing that he had no jurisdiction to do it.

This principle should cover the justices of the peace also. They should no longer be subject to 'strokes of the rodde, or spur'. Aided by their clerks, they do their work with the highest degree of responsibility and competence—to the satisfaction of the entire community. They should have the same protection as other judges.

(iv) The Crown Court

Today we are concerned with judges of a new kind. The judges of the Crown Court. It is, by definition, a superior court of record: see section 4(1) of the Act of 1971. The judges of it should, in principle, have the same immunity as all other judges, high or low. The Crown Court is manned by judges of every rank. Judges of the High Court, circuit judges, recorders, justices of the peace, all sit there. No distinction can or should be drawn between them. Each one shares responsibility for the decisions given by the court. If the High Court judge is not liable to an action, it should be same with the circuit judge, the recorder or the justice of the peace. No distinction can be taken on the seriousness of the case. Any one of them may sit on one day on a case of trifling importance, on the next on a case of the utmost gravity. No distinction can be taken as tot he nature of the case. It may be a matter triable only in indictment, or it may be a man up for sentence, or an appeal from magistrates. If they are not liable in trials on indictment, they should not be liable on other matters. But, whatever, it is, the immunity of the judges—and each of them—should rest on the same principle. Not liable for acts done by them in a judicial capacity. Only liable for acting in bad faith, knowing they have no jurisdiction to do it.

Conclusion

The judge had no jurisdiction to detain Sirros in custody. The Divisional Court were right to release him on habeas corpus. Though the judge was mistaken, yet he acted judicially and for that reason no action will lie against him. Likewise, no action will lie against the police officers. They are protected in respect of anything they did at his direction, not knowing it was wrong: see *London Corp v Cox* (1867) LR 2 HL 239, 269. I would therefore dismiss the appeal.

[7:2] Criminal Procedure Rules 2005/384

Parts 1–3

Part 1 THE OVERRIDING OBJECTIVE

1.1 The overriding objective

(1) The overriding objective of this new code is that criminal cases be dealt with justly.

(2) Dealing with a criminal case justly includes—

   (a) acquitting the innocent and convicting the guilty;

   (b) dealing with the prosecution and the defence fairly;

   (c) recognising the rights of a defendant, particularly those under Article 6 of the European Convention on Human Rights;

   (d) respecting the interests of witnesses, victims and jurors and keeping them informed of the progress of the case;

   (e) dealing with the case efficiently and expeditiously;

   (f) ensuring that appropriate information is available to the court when bail and sentence are considered; and

   (g) dealing with the case in ways that take into account—

      (i) the gravity of the offence alleged,

      (ii) the complexity of what is in issue,

      (iii) the severity of the consequences for the defendant and others affected, and

      (iv) the needs of other cases.

1.2 The duty of the participants in a criminal case

(1) Each participant, in the conduct of each case, must—

(a) prepare and conduct the case in accordance with the overriding objective;

(b) comply with these Rules, practice directions and directions made by the court; and

(c) at once inform the court and all parties of any significant failure (whether or not that participant is responsible for that failure) to take any procedural step required by these Rules, any practice direction or any direction of the court. A failure is significant if it might hinder the court in furthering the overriding objective.

(2) Anyone involved in any way with a criminal case is a participant in its conduct for the purposes of this rule.

1.3 The application by the court of the overriding objective

The court must further the overriding objective in particular when—

(a) exercising any power given to it by legislation (including these Rules);

(b) applying any practice direction; or

(c) interpreting any rule or practice direction.

Part 2 UNDERSTANDING AND APPLYING THE RULES

2.1 When the Rules apply

(1) In general, the Criminal Procedure Rules apply—

(a) in all criminal cases in magistrates' courts and in the Crown Court; and

(b) in all cases in the criminal division of the Court of Appeal.

(2) If a rule applies only in one or two of those courts, the rule makes that clear.

(3) The Rules apply on and after 4th April, 2005, but do not affect any right or duty existing under the rules of court revoked by the coming into force of these Rules.

(4) The rules in Part 33 apply in all cases in which the defendant is charged on or after 6 November 2006 and in other cases if the court so orders.

(5) The rules in Part 14 apply in cases in which one of the events listed in sub-paragraphs (a) to (d) of rule 14.1(1) takes place on or after 2nd April 2007. In other cases the rules of court replaced by those rules apply.

(6) The rules in Part 28 apply in cases in which an application under rule 28.3 is made on or after 2nd April 2007. In other cases the rules replaced by those rules apply.

(7) The rules in Parts 65, 66, 67, 68, 69 and 70 apply where an appeal, application or reference, to which one of those Parts applies, is made on or after 1st October 2007. In other cases the rules replaced by those rules apply.

2.2 Definitions

(1) In these Rules, unless the context makes it clear that something different is meant:

"business day" means any day except Saturday, Sunday, Christmas Day, Boxing Day, Good Friday, Easter Monday or a bank holiday;

"court" means a tribunal with jurisdiction over criminal cases. It includes a judge, recorder, District Judge (Magistrates' Court's), lay justice and, when exercising their judicial powers, the Registrar of Criminal Appeals, a justices' clerk or assistant clerk;

"court officer" means the appropriate member of the staff of a court;

"live link" means an arrangement by which a person can see and hear, and be seen and heard by, the court when that person is not in court;

"Practice Direction" means the Lord Chief Justice's Consolidated Criminal Practice Direction, as amended[; and][1]

"public interest ruling" means a ruling about whether it is in the public interest to disclose prosecution material under sections 3(6), 7A(8) or 8(5) of the Criminal Procedure and Investigations Act 1996.[2]

(2) Definitions of some other expressions are in the rules in which they apply.

2.3 References to Acts of Parliament and to Statutory Instruments

In these Rules, where a rule refers to an Act of Parliament or to subordinate legislation by title and year, subsequent references to that Act or to that legislation in the rule are shortened: so, for example, after a reference to the Criminal Procedure and Investigations Act 1996 that Act is called "the 1996 Act"; and after a reference to the Criminal Procedure and Investigations Act 1996 (Defence Disclosure Time Limits) Regulations 1997 those Regulations are called "the 1997 Regulations".

2.4 The glossary

The glossary at the end of the Rules is a guide to the meaning of certain legal expressions used in them.

Part 3 CASE MANAGEMENT

3.1 The scope of this Part

This Part applies to the management of each case in a magistrates' court and in the Crown Court (including an appeal to the Crown Court) until the conclusion of that case.

[Note. Rules that apply to procedure in the Court of Appeal are in Parts 65 to 73 of these Rules.]

3.2 The duty of the court

(1) The court must further the overriding objective by actively managing the case.

(2) Active case management includes—

    (a) the early identification of the real issues;

    (b) the early identification of the needs of witnesses;

    (c) achieving certainty as to what must be done, by whom, and when, in particular by the early setting of a timetable for the progress of the case;

    (d) monitoring the progress of the case and compliance with directions;

    (e) ensuring that evidence, whether disputed or not, is presented in the shortest and clearest way;

    (f) discouraging delay, dealing with as many aspects of the case as possible on the same occasion, and avoiding unnecessary hearings;

    (g) encouraging the participants to co-operate in the progression of the case; and

    (h) making use of technology.

(3) The court must actively manage the case by giving any direction appropriate to the needs of that case as early as possible.

3.3 The duty of the parties

Each party must—

    (a) actively assist the court in fulfilling its duty under rule 3.2, without or if necessary with a direction; and

    (b) apply for a direction if needed to further the overriding objective.

3.4 Case progression officers and their duties

(1) At the beginning of the case each party must, unless the court otherwise directs—

  (a) nominate an individual responsible for progressing that case; and

  (b) tell other parties and the court who he is and how to contact him.

(2) In fulfilling its duty under rule 3.2, the court must where appropriate—

  (a) nominate a court officer responsible for progressing the case; and

  (b) make sure the parties know who he is and how to contact him.

(3) In this Part a person nominated under this rule is called a case progression officer.

(4) A case progression officer must—

  (a) monitor compliance with directions;

  (b) make sure that the court is kept informed of events that may affect the progress of that case;

  (c) make sure that he can be contacted promptly about the case during ordinary business hours;

  (d) act promptly and reasonably in response to communications about the case; and

  (e) if he will be unavailable, appoint a substitute to fulfil his duties and inform the other case progression officers.

3.5 The court's case management powers

(1) In fulfilling its duty under rule 3.2 the court may give any direction and take any step actively to manage a case unless that direction or step would be inconsistent with legislation, including these Rules.

(2) In particular, the court may—

  (a) nominate a judge, magistrate, justices' clerk or assistant to a justices' clerk to manage the case;

  (b) give a direction on its own initiative or on application by a party;

  (c) ask or allow a party to propose a direction;

  (d) for the purpose of giving directions, receive applications and representations by letter, by telephone or by any other means of electronic communication, and conduct a hearing by such means;

  (e) give a direction without a hearing;

  (f) fix, postpone, bring forward, extend or cancel a hearing;

  (g) shorten or extend (even after it has expired) a time limit fixed by a direction;

  (h) require that issues in the case should be determined separately, and decide in what order they will be determined; and

  (i) specify the consequences of failing to comply with a direction.

(3) A magistrates' court may give a direction that will apply in the Crown Court if the case is to continue there.

(4) The Crown Court may give a direction that will apply in a magistrates' court if the case is to continue there.

(5) Any power to give a direction under this Part includes a power to vary or revoke that direction.

  . . .

[7:3] *R v Jisl*

[2004] EWCA Crim 696

Judge LJ finishes his judgement with the following advice:

Case Management

113. After an earlier trial which had taken place in 1998, this trial took place in the summer of 2001. By the time the retrial started we recognise that its management had already been fixed, virtually immutably, into pre-determined patterns. The observations which follow are not intended to be critical of the trial judge. Rather, they are an attempt to explain that since the date of this trial arrangements for case management by trial judges have changed, and to emphasise the urgent necessity that these changes and their potential impact are fully and widely understood.

114. The starting point is simple. Justice must be done. The defendant is entitled to a fair trial: and, which is sometimes overlooked, the prosecution is equally entitled to a reasonable opportunity to present the evidence against the defendant. It is not however a concomitant of the entitlement to a fair trial that either or both sides are further entitled to take as much time as they like, or for that matter, as long as counsel and solicitors or the defendants themselves think appropriate. Resources are limited. The funding for courts and judges, for prosecuting and the vast majority of defence lawyers is dependent on public money, for which there are many competing demands. Time itself is a resource. Every day unnecessarily used, while the trial meanders sluggishly to its eventual conclusion, represents another day's stressful waiting for the remaining witnesses and the jurors in that particular trial, and no less important, continuing and increasing tension and worry for another defendant or defendants, some of whom are remanded in custody, and the witnesses in trials which are waiting their turn to be listed. It follows that the sensible use of time requires judicial management and control.

115. Almost exactly a year ago in *R v Chaaban* [2003] EWCA Crim. 1012 this Court endeavoured to explain the principle:

> "35. ...The trial judge has always been responsible for managing the trial. That is one of his most important functions. To perform it he has to be alert to the needs of everyone involved in the case. That obviously includes, but it is not limited to, the interests of the defendant. It extends to the prosecution, the complainant, to every witness (whichever side is to call the witness), to the jury, or if the jury has not been sworn, to jurors in waiting. Finally, the judge should not overlook the community's interest that justice should be done...without unnecessary delay. A fair balance has to be struck between all these interests.

> 37. ...nowadays, as part of his responsibility for managing the trial, the judge is expected to control the timetable and to manage the available time. Time is not unlimited. No one should assume that trials can continue to take as long or use up as much time as either or both sides may wish, or think, or assert, they need. The entitlement to a fair trial is not inconsistent with proper judicial control over the use of time. At the risk of stating the obvious, every trial which takes longer than it reasonably should is wasteful of limited resources. It also results in delays to justice in cases still waiting to be tried, adding to the tension and distress of victims, defendants, particularly those in custody awaiting trial, and witnesses. Most important of all it does nothing to assist the jury to reach a true verdict on the evidence.

> 38. In principle, the trial judge should exercise firm control over the timetable, where necessary, making clear in advance and throughout the trial that the timetable will be subject to appropriate constraints. With such necessary even-handedness and flexibility as the interests of the justice require as the case unfolds, the judge is entitled to direct that the trial is expected to conclude by a specific date and to exercise his powers to see that it does."

116. The principle therefore, is not in doubt. This appeal enables us to re-emphasise that its practical application depends on the determination of trial judges and the co-operation of the legal profession.

Active, hands on, case management, both pre-trial and throughout the trial itself, is now regarded as an essential part of the judge's duty. The profession must understand that this has become and will remain part of the normal trial process, and that cases must be prepared and conducted accordingly.

117. The issues in this particular trial were identified at a very early stage, indeed during the course of the previous trial itself. In relation to each of the defendants, in a single word, the issue was knowledge. And indeed, the issue in most trials is equally readily identified.

118. Once the issue has been identified, in a case of any substance at all, (and this particular case was undoubtedly a case of substance and difficulty) the judge should consider whether to direct a timetable to cover pre-trial steps, and eventually the conduct of the trial itself, not rigid, nor immutable, and fully recognising that during the trial at any rate the unexpected must be treated as normal, and making due allowance for it in the interests of justice. To enable the trial judge to manage the case in a way which is fair to every participant, pre-trial, the potential problems as well as the possible areas for time saving, should be canvassed. In short, a sensible informed discussion about the future management of the case and the most convenient way to present the evidence, whether disputed or not, and where appropriate, with admissions by one or other or both sides, should enable the judge to make a fully informed analysis of the future timetable, and the proper conduct of the trial. The objective is not haste and rush, but greater efficiency and better use of limited resources by closer identification of and focus on critical rather than peripheral issues. When trial judges act in accordance with these principles, the directions they give, and where appropriate, the timetables they prescribe in the exercise of their case management responsibilities, will be supported in this Court. Criticism is more likely to be addressed to those who ignore them.

119. If these principles had been applied to this trial, it seems to us inconceivable that it would have taken 70 days before the jury reached its verdict, or given the issue in Tekin's case, that his evidence would have lasted four days in chief, and part of a further ten days in cross-examination by counsel for the Crown, or that Tekin himself should have been permitted without warning, to produce a bundle of documents some four hundred pages long and seek to adduce it in evidence. Equally, we doubt whether the repeated recall of prosecution witnesses, some twice, several three times, would have taken place, or that the judge would have been invited time after time to break off the hearing of the evidence in order to give legal rulings. We are not seeking to analyse each and every aspect of the present trial where modern case management would have avoided delay. We are simply illustrating some of the more obvious areas where the modern approach would probably have saved time.

120. The proper progress of this case was also interrupted by additional administrative burdens on the judge, performed and eating into the ordinary sitting hours of the court. Experience shows that once the forward impetus has been lost, it becomes extremely difficult to recover it. Imperceptibly at first, drift infiltrates the proceedings and develops into unacceptable delay. Again, we shall simply illustrate the phenomenon by example. If the jury is asked to be ready for the trial to start at 10.00 am or 10.30 am, and the start is delayed by even a few minutes, a pattern of late sitting eventually engulfs everyone. The ten minute break for the jury then lasts fifteen minutes. Counsel or the defendants, or one or other of them, is then not quite ready for the court to sit at 2.00 pm sharp. And so on. Witnesses whose evidence should have been completed on one particular day have to return on the next. Then, as by definition their evidence is not completed, the next day's hearing inevitably involves some repetition of what has already been explored on the previous day—sometimes inadvertently, sometimes to enable a particular forensic point to be repeated. The inconvenience to the witness, and the problem of repetition would both have been avoided if the evidence had been completed by the end of the previous day. The trial judge is responsible for providing the necessary example and leadership to prevent accumulating drift. In the longer cases in particular, the organisation of his administrative and other judicial burdens should, so far as practical, be reduced or organised to start at times which enable him to sit every day for full court days.

121. As already explained, these observations are directed to future arrangements for case management of criminal trials. They do not impinge on the safety of these convictions, or the appropriate levels of sentence.

[7:4] Sentencing Guidelines Council, *Reduction in Sentence for a Guilty Plea: Definitive Guideline*

(Revised 2007)

B. Statement of Purpose

2.1 When imposing a custodial sentence, statute requires that a court must impose the shortest term that is commensurate with the seriousness of the offence(s).[4] Similarly, when imposing a community order, the restrictions on liberty must be commensurate with the seriousness of the offence(s).[5] Once that decision is made, a court is required to give consideration to the reduction for any guilty plea. As a result, the final sentence after the reduction for a guilty plea will be less than the seriousness of the offence requires.

2.2 A reduction in sentence is appropriate because a guilty plea avoids the need for a trial (thus enabling other cases to be disposed of more expeditiously), shortens the gap between charge and sentence, saves considerable cost, and, in the case of an early plea, saves victims and witnesses from the concern about having to give evidence. The reduction principle derives from the need for the effective administration of justice and not as an aspect of mitigation.

2.3 Where a sentencer is in doubt as to whether a custodial sentence is appropriate, the reduction attributable to a guilty plea will be a relevant consideration. Where this is amongst the factors leading to the imposition of a non-custodial sentence, there will be no need to apply a further reduction on account of the guilty plea. A similar approach is appropriate where the reduction for a guilty plea is amongst the factors leading to the imposition of a financial penalty or discharge instead of a community order.

2.4 When deciding the most appropriate length of sentence, the sentencer should address separately the issue of remorse, together with any other mitigating features, before calculating the reduction for the guilty plea. Similarly, assistance to the prosecuting or enforcement authorities is a separate issue which may attract a reduction in sentence under other procedures; care will need to be taken to ensure that there is no "double counting".

2.5 The implications of other offences that an offender has asked to be taken into consideration should be reflected in the sentence before the reduction for guilty plea has been applied.

2.6 A reduction in sentence should only be applied to the punitive elements of a penalty.[6] The guilty plea reduction has no impact on sentencing decisions in relation to ancillary orders, including orders of disqualification from driving.

C. Application of the Reduction Principle

Recommended Approach

The court decides sentence for the offence(s) taking into account aggravating and mitigating factors and any other offences that have been formally admitted (TICs)

The court selects the amount of the reduction by reference to the sliding scale

The court applies the reduction

When pronouncing sentence the court should usually state what the sentence would have been if there had been no reduction as a result of the guilty plea.

D. Determining the Level of Reduction

4.1 The level of reduction should be a proportion of the total sentence imposed, with the proportion calculated by reference to the circumstances in which the guilty plea was indicated, in particular the stage in the proceedings. The greatest reduction will be given where the plea was indicated at the "first reasonable opportunity".

4.2 Save where section 144(2) of the 2003 Act applies,[7] the level of the reduction will be gauged on a sliding scale ranging from a recommended one third (where the guilty plea was entered at the first reasonable opportunity in relation to the offence for which sentence is being imposed), reducing to a recommended one quarter (where a trial date has been set) and to a recommended one tenth(for a guilty plea entered at the 'door of the court' or after the trial has begun). See diagram below.

4.3 The level of reduction should reflect the stage at which the offender indicated a willingness to admit guilt to the offence for which he is eventually sentenced:

(i) the largest recommended reduction will not normally be given unless the offender indicated willingness to admit guilt at the first reasonable opportunity; when this occurs will vary from case to case (see Annex 1 for illustrative examples);

(ii) where the admission of guilt comes later than the first reasonable opportunity, the reduction for guilty plea will normally be less than one third;

(iii) where the plea of guilty comes very late, it is still appropriate to give some reduction;

(iv) if after pleading guilty there is a Newton hearing and the offender's version of the circumstances of the offence is rejected, this should be taken into account in determining the level of reduction;

(v) if the not guilty plea was entered and maintained for tactical reasons (such as to retain privileges whilst on remand), a late guilty plea should attract very little, if any, discount.

In each category, there is a presumption that the recommended reduction will be given unless there are good reasons for a lower amount.

First resonable opportunity	After a trial date is set	Door of the court after trial has begun
=======	============	============
recommended 1/3	**recommended** 1/4	**recommended** 1/10

[7:5] Zander, M and Henderson, P, *The Crown Court Study*

(1993) RCCJ Research Study No 19, HMSO (at page 138)

4.11 'Innocent pleading guilty' cases

4.11.1 Was this a case of an innocent person pleading guilty?

In cases where the defendant pleaded guilty to all charges, defence barristers were asked (Db184): 'An innocent defendant sometimes decided to plead guilty to achieve a sentence discount or reduction in the indictment. Were you concerned that this was such a case?' (According to the Bar's Code of Conduct, counsel's duty in such a situation is to advise his client that he should not plead guilty unless he is guilty. But the decision as to plea is for the client.)

There were 846 substantive replies to this question—not counting 368 non-replies, most probably signifying Don't know or No view. In 793 (94%) the reply was No. But 53 (6% of the 846) the reply was

Yes. These 53 cases 'grossed up' represent close to 1,400 cases a year. This appeared to be a cause for concern. It was clear that further analysis of the cases should be undertaken.

The further analysis showed that few (if any) of these cases could safely be characterised as clear examples of what Q184 in the defence barrister's questionnaire was intended to reveal—namely cases where a person, who in the view of his lawyers could have been innocent of all the charges he faced, nevertheless pleaded guilty because of the sentence discount. It was plain that in many of the 53 cases the defence barristers had misunderstood the thrust of the question—no doubt due to the imperfect drafting of the question and the absence of guidance to respondents as to what it was intended to mean.

In regard to 15 of the 53 cases, the defendant also returned a questionnaire. In six of these cases he pleaded guilty though he was not guilty of the offence. In nine he said he had been guilty of the offence(s) charged or similar offences. The other side of the same coin was the response made by defendants themselves to a somewhat similar question we put to them. We did not think we could fairly ask defendants who pleaded not guilty whether they were actually guilty of the offence. But we asked those who pleased guilty (Def38): 'Did you actually commit the offence(s) for which you pleaded guilty, or a similar offence?'

There were 269 effective replies. Of these, 71% said they had committed the offence as charged and another 17% said they had committed a similar offence.

But there were 31 cases (11%) where the defendant claimed that he had not committed the offence. In 26 of these 31 cases the defence barrister had also returned a questionnaire. In 20 of the 26 cases the barrister gave no indication in answering Q184 that he took the view that his client might have been an innocent person pleading guilty because of the sentence discount.

But in six, as has been seen, the barrister did give this indication. (In none of these six cases did the defendant go to prison.)

- Case No 46—D, aged 21, no previous convictions, charged with theft from his employer, got a community service order. He had simply helped a friend but had not done much and had not benefited from the crime. Db thought it was too trivial to warrant prosecution. Def. said 'I didn't commit the offence but pleaded guilty because of the credit factor which was explained to me because of the statement of my co-defendant'. He had confessed in a tape-recorded interview.

- Case No 50—D, no previous convictions, charged with gross indecency, given a conditional discharge. Def. said he did not commit the offence but pleaded guilty 'to get it over as quickly as possible'. He agreed with the advice of his lawyers to plead guilty. Db said the Def. had had no faith that his evidence would be believed.

- Case No 9—D, aged 22, several previous convictions, charged with assault occasional actual bodily harm and theft, put on probation and ordered to pay compensation of £400. Db said: 'The prosecution was intending to add a charge of blackmail. D refused to run the risk.' Def. said 'I pleaded guilty because of threat to amend the charges to assault with intent to rob and blackmail, theft and actual bodily harm. I was blackmailed into pleading guilty. Disgusting. By the time you read this paper I will probably be in prison for two crimes—one of which I did not commit'.

- Case No 23—D, female aged 49, three Class B drugs' charges, one of supplying, two of possession. Three previous convictions for similar offences in 1977, 1986, 1987. Given a suspended sentence of 12 months imprisonment. Def. said 'Knew I was guilty of the offences I was accused for. I was lucky to get away with a suspended sentence.' Db said a conference with the client satisfied him that hers was not a case of an innocent person pleading guilty. She was facing her first custodial penalty.

- Case No 24—D, female aged 25, charged with theft and 1 other offence taken into consideration (TIC). Previous convictions for shoplifting in 1983, 1987 and 1991. Given a suspended sentence of 3 months. Def. said 'I was advised to plead guilty by my barrister to get it over and done with. Otherwise we would of (sic) come back for a hearing.' She agreed with this advice. Db said D's instructions revealed a good defence. Crown offered to drop a further charge currently in the magistrates' court on a similar matter of a guilty plea.'

- Case No 16—D, male aged 25, no previous convictions, charged with shoplifting from WH Smith's and Woolworth's. His co-defendant had a string of previous convictions for shoplifting. Def. admitted the WH Smith's offence but initially denied the Woolworth's one. Pleaded guilty to both. Given conditional discharge. Def. said 'Pleaded guilty although I was not guilty—to keep myself in one piece. I decided my plea on advice from the barrister and solicitor. I did not agree with the advice. I was only being used.' He had made a confession in the police car and at the police station. He had signed it, but it was not accurate: 'I signed under the influence of drink and drugs.'

In the other 25 cases where the defendant said he was not guilty the following were typical of the reasons or explanations given:

- Case No 0014 'So I did not have to go through a trial. Also because of the advice of my barrister.' (Many previous convictions. Facing nine charges including burglary and assault occasioning actual bodily harm. Received 15 months.)
- Case No 0085 'If I had pleaded not guilty, I would have received a bigger sentence, I think.' (one previous conviction in 1988 for offences against the person. Charged with burglary. (Conditional discharge plus £75 prosecution costs.)
- Case No 0592 'I have been in prison for similar thefts. I was out to steal that day but I never actually attempted to steal what the store detective claimed. I pleaded guilty because my barrister spoke to the judge and got assurance that if I pleaded guilty I would not be sent to prison. However this guarantee did not extend if I pleaded not guilty and was found guilty.' (Many previous convictions. Charged with attempted theft. Conditional discharge.)
- Case No 0125 'Because the police bully you and it is pure hell.' (Many previous convictions. Facing four charges of burglary and theft. 9 months imprisonment.)
- Case No 0183 'I wanted to protect my co-accused.' (Many previous convictions. Charges of theft, taking a conveyance, driving whilst disqualified, driving without insurance, 6 months imprisonment on each charge concurrent.)
- Case No 0642 'Seemed easier at the time to get it over with.' Agreed with the lawyers' advice to plead guilty. (Many previous convictions. Charged with drugs and vehicle offences. 3 months imprisonment suspended.)
- Case No 0310 'Because my solicitor told me so.' (Several previous convictions. Charged with burglary. Probation.)
- Case No 0352 'To dispence (sic) with the case and lead a normal life.' (many previous convictions. Charged with theft, 3 months imprisonment, including 1 months for an activated previous conditional discharge.)
- Case No 0418 'To save time and taxpayer's money.' (Many previous convictions. Facing seven charges of burglary and theft. Three sentences of 2 years imprisonment concurrent and four of 3 months imprisonment.)
- Case No 0575 'I did not want to put the victim through a court ordeal.' (1 minor previous conviction. Charged with four counts of indecent assaults on a child. Two months imprisonment.)

[7:6] *Royal Commission on Criminal Justice*
(1993) Cm 2263, HMSO (at page 111)

45 Against the risk that defendants may be tempted to plead guilty to charges of which they are not guilty must be weighted the benefits to the system and to defendants of encouraging those who are in fact guilty to plead guilty. We believe that the system of sentence discounts should remain. But we do see reason to make the system more effective. In particular we believe that a clearer system of graduated discounts would help to alleviate the problem of 'cracked' trials. The Crown Court Study showed

that 'cracked' trials were 26% of all cases or 43% of cases other than those listed as guilty pleas. 'Cracked' trials create serious problems, principally for all the thousands of witnesses each year—police officers, experts and ordinary citizens—who come to court expecting a trial only to find that there is no trial because the defendant has decided to plead guilty at the last minute. This causes in particular unnecessary anxiety for victims whose evidence has up to that point been disputed.

46 At present, the sentence discount is available at any stage until the beginning of the trial but the Court of Appeal has stated in terms that, other things being equal, an earlier plea ought to attract a higher discount and that late tactical pleas should not attract the same discount:

> 'This court has long said that discounts on sentences are appropriate, but everything depends upon the circumstances of each case. If a man is arrested and at once tells the police that he is guilty and co-operates with them in the recovery of property and the identification of others concerned in the offence, he can expect to get a substantial discount. But if a man is arrested in circumstances in which he cannot hope to put forward a defence of not guilty, he cannot expect much by way of a discount. In between come this kind of case, where the court has been put to considerable trouble as a result of a tactical plea. The sooner it is appreciated that defendants are not going to get a full discount for pleas of guilty in these sort of circumstances, the better it will be for the administration of justice.'[1]

47 We agree with the view expressed by the Court of Appeal that, other things being equal, the earlier the plea the higher the discount. In broad terms, solicitors and barristers should advise their clients to that effect. Judges must, however, retain their discretion to deal appropriately with the particular circumstances of the individual case. Subject to these points, a system of graduated discounts might work broadly as follows:

(a) The most generous discount should be available to the defendant who indicates a guilty plea in response to the service of the case disclosed by the prosecution.

(b) The next most generous discount should be available to the defendant who indicates a guilty plea in sufficient time to avoid full preparation for trial. The discount might be less if the plea were entered only after a preparatory hearing.

(c) At the bottom of the scale should come the discount for a guilty plea entered on the day of the trial itself. Since resources would be saved by avoiding a contested trial even at this late stage, we think that some discount should continue to be available. But it should be appreciably smaller than for a guilty plea offered at one of the earlier stages.

We do not think that clearer articulation of the long accepted principle that there should be greater sentence discounts for earlier pleas will increase the risk that defendants may plead guilty to offences they did not commit. We would on the other hand expect that it would lead some who would at present plead guilty to do so earlier.

48 We believe, however, that still more could be done to reduce the incidence of 'cracked' trials. As the Seabrook Committee argued, the most common reason for defendants delaying a plea of guilty until the last minute is a reluctance to face the facts until they are at the door of the court. It is often said too that a defendant has a considerable incentive to behave in this way. The longer the delay, the more the likelihood of a witness becoming intimidated or forgetting to turn up or disappearing. And, if the defendant is remanded in custody, he or she will continue to enjoy the privileges of an unconvicted remand prisoner whereas, once a guilty pleas has been entered, the prisoner enters the category of convicted/unsentenced and loses those privileges. Although this last disincentive can be removed, as we recommend below, the problem of last minute changes of plea can never be completely eradicated. We believe, however, that a significant number of those who now plead guilty at the last minute would be more ready to declare their hand at an earlier stage if they were given a reliable early indication of the maximum sentence that they would face if found guilty.

49 The defendant will be interested not so much in the discount on sentence that he or she might receive as the actual sentence and in particular whether it will be custodial or not. It used to be possible for defence counsel to ask the judge for an indication of the sentence that his or her client might receive if found guilty after a contested trial, as opposed to the sentence that might be passed if the plea were changed to guilty. But the discussion of likely sentences with judges is now severely constrained by the Court of Appeal's judgment in *R v Turner*.[2] According to this, judges may say that, whether the accused pleads guilty or not guilty, the sentence will or will not take a particular form. They must not, however, state that on a plea of guilty they would impose one sentence while on conviction following a plea of not guilty they would impose a severer sentence. The court took the view that this would be placing undue pressure on defendants, depriving them of that complete freedom of choice which is essential.

50 Many witnesses, particularly from the judiciary and the Bar, urged on us the desirability of reverting, in essence, to the system as it applied before the judgment in the case of *Turner*. The Crown Court Study also showed that, among the judges and barristers who responded, there was overwhelming support for change. We do not support a total reversal of the judgment in *Turner*, since we agree that to face defendants with a choice between what they might get on an immediate plea of guilty and what they might get if found guilty by the jury does amount to unacceptable pressure. But the effect of *Turner* and related judgments appears to have been to make judges reluctant to discuss sentence with counsel at all. We think that there is a case for a change of approach. We recommend that, at the request of defence counsel on instructions from the defendant, judges should be able to indicate the highest sentence that they would impose at that point on the basis of the facts as put to them. A request for such an indication might be made at a preparatory hearing, at a hearing called specially for this purpose, or at the trial itself.

51 We envisage that the procedure which we recommend would be initiated solely by, and for the benefit of, defendants who wish to exercise a right to be told the consequences of a decision which is theirs alone. Where a defendant would need the protection of an appropriate adult during inquiries carried out at a police station, the system must be operated with particular care. The sentence 'canvass', as we have called it, should normally take place in the judge's chambers with both sides being represented by counsel. A shorthand writer should also be present. If none is available a member of the court staff should take a note to be agreed immediately by the judge and both counsel. The judge may give the answer to the question 'what would be the maximum sentence if my client were to plead guilty at this stage?' but to no other. The judge's indication should be based on brief statements from prosecution and defence of all the relevant circumstances, which should include details of the defendant's previous convictions if any and, if available, any pre-sentence report required by the Criminal Justice Act 1991.

Notes

1 *R v Hollington and Emmens* (1985) 82 Cr App Rep 281.

2 [1970] 2 WLR 1093. [See also **[7:4]**.]

[7:7] *R v Goodyear*

[2005] EWCA Crim 888, [2005] 1 WLR 2532

Lord Woolf, Chief Justice:

1. This is the judgment of the Court prepared by the Deputy Chief Justice, Lord Justice Judge.

2. On first analysis this is an unremarkable appeal against sentence by Karl Goodyear following his plea of guilty to an offence of corruption on 19th April 2004 at the Crown Court at Doncaster before His Honour Judge Jack.

3. In reality, the appeal raises important questions about the continuing applicability of the practice promulgated in R v Turner [1970] 2 QB 321, as underlined and applied in subsequent cases, which, save in the most exceptional circumstances, effectively prohibited the judge from giving any indication of sentence in advance of a guilty plea by the defendant. Accordingly, following the procedure adopted in Attorney General's Reference (No. 1 of 2004) 1 WLR 2111 and R v Simpson [2004] QB 118, a five-judge court, presided over by the Lord Chief Justice, was convened to consider whether what we shall compendiously summarise as the Turner rule of practice may now properly be modified, and if so, to what extent.

. . .

Guidelines

53. The objective of these Guidelines is to ensure common process and continuing safeguards against the creation or appearance of judicial pressure on the defendant. The potential advantages include, first and foremost, that the defendant himself would make a better informed decision whether to plead, or not. Experience tends to suggest that this would result in an increased number of early guilty pleas, which a consequent reduction in the number of trials, and the number of cases which are listed for trial, and then, to use current language, "crack" at the last minute, usually at considerable inconvenience to those involved in the intended trial, and in particular, victims and witnesses. Properly applied, too, there may be a reduced number of sentences to be considered by the Attorney General, and where appropriate, referred to this Court as unduly lenient. In short, an increase in the efficient administration of justice will not impinge on the defendant's entitlement to tender a voluntary plea.

54. In our judgment, any advance indication of sentence to be given by the judge should normally be confined to the maximum sentence if a plea of guilty were tendered at the stage at which the indication is sought. In essence we accept the recommendation of the Report of the Royal Commission that the judge should treat the request for a sentence indication, in whatever form it reaches him, as if he were being asked to indicate the maximum sentence on the defendant at that stage. For the process to go further, and the judge to indicate his view of the maximum possible level of sentence following conviction by the jury, as well as its level after a plea of guilty, would have two specific disadvantages. First, by definition, the judge could not be sufficiently informed of the likely impact of the trial on him (or the trial judge) in the sentencing context. It would be unwise for him to bind himself to any indication of the sentence after a trial in advance of it, in effect on a hypothetical basis. If he were to do so, to cover all eventualities he would probably have to indicate a very substantial possible maximum sentence. This would lead to a second problem, arising from the comparison between the two alternatives available to the defendant, that is the maximum level after a trial, and the maximum level following an immediate plea. With some defendants at any rate, the very process of comparing the two alternatives create pressure to tender a guilty plea.

The Judge

55. The judge should not give an advance indication of sentence unless one has been sought by the defendant.

56. He remains entitled, if he sees fit, to exercise the power recognised in Turner to indicate, that the sentence, or type of sentence, on the defendant would be the same, whether the case proceeded as a plea of guilty or went to trial, with a resulting conviction. Nowadays, given the guidance published by the Sentencing Guidelines Council on the credit to be given for a guilty plea, this would be unusual. He is also entitled in an appropriate case to remind the defence advocate that the defendant is entitled to seek an advance indication of sentence.

57. In whatever circumstances an advance indication of sentence is sought, the judge retains an unfettered discretion to refuse to give one. It may indeed be inappropriate for him to give any indication at all. For example, he may consider that for a variety of reasons the defendant is already under pressure (perhaps from a co-accused), or vulnerable, and that to give the requested indication, even in answer to a request, may create additional pressure. Similarly, he may be troubled that the particular

defendant may not fully have appreciated that he should not plead guilty unless in fact he is guilty. Again, the judge may believe that if he were to give a sentence indication at the stage when it is sought, he would not properly be able to judge the true culpability of the defendant, or the differing levels of responsibility between defendants. In a case involving a number of defendants, he may be concerned that an indication given to one defendant who seeks it, may itself create pressure on another defendant. Yet again, the judge may consider that the application is no less than a "try on" by a defendant who intends or would be likely to plead guilty in any event, seeking to take a tactical advantage of the changed process envisaged in this judgment. If so, he would probably refuse to say anything at all, and indeed, a guilty plea tendered after such tactical manoeuvrings may strike the judge as a plea tendered later than the first reasonable opportunity for doing so, with a consequent reduction in the discount for the guilty plea.

58. Just as the judge may refuse to give an indication, he may reserve his position until such time as he feels able to give one, for example, until a pre-sentence report is available. There will be occasions when experience will remind him that in some cases the psychiatric or other reports may provide valuable insight into the level of risk posed by the defendant, and if so, he may justifiably feel disinclined to give an indication at the stage when it is sought. Another problem may simply be that the judge is not sufficiently familiar with the case to give an informed indication, and if so, he may defer doing so until he is.

59. In short, the judge may refuse altogether to give an indication, or may postpone doing so. He may or may not give reasons. In many cases involving an outright refusal, he would probably conclude that it would be inappropriate to give his reasons. If he has in mind to defer an indication, the probability is that he would explain his reasons, and further indicate the circumstances in which, and when, he would be prepared to respond to a request for a sentence indication.

60. If at any stage the judge refuses to give an indication (as opposed to deferring it) it remains open to the defendant to seek a further indication at a later stage. However once the judge has refused to give an indication, he should not normally initiate the process, except, where it arises, to indicate that the circumstances had changed sufficiently for him to be prepared to consider a renewed application for an indication.

61. Once an indication has been given, it is binding and remains binding on the judge who has given it, and it also binds any other judge who becomes responsible for the case. In principle, the judge who has given an indication should, where possible, deal with the case immediately, and if that is not possible, any subsequent hearings should be listed before him. This cannot always apply. We recognise that a new judge has his own sentencing responsibilities, but judicial comity as well as the expectation aroused in a defendant that he will not receive a sentence in excess of whatever the first judge indicated, requires that a later sentencing judge should not exceed the earlier indication. If, after a reasonable opportunity to consider his position in the light of the indication, the defendant does not plead guilty, the indication will cease to have effect. In straightforward cases, once an indication has been sought and given, we do not anticipate an adjournment for the plea to be taken on another day.

62. Later in this judgment we will deal with the obligations of the defence and the prosecution, and to the extent that they may be relevant to the judge's decision, they should be applied. For example, an indication should not be sought on a basis of hypothetical facts. Where appropriate, there must be an agreed, written basis of plea. Unless there is, the judge should refuse to give an indication: otherwise he may become inappropriately involved in negotiations about the acceptance of pleas, and any agreed basis of plea.

The Defence

...

65. The advocate is personally responsible for ensuring that his client fully appreciates that:

*(a) he should not plead guilty unless he is guilty;

* (b) any sentence indication given by the judge remains subject to the entitlement of the Attorney General (where it arises) to refer an unduly lenient sentence to the Court of Appeal;

* (c) any indication given by the judge reflects the situation at the time when it is given, and that if a "guilty plea" is not tendered in the light of that indication the indication ceases to have effect;

* (d) any indication which may be given relates only to the matters about which an indication is sought. Thus, certain steps, like confiscation proceedings, follow automatically, and the judge cannot dispense with them, nor, by giving an indication of sentence, create an expectation that they will be dispensed with.

The Prosecution

. . .

70. We must expressly identify a number of specific matters for which the advocate for the prosecution is responsible.

* (a) If there is no final agreement about the plea to the indictment, or the basis of plea, and the defence nevertheless proceeds to seek an indication, which the judge appears minded to give, prosecuting counsel should remind him of this guidance, that normally speaking an indication of sentence should not be given until the basis of the plea has been agreed, or the judge has concluded that he can properly deal with the case without the need for a Newton hearing.

* (b) If an indication is sought, the prosecution should normally enquire whether the judge is in possession of or has had access to all the evidence relied on by the prosecution, including any personal impact statement from the victim of the crime, as well as any information of relevant previous convictions recorded against the defendant.

* (c) If the process has been properly followed, it should not normally be necessary for counsel for the prosecution, before the judge gives any indication, to do more than, first, draw the judge's attention to any minimum or mandatory statutory sentencing requirements, and where he would be expected to offer the judge assistance with relevant guideline cases, or the views of the Sentencing Guidelines Council, to invite the judge to allow him to do so, and second, where it applies, to remind the judge that the position of the Attorney General to refer any eventual sentencing decision as unduly lenient is not affected.

* (d) In any event, counsel should not say anything which may create the impression that the sentence indication has the support or approval of the Crown.

. . .

Process

73. We anticipate that any sentence indication would normally be sought at the plea and case management hearing. In cases "sent" to the Crown Court under s 51 of the Crime and Disorder Act 1998, or transferred under s 4 of the Criminal Justice Act 1987 or s 53 of the Criminal Justice Act 1991, this is usually the first opportunity for the defendant to plead guilty and therefore the moment when the maximum discount for the guilty plea will be available to the defendant. For victims and witnesses, too, there is a huge advantage in the earliest possible conclusion to the case. That said, as the judgment makes clear, we do not rule out the entitlement of a defendant to seek an indication at a later stage, or even, in what we know would be a rare case, during the course of the trial itself.

74. The judge is most unlikely to be able to give an indication, even if it is sought, in complicated or difficult cases, unless issues between the prosecution and the defence have been addressed and resolved. Therefore in such cases, no less than seven days' notice in writing of an intention to seek an indication should normally be given in writing to the prosecution, and the court. If an application is made without notice when it should have been given, the judge may conclude that any inevitable adjournment should

have been avoided and that the discount for the guilty plea should be reduced accordingly. It may be that in due course the Criminal Procedure Rules Committee will wish to consider the question of notice, and its length, and indeed whether either of the relevant case progression forms should be amended.

75. The hearing should normally take place in open court, with a full recording of the entire proceedings, and both sides represented, in the defendant's presence.

76. As already indicated, in cases of any complexity or difficulty, proper notice should be given to the Crown that a sentence indication will be sought. The fact that notice has been given, and any reference to a request for a sentence indication, or the circumstances in which it was sought, would be inadmissible in any subsequent trial.

77. If the process we envisage is properly followed, there should be very little need for the judge to involve himself in the discussions with the advocates, although obviously he may wish to seek better information on any aspect of the case which is troubling him. We do not anticipate an opening by the Crown, or a mitigation plea by the defence. That must be postponed until after the defendant has pleaded guilty. Generally speaking, we assume that the process will be very short, the judge bearing in mind that the defendant and the public are present, and that he (the judge) may be the trial judge, and that he is simply deciding whether to respond, and if so how, to a request that he give an indication of the maximum sentence he would pass if the defendant pleaded guilty at that stage. The fact that the case may yet proceed as a trial, and that if it does so, no reference may be made to the request for a sentence indication, leads to the conclusion that reporting restrictions should normally be imposed, to be lifted if and when the defendant pleads or is found guilty.

Magistrates' Court

78. In our judgment it would be impracticable for these new arrangements to be extended to proceedings in the Magistrates' Court. We are not at present satisfied that an advance sentence indication can readily be applied to and processed there. We believe that it would be better for the new arrangements in the Crown Court to settle in for some time before considering whether and, if so how, similar arrangements can be made in the context of summary trials. Accordingly, for the time being, the magistrates should confine themselves to the statutory arrangements in Schedule 3 of the 2003 Act.

…

[7:8] *R v McDonald*
[2007] Crim LR 737

The appellant pleaded guilty to burglary and to making a threat to kill. The appellant entered an address late at night. When one of the occupiers awoke, he made his way into the kitchen where the appellant grabbed him from behind around the throat and said "don't make a sound or I will kill you". The occupier fought off the appellant, who eventually ran away. The appellant had 19 previous convictions for 65 offences, including rape and aggravated burglary. Before the appellant entered a plea to the count charging threatening to kill, the appellant's counsel asked the sentencing judge for an advance indication of sentence in accordance with *Goodyear*. The proceedings were conducted in open court and eventually the sentencing judge indicated that for the two offences of burglary and threatening to kill, the total sentence would involve five years' custody. Following this indication the appellant pleaded guilty to threatening to kill. The case was adjourned for a pre-sentence report to be obtained. The pre-sentence report indicated that the appellant represented a high degree of risk of harm to the public. When the appellant again appeared before the court, prosecuting counsel indicated that the offence of threatening to kill was one in respect of which a court was obliged to consider whether or not to impose a sentence of imprisonment for public protection. Defence counsel did not remind the judge of the advance indication given on the previous appearance. The sentencing judge imposed a sentence of imprisonment for public protection, with a minimum period of $4\frac{1}{2}$ years, less 213 days.

Held, the appellant submitted that as the judge had given an indication that the maximum sentence he would impose would be a determinate sentence of five years' imprisonment, he ought not to have imposed an indeterminate sentence in the form of a sentence of imprisonment for public protection. Counsel had requested an advance indication of sentence in accordance with *Goodyear*. The sentencing judge was not bound to give any indication at all and might have reserved his position until such time as he felt able to give one. Once an indication had been given it was binding on the judge and remained binding on the judge who gave it and any other judge who became responsible for the case. The court was confident that if the judge had been reminded by counsel of the indication that he had given, he would not have imposed a sentence of imprisonment for public protection and would have felt himself bound by the indication he had given on the previous appearance. In the court's view it would be unjust for the sentence of imprisonment for public protection to remain. Accordingly, the appropriate course was to quash that sentence and substitute a determinate sentence of $4\frac{1}{2}$ years.

Commentary [By David Thomas QC] The implication of this decision seems to be that the expectation raised by a *Goodyear* indication overrides a statutory obligation to impose a sentence of imprisonment for public protection, which is a mandatory sentence where the court is of the opinion that there is a significant risk to the public from future specified offences. The case makes an interesting contrast with Attorney-General's Reference (No. 112 of 2006) [2007] 2 Cr. App. R. (S.) 39 (p.150). There, the offender pleaded guilty to wounding with intent on the morning of the trial following an advance indication of sentence in accordance with *Goodyear*, and was sentenced to three years' imprisonment. On a reference by the Attorney-General, the court stated that the sentencer was obliged by statute to consider the question whether there was a "significant risk of serious harm" as required by s.224 of the Criminal Justice Act 2003. As there were previous specified offences, s.229(3) required the sentencing judge to assume that there was a significant risk of serious harm from future specified offences unless it was unreasonable to do so. If the judge had addressed the question of risk, he would inevitably have concluded that there was such a risk. The court accordingly substituted a sentence of imprisonment for public protection. What would have happened in *McDonald* if the sentencing judge had passed a sentence in accordance with the *Goodyear* indication? Would a reference by the Attorney-General have succeeded? *Goodyear* states that an indication, although binding on the sentencing judge and other judges in the Crown Court, does not prevent a reference by the Attorney-General. What would have happened in *Glover* if the sentencing judge had gone back on his indication and passed a sentence of imprisonment for public protection? Presumably it would have been quashed on the same principle as *McDonald*. The moral seems to be that *Goodyear* indications should never be given in respect of a specified offence unless the judge is satisfied that there will be no question of the imposition of a sentence of imprisonment for public protection, or at least given in qualified terms which do not exclude the possibility of a sentence of imprisonment for public protection if the information before the court indicates that such a sentence is required.

[7:9] Hood, R, *Race and Sentencing: A Study in the Crown Court*
(1992) Oxford UP

Offenders of Afro-Caribbean origin comprise over 10 per cent of the male sentenced population, between eight and nine times their proportion in the population at large. Almost a quarter of female prisoners are black: a substantial number are foreigners imprisoned for importing drugs (and see [1:11]). This study was carried out in the Crown Court Centres which service the region covered by the West Midlands Police, and was based on a sample of 2,884 male offenders sentenced in 1989 (886 black, 536 Asian, 1,443 white, and 16 from other backgrounds) as well as all 433 women sentenced in these courts over the same period.

The following extracts are taken from Chapter 12: Discrimination in the Courts? (pages 179–192):

This study has confirmed what has for long been suspected, namely that, to a very substantial degree, the over-representation of Afro-Caribbean males and females in the prison system is a product of their over-representation among those convicted of crime and sentenced in the Crown Courts. The best evidence that it is possible to make from this study is that 80% of the over-representation of black male offenders in the prison population was due to their over-representation among those convicted at the Crown Court and to the type and circumstances of the offences of which black men were convicted. The remaining 20%, in the case of males but not females, appeared to be due to differential treatment and other factors which influence the nature and length of the sentences imposed: two thirds of it resulting from the higher proportion of black defendants who pleaded not guilty and who were, as a consequence, more liable on conviction to receive longer custodial sentences.

From Crown Court records it was not possible to shed much light on the circumstances and factors which might produce a higher rate of convictions amongst the black population, but there were some clues which are worthy of further investigation. A higher proportion of black people were charged with offences which could only be dealt with on indictment at the Crown Court: considerably more being charged with robbery, often of the kind normally referred to as 'mugging'. One should not minimise the distress caused by such behaviour, especially when women are the victims, nor the general sense of unease which it breeds, but as a form of violent or property crime it is often not more serious in its consequences than grievous bodily harm or housebreaking, both of which can be dealt with summarily if the court and defendant consent. This would not, of course, have meant that all of these black defendants would have accepted summary trial. The reason is that considerably more of them had, early on in the procedure, signified their intention to plead not guilty: 46% of blacks and Asians compared with 34% of whites charged with robbery. Nevertheless, the unavailability of discretion to deal with these offences either-way inevitably brings more black defendants into the arena of the Crown Court and its greater propensity to inflict a custodial penalty.

Black offenders were also disproportionately involved in the supply of drugs, usually cannabis, and these convictions regularly arose from police activity rather than from a complaint by citizens. This is not the place to open the debate about the seriousness of illegal dealings at street level in cannabis. It is only to say that if these offences were excluded the proportion of black males dealt with at the West Midlands courts would have been 13.7% rather than 17.2%, equivalent to 20% lower. By contrast, excluding such cases amongst white and Asians would have reduced their number by only 0.6% and 0.9% respectively. Of course, it is impossible to say whether these persons would have committed other offences but it is incontrovertible that the continued legal proscription of cannabis and the insistence that trading in it, even on a small or moderate scale, is an offence which should always be committed to the Crown Court for trial,30 is a substantial factor influencing the number of black persons in the prison population.

Furthermore, black defendants were at a disadvantage both because of decisions they made and decisions made about them during the processing of cases before they appeared for sentence. They were more likely to be remanded in custody by magistrates who committed them for trial, even taking into account the seriousness of the charges against them and other factors which might legitimately have had an effect on the decision whether to give bail. They were much less likely to have had a social inquiry report prepared on their background, mainly because a considerably high proportion of them signified their intention to plead not guilty, but also because fewer who pleaded guilty were reported on, although, the reasons for this are not known.

Being already in custody, pleading not guilty, and not having a report were all associated with a higher probability of receiving a custodial sentence or with a lengthier sentence. And all of them, of course, limit the possibilities for effective pleas in mitigation. Those who have been in custody have less opportunity to show that they have been of exemplary behaviour or have sought to make amends by, say, entering regular employment since they were charged with the offence. Those who deny the offence cannot suddenly, on being found guilty, convincingly express remorse. For those without social inquiry reports there is often insufficient information on hand to put the offence in its social context, and no opportunity to take advantage of a specific proposal from a probation officer for an alternative sentence to custody. It would appear, therefore, that ethnic minority defendants were inadvertently subjected to a form of indirect discrimination at the point of sentence due to the fact that they chose more often to contest the case against them. Because of the way that the system works to encourage guilty pleas through a 'discount' on sentence, which has been shown to produce a substantial reduction, and because it is the policy of the Probation Service not generally to make social inquiry reports on those who intend to contest the case against them, black defendants obviously put themselves at greater risk of custody and longer sentences.

. . .

Black defendants at the Dudley courts got a sentence greater than that recommended by a probation officer much more often than did blacks at Birmingham. Moreover, blacks at the Dudley courts received sentences generally further up the scale of penalties; and if they were recommended for probation or community service they were more likely to get a more severe penalty than was a white defendant.

In attempting to understand what may have produced this divergent pattern, it was at once noticeable that the differences were greatest not in the mid to upper band of cases where difficult decisions were being made about whether to use custody or not, but in the range of cases at the lower end of the scale of severity. There was strong evidence to suggest that factors which would have been regarded as mitigating the seriousness of the case if the defendant was white were not given the same weight if the defendant was black in the cases dealt with at Dudley courts. Yet, they were given a similar weight for black offenders dealt with at Birmingham. For instance, blacks at the Dudley courts were sentenced to custody in a significantly higher proportion of cases whether they were employed or unemployed, whether they were under 21 or over 21, whether they had only one prior conviction or two or more, whether they pleaded guilty or not guilty.

A much higher proportion of the black offenders at the Dudley courts (amongst those in the lower band of seriousness) who had been convicted with at least one other black defendant were sentenced to custody at the Dudley courts. Here the difference between the observed and expected rate, given the nature of the cases, was so big that it explained half of the difference between the observed and expected rate of custody for all black cases at the Dudley courts. An examination of these cases failed to find any distinctive differences between them and the cases where whites had been convicted with other whites. Nor were the black cases at Birmingham, where custody was, in contrast, rarely used, substantially different in character. It appears reasonable to assume that the judges at the Dudley courts viewed these cases in a different light to those involving groups of whites. While it is true that there were slightly more black offenders who were committed with other black offenders at the Dudley courts than at Birmingham, there were substantially more white at the Dudley courts who had been convicted alongside other whites. Furthermore, blacks were sentenced more often to custody than either whites at the Dudley courts or blacks at Birmingham, when they were the sole offender. On the whole, there was nothing to suggest that the judges who dealt with the Dudley courts' cases were confronted with a worse impression of black criminality than were the far more lenient judges at Birmingham. On the contrary, black defendants were a lower proportion of the caseload of the Dudley courts, and the seriousness of the cases dealt with, as measured by their risk of custody score, was no different from the cases in Birmingham.

. . .

When one contrasts the overall treatment meted out to black Afro-Caribbean males one is left wondering whether it is not a result of different racial stereotypes operating on the perceptions of some judges. The greater involvement of black offenders in street crime and in the trade in cannabis, their higher rate of unemployment, their greater resistance to pressures to plead guilty, and possibly a perception of a different, less deferential, demeanor in court may all appear somewhat more threatening. And, if not threatening, less worthy of mitigation of punishment. It was significant that being unemployed increased the risk of a black male getting a custodial sentence, but not, in general, for a white or an Asian offender. In contrast, the better financial and employment status of the Asians and their more socially integrated households, when judged by white standards, as well as the fact that they were much more likely to be first-time offenders, may have meant that they were probably able to present themselves as less threatening, and more worthy of mitigation than either white or blacks. Only in respect of the length of sentences received by those who were sentenced to prison did Asian adult males fare worse. But without research which would allow the investigation of judicial attitudes towards, and perceptions of, racially related differences in crime patterns and in cultural responses to the criminal justice system, all this for the moment must remain speculation. It cannot be doubted that such a programme of research is now needed.

The findings regarding women will surprise many, especially given the very large over-representation of black women in penal institutions. The evidence in general supports the so-called 'chivalry' or 'paternalistic' hypothesis that judges give much more weight to mitigating features of the case in sentencing women offenders, whether white or black. No differences were found between the use of custody, of alternatives, or in sentence length between white and black women when variables relating to the seriousness of the offences were controlled for. Black women were just as likely as the whites to have had a social inquiry report prepared about them prior to sentence and were no more likely than the white to have been given a sentence greater than that recommended by the probation officer. Furthermore, compared with black men, black women were dealt with relatively leniently just as white women were dealt with leniently compared with white men. Nevertheless, when a particularly disadvantaged group were singled out—those who had various attributes which could be associated with failure to conform to female stereotypes—a relatively high proportion of them were sentenced to custody: yet, no more blacks than whites and no more females than males. One thing is certain. If considerations relating to their gender did not mitigate the punishment of women, and they were treated as men are, there would be many more in custody than at present.

What conclusions of a practical kind can be drawn from this study? First, that the research has revealed a complex picture of the way in which race appears to have affected the pattern of sentencing. In doing so, it has led to some uncomfortable conclusions for those whose duty it is to sentence offenders. It will not be possible any more to make the claim that all the differences in the treatment of black offenders occur elsewhere in the criminal justice system. At least some of it occurs in the courts, and more often in some localities than others. Much will be achieved if judges recognise this. One aim of studying sentencing by empirical methods is to help stimulate reassessment of attitudes and judicial responses. Previous research has shown how unaware judges may be of their own practices, let alone those of their colleagues. It may be that some are not yet sufficiently sensitive to the way in which racial views and beliefs may influence their judgment. If this research can stimulate such self-awareness and re-evaluation it will have made a modest contribution towards the positive self conscious appreciation of the need to take the question of race seriously which the Judicial Studies Board has now recognised by the setting up of its Ethnic Minorities Advisory Committee.

Secondly, this study draws attention to the way in which the criminal process may contribute to indirect discrimination against black people. There is clearly a need to consider the implications of the policy which favours so strongly those who plead guilty, when ethnic minorities are less willing to let a prosecution go unchallenged. This has implications, in particular, for the range and value of the information available to the courts in deciding whether or not to impose a custodial sentence as well as the type of non-custodial sentence. And, for the reason already mentioned, it will be necessary to monitor carefully the way in which the courts exercise their discretion, under the Criminal Justice Act 1991, to pass sentence without a pre-sentence report when the case is one triable only on indictment.

Thirdly, there are obvious implications relating to the duty placed on the Secretary of State by Section 95(1)(b) to 'publish such information as he considers expedient for the purpose of … facilitating the performance...[by persons engaged in the administration of criminal justice]...of their duty to avoid discriminating against any person on the grounds of race or sex or any other improper ground.' To do this it will be essential for the Crown Courts to monitor the ethnic origin of all persons appearing before them. If the self-reflection on sentencing performance mentioned above is to be achieved, information on sentencing dispositions, analysed by ethnic origin, should be communicated to each judge and to the court as a whole annually. Only then will it be possible to detect whether sentencing patterns which might prove to be unfavourable to any ethnic minority are becoming established.

[7:10] *R v Christou*
[1992] QB 979

In an undercover police operation in London, a shop was set up purportedly to buy and sell jewellery. It was staffed solely by undercover officers purporting to be shady jewellers willing to buy stolen property. Discreetly sited cameras and sound equipment recorded all that occurred over the counter. The appellants who each made repeated sales at the shop pleaded not guilty to indictments charging burglary and handling stolen goods as alternatives. The trial judge ruled that the evidence obtained was not unfairly obtained.

The Court of Appeal dismissed the appeals, and held that the judge had exercised his discretion correctly.

Lord Taylor CJ (at page 989):

...the trick was not applied to the appellants; they voluntarily applied themselves to the trick. It is not every trick producing evidence against an accused which results in unfairness. There are, in criminal investigations, a number of situations in which the police adopt ruses or tricks in the public interest to obtain evidence. For example, to trap a blackmailer, the victim may be used as an agent of the police to arrange an appointment and false or marked money may be laid as bait to catch the offender. A trick, certainly; in a sense too, a trick which results in a form of self-incrimination; but not one which could reasonably be thought to involve unfairness.

In our view, although the Code extends beyond the treatment of those in detention, what is clear is that it was intended to protect suspects who are vulnerable to abuse or pressure from police officers or who may believe themselves to be so. Frequently, the suspect will be a detainee. But the Code will also apply where a suspect, not in detention, is being questioned about an offence by a police officer acting as a police officer for the purpose of obtaining evidence. In that situation, the officer and the suspect are not on equal terms. The officer is perceived to be in a position of authority; the suspect may be intimidated or undermined.

The situation at Stardust Jewellers was quite different. The appellants were not being questioned by police officers acting as such. Conversation was on equal terms. There could be no question of pressure or intimidation by Gary or Aggi as persons actually in authority or believed to be so. We agree with the judge that the Code simply was not intended to apply in such a context.

In reaching that conclusion, we should ourselves administer a caution. It would be wrong for police officers to adopt or use an undercover pose or disguise to enable themselves to ask questions about an offence uninhibited by the requirements of the Code and with the effect of circumventing it.

Were they to do so, it would be open to the judge to exclude the questions and answers under section 78 of the Act of 1984. It is therefore necessary here to see whether the questioning by Gary and Aggi was such as to require the judge in his discretion to exclude the conversation. The judge carefully reviewed the evidence on this issue. He concluded that the questions and comments from Gary and Aggi were for the most part simply those necessary to conduct the bartering and maintain their cover. They were not questions 'about the offence.' The only exception was the questioning about which area should be avoided in reselling the goods. However, even that was partly to maintain cover since it was the sort of questioning to be expected from a shady jeweller.

We are of the view that the judge's approach to the aspect of the case concerned with the Code cannot be faulted.

Before parting with the case, we should refer to a further argument mounted by Mr Thornton. He submitted that the undercover exercise, lasting as it did for some three months, was contrary to public policy. The basis for that submission was that the officers ought to have arrested offenders as soon as they had sufficient evidence. Instead, they allowed offenders such as these two appellants to return again and again with further stolen properties. Only when the shop was wound up were charges brought. The mischief alleged is that offenders were allowed to commit further offences which would or may have been obviated had they been arrested earlier. The existence of the shop was therefore facilitating, if not encouraging, the commission of crime.

Clearly, it must be a matter for policy and operational decision by the police as to how they reconcile and balance the need on the one hand to bring an individual offender swiftly to book and deter crime.

[7:11] *R v Bryce*
[1992] 4 All ER 567

The appellant was charged with handling stolen goods and theft. At his trial, the evidence against him included a conversation alleged to have taken place when an undercover policeman using a false name and posing as a potential buyer for a car telephoned the appellant and agreed to buy a stolen car, another conversation which took place when the two later met, and an unrecorded interview which came after a recorded interview in which the appellant had made no comments. The Court of Appeal quashed his conviction.

Lord Taylor CJ (at page 571):

[Counsel for the appellant] submits the evidence that the appellant turned up in a stolen car at Smithfield as a result of a telephone call was admissible. However, the conversation on the telephone and at Smithfield should, he submits, have been excluded because 'Pearson' asked questions which were in the nature of an interrogation. They deprived the appellant of his right not to incriminate himself by answering questions which, had they been put by a police officer acting overtly as such, would have required a caution under the code. In particular, [Counsel] points to the question and answer on the telephone: 'Pearson. How warm it is? Paul. It is a couple days old' and the question and answer at Smithfield: 'Pearson. How long has it been nicked? Paul. Two or three days.'

Those questions went to the heart of the vital issue of dishonesty. They were not even necessary to the undercover operation, which was designed to provide evidence of the appellant in possession of a recently stolen car offering it for sale at a knock-down price. Moreover, the second question simply invited the appellant to repeat his answer to the first in more specifically incriminating terms. On the voire dire 'Pearson' was asked in cross-examination what he would have done had the appellant said the car was not stolen. He replied:

'If he had said, "It is not stolen", I would have asked other questions, Sir. What are you doing selling a motor car like that? What is wrong with it? Is it an import? Has it come from abroad?'

In our judgment, that series of questions by an undercover officer would clearly offend against the caveat this court stated in *R v Christou*. It would blatantly have been an interrogation with the effect, if not the design, of using an undercover pose to circumvent the code.

The two questions of which [Counsel] makes strongest complaint did not go as far as that. They were single, isolated questions in separate conversations. There was no extended interrogation. However, they did go directly to the critical issue of guilty knowledge. Moreover, they were hotly disputed and there was no contemporary record. In *R v Christou* there were questions from the undercover officers as to the area where it would be unwise to resell the goods, the answers being obliquely an indication that the goods had been or may have been stolen from that area to the knowledge or belief of the suspect. However, in that case the whole interview was recorded both on tape and on film. The circumstances to be considered by the learned judge in that case in deciding whether the admission of the evidence would have an adverse effect on the fairness of the trial and how adverse where therefore quite different from those in the present case. The film and sound record eliminated any question of concoction. Not so here. The questions asked were direct, not oblique, the conversation was challenged and the appellant had no means of showing by a neutral, reliable record what was or was not said. For those reasons we consider that the learned judge erred here in admitting those answers.

We turn to the second ground. At the police station, an interview was properly set up and conducted in accordance with the code. It was tape-recorded, timed and it began with a caution. However, its only yield was a succession of 'No comment's from the appellant. It is submitted that what followed was clearly in breach of the code. The officers assert that after the tape recorder was switched off the appellant said he did not wish anything written down, but then proceeded to volunteer an account which in effect contained an admission.

Mr Thomas submits, first, that the appellant ought to have been cautioned again or reminded of the caution in accordance with para 10.5 of Code C, which provides:

'When there is a break in questioning under caution the interviewing officer must ensure that the person being questioned is aware that he remains under caution. If there is any doubt the caution should be given again in full when the interview resumes.'

The tape-recorded interview had concluded; what followed was therefore at the very least 'a break in questioning'. In our judgment, that submission is unanswerable. The failure to caution the appellant again was not just a technical breach in the circumstances of this case. According to the police, once the recorder was switched off, the appellant said he wanted nothing written down. He repeated that, saying 'If you record it, I won't say anything.' The officer's reply, 'Well, what happened then?' might reasonably have been taken as an acceptance of the appellant's terms. The appellant may well therefore have believed that what was not recorded could not be given in evidence. Hence the importance of a fresh caution or reminder of it. Significantly, as [Counsel] for the Crown fairly pointed out, the officer does not claim to have asked the question, 'Is that everything Paul?' until he was already sealing the tapes. One might have expected the question to have been asked before the recorder was switched off.

Mr Thomas further submits that the alleged admissions by the appellant were not recorded contemporaneously and, for that reason too, they should have been excluded. It was strenuously denied by the appellant that any such admissions were made and indeed that any interview, on or off the record, occurred after the tape recorder was switched off.

If this interview was correctly admitted, the effect would be to set at nought the requirements of the Police and Criminal Evidence Act 1984 and the code in regard to interviews. One of the main purposes of the code is to eliminate the possibility of an interview being concocted or of a true interview being falsely alleged to have been concocted. If it were permissible for an officer simply to assert that, after a properly conducted interview produced a nil return, the suspect confessed off the record and for that confession to be admitted, then the safeguards of the code could readily be bypassed.

In our judgment there would have to be some highly exceptional circumstances, perhaps involving cogent corroboration, before such an interview could be admitted without its having such an adverse effect on the fairness of the trial that it ought to be excluded under s 78.

Here the situation was a classic example of that suspicious sequence—a total denial or refusal to comment, followed by an alleged confession, followed in its turn by a refusal to sign the notes and a denial that the confession was made. We have no doubt that the alleged interview should in the circumstances of this case have been excluded.

Since the conversations and interviews with the police, both undercover and in uniform, formed such a major part of the prosecution case, we were bound to hold that the irregularities identified above rendered the conviction unsafe and unsatisfactory. Accordingly we quashed the conviction.

[7:12] *R v Khan*

[1997] AC 558

The appellant was charged with being knowingly concerned in the fraudulent evasion of the prohibition on the importation of a class A drug, heroin. The evidence included a record of the appellant's conversation with several people in a house to which, unknown to the occupants, the police had attached an electronic surveillance device. He appealed on the grounds that the evidence of his conversation should not have been admitted in evidence.

The appeal was dismissed.

Lord Nicholls (at page 582):

My Lords, I have had the opportunity to read in advance a draft of the speech of my noble and learned friend, Lord Nolan. I agree that this appeal should be dismissed. I add only two observations of my own. First, the appellant contended for a right of privacy in respect of private conversations in private houses. I prefer to express no view, either way, on the existence of such a right. This right, if it exists, can only do so as part of a larger and wider right of privacy. The difficulties attendant on this controversial subject are well known. Equally well known is the continuing, widespread concern at the apparent failure of the law to give individuals a reasonable degree of protection from unwarranted intrusion in many situations. I prefer to leave open for another occasion the important question whether the present, piecemeal protection of privacy has now developed to the extent that a more comprehensive principle can be seen to exist. It is not necessary to pursue this question on this appeal. Even if the right for which the appellant contended does exist, this would not lead to the consequence that obtaining evidence for the purpose of detecting or preventing serious crime was an infringement of the right or, even if it were, that the evidence was inadmissible at the trial.

Second, the discretionary powers of the trial judge to exclude evidence march and in hand with article 6(1) of the European Convention on Human Rights and Fundamental Freedoms. Both are concerned to ensure that those facing criminal charges receive a fair hearing. Accordingly, when considering the common law and statutory discretionary powers under English law the jurisprudence on article 6 can have a valuable role to play. English law relating to the ingredients of a fair trial is highly developed. But every system of law stands to benefit by an awareness of the answers given by other courts and tribunals to similar problems. In the present case the decision of the European Court of Human Rights in *Schenk v Switzerland* 13 EHRR 242 confirms that the use at a criminal trial of material obtained in breach of the rights of privacy enshrined in article 8 does not of itself mean that the trial is unfair. Thus the European Court of Human Rights case law on this issue leads to the same conclusion as English law.

[7:13] *R v Davis; R v Ellis, Gregory, Simms and Martin*

[2006] EWCA Crim 1155 (report taken from (2006) 6 Archbold News 6)

Two unrelated cases were heard together. Both involved appeals from murder convictions, and both had involved anonymous witnesses. In each case, there was non-disclosure of the true identity of witnesses, together with voice modulation to give the witnesses anonymity.

The Court of Appeal, led by the President of the Queen's Bench Division, dismissed the appeals. The court undoubtedly possessed an inherent jurisdiction at common law to control its own proceedings 'to defeat any attempted thwarting of its process' (per Lord Morris in *Connelly v DPP* (1964) 2 AC 1254). The President reviewed the European jurisprudence, including *Osman v United Kingdom* [1999] 1 FLR 193, *Ludi v Switzerland* (1993) 15 EHRR 173 and *Doorson v Netherlands* (1996) 22 EHRR 330, as well as domestic cases (*R (Al-Fawwaz) v Governor of Brixton Prison* [2001] UKHL 69).

> In our judgment the discretion to permit evidence to be given by witnesses whose identity may not be known to the defendant is now beyond question. The potential disadvantages to the defendant require the court to examine the application for witness anonymity with scrupulous care, to ensure that it is necessary and that the witness is indeed in genuine and justified fear of serious consequences if his true identity became known to the defendant or the defendant's associates. It is in any event elementary that the court should be alert to potential or actual disadvantages faced by the defendant in consequence of any anonymity ruling, and ensure that necessary and appropriate precautions are taken to ensure that the trial itself will be fair. Provided that appropriate safeguards are applied, and the judge is satisfied that a fair trial can take place, it may proceed. If not, he should not permit anonymity. If he does so, and there is a conviction, it is not to be regarded as unsafe simply because the evidence of anonymous witnesses may have been decisive.
>
> Among the safeguards, first, is the decision of the trial judge whether to exercise his discretion to allow some or all the witnesses against to the defendant to give their evidence anonymously. If the only evidence against the defendant consists of wholly unsupported anonymous witnesses, whose evidence is demonstrably suspect, the judge may decide, as Hughes J did in *R v Bola*, that the Crown should not adduce it.... these are issues for judicial decision in case specific situations, after allowing for the disclosure process, any PII decisions, and the ability to cross-examine together with the deployment of material helpful to the defendant in the course of cross-examination, or even when cross-examination may not be possible...At the end of the prosecution case, the judge may decide that it would be unsafe for the evidence of the anonymous witnesses to be considered further by the jury, or indeed, that the case as a whole should be withdrawn from their consideration. We are not seeking to formulate a scheme, merely to identify appropriate safeguards currently in place to ensure the fairness of the trial... The judge would probably suggest that the jury should consider whether there is any independent, supporting evidence, tending to confirm the credibility of the anonymous witnesses, and the incriminating evidence they have given. We are not reinstating outdated principles relating to corroboration, nor implying that such independent evidence is a pre-requisite to conviction. We are simply reflecting the obvious consideration that independent evidence consistent with the defendant's guilt would be likely to increase confidence in the truthfulness and accuracy of incriminating anonymous witnesses. We should perhaps finally underline that these appeals themselves demonstrate the effectiveness of the safeguards. As we shall see, in the context of the Davis appeal, the defendant in a linked trial, Harvey, was acquitted by the jury after anonymous witnesses gave evidence incriminating him, and in the Ellis appeal, the cross-examination of the anonymous witnesses wholly undermined their evidence (paras 59–61).

The Court of Appeal would not interfere with the judge's decision unless, at the time it was made, it was plainly wrong.

> However, once leave to appeal is given, it may not be sufficient for the court to dispose of the appeal on the basis that there are no grounds to justify interfering with a decision made by the judge at the time when he made it. After conviction, on appeal, this court may conclude that the order for witness anonymity had the effect of producing what in all the circumstances was an unfair trial. If so, even if the original decision of the trial judge would not be open to criticism, the conviction would be unsafe, and it would be quashed (para 64).

The President acknowledged that witness anonymity raised a distinct problem for trial counsel in deciding whether or not they should observe the witness, when their client may not.

> Our pragmatic solution...is that counsel should identify the issues for his client, and explain the alternatives. The choice is stark, and should be made by the client, on advice...Whether or not counsel decides to observe the witness personally, at the trial each member of the jury, as well as the judge, remains able to see and observe the witness for himself. They are also able to hear the unmodulated voices of the witnesses, even if they are mechanically disguised for the defendant and public, as well as counsel...If...the decision is made that counsel shall not observe the witness, the defendant cannot subsequently make a complaint to this court based on his, or his counsel's, rejection of the opportunity to do so (paras 70–73).

With the encouragement of both sides, the Court had invited the Attorney General to appoint a Special Advocate to assist the Court with the disclosure/PII matters which had been raised with the trial judge in the absence of the defence in the case of Davis. The Court concluded that no error had occurred which caused any significant disadvantage to the conduct of the defence. It had not been 'an entirely wrinkle free process' but the trial was fair.

[7:14] *R v Newton*
(1982) 77 Cr App R 13

The appellant pleaded guilty to buggery of his wife. The appellant maintained that the acts complained of were consensual, the victim that they were violent and non-consensual. The Court of Appeal allowed his appeal against sentence.

The Lord Chief Justice (at page 15):

There are three ways in which a judge in these circumstances can approach his difficult task of sentencing. It is in certain circumstances possible to obtain the answer to the problem from a jury. For example, when it is a question of whether the conviction should be under section 18 or section 20 of the Offences against the Person Act 1861, the jury can determine the issue on a trial under section 18 by deciding whether or not the necessary intent has been proved by the prosecution.

The second method which could be adopted by the judge in these circumstances is himself to hear the evidence on one side and another, and come to his own conclusion, acting so to speak as his own jury on the issue which is the root of the problem.

The third possibility in these circumstances is for him to hear no evidence but to listen to the submissions of counsel and then come to a conclusion. But if he does that, then, as Judge Argyle himself said in a passage to which reference will be made in a moment, where there is a substantial conflict between the two sides, he must come down on the side of the defendant. In other words where there has been a substantial conflict, the version of the defendant must so far as possible be accepted.

It is plain from what I have read, and indeed as accepted by learned counsel for the Crown, that the judge failed to adopt one of the three courses open to him, or the one that he did adopt was wrongly performed by him. The answer is, so far as the sentence of eight years is concerned, that that must be quashed. It is plain that in the circumstances of this case the appellant has already served too long in prison, and we propose therefore to substitute for the sentence of eight years' imprisonment such sentence as will result in his release today.

[7:15] *R v Underwood, R v Arobieke, R v Khan, R v Connors*
[2004] EWCA Crim 2256, [2005] 1 Cr App R 13, [2005] 1 Cr App R (S) 90

1. In these appeals, which we heard and decided earlier this week, we are concerned with what can compendiously be described as Newton hearings. Although the principle are clear, they are not always fully understood or applied. These appeals have therefore been listed together to enable this Court to repeat and emphasise general guidance about the procedure to be adopted where the defendant pleads guilty on a factual basis different to that which appears from the Crown's case, or, indeed, a study of the papers. In short, we are concerned with the process which will achieve the sentence appropriate to reflect the justice of the case where there is plea of guilty, but some important fact or facts relating to the offence which the defendant is admitting, of potential significance to the sentencing decision, are in dispute.

2. The essential principle is that the sentencing judge must do justice. So far as possible the offender should be sentenced on the basis which accurately reflects the facts of the individual case...

3. The starting point has to be the defendant's instructions. His advocate will appreciate whether any significant facts about the prosecution evidence are disputed and the factual basis on which the defendant intends to plead guilty. If the resolution of the facts in dispute may matter to the sentencing decision, the responsibility for taking any initiative and alerting the prosecutor to the areas of dispute rest with the defence. The Crown should not be taken by surprise, and if it is suddenly faced with a proposed basis of plea of guilty where important facts are disputed, it should, if necessary, take time for proper reflection and consultation to consider its position and the interests of justice. In any event, whatever view may be formed by the Crown on any proposed basis of plea, it is deemed to be conditional on the judge's acceptance of it.

   ...

6. After submissions from the advocates the judge should decide how to proceed. If not already decided, he will address the question whether he should approve the Crown's acceptance of pleas. Then he will address the proposed basis of plea. We emphasise that whether or not the basis of plea is "agreed", the judge is not bound by any such agreement and is entitled of his own motion to insist that any evidence relevant to the facts in dispute should be called before him. No doubt, before doing so, he will examine any agreement reached by the advocates, paying appropriate regard to it, and any reasons which the Crown, in particular, may advance to justify him proceeding immediately to sentence. At the risk of stating the obvious, the judge is responsible for the sentencing decision and he may therefore order a Newton hearing and to ascertain the truth about disputed facts.

7. The prosecuting advocate should assist him by calling any appropriate evidence and testing the evidence advanced by the defence. The defence advocate should similarly call any relevant evidence and, in particular, where the issue arises from facts which are within the exclusive knowledge of the defendant and the defendant is willing to give evidence in support of his case, be prepared to call him. If he is not, and subject to any explanation which may be proffered, the judge may draw such inferences he thinks fit from that fact. An adjournment for these purposes is often unnecessary. If the plea is tendered late when the case is due to be tried the relevant witnesses for the Crown are likely to be available. The Newton hearing should proceed immediately. In every case, or virtually so, the defendant will be present. It may be sufficient for the judge's purpose to hear the defendant. If so, again, unless it is impracticable for some exceptional reason, the hearing should proceed immediately.

8. The judge must then make up his mind about the facts in dispute. He may, of course, reject evidence called by the prosecution. It is sometimes overlooked that he may equally reject assertions advanced by the defendant, or his witnesses, even if the Crown does not offer positive contradictory evidence.

9. The judge must, of course, direct himself in accordance with ordinary principles, such as, for example, the burden and standard of proof. In short, his self-directions should reflect the relevant directions he would have given to the jury. Having reached his conclusions, he should explain them in a judgment.

10. Again, by way of reminder, we must explain some of the limitations on the Newton hearing procedure.

(a) There will be occasions when the Newton hearing will be inappropriate. Some issues require a verdict from the jury. To take an obvious example, a dispute whether the necessary intent under section 18 of the Offences against the Person Act 1861 has been proved should be decided by the jury. Where the factual issue is not encapsulated in a distinct count in the indictment when it should be, then, again, the indictment should be amended and the issue resolved by the jury. We have in mind, again for example, cases where there is a dispute whether the defendant was carrying a firearm to commit a robbery. In essence, if the defendant is denying that a specific criminal offence has been committed, the tribunal for deciding whether the offence has been proved is the jury.

(b) At the end of the Newton hearing the judge cannot make findings of fact and sentence on a basis which is inconsistent with the pleas to counts which have already been accepted by the Crown and approved by the court. Particular care is needed in relation to a multi-count indictment involving one defendant, or an indictment involving a number of defendants, and to circumstances in which the Crown accepts, and the court approves, a guilty plea to a reduced charge.

(c) Where there are a number of defendants to a joint enterprise, the judge, while reflecting on the individual basis of pleas, should bear in mind the relative seriousness of the joint enterprise on which the defendants were involved. In short, the context is always relevant. He should also take care not to regard a written basis of plea offered by one defendant, without more, as evidence justifying an adverse conclusion against another defendant.

(d) Generally speaking, matters of mitigation are not normally dealt with by way of a Newton hearing. It is, of course, always open to the court to allow a defendant to give evidence of matters of mitigation which are within his own knowledge. From time to time, for example, defendants involved in drug cases will assert that they were acting under some form of duress, not amounting in law to a defence. If there is nothing to support such a contention, the judge is entitled to invite the advocate for the defendant to call his client rather than depend on the unsupported assertions of the advocate.

(e) Where the impact of the dispute on the eventual sentencing decision is minimal, the Newton hearing is unnecessary. The judge is rarely likely to be concerned with minute differences about events on the periphery.

(f) The judge is entitled to decline to hear evidence about disputed facts if the case advanced on the defendant's behalf is, for good reason, to be regarded as absurd or obviously untenable. If so, however, he should explain why he has reached this conclusion.

11. The final matter for guidance is whether the defendant should lose the mitigation available to him for his guilty plea if, having contested facts alleged by the prosecution, the issues are resolved against him. The principles are clear. If the issues at the Newton hearing are wholly resolved in the defendant's favour, the credit due to him should not be reduced. If for example, however, the defendant is disbelieved, or obliges the prosecution to call evidence from the victim, who is then subjected to a cross-examination, which, because it is entirely unfounded, causes unnecessary and inappropriate distress, or if the defendant conveys to the judge that he has no insight into the consequences of his offence and no genuine remorse for it, these are all matters which may lead the judge to reduce the discount which the defendant would otherwise have received for his guilty plea, particularly if that plea is tendered at a very late stage. Accordingly, there may even be exceptional cases in which the normal entitlement to a credit for a plea of guilty is wholly dissipated by the Newton hearing. In such cases, again, the judge should explain his reasons.

[7:16] Sentencing Guidelines Council; Sexual Offences Act 2003: Definitive Guideline

Applicable to all those sentenced on or after 14 May 2007

This Guideline has 139 pages, so we have included only short extracts here, by way of examples. The first 20 pages deal with General Principles, such as (at pages 9–10):

THESE FACTORS APPLY TO A WIDE RANGE OF OFFENCES AND NOT ALL WILL BE RELEVANT TO SEXUAL OFFENCES

Factors indicating higher culpability:

- Offence committed whilst on bail for other offences
- Failure to respond to previous sentences
- Offence was racially or religiously aggravated
- Offence motivated by, or demonstrating, hostility to the victim based on his or her sexual orientation (or presumed sexual orientation)
- Offence motivated by, or demonstrating, hostility based on the victim's disability (or presumed disability)
- Previous conviction(s), particularly where a pattern of repeat offending is disclosed
- Planning of an offence
- An intention to commit more serious harm than actually resulted from the offence
- Offenders operating in groups or gangs
- 'Professional' offending
- Commission of the offence for financial gain (where this is not inherent in the offence itself)
- High level of profit from the offence
- An attempt to conceal or dispose of evidence
- Failure to respond to warnings or concerns expressed by others about the offender's behaviour
- Offence committed whilst on licence
- Offence motivated by hostility towards a minority group, or a member or members of it
- Deliberate targeting of vulnerable victim(s)
- Commission of an offence while under the influence of alcohol or drugs
- Use of a weapon to frighten or injure victim
- Deliberate and gratuitous violence or damage to property, over and above what is needed to carry out the offence
- Abuse of power
- Abuse of a position of trust

Factors indicating a more than usually serious degree of harm:

- Multiple victims
- An especially serious physical or psychological effect on the victim, even if unintended
- A sustained assault or repeated assaults on the same victim
- Victim is particularly vulnerable
- Location of the offence (for example, in an isolated place)

- Offence is committed against those working in the public sector or providing a service to the public
- Presence of others e.g. relatives, especially children or partner of the victim
- Additional degradation of the victim (e.g. taking photographs of a victim as part of a sexual offence)
- In property offences, high value (including sentimental value) of property to the victim, or substantial consequential loss (e.g. where the theft of equipment causes serious disruption to a victim's life or business)

Factors indicating significantly lower culpability:

- A greater degree of provocation than normally expected
- Mental illness or disability
- Youth or age, where it affects the responsibility of the individual defendant
- The fact that the offender played only a minor role in the offence

Personal mitigation

Section 166(1) Criminal Justice Act 2003 makes provision for a sentencer to take account of any matters that 'in the opinion of the court, are relevant in mitigation of sentence'. When the court has formed an initial assessment of the seriousness of the offence, then it should consider any offender mitigation. The issue of remorse should be taken into account at this point along with other mitigating features such as admissions to the police in interview.

...

Summary of general principles

(i) Except where otherwise indicated, the offence guidelines all relate to sentencing on conviction for a first-time offender after a plea of not guilty.

(ii) Starting points are based on a basic offence[17] of its category. Aggravating and mitigating factors that are particularly relevant to each offence are listed in the individual offence guidelines. The list of aggravating factors is not exhaustive and the factors are not ranked in any particular order. A factor that is an ingredient of an offence cannot also be an aggravating factor. Sexual offences will often involve some form of violence as an essential element of the offence and this has been included in fixing the starting points. Where harm is inflicted over and above that necessary to commit the offence, that will be an aggravating factor.

(iii) In relation to sexual offences, the presence of generic and offence-specific aggravating factors will significantly influence the type and length of sentence imposed. The generic list of aggravating and mitigating factors identified by the Sentencing Guidelines Council in its guideline on seriousness is reproduced at paragraph 1.20 above but not for each offence. These factors apply to a wide range of offences and not all will be relevant to sexual offences.

(iv) Unless specifically stated, the starting points assume that the offender is an adult. Sentences will normally need to be reduced where the offender is sentenced as a youth, save in the most serious cases (see paragraph 1.17 above).

(v) Specific guidance on sentencing youths for one of the child sex offences that attracts a lower statutory maximum penalty where the offender is under 18 can be found in Part 7.

(vi) There are a large number of new or amended offences in the SOA 2003 for which there is no sentencing case law. The guidelines use the starting point of 5 years for the rape of an adult with no aggravating or mitigating factors (derived from Millberry and others[18]) as the baseline from which all other sentences have been calculated.

(vii) Where a community order is the recommended starting point, the requirements to be imposed are left for the court to decide according to the particular facts of the individual case. Where a community order is the proposed starting point for different levels of seriousness of the same offence or for a second or subsequent offence of the same level of seriousness, this should be reflected by the imposition of more onerous requirements.[19]

(viii) Treatment programmes are not specifically mentioned in the guidelines. A sentencer should always consider whether, in the circumstances of the individual case and the profile of the offending behaviour, it would be sensible to require the offender to take part in a programme designed to address sexually deviant behaviour.

(ix) Reference to 'non-custodial sentence' in any of the offence guidelines (save for those in Part 7) suggests that the court consider a community order or a fine. In most instances, an offence will have crossed the threshold for a community order. However, in accordance with normal sentencing practice, even in those circumstances a court is not precluded from imposing a financial penalty where that is determined to be the appropriate sentence.

(x) In all cases, the court must consider whether it would be appropriate to make any ancillary orders, such as an order banning the offender from working with children, an order requiring the offender to pay compensation to a victim, or an order confiscating an offender's assets or requiring the forfeiture of equipment used in connection with an offence.

Notes

17 A 'basic offence' is one in which the ingredients of the offence as defined are present, and assuming no aggravating or mitigating factors

18 [2003] 2 Cr App R (S) 31

19 For further information, see the Council guideline New Sentences: Criminal Justice Act 2003, section B: 'Imposing a Community Sentence—The Approach'

. . .

The decision making process

The process set out below is intended to show that the sentencing approach for sexual offences is fluid and requires the structured exercise of discretion.

1. Identify dangerous offenders

Most sexual offences are specified offences for the purposes of the public protection provisions in the CJA 2003. The court must determine whether there is a significant risk of serious harm by the commission of a further specified offence. The starting points in the guidelines are a) for offenders who do not meet the dangerous offender criteria and b) as the basis for the setting of a minimum term within an indeterminate sentence for those who do meet the criteria.

2. Identify the appropriate starting point

Because many acts can be charged as more than one offence, consideration will have to be given to the appropriate guideline once findings of fact have been made. The sentence should reflect the facts found to exist and not just the title of the offence of which the offender is convicted.

3. Consider relevant aggravating factors, both general and those specific to the type of offence

This may result in a sentence level being identified that is higher than the suggested starting point, sometimes substantially so.

4. Consider mitigating factors and personal mitigation

There may be general or offence-specific mitigating factors and matters of personal mitigation which could result in a sentence that is lower than the suggested starting point (possibly substantially so), or a sentence of a different type.

5. Reduction for guilty plea

The court will then apply any reduction for a guilty plea following the approach set out in the Council's guideline Reduction in Sentence for a Guilty Plea.

6. Consider ancillary orders

The court should consider whether ancillary orders are appropriate or necessary. These are referred to in some of the offence guidelines.

7. The totality principle

The court should review the total sentence to ensure that it is proportionate to the offending behaviour and properly balanced.

. . .

The Guideline then deals with each sexual offence separately. For example:

Rape

THESE ARE SERIOUS OFFENCES FOR THE PURPOSES OF SECTION 224 CJA 2003

1. Rape (section 1): Intentional non-consensual penile penetration of the vagina, anus or mouth
2. Rape of a child under 13 (section 5): Intentional penile penetration of the vagina, anus or mouth of a person under 13

Maximum penalty for both offences: Life imprisonment

Type/nature of activity	Starting points	Sentencing ranges
Repeated rape of same victim over a course of time or rape involving multiple victims	15 years custody	13–19 years custody
Rape accompanied by any one of the following: abduction or detention; offender aware that he is suffering from a sexually transmitted infection; more than one offender acting together; abuse of trust; offence motivated by prejudice (race, religion, sexual orientation, physical disability); sustained attack	13 years custody if the victim is under 13	11–17 years custody
	10 years custody if the victim is a child aged 13 or over but under 16	8–13 years custody
	8 years custody if the victim is 16 or over	6–11 years custody
Single offence of rape by single offender	10 years custody if the victim is under 13	8–13 years custody
	8 years custody if the victim is 13 or over but under 16	6–11 years custody
	5 years custody if the victim is 16 or over	4–8 years custody

Additional aggravating factors	Additional mitigating factors
1. Offender ejaculated or caused victim to ejaculate	*Where the victim is aged 16 or over*
2. Background of intimidation or coercion	Victim engaged in consensual sexual activity with the offender on the same occasion and immediately before the offence
3. Use of drugs, alcohol or other substance to facilitate the offence	
4. Threats to prevent victim reporting the incident	*Where the victim is under 16*
5. Abduction or detention	• Sexual activity between two children (one of whom is the offender) was mutually agreed and experimental
6. Offender aware that he is suffering from a sexually transmitted infection	
7. Pregnancy or infection results	• Reasonable belief (by a young offender) that the victim was aged 16 or over

An offender convicted of these offences is automatically subject to notification requirements.

[7:17] *R v Webbe*
[2001] EWCA Crim 1217, [2002] 1 Cr App R (S) 82

Rose LJ:

These four appeals and one renewed application for leave to appeal against sentence have been listed together to enable the Court to consider the proposal of the Sentencing Advisory Panel, in their advice to this Court in March 2001, that sentencing guidelines should be framed in relation to offences of handling dishonestly obtained goods, contrary to section 22 of the Theft Act 1968.

...

The difficulty of issuing guidelines in relation to handling arises from the enormous variety of possible sentences according to the circumstances, as pointed out by Lord Lane C.J., in *Patel* (1984) 6 Cr.App.R.(S.) 191 at pages 192–193. The offence is triable either way and can attract a penalty within the range from a conditional discharge or modest fine at one end, to many years' imprisonment, up to the maximum of 14 provided by Parliament, at the other.

The particular feature of handling which marks it out from most other offences is that it is, by definition, ancillary to another offence in a way which can conveniently be described as secondary to a primary offence. Because the primary offence may be, for example, shoplifting or armed robbery, the degree of gravity of the secondary offence can vary accordingly.

...

We have therefore concluded that, although there is, as it seems to us, no clear evidence of inconsistency in the court's current sentencing practice, it will be helpful in promoting consistency to adopt the Sentencing Advisory Panel's proposal that guidelines should be given. We stress, however, as this Court has stressed in earlier cases, that what we suggest is not to be regarded as mandatory, but is by way of guidance only.

There are a number of authorities to which reference can conveniently be made, which show the range of sentences which may be appropriate in relation to handling.

...

In *Bloomfield* (1995) 16 Cr.App.R.(S.) 221, the Court of Appeal noted that the appropriate sentencing bracket for a receiver, who dealt regularly with thieves and burglars providing a regular outlet, was between two and four years' imprisonment, although, in that particular case, which was a one-off offence, a significantly lower sentence was imposed, namely 15 months for receiving three stolen caravans, for which he, a caravan dealer, had paid £9,000.

In *Attorney-General's Reference No. 70 of 1999* [2000] 2 Cr.App.R.(S.) 28, sentences totalling 12 months' imprisonment were increased to 30 months in relation to an offender convicted of conspiracy to handle and steal computers, which he sold through his business. In the course of the judgment of the Court, reference was made, at page 30, to a number of authorities, to at least one of which we have already referred.

In that context, we turn to the advice of the Sentencing Panel with which, as will emerge, we largely although not entirely agree. Paragraph 11 of that advice, with which we agree, is in these terms:

> "The relative seriousness of a particular case of handling depends upon the interplay of different factors. One important issue is whether the handler has had advance knowledge of the original offence; or has directly or indirectly made known his willingness to receive the proceeds of the original offence, as compared with a handler who has had no connection with the original offence but who has dishonestly accepted the stolen goods at an undervalue. Where the handler has had knowledge of the original offence, the seriousness of the handling is inevitably linked to the seriousness of that original offence. The link to the original offence explains the need for the high maximum penalty of 14 years' imprisonment for handling, which might otherwise look anomalous. Sentences approaching the maximum should clearly be reserved for the most serious and unusual cases where the handler had previous knowledge of a very serious offence such as an armed robbery, which itself carries life imprisonment as its maximum."

Paragraph 12, with the terms of which we also agree, and says as follows:

> "The replacement value of the goods involved is often a helpful indication of the seriousness of the offence. (In this context the Mode of Trial guidelines suggest that cases of handling should normally be dealt with in the magistrates' court, and hence attract a maximum sentence of six months' imprisonment, if the value of the property is under £10,000.) We do not, however, believe that monetary value itself should be regarded as the determining factor."

We interpose the comment that it is important for sentencers to bear in mind that value would not be regarded as prescriptive. There is an obvious difference, for example, between the gravity of receiving in a public house £100 worth of stolen television sets, and the gravity of receiving £100 in cash from the proceeds of a robbery which has taken place in the receiver's presence. Furthermore, accurate values in relation to the property received may very often be extremely difficult to ascertain.

The Panel, in paragraph 12 of their advice, go on to identify other factors significantly affecting the relative seriousness of the handling offence, namely the level of sophistication of the handler, the ultimate designation of the goods, the criminal origin of the goods, the impact on the victim, the level of profit made or expected by the handler, and, especially in cases of actual or intended disposal of goods, the precise role played by the handler. In our judgment, those factors are rightly identified.

We also agree, in relation to paragraph 13 of the panel's advice, that handling cases at or towards the lower end of the scale are characterised by the handler having no connection with the original offence, an absence of sophistication on the part of the handler, the less serious nature of the original offence, the relatively low value of the goods and the absence of any significant profit.

The Sentencing Panel, in paragraph 14, go on to identify nine factors, which may be regarded as aggravating the offence. With each of these factors we agree. They are as follows:

1 The closeness of the handler to the primary offence. (We add that closeness may be geographical, arising from presence at or near the primary offence when it was committed, or temporal, where the handler instigated or encouraged the primary offence beforehand, or, soon after, provided a safe haven or route for disposal).

2 Particular seriousness in the primary offence.

3 High value of the goods to the loser, including sentimental value.

4 The fact that the goods were the proceeds of a domestic burglary.

5 Sophistication in relation to the handling.

6 A high level of profit made or expected by the handler.

7 The provision by the handler of a regular outlet for stolen goods.

8 Threats of violence or abuse of power by the handler over others, for example, an adult commissioning criminal activity by children, or a drug dealer pressurizing addicts to steal in order to pay for their habit.

9 As is statutorily provided by section 151(2) of the Powers of Criminal Courts (Sentencing) Act 2000, the commission of an offence while on bail.

We also agree with the mitigating factors identified as being among those relevant by the sentencing panel: namely, low monetary value of the goods, the fact that the offence was a one-off offence, committed by an otherwise honest defendant, the fact that there is little or no benefit to the defendant, and the fact of voluntary restitution to the victim.

We also agree with the Panel that other factors to be taken into account include personal mitigation, ready co-operation with the police, previous convictions, especially for offences of dishonesty and, as statutorily provided by section 152 of the Powers of Criminal Courts (Sentencing) Act 2000, a timely plea of guilty.

The Panel, in paragraph 21 of their advice, helpfully identify four possible levels of seriousness of the offence. They suggest that a distinction can be drawn between offences first, for which a fine or a discharge is appropriate; second, for which a community sentence is appropriate; third for those which cross the custody threshold and, fourth, more serious offences.

We agree that offences do fall into those four categories. We do not, however, take the view that it is always possible to draw a distinction between the first two categories of offence with quite the clarity which the Panel suggest.

In our judgment, the Panel are right to say that, where the property handled is of low monetary value and was acquired for the receiver's own use, the starting point should generally be a moderate fine or, in some cases (particularly, of course, if a fine cannot be paid by a particular defendant) a discharge. Such an outcome would, in our judgment be appropriate in relation to someone of previous good character handling low value domestic goods for his own use. By low value we mean less than four figures.

We agree that, irrespective of value, the presence of any one of the aggravating features to which we have referred is likely to result in a community sentence rather than a fine or discharge. We agree that a community sentence may be appropriate where property worth less than four figures is acquired for resale, or where more valuable goods are acquired for the handler's own use. Such a sentence may well be appropriate in relation to a young offender with little criminal experience, playing a peripheral role. But adult defendants with a record of dishonesty are likely to attract a custodial sentence.

Thus far, as we have indicated, we agree with the factors which the Panel identifies in relation to the sentencing process for less serious offences. But we do not believe that a clear dividing line is capable of being drawn between those offences which, appropriately attract, on the one hand, a discharge or fine and, on the other, a community sentence.

So far as the custody threshold is concerned, we agree that a defendant either with a record of offences of dishonesty, or who engages in sophisticated law breaking, will attract a custodial sentence. It is in relation to the length of that sentence that the aggravating and mitigating features which we have earlier identified will come into play, as will the personal mitigation of the offender, who may appropriately, in accordance with *Ollerenshaw* [1999] 1 Cr.App.R.(S.) 65, be dealt with by a somewhat shorter sentence than might, at first blush, otherwise have seemed appropriate.

We also agree with the panel that, in relation to more serious offences, there will be some for which a sentence within the range of 12 months to four years will be appropriate and there will be others for which a sentence of considerably more than four years, up to the maximum, may be appropriate. In this regard, the factors to be taken into consideration will include whether an offence is committed in the context of a business, whether the offender is acting as an organiser or distributor of the proceeds of crime and whether the offender has made himself available to other criminals as willing to handle the proceeds of thefts or burglaries.

In all of these more serious cases, according to the other circumstances, sentences in the range of 12 months to four years are likely to be appropriate if the value of the goods involved is up to around £100,000. Where the value of the goods is in excess of £100,000, or where the offence is highly organised and bears the hallmarks of a professional commercial operation, a sentence of four years and upwards is likely to be appropriate, and it will be the higher where the source of the handled property is known by the handler to be a serious violent offence such as armed robbery. As we have earlier indicated, sentences significantly higher than four years also may be appropriate where a professional handler, over a substantial period of time, demonstrated by his record or otherwise, has promoted and encouraged, albeit indirectly, criminal activity by others.

The sentences which we have indicated will, of course, be subject to discount in appropriate cases for a plea of guilty.

We should also add that a court passing sentence in handling cases should always have in mind the power to make restitution orders under sections 148 and 149 of the Powers of Criminal Courts (Sentencing) Act 2000, to make compensation orders under section 130 of the Powers of Criminal Court (Sentencing) Act 2000, and to make confiscation orders in relation to profits, under the Criminal Justice Act 1988 and the Proceeds of Crime Act 1995. A magistrates' court cannot, of course, make a confiscation order in a case of handling. But it is open to magistrates, in such a case, where appropriate, to commit to the Crown Court for sentence.

It is implicit, in what we have said, that this Court is greatly indebted to the sentencing Advisory Panel for the advice which they have tendered.

In the context of those observations, we turn to the particular cases before this Court.

Bernard Webbe, who is 33, pleaded guilty at Manchester Crown Court on December 11, 2000 to an offence of attempting to handle and an offence of handling stolen watches. He was sentenced on January 8, 2001 by his Honour Judge Owen to 15 months' imprisonment concurrently on each count. He appeals against sentence by leave of the single judge.

The offences came to light on August 17, 2000 when, in the course of a search being made at an address in Stretford, by police officers in relation to drugs offences, the officers asked to search the appellant's car. In the boot there were three watches and £250 in cash. The appellant said they were Christmas presents which he had bought the day before through his company. One of the watches was an 18 carat gold watch with a retail value of £7,700. It had, on its journey from Switzerland to a Malaysian agent in Singapore in 1996, gone missing. That was the subject of count 1. Count 2 related to two other link chronographs, each with a retail value of £1,150 which had been stolen in transit to a shop in Northern Ireland. That gave rise to count 2. In interview the appellant made no comment. But later, he said·that he had paid £200 for the watches, to a man he had met in the street.

The appellant is of previous good character, and there was before the sentencing judge, as there is before this Court, a pre-sentence report which indicated the appellant's regret and that he was not a man who had criminal attitudes or a general disrespect for the law. He seemed to be genuinely ashamed and the risk of reoffending was minimal.

On his behalf, Mr Whelan submits that the sentence passed failed to take proper account of the plea of guilty, the good character of the appellant, the fact that he was unaware of the true value of the watches, and the absence of any professional hallmarks in this offence.

It is apparent that the total retail value of these goods was only slightly in excess of £10,000. It is also apparent that the appellant was not forthcoming in interview and could have provided the police with more help than he did as to the source and circumstances of his acquisitions. That being so, it seems to us that the custody threshold was passed, though the case could, in our judgment, properly have been dealt with, in all the circumstances, in the magistrates' court.

Taking into account the appellant's good character, the fact that the goods were apparently for the appellant's own use, the plea of guilty and the observations made in *Ollerenshaw*, we take the view that a sentence of 15 months, was manifestly excessive. We quash it. The appeal is allowed to the extent that, in substitution for that sentence, we impose a sentence of four months' imprisonment concurrently on each count.

...

Robert John Moore pleaded guilty at Northampton Crown Court on September 19, 2000 to two offences of handling stolen property. He asked for 47 other offences, predominantly of burglary and theft, to be taken into consideration. He was sentenced by His Honour Judge Allen, sitting with justices, to 4 years' imprisonment concurrently on each account.

The total value of the goods in the indictment was somewhat less than £2,000. On the other hand, the value of the property involved in the other offences, almost none of which was recovered, was some £20,000.

The appellant appeals by leave of the single judge.

The facts can be very briefly stated. On the evening of February 12/13, 2000, a dwelling house in Kiln Way, Wellingborough, was entered through an open window and jewellery stolen. On the same evening, another dwelling house, not far away, was entered by breaking a rear kitchen window while the occupants were in bed and a considerable number of compact discs and computer equipment was stolen.

On February 15, that is to say a day or two after the burglary in Kiln Way, the appellant visited a pawnbrokers and presented a stolen necklace and ring, for which he was paid cash. As evidence of identity, he produced a tenancy agreement in his own name.

A few days later, on February 21, the appellant handed to his girlfriend stolen rings which she took and converted into cash at the same pawnbrokers. On March 22 the appellant went to another pawnbrokers to sell compact discs and he was arrested by police officers. His home was searched and a number of stolen items were seized. It emerged that the appellant and his girlfriend had tried to sell computer parts at other shops in Wellingborough. At about the same time, the victims of the Kiln Way burglary saw some of the stolen property in the window of the pawnshop.

The appellant was interviewed on three occasions. On the first, he claimed that the CDs were his own and the jewellery belonged to his girlfriend. He denied involvement in the Kiln Way burglary and was unable to explain the other stolen items at his premises. On the second occasion, some six weeks later, he refused to be any more forthcoming but, on April 28, he effectively admitted having carried out the burglary at Kiln Way, saying the window was open and he climbed in, went upstairs and found the jewellery.

The 47 offences which he asked to have taken into consideration included some 27 of theft and some 17 or so of burglary.

The learned judge, in passing sentence, said he gave credit for the plea and such frankness as the appellant had shown, but the handling of the stolen property, soon after the burglaries, and the other offences involving many dwelling-house burglaries, called for the sentence which he imposed.

The appellant is 26. He has 18 previous convictions involving 60 offences. He has been sentenced to immediate custody on seven previous occasions. His record includes many offences of dishonesty, including burglary, theft and handling.

The submission which is made on his behalf, by Miss Hales, is that the weight of offences taken into consideration was very much greater than the two offences to which the appellant pleaded guilty on the indictment. The learned judge, in passing the sentence which he did, inadequately reflected the credit which needed to be given by the court for the frankness which the appellant had shown in admitting these other offences, and asking for them to be taken into consideration. She submits, rightly, that the convention of taking offences into consideration, is pragmatically based and is of benefit to the police and to a defendant. It is of benefit for the police in clearing up offences. It is of benefit to the defendant because he avoids the need to have to appear on another occasion to be dealt with for offences which he now admits. Miss Hales does not submit that, if the appellant were being sentenced for the many offences of burglary which he had taken into consideration, four years would be otherwise than appropriate. But she submits that it did not adequately reflect the degree of co-operation by the appellant, in all these circumstances of this case.

In our judgment, it is not generally desirable that a very large number of offences should be taken into consideration when there are comparatively few offences in the indictment and when the offences taken into consideration are of a different kind from those in the indictment. It is a far preferable course for the indictment, so far as possible, to reflect the general level of criminality of a particular defendant.

There are, of course, cases where it is entirely appropriate for there to be many similar offences to be taken into consideration, for example, in social security frauds; and many other examples can be thought of.

That said, in the present case, all the offences taken into consideration were offences of dishonesty. They were not offences, in that sense, dissimilar from those in the indictment. Furthermore, the burglary offences were ones to which the same maximum sentence as for handling applies, that is 14 years.

In our judgment, the learned judge fully recognised that the appellant was entitled to credit, not only for his pleas of guilty, but also for the co-operation which he had shown in disclosing and admitting his part in the other offences which were taken into consideration. We have no hesitation in concluding that, had the learned judge been called upon to sentence the offender for 17 domestic burglaries, in the light of his record, the sentence would have been very considerably longer than four years' imprisonment. Despite Miss Hales' submission, therefore, we are unpersuaded that the sentence of four years failed to reflect the degree of co-operation displayed by the appellant.

So far as the receiving offences themselves are concerned, it is apparent, in relation to at least one of them, that the appellant was, to put it no higher, extremely close to the commission of the primary offence. The total sentence was not excessive. In our judgment, there is no merit in this appeal and accordingly it is dismissed.

...

[7:18] *Attorney-General's Reference No 111 of 2006 (Ghulam Hussain)*
[2006] EWCA Crim 3269

Lord Justice Keene:

1 This is an application, under section 36 of the Criminal Justice Act 1988 , by Her Majesty's Attorney-General for leave to refer a sentence to this Court because it appears to him to be unduly lenient. We grant leave and we treat this therefore as the hearing of the Reference.

2 This offender pleaded guilty to manslaughter on 14th August 2006 in the Crown Court at Wolverhampton on an indictment charging him with murder. He was sentenced on 18th September 2006 by His Honour Judge Chapman to 3 years' imprisonment and was disqualified from driving for 5 years and ordered to take an extended driving test.

3 The offender was at the time a 44-year old taxi driver. The offence arose out of events just after 2.00 am on Sunday 26th February 2006, in West Bromwich. Around that time the victim, a 17-year-old student called Scott Poll, was with two friends of about the same age, walking along a road called Hollyhedge Road within the built-up area. They had been enjoying a Saturday evening out and had undoubtedly had some drinks. By 2.00 am they were trying to find a taxi. They were passed by the offender driving his black cab. As he passed the three young men, Scott Poll attempted, unsuccessfully, to flag him down, and then shouted "Paki" at him, a shout which it appears the offender did not hear.

The offender did a U-turn a little way up the road and travelled back the way he had come. As he did so the group crossed the road so as to be on the same side as the taxi but Scott Poll remained in the carriageway while his friends stood on the footway. As the offender approached Scott Poll, he slowed his vehicle down to a walking pace. There was evidence that at the same time the victim's friends began shouting. The offender then steered to go round Scott Poll, who moved in the same direction, with the result that he remained in front of the taxi. Scott Poll also put his hands onto the bonnet. The offender continued to drive slowly forwards and Scott Poll was moving backwards as he did so. Scott Poll then lost his footing and fell under the front of the taxi.

4 The offender, however, did not stop when Scott Poll went under the front of the vehicle, but instead accelerated away. It is clear, as the judge found, that he realised immediately after the initial collision that something was very wrong. The judge said that he must have realised that the victim was under the taxi because he must have felt the resistance in attempting to steer the taxi; he admitted that the steering felt wrong and heavy—that admission was made in interview—and because of the screams and shouts from the victim. Those screams were sufficiently loud to be audible to other people who were asleep in their beds in nearby properties.

5 Scott Poll became trapped under the front of the vehicle and he was dragged along screaming, including, for part of the time, being driven onto the pavement and over road humps. The offender carried on in this fashion for more than a mile at normal road speeds, despite being aware, as I have indicated, that he was dragging someone beneath his cab, until the body of Scott Poll eventually became dislodged at a roundabout and was left in the road. The offender then continued driving on.

6 The police were alerted and they found the body of Scott Poll. He had died from multiple injuries caused by being dragged against the ground as the vehicle travelled along. The next day the offender had the underside of his taxi steam cleaned. He eventually went to police on Wednesday, 1st March, admitting he had been the driver but initially denying knowing that he had hit anyone. In his second interview, he admitted that when he drove off, he had felt someone under his car for some distance but that he had not stopped out of panic, thinking that he had killed someone.

7 In his basis of plea it was said that the deceased's companions had began shouting and that as a result of that the offender drove off in a blind panic.

8 On the eve of the trial, 11th August 2006, the offender offered a plea of guilty to manslaughter on the basis of gross negligence, the negligence being that he had acted as he had done from the moment Scott Poll had gone under the front of the taxi. Initially the prosecution declined to accept that plea, and the trial began. However, on the second day the prosecution decided to accept the plea and the defendant then entered formally a plea of guilty to manslaughter.

9 The judge indicated in his sentencing remarks that he would allow a 25 per cent reduction in sentence for the plea of guilty. He emphasised that the offender must have seen Mr Poll in the carriageway and, as I have indicated, must have realised that he had fallen beneath the cab.

10 The judge did not suggest that the offender deliberately drove into the victim, but he stressed that the offender had then driven on, knowing that Scott Poll was trapped beneath the vehicle. The judge, at page 26 of his sentencing remarks said that:

"...the further you drove, the longer you continued driving knowing that he was trapped beneath you, the more culpable your actions became, so that after a time I am satisfied that you continued to drive with an utterly reckless disregard for the safety of Scott Poll, and that as a result he died."

....

14 We acknowledge that sentencing for offences of manslaughter by gross negligence is never an easy process. The guidance on causing death by dangerous driving in a case such as this may be of some relevance because the mitigating and aggravating factors identified in the guidelines for those cases may sometime apply; but their value tends to be somewhat limited, and such is the case here. It is to be borne in mind that death by dangerous driving has a maximum sentence, even now, of 14 years, whereas the maximum for manslaughter is life imprisonment. Manslaughter when using a

vehicle can vary considerably in its characteristics, and various factors may be relevant in the individual case. Whether there was any animosity by the defendant towards the deceased will be relevant, as will whether the gross negligence was prolonged or shortlived and whether it took place in the context of some other offence, such as seeking to steal the vehicle. The consequences, such as the number of deaths, would also be relevant.

15 There are a number of decided cases concerned with sentencing for motor manslaughter in recent years, but none purport to be guideline cases. The facts vary hugely, but on a plea of guilty the sentences at first instance tend to suggest a bracket of between 4 and 7 years, with most tending to be in the upper half of that range (see the decisions in R v Sherwood (1995) 16 Cr App R(S) 513 , R v Gault (1995) 16 Cr App R(S) 1013 , Attorney-General's Reference 68 of 1995 [1996] 2 Cr App R(S) 358 , R v Ripley (1997) 1 Cr App R(S) 19 , and the Attorney-General's References No 16 of 1999 and 14 of 2001 [2000] 1 Cr App R(S) 524 and [2002] 1 Cr App R(S) 106).

16 In the present case one is faced with an offender of good character and mature years. We entirely accept that. He was not at the time engaged in any unlawful activity and he pleaded guilty. We are unpersuaded that the judge should have given any greater discount than the 25 per cent which he allowed here. This offender had ample opportunities to offer a plea to manslaughter at the various earlier hearings in this case. He was at that time advised by counsel. In all those circumstances a plea offered on the eve of trial merited no more than the 25 per cent discount which the judge allowed him.

17 Coming to the circumstances of the case, we accept that the offender here did panic. The consequences of his actions, however, were quite devastating, not only for his victim but also for the victim's family. A relatively young life was cut short by the offender's action.

18 Three factors seem to this Court to make this offence particularly serious within the sort of range to which we have referred. The first is that this offender put his own fear ahead of the life of another person. He may have acted instantaneously, as is submitted, but he was aware that Scott Poll had gone under the cab and was trapped there but, in that knowledge, he accelerated away, choosing to risk Mr Poll's life. As the judge said, this exhibited an utterly reckless disregard. Secondly, even though the offender may have driven initially because of fear or panic, he persisted in driving with his victim being dragged along under the vehicle for over a mile. That is a factor which weighs particularly heavily in this Court's assessment of the appropriate sentence. The offender must have been well away, from the victim's two friends long before that point was reached. Thirdly, even when the body of Scott Poll fell from beneath the cab, the offender did not stop and try to render any assistance in case assistance might have been of value at that stage. Instead, he simply drove on. All these actions show a wanton disregard for the life of another person.

19 We are satisfied that, even taking account of the late plea of guilty and the other mitigating factors in this case, the sentence of 3 years' imprisonment was unduly lenient. At first instance the sentence here, on this late plea, should have been one of 6 years' imprisonment. As this is a reference, we have to make allowance for what often is called double jeopardy, in other words for the fact that this man is being sentenced a second time for this offence.

20 For that reason, we quash the sentence of 3 years' imprisonment, but we put in its place a term of imprisonment of 5 years. The 12 days spent on remand will still count towards the serving of the sentence. The other parts of the sentence passed by the judge below stand as they were.

[7:19] Ashworth, A, Genders, E, Mansfield, G, Peay, J, and Player, E, *Sentencing in the Crown Court: Report of an Exploratory Study*

(1984) Oxford Centre for Criminological Research Occasional Paper No 10 (at page 60)

All the judges whom we consulted insisted that the right to determine the form and length of sentence in each case should be theirs, and firmly opposed any suggestion of 'interference' by Parliament in the form of legislative restrictions on sentencing. 'The Judges should be trusted', as one judge put it. A wise sentencing discretion was defended as necessary to give proper effect to the varying facts of individual cases. This pre-occupation with variations of facts in individual cases leads many judges to regard sentencing as 'an art rather than a science'. It is generally thought inappropriate to require a judge to give reasons for his choice of sentence, and such 'reasons' as are given tend to consist of general references to factors taken into account rather than a detailed explanation of how the judge weighted those factors in arriving at the precise sentence. There is judicial ambivalence about the implications of the view that sentencing is 'an art rather than a science'. The grip of the maxim that 'each case depends on its own facts' leads many judges to considerable scepticism about the very enterprise of formulating and stating principles of sentencing. Indeed, even if general principles were clearly articulated, a particular judge's interpretation of the material presented to him might lead him to categorise the facts in one way whilst another judge classified them differently. On the other hand, the 'pilot study' found no shortage of judicial requests for more guidance on some issues which seem capable of resolution or which raise particular difficulties. It is elementary to point out that maxims such as 'each case depends on its own facts' do not sit comfortably with a judicial commitment to consistency and to 'uniformity of approach'. The Lord Chief Justice, in his judgment in *R v Bibi* (1980) 71 Cr App Rep 360 and in other judgments since the 'pilot study' was completed, has shown his firm belief that more guidance is necessary and, by implication, that it can be helpful to Crown Court sentencers in dealing with their cases.

Research could go much further than simply showing that the 'facts of the case' are not objective matters but are the result of a subtle reconstruction by the individual judge, and that judges do draw upon general views or propositions when arriving at sentences. it could identify key factors which tend to be interpreted differently by individual judges, and could identify salient variations in the attitudes of judges to certain types of offence, types of offenders and types of sentence. This information could be used in framing the guidance given to sentencers at judicial seminars or by the Court of Appeal. It could make a major contribution to the development of consistency in sentencing, by ensuring not only that the guidance meets and takes account of the needs of sentencers but also that the guidance is likely to be effective. The possibility of judges interpreting similar cases in different ways ought to be reduced if clear guidance on the significance is to be found in *Bibi* (1980), where the Lord Chief Justice identified classes of case in which sentences might be lowered but made no reference to the effect on sentence of the offender's previous record, the number of offences, and so on. Is it realistic to call for 'uniformity of approach' when no reference is made to the effect on sentence of matters which sentencers clearly regard as important? Policy initiatives aimed at altering practice in a particular sphere of sentencing may meet with little success, as did the *Bibi* initiative, or have unintended side-effects, unless they are grounded upon systematic knowledge of judicial approaches to sentencing.

Some might argue that the diversity of approaches we found among the small numbers of 'experienced' judges interviewed in this 'pilot study' raises a powerful case for greater control over the use of sentencing powers by judges, whether by legislative restrictions or otherwise. That might be the correct conclusion, but it need not be. Another possibility would be to use the results of research in framing study programmes for judges. The 'pilot study' found that many judges appeared to have devoted little thought to the principles on which they act. The Judicial Studies Board might be willing to use research findings on judges' awareness of their own sentencing practices, on judges' feelings of constraint, on different interpretations of the facts of cases, and generally on judicial attitudes towards various factors in sentencing. It might be profitable if the divergent practices were discussed and debated at judicial seminars, with a view to formulating general policies on some matters and modifying attitudes. If, as the 'pilot study' suggests, one reason why guidance from Parliament or from the Court of Appeal might have limited effect lies in the resilience of individual judicial attitudes, then it might be best to tackle these individual differences directly in the context of a judicial seminar. Systematic research into Crown Court sentencing could supply the basis for such an approach.

Research findings also have implications for the concept of judicial independence. On the one hand, despite judges' opposition to any encroachment upon their independence by members of the executive such as the Home Office, some judges seem quite unaware of the influence upon the listing of cases exerted by certain administrators. Research which is able to identify influences of this kind may enhance rather than challenge the independence of the judiciary. On the other hand, there are respects in which the concept of judicial independence seems to be used inappropriately: greater contact with the probation service would not necessarily threaten, either apparently or in reality, the impartiality of the judiciary and might well improve understanding of the expectations of each party. Perhaps the most forceful manifestation of judicial independence, however, lies in the substantial autonomy of the individual judge. In theory, of course, each judge is subject to the law, to the appeal process, and to the undertaking in his judicial oath. In practice, the paucity of legal rules and principles on sentencing and the limitations of their enforcement set by the appeal system (with no prosecution appeals, and few defence appeals actually coming before the Court of Appeal) leave the individual judge with considerable room to gall into idiosyncrasies in sentencing. Whilst assistant recorders and recorders will know that their appointment to a higher judicial office may to some extent depend upon reports of their 'performance', there appear to be few controls on the approach to sentencing of a circuit judge. Sentences which are grossly out of line are likely to be corrected if the excess is one of severity rather than leniency, and there is the possibility of a 'word in the ear' from a presiding judge on the circuit, but in general judges have considerable leeway. They appear also to have developed techniques for the neutralisation of criticism. Apparent inconsistencies in sentencing are explained by reference to the facts of the particular case; the press, the public and politicians are believed to be generally ill-informed about the full facts of cases and thus their criticisms are discounted; indeed, individual judges may attempt to neutralise criticism from the Court of Appeal, in a case in which it varies a sentence passed at the trial, by maintaining that the Court is out of touch with current practice. One consequence of all this is that the principle of judicial independence may have become a cloak behind which the idiosyncrasies of an individual judge go substantially unchallenged, thus undermining the 'uniformity of approach' which the Lord Chief Justice has declared to be his aim.

At the end of our report to the Lord Chief Justice on the 'pilot study', we outlined the proposal for a full research project which would continue the attempt 'faithfully to reflect the realities of Crown Court sentencing and the system within which it takes place, and to explore the reasons why judges approach sentencing as they do'. Within the study we propose to pursue certain particular lines of enquiry:

- the attitudes of judges to certain kinds of crime and certain kinds of sentence;
- the interpretations which judges place upon evidence before them, in order to arrive at the 'facts of the case' which they consider relevant for the purpose of sentencing;
- what judges expect of the Court of Appeal and, if permission were given, how the Court of Appeal views its functions in relation to the lower courts;
- what judges seek from social enquiry reports and speeches in mitigation;
- how the practices of probation officers, counsel and court administrators can influence the course which a case takes;
- how it is that judges sometimes feel they have no alternative but to pass a particular sentence, when other judges would pass different sentences;
- how well judges understand their own sentencing practices, and whether it is possible for a judge to believe that he is passing a reduced sentence when, by his own standards, he is not.

In December 1981, the Lord Chief Justice, Lord Lane, informed us that the research would not be allowed to go ahead.

CHAPTER EIGHT

JURIES

Since Gerry Good was charged with an offence under the Offences Against the Person Act 1861 (OAPA 1861), section 18, he is triable only on indictment. He will therefore be tried in the Crown Court before a judge and jury. It is the jury who decide whether or not he is guilty. Juries are often seen as the 'bulwark of our liberty', yet the reality may be very different: there is increasing scepticism about what is clearly an expensive and under-researched method of trial. Perhaps the most interesting question is how juries reach their decisions, but little is known about how juries work in practice. The Contempt of Court Act 1981, section 8 **[8:1]** effectively banned any research into jury decision making. No action has yet been taken on the recommendation of the Royal Commission on Criminal Justice (1993) that it should be possible for properly authorized research to be carried out into the way in which juries reach their verdicts and that section 8 should be amended (although Lord Justice Auld **[1:5]** was more ambivalent about the need for this). Some research into how juries actually carry out their task has been done using shadow or mock juries (see, for example, McCabe and Purves (1974)), and there have been a number of television programmes using this technique. However, since the mock jury knows that that is all it is, the value of such studies is limited. Darbyshire (2001) provides a useful review of the literature.

(i) SELECTING THE JURY

The basic rules governing juries are found in the Juries Act 1974 **[8:2]**, though the Criminal Justice Act 1988, section 119 raised the maximum age of jurors to 70 (but jury service is voluntary after the age of 65) and the Criminal Justice and Public Order Act (CJPOA) 1994, sections 40–43, the Courts Act 2003, the Criminal Justice Act 2003, section 321 and Schedule 33, the Constitutional Reform Act 2005, and the Electoral Administration Act 2006 have all amended the rules on disqualification and excusal. Even today, the jury does not necessarily reflect the community as a whole: the initial summoning is done at random from names on the electoral roll, and many people may not be registered on the roll. Of those summoned, a high proportion successfully avoid or evade service (see Darbyshire, 2001). The Royal Commission on Criminal Justice **[1:4]** urged electoral registration officers to take every possible step to ensure that electoral rolls are as comprehensive as possible. It pointed out that it is particularly important that efforts are made to persuade people from ethnic minorities to register. How are electoral officers to achieve this? Is there any convincing alternative to using the electoral roll?

Those who are mentally ill are ineligible for jury service. The people disqualified are those on bail; those who have at any time been sentenced to indeterminate, or more than five years, imprisonment; those who have served any period of imprisonment, suspended sentence, or community order within the last ten years. Those with minor criminal convictions may sit on a jury—but is it right to disqualify those on bail? The Royal Commission was not convinced that the jury service rules are the best that could be devised, but it concluded that, before they were changed, there should be proper research into their possible influence on jury trials. Auld **[1:5]** suggested the law should be amended to substitute for the condition of registration on an electoral roll 'inclusion in such a roll and/or on any one or more of a number of specified publicly maintained lists or directories, but excluding anyone listed, who, on investigation at the summons stage, is found not to be entitled to registration as an elector'. Until the Criminal Justice Act (CJA) 2003, judges, those 'concerned with the administration of justice', and the clergy were ineligible for jury service. At **[8:3]** we discuss *R v Abdroikov* [2007] UKHL 37 where, in three joined appeals, the House of Lords had to decide whether the presence of a police officer or a Crown Prosecution Service (CPS) solicitor on a jury would lead a fair-minded and informed observer to conclude that there was a real possibility of bias. Which way would you have decided the case?

Between the ages of 18 and 65 jury service is compulsory: this can be both inconvenient and expensive to the individual juror. When the jury summonses have been issued, many people return them, pleading a wide variety of reasons for being unable to sit on a jury on the dates in question, such as a booked holiday or an important work commitment. The Divisional Court in *R v Guildford Crown Court, ex p Siderfin* [1990] 2 QB 683 held that there was no excusal as of right on religious grounds. However, the Royal Commission's recommendation **[1:4]** that practising members of religious societies or orders who find jury service to be incompatible with their tenets or beliefs should be excused was enacted by CJPOA 1994, section 42. But the CJA 2003 abolished the right to be excused: now anyone who wishes to be excused must show 'good reason'. An important deterrent may well be the risk of loss of earnings. The Royal Commission recommended an urgent review of financial loss allowances, but this raises the bigger question of how this compulsory community service can be justified. In a typical short case like Gerry Good's, the jury will have been summoned for a two-week period. Several jurors may have sat together on a jury the day before, but much time will have been spent hanging around—the facilities are often poor: uncomfortable chairs, no TV or newspapers, unattractive refreshment facilities. It is not surprising that Auld **[1:5]** argued strongly for improved court facilities for jurors, including facilities to enable jurors-in-waiting to conduct their own affairs. In section (iii) below some attempt will be made to assess the value of the lay jury in deciding questions of fact in certain criminal trials. An important associated question is whether 12 is too high a number—fewer people's time would be wasted if the jury had fewer members. Would a jury made up of nine, or even six, people be as satisfactory?

Are jurors truly representative? Zander and Henderson's famous Crown Court study (1993) (and see **[7:2]**) found that neither women nor people from ethnic minorities were badly under-represented. Women made up 47 per cent of all jurors (but only 22 per cent of jury foremen) and non-white jurors made up 5 per cent of jurors, as compared with 5.9 per cent of the total population. Perhaps of more concern is the distribution of non-white jurors in individual cases. In 65 per cent of cases there were no non-whites on the jury (and in one, no white jurors). The Court of Appeal held in *Ford* **[8:4]** that there is no right to a multiracial jury. However, the Royal Commission believed that in some cases race should be taken into account. It accepted the proposal of the Commission for Racial Equality that, before trial, the prosecution or defence should be able to apply to the judge for a multiracial jury, including up to three people from ethnic minorities. This the judge would grant only if the applicant's case was reasonable because of some special feature. Auld **[1:5]** also advocated a scheme for cases in which the court considers that race is likely to be relevant to an important issue in the case, for the selection of a jury consisting of, say, up to three people from any ethnic minority group. But the decision in *Ford* has not been overruled.

There are other criticisms of the composition of juries. The longer a trial, the more complicated it is likely to be. Yet the longer the trial, the more jurors will find legitimate grounds for excusal, and the less representative they will be. There are those who suggest that 18 is too young a minimum age for jurors, since they will be too inexperienced. However, Zander and Henderson (1993) found that age had little or no effect on jury verdicts: if anything, older age-group juries were more likely to acquit than the younger. Should there be physical or educational (reading and writing?) tests, as recommended by Lord Denning (1982)?

Those summoned for jury service constitute the jury panel, and from the panel the jury for an individual case will be selected. The parties to the case are entitled to inspect the list, but it contains only names and addresses. From the jury panel, the jury is selected randomly in open court, by the clerk of the court reading out the names from a pile of cards. Thus, in Gerry Good's case, once he has been arraigned (asked if he pleads guilty or not guilty) perhaps 20 jurors will be led into the back of the courtroom. The clerk will read out one name at a time. As they enter the jury box, each juror may be challenged by the prosecution or the defence. Probably Gerry Good keeps his eyes down, vaguely irritated, and vaguely embarrassed by the whole process. The defence used to have a right of peremptory challenge (the right to challenge prospective jurors without having to give reasons) but this was reduced from seven to three challenges per defendant by the Criminal Law Act 1977 and abolished by the Criminal Justice Act 1988. The main objection to these challenges was that they interfered with the random selection of the jury, but there was no evidence that peremptory challenges had any effect on acquittals, and they were rarely used. What peremptory challenges did allow was the exclusion of those who defendants, or their counsel, felt by their appearance were unlikely to reach a fair verdict.

Thus, today the defence only has the right to 'challenge for cause', which means the right to ask that a prospective juror be dismissed because there is reason to believe that he or she will be biased or incapable. Since, unlike in the United States, potential jurors cannot be questioned in order to discover whether there is any ground for a challenge, challenges for cause are rare. The prosecution has the right to challenge for cause, or to require a juror to 'stand by for the Crown', which is similar to a peremptory challenge. This right was not abolished by the Criminal Justice Act 1988, but the following year the Attorney-General issued guidelines stating that the Crown should assert its right to stand by 'only sparingly and in exceptional circumstances' **[8:5]**. The guidelines allow the search of criminal records for the purpose of ascertaining whether or not a member of the panel is a disqualified person, and some further investigations of members of the panel in security or terrorist cases. This practice, known as 'jury vetting', remains controversial, perhaps mainly because it is unclear how widespread the practice is.

(ii) THE FUNCTION OF THE JURY

This is a book on criminal processes, but it is worth remembering that juries have a role elsewhere in the legal system. The Court of Appeal confirmed in *H v Ministry of Defence* **[8:6]** that juries are rarely available in civil personal injury cases. Controversy surrounds the use of juries in libel cases, where the jury not only decide liability but also award damages, often in a way which can be both unpredictable and unjust. A jury is also summoned in some inquests in coroners' courts (particularly where there has been a death in custody). In criminal cases, the jury's role is limited to determining guilt, and they have no role in sentencing. Juries have to decide issues of fact, and on those facts decide whether or not the defendant is guilty of the crime charged. They give no reasons for their decisions, with the result that it is extremely difficult to challenge a verdict. Does this undermine a defendant's right to a fair trial?

During the course of a trial the jury sit together in the jury box and listen to the evidence. It is widely acknowledged that juries are likely to perform better if they know what to expect and if they receive full, clear guidance and assistance. They therefore receive written notes explaining the procedure of jury service, and usually see an introductory video, before the case begins. Perhaps they should be encouraged by judges to take notes if they want to? At a time when juries are increasingly being asked to study lengthy and complicated written evidence, the Royal Commission (1993) sensibly recommended that the provision of writing materials should be standard, which it now is. Note Madge (2006)—a judge's view that jury's should receive more guidance in writing.

In Gerry Good's case, four witnesses for the prosecution are called, and none for the defence. Gerry chooses, as he is entitled to, not to give evidence. It may not be a very wise decision: since 1995, the jury has been entitled to draw 'such inferences as appear proper' from a defendant's failure to testify in court (see CJPOA 1994, section 35). The Crime and Disorder Act 1998, section 35, extends this provision to allow adverse inferences to be drawn against defendants under the age of 14. Although a person cannot be convicted solely on an inference drawn from silence, this change in the law can be seen to undermine the presumption of innocence. How it works in practice can be seen in *Cowan* [1996] 1 Cr App R 1. A rather harsh example is *Friend* [1997] 2 Cr App R 231, where the jury were entitled to draw adverse inferences from the decision of a mentally disabled 15-year-old not to give evidence. However, the drawing of adverse inferences from silence in the police station is a much greater threat to due process than inferences drawn from silence at trial (see Chapter 2).

After counsel for both sides have made their closing speeches, the judge gives the summing up, the importance of which was discussed in Chapter 7. The jury will be told that they have to reach a unanimous verdict, although they may well know that eventually a majority verdict may be permitted. At the end of the summing up they retire to a jury room to consider their verdict, and will then be kept together privately until either they reach a verdict or they are discharged because they find themselves unable to do so. Sometimes jurors wish to ask the judge questions or to be reminded of a piece of evidence, in which case they will be brought back into open court. Occasionally, when the jury have been unable to reach a verdict swiftly, it has been necessary to keep them in a hotel overnight, but nowadays they will usually be permitted to separate for the night, even once they have retired to consider their verdict. Remember that the verdict is simply 'guilty' or 'not guilty'. Juries do not give reasons for their decisions. How does this stand up to scrutiny in the light of the right to a fair trial in Article 6 of the European Convention on Human Rights **[1:12]**? As Spencer (2001) shows, the European case law is not altogether helpful on the point.

Majority verdicts, first introduced by the Criminal Justice Act 1967, are now governed by the Juries Act 1974, section 17 **[8:2]**. The jury are sent out to reach a unanimous verdict and it is left to the judge's discretion whether, after at least two hours have passed, they are prepared to accept a majority verdict. If a majority verdict is guilty, the foreman must state in open court the number of jurors who agreed to, and the number who dissented from, the verdict.

TABLE 8.1 Jury verdicts and majority verdicts

	Defendants convicted after a plea of not guilty	Percentage after a majority verdict
1993	12,460	15%
1997	11,510	20%
2001	16,605	14%
2006	11, 839	18%

Source: Judicial Statistics 1997–2001, Table 6.11; Judicial Statistics 2006, Table 6.9

Are majority verdicts a dangerous inroad into the principle that no one should be convicted unless the prosecution has proved their guilt beyond reasonable doubt, or are they a sensible pragmatic compromise? Are there adequate due process safeguards? The main justification for introducing the majority verdict was said at the time to be that a majority verdict would reduce the risk of improper pressure being put on individual jurors and reduce the likelihood of 'jury nobbling'. Today the main justification would probably be the costs saved in avoiding a retrial, but the risks of corrupt influences and jury intimidation still remain.

Is the function of the jury to apply a clearly established legal definition to the facts that they have found to be proved, or do they have an additional function of introducing lay values into the administration of justice (see Andrews (1978))? Is it part of their function to prevent the unjust use of the criminal law, exercising what is sometimes called 'jury equity'? Drawing the line between the proper functions of judge and jury can be very difficult. The criminal law reflects an ambivalence: some words—such as, for example, 'insulting' or 'dishonest'—are left for the jury to interpret according to their common sense, while others—such as 'intention', 'recklessness' or 'provocation'—have been rigidly judicially defined such that, at times, as a matter of law, they no longer mean what ordinary English suggests *Brutus v Cozens* [8:7] is a classic example: whilst the House of Lords says that it is for the magistrates (or jury) to decide the meaning of 'insulting behaviour', the real question is whether it should be the judge or the jury who should decide whether the protester was infringing the law set out in the Public Order Act 1936. The meaning of an ordinary word may not be a question of law, but the proper construction of a statute clearly is. Does the distinction between law and fact in this context make sense, or is it just a technique that allows judges to avoid ruling on difficult questions? Another example: a sewage company unknowingly causes pollution, because an unauthorized person had dumped a chemical into the sewers: do they 'cause' the pollution? Should the judge or jury decide this? (An answer to this question can be found in *National Rivers Authority v Yorkshire Water Services Ltd* [1995] 1 AC 444.)

(iii) ASSESSING THE JURY

A fundamental question is whether the jury or the judge is better equipped to deal with the meaning of ordinary words (or the ordinary meaning of words, as Guest (1986) prefers to put it). The jury are often said to have an important constitutional role: 'the lamp that shows that freedom lives', as Lord Devlin famously said. Certainly a jury can acquit someone against the evidence, when their conscience leads them so to do. One reason why sheep-stealing stopped being a capital offence was that juries were refusing to convict sheep-stealers, and in the 1930s Parliament was forced to introduce a new offence of causing death by reckless driving when juries showed a marked reluctance to convict for manslaughter those who killed by dangerous driving. The acquittal in 1984 of Ponting—a senior civil servant who passed secret documents to an MP and was prosecuted under the Official Secrets Act 1911—is said to show the constitutional importance of the jury, with their freedom to disagree with both the judge and the Government. Lord Devlin **[8:8]** describes the jury as a democratic veto on law enforcement.

But this argument is debunked by Darbyshire **[8:9]**. Juries are used in relatively few cases: the Crown Court deals with less than 3 per cent of all criminal cases.

TABLE 8.2 Acquittals of defendants by juries

	Acquittals (as percentage of those pleading not guilty)	Percentage of those acquitted who are acquitted by jury (as opposed to on direction of judge)
1993	58%	43%
1997	64%	35%
2001	66%	33%
2005	59%	30%

Source: Judicial Statistics (various years), Chapter 6

Let us look a bit more closely at the acquittal rate: during 2006, 59 per cent (16,982) of the defendants who pleaded not guilty in the Crown Court (28,821) were acquitted, representing 21 per cent of the total 80,947 dealt with who recorded a plea. Of those 16,982, 58 per cent were discharged by the judge, 10 per cent were acquitted on the direction of the judge, 1 per cent were otherwise acquitted, and 30 per cent were acquitted by a jury (Judicial and Court Statistics 2006, page 103). How can we know if these people were wrongly acquitted? It is very difficult to assess the jury. Are they too easily swayed, susceptible to rhetoric? Are they prone to leniency? Are they too doubtful nowadays of police evidence? The acquittal of Ponting can be seen as inappropriate—the proper means for amending the Official Secrets Act was through the ballot box, not via the jury room—and one has to remember that in all 'miscarriage of justice' cases it was the jury who decided to convict.

It is clear that defendants and their legal advisers prefer trial by jury and consider it fairer than trial by magistrates (and not simply more likely to result in an acquittal: see **[6:2]**). But is this belief justified? Zander and Henderson (1993) (and see **[7:5]**) asked the various participants in the trial process whether they were surprised by the jury's verdict. Prosecution barristers were surprised in 15 per cent of cases, defence barristers and judges in 14 per cent, defence solicitors in 18 per cent, police in 25 per cent, and the CPS in 27 per cent of cases. They were not necessarily surprised by the same verdicts, and acquittals gave rise to surprise more frequently than convictions. The police and CPS were surprised by 44–47 per cent of acquittals. Judges were surprised by 25 per cent of acquittals, though most of these were 'understandable in the light of the evidence'. However, according to judges, 29 per cent of all acquittals were against the weight of the evidence, against the judge's direction on the law, or simply inexplicable to judges. The number of 'problematic acquittals', according to prosecution barristers, was 31 per cent, and for defence barristers the figure was 16 per cent. Does this suggest that a quarter of all acquittals are wrong? Thomas (2007) revealed that mixed ethnicity juries in London did not discriminate against defendants based on their ethnicity but that most juries in most Crown Courts are likely to be all-white juries. The crucial question being addressed in the next research is whether all-white juries discriminate against ethnic minority defendants.

Even more worryingly, judges and prosecution barristers thought that the jury's decision to convict was against the evidence or against the law in 2 per cent of cases. For defence barristers the percentage of problematic convictions was 17 per cent—2 per cent of jury convictions a year would be 250 cases; 17 per cent would be 2,000 cases. Are juries more reliable than judges? Even if the jury are getting it wrong in some cases, the fault may be with the legal process rather than with the jury. As Griew (1985) pointed out, 'A jury without stars or a compass cannot be accused of bad navigation' (at page 346). In assessing the case, they are reliant on the information presented to them and on the performance of counsel, and are doubtless influenced by the formidable courtroom, the formal procedure, and status of the trial judge.

Are juries capable of understanding the evidence and making decisions in complex cases? Stockdale (1967) questioned why judge and jury are kept so rigorously separated 'and free to make their own mistakes'. Should they have their own legal adviser (or even the judge) present to steer their deliberations? Jackson and Doran (1997) argue that the traditional division of labour between judges and juries should be redrawn in order to enable judges to take greater responsibility for areas where their fact-finding strengths are located (for example, identification and scientific evidence). As we see in *H v Ministry of Defence* **[8:6]**, juries are now rarely used in civil cases. The Roskill Committee on Fraud Trials **[8:10]** had little difficulty in concluding that juries should be abolished for complex fraud trials, and that trials should take place before a Fraud Trials Tribunal. The extract refers to a study that cast grave doubts on a jury's fact-finding ability. But if one accepts that some cases are too difficult for a jury, where should the line be drawn? Many cases hang on complicated scientific evidence, and it is difficult to argue that fraud is necessarily more 'difficult' than, say, murder or rape.

There have been a few scandals involving juror misbehaviour. *Young* [1995] QB 324 involved a jury consulting an ouija board. Then in *Mirza* [2004] 1 AC 1118 the House of Lords had to consider a case where a juror had written to counsel suggesting that there had been a racial element in the jury's verdict; in *Smith* [2005] 1 WLR 704, after the jury had begun their deliberations, the judge received a letter from one juror alleging that certain jurors were disregarding the judge's directions on the law, were indulging in speculation, and were engaging in improper bargaining over verdicts on several counts; in *Charnley* [2007] 2 Cr App R 33 a juror alleged that the verdicts had not been unanimous as directed by the judge. What should happen in such cases? The summary and comment on the decision of the House of Lords in *Attorney-General v Scotcher* [2005] UKHL 36 **[8:11]** raises some important questions. The Government issued a consultation in 2005 inviting comments on on options for allowing research into jury deliberations and to consider investigations into alleged juror impropriety. On the issue of juror impropriety the Government decided to maintain the status quo and allow the common law to develop on a case by case basis (see <http://www.dca.gov.uk/consult/juryresearch/juryresearch_cp0405.htm#paper>). Was this an adequate response?

Most discussions of trial by jury conclude by looking at the alternatives—and deciding that no other system is better. Useful discussion of the alternatives are to be found in Cornish (1968), in the Roskill Committee report, and in Levi's report **[8:12]**, which summarizes some of the disadvantages of the possible alternatives in fraud trials. One option, which seems to be the one preferred by governments in recent years, is to limit the number of cases for which trial by jury is available, and to transfer an increasing number of offences to the magistrates' courts. Thus, the Criminal Justice Act 1988 reduced four offences to the summary-only category (driving whilst disqualified, taking a car without the owner's consent, common assault, and criminal damage to a value less than £2,000); and the CJPOA 1994, section 46 raised the upper limit in the case of criminal damage to £5,000. Part of the function of the mode of trial guidelines, discussed in Chapter 6, is to encourage magistrates to keep more either-way offences in their own courts. The heated political debate that erupted over the failed Criminal Justice (Mode of Trial) Bill 1999, which was seen by many as an erosion of a fundamental right, recurred when the Criminal Justice Act 2003 changed the law to allow trials without jury on grounds of length or complexity, or where there is a real danger of jury tampering (no cases yet). The Domestic Violence, Crime and Victims Act 2004, section 17 allows applications by the prosecution for certain counts to be tried without a jury: although this was brought into force on 8 January 2007, there has been (to my knowledge!) no use made of this procedure. The change resulted from the Law Commission's report, *The Effective Prosecution of Multiple Offending* (2002), Law Com No 277, and the jury would still have to try key specimen charges. Is this compromise of the principle of jury trial for serious offences justified given the continuance of jury trial for the specimen charges and the consequential benefit of the two-stage procedure of the judge being able to sentence according to the proved sum of the defendant's criminality (as the Editor of the Criminal Law Review argued at [2005] Crim LR 83)? It all depends on how important you think the principle of trial by jury is. Perhaps another solution would be to give the defendant the right to choose trial by judge alone.

But is trial by jury in practice all that it is held up to be? What are the jury actually doing when considering their verdict? More research is needed into the methods used by juries to evaluate the evidence, although Professor Sir John Smith warns (1998, at page 105):

Much of our law of evidence is based on assumptions about the behaviour of juries which are mere guesswork and, of course, I recognize that it is highly desirable that we should know whether these assumptions are well founded or not. But I fear that there is a price to be paid—namely the revelation that many cases are decided in consequence of material irregularities in the jury room with the consequent undermining of public confidence in jury trial. If we are to keep jury trial—and there is an overwhelming sentiment in favour of doing so—it is perhaps better not to know. Is this a case where ignorance is bliss?

This author rejects that approach, and indeed hopes were raised when the Department for Constitutional Affairs consulted in 2005 on options for allowing research into jury deliberations. Particularly worrying is, of course, the fact that juries do not have to give reasons for their decisions (unlike most other decision-making bodies). Most disappointingly, the Government decided that, although most respondents were supportive of the idea of further research into jury deliberations, it would support research only 'within the confines of the current law'. Section 8 of the Contempt of Court Act 1981 **[8:1]** continues to provide a barrier to understanding jury decision making.

FURTHER READING

Andrews, J A, 'Uses and Abuses of the Jury' in Glazebrook, P R (ed), *Reshaping the Criminal Law* (1978) Sweet & Maxwell

Baldwin, J and McConville, M, *Jury Trials* (1979) Clarendon Press

Cornish, W R, *The Jury* (1968) Allen Lane

Darbyshire, P, et al, 'What can the English Legal System Learn from Jury Research Published up to 2001?' (<http://www.criminal-courts-review.org.uk>)

Denning, Lord, *What Next in the Law?* (1982) Butterworths

Department for Constitutional Affairs, *Jury Research and Impropriety: a consultation* (2005)

Devlin, P, *Trial by Jury* (1956) Stevens

Enright, S and Morton, J, *Taking Liberties: The Criminal Jury in the 1990s* (1990) Weidenfeld & Nicolson

Findlay, M and Duff, P (eds), *The Jury under Attack* (1988) Butterworths

Griew, E, 'Dishonesty: Objections to *Feely* and *Ghosh*' [1985] Crim LR 341

Guest, S, 'Law, Fact and Lay Questions' in Dennis, I H (ed), *Criminal Law and Justice* (1986) Sweet & Maxwell

Hans, V P and Vidmar, N, *Judging the Jury* (1986) Plenum Press

Hastie, R, *Inside the Juror: the psychology of juror decision making* (1983) Cambridge UP

Jackson, J and Doran, S, *Judge without Jury: Diplock Trials in the Adversary System* (1995) Clarendon Press

Jackson, J and Doran, S, 'Judge and Jury: Towards a new division of labour in criminal trials' (1997) 60 MLR 759

Madge, N, 'Summing up—a judge's perspective' [2006] Crim LR 817

McCabe, S, *The Jury at Work* (1972) Blackwell: OUP RU Paper No 4

McCabe, S and Purves, R, *The Shadow Jury at Work* (1974) Blackwell: OUP RU Paper No 8

Smith, J C, 'Is Ignorance Bliss? Could Jury Trial Survive Investigation?' (1998) 38 Med Sci Law 98

Spencer, J R, 'Inscrutable Verdicts, the duty to give reasons and Art. 6 of the European Convention on Human Rights' (2001) 1 Archbold News 5

Stockdale, E, *The Court and the Offender* (1967) Gollanz

Thomas, C, *Diversity and Fairness in the Jury System* (2007) Ministry of Justice Research Series 2/07

Vidmar, N (ed), *World Jury Systems* (2000) Oxford UP

Zander, M and Henderson, P, *The Crown Court Study* (1993) RCCJ Research Study No 19, HMSO

DOCUMENTS

[8:1] Contempt of Court Act 1981

Section 8

8 Confidentiality of jury's deliberations

(1) Subject to subsection (2) below, it is a contempt of court to obtain, disclose or solicit any particulars of statements made, opinions expressed, arguments advanced or votes cast by members of a jury in the course of their deliberations in any legal proceedings.

(2) This section does not apply to any disclosure of any particulars—

    (a) in the proceedings in question for the purpose of enabling the jury to arrive at their verdict, or in connection with the delivery of that verdict, or

    (b) in evidence in any subsequent proceedings for an offence alleged to have been committed in relation to the jury in the first mentioned proceedings,

    or to the publication of any particulars so disclosed.

(3) Proceedings for a contempt of court under this section (other than Scottish proceedings) shall not be instituted except by or with the consent of the Attorney General or on the motion of a court having jurisdiction to deal with it.

[8:2] Juries Act 1974 (as amended)

Sections 1; 3; 9; 17

1 Qualification for jury service

Subject to the provisions of this Act, every person shall be qualified to serve as a juror in the Crown Court, the High Court and county courts and be liable accordingly to attend for jury service when summoned under this Act, if—

    (a) he is for the time being registered as a parliamentary or local government elector and is not less than eighteen nor more than seventy years of age; and

    (b) he has been ordinarily resident in the United Kingdom, the Channel Islands or the Isle of Man for any period of at least five years since attaining the age of thirteen,

    (c) he is not a mentally disordered person; and

    (d) he is not disqualified for jury service.

(2) In subsection (1) above "mentally disordered person" means any person listed in Part 1 of Schedule 1 to this Act.

(3) The persons who are disqualified for jury service are those listed in Part 2 of that Schedule.

3 Electoral register as basis of jury selection

    (1) Every electoral registration officer under the Representation of the People Act 1983 shall as soon as practicable after the publication of any register of electors for his area deliver to such officer as the Lord Chancellor may designate such number of copies of the register as the designated officer may require for the purpose of summoning jurors, and on each copy there shall be indicated those persons on the register whom the registration officer has ascertained to be, or to have been on a date also indicated on the copy, less than eighteen or more than seventy years of age.

    (1A) If a register to be delivered under subsection (1) above includes any anonymous entries (within the meaning of that Act of 1983) the registration officer must, at the same time as he delivers the register, also deliver to the designated officer any record prepared in pursuance of provision made as mentioned in paragraph 8A of Schedule 2 to that Act which relates to such anonymous entries.

    (2) The reference in subsection (1) above to a register of electors does not include a ward list within the meaning of section 4(1) of the City of London (Various Powers) Act 1957.

9 Excusal for certain persons and discretionary excusal

    (1) A person summoned under this Act shall be entitled, if he so wishes, to be excused from jury service if he is among the persons listed in Part III of Schedule 1 to this Act but, except as provided by that Part of that Schedule in the case of members of the forces...a person shall not by this section be exempt from his obligation to attend if summoned unless he is excused from attending under subsection (2) below.

(2) If any person summoned under this Act shows to the satisfaction of the appropriate officer that there is good reason why he should be excused from attending in pursuance of the summons, the appropriate officer may excuse him from so attending and shall do so if the reason shown is that the person is entitled under subsection (1) above to excusal.

(3) Crown Court rules shall provide a right of appeal to the court (or one of the courts) before which the person is summoned to attend against any refusal of the appropriate officer to excuse him under subsection (2) above.

(4) Without prejudice to the preceding provisions of this section, the court (or any of the courts) before which a person is summoned to attend under this Act may excuse that person from so attending.

...

17 Majority verdicts

(1) Subject to subsections (3) and (4) below, the verdict of a jury in proceedings in the Crown Court or the High Court need not be unanimous if—

(a) in a case where there are not less than eleven jurors, ten of them agree on the verdict; and

(b) in a case where there are ten jurors, nine of them agree on the verdict.

(2) Subject to subsection (4) below, the verdict of a jury (that is to say a complete jury of eight) in proceedings in a county court need not be unanimous if seven of them agree on the verdict.

(3) The Crown Court shall not accept a verdict of guilty by virtue of subsection (1) above unless the foreman of the jury has stated in open court the number of jurors who respectively agreed to and dissented from the verdict.

(4) No court shall accept a verdict by virtue of subsection (1) or (2) above unless it appears to the court that the jury have had such period of time for deliberation as the court thinks reasonable having regard to the nature and complexity of the case; and the Crown Court shall in any event not accept such a verdict unless it appears to the court that the jury have had at least two hours for deliberation.

(5) This section is without prejudice to any practice in civil proceedings by which a court may accept a majority verdict with the consent of the parties, or by which the parties may agree to proceed in any case with an incomplete jury.

[8:3] *R v Abdroikov*

[2008] Crim LR 134

Under the Criminal Justice Act 2003, rules formerly governing the qualification and disqualification of jurors were changed so that police officers and employees of the Crown Prosecution Service (the CPS) were no longer exempt from jury service. The three appellants were tried on an indictment in different courts and on unrelated charges and were convicted. In the first case, the appellant was charged with attempted murder and there was a minor issue concerning one aspect of the evidence of a police witness. When the jury were considering their verdicts the foreman of the jury sent a note to the judge revealing that he was a serving police officer. He was concerned that if required to report for duty on the following Bank Holiday Monday, when the court was not sitting, he might meet one or more of the police officers who had been called to give evidence at the trial. With the acquiescence of defending counsel, the juror was directed not to report for duty on the Monday. The second appellant had been stopped by police officers and searched. In the course of the search one of the officers put his hand into the appellant's pocket and was pricked on the finger by a used syringe. The second appellant was charged with assault occasioning actual bodily harm. At trial there was a dispute on the evidence between the second appellant and the police officer concerning the manner in which he had been searched and what he and the officer had subsequently said. He was convicted. Some time after the trial, the appellant's solicitor became aware that a police officer had been a member of the trial jury. That police officer was at the time posted to a station within the operational command unit which committed its work to the Crown Court at which the second appellant had been tried. Moreover, both the juror and the police officer giving evidence were both serving in the same borough at the time of the incident and had once served in the same police station at the same time. The two officers were not, however, known to one another. The third appellant had been charged with two very serious charges of rape. The jury which convicted him included among its members a solicitor who worked for the CPS. Before the trial he had written to the Crown Court, in accordance with the guidance given to those working in the CPS who were to serve on juries, that he had had worked for the CPS since its inception and was a Higher Court Advocate who had practised in many local courts although he had not conducted a trial in the Crown Court where he was to sit as a juror. Defence counsel objected but the judge ruled that he had to operate within the law passed by Parliament and he could see no objection to the solicitor sitting as a juror in the light of the current legislation. The solicitor thereafter became foreman of the jury and the third appellant was convicted. Each appellant appealed and the cases were joined before the Court of Appeal. The Court of Appeal concluded that the convictions were safe as the fact that there were 12 members of the jury of which at least 10 had to be agreed was a real protection against the prejudices of an individual juror resulting in unfairness to a defendant and that the fair-minded and informed observer would not conclude that there was a real possibility that a jury was biased merely because his occupation was one which meant that he was involved in some capacity or other in the administration of justice. The appellants all appealed.

Held, dismissing the first appeal and (Lord Rodger and Lord Carswell dissenting) allowing the second and third appeals, it had to be accepted that most adult human beings, as a result of their background, education and experience, harboured certain prejudices and predilections of which they might be conscious or unconscious, but that safeguards established to protect the impartiality of the jury, when properly operated, did all that could reasonably be done to neutralize those prejudices and predilections to which everyone was prone. However, it was not possible to dismiss the argument that there was the possibility of bias, possibly unconscious, which inevitably flowed from the presence on a jury of professional persons committed to one side only of an adversarial trial process. Nevertheless, Parliament had declared that in England and Wales police officers were eligible to sit, perhaps envisaging that their identity would be known and any objection would be the subject of judicial decision. The first case did not turn on a contest between the evidence of the police and that of the appellant and, therefore, it was hard to suggest that the case was one in which unconscious prejudice, even if present, would have been likely to operate to the disadvantage of the appellant, and it made no difference that the officer was the foreman of the jury. It followed that the Court of Appeal had reached the right conclusion in that case. The second appellant's case, however, was different as there was a crucial dispute on the evidence between the appellant and the police officer, and the officer and the juror, although not personally known to each other, had shared the same local background. In those circumstances, the instinct of a police officer, even if it was unconscious, to prefer the evidence of a fellow brother officer to that of a drug-addicted defendant would be judged by the fair-minded and informed observer to be a real and possible source of unfairness, beyond the reach of standard judicial warnings and directions. Thus, the second appellant was not tried by a tribunal which was and appeared to be impartial and his conviction would be quashed. In the case of the third appellant, no possible criticism was to be made of the CPS lawyer, but the judge had given no serious consideration to the objection of defence counsel, who himself had little opportunity to review the law. It had to be doubted whether Parliament had contemplated that employed Crown prosecutors would sit as jurors in prosecutions brought by their own authority. It was clear that justice was not seen to be done if one discharging the very important neutral role of juror was a full-time salaried, long-serving employee of the prosecutor. The third appellant had been entitled to be tried by a tribunal that was, and appeared to be, impartial and he had not been. That appeal, therefore, would be allowed and the matter remitted to the Court of Appeal with an invitation to quash the convictions and rule on any application which might be made for a retrial.

(Case considered: Pullar v United Kingdom (1996) 22 E.H.R.R. 391).

Commentary (by Nick Taylor): For many years the position was that serving police officers and those professionally concerned in the administration of law were not eligible to serve as jury members. Their non-qualification under s.1 of the Juries Act 1974 was based on the concern that persons with specialist knowledge of the system, and the prestige attached to their position would unduly influence other jurors (see Report of the Departmental Committee on Jury Service (1965, Cmnd.2627, para.103) (The Morris Report)). The Morris Report stated (at para.103) that: "It seems to us clearly right that such persons...should be specifically excluded from juries." The Royal Commission on Criminal Justice (1993, Cm.2263, Ch.8, para.57) recommended no change to this aspect of the exclusionary rule. The Auld Report (Review of the Criminal Courts of England and Wales, Home Office, 2001) argued that it would today be unlikely that jurors simply on the basis of their status or position would influence other jurors (Ch.5, para.30). Auld L.J. suggested that people no longer deferred to professionals as was once the case and to support this point he drew attention to the position in the United States where there was no evidence that criminal justice professionals dominated jury deliberations to which they were a party. As such, Sch.33 to the Criminal Justice Act 2003 provided that both police officers and prosecuting solicitors could qualify for jury service. Whilst the position adopted in the Criminal Justice Act can be defended, it can be argued that as the Morris Report was so clear in its position that it is difficult to see how such a change could be made in the absence of clear tangible evidence that the problem of bias or perceived bias could in future be catered for. As such, there are those who might consider that there will indeed be at least a perception of bias when serving police officers or those professionally concerned in the administration of law sit on juries. Nevertheless, the statute is clear and the courts must give effect to the intention of Parliament. Even so, as Baroness Hale stated:

> "The fact that Parliament has said that they are eligible to serve does not mean that Parliament intended that they should do so in any case to which they were summoned." (at [46])

What this case seeks to clarify is not whether such professionals can sit on juries, that answer is clear, but that there are occasions when it might be inappropriate for them to do so. In considering the legislative change, Auld L.J. anticipated that doubtful cases would be resolved by the trial court judge on a case-by-case basis. This can only be effective if that judge is aware of the presence of such jurors or the exact nature of their links to the case. In the case of the first appellant this clearly did not happen. However, in light of the clear wording of the legislation the House of Lords were unanimous in dismissing the appeal. Lord Bingham recognised that this case did not turn on evidence that was contested between the appellant and the police officer and as such there was no reason to believe that any unconscious prejudice would disadvantage the appellant. The only ground on which a perception of bias could be pinned would be the mere presence of a police officer on the jury and to find prejudice on this ground alone would be clearly contrary to the legislation. Lord Bingham reached this conclusion with a degree of "unease" (at [25]).

The cases relating to the second and third appellants had crucial features that enabled the majority to distinguish them from the first appellant in that there were links between the particular jurors and specific features of the case. These were not particularly direct links and thus differ from the more straightforward scenario in *Pintori* [2007] Crim. L.R. 997 (see also *Pullar v United Kingdom* (1996) 22 E.H.R.R. 391). In the case of the second appellant the police officer on the jury shared the same local service background as a sergeant in the case though they were not personally known to each other. One can see how the appearance of bias might arise here and Parliament cannot have intended that this should be ignored. This falls within the area identified by Baroness Hale that whilst the police officer is eligible that does not mean that he or she must sit in any case to which they are summoned. In the third case it was suggested that neither Auld L.J. nor Parliament could have intended that Crown prosecutors would sit as jurors in cases brought by their own authority. Lord Rodger in a dissenting opinion stated that such indirect links as occurred in these cases suggested a potential for bias that was no greater than in many other situations that would arise and are catered for by the law, for example, through the oath (or affirmation) by the jury that they will, "give a true verdict according to the evidence". Whilst this does focus the mind of the individual juror and requires them to assess the evidence individually, it is difficult to see how this might impact upon subconscious bias or indeed the outside perception that an individual juror might be biased.

The fact that this was a majority decision emphasises that these are relatively fine distinctions that are being drawn. For example, it is well recognised that police officers share a very strong occupational culture. Can it really be said that the potential for bias, or the perception of bias, only arises when a link can be established between the juror and someone involved in the prosecution, albeit one that, in this case, is based merely on the fact that the two individuals concerned were once based at the same station though did not know each other? Is this any stronger than the already strong occupational culture between all officers, or indeed the perception that officers are more likely to favour the prosecution given that their professional lives are served to supporting one particular side in the prosecution process? Such questions are undoubtedly very difficult to answer, particularly for a trial judge who must make the decision. However, the legislation ensures that such difficult questions must be answered and fine distinctions must be made if the plain meaning of the Act is not to be frustrated and the perception of bias is to be avoided.

[8:4] *R v Ford*

[1989] QB 868

The appellant, who was of mixed race and preferred to be called black, was chased and arrested by a police constable, also of mixed race. He was charged with six offences arising from the unlawful use of a motor car and from his subsequent arrest. At the Crown Court he pleaded guilty to one count, and at the outset of the trial he applied to the judge, through counsel, for a multiracial jury. The judge, under the misapprehension that counsel was about to use the case as a platform for racial haranguing, refused the application. The appellant was convicted on two counts.

The Court of Appeal, allowing his appeal on other grounds, confirmed that there is no right to a multiracial jury.

Lord Lane CJ (at page 871):

At common law a judge has a residual discretion to discharge a particular juror who ought not to be serving on the jury. This is part of the judge's duty to ensure that there is a fair trial. It is based on the duty of a judge expressed by Lord Campbell CJ in *R v Mansell* (1857) 8 E & B 54 as a duty 'to prevent scandal and the perversion of justice'. A judge must achieve that for example by preventing a juryman from serving who is completely deaf or blind or otherwise incompetent to give a verdict.

It is important to stress, however, that that is to be exercised to prevent individual jurors who are not competent from serving. it has never been held to include a discretion to discharge a competent juror, or jurors, in an attempt to secure a jury drawn from particular sections of the community, or otherwise to influence the overall composition of the jury. For this latter purpose the law provides that 'fairness' is achieved by the principle of random selection.

The way in which random selection should take place is a matter not for the judge but for the Lord Chancellor, as we endeavoured to point out in the course of argument to Mr. Herbert by citing the relevant portion of the Juries Act 1974, which is section 5(1). That provides:

'The arrangements to be made by the Lord Chancellor under this Act shall include the preparation of lists (called panels) of persons summoned as jurors, and the information to be included in panels, the court sittings for which they are prepared, their division into parts or sets (whether according to the day of first attendance or otherwise), their enlargement or amendment, and all other matters relating to the contents and form of the panels shall be such as the Lord Chancellor may from time to time direct.'

There are several cases which give examples of this residual discretion. It may be exercised even in the absence of any objection by any of the parties. The basic position is that a juror may be discharged on grounds that would found a challenge for cause. In addition jurors who are not likely to be willing or able properly to perform their duties may also be discharged.

The most common cases which this question has arisen have involved questions of ethnic groups where it has been suggested that the jury should consist partly or wholly of members of that same ethnic group. Those applications provide particular difficulty for the judge and the present case is a very good example. They arise without warning and are usually argued without any reference to authority, as indeed was very largely the case in the present instance.

It has never been suggested that the judge has a discretion to discharge a whole panel or part panel on grounds that would not found a valid challenge. Similarly, in the absence of evidence of specific bias, ethnic origins could not found a valid ground for challenge to an individual juror. The alleged discretion of the judge to intervene in the selection of the jury does not therefore fall within any acknowledged category of judicial power or discretion.

There are, moreover, strong reasons why such a discretion should not be recognised. The whole essence of the jury system is random selection, as the passage from *R v Crown Court at Sheffield, ex p Brownlow* [1980] QB 530, from Lord Denning's judgment cited in the course of argument, shows. He said, at p 541: 'Our philosophy is that the jury should be selected at random—from a panel of persons who are nominated at random. We believe that 12 persons selected at random are likely to be a cross-section of the people as a whole—and thus represent the views of the common man...The parties must take them as they come.'

The judgment was supported by Shaw LJ, sitting with Lord Denning MR.

Secondly, it is worth noting that on occasions in the past when it has been thought desirable that the court should have a power of this kind, it has been expressly granted by statute and equally subsequently abolished by statute.

Thirdly, such an application is in effect a request to the judge either to give directions as to the constitution of the panel or to order some individual jurors to be replaced without assigning a cause, that is peremptorily. It is true that in *R v Bansall* [1985] Crim LR 151, in response to an application of this type, Woolf J did give directions that the jury panel should be selected from a particular area known to contain members of the Asian community, but the judge does not appear to have had the benefit of full argument on the point.

Responsibility for the summoning of jurors to attend for service in the Crown Court and the High Court is by statute clearly laid upon the Lord Chancellor. That is clear from section 2 and section 5 of the Juries Act 1974 which has already been cited in this judgment. It is not the function of the judge to alter the composition of the panel or to give any directions about the district from which it is to be drawn. The summoning of panels is not a judicial function, but it is specifically conferred by statute on an administrative officer. That fact may not have been drawn to the attention of the court in the cases we have cited and others which have suggested that the judge has power to give directions as to the composition of the panel of jurors.

It should also be remembered that the mere fact that a juror is, for instance, of a particular race or holds a particular religious belief cannot be made the basis for a challenge for cause on the grounds of bias or on any other grounds. If therefore a judge were to exercise his discretion to remove a juror on either of these grounds, he would be assuming bias where none was proved, Such a course is not only unjustified in law, but also indeed might be thought to be seriously derogatory of the particular juror. Further, any attempt to influence the composition of the jury on these grounds would conflict with the requirement that the jury to try an issue before a court shall be selected by ballot in open court from the panel as summoned: see Juries Act 1974, section 11.

The conclusion is that, however well-intentioned the judge's motive might be, the judge has no power to influence the composition of the jury, and that it is wrong for him to attempt to do so. If it should ever become desirable that the principle of random selection should be altered, that will have to be done by way of statute and cannot be done by any judicial decision.

[8:5] *Attorney-General's Guidelines: Juries: The Exercise by the Crown of its Right of Stand By*
(1989) 88 Cr App R 124

The Attorney-General has issued the following guidelines on the exercise by the Crown in England and Wales of its right to stand by. The guidelines are to have effect from 5 July 1989, to coincide with the implementation of section 118 of the Criminal Justice Act 1988, which abolished the right of peremptory challenge. The Attorney-General has also reissued his guidelines on giving checks. These incorporate amendments made in 1986, together with a new amendment to paragraph 9 whereby the Attorney-General's personal authority is required before the right to stand by can be exercised on the basis of information obtained as a result of an authorised check.

1 Although the law has long recognised the right of the Crown to exclude a member of a jury panel from sitting as a juror by the exercise in open court of the right to request a stand by or, if necessary, by challenge for cause, it has been customary for those instructed to prosecute on behalf of the Crown to assert that right only sparingly and in exceptional circumstances. it is generally accepted that the prosecution should not use its right in order to influence the overall composition of a jury or with a view to tactical advantage.

2 The approach outlined above is founded on the principles that:

(a) the members of a jury should be selected at random from the panel subject to any rule of law as to right of challenge by the defence; and

(b) the Juries Act 1974 together with the Juries (Disqualification) Act 1984 identified those classes of persons who alone are disqualified from or ineligible for service on a jury. No other class of person may be treated as disqualified or ineligible.

3 The enactment by Parliament of section 118 of the Criminal Justice Act 1988 abolishing the right of defendants to remove jurors by means of peremptory challenge makes it appropriate that the Crown should assert its right to stand by only on the basis of clearly defined and restrictive criteria. Derogation from the principle that members of a jury should be selected at random should be permitted only where it is essential.

4 Primary responsibility for ensuring that an individual does not serve on a jury if he is not competent to discharge properly the duties of a juror rests with the appropriate court officer and, ultimately, the trial judge. Current legislation provides, in sections 9 and 10 of the Juries Act 1974, fairly wide discretions to excuse or discharge jurors either at the person's own request, where he offers 'good reason why he should be excused', or where the judge determines that 'on account of physical disability or insufficient understanding of English there is doubt as to his capacity to act effectively as a juror...'

5 The circumstances in which it would be proper for the Crown to exercise its right to stand by a member of a jury panel are:

(a) where a jury check authorised in accordance with the Attorney-General's Guidelines on Jury Checks reveals information justifying exercise of the right to stand by in accordance with paragraph 9 of the guidelines and the Attorney-General personally authorises the exercise of the right to stand by; or

(b) where a person is about to be sworn as a juror who is manifestly unsuitable and the defence agree that, accordingly, the exercise by the prosecution of the right to stand by would be appropriate. An example of the sort of exceptional circumstances which might justify stand by is where it becomes apparent that, despite the provisions mentioned in paragraph 4 above, a juror selected for service to try a complex case is in fact illiterate.

Jury checks

1 The principles which are generally to be observed are:

   (a) that members of a jury should be selected at random from the panel;

   (b) the Juries Act 1974 together with the Juries (Disqualification) Act 1984 identified those classes of persons who alone are either disqualified from or ineligible for service on a jury. No other class of person may be treated as disqualified or ineligible;

   (c) the correct way for the Crown to seek to exclude a member of the panel from sitting as a juror is by the exercise in open court of the right to request a stand by or, if necessary, to challenge for cause.

2 Parliament has provided safeguards against jurors who may be corrupt or biased. In addition to the provision for majority verdicts, there is the sanction of a criminal offence for a disqualified person to serve on a jury. The omission of a disqualified person from the panel is a matter for Court officials but any search of criminal records for the purpose of ascertaining whether or not a jury panel includes any disqualified person is a matter for the police as the only authority able to carry out such a search and as part of their usual function of preventing the commission of offences. The recommendations of the Association of Chief Police Officers respecting checks on criminal records for disqualified persons are annexed to these guidelines.

3 There are however certain exceptional types of case of public importance for which the provisions are to majority verdicts and the disqualification of jurors may not be sufficient to ensure the proper administration of justice. In such cases it is in the interests both of justice and the public that there should be further safeguards against the possibility of bias and in such cases checks which go beyond the investigation of criminal records may be necessary.

4 These classes of case may be defined broadly as:

   (a) cases in which national security is involved and part of the evidence is likely to be heard in camera;

   (b) terrorist cases.

5 The particular aspects of these cases which may make it desirable to seek extra precautions are:

   (a) in security cases a danger that a juror, voluntarily or under pressure, may make an improper use of evidence which, because of its sensitivity has been given in camera;

   (b) in both security and terrorist cases the danger that a juror's political beliefs are so biased as to go beyond normally reflecting the broad spectrum of views and interests in the community to reflect the extreme views of sectarian interest or pressure groups to a degree which might interfere with his fair assessment of the facts of the case or lead him to exert improper pressure on his fellow jurors.

6 In order to ascertain whether in exceptional circumstances of the above nature either of these factors might seriously influence a potential juror's impartial performance of his duties or his respecting the secrecy of evidence given in camera, it may be necessary to conduct a limited investigation of the panel. In general, such further investigation beyond one of criminal records made for disqualifications may only be made with the records of Police Special Branches. However, in cases falling under paragraph 4(a) above (security cases), the investigation may, additionally, involve the security services. No checks other than on these sources and no general inquiries are to be made save to the limited extent that they may be needed to confirm the identity of a juror about whom the initial check has raised serious doubts.

7 No further investigation, as described in paragraph 6 above, should be made save with the personal authority of the Attorney-General on the application of the Director of Public Prosecutions and such checks are hereafter referred to as 'authorised checks'. When a Chief Officer of Police has reason to believe that it is unlikely that an authorised check may be desirable and proper in

accordance with these guidelines he should refer the matter to the Director of Public Prosecutions with a view to his having the conduct of the prosecution from an early stage. The Director will make any appropriate application to the Attorney-General.

8 The result of any authorised check will be sent to the Director of Public Prosecutions. The Director will then decide, having regard to the matters set out in paragraph 5 above, what information ought to be brought to the attention of prosecuting Counsel.

9 No right of stand by should be exercised by Counsel for the Crown on the basis of information obtained as a result of an authorised check save with the personal authority of the Attorney-General and unless the information is such as, having regard to the facts of the case and the offences charges, to afford strong reason for believing that a particular juror might be a security risk, be susceptible to improper approaches or be influenced in arriving at a verdict for the reasons given above.

10 Where a potential juror is asked to stand by the Crown, there is no duty to disclose to the defence the information upon which it was founded, but Counsel may use his discretion to disclose it if its nature and source permit it.

11 When information revealed in the course of an authorised check is not such as to cause Counsel for the Crown to ask for a juror to stand by, but does give reason to believe that he may be biased against the accused, the defence should be given, at least, an indication of why that potential juror may be inimical to their interests; but because of its nature and source it may not be possible to give the defence more than a general indication.

12 A record is to be kept by the Director of Public Prosecutions of the use made by Counsel of the information passed to him and of the jurors stood by or challenged by the parties to the proceedings. A copy of this record is to be forwarded to the Attorney-General for the sole purpose of enabling him to monitor the operation of these guidelines.

13 No use of the information obtained as a result of an authorised check is to be made except as may be necessary in direct relation to or arising out of the trial for which the check was authorised.

Annex to the Attorney-General's guidelines on jury checks; recommendations of the Association of Chief Police Officers

1 The Association of Chief Police Officers recommends that in the light of observations made in *Mason* (1980) 71 Cr App Rep 157 the police should undertake a check of the names of potential jurors against records of previous convictions in any case when the Director of Public Prosecutions or a chief constable considers that in all circumstances it would be in the interests of justice so to do, namely:

  (i) in any case in which there is reason to believe that attempts are being made to circumvent the statutory provisions excluding disqualified persons from service on a jury, including any case when there is reason to believe that a particular juror may be disqualified;

  (ii) in any case in which it is believed that in a pervious related abortive trial an attempt was made to interfere with a juror or jurors;

  (iii) in any other case in which in the opinion of the Director of Public Prosecutions or the Chief constable it is particularly important to ensure that no disqualified person serves on the jury.

2 The association also recommends that no further checks should be made unless authorised by the Attorney-General under his guidelines and no inquiries carried out save to the limited extent that they may be needed to confirm the identity of a juror about whom the initial check has raised serious doubts.

3 The Association of Chief Police Officers further recommends that chief constables should agree to undertake check of jurors, on behalf of the defence only if requested to do so by the Director

of Public Prosecutions acting on behalf of the Attorney-General. Accordingly if the police are approached directly with such a request they will refer it to the Director.

4 When, as a result of any checks of criminal Records, information is obtained which suggests that, although not disqualified under the terms of the Juries Act 1974 a person may be unsuitable to sit as a member of a particular jury the police or the Director may pass the relevant information to prosecuting counsel, who will decide what use to make of it.

[8:6] *H v Ministry of Defence*
[1991] 2 All ER 834

The Ministry of Defence admitted liability for personal injuries caused by negligence in the treatment of a 27-year-old soldier, who had had a major part of his penis amputated without his consent. The Court of Appeal allowed the Ministry's appeal against the trial judge's decision that a trial by jury should be allowed.

Lord Donaldson (at page 839):

Finally, Mr Sedley draws attention to the fact that it is not for this court to disturb a discretionary decision of a judge sitting at first instance, unless it is satisfied that he has misdirected himself or his decision is clearly wrong. This, of course, we unreservedly accept.

We have reluctantly, but firmly, come to the conclusion that the judge's discretionary order was wrong and we think that he basis of the error was either a failure to appreciate the significance of the shift in emphasis created by the enactment of section 69 of the 1981 Act in place of section 6 of the 1933 Act or his acceptance of the submission that the retention of a judicial discretion necessarily involved the proposition that there must be some claims for compensatory damages in personal injury cases which were appropriate to be tried by jury or both. It follows that we are entitled, and indeed bound, to exercise a fresh discretion.

There was some discussion in argument as to the propriety of an appellate court declaring a policy or guidelines for the exercise of a judicial discretion, but it was rightly accepted that this could and should be done, provided that it was made clear that every case had to be considered on its own merits and that, if the rationale of the policy was not wholly applicable, even if the case fell within the terms of that policy, a judge was always free to depart from it. This too was unreservedly accept.

The policy should be that stated in *Ward v James* [1965] 1 All ER 563; [1966] 1 QB 273, namely that trial by jury is normally inappropriate for any personal injury action in so far as the jury is required to assess compensatory damages, because the assessment of such damages must be based upon or have regard to conventional scales of damages. the very fact that no jury trial of a claim for damages for personal injuries appears to have taken place for over 25 years affirms how exceptional the circumstances would have to be before it was appropriate to order such a trial and the enactment of section 69 of the 1981 Act strengthens the presumption against making such an order.

[8:7] *Brutus v Cozens*
[1973] AC 854

During a Wimbledon tennis match the appellant ran onto the court blowing a whistle and attempted to distribute leaflets. He sat down on the court and play was disrupted. He was charged with using insulting behaviour whereby a breach of the peace was likely to be occasioned, contrary to section 5 of the Public Order Act 1936. The magistrates held that his behaviour had not been insulting and dismissed the information. The House of Lords upheld this decision, stating that the magistrates' decision was one of fact, and there was no evidence that they had misdirected themselves.

Lord Reid (at page 861):

The meaning of an ordinary word of the English language is not a question of law. The proper construction of a statute is a question of law. If the context shows that a word is used in an unusual sense the court will determine in other words what that unusual sense is. But here there is in my opinion no question of the word 'insulting' being used in any unusual sense. It appears to me, for reasons which I shall give later, to be intended to have its ordinary meaning. It is for the tribunal which decides the case to consider, not as law but as fact, whether in the whole circumstances the words of the statute do or do not as a matter of ordinary usage of the English language cover or apply to the facts which have been proved. If it is alleged that the tribunal has reached a wrong decision then there can be a question of law but only of a limited character. The question would normally be whether their decision was unreasonable in the sense that no tribunal acquainted with the ordinary use of language could reasonably reach that decision.

Were it otherwise we should reach an impossible position. When considering the meaning of a word one often goes to a dictionary. There one finds other words set out. And if one wants to pursue the matter and find the meaning of those other words the dictionary will give the meaning of those other words in still further words which often include the word for whose meaning one is searching.

No doubt the court could act as a dictionary. It could direct the tribunal to take some word or phrase other than the word in the statute and consider whether that word or phrase applied to or covered the facts proved. But we have been warned time and again not to substitute other words for the words of a statute. And there is very good reason for that. Few words have exact synonyms. The overtones are almost always different.

Or the court could frame a definition. But then again the tribunal would be left with words to consider. No doubt a statute may contain a definition—which incidentally often creates more problems than it solves—but the purpose of a definition is to limit or modify the ordinary meaning of a word and the court is not entitled to do that.

So the question of law in this case must be whether it was unreasonable to hold that the appellant's behaviour was not insulting. To that question there could in my view be only one answer—No.

But as the Divisional Court [1972] 1 WLR 484, have expressed their view as to the meaning of 'insulting' I must, I think, consider it. It was said, at p 487:

'The language of section 5, as amended, of the Public Order Act 1936, omitting words which do not matter for our present purpose, is: "Any person who in any public place...uses...insulting...behaviour...with intent to provoke a breach of the peace or whereby a breach of the peace is likely to be occasioned, shall be guilty of an offence." It therefore becomes necessary to consider the meaning of the word "insulting" in its context in that section. In my view it is not necessary, and is probably undesirable, to try to frame an exhaustive definition which will cover every possible set of facts that may arise for consideration under this section. It is, as I think, quite sufficient for the purpose of this case to say that behaviour which affronts other people, and evidence a disrespect or contempt for their rights, behaviour which reasonable persons would foresee is likely to cause resentment or protest such as was aroused in this case, and I rely particularly on the reaction of the crowd as set out in the case stated, is insulting for the purpose of this section.'

I cannot agree with that. Parliament had to solve the difficult question of how far freedom of speech or behaviour must be limited in the general public interest. It would have been going much too far to prohibit all speech or conduct likely to occasion a breach of the peace because determined opponents may not shrink from organising or at least threatening a breach of the peace in order to silence a speaker whose views they detest. Therefore vigorous and it may be distasteful or unmannerly speech or behaviour is permitted so long as it does not go beyond any one of three limits. It must not be threatening. It must not be abusive. It must not be insulting. I see no reason why any of these should be construed as having a specially wide or a specially narrow meaning. They are all limits easily recognisable by the ordinary man. Free speech is not impaired by ruling them out. But before a man can be convicted it must be clearly shown that one or more of them has been disregarded.

We were referred to a number of dictionary meanings of 'insult' such as treating with insolence or contempt or indignity or derision or dishonour or offensive disrespect. Many things otherwise unobjectionable may be said or done in an insulting way. There can be no definition. But an ordinary sensible man knows an insult when he sees or hears it.

Taking the passage which I have quoted, 'affront' is much too vague a word to be helpful; there can often be disrespect without insult, and I do not think that contempt for a person's rights as distinct from contempt of the person himself would generally be held to be insulting. Moreover, there are many grounds other than insult for feeling resentment or protesting. I do not agree that there can be conduct which is not insulting in the ordinary sense of the word but which is 'insulting for the purpose of this section'. If the view of the Divisional Court was that in this section the word 'insulting' has some special or unusually wide meaning, then I do not agree. Parliament has given no indication that the word is to be given any unusual meaning. Insulting means insulting and nothing else.

If I had to decide, which I do not, whether the appellant's conduct insulted the spectators in this case, I would agree with the magistrates. the spectators may have been very angry and justly so. the appellant's conduct was deplorable. Probably it ought to be punishable. But I cannot see how it insulted the spectators.

[8:8] Devlin, P, 'The Conscience of the Jury'
(1991) 107 Law Quarterly Review 398 (at page 402)

These are the mundane reasons for preserving trial by jury, especially in crime. It exhibits, especially in the criminal verdict, the element of popularity that is appropriate in a democracy; it will be a long time before the judiciary ceases to be associated in the public mind with the upper classes.

But the paramount reason for it is that in defiance of regularity and of the disapproval of Lord Mansfield it lets the workings of conscience into the system. Judges are sworn to uphold the law; the jury is not. Sooner or later in life a man may be confronted with a struggle between what the law demands and what conscience urges. It is not a struggle that is peculiar to the jury box.

When juries fail to punish those whom they do not believe to deserve it, who is to say that they have not done what Lord Mansfield told them to do and answered to God? It is not they who are being perverse. The perversity is in the judges and bureaucrats who are so slow to see that when a procession of different juries refuses to convict of a particular crime, there is more likely to be something wrong with the law than with the juries.

This is the situation which gives the jury its peculiar place in our Constitution. It gives it what is tantamount to a democratic veto on law enforcement.

It is true that the law is made by Parliament which is a democratic body. But the function of Parliament in modern times is to approve, reject or modify the plans of the Executive. Members of Parliament are made of the same stuff as jurors. But they operate at planning headquarters behind the lines. Juries are in the front line. They see the impact of the law on its subjects and they have to decide when to use its weapons. They exercise the discretion of the man on the spot. This is as far as military analogy can be pushed. Put into constitutional terms, the jury is invested with a dispensing power to be used when their respect for law is overridden by the conviction that to punish would be unjust.

It is not only in individual cases that they act. Though they themselves have no legislative power, they can decisively influence those who have. For it is no use making laws which juries consistently fail to enforce.

It is not our great liberties that are threatened today. If they were, they would be guarded by judges. It is the little liberties which are infringed. Since the infringements are embedded in the statute the judges are powerless; the jury is not. It respects the law but it will not put it above the justice of the case.

Is this a picture of Lord Denning institutionalised? Perhaps so, but with one very big difference. The power that puts the jury above the law can never safely be entrusted to a single person or to an institution, no matter how great or how good. For it is an absolute power and, given time, absolute power corrupts absolutely. But jurors are anonymous characters who meet upon a random and unexpected summons to a single task (or perhaps a few), whose accomplishment is their dissolution. Power lies beneath their feet but they tread on its so swiftly that they are not burnt.

[8:9] Darbyshire, P, 'The Lamp that Shows that Freedom Lives—Is it Worth the Candle?'
[1991] Crim LR 740 (at page 741)

The symbolic function of the jury far outweighs its practical significance. I shall argue in this paper that this sentimental attachment to the symbol of the jury is dangerous. Adulation of the jury is based on no justification or spurious justification. It has fed public complacency with the English legal system and distracted attention from its evils; a systematic lack of due process pre-trial and post-trial and certain deficiencies in the trial process itself. It has distorted the truth. The truth is that for most people who pass through a criminal justice system this palladium is simply not available and for those who can and do submit themselves to its verdict, it will not necessarily safeguard their civil liberties.

A 'Constitutional Right' to jury trial

This justification for the jury is perhaps the best known and the most often served up without explanation, as a self-evident truth. Three problems arise under this heading:

(a) the supposed guarantee of a right to jury in Magna Carta;

(b) what is meant by a constitutional right to jury trial in the English legal system; and

(c) what is meant, in jurisprudential terms, by asserting that there is a right to jury trial.

(a) Magna Carta

Many writers claim that jury trial was enshrined as a constitutional right in Magna Carta 1215, clause 39, which provided for a 'trial by peers'.[1] Later authors undoubtedly derived this myth from Devlin, who perpetuated it in 1956, having taken it from Blackstone's Commentaries.

Whilst Blackstone's grandiloquent account of the English legal system in the eighteenth century is of great entertainment value, few later legal historians or constitutional lawyers would accept it as historically accurate. Some of his assertions have been used to quite an alarming extent, however, in establishing the constitutional foundations of newer common law jurisdictions.

The famous clause 39 of Magna Carta reads: 'Nullus liber homo capiatur vel imprisonetur, aut disseisiatur aut utlagetur, aut utlagetur, aut exuletur, aut aliquo modo destruatur, nec super eum ibimus nec super eum mittemus, nisi per legale judicium parium vel per legum terrae'; which Holdsworth[2] translates as: 'No freeman shall be taken or/and imprisoned, or disseised, or exiled, or in any way destroyed, nor will we go upon him nor will we send upon him, except by the lawful judgment of his peers or/and by the law of the land'.

Legal historians have been at pains to point out that clause 39 has nothing to do with trial by jury and, as Cornish said[3] 'It has always been bad history to trace the system back to Magna Carta.' Holdsworth acknowledges that the mis-interpretation of clause 39 has had sweeping effects on English constitutional history but explains: '. . . it is also clear that the words judicium parium do not refer to trial by jury. A trial by a royal judge and a body of recognitors was exactly what the barons did not want. What they did want was firstly a tribunal of the old type in which all the suitors were judges of both law and fact, and secondly a tribunal in which they would not be judges by their inferiors. Some of them did not consider that the royal judge, none of them would have considered that a body of recognitors, were their peers.'

Earlier, in his History of Trial By Jury[4] Forsyth had said that it was a common but erroneous opinion that judicium parium or trial by one's peers had reference to the jury and had misled many, including Blackstone. He explains that judicium implies the decision of a judge, not a jury verdict. I would add that it is crucial to remember that, in 1215, the jury was still a group of oathswearing witnesses, or compurgators. They did not pronounce judgment. The *pares*, suggests Forsyth, were: 'members of the county and other courts, who discharged the function of judges, and who were the peers or fellows of the parties before them.'[5]

As these and other historians have pointed out, by Magna Carta the barons simply sought to secure a deal from King John, within which they safeguarded their right to be judged by judges of no lesser rank than themselves. Liber homo has been translated as either 'freeman' or 'freeholder' and 'freeman' did not mean what it does today. As we should remember from school history, freemen were a limited class in the feudal system.

(b) A constitutional right?

Even if one were to concede that it has become a constitutional convention, since the fourteenth century, when statute prescribed that jurors be independent, that juries be used in certain criminal trials, I balk at the concept of trial by jury's being 'more than one wheel of the constitution'.[6] Devlin and others speak as if there were an entrenched right to jury trial, as there is in the United States Constitution or the Canadian Bill of Rights. The concept of a 'constitutional right; has, historically, been so alien to British constitutional lawyers, that the phrase seldom appeared in textbooks before the 1980s and now it only appears in the context of the debate over the need for a Bill of Rights. Indeed, the call for a Bill of Rights has arisen for this very reason: the sovereignty of parliament dictates that we do not have any entrenched rights, especially in issues beyond the grasp of EC or international law. This is manifest in relation to jury trial. Parliament has almost rendered the civil jury extinct and has continually eroded the use and availability of the jury in the criminal trial.

(c) A right?

There is also a jurisprudential problem with those who justify the use of jury trial as a right. the term 'right' at least to 'will' theorists, implies a choice. When we speak of procedural rights in the criminal justice system, we imply a choice. For example, I do not have to exercise my right of silence. Similarly, if I am charged with an offence which is triable either way, I can choose to be tried by judge and jury or magistrates. This choice can properly be called a 'right' to jury trial. What of indictable offences? Here, I must appear before the Crown Court, where my only choice is as to plea. My only right is as to trial. I cannot choose to be tried by judge alone, as I could in the United States. Thus, it is correct to speak of a 'right to jury trial' in the United States but not to speak of jury trials being a 'right', in general terms, in the English legal system, as so many defenders of the jury are wont to do.

By reasoning thus, I am accepting that the essence of a right must be a power of waiver, MacCormick would take issue with this and argue that restricting my power of waiver does not negate my right. To this, I would repeat Simmonds' reply 'It is doubtful if paternalism of this kind is best interpreted as a protection of the part's rights'.

Not only does the concept of a right to jury trial in indictable offences fail to accord with 'will' theories of rights, it also fails to satisfy classical 'interest' theories of rights and I would extend my argument here to include triable either way offences. According to interest theories, as I would apply them here, jury trial can only be described as a 'right' if the intended beneficiary of the court's duty to provide that right is the defendant. If the purpose of jury trial is primarily ideological, as I argue here, as a symbol to legitimate the criminal justice system, then the defendant is the unintended beneficiary and thus cannot be said to have real right to jury trial.

Notes

1 Eg Devlin, P *Trial by Jury* 1956 at page 164; Blake, N 'The Case For The Jury'; Brown, D and Neal, D 'Show Trials: the Media and the Gang of Twelve'; Frieberg, A 'Jury Selection in Trials of Commonwealth Offences'; all in Findlay, M and Duff, P *The Jury under Attack* (1988) Butterworths.

2 Holdsworth, W R A *History of English Law* vol 1 (7th edition, 1903) (1956) at page 59.

3 Cornish, W R *The Jury* (1968) at page 12.

4 Forsyth *History of Trial by Jury* (1852) at page 108.

5 Forsyth *History of Trial by Jury* (1852) at page 110.

6 Devlin, P *Trial by Jury* 1956 at page 164.

[8:10] *Roskill Committee on Fraud Trials*
(1986) HMSO (at page 138)

The anomaly

8.21 We draw attention to an astonishing development in the administration of the law. In the vast majority of legal cases in England and Wales today the persons selected to hear them are skilled people with particular knowledge and attributes, as opposed to a random selection drawn from the public at large which is the principle on which jury trials are at present founded. By 1984 magistrates' courts were handling about 2.2 million criminal cases a year. In the same year there were over 22,000 trials in the county courts and about 2,200 trials of civil actions in the Queen's Bench Division of the High Court, and only a handful of cases was tried with a jury. Tribunals, typically composed of a legal Chairman sitting with two lay members, also deal with disputes in immigration, rates, social benefits, industrial problems and many other fields. There are now over 60 specialist tribunals dealing with hundred of thousands of cases a year. Out of all the citizens (possibly some 3 million) who, in the course of any year, find themselves in difficulty with the law, only a small proportion (32,300 in 1984) will be tried by a jury.

8.22 The underlying logic of this situation, we find puzzling in the extreme. If society believes that trial by jury is the fairest form of trial, is it too costly and troublesome to be universally applied? If so, the millions of people convicted of summary offences before magistrates' courts in recent years, some of them facing imprisonment as a result, have a legitimate grievance, since they have been denied, on grounds of expediency, what is deemed to be the fairest form of trial. But if jury trial is not inherently more fair, given its extra cost and trouble, what are the merits which justify its retention? Society appears to have an attachment to jury trial which is emotional or sentimental rather than logical.

8.23 The most important conclusion to draw from these considerations, however, is that in almost every area of the law, society has accepted that just verdicts are best delivered by persons qualified by training, knowledge, experience, integrity or by a combination of these four qualifications. Only in a minority of cases is the delivery of a verdict left in the hands of jurors deliberately selected at random without any regard for their qualifications. Thus, those who advocate that complex fraud trials should be conducted before a select, as opposed to a random, tribunal are arguing not that such cases should be treated in any special or unique fashion, but that they should be treated in a manner more akin to the way the vast majority of all other legal cases are treated today.

8.24 In our opinion the absence from the jury box in a complex fraud case, except by chance, of persons with the qualities described in the preceding paragraph seriously impairs the prospect of a fair trial. We draw attention to other impediments to justice in succeeding paragraphs.

At page 142:

The limits of comprehension

8.33 Because direct research on jurors' comprehension of actual fraud cases would amount to a contempt of court, we commissioned a research project of a more indirect nature from the MRC Applied Psychology Unit at Cambridge. The research was conducted with individual volunteers, not with actual members of a jury. Sometimes these volunteers were classified so as to resemble members of a jury. The detailed research findings of this project are published separately.[7] Only a broad conclusion needs to be quoted here.

8.34 The research posed the question, when complex information is communicated to individuals in a manner designed to resemble courtroom procedure, how much of it is retained? And the answer is, very little indeed. By definition, the research cannot be conclusive, since it cannot be conducted on actual jurors. Nevertheless, the research findings strongly support the view of experienced observers and the promptings of commonsense, that the most complex of fraud cases will exceed the limits of comprehension of members of a jury. We have no doubt that most ordinary jurors experience grave difficulties in following the arguments and retaining in their minds all the essential points at issued, particularly in a long hearing of a complex character. This creates the serious risk wither that the jury will acquit a defendant because they have not understood the evidence or will convict him because they mistakenly think they have understood it when they have in fact done little more than applied the maxim 'there's no smoke without fire'.

Conclusions on complex fraud trials

8.35 There is no accurate evidence which we have been able to obtain to suggest that there has been a higher proportion of acquittals in complex fraud cases than in fraud cases or other criminal cases generally. Nevertheless, we do not find trial by a random jury a satisfactory way of achieving justice in cases as long and complex as we have described. We believe that many jurors are out of their depth. The breadth of experience of these cases of many of our witnesses leads us to accept their evidence.

8.36 There is another factor to which we attach great importance. We made inquiries whether prosecuting authorities refrained from prosecuting in some cases because of the difficulty of presenting them to juries selected at random in a way which the juries would be able to comprehend. We were told that this was rarely the sole reason, but that it was sometimes a major contributory factor in deciding not to proceed with a prosecution. We also had evidence that the difficulty of presenting a complex case often resulted in a decision to opt for less serious charges than the facts warranted.

8.37 We regard this as a serious situation. All the available evidence indicates that, in the United Kingdom, fraud is a growth industry and attention is directed to the statistics furnished in Appendix K. Unless all fraud cases are vigorously pursued the number will increase. For example, at the end of 1984, in London alone, there were 636 cases under investigation by the Metropolitan and City Police Company Fraud Department and £776 millions at risk. The prizes for success in such criminal ventures are so large that a growing number of people are being attracted into fraudulent dealings. We have observed moreover that there is public disquiet when company failures occur under conditions which suggest fraud or wrongdoing and no prosecution follows. We hope that the gravity of this situation will not be underestimated. Fraud is posing a threat to London as a financial centre and to the considerable volume of invisible exports which represents a major factor in the economy of the country.

8.38 Elsewhere in this report we recommend improvements in the investigation and preparation of cases; changes in the remuneration structure for the Bar designed to favour proper case preparation; an alternative procedure designed to bring cases more quickly to the Crown Court pending the government's decision on the abolition of committal proceedings; further development of the pre-trial review designed to simplify cases and isolate the real grounds of difference; the abolition of the right of peremptory challenge; substantial changes in the rules of evidence; a higher standard of presentation of the hearing; the use of visual aids; and the selection of judges with special experience. In sum, these proposals represent a fundamental overhaul of the courtroom process, which most of our witnesses regard as long overdue.

8.39 These changes would be a great assistance to juries and we would expect them to result in increased comprehensibility by them. But in the light of the foregoing analysis of the nature of a complex fraud case and the uncertain quality of a jury of 12 persons selected at random, we are satisfied that a different form of tribunal is necessary to try cases which fall within the Guidelines. Any such tribunal should we think have two basic characteristics in order to ensure that it would arrive at a fair and just verdict. First, it should be comprised of persons who are able to comprehend without difficulty the kind of complex transactions which are under inquiry. Second, the persons should be chosen, like all other persons who are appointed to judicial or quasi-judicial positions in the United Kingdom in criminal, civil, and other tribunals, because they are believed to uphold a high standard of integrity and to have a general competence which fits them to discharge their responsibilities.

8.40 The numerous changes we propose are long overdue and we think they are necessary in any event, for the proper administration of justice and the conduct of the different tribunal. It is impossible to ascertain how many cases would arise each year which fall within the Guidelines. It seems inevitable that there will be an increase of complex fraud cases and in any case we have not been able to assess the increased number of cases which will come to trial as a result of the improvements we proposed. The figures in paragraph 8.30 show that there has been an average of 26 fraud trials each year lasting more than 20 working days. The magnitude of the load will become clearer when experience has been gained with improved jury trials in cases in which they will still adjudicate. But we have no doubt about the immediate need for a different tribunal for complex fraud cases.

Notes

7 Improving the presentation of information to juries in fraud cases (1986) HMSO.

[8:11] *Attorney-General v Scotcher*

[2005] UKHL 36 (this summary is taken from (2005) 6 Archbold News 3)

The appellant was convicted of contempt of court. After serving as a juror at a trial in February 2000, he had written to the defendants' mother explaining how, amongst other things, other jurors had changed their votes simply because they wanted to get out of the court room, and wishing her luck in her further efforts to get the conviction of her sons quashed. It was not disputed that the appellant genuinely believed that there had been a miscarriage of justice due to what he perceived to be failings on the part of his fellow jurors. The mother had passed the letter to her solicitors, who passed the letter to the Court of Appeal, who contacted the police. In July 2002 the Attorney General informed the appellant that he had given his consent to proceedings being instituted. In October 2002 the Divisional Court granted the Attorney General permission to apply for a committal order against the appellant. When the matter came before the court again on May 2003, the court decided to hear argument on whether a defence was available to a juror who disclosed the deliberations of the jury if the juror was motivated by a desire to expose a miscarriage of justice. The Divisional Court held that no such defence was available. The appellant then accepted that he had committed a contempt of court in terms of section 8(1), which provides:

> Subject to subsection (2) below, it is a contempt of court to obtain, disclose or solicit any particulars of statements made, opinions expressed, arguments advanced or votes cast by members of a jury in the course of their deliberations in any legal proceedings

The Divisional Court ordered that the appellant should serve a two-month prison sentence suspended for one year and should pay costs of £2500. He appealed.

The House of Lords unanimously dismissed the appeal, Lord Rodger giving the only speech. He explored the reasoning in *Mirza* [2004] 1 AC 1118 at length, including the speech of Lord Steyn, who had dissented in that case. He concluded that the decision in *Mirza* is

> authority for the proposition that section 8(1) of the 1981 Act does not apply to a court when it considers a juror's complaints about misconduct during the jury's deliberations, since a court cannot be in contempt of itself. By necessary implication, the complaint which the court may lawfully consider must itself be lawful. Therefore, as Lord Hobhouse held, a juror who discloses to the court what is said or done during the jury's deliberations with the intention of prompting an investigation is not, without more, e g malice, dishonesty or improper motive, in contempt of court in terms of section 8(1). The subsection no more applies to the juror than to the court. The background to the enactment of the provision is wholly consistent with that interpretation, which can be reached on ordinary principles of statutory construction without resort to section 3 of the 1998 Act. (para 25)

Thus, had the juror written to the court he would not have been guilty of contempt. Lord Rodger accepted that

> frequently, what can be done directly can also be done indirectly and to hold otherwise would be to promote form over substance. For example, if instead of writing to the trial judge or to the appeal court, the appellant had spoken or written to the jury bailiff or to the clerk of court, he would not have been in contempt. Similarly, if he had sent a sealed letter containing his complaint to the defendants' solicitors or counsel, or even to a citizens' advice bureau or similar organisation, and had asked them to forward it unopened to the appropriate court authorities, any disclosures in the letter would have been disclosures to the court and so outside the terms of section 8(1). (para 27)

However, what this juror had done was very different. Section 3 of the Human Rights Act 1998 did not apply as section 8(1) is compatible with Article 10 of the European Convention on Human Rights.

Comment: It would not be surprising if the appellant in this case felt rather sore at Lord Rodger's reasoning. No one, at the time of the trial in which he served as a juror, had informed him that he could complain to the court. He had simply been told it was a contempt to discuss the jurors' deliberations at all. Now that all jurors should be made well aware of their right (duty?) to bring inappropriate decision making to the attention of the proper authorities (see *Mirza*), it would be interesting to know if jurors have become more active in this regard.

[8:12] Levi, M, *The Investigation, Prosecution and Trial of Serious Fraud*
(1993) RCCJ Research Study No 14, HMSO (at page 190)

Though the cultural and political obstacles to jury abolition in fraud cases are powerful, it may be useful to summarise some problems with alternative modes of trial of fraud. These could take place at the election of (a) the prosecution, as in transfer proceedings; (b) the defence, as in the US, Canada, and some Australian jurisdictions; (c) both, if they agree; and (d) the judge. If defendants had the right to elect for trial without jury, there would have to be provisions should they disagree. The possible alternative modes of trial are:

(1) Trial by judge(s) alone

Judges sit alone in long civil trials—themselves a demonstration of the way in which the inherent complexity of some frauds takes a long time to examine—but in my judgment, the stress of doing so in criminal trials is enormous. Judges might benefit from the presence of people of some expertise—greater, perhaps, than those recruited as clerks in recent long cases, whom judges have found very useful—to bounce arguments against, and that is an argument for there being three (or, more riskily, two) judges. This will cost money and cause listing problems, as dual arrangements have to be made. The advantage of judicial trial is that oral prolixity will be discouraged, the hearsay rule can be abandoned, and a much more businesslike atmosphere engendered. The disadvantage is that if the moral standards of ordinary people are the baseline, how are judges to know what those standards are? Chancery judges may be viewed by some as too tolerant using practitioners' views as the standard, as allegedly happened in the trial arising out of the failure of secondary bank London and Country Securities—while 'criminal judges' may be seen as too severe (and as lacking detailed knowledge of commercial systems and values). Trial by judge alone exposes the judiciary to accusations of political bias, as may be seen from the conviction (and jailing for six years) of the Olivetti Chairman Carlo de Benedetti by the Milan court in April 1992 in connection with the Banco Ambrosiano fraud. It could be countered that judges often direct acquittals at present, and that this has not received much adverse comment: there would certainly be a greater risk of this, however, if juries were not involved at all. A further counter is that we should go for what is objectively 'the right system'.

(2) Trial by judge with assessors

This may look like an attractive option. It would take some of the political 'heat' off the judiciary should there be an acquittal and would inject some market expertise into the judgment process. However, how are the assessors to be chosen? From a 'fit and proper' general panel, as they are at Lloyd's and other regulators' disciplinary hearings? Are the defence going to be allowed to propose persons or if not, to object for cause, and on what criteria? Will there be a voir dire of the assessors? What if the defendants disagree among themselves about the suitability of assessors, as is quite plausible, either genuinely or as a tactic? What if, in Guinness, the prosecution had wanted people from the Takeover panel, Saunders had opted for marketing people, Parnes for other 'dynamic' stockbrokers, etc?

The trial may not be shortened by the presence of expert assessors, if the experts become entangled in technical debates or argue as long as the accountancy profession have done about the correct standards in SSAPs, or how one judges what is a 'true and fair view' of accounts! How will the defendants and the general public view the objectivity of the verdicts, irrespectively of how fairly the assessors have actually approached the issues? To satisfy this populist concern, the assessors could be substituted by two or more ordinary people drawn as jurors presently are, who would sit with the judge at the end, or even during the case.

(3) Trial by special jury

In some respects, this is more consistent that present jury trials with the original concept of the jury as persons who were familiar with the accused and the general environment in which the offence occurred. This solution suffers from the problems noted in the section on assessors, and special jurors may be no more inclined than present jurors to follow the judge's legal directions. In some respects, the legitimacy problems are even worse. Let us imagine that a jury of merchant bankers or of City folk, however distinguished, had acquitted in Blue Arrow: would the public have believed it was anything other than a 'fix' by 'the City looking after their own kind'? If they had convicted, the defendants might well have represented that it was a vendetta against them (to eliminate a competitor) or that it was an attempt to sanitise the image of the City by throwing some sacrifices to the courts. (Imagine if a special jury of Lloyd's brokers had tried Ian Posgate in his criminal trial: who would have accepted that no prejudice was involved?) Some jurors interviewed certainly took the view that trial other than by jury would be 'a fix'. To reveal that alternative proposals have problems is not to rule them out, but my object here is to make it clear that public policy should not assume that simply because judges and assessors are persons of rectitude, their decisions will be viewed with legitimacy.

(4) Other alterations to trial by jury

One possible 'mixed' system would be to have a tribunal composed of a judge, two assessors, and two lay persons, with a requirement that at least one of each would have to agree before someone could be convicted. (Perhaps a conviction might require the agreement of the judge.) In France, the Cour d'Assises which deals with major crimes which have a maximum penalty of five years or more—currently excluding frauds, which have maxima under five years and are tried by judges alone in the Tribunal Correctionel—has a jury composed of three judges and nine persons drawn from the electoral register. An alternative, more modest, approach would not violate the essential principle of jurors being representative sample of the population: a 'quota system' would ensure a more statistically proportionate number of middle-class persons than one often observes. Given their numbers in the general population, there ought to be some five 'middle-class' persons on a jury, and there could be a special jury panel to make up that proportion of the whole. This would ensure some spread of opinion and debate, and allay the fears of the political conspiracy theorists. Despite the shake-out in the financial services industry, unless fraud trials are greatly reduced in length, there are bound to be difficulties in getting people with current commercial expertise, not least because the pay limits are so low and many of them live outside the catchment area of the major fraud trial centres.

A further possibility is to give defendants the right to elect trial without a jury, as in North America and New Zealand and some parts of Australia. It is notable that the defendants in the Equiticorp case, a New Zealand SFO prosecution which is expected to last two years, have elected trial by judge, as reportedly as common in North America in cases where defendants have technical defences and wish a verdict to be accompanied by appealable reasoning. It also offers a bulwark against jury prejudice, particularly if inflamed by the media. If defendants are given the right of electing trial without jury, there would have to be procedures for solving inter-defendant disputes. One way forward might be to allow for trial without jury only if all defendants in one trial were agreed: this would enable severed components of one 'case' to undergo different modes of trial if the defendants wished it.

CHAPTER NINE
APPEAL AND REVIEW DECISIONS

The ease and speed with which a decision can be challenged in a higher court is one yardstick by which to measure a criminal justice system. In England and Wales, the role of the Court of Appeal in correcting errors and miscarriages of justice must be scrutinized. In our story, Gerry Good has now been convicted of an offence under the Offences Against the Person Act 1861 (OAPA 1861), section 20 and has been sentenced to three years in prison. This chapter will show how unlikely he is to appeal successfully against either conviction or sentence. The Court of Appeal takes a very cautious approach, reluctant to interpret its powers too widely. And yet, as we will see, the Government is urging yet more caution upon it.

The appeal process has a number of functions. First, and perhaps most obviously, it has to correct mistakes. An appeal court checks that the court of first instance reached an appropriate result, and should put the matter right if it did not. Secondly, it has a due process function. The appellate courts should quash decisions reached unfairly, in order to safeguard the integrity of the criminal justice system as a whole. Finally, it has a consistency function: it allows the judiciary to develop clear legal rules, so providing for the harmonious development of the law.

However, these functions are not always achieved, nor are they all considered to be equally important. Thus, in appeals against conviction, the Court of Appeal is reluctant to interfere with the jury's fact-finding role; and in appeals against sentence it has always held that there is no such thing as a correct sentence—only if the sentence was 'wrong in principle' will the Court of Appeal interfere. The due process function is weighted more strongly by some than by others: Zander's dissent **[9:1]** in the report of the *Royal Commission of Criminal Justice* (1993) is a strong affirmation of due process values. Note what he says at paragraph 68: 'the moral foundation of the criminal justice system requires that if the prosecution has employed foul means the defendant must go free even though he is plainly guilty'. Read the passage carefully before you assess the Government's latest proposals (summarized and criticized at **[9:1]**). The consistency function is no more clear-cut, raising many of the fundamental dilemmas facing any legal system: in order to be fair, a legal system must be certain and predictable; but in order to be fair, it must also show some flexibility. Does our criminal justice system correctly balance certainty and flexibility?

(i) USUAL APPEAL ROUTES

(a) After summary trial

Summary appeals, from convictions in the magistrates' courts, are governed by the Magistrates' Courts Act 1980, section 108 **[9:2]** and are heard in the Crown Court. The judge will normally sit with two lay magistrates. The appeal takes the form of a rehearing, with all the witnesses being recalled. Historically, this is because the records of proceedings in the magistrates' court were inadequate, and so there was no option but to hear the case again. But, ironically, this has the effect today that an appeal from a conviction for a summary offence, which normally has less important consequences for the offender than a conviction for an indictable offence, is often dealt with more thoroughly than an appeal from the verdict of a jury. The powers of the Crown Court are governed by the Supreme Court Act 1981, section 48 **[9:3]**. The court may impose any sentence which was available to the original court. Unmeritorious appellants are deterred by the knowledge that the court may (although it rarely does) increase the sentence imposed on the offender.

TABLE 9.1 Appeals in the Crown Court

	Number heard	Percentage successful
1993	23,722	47%
1997	16,199	23%
2001	12,679	44%
2005	12,805	43%
2006	12,992	42%

Source: Judicial Statistics (for 2005, Judicial Statistics Revised, Cm 6903:page 91; 2006: Judicial Statistics, page 104

Less than 1 per cent of cases dealt with in the magistrates' courts are appealed. Does this reflect satisfaction with summary justice, a lack of legal aid, or a fear of an increased penalty? For Auld **[1:5]** the answer was to remove appeals as of right from the magistrates' courts: but is this really necessary?

There is no further appeal from the Crown Court (except appeals by way of case stated to the High Court: see (ii) below). Diagram 9.1 explains the structure of English courts:

(b) After trial in the Crown Court

For those tried in the Crown Court, an appeal lies to the Court of Appeal (Criminal Division). A formal system of criminal appeals was introduced only in 1907. Important reforms were effected, as a result of the Tucker Report (1954), in the Criminal Appeal Act 1966—which replaced the old Court of Criminal Appeal with the current Court of Appeal (Criminal Division)—and in the Criminal Appeal Act 1968. This was then substantially amended in 1995 **[9:4]**. For a critique of Auld's comments **[1:5]** on the inefficient use of judicial resources in the appellate process, see Malleson and Roberts (2002).

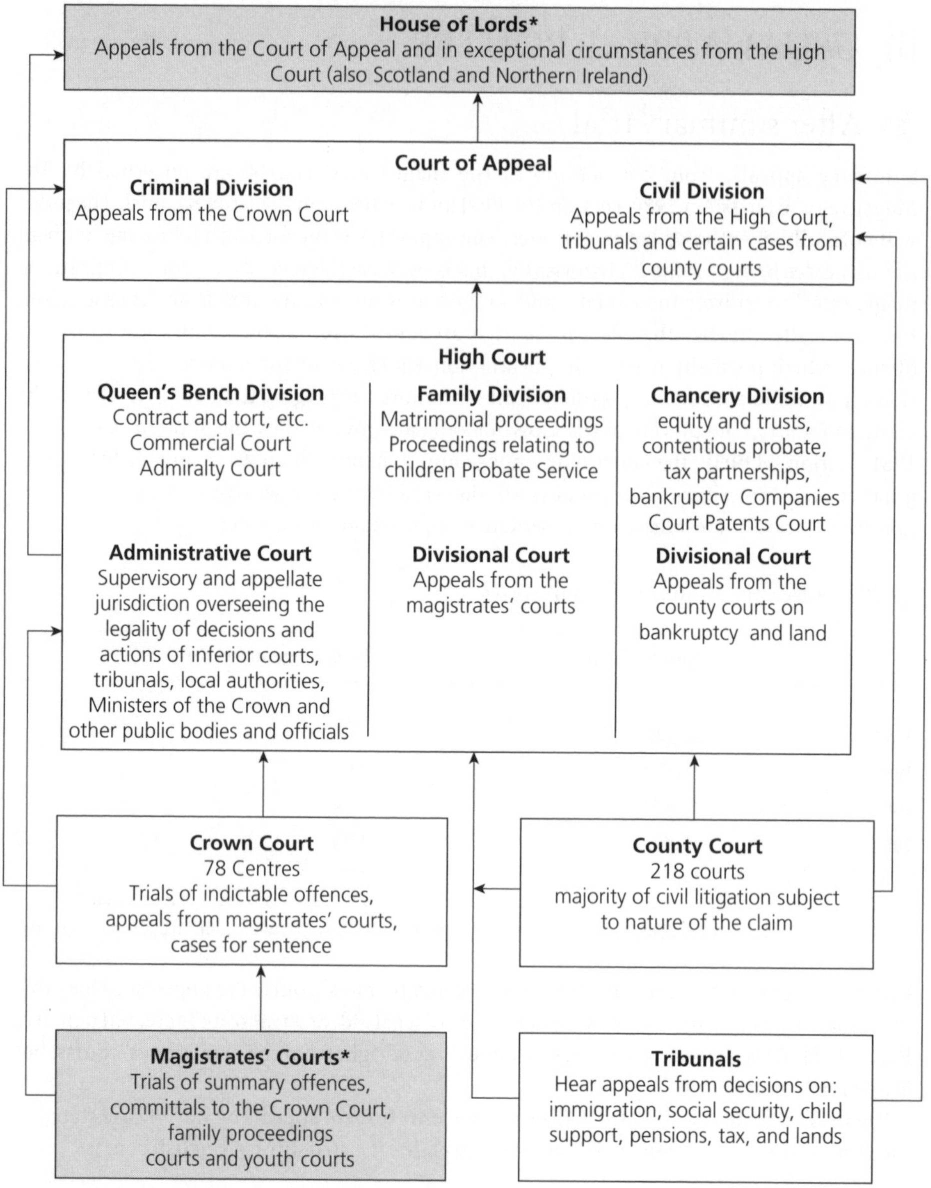

House of Lords*
Appeals from the Court of Appeal and in exceptional circumstances from the High Court (also Scotland and Northern Ireland)

Court of Appeal

Criminal Division	**Civil Division**
Appeals from the Crown Court	Appeals from the High Court, tribunals and certain cases from county courts

High Court

Queen's Bench Division	**Family Division**	**Chancery Division**
Contract and tort, etc. Commercial Court Admiralty Court	Matrimonial proceedings Proceedings relating to children Probate Service	equity and trusts, contentious probate, tax partnerships, bankruptcy Companies Court Patents Court
Administrative Court Supervisory and appellate jurisdiction overseeing the legality of decisions and actions of inferior courts, tribunals, local authorities, Ministers of the Crown and other public bodies and officials	**Divisional Court** Appeals from the magistrates' courts	**Divisional Court** Appeals from the county courts on bankruptcy and land

Crown Court 78 Centres Trials of indictable offences, appeals from magistrates' courts, cases for sentence	**County Court** 218 courts majority of civil litigation subject to nature of the claim

Magistrates' Courts* Trials of summary offences, committals to the Crown Court, family proceedings courts and youth courts	**Tribunals** Hear appeals from decisions on: immigration, social security, child support, pensions, tax, and lands

* To be renamed Supreme Court.

DIAGRAM 9.1 The court structure in England and Wales
Source: <http://www.dca.gov.uk/deprep0102/downloads/a01-chart.pdf>

Appeals in the Court of Appeal (Criminal Division) are normally heard by Lords Justices of Appeal and High Court judges. Curiously, these judges may have had little experience of criminal trials. The recommendation of the *Royal Commission on Criminal Justice* (1993)—that it would be beneficial if senior circuit judges, often with greater experience and knowledge of criminal trials, should be able to sit as members of the court—was adopted in the Criminal Justice and Public Order Act (CJPOA) 1994, section 52. It is also arguable that there should be lay members of the court, an issue we will return to later in this chapter.

Initially the defendant applies to a single judge for permission (or leave) to appeal, unless the appeal raises a question of law alone. This is a written application, and there is normally no hearing. Even where there is a hearing, witnesses are rarely called. Permission is required when the appeal turns on questions of fact, because of the reluctance of the judiciary to upset jury verdicts. Since most miscarriages of justice hang on questions of fact, such as the alleged police fabrication of evidence or mistaken identification, is this 'permission hurdle' appropriate?

TABLE 9.2 Applications for leave (permission) to appeal against conviction

	Number of applications	Granted leave by single judge	Application granted by Full Court	Appeals allowed
1993	2,134	601		402
1997	2,318	589	131	236
2001	1,943	438	150	135
2005	1,661	360	141	228
2006	1,596	291	137	181

Source: Judicial Statistics 1993, pages 11–12; 1997, pages 13–14; 2001, page 14; 2005, page 17–18, 2006, page 21

Thus, few defendants make an application to appeal, and many fewer are successful. The role of lawyers is vital: Chapter 5 looked at the need for good quality legal advice throughout the legal process, and an extract from Plotnikoff and Woolfson **[5:9]** described their findings and outlined their recommendations on good practice and the responsibilities of legal advisers in the 28 days following conviction. The *Royal Commission* (1993) gave considerable space to recommendations for improvements to the practical procedures, in order to help applicants apply for permission to appeal. What has happened?

The grounds of appeal were reformed in 1995, following the recommendations of the majority of the *Royal Commission*. Malleson **[9:5]** showed how the grounds of appeal overlapped confusingly. The Commission accepted that the Court of Appeal was too narrow in its approach, too heavily influenced by the role of the jury, which led it to concentrate too much on assessing errors of law or procedural irregularities. The *Royal Commission* was split as to what form the new powers should take: the majority suggested that a single broad ground, that the conviction 'is or may be unsafe', would be adequate. A minority (of three) were concerned that an umbrella formula would not give the Court of Appeal sufficient guidance towards adopting a less restrictive approach. In Chapter 1 we noted that the managerial and efficiency concerns of the *Royal Commission* allowed it to avoid developing a coherent philosophy or vision. The differences of opinion within it, on reforming the powers of the Court of Appeal, is another example of the *Commission*'s failure adequately to debate fundamental principles (in this case, the function of the appeal process). Note the wording of section 2:

TABLE 9.3 The wording of section 2 of the Criminal Appeal Act 1968

Old section 2 Criminal Appeal Act 1968	New section 2 Criminal Appeal Act 1968 (after CAA 1995)
Except as provided by this Act, the Court of Appeal shall allow an appeal against conviction if they think:	Subject to the provisions of this Act, the Court of Appeal:
(a) that the conviction shall be set aside on the ground that under all the circumstances of the case it is unsafe or unsatisfactory; or	(a) shall allow an appeal against conviction if they think that the conviction is unsafe; and
(b) that the judgment of the court of trial should be set aside on the ground of a wrong decision of any question of law; or	(b) shall dismiss such an appeal in any other case.
(c) that there was a material irregularity in the course of the trial;	
and in any other case shall dismiss the appeal.	
Provided that the court may, notwithstanding that they are of opinion that the point raised in the appeal might be decided in favour of the appellant, dismiss the appeal if they consider that no miscarriage of justice has actually occurred.	

What difference has the change in the law made in practice? Look again at Malleson's conclusions from her research into the Court of Appeal at the beginning of the 1990s. The Court of Appeal remains reluctant to 'upset' a jury's verdict and the question of limited resources is ever more pressing. It is, of course, very difficult for a defendant such as Gerry Good to establish that his conviction is unsafe. He will have to rely on the transcript of the trial, and he will bear a heavy burden of proof. The Court of Appeal in *Chalkley and Jeffries* [1998] **[9:6]** held that a conviction is safe if there is no possibility that the defendant was convicted of a crime of which he was in fact innocent. But the Court of Appeal in *Mullen* [1999] **[9:7]** seemed to suggest that 'unsafe' bears a meaning wider than simply factually unsafe. Surely if a defendant is convicted following grossly unfair prosecution practices, he should have his conviction quashed. The Court of Appeal in *Togher* [2001] 3 All ER 463 preferred the approach in *Mullen*. That is the position today.

But now look at the Government's consultation paper *Quashing Convictions*, published in September 2006 (and available at <http://www.homeoffice.gov.uk/documents/cons-2006-quashing/cons-2006-quashing-convictions2>) and John Spencer's critique of it **[9:8]**. Spencer criticizes the proposal to modify the Criminal Appeal Act 1968 section 2 to remove the Court of Appeal's power to quash convictions on 'purely procedural grounds' where the defendant's guilt on the facts is not in question. He defends the Court of Appeal's record in exercising its discretion, as exemplified by Mullen, and explores how such cases might be decided were the proposals to become law. Do you agree that the Government should refrain from attempting to tie the hands of the Court of Appeal? The Government certainly intends to use the Criminal Justice and Immigration Bill 2007 currently going through Parliament to limit the powers of the Court of Appeal, but many changes are still afoot as it makes it way through Parliament: we leave further comment to our next edition!

Much controversy has surrounded the Court of Appeal's power to hear fresh evidence under the Criminal Appeal Act 1968, section 23 **[9:4]**. This section (amended by the Criminal Appeal Act 1995, section 4) gives the Court of Appeal a wide mandate, but the court remains hesitant about becoming involved. Thus, the Court of Appeal in *McIlkenny* **[9:9]**, the case of the 'Birmingham Six', set out its vision of its role. Is the Court of Appeal construing its role too conservatively? If the Court of Appeal too easily accepts fresh evidence, there is a danger that defendants might 'save up' evidence for the appeal, and the court would be usurping the role of the jury. Yet Pattenden (1996) argues that 'an appellate court genuinely concerned to avoid miscarriages of justice should admit all evidence which could be believed by a reasonable jury, which could have affected the outcome of the case [and] that has not been deliberately saved up for appeal, should the accused be convicted' (at page 138).

There have been a number of legislative attempts to encourage appellate judges to use their powers to order retrials more frequently. Section 43 of the Criminal Justice Act 1988 **[9:10]** gave them power to order a retrial where this appears to be 'in the interest of justice'. Previously, this power had been restricted to cases where there was fresh evidence.

TABLE 9.4 Numbers of retrials ordered by Court of Appeal

Year	Number of retrials ordered	Year	Number of retrials ordered
1989	1	1999	70
1990	3	2000	72
1991	15	2001	58
1992	12	2002	50
1993	20	2003	45
1996	53	2004	66
1997	33	2005	77
1998	73	2006	58

Source: Judicial Statistics 1995; 1997, page 12; 2001, page 14; 2005, page 18 (+ personal communication for 2005 (not in stats)

But retrials are not a panacea: they are expensive, often impractical, and burdensome on both witnesses and defendants. Perhaps an awareness of these concerns explains why the Court of Appeal does not order retrials as often as one might have expected?

Appeals against sentence are more common than appeals against conviction, because many of those who plead guilty still seek to challenge the sentence imposed by the Crown Court. Although the Court of Appeal will only vary a sentence if it was 'wrong in principle' **[9:4]** (and remember that defendants require permission to appeal), appeals against sentence are statistically a little more likely to be successful than appeals against conviction.

TABLE 9.5 Appeals against sentence

	Applications for permission to appeal	Leave granted by single judge	Leave granted by Full Court	Appeal successful
1993	4,848	1,597		1,309
1998	6,550	1,909	377	1,589
2001	5,497	1,551	240	1,101
2005	5,178	1,541	326	1,534
2006	5,082	1,261	425	1,391

Source: Judicial Statistics 1993, pages 11–12; 1997, page 12; 2001, page 14; 2005, page 17–18

The 'loss of time' rule, developed in two Practice Statements—[1970] 1 WLR 663 and [1980] 1 All ER 555 and now to be found in the Consolidated Criminal Practice Direction, Rule II.16—allows the Court of Appeal to order that time spent in prison pending an appeal should not count towards sentence. In *Monnell and Morris v United Kingdom* **[9:11]**, the European Court of Human Rights considered whether the rule infringed the European Convention on Human Rights, and held by a majority that there had been no such infringement. Extracts from both the majority and dissenting judgments are included in order to illustrate how the approach of the European Court of Human Rights to its task is somewhat different from the approach of a domestic appellate court (another example is at **[1:13]**). The *Royal Commission* (1993) considered the power to order loss of time 'to be necessary as a means of discouraging appeals that have no merit' (at page 167). In practice, it is true, the Court of Appeal rarely orders that time spent on appeal should not count towards sentence, but does this excuse such an erosion of due process rights?

We saw in Chapter 7, how the trial judge's discretion in sentencing is constrained not only by statute but also by decisions of the Court of Appeal. Remember too that the courts (trial courts and appellate courts) are constrained by the guidelines of the Sentencing Guidelines Council (SGC) (see, for example, **[7:4]**). Before the creation of the SGC, it was the Sentencing Advisory Panel (created by the Crime and Disorder Act 1998), which provided advice directly to the Court of Appeal: the first advice, on environmental offences, was issued in 2000. But this was merely advice. The Court of Appeal has confirmed (in *Oosthuizen* [2005] EWCA Crim 1978, [2005] Crim LR 979) that a judge who does not follow the guidance must give reasons why he or she is not doing so. As we noted in Chapters 6 and 7, the extent to which judges and magistrates should be bound by external 'advice' remains contentious: the Government has appointed a working party chaired by Gage LJ to explore the proper role of a Sentencing Commission.

(ii) UNUSUAL METHODS OF APPEAL AND REVIEW

Another way in which a party may appeal is by way of case stated. Under the Summary Jurisdiction Act 1857, section 6, the Divisional Court of the Queen's Bench Division of the High Court may 'reverse, affirm or amend the determination in respect of which the case has been stated, or remit the matter to the justices, with the opinion of the court thereon'. This procedure is normally used where the magistrates made an error of substantive law or acted in excess of jurisdiction, and the prosecution states a case for the opinion of the Divisional Court in order that that court (and the House of Lords, if the decision is further appealed) can stamp on a wrong ruling on a point of law before it spreads dangerously around the lower courts.

TABLE 9.6 Appeals by way of case stated

	Appeals received from magistrates' courts	Appeals received from Crown Courts	Appeals allowed from magistrates' courts	Appeals allowed from Crown Courts
1993	182	34	72	13
1997	144	32	62	7
2001	112	24	40	8
2005	98	23	39	6
2006	113	24	42	3

Source: Judicial Statistics, 1993, page 16; 1997, page 17; 2001, page 19; 2005, page 24; 2006, page 27

The procedure is useful for correcting inappropriate rulings on the substantive law, but it may well be time to modernize the procedure and terminology.

Judicial review by the High Court of criminal justice decisions is not common (see Table 9.6), but the importance of judicial review of criminal proceedings is not revealed by the small number of cases involved: look at the number of such cases extracted in this book, which have included reviews of decisions taken by the Home Secretary **[2:3]**, the police, the Crown Prosecution Service (CPS) **[3:2]** and the Serious Fraud Office (SFO) **[4:10]**. Judicial review is a vital constitutional safeguard, especially where statutory rights of appeal are inadequate. A further example is provided by the case of *R v Secretary of State for Home Affairs, ex p Bentley* **[9:14]**. (Bentley was convicted and executed in 1952: the case we report is a judicial review hearing: it was not until 1998 that the Court of Appeal eventually quashed

TABLE 9.7 Applications for judicial review in criminal proceedings

	Applications	Applications allowed
1993	472	68
1997	284	45
2001	330	53
2005	251	29
2006	253	38

Source: Judicial Statistics 1993, page 15; 1997, page 16; 2001, page 18; 2005, page 23; 2006, page 26

his conviction.) Judicial review differs from an appeal in three important ways: first, it is a review of the law and not an investigation of the facts; secondly, judicial review results either in a decision being quashed or upheld (the reviewing court will not substitute its own decision); and thirdly, judicial review is based in common law and is not a creation of statute. Judicial review of court decisions is rare, because where an appeal procedure is available, that will be the appropriate route for the appellant to pursue.

In the past, judicial review was usually only applied for if there had been some illegality, for example, if magistrates had failed to comply with the rules of criminal procedure. Today, despite the greater willingness of the courts to review cases, it remains very difficult to succeed in challenging any alleged misuse of discretion. Lord Diplock summarized the grounds upon which judicial review can be successfully sought as 'illegality, irrationality and procedural irregularity' (*Council of Civil Service Unions v Minister for the Civil Service* [1985] AC 374). Errors of law generally create illegality, and so are challengeable. The scope of irrationality is more difficult: it is difficult to find examples in the criminal context of the High Court quashing a decision for being 'irrational'. Even procedural irregularities will not necessarily lead to the quashing of a decision, since judicial review is itself discretionary. Any matters arising from the trial itself are dealt with through the usual appeal process: because in judicial review proceedings, the court is reviewing the manner in which a decision is taken, and not the merits of the decision, such proceedings are no substitute for a 'real' appeal process.

(iii) THE ROLE OF THE ATTORNEY-GENERAL

We saw in Chapter 3 how the Attorney-General exercises ministerial responsibility for the CPS and SFO. Her power to enter a plea of *nolle prosequi*, which has the effect of stopping proceedings, was noted in Chapter 4. She also has an important role in the appellate process. In general terms, the Attorney-General has three key roles:

(1) Legal adviser to the Crown (in the wider sense, i.e. to the Government and, on some issues, Parliament and the Queen) and the Crown's representative in the courts. The Attorney General also oversees the Government's in-house legal advisers and is the Minister responsible for the Treasury Solicitor's Department.

(2) Minister of the Crown with responsibility for superintending the Crown Prosecution Service, Serious Fraud Office, Revenue and Customs Prosecutions Office, the Army, Royal Navy and Royal Air Force prosecuting authorities, HM CPS Inspectorate and (with the Home Secretary and Secretary of State for Justice) the Office of Criminal Justice Reform. The Attorney-General is also, with the Home Secretary and Secretary of State for Justice, responsible for criminal justice policy.

(3) Guardian of the public interest, in particular in certain kinds of legal proceedings—such as decisions on the bringing or termination of criminal prosecutions, charity matters, and the appointment of 'advocates to the court' to act as neutral advisers to the court in litigation and 'special advocates' to represent the interests of parties in certain national security cases. The Attorney-General's independent public interest role includes consultation by the prosecuting authorities on individual criminal cases as part of the superintendence role.

As we go to press, the Government is consulting on whether the current role of the Attorney-General is fit for purpose in the twenty-first century: particularly in view of the tension between the Attorney-General's political status as a Government minister and his other functions (see **[3:9]**). Can the Attorney-General be seen to be impartial in weighing up or advising on the public interest on matters in which the Government may itself have a strong policy interest (for example in the protection of jobs)? The Law Commission concluded (in Law Com No 255) that the existing functions of the Attorney-General to give consent to prosecutions should (if not abolished altogether) be transferred to the Director of Public Prosecutions (DPP) except where the offence involves national security or has some international element.

The prosecution has no general right of appeal in English law. There is an argument for giving the prosecution a right of appeal—for example, where the acquittal is perverse and flies in the face of the evidence, or where the acquittal is due to an error on the part of the prosecution. The *Royal Commission on Criminal Justice* (1993) rejected such proposals, suggesting only that where it can be shown that the jury was bribed or intimidated, the prosecution should be able to apply for a retrial. However, the Criminal Justice Act 2003 gave the prosecution, in very serious cases (defined in this context as offences which carry a maximum sentence of life imprisonment, and for which the consequences for victims or for society as a whole are particularly serious), the right to apply for a retrial where there is new evidence that makes it 'highly probable' that the person is guilty. This undermining of the double jeopardy rule (that no one should stand trial on the same facts twice) has, unsurprisingly, been very controversial.

Under the Criminal Justice Act 1972, section 36 **[9:12]**, the Attorney-General may refer an acquittal for the opinion of the Court of Appeal. Whilst the judgment of the Court of Appeal in the case has no effect on the actual trial or acquittal of the defendant, it is used as a procedure to correct inappropriate rulings on the substantive criminal law. An example is provided at **[9:12]**. Jocosely (1981) argues that hypothetical disputes should not be a means of clarifying controversial points of law. This view should be contrasted with that of A T H Smith (1984), who suggested that the Attorney-General's reference procedure should be extended to replace appeals to the House of Lords in criminal matters (see (vi) below).

The Criminal Justice Act 1988, sections 35, 36 **[9:10]** then gave the Attorney-General the power to appeal against an 'unduly lenient' sentence, and in these cases the Court of Appeal may actually increase the sentence (see **[7:18]** for an example). However, the Court of Appeal has again interpreted its role very narrowly here. As Lord Lane CJ said in *A-G's Reference (No 4 of 1989)* 11 Cr App R (S) 517, at page 531: 'A sentence is unduly lenient, we would hold, where it falls outside the range of sentences which the judge, applying his mind to all the relevant facts, could reasonably consider appropriate'. Little research has been done into which cases are reviewed, and it may well be that the media exert an improper influence over which cases are referred to the Court of Appeal. Henham (1994) argued that the procedure should either be abolished or replaced by a general prosecution right of appeal free from the limitations of the present system. A long time ago, Thomas (1972) argued that a few prosecution appeals in test cases 'would lead to a more careful articulation of principles in the area of sentencing which would lead in turn to an improvement in the performance of trial courts generally' (at page 306). Can this argument be taken so far as to suggest a mechanism for the review of all sentences, or simply that the CPS should be involved at the trial stage in suggesting a suitable sentence (see Chapter 3)?

(iv) THE ROLE OF THE HOME SECRETARY AND MINISTER OF JUSTICE

We have seen many examples of the powers of both the Home Secretary and Minister of Justice (the Lord Chancellor) in criminal justice. Their role in the development of policy is, of course, crucial. They are the driving forces behind most legislative change. But their role in deciding individual cases has been declining fast in recent years, in recognition of the constitutional doctrine of the separation of powers. Parliament may make the law, but it is for judges to apply it.

The royal prerogative of mercy is still granted occasionally. This may take one of three forms: a free pardon, a conditional pardon, or remission of all or part of the penalty imposed by the court. Although a pardon is normally granted because the guilt of the defendant can no longer be accepted beyond all reasonable doubt, the conviction itself stands. This is because only a court can quash a judicial decision. The High Court held that the courts have jurisdiction to review the exercise of the royal prerogative of mercy in *R v Secretary of State for Home Affairs, ex p Bentley* **[9:13]**. (That the prerogative lives on is clear from PSO 6650—see Chapter 10; the only case to cite *Bentley* is *R (Page) v Minister of Justice* [2007] EWHC (Admin) 2026, where a prisoner successfully relied on that earlier decision.) A person who has been pardoned may, however, be given compensation under the Criminal Justice Act 1988, section 133 **[9:10]**: in *R (Mullen) v Secretary of State for the Home Department* [2002] EWCA Civ 1882, [2003] 1 All ER 613 the Court of Appeal held that Mullen (see **[9:7]**) was entitled to compensation under this provision.

Perhaps the most controversial role that the Home Secretary has had has been in the area of early release from prison, in particular in fixing the length of time that those sentenced to life sentences must serve before the Parole Board reviews their detention. There were many rulings against these practices by both domestic courts and the European Court of Human Rights—see, for example: *V and T v United Kingdom* (1999) 30 EHRR 121; *Stafford v United Kingdom* (2002) 35 EHRR 1121 **[10:15]**; *R (Anderson) v Secretary of State for the Home Department* [2002] UKHL 46, [2003] 1 AC 837—but the Home Secretary was reluctant to give up these powers (see Chapter 10 on early release rules). Now that many of the powers of the Home Secretary have been transferred to the new Ministry of Justice (May 2007), we may see more constitutional change.

(v) THE CRIMINAL CASES REVIEW COMMISSION

Since the Court of Appeal has no power to entertain second applications for permission to appeal, there needs to be a mechanism to reopen cases which turn out to be miscarriages of justice. Until 1995, the Home Secretary could refer a case back to the Court of Appeal. The Home Secretary sat on the horns of a dilemma: on the one hand, he was criticized for his reluctance to use his powers; and on the other he was also criticized, being essentially a political figure, for having a role in the court process at all. In most cases a convicted person had to attract the support of a public figure or a newspaper before the Home Secretary would refer a case back to the Court of Appeal. The power of the media was very clear.

The *Royal Commission* (1993) **[1:4]** recommended that the Home Secretary's power be given instead to a Criminal Cases Review Authority. This was adopted in the Criminal Appeal Act 1995, section 8 **[9:16]**, though the authority was named the Criminal Cases Review Commission (CCRC). The CCRC is made up of 14 members, and started work in 1997. Its powers are set out in the Criminal Appeal Act 1995, section 13 **[9:16]**: a case may be referred by the CCRC to the Court of Appeal if there is a 'real possibility' that the conviction will be overturned because there exists evidence/arguments which were 'not raised in the proceedings which led to it or on any appeal or application for leave to appeal'. There is a safety valve built into section 13(2) of the Act: the CCRC is not prevented from making a reference 'if it appears to [it] that there are exceptional circumstances which justify making it'.

The CCRC is given powers of investigation by sections 17–21 of the 1995 Act, but its powers are in reality controlled by its budget. It has faced many problems of case backlog and delay (see James, Taylor, and Walker (2000), Elks (2008)). The annual reports give a clear picture of the sort of cases with which the CCRC deals, and of its working practices. Even if the CCRC was adequately resourced, how can we measure its 'independence' and its 'efficacy'? We saw in Chapter 2 the problems, in relation to the police, of maintaining a force which is simultaneously both independent and truly accountable for its actions. The same issues arise here. Another way forward would have been to enhance the powers of the judiciary to refer cases back to the Court of Appeal, and to strengthen the resolve of the Court of Appeal itself to correct miscarriages of justice.

(vi) THE ROLE OF THE HOUSE OF LORDS

The House of Lords in its judicial capacity plays a relatively minor role in the criminal justice system. Under the Criminal Appeal Act 1968, section 33 **[9:4]** there are two requirements before there can be a further appeal to the House of Lords: (a) the court from which the appeal is brought (either the Divisional Court or the Court of Appeal) must certify that the case involves a point of law of general public importance; and (b) that court, or the House of Lords itself, must give permission to appeal. The *Royal Commission* (1993) recommended the removal of the requirement that the Court of Appeal certifies that the case involves a point of law of general public importance, on the basis that it is unduly

TABLE 9.8 Petitions to the House of Lords

	Petitions received	Refused permission to appeal	Successful appeals
1993	16	11	0
1998	12	11	2
2001	34	13	13
2005	39	25	13
2006	37	26	5

Source: Judicial Statistics 1993, page 9; 1998, page 9; 2001, page 10; 2005, page 14; 2006, pages 18–19

restrictive, but this has not happened. Having both hurdles to overcome reflects the priority given to limiting the number of cases that reach the House of Lords. Yet Auld **[1:5]** recommended that on points of law of general public importance, consideration should be given to allowing a 'leapfrog' appeal from the Crown Court to the House of Lords when the law is in such an unsatisfactory state that only the House of Lords can resolve it. Auld also recommended that distinguished academics should sometimes be invited to help the House of Lords.

Why do we need two levels of appeal in criminal matters? Having reviewed the House of Lords' unimpressive record in clarifying the criminal law, Glanville Williams said, in a letter published at (1981) Crim LR 581, that 'it is a nice question whether, with this sort of balance sheet, the appellate jurisdiction of the House of Lords in criminal cases is worth the expense to the community'. The question is just as pertinent today. A T H Smith (1984) also concluded that appeals to the House of Lords should be abolished, though he would continue to give the House of Lords a role by means of Attorney-General's references to consider hypothetically whether or not any particular activity is within the ambit of the criminal law. (Readers should be aware that the House of Lords will be renamed the Supreme Court once it moves to its new premises, probably in 2009 (see the Constitutional Reform Act 2005.)

FURTHER READING

Criminal Cases Review Commission Annual Reports

Elks, L, *The Criminal Cases Review Commission* (2008) Justice

Foot, P, *Murder at the Farm: Who Killed Carl Bridgwater?* (1988) Penguin

Henham, R, 'Attorney-General's References and Sentencing Policy' [1994] Crim LR 499

Jaconelli, J, 'Attorney-General's References—a Problematic Device' [1981] Crim LR 543

James, A, Taylor, N, and Walker, C, 'The Criminal Cases Review Commission: Economy, Effectiveness and Justice' [2000] Crim LR 140

Justice, *Miscarriages of Justice* (1989)

Justice, *Remedying Miscarriages of Justice* (1994)

Kennedy, L, *Wicked Beyond Belief: the Luton Murder Case* (1980) Panther

Malleson, K and Roberts, S, 'Streamlining and Clarifying the Appellate Process' [2002] Crim LR 272

Mullin, C, *Error of Judgement: the Birmingham Bombings* (1986) Chatto & Windus

Pattenden, R, *Judicial Discretion and Criminal Litigation* (1990) Clarendon Press

Pattenden, R, *English Criminal Appeals 1844–1994* (1996) Clarendon Press

Pattenden, R, 'Prosecution Appeals' [2000] Crim LR 971

Smith, A T H, 'Criminal Appeals in the House of Lords' (1984) 47 MLR 133

Spencer, J N, 'Judicial Review of Criminal Proceedings' [1991] Crim LR 259

Spencer, J R, 'Does our present criminal appeal system make sense?' [2006] Crim LR 677

Stevens, R, *Law and Politics: the House of Lords as a judicial body* (1979) Weidenfeld & Nicolson

Thomas, D A, 'Increasing Sentences on Appeal' [1972] Crim LR 288

Tregilgas-Davey, M, 'Miscarriages of justice within the English legal system' (1991) 141 NLJ 668

DOCUMENTS

[9:1] *Royal Commission on Criminal Justice: Professor Zander's Dissent*
(1993) Cmnd 2263, HMSO

Professor Zander dissented on three topics: defence disclosure, pre-trial procedures, and the powers of the Court of Appeal. Only the third part of his dissent is included here.

(At page 223:)

III The Court of Appeal's power to quash a conviction (or order a retrial) on account of error at trial or malpractice by the prosecution.

62 When convictions are quashed by the Court of Appeal it is usually because there has been some error or irregularity at the trial or some procedural or legal defect in the pre-trial process, or there has been serious malpractice by the prosecution. Typically, the trial judge misdirected the jury on the law or the evidence, or his summing up was unbalanced, or he wrongly admitted inadmissible evidence.[1] The Commission is unanimous in believing that the Court of Appeal's past practice of allowing many guilty persons to escape their just deserts simply because there has been a defect in the process leading to their conviction requires consideration. But the Commission is not unanimous as to how the problem should be addressed.

63 The majority of the Commission propose that, where there is an appeal against conviction, the conviction should be upheld unless the ground of appeal is such as to undermine the conviction—in the sense that the Court of Appeal concludes that the verdict is no longer safe. In that event, it would quash the conviction. The gravity of the defect on its own would no longer carry any weight. The question would always be only whether the verdict was safe. If the Court of Appeal thinks the defect may make the conviction unsafe, it would order a retrial. (One of the consequences of such a change of approach would be significantly, perhaps drastically, to reduce the number of successful appeals against conviction.)

64 Two Commissioners and I would go further in regard to errors of law or procedure at the trial, other than minor errors or irregularities. As stated in chapter ten of the Report, paragraph 37, we would in addition give the Court of Appeal the power to order a retrial in such cases even though the error or defect cannot be said to make the verdict unsafe. In our view defendants should not be serving prison sentences on the basis of trials that are seriously flawed. If the court holds that the error at the trial is a serious one but that for any reason a retrial is not a practicable or desirable option, it would have to quash the conviction.

65 Where, however, the basis of the appeal is something that occurred pre-trial the view taken by the minority depends on the gravity of the defect. If the defect is minor or 'harmless' error, we agree with the majority that the appeal should fail. On this the Commission is therefore unanimous. If the defect, though not of the gravest kind, is of the level of gravity that now leads the court to quash

the conviction, I and another Commissioner believe that the Court of Appeal should continue to be empowered to deal with such a defect even though it may not render the conviction unsafe. The typical case would be a serious breach of PACE or of its Codes of Practice. Since the introduction of PACE in January 1986 there have been dozens of cases that have gone to the Court of appeal where the substance of the appeal has been that the police broke one or other of the PACE rules. Many have concerned failure to comply with the rules regarding access to a solicitor, or provision of an appropriate adult or with the rules regarding recording of interviews. In a proportion of such cases the Court of Appeal has held that the defect was sufficiently serious to require that the conviction be quashed.

66 The majority would limit the Court of Appeal's power to deal with breaches of PACE to those cases where the breach rendered the jury's verdict unsafe. In my view this is insufficient because it ignores the important role that the Court of Appeal plays in upholding the PACE rules—quite apart from the question whether the breach affected the verdict. Breaches of PACE are automatically breaches of police disciplinary rules but as the Report states[2] 'there are hardly any formal disciplinary proceedings for breaches of PACE'. If any action is taken, even for serious breaches of PACE, it virtually never goes beyond mere 'advice' to the officer concerned. The role of the Court of Appeal in promoting observance of the complex and crucial network of PACE rules is therefore of great importance. The majority's approach would weaken this role. I would however wish to see the Court of Appeal, wherever possible, deal with a serious breach of PACE by ordering a retrial rather than by allowing a guilty person to go free by quashing the conviction. Retrials are not ideal[3] but where there has been a serious breach of PACE they can be preferable to allowing a guilty person to go free.

67 If, however, the pre-trial malpractice is of the most serious kind, the Court of Appeal must be able not simply to order a retrial but to quash the conviction. This is the only appropriate response where prosecution agencies have fabricated or suppressed important evidence or where the defendant has been subjected to serious violence in the course of interrogation. Obviously, if the fabricated or suppressed evidence or the confession produced by violent means was the only or the main evidence for the prosecution, the Court of Appeal would have no difficulty in quashing the conviction. In such a case the Commission is unanimous as to the outcome. But it may be that there is other, reliable evidence showing that the defendant committed the offence. Nine of my ten colleagues believe that if there is sufficient sound evidence, even the most serious misconduct by the prosecution should not result in the conviction being quashed.

68 I cannot agree. The moral foundation of the criminal justice system requires that if the prosecution has employed foul means the defendant must go free even though he is plainly guilty. Where the integrity of the process is fatally flawed, the conviction should be quashed as an expression of the system's repugnance at the methods used by those acting for the prosecution.

69 The majority's position would, I believe, encourage serious wrongdoings from some police officers who might be tempted to exert force or fabricate or suppress evidence in the hope of establishing the guilt of the suspect, especially in a serious case when they believe him to be guilty. There have unfortunately been some gross examples of such conduct.

70 The position adopted by the majority also seems to me to risk undermining the principle at the heart of section 78 of PACE which explicitly gives the court the power to exclude evidence on the ground that it renders the proceedings 'unfair'. The word 'unfair' expresses the underlying moral principle and the Court of Appeal has repeatedly used this new statutory power very broadly to express its refusal to uphold convictions based on unacceptable police practices even when it could not be said that the misconduct had any impact on the jury's verdict.

71 Section 78 would of course remain—but the majority would in effect be encouraging the Court of Appeal to undercut a part of its moral force by saying that the issue of 'unfairness' can be ignored where there is sufficient evidence to show that the defendant is actually guilty. Any judge concerned to discourage prosecution malpractice would I believe be dismayed by the majority's position. In terms of the message sent to the police service and other prosecution agencies it could undo much of the good effect being achieved by the attitude of the judges to section 78 of PACE.

72 But the matter goes beyond discouraging prosecution malpractice. At the heart of the criminal justice system there is a fundamental principle that the process must itself have integrity. The majority suggest that the answer to prosecution wrongdoing in the investigation of crime is to deal with the wrongdoers through prosecution or disciplinary proceedings. Even were this to happen (and often in practice it would not), the approach is not merely insufficient, it is irrelevant to the point of principle. The more serious the case, the greater the need that the system upholds the values in the name of which it claims to act. If the behaviour of the prosecution agencies has deprived a guilty verdict of its moral legitimacy the Court of Appeal must have a residual power to quash the verdict no matter how strong the evidence of guilt. The integrity of the criminal justice system is a higher objective than the conviction of any individual.

Notes

1 See Malleson, K *Review of the Appeal Process* Royal Commission on Criminal Justice Research Study No 17 (1993) Table 1.1, which showed that 60% of successful appeals were based on errors by the trial judge.

2 Chapter three, paragraph 102.

3 They are, however, frequent in many common law jurisdictions, including Australia, Canada, Ireland and New Zealand. Michael Knight, in *Criminal Appeals* (1970, Stevens) reports that, for instance, in Ireland in the period 1954–64 retrials were ordered in three-quarters of all quashed conviction cases.

[9:2] Magistrates' Courts Act 1980 (as amended)

Section 108

108 Right of appeal to the Crown Court

(1) A person convicted by a magistrates' court may appeal to the Crown Court—

    (a) if he pleaded guilty, against his sentence;

    (b) if he did not, against the conviction or sentence.

(1A) Section 14 of the Powers of Criminal Courts (Sentencing) Act 2000 (under which a conviction of an offence for which…an order for conditional or absolute discharge is made is deemed not to be a conviction except for certain purposes) shall not prevent an appeal under this section, whether against conviction or otherwise.

(2) A person sentenced by a magistrates' court for an offence in respect of which…an order for conditional discharge has been previously made may appeal to the Crown Court against the sentence.

(3) In this section "sentence" includes any order made on conviction by a magistrates' court, not being—

    (b) an order for the payment of costs;

    (c) an order under section 37(1) of the Animal Welfare Act 2006 (which enables a court to order the destruction of an animal); or

    (d) an order made in pursuance of any enactment under which the court has no discretion as to the making of the order or its terms;

and also includes a declaration of relevance under the Football Spectators Act 1989.

[9:3] Supreme Court Act 1981 (as amended)

Section 48

48 Appeals to Crown Court

(1) The Crown Court may, in the course of hearing any appeal, correct any error or mistake in the order or judgment incorporating the decision which is the subject of the appeal.

(2) On the termination of the hearing of an appeal the Crown Court—

    (a) may confirm, reverse or vary any part of the decision appealed against, including a determination not to impose a separate penalty in respect of an offence; or

    (b) may remit the matter with its opinion thereon to the authority whose decision is appealed against; or

    (c) may make such other order in the matter as the court thinks just, and by such order exercise any power which the said authority might have exercised.

(3) Subsection (2) has effect subject to any enactment relating to any such appeal which expressly limits or restricts the powers of the court on the appeal.

(4) Subject to section 11(6) of the Criminal Appeal Act 1995, if the appeal is against a conviction or a sentence, the preceding provisions of this section shall be construed as including power to award any punishment, whether more or less severe than that awarded by the magistrates' court whose decision is appealed against, if that is a punishment which that magistrates' court might have awarded.

(5) This section applies whether or not the appeal is against the whole of the decision.

(6) In this section "sentence" includes any order made by a court when dealing with an offender, including—

    (a) a hospital order under Part III of the Mental Health Act 1983, with or without a restriction order, and an interim hospital order under that Act; and

    (b) a recommendation for deportation made when dealing with an offender.

(7) The fact that an appeal is pending against an interim hospital order under the said Act of 1983 shall not affect the power of the magistrates' court that made it to renew or terminate the order or to deal with the appellant on its termination; and where the Crown Court quashes such an order but does not pass any sentence or make any other order in its place the Court may direct the appellant to be kept in custody or released on bail pending his being dealt with by that magistrates' court.

(8) Where the Crown Court makes an interim hospital order by virtue of subsection (2)—

    (a) the power of renewing or terminating the order and of dealing with the appellant on its termination shall be exercisable by the magistrates' court whose decision is appealed against and not by the Crown Court; and

    (b) that magistrates' court shall be treated for the purposes of section 38(7) of the said Act of 1983 (absconding offenders) as the court that made the order.

[9:4] Criminal Appeal Act 1968 (as amended)

Sections 2; 23; 33

2 Grounds for allowing an appeal under s 1

(1) Subject to the provisions of this Act, the Court of Appeal—

    (a) shall allow an appeal against conviction if they think that the conviction is unsafe; and

    (b) shall dismiss such an appeal in any other case.

(2) In the case of an appeal against conviction the Court shall, if they allow the appeal, quash the conviction.

(3) An order of the Court of Appeal quashing a conviction shall, except when under section 7 below the appellant is ordered to be retried, operate as a direction to the court of trial to enter, instead of the record of conviction, a judgment and verdict of acquittal.

23 Evidence

(1) For the purposes of an appeal under this Part of this Act the Court of Appeal may, if they think it necessary or expedient in the interests of justice—

    (a) order the production of any document, exhibit or other thing connected with the proceedings, the production of which appears to them necessary for the determination of the case;

    (b) order any witness who would have been a compellable witness in the proceedings from which the appeal lies to attend for examination and be examined before the Court, whether or not he was called in those proceedings; and

    (c) receive any evidence which was not adduced in the proceedings from which the appeal lies.

(2) The Court of Appeal shall, in considering whether to receive any evidence, have regard in particular to—

    (a) whether the evidence appears to the Court to be capable of belief;

    (b) whether it appears to the Court that the evidence may afford any ground for allowing the appeal;

    (c) whether the evidence would have been admissible in the proceedings from which the appeal lies on an issue which is the subject of the appeal; and

    (d) whether there is a reasonable explanation for the failure to adduce the evidence in those proceedings.

(3) Subsection (1)(c) above applies to any evidence of a witness (including the appellant) who is competent but not compellable . . .

(4) For the purposes of an appeal under this Part of this Act, the Court of Appeal may, if they think it necessary or expedient in the interests of justice, order the examination of any witness whose attendance might be required under subsection (1)(b) above to be conducted, in manner provided by rules of court, before any judge or officer of the Court or other person appointed by the Court for the purpose, and allow the admission of any depositions so taken as evidence before the Court.

(5) A live link direction under section 22(4) does not apply to the giving of oral evidence by the appellant at any hearing unless that direction, or any subsequent direction of the court, provides expressly for the giving of such evidence through a live link.

33 Right of appeal to House of Lords

(1) An appeal lies to the House of Lords, at the instance of the defendant or the prosecutor, from any decision of the Court of Appeal on an appeal to that court under Part I of this Act or section 9 (preparatory hearings) of the Criminal Justice Act 1987 or section 35 of the Criminal Procedure and Investigations Act 1996.

(1B) An appeal lies to the House of Lords, at the instance of the acquitted person or the prosecutor, from any decision of the Court of Appeal on an application under section 76(1) or (2) of the Criminal Justice Act 2003 (retrial for serious offences).

(2) The appeal lies only with the leave of the Court of Appeal or the House of Lords; and leave shall not be granted unless it is certified by the Court of Appeal that a point of law of general public

importance is involved in the decision and it appears to the Court of Appeal or the House of Lords (as the case may be) that the point is one which ought to be considered by that House.

(3) Except as provided by this Part of this Act and section 13 of the Administration of Justice Act 1960 (appeal in cases of contempt of court), no appeal shall lie from any decision of the criminal division of the Court of Appeal.

(4) In relation to an appeal under subsection (1B), references in this Part to a defendant are references to the acquitted person.

[9:5] Malleson, K, *Review of the Appeal Process*
(1993), RCCJ Research Study No 17, HMSO (at page 15)

From these findings, the work of the Court of Appeal can be summarised as follows. Most of its time is spent reviewing the decisions of the trial judge, considering whether his summing up was adequate, whether or not he misdirected the jury as to the application of the law or evidence, or whether he erred in exercising his discretion to include or exclude a piece of evidence. It is rare for the court to hear fresh evidence, consider the existence of a 'lurking doubt' about the conviction or order a retrial. Thus, the court performs, in practice, a relatively limited function. With the exception of the retrial, this cannot be explained as a result of the restrictions of the provisions of the CAA. The rarity of the use of a retrial must, as least party, be explained by the wording of s 7, but the courts interpretation of the grounds set out in s 2(1) and particularly the phrase 'unsafe and unsatisfactory' seems to be quite wide enough to cover a broad range of cases.

The fact that the sample did include fresh evidence cases, lurking doubt and retrial cases shows that the court is quite capable of taking a broad view of its powers and applying them to a wide range of cases if it so chooses. The evidence of both forensic experts and witnesses of fact were considered in cases involving a diverse range of issues and circumstances. The presence of a small number of such cases is evidence that the court considers that it does possess wide powers but that it is reluctant to use them very often.

There are three main explanations which may account for the fact that the court exercises the full range of its powers so infrequently:

(i) The court is very concerned that as far as possible the jury's decision should be final and the trial should not come to be seen as an 'initial skirmish'[4] The court's anxiety not to undermine the principle of the sovereignty of the jury was referred to directly or indirectly in many of the cases reviewed. When assessing a witness's credibility or the soundness of the conviction the court appeared to be considering questions of fact and placing itself in the position of the jury, so threatening the principle which it claims to be reinforcing.

(ii) The court is keen to limit the flow of cases into the appeal system. A number of the cases reviewed commented on the length of time which the appeal had taken to be heard and the court is conscious that delays can amount to a fresh source of injustice. In limiting the type of cases which it hears, the court contributes to the task of holding closed the 'floodgates' to keep out the tide of cases which it fears will swamp the already overstretched resources of the Court of Appeal. Lawyers and appellants know that they are very unlikely to persuade the court to hear fresh evidence or find that there is a 'lurking doubt' about the conviction. This knowledge may help to ensure that few such cases come into the appeal system. The court's decision that errors of an appellant's legal advisers are not generally valid grounds of appeal is an important example of this process of keeping down the numbers of appeals. The fact that many appeals are submitted on the basis of lawyer's errors, despite the ruling, only to be weeded out by the single judge[5] suggests that many more are kept from appealing by the knowledge that it would be hopeless to do so. This process may also be assisted by fear of the time loss rules which keep many potential appellants out of the system. It is likely that they are so rarely applied because the threat alone is sufficient to keep down the numbers of appeals. Possibly, if it came to be widely known that this power is hardly ever exercised, causing numbers of applications for leave to appeal to rise, its use would increase.

(iii) The resources which the court has at its disposal do not equip it to review all the circumstances of alleged injustice, before during and after trial, which can be raised at appeal. From the papers provided by the CAO the court is relatively well placed to effectively assess the quality of the summing up or the judges decisions on law or procedure but is ill-equipped to look into the surrounding circumstances of the cases. Although it has the power to call for documents, exhibits or other thing connected with the case, this is rarely exercised and it has no facilities for investigating the full range of issues which may be raised at the appeal and is in a weak position to assess the actions and integrity of individuals and institutions such as the police, witnesses, lawyers or forensic experts.

The research findings indicate that the court is reluctant to exercise frequently its full range of powers. Three factors can be identified as affecting the court's approach to reviewing appeals against conviction. These are, firstly, the principle of the sovereignty of the jury which is perceived by the court to limit its role in the criminal justice process, secondly, the limited resources of the appeal system which demands that the court contributes to keeping the 'floodgates' closed and, lastly, the court's limited investigative resources for reviewing individual cases.

[See also **[5:9]**.]

Notes

4 See *R v Shields and Patrick* [1977] Crim LR 281.

5 See comparison of own-grounds and legally assisted application for leave to appeal.

[9:6] *R v Chalkley and Jeffries*
[1998] QB 848

Police officers considered that there was a serious threat that the appellants were planning robberies involving firearms. Having obtained permission from an authorizing officer, they arrested the first appellant in connection with an unrelated matter, which allowed them to take his keys and let themselves into his home without his knowledge and to install a listening device in his home. Defence counsel submitted that the evidence of the listening device had been obtained unlawfully and should not have been admitted. The trial judge ruled that the police had acted in good faith and that the evidence was therefore admissible. The appellants changed their plea to guilty. They appealed against conviction on the ground that the judge's ruling was wrong.

The Court of Appeal dismissed the appeals.

Auld LJ (at page 98):

In our view, whatever may have been the use by the Court of the former tests of 'unsatisfactor[iness]' and 'material irregularity' (see the penetrating and engaging analysis of Sir Louis Blom-Cooper QC in 'The Birmingham Six' and other cases, *Victims of Circumstance*, 1997, Duckworth, Cap V), they are not available to it now, save as aids to determining the safety of a conviction. The Court has no power under the substituted section 2(1) to allow an appeal if it does not think the conviction unsafe but is dissatisfied in some way with what went on at the trial. The editors of the third supplement to the current edition of *Archbold* (1997) refer to this as a 'minor, but important, respect' in which the 1995 substitution has done more than just change the wording of the 1968 Act. Whilst we agree that it is an important change, it may not be 'minor', particularly in those cases where, although the Court is of the view that justice has not been seen to be done, it is satisfied that it has been done—that is, that the conviction is safe. All of this is, however, subject to what the Court will make of Article 6(1) of the European Convention on Human Rights, entitling everyone charged with a criminal offence to a fair trial, when it becomes part of our domestic law. Such European Court of Human Rights jurisprudence on the point as there is suggests that procedural unfairness not resulting in unsafety of a conviction may be marked in some manner other than by quashing the conviction. (See *Murray v United Kingdom* [1996] 23 EHRR 29; *Saunders v United Kingdom* [1996] 1 Cr App Rep 463, [1996] 23 EHRR 313, 342, para 86; *Staines and Morrissey* [1997] 2 Cr App Rep 426, and *Coyne v United Kingdom* 26 September 1997.) For a helpful summary of these recent authorities and the light that they may shed on the notion and effect of unsatisfactoriness of a conviction regardless of its safety, see Sir Louis Blom-Cooper QC, op cit pp 74–77) who suggests that procedural unfairness not resulting in unsafety of a conviction may be marked in some manner other than quashing the conviction.

...

We hold that the appellants' appeals against conviction fail because, by their pleas of guilty, they intended to admit and have admitted their guilt, and that their convictions are, therefore, safe.

At page 107:

[W]e consider that the proper course is to make our own decision about the fairness of admitting this evidence. We have no doubt whatever about the fairness of doing so. As we have said, there was no dispute as to its authenticity, content or effect; it was relevant, highly probative of the appellants' involvement in the conspiracy and otherwise admissible; it did not result from incitement, entrapment or inducement or any other conduct of that sort; and none of the unlawful conduct of the police or other of their conduct of which complaint is made affects the quality of the evidence. In the circumstances, we can see no basis for concluding that the admission of this evidence would, in the words of section 78, have had such an adverse effect on the fairness of the proceedings that the Judge should not have admitted it. Accordingly, we would dismiss the appeals on that ground also.

[9:7] *R v Mullen*
[1999] 2 Cr App R 143

The defendant, who was wanted by the police in England, was brought back to England from Zimbabwe by a Zimbabwean immigration officer in 1988. He was arrested and in due course convicted of conspiracy to cause explosions and sentenced to 30 years' imprisonment. He was refused permission to appeal against sentence. In 1998, he was granted an extension of time and permission to appeal against conviction. Evidence disclosed revealed that the security services in England and Zimbabwe had colluded in order to procure the defendant's deportation from Zimbabwe in circumstances in which he was denied access to a lawyer, contrary to Zimbabwean law and internationally recognized human rights.

Although there was no complaint about the fairness of the trial itself, the Court of Appeal allowed his appeal.

Rose LJ (at page 159):

This court's jurisdiction is statutory and depends for present purposes on the meaning properly to be attributed to the word 'unsafe'. In particular, is it apt to confer jurisdiction to quash a conviction when no complaint is made about the conduct of the trial and the sole ground of appeal is that no trial should have taken place, because of the prosecution's abuse of the process of the court prior to trial?

In *R v Chalkley* [1998] QB 848, 859, Auld LJ, giving the judgment of the court, referred to the amended test as being much simpler than the old test in the Act of 1968 prior to amendment. At page

869 he expressly agreed with a passage in *Archbold, Criminal Pleading, Evidence & Practice*, 1997 edn, 3rd supplement, page 99, paragraph 7–45, which contains the following:

'Neither the misconduct of the prosecution, nor the fact that there has been a failure to observe some general notion of "fair play" are in themselves reasons for quashing a conviction... "unsafe"... is clearly intended to refer to the correctness of the conviction (ie a conviction is unsafe if there is a possibility that the defendant was convicted of an offence of which he was in fact innocent).'

At first blush, this passage in the court's judgment might be understood as precluding this court from regarding the present conviction as unsafe. But it is to be noted that *R v Horseferry Road Magistrates' Court, ex p Bennett* [1994] 1 AC 42 was not referred to and, in *R v MacDonald* [1998] Crim LR 808 Auld LJ, giving the judgment of a differently constituted division of this court, said:

'Before parting with the matter we express some reservation about the jurisdiction of the Court to quash a conviction where there has been an abuse of process of the *ex parte Bennett* kind, that is, where a fair trial was possible and in the event resulted in a safe conviction, but where, on a proper view of the matter, the prosecution should have been stayed as an affront to justice. The question does not arise for our determination in the light of our conclusion that a fair trial was possible and took place, that it was not unfair to try the defendants and that safe convictions resulted. And the matter was only touched on briefly in argument. However, if our view had been that it was an abuse of the *ex parte Bennett* kind, we do not know where we could have found the power to quash what we regard as a safe conviction. The court's jurisdiction is entirely statutory, and the single criterion for interference with a conviction is now—since its recent amendment of section 2 of the Criminal Appeal Act 1968—its unsafety. The court seems to have assumed such jurisdiction in *R v Bloomfield* [1997] 1 Cr App Rep 125 [135] and *R v Hyatt* (1977) 3 Archbold News 2, but as the editors of *Criminal Law Week* comment in their Issue 2 of 1998, it is far from obvious as to why this should be so. See the observation of Lord Lloyd in *R v Martin* [1998] AC 917, 928–929, and the judgment of this court in *R v Chalkley* [1998] QB 848, 868–870. It may be that a conviction in a trial which should never have taken place is to be regarded as unsafe for that reason. It may be that, despite the statutory basis of the court's jurisdiction, it has also some inherent or ancillary jurisdictional basis for intervening to mark abuse of process by quashing a conviction when it considers that the court below should have stayed the proceeding. Or it may be that the recent amendment to the Act of 1968 has removed the supervisory role of this court over abuse of criminal process where the affront to justice, however outrageous, has not so prejudiced the defendant in his trial as to render his conviction unsafe. All that is for decision by another court in an appropriate case.'

In the light of these observations, *R v Chalkley* [1998] QB 848 cannot, in our judgment, properly be regarded as having concluded the matter. On the contrary, it is apparent from what he said in the passage cited in *R v MacDonald* [1998] Crim LR 808 that Auld LJ regarded the point as still open. A similar view was expressed in *R v Simpson* [1998] Crim LR 481 by Garland J in the passage cited earlier.

However, in *R v Martin* [1998] AC 917, which was referred to in *R v MacDonald* [1998] Crim LR 808 but not in *R v Simpson* [1998] Crim LR 481, Lord Lloyd of Berwick said [1998] AC 917, 928–929:

'Even if the Courts-Martial Appeal Court had been satisfied that there was an abuse of process, it would still have been necessary for the court to dismiss the appeal, unless persuaded that the conviction was unsafe. For the Courts-Martial Appeal Court is a creature of statute, and has no power to allow appeals save in accordance with section 12(1) of the Courts-Martial (Appeals) Act 1968 as substituted by section 29(1) of and paragraph 5 of Schedule 2 to the Criminal Appeal Act 1995. (These provisions are identical to those amending section 2 of the Act of 1968 in relation to this court).'

Lord Browne-Wilkinson and Lord Slynn both agreed with Lord Lloyd's reasons for dismissing the appeal. Lord Hope of Craighead said, at page 930:

'...I do not think it can be doubted that the appeal court—in this particular case, the Courts-Martial Appeal Court—have power to declare a conviction to be unsafe and to quash the conviction if they find that the course of proceedings leading to what would otherwise have been a fair trial has been such as to threaten either basic human rights or the rule of law.'

It seems plain that these conflicting observations by Lord Lloyd and Lord Hope were obiter and formed no part of the reasoning which led to the decision in *R v Martin* [1998] AC 917. Furthermore, it does not appear that their Lordships were invited to consider what was said in Parliament when the Act of 1968 was amended or what the pre-amendment practice of this court was, as exemplified by *R v Heston-Francois* [1984] QB 278 and *Attorney-General's Reference (No 1 of 1990)* [1992] QB 630, 643–644. It is also pertinent that Sir John Smith's article in [1995] Crim LR 920 was not before the House of Lords in *R v Martin* [1998] AC 917.

In our judgment the conflicting views expressed in *R v Martin* [1998] AC 917 in themselves afford a sufficient demonstration of the ambiguity of 'unsafe' to permit this court, in accordance with *Pepper v Hart* [1993] AC 593, to have recourse to Hansard. Furthermore, if the construction of Lord Lloyd is correct, it will, with respect, lead to absurdity, which provides a further reason for recourse to Hansard: in relation to a minor offence triable by justices, abuse arguments can lead to redress by judicial review in the Divisional Court, but, in relation to a serious offence tried at the Crown Court, abuse arguments could not lead to appellate success.

Accordingly, we turn to Hansard (HC Debates), 6 March 1995, col 24, the relevant passages from which are conveniently set out in Sir John Smith's article [1995] Crim LR 920, 924. It is unnecessary to rehearse what was said on second reading and in standing committee. But it is apparent that the amended form of section 2 of the Act of 1968 was intended by the Home Secretary, by Lord Taylor of Gosforth CJ and, crucially, by Parliament, to restate the existing practice of the Court of Appeal; although there is nothing to suggest that express consideration was then given by anyone to whether 'unsafe' was apt to embrace abuse of the *Bennett* or any other type. It is common ground that *R v Heston-Francois* [1984] QB 278 and *Attorney-General's Reference (No 1 of 1990)* [1992] QB 630 show the pre-amendment practice of this court, namely that abuse can be a ground for quashing a conviction.

Furthermore, in our judgment, for a conviction to be safe, it must be lawful; and if it results from a trial which should never have taken place, it can hardly be regarded as safe. Indeed the *Oxford English Dictionary* gives the legal meaning of 'unsafe' as 'likely to constitute a miscarriage of justice'.

Sir John Smith's article does not deal with 'unsafe' in relation to abuse, though his commentary on *R v Simpson* [1998] Crim LR 481, raises directly pertinent questions. But, for the reasons which we have given, we agree with his 1995 conclusion that 'unsafe' bears a broad meaning and one which is apt to embrace abuse of process of the *Bennett* or any other kind.

It follows that, in the highly unusual circumstances of this case, notwithstanding that there is no criticism of the trial judge or jury, and no challenge to the propriety of the outcome of the trial itself, this appeal must be allowed and the defendant's conviction quashed.

[9:8] Professor J R Spencer QC, 'Quashing Convictions, and Squashing the Court of Appeal'
(2006) 170 JP 790–793

In its latest consultation paper, entitled 'Quashing Convictions',[1] the Government proposes legislation to curtail the powers of the Court of Appeal, so that it will no longer be able to quash convictions on 'purely procedural grounds' in cases where it is sure that the defendant is factually guilty; and it invites comments on three possible modifications to section 2 of the Criminal Appeal Act 1968 designed to achieve this end.

Painful as it is to have to say so, this paper is marked by two particularly bad qualities: arrogance, and shallowness.

The first emerges from the Home Secretary's foreword, in which he tells readers not to argue about the basic proposal, because the Government has already made up its mind to do it. 'However, whilst the Government is open to suggestions about *how* we achieve the aims, we are not consulting on the aims themselves or therefore *whether* the law should be changed.' And the second emerges from the later pages, in which we find no serious attempt to make the case for the change, and not the slightest recognition that there might be any case against it—let alone an attempt to answer it.[2] The present system, we are simply told, 'risks outcomes which are unacceptable to the law-abiding majority'; the Government is committed 'to rebalancing the criminal justice system in favour of the victim and the law-abiding majority': and that is that.

I believe that the basic proposal set out in this document is objectionable, and for reasons which should be obvious to any member of 'the law-abiding majority' in whose supposed interests this proposal has been made. But as the Home Secretary has made it clear that he is not prepared to listen to arguments of principle, it is presumably a waste of time for me to engage with him in the official consultation process—or with the Lord Chancellor, or the Attorney General, both of whom (surprisingly) have put their names on the document as well. So this response is written for the wider public, in the hope that Parliament may eventually be persuaded to reject the Government's proposal when, having 'consulted', it introduces it as part of its next Bill to 'rebalance' criminal justice.

Put simply, the objection to the proposal is that, in a democratic society which expects certain minimum standards to be respected in the way its citizens are treated, there are values which are higher than inflicting punishment upon the wicked. For this reason, there are limits to the steps that we are prepared to allow the police to take when catching and collecting evidence against criminals, however wicked and however clearly guilty, and there are also limits to the steps that we are prepared to allow the public prosecutor to go in ensuring trial courts convict them. Thus to take some extreme examples, we do not allow the police to put them on the rack, or throw them into rat-infested dungeons without food until at length they talk; and we do not allow the Attorney General or the Home Secretary to threaten jurors if they dare acquit, or intimidate defence witnesses to make them stay away. In a country which respects the rule of law, we simply cannot allow convictions to stand if they have been obtained by methods such as these, however sure the appeal court is that those concerned are really guilty. And this is for two reasons, one theoretical, and the other practical.

The theoretical reason is that a conviction obtained by such methods is deprived of one of its essential ingredients: moral authority.

> …a criminal conviction serves three functions: to make a public finding of the defendant's factual commission of the offence, to make a moral statement of the defendant's guilt and fitness for punishment, and to make a public expression of the continuing validity of the norms of the criminal law and the consequences of its breach. In order for the verdict to discharge these functions it must be factually accurate, morally authoritative, and founded itself on the rule of law.[3]

The practical reason is that, if convictions can be upheld in cases where the authorities have flouted the basic rules of criminal procedure, this will undermine the self-restraint that we expect the authorities to show in keeping to the rules. 'If at the end of the day a conviction obtained by these means will be appeal-proof if it is clear that the defendant committed the offence, why shouldn't we take the risk and break the rules?'

...

The particular butt of the Home Secretary's wrath is the Court of Appeal decision in *Mullen*.[4] In 1990, Mullen was convicted of conspiracy to cause explosions in the context of an IRA bombing campaign in mainland Britain, and sentenced to 30 years' imprisonment. Before arrest he had fled to Zimbabwe, whence the British authorities, unwilling to go through the formalities of extradition, got him back by persuading the Zimbabwe authorities to unlawfully expel him.

In another case four years later, in which the Metropolitan Police had conspired with their South African colleagues to (in effect) kidnap a fugitive suspect and put him on a plane to Heathrow, the House of Lords ruled that where the authorities committed this sort of blatant illegality, the resulting proceedings are irremediably tainted, and cannot go ahead; to prosecute after this illegal start would constitute an 'abuse of process'.[5] It did so because, as Lord Griffiths explained, '...the judiciary accept a responsibility for the maintenance of the rule of law that embraces a willingness to oversee executive action and to refuse to countenance behaviour that threatens either basic human rights or the rule of law.' At this point Mullen appealed, and the Court of Appeal felt obliged to quash his conviction: irrespective of the fact that evidence against him was extremely strong, and had evidently convinced the jury that convicted him. With considerable chuzpah (or its Irish equivalent) Mullen then sued the Home Secretary for compensation for the period he had spent in prison, in which attempt he failed.[6] It seems to have been this unsuccessful attempt that provoked the previous Home Secretary, earlier this year, to announce the immediate abolition of the then-existing discretionary scheme under which the Home Office occasionally (and grudgingly) paid compensation to those whose convictions were quashed upon appeal.[7] And now it is the same case which has led the current Home Secretary to attempt to change the law so that, should the same facts occur in future, the Court of Appeal would be unable to quash the conviction.

If the proposal announced in this Consultation Paper is carried out, then not only would the Court of Appeal be obliged to uphold the conviction of an obviously guilty Mullen in the circumstances of that case; it would also be obliged to uphold the conviction in the following circumstances, if it was convinced that he had committed the offence for which he had been convicted:

(1) Mullen, instead of being illegally expelled by the authorities in Zimbabwe in collusion with our own, is kidnapped there by our secret service and brought back to London, drugged and shackled, in a crate;

(2) Mullen, when arrested, is interrogated under torture, and confesses; facts discovered as a result of what he said under torture enable his guilt to be established beyond any doubt; at trial the judge, in disregard of sections 76 and 78 of the Police and Criminal Evidence Act 1984, allows the evidence to go to the jury, which convicts;

(3) Mullen, a previously law-abiding citizen, was blackmailed into joining the conspiracy by people posing as members of the IRA, who were in fact agents of the secret service;[8]

(4) at trial, the judge refuses to allow Mullen to have a barrister to defend him, or refuses to allow him to give evidence in his defence (or both);

(5) when summing up, the trial judge directs the jury that on the evidence Mullen is clearly guilty and has no conceivable defence, and it is their duty to return an immediate verdict to that effect—which they promptly do, without retiring;[9]

(6) during the trial, the jurors receive letters from the Home Office warning them that if they acquit this dangerous terrorist, they will be viewed as threats to national security and may find themselves subjected to control orders under the Terrorism Act 2006;

(7) after the trial, it emerges that the judge received a letter from the Prime Minister's office, telling him that the Government believed it to be in the national interest that Mullen should be convicted—to which the judge replied 'You can count on me: but remember that one good turn deserves another.'

Some of these examples are real cases, in which the Court of Appeal, applying the present rules, has actually quashed the conviction—in some cases ordering a retrial, and in other cases not. Some, by contrast, are imaginary. Ten years ago, I would have described the imaginary ones as purely fanciful, but in the oppressive political climate of today I am not so sure they are. Who would have thought, even ten years ago, the President of the USA would publicly admit that terrorist suspects are being held for interrogation in secret prisons—and that when he did so, it would provoke little or no comment? Who would have thought, ten years ago, that we would have a Home Secretary who made a habit of publicly abusing members of the judiciary in the coarsest terms: and that far from being sacked for this, was smiled upon by the Prime Minister, until a scandal about a different matter forced him to resign? Or that his successor-but-one would join the tabloid newspapers in publicly condemning a judge for imposing a sentence which the law required him to impose? Or that, in the land of Magna Carta, a government in time of peace would first try to introduce indefinite administrative detention for suspected terrorists, and when that was struck down by the courts, house-arrest?

To remain the sort of society in which it is safe for the 'law abiding majority' to live, the citizens of this country need to be protected not only from being blown to pieces by the likes of Mullen, but also from being convicted and sent to prison after outrageously illegal conduct by the police and the other agencies of the state. As the law stands at present, happily, they are. But if the Government succeeds in its attempt to 'rebalance' the Criminal Appeal Act, this will no longer be the case.

If a Bill is introduced to make the change the Government now has in mind, I fail to see how the Minister will be able truthfully to make the necessary declaration to Parliament that its terms are 'compatible with Convention rights'.[10] And if it is enacted, we shall (I believe) be the only country in Europe in which convictions are not automatically set aside for grave procedural errors, irrespective of the guilt of the accused—and we can expect a further string of embarrassing condemnations from Strasbourg a few years down the line.

Is there really anything to be said for the Government's position?

There is this much: that it is possible to disagree with the Court of Appeal (and indeed the House of Lords) about the details of which procedural irregularities are sufficiently serious to justify the conviction of an obviously guilty person being set aside.

...

But the fact that two views are possible about some of the cases in which the higher courts have felt it necessary to quash the conviction of an obviously guilty person is no good reason for abolishing their power to do so altogether. If there is room for argument about the cases mentioned in the previous paragraph, no one, I believe—or at any rate, profoundly hope—would wish to see the Court of Appeal constrained to uphold a conviction in the hypothetical cases numbered (2), (3) (4), (6) or (7) on pages 4–5 above, however convincing the evidence of the defendant's guilt might be.

So if what the Government currently proposes is unacceptable, could the problem (if it is one) be resolved by a watered-down version of it, in which the Court of Appeal's power to quash the conviction of an obviously guilty person is restricted to certain stated cases, or in which certain specific cases are put beyond its reach? I do not think so. Decisions of this sort, I believe, are best made as they are now: by our senior judges, after argument, on a case-by-case basis. As the law stands, I believe they are making a reasonably good job of it. And there is no reason to tie their hands with yet more prescriptive legislation, passed with an eye to reversing particular decisions that happen to have attracted the attention of the tabloid newspapers.

At the beginning of this Consultation Paper, the Home Secretary, Lord Chancellor and Attorney-General did me the honour of quoting from the first page of an article of mine about criminal appeals which was published in the *Criminal Law Review* in August.[11] Had they read to the end, they would have seen that my concluding words were these: 'The message I hope this article has conveyed is that we should stop tinkering with the appeal system, stand back from it, and try to re-plan it as a coherent whole.' If the Government persists with this deplorable proposal, I hope that Parliament will bear these words in mind and resoundingly reject it.

Notes

1 Office for Criminal Justice Reform, September 2006; available on the Home Office website at http://www.homeoffice.gov.uk/documents/cons-2006-quashing-convictions2?view=Binary

2 The attentive reader will also be disquieted to notice that, when discussing the background to the current law, it makes repeated reference to "the 1985 (sic) Royal Commission on Criminal Justice".

3 Ian Dennis, "Fair trials and safe convictions", [2003] Current Legal Problems 211, at 235–6.

4 [1999] 2 CrAppR 143.

5 R v Horseferry Road JJ ex pte Bennett [1994] AC 42, and [1995] 1 CrAppR 147.

6 R (Mullen) v Secretary of State for the Home Department [2004] UKHL 18, [2005] 1 AC 1.

7 See the written Ministerial statement, 19 April 2006, available on the Home Office website.

8 c.f. Loosely and A-G's Reference (No.3 of 2000) [2001] UKHL 53, [2001] 1 WLR 2060.

9 Wang [2005] UKHL 9, [2005] 1 WLR 661.

10 As required by s.19 of the Human Rights Act 1998.

11 Does our present criminal appeal system make sense?, [2006] CrimLR 677–694.

[9:9] *R v McIlkenny*
(1992) 93 Cr App R 287

This is the famous judgment of the Court of Appeal in the 'Birmingham Six' case. In 1975 the appellants were convicted of 21 counts of murder, arising out of the IRA bombing of two pubs in Birmingham in which 21 people were killed and 162 injured. Their appeals against conviction were dismissed. In 1987 the Home Secretary referred the case to the Court of Appeal on the ground that there was fresh scientific evidence and fresh evidence that the appellants had been beaten following their arrests, and this was likewise dismissed. On a second reference in 1990, the court held that the convictions were now unsafe and unsatisfactory, as a result of both the fresh scientific evidence and the fresh investigation into the police evidence. The court stressed that they were saying nothing about the innocence or otherwise of the applicants, and indeed stressed the strengths as well as the weaknesses in the prosecution case.

Lloyd LJ (at page 310):

The Role of the Court of Appeal

Since the present appeal has given rise to much public discussion as to the powers and duties of the Court of Appeal (Criminal Division), and since the Home Secretary has set up a Royal Commission to investigate and report, it may be helpful if we set out our understanding of the present state of the law.

(1) The Court of Appeal (Criminal Division) is the creature of statute. Our powers are derived from, and confined to, those contained in the Supreme Court Act 1981, the Criminal Appeal Act 1968 and the Criminal Justice Act 1988. We have no inherent jurisdiction apart from statute: see *Jeffries* (1968) 52 Cr App Rep 654, [1969] 1 QB 120, *R v Collins* (1969) 54 Cr App Rep 19, [1970] 1 QB 710 and *DPP v Shannon* (1974) 59 Cr App Rep 250, [1975] AC 717. Thus we have no power to conduct an open-ended investigation into an alleged miscarriage of justice, even if we were equipped to do so. Our function is to hear criminal appeals, neither more or less.

(2) Just as we have no powers other than those conferred on us by Parliament, so we are guided by Parliament in the exercise of those powers. Thus by section 2(1) of the 1968 Act we are directed to allow an appeal against conviction if, but only if, (a) we think that the conviction is unsafe or unsatisfactory; (b) there has been a wrong decision on a question of law or, (c) there has been a

material irregularity. In all other cases we are obliged to dismiss the appeal. Where we allow an appeal, we are directed by section 2(2) to quash the conviction. Where we quash the conviction, the other operates, by virtue of section 2(3) as a direction to the trial court to enter a verdict of acquittal, except where a retrial is ordered under section 7 of the Act. Nothing in section 2 of the Act, or anywhere else obliges or entitles us to say whether we think that the appellant is innocent. This is a point of great constitutional importance. The task of deciding whether a man is guilty falls on the jury. We are concerned solely with the question whether the verdict of the jury can stand.

(3) Rightly or wrongly (we think rightly) trial by jury is the foundation of our criminal justice system. Under jury trial juries not only find the facts; they also apply the law. Since they are not experts in the law, they are directed on the relevant law by the judge. But the task of applying the law to the facts, and so reaching a verdict, belongs to the jury, and the jury alone. The primacy of the jury in the English criminal justice system explains why, historically, the Court of Appeal had so limited a function. Until 1907, there was no Court of Criminal Appeal at all. If, before then, a point of law arose in the course of a trial, the judge could 'reserve' the point, if he thought fit, for consideration by the Court for Crown Cases Reserved. In the event of the point being decided in favour of the accused, the conviction would be quashed. But there was no right of appeal as such. The Criminal Appeal Act 1907 created the right of appeal for the first time. It also enabled the Court of Criminal Appeal to receive fresh evidence. There was no power to order a retrial, except by way of the writ of venire de novo. But that writ only issued when the trial had been a nullity. There was no general power to order a retrial until the Criminal Appeal Act 1964, and then only in fresh evidence cases. The power has since been greatly extended.

(4) The primacy of the jury in the criminal justice system is well illustrated by the difference between the Criminal and Civil Divisions of the Court of Appeal. Like the Criminal Division, the Civil Division is also a creature of statute. But its powers are much wider. A civil appeal is by way of re-hearing of the whole cases. So the court is concerned with fact as well as law. It is true the court does not re-hear the witnesses. But it reads their evidence. It follows that in a civil case the Court of Appeal may take a different view of the facts from the court below. In a criminal case this is not possible. Since justice is as much concerned with the conviction of the guilty as the acquittal of the innocent, and the task of convicting the guilty belongs constitutionally to the jury, not to us, the role of the Criminal Division of the Court of Appeal is necessarily limited. Hence it is true to say that whereas the Civil Division of the Court of Appeal has appellate jurisdiction in the full sense, the Criminal Division is perhaps more accurately described as a court of review. In the 1907 Act there was a power to set aside a verdict if the court thought it unreasonable, or that it could not be supported having regard to the evidence. This power was very narrowly construed. The wording has now been changed. We have power to upset the verdict of a jury on a question of fact if we think a conviction unsafe or unsatisfactory under all the circumstances of the case. These words were substituted by section 4 of the Criminal Appeal Act 1966. We shall return to their meaning later.

(5) Another feature of our law, which goes hand in hand with trial by jury, is the adversarial nature of criminal proceedings. Clearly a jury cannot embark on a judicial investigation. So the material must be placed before the jury. It is sometimes said that the adversarial system leaves too much power in the hands of the police. But that criticism has been met, at least in part, by the creation of the Crown Prosecution Service. The great advantage of the adversarial system is that it enables the defendant to test the prosecution case in open court. Once there is sufficient evidence to commit a defendant for trial, the prosecution has to prove the case against him by calling witnesses to give oral testimony in the presence of the jury. We doubt whether there is a better way of exposing the weaknesses in the prosecution case, whether the witness be a policeman, a scientist or a bystander, than by cross-examination.

(6) A disadvantage of the adversarial system may be that the parties are not evenly matched in resources. As we have seen, one reason why the judge expressed his preference for Dr Skuse

was that Dr Black had carried out no experiments to prove his theory. Experiments presumably cost money. Whether Dr Black could have carried out any experiments within the limitation of legal aid, or the time available, we do not know. But the inequality of resources is ameliorated by the obligation on the part of the prosecution to make available all material which may prove helpful to the defence. The later history of the present appeal shows how well the prosecution can perform that obligation.

(7) No system is better than its human input. Like any other system of justice the adversarial system may be abused. The evidence adduced may be inadequate. Expert evidence may not have been properly researched or there may have been a deliberate attempt to undermine the system by giving false evidence. If there is a conflict of evidence there is no way of ensuring the jury will always get it right. This is particularly so where there is a conflict of expert evidence, such as there was here. No human system can expect to be perfect.

(8) Just as the adversarial system prevails at the trial, so also it prevails in the Court of Appeal. It is for the appellants to raise the issues which they wish to lay before the court. Those issues are set out in the grounds of appeal. It will be remembered that at the initial application for leave to appeal, virtually the only issue before the court was the fairness of the summing-up. If the appellants had insisted on raising other issues, they could have done so. The same applies when the case was referred back to the court in 1987. A number of distinguished scientists were called on both sides. But as we have seen, the scientific issues before the court in 1987 were not the same as they are now. Thus nobody suggested in 1987 that Dr Skuse's results could have been due to nitrite contamination from the soap he was using to clean his bowls. Nobody knew that Dr Drayton would modify her view in the light of later scientific research. Nobody knew that the 'contemporaneous' notes taken by DC Woodwiss of the two McIlkenny interviews were written on four different pads of paper. So the issues were very different.

(9) For an adversarial system to work, there must be an adversary. One of our difficulties in the present appeal has been that we have listened to the fresh evidence of Dr Scaplehorn and Dr Baxendale, without the benefit of hearing any cross-examination. We say at once, and as emphatically as we can, that this is not criticism of the Director or Mr Boal. They have acted with perfect propriety. The concluding paragraphs of the Farquharson's Committee's Report on The Role of Prosecuting Counsel, May 1986 (Archbold 43rd ed para 4–47a) deals with prosecution counsel's function in the Court of Appeal in this way:

> 'If prosecution counsel has formed the view that the appeal should succeed he should acquaint the court with the view and explain the reasons for it. If the court disagrees with him counsel is entitled to adhere to his view and is not obliged to conduct the appeal in a way which conflicts with his own judgment. At the same time it remains counsel's duty to give assistance to the court if requested to do so.'

Mr Boal and the DPP had a number of very difficult decisions to take in the abnormal circumstances of the present appeal. Having decided that they could not support the scientific evidence on which the prosecution was based, or the police evidence, it was their duty to. They have since given us every possible assistance. But the effect of their decision was, inevitably, that we have not heard the other side put, if indeed there is another side.

(10) This has led us to consider whether some other system might be devised in the very exceptional class of case, of which this is one, where fresh evidence comes to light long after the conviction. In the ordinary case, not depending on fresh evidence, there is no difficulty. Nor is there any difficulty in fresh evidence cases, where the fresh evidence is discovered soon after the trial. If the evidence is incredible, or inadmissible, or would not afford a ground for allowing the appeal, we decline to receive it. If the fresh evidence surmounts that preliminary hurdle, we first quash the conviction, if we think it unsafe or unsatisfactory, and then order a retrial under section 7 of the Act, if the interests of justice so require. Where new evidence is conclusive, we quash the conviction without

ordering a retrial: see *R v Flower* (1965) 50 Cr App Rep 22, [1966] 1 QB 146. There is a view, put forward notably by Lord Devlin in The Judge, that we should always quash a conviction where fresh evidence has been received, since a conviction is bound to be unsafe, or at least unsatisfactory, where it has not been based on all the evidence. But this view did not find favour with the House of Lords in *Stafford and Luvaglio v DPP* (1973) 58 Cr App Rep 256, [1974] AC 878.

The difficulty in fresh evidence cases arises where a retrial is no longer practicable, as in the present case. The difficulty becomes acute when there is no contest. For we then have to make up our own minds whether the convictions are unsafe or unsatisfactory without having the benefit of hearing the evidence tested by cross-examination. Where a retrial is still possible, the quashing of the conviction is, as it were, only the first half of a two stage process. Where a retrial is no longer possible, it is the end of the road. This is not the occasion to offer a solution to the difficulty ourselves. No doubt all these problems will be reviewed by the Royal Commission.

[9:10] Criminal Justice Act 1988 (as amended)

Sections 36; 133

36 Reviews of sentencing

(1) If it appears to the Attorney General—

    (a) that the sentencing of a person in a proceeding in the Crown Court has been unduly lenient; and

    (b) that the case is one to which this Part of this Act applies,

    he may, with the leave of the Court of Appeal, refer the case to them for them to review the sentencing of that person; and on such a reference the Court of Appeal may—

    (i) quash any sentence passed on him in the proceeding; and

    (ii) in place of it pass such sentence as they think appropriate for the case and as the court below had power to pass when dealing with him.

(2) Without prejudice to the generality of subsection (1) above, the condition specified in paragraph (a) of that subsection may be satisfied if it appears to the Attorney General that the judge;

    (a) erred in law as to his powers of sentencing; or

    (b) failed to impose a sentence required by—

        (i) section 51A(2) of the Firearms Act 1968;

        (ii) section 110(2) or 111(2) of the Powers of Criminal Courts (Sentencing) Act 2000;

        (iii) any of sections 225 to 228 of the Criminal Justice Act 2003; or

        (iv) under section 29(4) or (6) of the Violent Crime Reduction Act 2006.

(3) For the purposes of this Part of this Act any two or more sentences are to be treated as passed in the same proceeding if they would be so treated for the purposes of section 10 of the Criminal Appeal Act 1968.

(4) No judge shall sit as a member of the Court of Appeal on the hearing of, or shall determine any application in proceedings incidental or preliminary to, a reference under this section of a sentence passed by himself.

(5) Where the Court of Appeal have concluded their review of a case referred to them under this section the Attorney General or the person to whose sentencing the reference relates may refer a point of law involved in any sentence passed on that person in the proceeding to the House of Lords for their opinion, and the House shall consider the point and give their opinion on it accordingly, and either remit the case to the Court of Appeal to be dealt with or deal with it themselves; and section 35(1) of the Criminal Appeal Act 1968 (composition of House for appeals) shall apply also in relation to any proceedings of the House under this section.

(6) A reference under subsection (5) above shall be made only with the leave of the Court of Appeal or the House of Lords; and leave shall not be granted unless it is certified by the Court of Appeal that the point of law is of general public importance and it appears to the Court of Appeal or the House of Lords (as the case may be) that the point is one which ought to be considered by that House.

(7) For the purpose of dealing with a case under this section the House of Lords may exercise any powers of the Court of Appeal.

(8) The supplementary provisions contained in Schedule 3 to this Act shall have effect.

(9) In the application of this section to Northern Ireland—

   (a) any reference to the Attorney General shall be construed as a reference to the Attorney General for Northern Ireland;

   (ab) the reference to section 29(4) or (6) of the Violent Crime Reduction Act 2006 shall be construed as a reference to paragraph 2(4) or (5) of Schedule 2 to that Act; and

   (b) the references to sections 10 and 35(1) of the Criminal Appeal Act 1968 shall be construed as references to sections 10(2) and 33(1) of the Criminal Appeal (Northern Ireland) Act 1980, respectively.

133 Compensation for miscarriages of justice

(1) Subject to subsection (2) below, when a person has been convicted of a criminal offence and when subsequently his conviction has been reversed or he has been pardoned on the ground that a new or newly discovered fact shows beyond reasonable doubt that there has been a miscarriage of justice, the Secretary of State shall pay compensation for the miscarriage of justice to the person who has suffered punishment as a result of such conviction or, if he is dead, to his personal representatives, unless the non-disclosure of the unknown fact was wholly or partly attributable to the person convicted.

(2) No payment of compensation under this section shall be made unless an application for such compensation has been made to the Secretary of State.

(3) The question whether there is a right to compensation under this section shall be determined by the Secretary of State.

(4) If the Secretary of State determines that there is a right to such compensation, the amount of the compensation shall be assessed by an assessor appointed by the Secretary of State.

(4A) In assessing so much of any compensation payable under this section to or in respect of a person as is attributable to suffering, harm to reputation or similar damage, the assessor shall have regard in particular to—

   (a) the seriousness of the offence of which the person was convicted and the severity of the punishment resulting from the conviction;

   (b) the conduct of the investigation and prosecution of the offence; and

   (c) any other convictions of the person and any punishment resulting from them.

(5) In this section "reversed" shall be construed as referring to a conviction having been quashed—

   (a) on an appeal out of time; or

   (b) on a reference—
      (i) under the Criminal Appeal Act 1995; or
      (ii) under section 263 of the Criminal Procedure (Scotland) Act 1975;

   (c) on an appeal under section 7 of the Terrorism Act 2000; or

   (d) on an appeal under section 12 of the Prevention of Terrorism Act 2005.

(6) For the purposes of this section a person suffers punishment as a result of a conviction when sentence is passed on him for the offence of which he was convicted.

(7) Schedule 12 shall have effect.

[9:11] *Monnell and Morris v United Kingdom*
(1987) 10 EHRR 205

The two applicants had applied unsuccessfully to the Court of Appeal for leave to appeal against both their convictions and sentences. The Court of Appeal, although neither applicant had been present or represented at the hearing, had ordered that part of the time already spent by the applicants in custody since conviction should not count towards the service of the sentences. The applicants argued that the periods of detention which the court ordered not to count towards their sentence was not covered by any of the categories of permitted detention set out in Article 5(1) of the European Convention on Human Rights (see **[1:12]**), and that the procedure followed did not comply with Articles 6(1), (3)(c), and 14. The court held, by a majority of five to two, that there had been no violation of Article 5 or 6, and unanimously that there had been no violation of Article 14.

The following extract is taken from the majority judgment (at page 217):

The power of the Court of Appeal to order loss of time, as it is actually exercised, is a component of the machinery existing under English law to ensure that criminal appeals are considered within a reasonable time and, in particular, to reduce the time spent in custody by those with meritorious grounds waiting for their appeal to be heard; this is made patently clear in the 1965 report of the Interdepartmental Committee on the Court of Criminal Appeal and in the two Practice Directions issued by the Lord Chief Justice. In sum, it is a power exercised to discourage abuse of the court's own procedures. As such, it is an inherent part of the criminal appeal process following conviction of an offender and pursues a legitimate aim under sub-paragraph (a) of Article 5(1).

47 It was pointed out in argument that under the law of many of the convention countries detention pending a criminal appeal is treated as detention on remand and a convicted person does not start to serve his or her sentence until the conviction has become final. In such systems, the appellate court itself determines the sentence and, in some of them, exercises a discretion in deciding whether or to what extent detention pending appeal shall be deducted from the sentence. The Delegate of the Commission was of the opinion that such systems, unlike the English system at issue in the present case, would be compatible with Article 5(1).

The difference between the two approaches to sentencing procedures is, however, one of form and not of substance as far as the effect on the convicted person is concerned. Sub-paragraph (a) of Article 5(1), which is silent as to the permissible forms of legal machinery whereby a person may lawfully be ordered to be detailed after conviction, must be taken to have left the Contracting States a discretion in the matter. Sentencing procedures may legitimately vary from Contracting State to Contracting State, whilst still complying with the requirements of Article 5(1)(a). The court considers that the technical and formal difference in the way in which sentencing procedures are arranged in the United Kingdom as compared with other Convention countries is not such as to exclude the applicability of sub-paragraph (a) of Article 5(1) in the present case.

48 In the light of all the foregoing factors, the court finds that there was a sufficient and legitimate connection, for the purposes of the deprivation of liberty permitted under sub-paragraph (a) of Article 5(1), between the conviction of each applicant and the additional period of imprisonment undergone as a result of the loss-of-time order made by the Court of appeal. The time spent in custody by each applicant under this head is accordingly to be regarded as detention of a person under conviction by a competent court, within the meaning of sub-paragraph (a) of Article 5(1).

49 The applicants at certain points in their pleadings appeared to be arguing that their applications for leave to appeal were not in fact hopeless or frivolous. This was a matter of appreciation coming within the discretion conferred on the Court of Appeal by the terms of section 29(1) of the Criminal Appeal Act 1968. Save in so far as is necessary to review the contested measure of deprivation of liberty

for compatibility with the Convention, it is not within the province of the European Court to substitute its own assessment of the facts for that of the domestic courts.

50 More generally, the court is satisfied in the circumstances of the present case as to the lawfulness and procedural propriety of the contested periods of loss of liberty. To begin within, it has been disputed that the relevant rules and procedures under English law were properly observed by the English courts in relation to the making of the loss-of-time orders. Further, contrary to the submissions of the applicants, the court finds that these orders depriving the applicants of their liberty issued from and were executed by an appropriate authority and were not arbitrary.

The contested deprivation of liberty must therefore be found to have been both lawful and effected in accordance with a procedure prescribed by law, as those expressions in Article 5(1) have been interpreted in the court's case law.

51 There has accordingly been no breach of Article 5(1) in the present case in respect of either applicant.

(At page 223:)

In the opinion of the Court, Article 6 required that Mr Monnell and Mr Morris be provided, in some appropriate way, with a fair procedure enabling them adequately and effectively to present their case against the possible exercise to their detriment of the power under section 29(1) of the 1968 Act. The court will accordingly review the procedure followed to ascertain whether this condition was satisfied.

62 To begin with, the principle of equality of arms, inherent in the notion of fairness under Article 6(1), was respected in that the prosecution, like the two accused, was not represented before either the single judge or the full Court of appeal.

The principle of equality of arms is, however, only one feature of the wider concept of fair trial in criminal proceedings; in particular even in the absence of a prosecuting party, a trial would not be fair if it took place in such conditions as to put the accused unfairly at a disadvantage.

63 In this connection, it is to be noted that, pursuant to the legal aid scheme, Mr Monnell and Mr Morris had the benefit of free legal advice on appeal. Counsel who had represented them at the trial advised that there were no reasonable prospects of successfully appealing, but both men chose to ignore this advice and pressed ahead with applications for leave to appeal.

64 They were both also aware that, in the absence of arguable grounds of appeal, to lodge and then to renew their applications for leave to appeal might well result in loss-of-time orders. Warnings to this effect were given in the Forms AA and SJ. Nevertheless and despite the fact that the single judge had refused leave, they renewed their applications to the full court of Appeal on the same grounds as in their original applications.

65 As to the possible manner of presenting their case, the system whereby applications for leave to appeal are lodged and then renewed on official forms meant that Mr Monnell and Mr Morris, like all applicants for leave to appeal, were afforded the opportunity to submit written grounds of appeal.

Admittedly, their ancillary applications to be present before the Court of Appeal were unsuccessful, this being a matter within the discretion of the court. Consequently, neither man was able to formulate oral arguments in person before being penalised by an additional loss of liberty.

However, there is no reason why their written submissions should not have included considerations relevant to exercise of the power to direct loss of time, especially in view of the warnings given to them in Forms AA and SJ as to the importance of legal advice and the consequences of pursuing an application without arguable grounds. Indeed, arguments going to the issue of the unmeritorious character of the application will necessarily have been incorporated in their submissions in support of the grounds of appeal.

In accordance with the usual procedure, when considering Mr Monnell's and Mr Morris's applications, both the single judge and the full Court of Appeal had before them all the relevant papers, including the grounds of appeal, a transcript of the trial and, for Mr Monnell, the social inquiry and psychiatric reports prepared on him.

66 Mr Monnell and Mr Morris, like any applicant for leave to appeal, had the right to instruct counsel to appeal on their behalf and present oral argument at a hearing both before the single judge and the full Court of Appeal.

67 It can be presumed that neither Mr Monnell nor Mr Morris could afford to pay counsel out of his own pocket, and under English law they were not automatically entitled to legal aid for the preparation of the written grounds of appeal or for representation through counsel at an oral hearing. Under paragraph 3(c) of Article 6, they were guaranteed the right to be given legal assistance free only so far as the interests of justice so required. The interests of justice cannot, however, be taken to require an automatic grant of legal aid whenever a convicted person, with no objective likelihood of success, wishes to appeal after having received a fair trial in the first instance in accordance with Article 6. Each applicant, it is to be noted, benefited from free legal assistance both at his trial and in being advised as to whether he had any arguable grounds of appeal. In the court's view, the issue to be decided in relation to section 29(1) of the Criminal Appeal Act 1968 did not call, as a matter of fairness, for oral submissions on behalf of the applicants in addition to the written submissions and material already before the Court of Appeal.

68 In short, the interests of justice and fairness could, in the circumstances, be met by the applicants being able to present relevant considerations through making written submissions.

In coming to this conclusion, the court has also borne in mind that, as the power under section 29(1) is exercised in practice, the maximum loss of time risked is in the order of two months and not the whole of the period spent in custody between conviction and determination by the Court of Appeal. It is true, as the applicants' lawyers stressed before the court, that this practical restraint is not brought to the attention of prospective applicants for leave to appeal. However, in view of all the other considerations prevailing, this shortcoming cannot be decisive for present purposes.

69 Finally, the court has no cause to doubt that the Court of Appeal's decision to refuse the applicants leave to appeal and, further, to impose loss of time was based on a full and thorough evaluation of the relevant factors.

70 Having regard to the special features of the context in which the power to order loss of time was exercised and to the circumstances of the case, the court finds that neither Mr Monnell nor Mr Morris was denied a fair procedure as guaranteed by paragraphs 1 and 3(c) of Article 6. There has accordingly been no breach of either of these provisions of the Convention.

The following extract is taken from the dissenting opinion (of judges Pettit and Spielmann):

I Article 5(1) of the Convention

As opposed to the majority, we voted for the violation of Article 5(1) of the Convention.

Quite correctly the court considered that formal differences in the judicial process for ordering detention after conviction cannot render Article 5(1) inapplicable.

In our opinion, however, the majority of the court was wrong in concluding that the aforementioned provision was not violated in the present case.

Generally speaking, it should be observed that, quite significantly, the vast majority of the member States of the Council of Europe do not possess a system of loss of time similar to the one submitted to the examination of the court.

As a matter of fact, the aforementioned system as regulated by an Act of 1968 provides that when an application for leave to appeal is rejected the single judge may order part or all of the time spent in custody awaiting the determination of the application not to count towards the prospective appellants' sentence. The same applies when the application is renewed before the full court which, moreover, may order a longer loss of time.

This entails a later date of release.

On a purely humanitarian level one may wonder about the validity of an institution which requires authorisation for the lodging of an appeal providing for sanctions in the case of refusal.

More particularly, this being the system of the respondent State, the court had to inquire whether, in the circumstances of the case, such as institution was compatible with the provisions of the Convention.

The Government submitted that the Court of Appeal merely gives directions as to the manner of execution of the sentences of those who persist in lodging an appeal, which the court itself considers as futile.

We cannot share this reasoning.

Even if we were to accept in principle the system of loss of time, it should have been hedged about with a number of elementary guarantees.

We believe that the impugned legislation is in breach of Article 5.

The time lost may comprise the entire period spent in custody between conviction and rejection of the application for leave to appeal.

Within these limits the competent authority decides according to no fixed criteria and no objective reasons.

In the two cases submitted to the court the loss of time at risk was in the range of 8 and 14 months.

The loss of time ordered was 28 and 46 days.

In practice apparently the average time lost would be 64 days.

What is more serious, however, is that the risk run in theory is of a nature to deter even an innocent person, or someone who considers himself to be innocent, from lodging an appeal.

In fact, as the Government itself recognises, the impugned system is used to dissuade convicted persons in custody from lodging appeals in order not unnecessarily to increase the workload of the court.

In our opinion it is inconceivable that the demands of the administration of the courts (shortage of judges, personnel, etc) should be given pre-eminence in a system of penalties involving deprivation of liberty.

Such a deviation, in the short or medium term, runs the risk of exposing the detained person, or anyone amenable to justice, to an instrument of a criminal policy, which is subject to political variations as to what should be, or should have been, the administration of justice.

In these conditions we concur with the opinion of the overwhelming majority of the Commission that there was a violation of Article 5(1) of the Convention.

In fact, as observed by the Commission, we consider that the period of time ordered not to count towards the applicants' sentences imposed by the trial judge cannot be regarded as forming part of their detention after conviction at first instance. The express terms of the loss of time orders exclude this hypothesis.

Quite correctly the majority of the Commission so concluded (...) bearing in mind the purpose for which the loss of time orders were made, which was unconnected with the original sentences imposed on the applicants or with the offences for which they were convicted.

In our opinion, the periods of detention which have been ordered not to count towards the service of the applicants' sentence cannot be considered as detention coming within the terms of Article 5 of the Convention.

II Article 6 of the Convention

The court considered, quite wrongly in our opinion, that there was no violation of Article 6 of the Convention.

In fact, even if we were to admit that the impugned system was compatible with Article 5 of the Convention, the additional prison sentence imposed on the two applicants remained the consequence of the refusal of leave to appeal.

In these conditions, we consider that the principle of fair trial would require the applicants to be heard by the competent authorities to enable them to present their arguments in person.

Could one seriously support that a written submission by the applicant—composed in the isolation of a prison—could satisfy the requirements of Article 6?

The importance of an additional prison sentence at stake raises objections to such an argument.

Is it not true that on that score the requirements of Article 6, which were applied in the case of Öztürk—where only a fine was at stake—should also be afforded when several months in prison were in issue?

In accordance with the opinion of the Commission, we consider that the applicants' absence from the determination of their applications for leave to appeal, which resulted in the making of the orders that they lost time in the calculation of their service of sentence, deprived them of a fair hearing in the determination of the criminal charges against them as guaranteed by Article 6(1) and of the right to defend themselves in person as guaranteed by Article 6(3)(c) of the Convention.

We believe that where the liberty of the individual is at stake it is necessary that all decisions are taken in the presence of the person affected in the course of a fully adversarial hearing.

[9:12] Criminal Justice Act 1972 (as amended)

Section 36

36 Reference to Court of Appeal of point of law following acquittal on indictment

(1) Where a person tried on indictment has been acquitted (whether in respect of the whole or part of the indictment) the Attorney General may, if he desires the opinion of the Court of Appeal on a point of law which has arisen in the case, refer that point to the court, and the court shall, in accordance with this section, consider the point and give their opinion on it.

(2) For the purpose of their consideration of a point referred to them under this section the Court of Appeal shall hear argument—

(a) by, or by counsel on behalf of, the Attorney General; and

(b) if the acquitted person desires to present any argument to the court, by counsel on his behalf or, with the leave of the court, by the acquitted person himself.

(3) Where the Court of Appeal have given their opinion on a point referred to them under this section, the court may, of their own motion or in pursuance of an application in that behalf, refer the point to the House of Lords if it appears to the court that the point ought to be considered by that House.

(4) If a point is referred to the House of Lords under subsection (3) of this section, the House shall consider the point and give their opinion on it accordingly; and section 35(1) of the Criminal Appeal Act 1968 (composition of House for appeals) shall apply also in relation to any proceedings of the House under this section.

(5) Where, on a point being referred to the Court of Appeal under this section or further referred to the House of Lords, the acquitted person appears by counsel for the purpose of presenting any argument to the court or the House, he shall be entitled to his costs, that is to say to the payment out of central funds of such sums as are reasonably sufficient to compensate him for expenses properly incurred by him for the purpose of being represented on the reference or further reference; and any amount recoverable under this subsection shall be ascertained, as soon as practicable, by the registrar of criminal appeals or, as the case may be, such officer as may be prescribed by order of the House of Lords.

(5A) Section 20(1) of the Prosecution of Offences Act 1985 (regulations as to scales and rates of payment of costs payable out of central funds) shall apply in relation to this section as it applies in relation to Part II of that Act.

(6) Subject to rules of court made under section 1(5) of the Criminal Appeal Act 1966 (power by rules to distribute business of Court of Appeal between its civil and criminal divisions), the jurisdiction

of the Court of Appeal under this section shall be exercised by the criminal division of the court; and references in this section to the Court of Appeal shall be construed accordingly as references to that division of the court.

(7) A reference under this section shall not affect the trial in relation to which the reference is made or any acquittal in that trial.

[9:13]   *Attorney-General's Reference (No 3 of 1994)*
[1997] 3 All ER 936

The defendant stabbed a young woman, who was to his knowledge pregnant with his child. No injury to the foetus was detected and the defendant pleaded guilty to a charge of wounding the woman with intent to cause her grievous bodily harm. A few weeks after the stabbing, and as a result of it, the woman went into labour and gave birth to a grossly premature child who was considered to have only a 50% chance of survival. At the time of the birth it was clear that, contrary to earlier belief, the knife had penetrated the foetus. The child died 121 days later from a lung condition which was due to her premature birth but unconnected with the knife wound and the defendant was thereafter charged with her murder. At the trial, the judge directed an acquittal on the ground that no conviction for either murder or manslaughter was possible in law. The Attorney General subsequently referred to the Court of Appeal under s 36(1) of the Criminal Justice Act 1972 the questions, inter alia, (i) whether, subject to proof of the requisite intent, the crimes of murder and manslaughter could be committed where unlawful injury was deliberately inflicted to a mother carrying a child in utero where the child was subsequently born alive, existed independently of the mother, and then died, the injuries while in utero either having caused or made a substantial contribution to the death, and (ii) whether the fact that the child's death resulted from injury to the mother rather than as a consequence of direct injury to the foetus could remove any liability for murder or manslaughter in those circumstances. The Court of Appeal answered the first question in the affirmative, on the ground that the foetus was to be treated as part of the mother until it had a separate existence of its own, but answered the second question in the negative. On the defendant's application the Court of Appeal referred the points to the House of Lords.

Held—(1) Murder could not be committed where unlawful injury was deliberately inflicted to a mother carrying a child in utero in circumstances where the child was subsequently born alive, enjoyed an existence independent of its mother and thereafter died, and where the injuries inflicted while in utero caused or contributed substantially to the death. Notwithstanding the dependence of the foetus on the mother for its survival until birth and the bond between them, the foetus could not be treated as part of the mother but was a unique organism. Accordingly, although there was no requirement that the person who died should be a person in being at the time the act causing the death was perpetrated, in the absence of an intention on the part of the defendant to injure either the foetus or the child which it would become, the required mens rea for murder was not present; it would be straining the concept of transferred malice too far to apply it in the circumstances since it would require the malice to be transferred not once but twice, namely from the mother to the foetus and from the foetus to the child.

(2) In those circumstances, however, manslaughter could be committed since the requisite mens rea to be proved in a case of manslaughter was an intention to do an act which was unlawful and which all sober and reasonable people would recognise as dangerous, ie likely to harm another person. Provided the defendant intended to do what he did, it was not necessary for him to know that his act was likely to injure the person who died as a result of it or to intend to injure that person. Since, in the instant case, the defendant intended to stab the child's mother and that was an unlawful and dangerous act, it followed that the requisite mens rea was established and although the child was a foetus at that time, on public policy grounds she was to be regarded as coming within that mens rea when she became a

living person. Accordingly, the fact that the child's death was caused solely as a consequence of injury to the mother, rather than injury to the foetus, did not negative any liability for manslaughter, provided the jury were satisfied as to causation.

Decision of the Court of Appeal, Criminal Division [1996] 2 All ER 10 affirmed in part.

Lord Mustill (at page 949):

My Lords, the purpose of this inquiry has been to see whether the existing rules are based on principles sound enough to justify their extension to a case where the defendant acts without an intent to injure either the foetus or the child which it will become. In my opinion they are not. To give an affirmative answer requires a double 'transfer' of intent: first from the mother to the foetus and then from the foetus to the child as yet unborn. Then one would have to deploy the fiction (or at least the doctrine) which converts an intention to commit serious harm into the mens rea of murder. For me, this is too much. If one could find any logic in the rules I would follow it from one fiction to another, but whatever grounds there may once have been have long since disappeared. I am willing to follow old laws until they are overturned, but not to make a new law on a basis for which there is no principle.

Moreover, even on a narrower approach the argument breaks down. The effect of transferred malice, as I understand it, is that the intended victim and the actual victim are treated as if they were one, so that what was intended to happen to the first person (but did not happen) is added to what actually did happen to the second person (but was not intended to happen), with the result that what was intended and what happened are married to make a notionally intended and actually consummated crime. The cases are treated as if the actual victim had been the intended victim from the start. To make any sense of this process there must, as it seems to me, be some compatibility between the original intention and the actual occurrence, and this is, indeed, what one finds in the cases. There is no such compatibility here. The defendant intended to commit and did commit an immediate crime of violence to the mother. He committed no relevant violence to the foetus, which was not a person, either at the time or in the future, and intended no harm to the foetus or to the human person which it would become. If fictions are useful, as they can be, they are only damaged by straining them beyond their limits. I would not overstrain the idea of transferred malice by trying to make it fit the present case.

[9:14] *R v Secretary of State for the Home Department, ex p Bentley*
[1993] 4 All ER 442

Bentley was hanged in 1952 for murder. The Divisional Court held that the Secretary of State's refusal to recommend a posthumous pardon was unlawful.

Watkins LJ (at page 452):

The CCSU case made it clear that the powers of the court cannot be ousted merely by invoking the word 'prerogative'. The question is simply whether the nature and subject matter of the decision is amenable to the judicial process. Are the courts qualified to deal with the matter or does the decision involve such questions of policy that they should not intrude because they are ill-equipped to do so? Looked at in this way there must be cases in which the exercise of the royal prerogative is reviewable, in our judgment. If, for example, it was clear that the Home Secretary had refused to pardon someone solely on the grounds of their sex, race or religion, the courts would be expected to interfere and, in our judgment, would be entitled to do so.

We conclude therefore that some aspects of the exercise of the royal prerogative are amenable to the judicial process. We do not think that it is necessary for us to say more than this in the instant case. It will be for other courts to decide on a case by case basis whether the matter in question is reviewable or not.

(At page 454:)

In an earlier part of the announcement of the decision, the Home Secretary, it will be recalled, stated that while he personally agreed that Derek Bentley should not have been hanged, he could not simply substitute his judgment for that of the then Home Secretary, Sir David Maxell Fyfe.

We understand the strength of the argument that, despite the fact that a free pardon does not eliminate the conviction, the grant of a free pardon should be reserved for cases where it can be established that the convicted person was morally and technically innocent. Furthermore, the policy of confining the grant of a free pardon to such cases has been followed by successive Secretaries of State for over a century. We therefore propose to set aside any question of a free (or full) pardon and look at the matter afresh.

The facts as disclosed by the contemporary papers are very striking. (1) Christopher Craig who fired the fatal shot, was not executed. (2) The jury recommended mercy in the case of Derek Bentley. (3) Both Mr Philip Allen, who wrote the memorandum dated 16 January 1953, and Sir Frank Newsam, the Permanent Under-Secretary, advised that effect should be given to the jury's recommendation for mercy. (4) The precedents established by the previous cases to which Mr Allen drew attention supported the argument for a reprieve. (5) Tests which had been carried out indicated that Bentley's mental state was 'just above the level of a feebleminded person'. He was aged 19. (6) It seems clear from the memorandum initialled by the Secretary of State dated 22 January 1953 that he consulted Lord Goddard CJ, the trial judge, before making his final decision. It will be remembered that in his letter to the Secretary of State dated 12 December 1952 Lord Goddard CJ had said that he could find 'no mitigating circumstances in Bentley's case'.

It is clear from the affidavit of Mr Wilson that one of the ways in which the prerogative of mercy can be exercised is by the grant of a conditional pardon, whereby the penalty is removed on condition that a lesser sentence is served. Had Bentley been reprieved in 1953, the substitution of a sentence of life imprisonment would have constituted a conditional pardon.

These questions, therefore, arise. (a) Is there any objection in principle to the grant of a posthumous conditional pardon? (b) Was the Home Secretary in error in failing to consider the grant of a conditional pardon in this case?

On the first question it may be objected that a conditional pardon is inappropriate where the full penalty has already been paid. The answer to this objection, however, is that it is an error to regard the prerogative of mercy as a prerogative right which is only exercisable in cases which fall into specific categories. The prerogative is a flexible power and its exercise can and should be adapted to meet the circumstances of the particular case. We would adopt the language used by the Court of Appeal in New Zealand in *Burt v Governor General* [1992] 3 NZLR 672 at 681:

> '... the prerogative of mercy [can no longer be regarded as] no more than an arbitrary monarchical right of grace and favour.'

It is now a constitutional safeguard against mistakes. It follows, therefore, that, in our view, there is no objection in principle to the grant of a posthumous conditional pardon when a death sentence has already been carried out. The grant of such a pardon is a recognition by the state that a mistake was made and that a reprieve should have been granted.

We return to the facts of the present case. We can well understand the decision of the Home Secretary in so far as it constituted a response to a free (or full) pardon. But we are far from satisfied that he gave sufficient consideration to his power to grant some other form of pardon which would be suitable to the circumstances of the particular case. It is true, as the Home Secretary pointed out in the announcement of his decision, that in 1953 the then Home Secretary was working in a different climate of opinion. But, as we have already underlined the facts of this case are very striking. There is a compelling argument that even by the standards of 1953 the then Home Secretary's decision was clearly wrong.

In these circumstances the court, though it has no power to direct the way in which the prerogative of mercy should be exercised, has some role to play. The Home Secretary's decision was directed to the grant of a free pardon. In these circumstances we do not think it would be right to make any formal order nor is this an appropriate case for the grant of a declaration. Nevertheless, we would invite the Home Secretary to look at the matter again and to examine whether it would be just to exercise the prerogative of mercy in such a way as to give full recognition to the now generally accepted view that this young man should have been reprieved.

It was submitted to the court that even a limited form of pardon might lead to a flood of other applications seeking to reopen past convictions. No doubt account has to be taken of such a risk. From our examination of the papers in this case, however, and in the light of our understanding of the broad scope of the prerogative of mercy, we are satisfied that the matter is exceptional and requires further consideration. The decision is, of course, one for the Home Secretary and not for the court, but it seems to us that it should be possible to devise some formula which would amount to a clear acknowledgement that an injustice was done.

[9:15] *Royal Commission on Criminal Justice*
(1993) Cmnd 2263, HMSO (at page 183)

Case for new body

2 In *R v Pinfold* the Court of Appeal held that it had no jurisdiction to entertain a second application for leave to appeal in the same case even where fresh evidence had emerged since the dismissal of the earlier appeal. The Court of Appeal can only consider such a case again if the Home Secretary uses his power under section 17 of the Criminal Appeal Act 1968 to refer it to the Court of Appeal, when the case is treated for all purposes as an appeal to the court by the convicted person. The power to refer cases in this way is limited to those tried on indictment; it does not include summary convictions by magistrates' courts.

3 If, therefore, an unsuccessful appellant wishes to reopen his or her case in the courts, the Home Secretary must be persuaded to refer it to the Court of Appeal. The only alternative course is to persuade the Home Secretary to recommend to the sovereign that the Royal Prerogative of Mercy be exercised. This alternative, which is described more fully in the next paragraph, is most often used when the case involves a summary conviction in the magistrates' courts. It is very seldom exercised when the option of a reference under section 17 is available, because successive Home Secretaries have been understandably reluctant to reverse a decision of the courts, preferring instead to ask the courts to reconsider the case as the statute envisages. The use of the Royal Prerogative to override convictions on indictment is limited to cases where there are convincing reasons for believing that a person is innocent but a reference to the Court of Appeal is not practicable, for example because relevant material would not be admissible in evidence. The Home Office told us in written evidence that such cases are extremely rare.

4 If the Royal Prerogative of Mercy is exercised by the grant of a free pardon, the effect is that so far as possible the person is relieved of all penalties and other consequences of the conviction. Alternatively, a sentence can be varied so as to give special remission of all or part of the penalty imposed by the court. This may be done for compassionate purposes, for example to give early release to prisoners with terminal illnesses, or in order to reward prisoners who have given exceptional assistance to prison staff, the police, or the prosecuting authorities. The exercise of the Royal Prerogative in this way is not the same as the grant of a free pardon. Nor does the exercise of the Royal Prerogative amount to the quashing of the conviction, even if a free pardon is granted. The conviction stands and can only be quashed by a separate application to the Court of Appeal.

5 The available figures for the number of cases referred by the Home Secretary to the Court of Appeal under section 17 of the Criminal Appeal Act 1968 show that the power is not often exercised.

From 1981 to the end of 1988, 36 cases involving 48 appellants were referred to the Court of Appeal as a result of the doubts raised about the safety of the convictions concerned. This represents an average of between 4 and 5 cases a year. In the years 1989–1992, 28 cases involving 49 appellants have been referred, including a number of cases stemming from the terrorist incidents of the early 1970s and inquiries into the activities of the West Midlands serious crimes squad. We were told by the Home Office that it receives between 700 and 800 cases a year which are no longer before the courts and where it is claimed that there has been a wrongful conviction. (The figure for 1992 was 790 of which 634 involved a custodial sentence). Plainly, therefore, a rigorous sifting process is applied, and only a small percentage of cases end in a reference to the Court of Appeal under section 17.

6 There is in theory no restriction on the numbers or categories of cases which the Home Secretary may refer to the Court of Appeal under section 17 since the section gives him discretion to refer cases 'if he thinks fit'. In practice, however, as Sir John May observed in his second report on the Maguire case, the Home Secretary and the civil servants advising him operate within strict self-imposed limits. These rest both upon constitutional considerations and upon the approach of the Court of Appeal itself to its own powers. The Home Secretary does not refer cases to the Court of Appeal merely to enable that court to reconsider matters that it has already considered. He will normally only refer a conviction if there is new evidence or some other consideration of substance which was not before the trial court. Successive Home Secretaries have adopted this approach, and not only because they have thought that it would be wrong for Ministers to suggest to the Court of Appeal that a different decision should have been reached by the courts on the same facts. They have also taken the view that there is no purpose in their referring a case where there is no real possibility of the Court of Appeal taking a different view than it did on the original appeal because of the lack of fresh evidence of some other new consideration of substance.

7 The effect of this second criterion was examined in depth by Sir John May as part of his inquiry into the case of the Maguires. We cannot do better than quote his conclusion:

> '...there is no doubt that the criterion so defined was and is a limiting one and has resulted in the responsible officials within the Home Office taking a substantially restricted view of cases to which their attention has been drawn...The very nature and terms of the self-imposed limits on the Home Secretary's power to refer cases have led the Home Office only to respond to the representations which have been made to it in relation to particular convictions rather than to carry out its own investigations into the circumstances of a particular case or the evidence given at trial...the approach of the Home Office was throughout reactive, it was never thought proper for the Department to become proactive.'

8 Sir John May refers later in his second report on the Maguires to the evidence that he heard from Home Office officials and from a former Home Secretary, Mr Hurd, expressing views on alternative machinery for considering alleged miscarriages of justice. This evidence led him to the conclusion that some alternative machinery was indeed required in place of the existing power of the Home Secretary to refer such cases to the Court of Appeal under section 17 of the Criminal Appeal Act 1968. We set out below our view of what the alternative machinery should be. First, however, we give our reasons for recommending (as we do in paragraph 11 below) the creation of a new body independent of both the Government and the courts to be responsible for dealing with allegations that a miscarriage of justice has occurred.

9 Our recommendation is based on the proposition, adequately established in our view by Sir John May's Inquiry; that the role assigned to the Home Secretary and his Department under the existing legislation is incompatible with the constitutional separation of powers as between the courts and the executive. The scrupulous observance of constitutional principles has meant a reluctance on the part of the Home Office to enquire deeply enough into the cases put to it and, given the constitutional background, we do not think that this is likely to change significantly in the future.

10 We have concluded that it is neither necessary nor desirable that the Home Secretary should be directly responsible for the consideration and investigation of alleged miscarriages of justice as well as

being responsible for law and order and for the police. The view that these two heavy responsibilities should be divided was expressed to Sir John May's Inquiry by a former Home Secretary and confirmed in oral evidence to us by the then Home Secretary and two of his predecessors.

11 We recommend therefore that the Home Secretary's power to refer cases to the Court of Appeal under section 17 of the Criminal Appeal Act 1968 should be removed and that a new body should be set up to consider alleged miscarriages of justice, to supervise their investigation if further inquiries are needed, and to refer appropriate cases to the Court of Appeal. We suggest that this body might be known as the Criminal Cases Review Authority. We refer to it in what follows as 'the Authority'.

Role of the authority

12 We recommend that the role of the Authority should be to consider allegations put to it that a miscarriage of justice may have occurred. The applicant's approach to the Authority would normally be made either after his or her conviction had been upheld by the Court of Appeal or after he or she had failed to obtain leave to appeal. In cases which seemed to the Authority to call for further investigation, it would ensure that that investigation was launched. Where the Authority instructed the police to conduct investigations, it would be responsible for supervising the investigation and would have the power to require the police to follow up those lines of inquiry that seemed to it necessary for the thorough re-examination of the case. Where the result of the investigation indicated that there were reasons for supposing that a miscarriage of justice might have occurred, the Authority would refer the case to the Court of Appeal, which would consider it as though it were an appeal referred to it by the Home Secretary under section 17 now. Where, in the Authority's view, the investigation revealed no grounds for such a reference, for example, because it revealed fresh material confirming the correctness of the conviction, an explanation with reasons would be given to the applicant.

Relationships of the authority with government and with Court of Appeal

13 We have already explained why we believe that the Authority should be independent of the Government. It will, however, be necessary for the Government to provide the resources to enable it to operate and a Government Minister will have to be responsible for appointing its members and accounting to Parliament for its activities. We recommend that the legislation which established it gives it operational independence but requires it to submit an annual report to the Minister concerned, who would in turn be required to lay the report before Parliament. The Minister would also be required to answer to Parliament for any suggestion that the Authority was inadequately resourced or not properly constituted for the task it was required to perform. We see these arrangements as necessary in order to ensure that the new system for correcting miscarriages of justice is working properly. We do not see them as compromising its independence.

14 We recommend that the Chairman of the Authority be appointed by the Queen on the advice of the Prime Minister as is done in the cases of Lords Justice of Appeal. Other members might be appointed by the Lord Chancellor. The Home Secretary, as the Minister responsible for criminal justice policy and for law and order, should be responsible for reporting to Parliament for the way in which the new arrangements are implemented.

15 We believe that there are cogent arguments for the Authority to be independent of the Court of Appeal. Their roles are different and, as we have said in the last chapter, we do not think that the Court of Appeal is either the most suitable or the best qualified body to supervise investigations of this kind. We have recommended in chapter ten that the Court of Appeal should be empowered if it thinks fit to refer cases to the Authority for investigation, and that the Authority should be required to report the outcome of any such investigation to the Court of Appeal. But we do not see the Authority as coming within the court structure. Nor, equally importantly, would it be empowered to take judicial decisions that are properly matters for the Court of Appeal.

16 When, therefore, an investigation is completed whose results the Authority believes should be considered by the Court of Appeal, we recommend that it should refer the case to that court, together with a statement of its reasons for so referring it. It should at the same time provide the court with such supporting material as it believes to be appropriate and desirable in the light of its investigations, and which in its view may be admissible, though without any recommendation or conclusion as to whether or not a miscarriage of justice has occurred. It would be for the Court of Appeal, on receiving a case referred in this way, to treat it as an appeal from the Crown Court. That is to say, it would ensure that the defence and the prosecution received a copy of the statement of reasons and supporting material sent to it, together with any additional material (see paragraph 31) that the Authority thought fit. It would then be for the appellant to present his or her case in whatever manner seemed best. As happens with references by the Home Secretary under section 17 now, it should continue to be open to the appellant to raise before the Court of Appeal any matter of law or fact, or mixed law and fact, as he or she wishes, regardless of whether or not it was included in the papers sent to the court by the Authority. The appellant should also be free to appear before the court if he or she so wishes.

17 As we have explained, we do not see the Home Secretary as continuing to have in general any function in relation to individual cases of miscarriage of justice. We do, however, assume that he or she will retain ministerial responsibility for the exercise of the Royal Prerogative of Mercy. For the reasons that the Home Office gave in oral evidence, and to which we refer above (paragraph 6), it will seldom if ever be necessary or desirable to exercise the Royal Prerogative in cases where it is concluded that a miscarriage of justice may have taken place To do so would be to override the decisions of the courts, whose function it properly is to determine such cases. Nevertheless, we do not entirely rule out the need in the very exceptional case for the Authority to refer the results of its consideration and investigation to the Home Secretary to consider the exercise of the Royal Prerogative. This should only be where the Court of Appeal is unlikely to be able to consider the case under the existing rules.

18 The one category of case that has been drawn to our attention where this might happen is if the Court of Appeal were to regard as inadmissible evidence which seemed to the Authority to show that a miscarriage of justice might have occurred. We have been told by the Home Office in written evidence that these cases are rare and we hope that, following the outcome of the review of the rules of evidence that we have recommended in Chapter Eight, they will become rarer still in the future. We cannot envisage any other circumstances in which the courts would be so far unable to provide a remedy that it ought to be suggested to the Home Secretary that he should recommend the exercise of the Royal Prerogative. There may, however, be unforeseeable circumstances where the need might arise. We therefore recommend that the possible use of the Royal Prerogative be kept open for the exceptional case. We emphasise, however, that it is undesirable for the courts to be deprived of powers to quash a conviction where the evidence, whatever its status, seems clearly to show that the appellant is innocent. We therefore, as we have already said, attach great importance to the Law Commission's review of the rules of evidence which we have recommended.

19 The primary function of the Authority will be to consider and if necessary investigate cases which have already passed through the criminal justice system and in which the right of appeal has been exercised. An applicant who is told by the Authority that it will not intervene in his or her case should always be free to try again, although he or she is likely to need to present flesh evidence or argument to stand any better chance of success. We therefore do not believe that there should be any right of appeal from the Authority's decisions to investigate or not to investigate the cases put to it and to refer or not to refer them to the Court of Appeal. In our view, the Authority's decisions should also not be subject to judicial review. We therefore recommend that there should be neither a right of appeal nor a right to judicial review in relation to decisions by the Authority, but that it should be free to consider a case more than once if that seems in the circumstances to be an appropriate course.

Composition and accountability of the authority

20 The Authority should consist of several members, the precise numbers depending on its workload at any particular time. Not all need be full-time. We do not favour a single person, however well qualified and eminent, filling the role on the model of the ombudsman, since we believe that the consideration of possible miscarriages of justice will benefit from bringing to bear several different points of view. Both lawyers and lay persons should be represented. We recommend that the Chairman should be chosen for his or her personal qualities rather than for any particular qualifications or background that he or she may have. We recommend, however, given the importance of the Authority being seen to be independent of the courts in the performance of its functions, that the Chairman should not be a serving member of the judiciary.

[9:16] Criminal Appeal Act 1995

Sections 8; 13

8 The Commission

(1) There shall be a body corporate to be known as the Criminal Cases Review Commission.

(2) The Commission shall not be regarded as the servant or agent of the Crown or as enjoying any status, immunity or privilege of the Crown; and the Commission's property shall not be regarded as property of, or held on behalf of, the Crown.

(3) The Commission shall consist of not fewer than eleven members.

(4) The members of the Commission shall be appointed by Her Majesty on the recommendation of the Prime Minister.

(5) At least one third of the members of the Commission shall be persons who are legally qualified; and for this purpose a person is legally qualified if—

(a) he has a ten year general qualification, within the meaning of section 71 of the Courts and Legal Services Act 1990, or

(b) he is a member of the Bar of Northern Ireland, or solicitor of the Supreme Court of Northern Ireland, of at least ten years' standing.

(6) At least two thirds of the members of the Commission shall be persons who appear to the Prime Minister to have knowledge or experience of any aspect of the criminal justice system and of them at least one shall be a person who appears to him to have knowledge or experience of any aspect of the criminal justice system in Northern Ireland; and for the purposes of this subsection the criminal justice system includes, in particular, the investigation of offences and the treatment of offenders.

(7) Schedule 1 (further provisions with respect to the Commission) shall have effect.

13 Conditions for making of references

(1) A reference of a conviction, verdict, finding or sentence shall not be made under any of sections 9 to 12 unless—

(a) the Commission consider that there is a real possibility that the conviction, verdict, finding or sentence would not be upheld were the reference to be made,

(b) the Commission so consider—

(i) in the case of a conviction, verdict or finding, because of an argument, or evidence, not raised in the proceedings which led to it or on any appeal or application for leave to appeal against it, or

(ii) in the case of a sentence, because of an argument on a point of law, or information, not so raised, and

(c) an appeal against the conviction, verdict, finding or sentence has been determined or leave to appeal against it has been refused.

(2) Nothing in subsection (1)(b)(i) or (c) shall prevent the making of a reference if it appears to the Commission that there are exceptional circumstances which justify making it.

CHAPTER TEN

SENTENCE MANAGEMENT

The sentenced offender is more vulnerable to the abuse of power than are most people, particularly if he or she is in custody. A variety of agencies, with different powers, may well be involved in the supervision and management of a sentenced prisoner, usually out of the view of the public, and in this chapter we will look at the role of these various different organizations. In our case study, Gerry Good has been sentenced to two years in prison. The National Offender Management Service, heralded with fanfares by the Government in January 2004, has limped slowly towards a constitutionally acceptable position (as we go to press most of the provisions of the Offender Management Act 2007 have still not been brought into force). In reality, the probation and prison systems are in a state of flux which has been going for some years. Several private prisons exist outside HM Prison Service. The probation service, which became a national service only in 2001, is being broken into new component parts, which work alongside an increasing number of private companies and charities. The purpose of this chapter is to raise questions about the powers and accountability of those who have such control over the lives of sentenced offenders. It provides only examples, not a definitive account, of the powers exercised by different bodies within the penal system. Thus, whilst most offenders are fined, fine enforcement—which can result in a fine defaulter serving a sentence of imprisonment—is not dealt with here in any detail. Two developments in recent years should perhaps be noted at the outset.

Procedural openness

The first is an increase in procedural openness. We will see in this chapter that sentence plans are often discussed with offenders and that procedures governing release from prisons or hospital are much more open than they were a decade or so ago. A fundamental question is whether this increased openness has led to increased substantive justice, or whether it sometimes disguises potential and real injustices. Procedural fairness does not necessarily lead to fairer outcomes. And fair hearings can mean very expensive hearings: we will take as an example the work of the Parole Board. The Board can get through a pile of paper hearings in a morning, but rarely more than three oral hearings in a day. Those who do not have the right to an oral hearing often suspect that the process applied to them is less fair, but this is of course not necessarily so. And at the moment, procedural concerns are leading to increased delays, which are certainly not fair. As we have seen elsewhere in this book (Chapter 5, for example), adequate funding is a prerequisite of fair processes. The Parole Board makes a fascinating case study.

Joined up services, or privatization and fragmentation?

The second development is more difficult to describe. Putting it positively, there has been a huge increase over the last 20 years in cooperation between different agencies, and a commitment by Government to 'joined up' thinking in criminal justice. The main example of this must be the creation of the National Offender Management Service. Originally proposed by Lord Carter, who reported in 2003 at the request of the Government (more precisely, at the request of the Prime Minister's Strategy Unit) on more 'effective' ways of managing offenders. In his Report *Managing Offenders Reducing Crime: a new approach* **[10:1]** he sought to focus all those involved on the key aim of crime reduction. He made interesting recommendations on sentencing law (which have not been adopted), and put great faith in the 'what works' agenda. But it was his recommendation that, in order to break down the 'silos of prison and probation' it was necessary to create a new National Offender Management Service (NOMS) responsible for reducing re-offending which caught the Government's imagination. Immediately, in a paper called *Reducing Crime—Changing Lives*, the Government accepted that they would separate the case management of offenders from the provision of prison places, treatment services, or community programmes (whether they are in the public, private, or voluntary sectors). NOMS started work in the summer of 2004, but, extraordinarily, the Government failed to enact any laws to create the legal basis for these changes. There was a Management of Offenders and Sentencing Bill in 2005, but it failed to get through the Parliamentary processes before the Government called the General Election that year: deeply controversial, the Conservative Opposition did not agree that it should rush through the Parliamentary process without significant debate (which is what happened to the Serious and Organised Crime and Police Act 2005). There were a few abortive attempts to legislate before the Offender Management Act 2007 finally reached the statute book in July 2007. The aim of the Act is to improve the 'delivery of probation services' by creating probation trusts (instead of probation boards); by encouraging the 'commissioning' of probation services; and enabling greater partnership working with voluntary, charitable, and private providers.

Under the Act, the commissioning of probation services will happen at national, regional, and local levels. The plan is that local 'lead providers' will work under contract to Regional Offender Managers (ROMs) for the delivery of services in a probation area. Provided their performance meets the requirements, the lead provider in a probation area will be the probation trust. The lead provider will concentrate on the delivery of offender management, while commissioning much of their interventions work from other providers based on what is most effective, and who is best placed to deliver, in their local community. Where interventions can be delivered more effectively across a region, ROMs will contract directly with providers, but this will be so as to complement, not replace, the local arrangements. Dates have not yet been set for when the various provisions will be brought into force.

Central to the Government's vision for NOMS are the concepts of 'commissioning' and 'contestability'. 'Providers' from the public, private, and voluntary and community sectors will by means of 'service level agreements' and contracts 'deliver services' to punish, support, and reform offenders. As we saw in Chapter 1, there remains concern about how this will work in practice: there are nine regional offender managers (ROMs) in England and a tenth director of offender management in Wales who are responsible for overseeing the management of services offered by service providers. But will small local initiatives survive in this deeply competitive world? Central Government is keeping close control: there are parallels here with our discussion of policing and how to get the balance right between local, central, and regional control. Note the Management of Offenders etc (Scotland) Act 2005 which established new Criminal Justice Authorities in Scotland to coordinate services for offenders and monitor joint working between local agencies to tackle re-offending: criminal justice agencies in local government have a duty to consult with partners, share information, and draw up plans to reduce re-offending. Is this cooperative structure 'better' than the 'contractual' structure being introduced in England and Wales?

The creation of NOMS came as no surprise: we had already seen two decades of managing criminal justice agencies through performance indicators, audits, framework and strategy documents, and a myriad of other 'performance tools' (see **[1:6]**). But perhaps it was a step too far: the Minister of Justice has suggested (January 2008) that a new structure will be developed. Of course, cooperation is essential at the post-sentence stage, where the different agencies are clearly interdependent. No one should doubt the need for a formal and standardized system of sentence planning, recognized in the Woolf Report **[10:2]** as long ago as 1991. This report examined the causes of riots in several prisons in 1990 and remains a valuable tool for those evaluating 'justice' in prisons. It was the Woolf Report which recommended that a national Criminal Justice Consultative Council, and 24 area committees, be set up to discuss matters affecting more than one agency. The membership of these committees included representatives of the police, the probation service, the Crown Prosecution Service (CPS), the prison service, judges, magistrates, and the legal profession. From 2003 the CJCC became the Criminal Justice Council and the area Committees are now 42 local Criminal Justice Boards (CJBs). It is difficult to assess the impact of these bodies: whilst they must indeed open up channels of communication, they may, for example, lead to a greater blurring of the lines of accountability. Look up your local CJB on the Internet: you will find performance figures, the minutes of its meetings open and so on all available for your study.

Privatization too is nothing new. It was not until the Prisons Act 1878 that prisons were all brought under the control of a national system run by the Prison Commission (later the Prison Department, then the Prison Service). Many of Charles Dickens' novels paint a picture of the early Victorian (nineteenth century) prison. And throughout the twentieth century many prison services, such as laundries, were run under private contract. It was the Conservative Government, in the Criminal Justice Act (CJA) 1991, which moved towards wholesale privatization. The Criminal Justice and Public Order Act 1994 allowed the privatization of prison escort duties (i.e. the delivery of prisoners to and from prison). Under section 94, where a court sentences someone too late in the day for that person to be admitted to prison, he can be held overnight by the escort company instead of by the police. Sections 96 and 99 allowed for the contracting out of part of a prison, or some of the functions within a prison, to the private sector.

The first privately run prison, the Wolds, a purpose-built remand prison, was opened in 1992, managed by Group 4 Remand Services Ltd. There are now 11 private prisons managed by private companies such as GSL, Serco, and G4S Justice Services. While privatization may lead to improved physical standards in prison, it raises questions of principle, discussed in Logan (1990), Padfield (2005), and Genders and Player (2007). Should the State delegate to private companies its right to punish those who break the law? In practice, the accountability of private prisons continues to be unclear. The Government is represented in the prison by a Comptroller, whilst the private company employs the Director (the equivalent of the governor in a State prison). But despite Government commitments in the 1990s that the Directors of private prisons would not be given powers which should 'properly' be in the hands of the State (the CJA 1991 provided specifically that Directors of private prisons were not allowed to conduct adjudications, segregate prisoners, apply restraints, or order confinement in a special cell, except in emergencies), these provisions have been repealed by the Offender Management Act 2007.

(i) PROBATION

Probation services were set up by the Probation of Offenders Act 1907. Before that, volunteer 'police court missionaries' had worked with offenders, using religion and moral education in an attempt to help people turn away from crime. The 1907 Act encouraged courts of summary jurisdiction to appoint probation officers to 'advise, assist and befriend' offenders, a service to be funded by local authorities. The Criminal Justice Act 1925 made it mandatory for every criminal court to appoint a probation officer. The duties of the 54 separate probation services were laid down in various pieces of legislation, consolidated in the Probation Service Act 1993. The Government published a stream of reports in 1998 and 1999 (*Joining Forces to Protect the Public*, the *Prisons Probation Review* and the *Correctional Policy Framework*, for example), which led to the creation of a National Probation Service for the first time. The Criminal Justice and Court Services Act 2000 created a unified system, the National Probation Service, based on 42 local areas, matching police areas. This started work in April 2001.

There was then a very short period when it felt as though the probation service had 'come of age', standing on an equal footing with the prison service (despite a much smaller budget, of course). But any growing confidence within the service has been undermined by the slow and uncomfortable birth of NOMS. The Offender Management Act 2007 has shaken up the organization of the probation service, abolished the existing local probation boards, and replaced them with trusts. The Act gives the Secretary of State responsibility for providing 'probation services' and the power to establish probation trusts. The first trusts are expected to be created from April 2008. Why is all this change necessary? The chief problem facing the probation service has been overload and a lack of resources to match their increasing responsibilities. **[10:3]** is an extract from the Annual Report of the Chief Inspector of Probation. He has been in the forefront of the drive for better management and so it is particularly interesting to note his concerns. As we go to press, there remains much uncertainty about the relationship between national, regional, and local probation structures. The reality of probation practice is governed by National Standards **[10:4]** and a mass of probation circulars, all available on the web, which communicate formal, significant, or long-term instructions, guidance, and requests for action or information from the Director of Probation to probation staff. This is another example of Government by 'informal decree' (see Chapter 2, page 70). The probation officer is surrounded by a bewildering amount of guidance: the Probation Rules have over the years been supplemented by Home Office circulars, Chief Probation Officer (CPO) letters, letters from HM Inspectorate of Probation, letters from the Probation Training Unit, probation circulars, guides and so on. The creation of the National Probation Service led briefly to greater clarity (see *A New Choreography: the Probation Service's Strategic Framework 2001–04*, which set out six 'stretch objectives', including improving the performance management framework), but we are now in a time of flux.

Probation officers have traditionally had two main roles: the provision of a service of social information and advice to the courts (and also to the CPS); and the supervision and rehabilitation of offenders in the community. Now 'probation purposes' are defined (in section 1 of the Offender Management Act 2007) as providing for—

(1) courts to be given assistance in determining the appropriate sentences to pass, and making other decisions, in respect of persons charged with or convicted of offences;

(2) authorized persons to be given assistance in determining whether conditional cautions should be given and which conditions to attach to conditional cautions;

(3) the supervision and rehabilitation of persons charged with or convicted of offences;

(4) the giving of assistance to persons remanded on bail;

(5) the supervision and rehabilitation of persons to whom conditional cautions are given;

(6) the giving of information to victims of persons charged with or convicted of offences.

Let us look at each of these in turn.

(a) Court reports

The CJA 1991 required sentencers to consult a pre-sentence report before sentencing someone to imprisonment, but this requirement was watered down by the CJA1993: the court had a discretion to dispense with a report where it is satisfied that it can properly pass sentence without one. The CJA 2003 sections 156–160 develop in detailed and complex language the rules on when a pre-sentence report (PSR) is required. In reality, a well-researched PSR is an invaluable help to the sentencer and as a basis for sentence planning. It should provide general information about an offender's background and some general circumstances surrounding the commission of the offence (see **[10:4]**). In the past, the emphasis might have been on their family circumstances, medical and psychiatric health, and employment situation, but today this information is directed towards assessing risk. A report on Gerry Good might look something like this.

This is a Pre-Sentence Report as defined in s. 158 of the Criminal Justice Act 2003 and has been prepared in accordance with the requirements of the National Standard for Pre-Sentence Reports. This report is a restricted document.	

OFFENDER'S DETAILS	
Name: Gerry Good	Date of Birth: 20/06/76
Address:	Age: 32
Postcode:	

COURT DETAILS	
Sentencing Court: Camford	
Court Type: Crown Court	
Local Justice Area	
Date Report Requested	
Date Report Required	
Purpose of Sentencing: Not stated	
Level of Seriousness: Not stated	
OFFENCE DETAILS	
Offence(s) (dealt with in this PSR)	Date of Offence(s): 13/01/07
1 x Assault occasioning actual bodily harm	
PSR WRITER'S DETAILS	
Name: Natalie Jones	
Office Title: Probation Officer	
Office Location: Camford Probation Office, Camford	
Date report completed and signed:	

1. Sources of Information.

1.1 For the purposes of writing this report I have interviewed Mr Good on one occasion at the Probation Office. I have read the CPS documents and seen a list of previous convictions. I have also contacted Mr Good's General Practitioner.

This report is underpinned and informed by an Offender Assessment System (OASys) in the identification of the risk of reconviction and the risk of harm presented by this defendant.

2. Offence Analysis

2.1 The court will be aware of the facts surrounding this case. Gerry Good was found guilty at trial of Actual Bodily Harm. Mr Good was remarkably frank in discussing the circumstances surrounding the offence with me and it is my assessment that he genuinely has little recall of what actually happened. His responses struck me as confused, rather than evasive. He does deny the seriousness of the offence and, although this may indicate a failure to take responsibility, it is also a reflection of the fact that he did not think he had committed an offence. Mr Good acknowledges that the major contributory factor behind this offence is his dependency on alcohol—in particular he tells me he had been drinking for most of the day before the offence took place.

2.2 Clearly the court will view this offence as particularly serious, not only because of its nature, but because it was committed whilst Mr Good was already subject to a Community Order imposed by Bleakham Magistrates' Court on 6 April 2005 for offences of theft. That Order had a requirement attached that Mr Good obtain treatment from the Alcohol Dependency Unit in Camford for his addiction. This offence therefore took place despite Mr Good's access to community resources relevant to his offending. It is my view that the circumstances in this case suggest that a further community disposal would not be effective in preventing re-offending. CPS information suggests that the victim required hospital treatment following the offence. CPS information could not, of course, capture the long-term psychological impact of such an offence, even though physical recovery may have been good. In my view Mr Good minimized the effect of the offence on the victim.

3. Offender Assessment and Likelihood of Re-offending

The OASys Chart below summarizes the relevant factors which have been identified as contributing to the defendant's risk of reconviction. The indicators which exceed the mid-way point on the bar chart are those which need to be addressed in order to reduce the likelihood of further offences being committed.

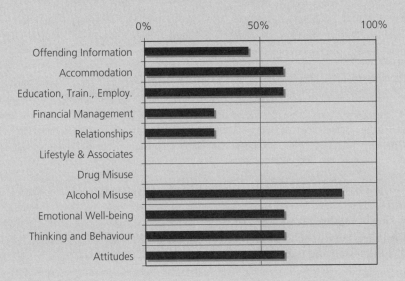

Factors Contributing to Offending

Likelihood of reconviction:	Risk is low	**Low-medium**	Medium	Medium high	High

3.1 Mr Good has lived in this area for two years. He has led an unsettled and chaotic life for the past five years, since his marriage broke up, when he became homeless. Mr Good does have occasional contact with his mother and with his daughter, who still live in the north of England. He has had no contact with his ex-partner for four years. He has had occasional relationships with women in recent years. He tells me that he had hoped that the victim of the offence was going to become his new partner.

3.2 Mr Good's criminal record reveals that he has previous convictions for dishonesty and minor offences of violence. The court has imposed a number of disposals aimed at reducing the risk of re-offending. None of these has been successful. Mr Good acknowledges that until and unless he addresses his dependency on alcohol he remains at risk of re-offending. At this stage I have not completed a detailed assessment of his attitude to women. His response to supervision has not been positive. He has reported when required during some of the current Order but when he has been drinking heavily he has neglected to fulfil these requirements. Furthermore he has not attended all the appointments offered to him by the Alcohol Dependency Unit.

3.3 At the time of his arrest, Mr Good was not working and was in receipt of Job Seekers Allowance. The fact that he has not been in employment for more than four years indicates further the effect his addiction to alcohol has had on his ability to lead a responsible lifestyle. He has been offered employment advice by a partnership agency of the Probation Service but did not sustain or take up the advice he was offered.

4. Assessment of the Risk of Harm

4.1 It is apparent that Mr Good deeply regrets what happened between him and the victim of the attack that evening. He considered her a friend, and is deeply hurt that she has, in his eyes, initiated proceedings against him. Although he acknowledges his dependency on alcohol (and occasionally drugs) he failed to complete a treatment programme at the Alcohol Dependency Unit in Camford. My impression is that he has considerable long-term personal issues which he attempts to disguise by consuming alcohol. The pessimism he expresses about the future is a reflection of the effects that his long-term drinking patterns have had on his ability to take responsibility for his own actions. Until Mr Good addresses his addiction he remains at risk of causing serious harm to members of the public.

4.2 He has previous offences for violence and the Probation Service assessment system assesses him as of medium risk of re-offending. He is at high risk of causing harm if he were to be in a similar situation to the one he was in when he committed this offence.

5. Conclusion

5.1 The court will have little option but to give consideration to a custodial sentence given the seriousness of the offence. Such a sentence would protect members of the public from further harm for its duration but it is unlikely that Mr Good would be offered anything other than a nominal introductory programme on the subject of alcohol dependency within the custodial setting. Therefore the likelihood is that he would be released posing a similar risk of harm and re-offending to that which he poses currently.

5.2 Should the court wish to give consideration to a community sentence the options are as follows:

5.3 Fine or Discharge:

Neither of these disposals would address the seriousness of the offence.

5.4 Supervision and Programme Requirements:

Mr Good could benefit from a general offending behaviour programme. In the course of that programme he would examine his own responses and attitudes to hopefully change his current methods of solving issues. Specific alcohol-related intervention could be sequenced following completion of the initial group work programme.

Mr Good would be expected to:

- report weekly to his supervising officer;
- attend the group work programme;
- be assessed for additional alcohol-related work;
- look at victim and relapse prevention issues;
- be assessed for employment/training.

5.5 If a custodial sentence is inevitable then Mr Good will be assessed for suitability for this programme as part of his licence conditions on release.

5.6 Mr Good could also be made subject to a community order comprising an unpaid work requirement with the number of hours appropriate to the court's view of the seriousness of this offence.

5.7 If however the court still judges the offence so serious that it must impose a custodial sentence, it might be possible for a Suspended Sentence to be considered. In that case, I would propose the court impose a Suspended Sentence Order with the same requirements of Unpaid Work and Supervision. I would further request that the amount of hours be reduced in recognition of the more onerous nature of the sentence as a whole.

(b) Assisting in determining whether conditional cautions should be given

As we saw in Chapters 1 and 2, an increasing number of offenders are cautioned or given warnings/reprimands rather than prosecuted. Traditionally probation officers had little involvement in non-court processes, though, as we shall see in (d) below, they have provided excellent support to those seeking to avoid being remanded in custody pre-trial, but this should not be seen as a diversion from the court process. But recently, they have become involved in diversionary schemes. As we saw in Chapter 2, the Criminal Justice Act (CJA) 2003 introduced 'conditional cautions,' i.e. conditions with cautions. The Act itself provides that probation officers should give assistance in determining whether conditional cautions should be given and which conditions should be attached, and to provide supervision and rehabilitation to those so cautioned. But the evidence seems to suggest that so far by far the most common condition has been a requirement to pay compensation. In the new NOMS world it would seem that unpaid work conditions are more likely to be managed using the voluntary sector as scheme managers.

(c) The supervision and rehabilitation of persons charged with or convicted of offences

This is the traditional 'core' probation role. Thus, if Gerry Good had been sentenced to a community order, his main contact would have been with a probation officer. The initial appointment with the supervising officer is, whenever possible, held within five working days of the making of the order, and the appointment is made before the offender leaves court. At the first meeting, the supervising officer gives the offender written information setting out what can be expected from the Probation Service, and what is expected of the offender. They are given a copy of the court order, with instructions to comply with its terms, and within two weeks a written supervision plan should have been drawn up. National Standards—first introduced in 1990, tightened in 1995, and re-issued in 2000 and again in 2005 **[10:4]**—suggest that at least one contact per week for the first 16 weeks of supervision. There will normally be a home visit made within the first 12 weeks of the order. Six appointments will be made within the second 12 weeks, after which appointments may reduce to monthly contact.

A probation officer is normally required to take breach action after no more than 'one unacceptable failure' by the offender to comply with the order (whereas the 1990 standards allowed 'three instances of failure'). This change reflects the pressure to move away from a welfare to a punishment model. The other great pressure is the financial squeeze. The average number of people supervised per main grade officer rose every year from 20.7 in 1992 to 34.6 in 1998, to 40.7 in 2001 (Probation Statistics, 2001). This reflects both rising caseloads and a falling or stable number of fully trained officers. Thus the number of people under probation service supervision was 235,000 in 2006, compared with a figure of 170,852 in 1996 (Offender Management Statistics, 2006, Table 1.2; the ratio of staff to offenders is more difficult to discover nowadays). Worrall **[10:5]** argues for what might be seen as 'traditional' probation values (advice, assistance, and befriending), rejecting the prevalent view that community sentences are simply alternatives to imprisonment: for her, prison should be seen as the alternative. We live in uncertain times: **[10:6]** is a concerned message from the voluntary sector. Who should be providing probation services: trained probation officers, or private and voluntary sector 'providers'? In the view of this author, whilst there is scope for innovative contributions from both the private and voluntary sectors, it is professionally well-qualified probation officers who should take a firm lead in work with offenders.

As we saw in Chapter 6, for *offences committed on or after* 4 April 2005, the new community order introduced under the CJA 2003 replaced all existing community sentences for those aged 18 years and over. The sentencing court must add at least one (but could potentially add all 12) of the following requirements: supervision; unpaid work; specified activities; prohibited activities; accredited programmes; curfew; exclusion; residence; mental health treatment; drug rehabilitation; alcohol treatment; or attendance centre requirement for under-25s. The CJA 2003 also introduced the new Suspended Sentence Order (SSO) for which the offender is given a custodial sentence suspended for between six months and two years. The court specifies a number of requirements from the set of options available for the community order, and these are supervised by the Probation Service. Data is more difficult to gather with the fragmentation of services (Community Orders or SSOs with single curfew requirements (standalone curfew orders) are not supervised by the Probation Service and are monitored separately and are not, surprisingly, included in the Offender Management Statistics). The statistics do tell us that half of all community orders starting in 2006 had one requirement, 35 per cent had two requirements, 14 per cent had three requirements, and 1 per cent had four requirements. Suspended Sentence Orders were more likely than Community Orders to have two or three requirements, with 44 per cent of SSOs having two requirements and 18 per cent having three requirements (compared with 35 per cent and 14 per cent respectively for Community Orders). The most frequently used combination of requirements commencing as part of a Community Order supervised by the probation service was 'unpaid work' as a single requirement on its own, accounting for 39,390 Community Orders commencing in 2006 (32 per cent of all Community Orders). Altogether 203,320 requirements were given with Community Orders (this and much more statistical data is available in the Offender Management Statistics, 2006). According to Mair et al (2007), who studied data from the first 16 months of the new regime, probation officers were worried about the lack of availability of some requirements, and the rise in the use of unpaid work. The use of suspended sentence orders was seen not to be diverting offenders from prison, but to be contributing to the prison population (because breaches are likely to lead to imprisonment). Readers are encouraged to read Gelsthorpe and Morgan (2007) to learn more on probation practice. The National Audit Office **[10:7]** raise concerns about the gaps in the Probation Service's knowledge about its management of sentence.

The Probation Service is of course not only concerned with the supervision of those serving community orders. Those released on licence from prison are subject to parole supervision by the probation service. In 2006/07, 28 per cent of those on licence were recalled to prison. This figure includes 11,230 determinate sentence offenders and 164 offenders on life licence (paragraphs 10.10 and 10.11 of the OM Statistics, 2006). Those people who think that early release from prison is a soft option are wrong: parole supervision can lead many people swiftly back to prison (Padfield and Maruna, 2005). Probation officers are thus increasingly involved in the management of the sentences of imprisoned offenders. In Gerry Good's case, he will be allocated to a supervising probation officer at the start of his sentence, and this officer should be fully involved in devising any sentence plan. Gerry will be automatically due for release at the halfway point in his sentence (and perhaps Home Detention Curfew (HDC)). His supervising officer has to provide a pre-discharge report at least one month before release. This will include recommendations to the prison governor on any extra licence conditions felt to be necessary, and will give instructions to Gerry Good on reporting once he is released from custody. After release, if the supervising officer wishes to add or delete a licence condition during the supervision period, they will have to apply to the prison establishment from which Gerry was discharged. If the request is approved, the prison issues a new licence (in duplicate) to the supervising officer.

Clearly, problems with the effective flow of information between the Probation Service, Social Services departments, the police, and the Prison Service remain. What happens if the different bodies disagree: if the governor imposes conditions that the probation officer believes to be unduly severe, are they obliged to bring breach proceedings? The picture has been complicated, first by the introduction of home detention curfew orders by the Crime and Disorder Act 1998, and then by the End of Custody Licence scheme introduced at the end of June 2007. The prison governor may release short-term prisoners on a 'home detention' curfew licence (enforced by electronic monitoring or 'tagging'). Initially this could be for up to two months before the normal date of release, but it was later increased to three months. The Release of Short-term Prisoners on Licence (Amendment of Requisite Period) Order 2003 (SI 2003/1602), which came into force in July 2003, increased the period of home detention curfew to 135 days. It is clear from the home detention curfew statistics that the power to release early in this way is exercised differently from prison to prison. It obviously makes a mockery of the precise calculation of short sentences by trial judges—now, anyone sentenced to, say, 18 months, may be released at some unpredictable time between five and nine months.

Then in June 2007, to deal with the problem of overcrowding, the Lord Chancellor announced a new scheme—the End of Custody Licence (ECL)—which introduced a presumption in favour of release on licence for prisoners serving between four weeks and four years for the final 18 days of their sentence subject to meeting strict eligibility criteria and providing a release address. Prisoners who would normally be subject to supervision on release (prisoners serving 12 months or more or under 22 years of age) are required to meet their probation officer after release and to have regular contact after that in line with their supervision plan. All prisoners released on ECL are liable to recall if they are reported to have misbehaved during the period of the licence. As we go to press, it is not clear whether this is a long-term measure, but it is yet another example of the bewildering complexity of the criminal justice process.

(d) The giving of assistance to persons remanded on bail

One of the most useful ways that probation officers can help offenders likely to be remanded in custody is by providing approved premises (which used to be known as probation or bail hostels). These may be run by probation staff, although increasingly 'approved' premises are likely to be managed under contract by voluntary bodies or private companies. The number of available beds in hostels declined during the 1990s, and a number of hostels closed. More recently the admissions criteria have been revised, reserving admission to those 'offenders or bailees posing a high or very high risk of harm' (see Probation Circular 37 of 2005). In 2007, in order to try and reduce the prison remand population, the Government decided, rather than to open new probation hostels, to give a private company, ClearSprings, a national contract to provide bail hostels (see Probation Circular 33 of 2007). Whether this proves to be an efficient and effective way forward remains to be seen.

(e) The supervision and rehabilitation of persons to whom conditional cautions are given

Despite this being a statutory probation service, the Code of Practice on Conditional Cautions (at <http://www.cps.gov.uk>) says little about the involvement of the probation service, though paragraph 5.5 says:

The police, CPS and National Probation Service (NPS) should take steps at local level (e.g. through the Local Criminal Justice Board or Crime & Disorder Reduction Partnership) to identify agencies, groups or organizations, voluntary or statutory, which provide courses or other activities that might form part of a Conditional Caution, and which it may be appropriate to consult when deciding whether a case is suitable for a Conditional Caution. The NPS could be approached in appropriate cases to assist in determining whether certain offenders are suitable for a Conditional Caution, for example where there are concerns about the health, behaviour or background of the offender.

As was suggested in Chapter 3, it is vital that we should soon have some independent research into how this new scheme is working.

(f) The giving of information to victims of persons charged with or convicted of offences

The National Standard **[10:4]** for victim contact work is that probation areas should offer face-to-face contact between the victim (or family) and a member of the probation service (or agent) within 40 working days of an offender being sentenced to a custodial sentence of 12 months or more for a violent or sexual offence. The National Probation Service target is to make initial contact within that timescale in 85 per cent of all eligible cases. In 2006/07, 93 per cent of the 15,490 known victims were contacted within the target time. This is another thorny area. It is vitally important that victims are supported though the criminal justice process, and it is clear that sometimes they are not treated with the respect they deserve. This is not to suggest that they should have any role in the fixing of the appropriate charges or sentences.

So how should we conclude this brief look at the role of the probation service? Clearly probation officers require discretionary powers: they are often managing difficult people in a problematic environment. It is not easy to monitor whether, for example, probation practice is non-discriminatory, as required by the Criminal Justice Act 1991, section 95 **[1:14]**. However, as central players within the system, they may serve to reinforce the bias evident elsewhere. For example, Chapter 6 included an extract from Eaton's study of the treatment of women by magistrates **[6:10]**. Her (1986) book concludes that 'the practices of probation officers serve to disadvantage women by an endorsement of a model of family life which involves the oppression and exploitation of women' (at page 61). How have things changed, and what will be the effect of the increased role for the voluntary and private sectors in the supervision of offenders? Considerable uncertainty surrounds issues of accountability when anything goes wrong with private or voluntary sector supervision. These are difficult days for the probation service, and doubtless therefore also for those that they supervise and 'manage'.

(ii) PRISONS

What happens when Gerry is sent to prison? If he were sentenced in Cambridge Crown Court in 2007, he would be likely to be sent to HMP Peterborough, which is run by the private company, Kalyx. This is one of 11 prisons run by private companies under contract to the NOMS. The other 126 prisons are run directly by the Prison Service (this number will change: some public service prisons are merging, and others may open).

What is the legal status of the Prison Service? In 1993 the Prison Service moved to executive agency status within the Home Office, to be run by a management board, chaired by a director-general who was directly accountable to the Home Secretary. Whilst agency status may have devolved more decision-making powers to individual prison governors, the audit and performance culture which has developed also led to more central control. Does agency status weaken the political accountability of the Home Secretary to Parliament? Of course, more controversial than agency status was the decision to privatize the management of individual prisons. From May 2007 the Prison Service became part of the new Ministry of Justice, and it remains an executive agency as well as part of the NOMS, which is therefore both its parent organization and its main commissioner. It continues to work closely with the re-structured Home Office as one of its key partners within the overall Criminal Justice System (CJS). The Prison Service receives funding from a number of different sources and manages a range of services and establishments. The Prison Service's main commissioner, NOMS, operates through Regional Offender Managers (ROMs) for each of the English regions and a Director of Offender Management for Wales (DOM). The ROMs/DOM commission work regionally both for offenders in custody and for those in the community, and have a close dialogue with Prison Service Areas and individual establishments. However, some specialist services, like high security prisons, continue to be provided and purchased on a nationwide basis. ROMs are not the only commissioners of services delivered by the Prison Service. Learning and Skills Councils (LSCs) are responsible, jointly with ROMs, for commissioning education and skills provision for prisoners; Primary Care Trusts (PCTs) are responsible for commissioning health services; and the Youth Justice Board (YJB) commissions services for those under 18 years old. The Prison Service also provides services for the Borders and Immigration Agency (BIA), which commissions services at Dover, Haslar, and Lindholme (these details have been obtained from the Prison Service's very detailed website). So, while HM Prison Service is perhaps not feeling quite as fractured as the probation service, it is equally being challenged by the private sector.

A short-term prisoner such as Gerry Good may serve the whole of his sentence in the local prison to which he is initially dispatched. Otherwise, during the initial period of assessment, the observation, classification, and allocation units of the prison decide on a classification for him, based on the crimes committed and the reports made on him by staff during the period of assessment. This determines to which prison he is allocated. Category A prisoners are those whose escape would be highly dangerous to the public; category B are those for whom the highest degree of security is not necessary but for whom escape must be made very difficult; category C are those who cannot be trusted in open conditions but who do not have the ability or resources to make a determined effort to escape; and category D are those who can reasonably be trusted to serve their sentences in open conditions. A review of categorization is carried out annually as part of sentence planning and as an incentive to good behaviour. Since this categorization decision has a direct impact on the date of a prisoner's ultimate release, the Divisional Court in *R v Secretary of State for the Home Department, ex p*

Duggan [1994] 3 All ER 277 held that, when categorization is reviewed, the gist of reports on which the decision is based should be given to the prisoner, as well as reasons for the decision (followed in *R (Lord) v Secretary of State for the Home Department* [2003] EWHC 2073). A category A prisoner may even have the right to an oral hearing (see *R (Williams) v Secretary of State for the Home Department* [2002] EWCA Civ 498, [2002] 4 All ER 872).

It is beyond the scope of this book to look in detail at the profile of the prison population, and life in prison. Students wanting a picture of prison conditions should read the inspection reports of HM Chief Inspector of Prisons. Better still, arrange to spend some time in a prison (voluntarily!). There are five main types of prison: local prisons (all closed establishments); training prisons; young offender institutions; remand centres; and dispersal prisons (high-security prisons where prisoners are sent to serve long sentences). There are currently 12 prisons for women and, of those, four hold women in only a part of the (otherwise male) prison. There are a small number of prisons with mother and baby units, but there are restrictions on how long young children can remain with their mothers in these institutions. An increasing number of prisons have several functions: not only do male prisons have small units for women, some adult prisons have a wing for young offenders, and training prisons may have a section for remand prisoners.

The riots in a number of prisons in April 1990 led to an investigation conducted by Lord Justice Woolf and Judge Stephen Tumin. Their report **[10:2]** painted a depressing picture and stressed the need for greater 'justice' within prisons. Some issues are only skimmed over by Woolf: for example, the over-representation of black prisoners in the prison populations.

TABLE 10.1 Percentage of prison population from ethnic minorities

	Male	Female
1990	15%	23%
1998	18%	24%
2001	21%	26%
2005	25%	29%

Source: Prison Statistics 2001, Chapter 6; Offender Management Caseload Statistics 2005 (HOSB 18/06), Chapter 8

Genders and Player (1999) carried out a study of race relations in three prisons. They looked in particular at four areas: disciplinary proceedings; the writing of assessments; the allocation of accommodation; and the allocation of jobs and training courses. They concluded that racial bias lay at the root of several of the pressing problems they identified. The problems facing women prisoners—partly caused, ironically, by their under-representation in the prison population—are not discussed in the Woolf Report, perhaps because the riots did not involve women prisoners. The most recent review of women in prison is the *Corston Report* (2007) **[10:8]**, which calls for a radical change in the way that we treat women throughout the whole of the criminal justice system. Somewhat depressingly, this call is far from original: see also HM Inspector of Prisons *Thematic Review of Women in Prison* (1997), the Prison Reform Trust's report on *Justice for Woman* (2000), as well as Eaton (1993).

As a result of the 1990 riots and the Woolf Report that followed it **[10:2]**, there were significant changes in the complaints and disciplinary procedures in prisons. Each prison has an

Independent Monitoring Board (known as Boards of Visitors until 2003, and the necessary statutory change of name happened in the Offender Management Act 2007), composed of lay volunteers, whose prime duty is to act as a watchdog on the prison, with each member having free access to the prison, prisoners, and prison records. A prisoner can now formally complain, either orally to the landing officer or the governor, or in writing to the governor or the Independent Monitoring Board. Another Woolf recommendation—that there should be an independent adjudicator at the apex of the system—resulted in the appointment of a Prison Ombudsman. He became the Prisons and Probation Ombudsman in 2001, but unsurprisingly his caseload remains dominated by complaints from those in prison rather than those under the supervision of the Probation Service. He also investigates deaths in custody. (The Criminal Justice and Immigration Bill 2007 proposes, rather curiously, to rename the office 'Her Majesty's Commissioner for Offender Management and Prisons'.) The reports of the Prisons and Probation Ombudsman are well worth reading, painting a good picture of the many difficulties facing prisoners within the penal system.

The prison disciplinary system underwent major reform in 1992. Until then, the Board of Visitors undertook adjudications over disciplinary matters within the prison. Woolf recommended that those responsible for monitoring conditions should not be responsible for discipline. Since then, the most serious offences against prison discipline, which are also serious criminal offences in themselves, are referred to the police with a view to prosecution in the criminal courts. In 1992, governors were given the power to deal with other offences themselves and to award up to 28 days' (increased to 42 in 1994) deferred release, known as ADAs, or 'additional days awarded'. The European Court of Human Rights, in *Ezeh and Connors v United Kingdom* (2002) 35 EHRR 691, held that disciplinary proceedings constituted criminal proceedings for the purposes of European Convention on Human Rights, Article 6 **[1:12]**, notwithstanding their classification as disciplinary proceedings. Therefore, prisoners not only had a right to legal representation, but the governor was not an 'independent and impartial tribunal'. As a result the Prison (Amendment) Rules 2002 (SI 2002/2116) changed the disciplinary process such that serious charges, which may result in ADAs, are referred to an independent adjudicator (normally a district judge). Also controversial are the administrative 'sanctions' available to the governor, such as the incentives and earned privileges scheme, segregation, or transfer to another prison to maintain discipline. Officially not part of the prison discipline system, being segregated or losing privileges feels like punishment: unsurprisingly, there is a large body of 'prison law' largely derived from judicial review proceedings imitated by prisoners (see Owen, Macdonald, and Livingstone, 2008).

English prisons in recent years have suffered dreadfully from overcrowding. There was some optimism in the early 1990s that the reforms of the Criminal Justice Act 1991 would lead to a reduction in the total number of prisoners. The male population reached a plateau at around 43,000 between 1990 and 1993. After 1993 it started to rise again and there was another plateau between 1999 and 2001; it has been rising steeply since then (nearly 76,000 as we go to press). The female population was at a fairly constant level throughout the twentieth century at around 1,000, until the mid-1980s, when it started to rise. But from the early 1990s it starting rising steeply to 4,450 in 2004, since when it seems to have remained more or less constant. The changes in release procedures and the continuing pressure on judges to treat 'serious' offenders 'seriously' means that there are an increasing number of long-term prisoners serving increasingly longer sentences. The number of prisoners has risen to over 81,883 on 30 November 2007.

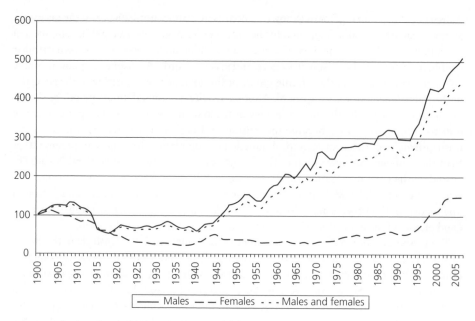

FIGURE 10.1 The average prison population
Source: Offender Management Caseload Statistics 2006 (HOSB 18/06)

The Woolf Report **[10:2]** adversely commented on the poor regimes in many local prisons and remand centres: how much has this improved in the last two decades? There have been many improvements, but the rising population of prisoners and financial squeezes have also taken their toll. The regime within prison is often tedious and unconstructive. Prisoners are paid derisory wages and have little incentive to work productively. Educational and work facilities are squeezed in times of financial stringency. In an attempt to improve performance, both the Prison Service and private prisons now follow service level agreements and Key Performance Indicators (see the Prison Service's annual corporate plans and annual reports). Of course, slavish adherence to such indicators can have a negative effect: perhaps, for example, an emphasis on unlocking prisoners without a corresponding rise in purposeful activities contributes to an increased number of assaults in prison. However, there can be no doubt that the current political emphasis on reducing offending has led to greater interest in 'what works' in prison, and much greater emphasis is being put on suitable courses, such as the Sex Offender Treatment Programme and other courses designed to encourage prisoners to confront their offending behaviour. However, the inevitable resources problem arises: budgets are limited, and the prison population goes ever upwards (see Morgan (2007)).

Clearly, prisoners are in the hands of the prison authorities (and their fellow prisoners) and are vulnerable to the abuse of power. The Prison Act 1952 **[10:9]** lays down the general duties of the prison authorities, and authorizes the Home Secretary to make rules for the management of prisons. The Prison Rules for adult prisoners date from 1964, and are regularly amended; the Young Offender Institution Rules are similar to the Prison Rules. The Rules rarely lay down specific rights, but they leave vast discretion to prison governors. Should breaches of the Prison Rules provide the basis for an action for breach of statutory duty? The courts have been reluctant to go this far: the House of Lords in *Hague* **[10:10]** overruled two different

decisions of the Court of Appeal, which had allowed prisoners' claims for false imprisonment, based on principles of 'residual liberty' and 'intolerable conditions'. However, this does
not mean that prisoners are without rights. The ordinary civil and criminal law applies in
prison, even though it may be difficult to enforce. Judicial review is also an avenue available to
the prisoner, though Loughlin (1993) warns that we should not assume that 'a greater degree
of legalism automatically leads to a better or more enlightened system' (at page 50). Whilst
the number of applications for judicial review by prisoners may increase, the breadth of the
powers of the prison authorities has meant that the vast majority are unsuccessful (see Valier
(2004)). The cry for enforceable minimum standards and a new Prison Act will not disappear
(see, for example, Owen, Macdonald, and Livingstone (2008) and the Prison Reform Trust).
The Human Rights Act 1998 **[1:12]** is having an impact in this area. As Lord Steyn said in *R
(Daly) v Secretary of State for the Home Department* [2001] UKHL 26, [2001] 2 AC 532, the
intensity of review in a public law case will depend on the subject matter in hand: 'In law,
context is everything'. The European Court of Human Rights remains important, as well.
In Chapter 1, we included a significant extract from the recent (and controversial) ruling of
the European Court of Human Rights in *Dickson v United Kingdom* (2007) that a prisoner
denied the opportunity to inseminate his wife artificially had had his rights under Article 8
breached **[1:13]**. Note that the reasoning of the Court is not that the prisoner necessarily has
a right to artificial insemination, but that the way it was banned in the UK was unlawful. Of
wider importance might be *Hirst v United Kingdom* (2004) 38 EHRR 40 where the European
Court held that the blanket ban on prisoners' right to vote was not proportionate.

Who decides when a prisoner comes out of prison? As we saw earlier, there is a confusing
array of different release rules. All sentences are now in effect partially suspended sentences,
served partly in prison and partly in the community, and all prisoners who commit an
imprisonable offence after release but before the end of their original sentences run the risk
of being returned to prison to complete their sentence. Let us first explain the rules for those
sentenced for *offences committed before* 4 April 2005. Those sentenced to less than 12 months'
imprisonment are eligible for automatic unconditional release at the halfway point in their
sentence. Prisoners are then at risk of being returned to serve the rest of their sentence if
they are convicted of a further imprisonable offence before their original sentence has fully
expired, but they are not subject to compulsory supervision. Those sentenced to between 12
months and four years are released at the halfway point on automatic *conditional* release.
They are supervised on licence, by a probation officer, until the point where three-quarters
of their sentence has passed. The Parole Board is only involved with the release of those
prisoners sentenced to more than four years, who become eligible for *discretionary* conditional release at the halfway point. If early release is not granted, these prisoners are released
automatically after two-thirds of their sentence has been served. They then remain under
supervision until the three-quarters point in their sentence, as above. Some sex offenders
remain on licence until the end of their sentence on the recommendation of the trial judge.
The system applicable to life sentence prisoners will be described in (iii) below, which looks
at the Parole Board. And for all those sentenced *for offences committed after* 4 April 2005,
there is a different system. Fixed (determinate) length sentenced prisoners are entitled to
release at the half-way point, and a possible earlier release on HDC or ELC (see page 456).
The Parole Board decides on the release of those serving indeterminate or extended sentences, and those recalled to prison having earlier been released. The prison authorities play
a vital role in all releases: fixing the terms of licences for those automatically released, and
deciding on HDC or ELC. They also have a crucial imput into the decision making of the
Parole Board by the creation of the prisoner's parole dossier, or file of reports.

(iii) THE PAROLE BOARD

Parole was first introduced in this country by the Criminal Justice Act 1967. There were originally two main objectives: to reduce the prison population, and to help in the rehabilitation of offenders by releasing them into the community at the 'right' time in their sentence, under the supervision of a probation officer to whom they were required to report regularly. Over the years many changes have been made to the system, both by Parliament (sweeping changes were made by the Criminal Justice Act 1991, the Criminal Justice and Public Order Act (CJPOA) 1994, and the Criminal Justice Act 2003) and change has also been forced on a reluctant Government by a stream of important decisions from the courts.

What is the status of the Parole Board? To give it a semblance of 'independence', in 1994 the Parole Board was made a non-departmental public body (see CJPOA 1994, section 149). But it has never been made a genuinely independent tribunal. Whether this will change soon remains to be seen: both the current Chairman (see Nichols, in Padfield (2007)) and the High Court (in *R (Brooke) v Parole Board* [2007] EWHC 2036 (Admin), [2007] HRLR 46) have been loud in their criticism of the Board's supposed compliance with Article 5(4) of the European Convention on Human Rights **[1:12]**. Is it time that a 'real' court made these decisions? What constitutes a 'real' court?

The members of the Parole Board include judges, psychiatrists, those with 'knowledge and experience of the supervision or aftercare of discharged prisoners', and those who have 'made a study of the causes of delinquency or the treatment of offenders' (see section 239 of and Schedule 19 to the Criminal Justice Act 2003). It carries out its functions in panels: sometimes three, sometimes two, and sometimes just one member panels. The work of the Parole Board is well described in its annual reports to Parliament, it has an excellent website, and it has encouraged a number of research projects. Thus, **[10:11]** and **[10:12]** provide two different historical 'snap shots'. Hood and Shute's (1994) work included the observation of almost 400 cases dealt with before the implementation of major changes in 1991, published as the first part of a study of the implementation of the 1991 changes. The task of the Parole Board is to predict and assess risk: it has to balance the need to protect the public from serious harm and to prevent further offending with the benefits of supervision. It seems curious that, while Parliament has attempted to structure judicial discretion in sentencing, the wide powers of the Parole Board—which decides the length of a sentence in practice—should be left wide open. Even if predictions of dangerousness could be made accurately, is it morally justifiable to keep some people in prison longer than others only because of the risk that they represent?

Today, the role of the Parole Board can be seen under three categories of case. First, life or indeterminate sentence cases. For many years, the most controversial parole procedures were those applicable to life sentence prisoners. The European Court of Human Rights in *Thynne* **[10:13]** ruled that once the 'tariff' period set by reference to the offence had expired, any subsequent detention on grounds of public protection should be capable of being challenged through proceedings in a court or tribunal that is independent of the executive. As a result, a much more open procedure was introduced in 1991 in relation to discretionary lifers. Slowly the right to an oral hearing was won by other life sentence prisoners. The European Court of Human Rights in *V and T v United Kingdom* (1999) 30 EHRR 121 held that the role of the Home Secretary in fixing the tariff of a juvenile murderer was unlawful; and in *Stafford v United Kingdom* (2002) 35 EHRR 1121 **[10:15]** it struck down the system for adult murderers (mandatory lifers). The House of Lords followed this in *R (Anderson)* *v Secretary of State for the Home Department* [2002] UKHL 46, [2003] 1 AC 837 (see page 411 of this book). All lifers now have the right to an oral hearing (see Padfield and Liebling, 2001; Padfield, 2006). In 2006/07, the Parole Board held 2,505 oral hearings (which included the first 50 IPP cases, the number of which will grow rapidly in the next few years (see page 326 of this book). Only 15 per cent were granted release on licence (the lowest release rate since 2001/02). In the same year, 97 prisoners on life licence were recalled during the year following allegations of further offences. This is out of a total of 1,622 life sentence prisoners under active supervision in the community during the year, or 6 per cent. This is a small rise on the figure for 2005/06 of 87 recalls for further offending out of 1,495 prisoners in the community, or 5.8 per cent.

The second category is the cases of determinate sentence prisoners. The Parole Board considers (at 'paper' panels) the release of all those sentenced to a fixed term of imprisonment for offences committed before 4 April 2005 (the old DCR scheme, studied by Hood and Shute). In 2006/07, the Parole Board considered 7,857 DCR cases (this figure will fall as these sentences get replaced by post-CJA 2003 sentences): 35.8 per cent of these were granted parole, down from 49.4 per cent in 2005/06 and the lowest release rate since 1996/97. As the Parole Board Annual Report 2006/07 states, 'the falling release rate appears to continue the trend in the last couple of years of a more cautious approach by panels to recommending release'.

Finally, there are the cases of the growing number of released prisoners recalled to prison. The system of recall (or back door sentencing) has undergone a particularly turbulent history. Until 1994 two systems of recall to custody ran in tandem: one operated by the Parole Board and one by the Home Secretary. The system has been changed radically several times (and is likely to be changed again by the Criminal Justice and Immigration Bill 2007). Currently, all decisions to recall people from licence or parole are taken by the Post Release Section of NOMS. The prisoner is then arrested by the police and taken to his nearest local prison. After a few days, Post Recall Section of NOMS writes to the prisoner and explains why he has been recalled (the prison will know no more than does the prisoner at this stage). A dossier, or recall pack, is then given to the prisoner who decides whether or not to make representations against his recall to the Parole Board. Even if the prisoner does not make representations, the case is considered by the Parole Board. They will either:

- order the immediate release of the prisoner on licence; or
- refuse immediate release but order release at a future date; or
- refuse immediate release and set a date for a further review the case; or
- refuse to release or review the case again (where there are less than 12 months to go on the sentence and the prisoner then serves what is left of the sentence in prison).

If dissatisfied, the prisoner can then ask for an oral hearing (fuller details are available on the Parole Board's website and in Padfield (2006)). In 2006/07, 28 per cent of those on licence were recalled, as well as 16 per cent of those on Home Detention Curfew (Offender Management Statistics 2006, Chapter 10). The Parole Board dealt with 14,669 recall cases that year. This compared with 9,296 in 2005/06, up a staggering 58 per cent in one year. This must be due to a more proactive recall policy being exercised by the probation service for reasons other than further offences, which, as the Parole Board Annual Report points out, actually fell for parolees during the year.

In this book, we can do no more than encourage students to look much more closely at the role of the Parole Board. At a time when much political discourse focuses on 'front door sentencing' (i.e. the decisions of judges and magistrates), it is the probation service, the prison authorities, NOMS, and the Parole Board who hold the keys to release, making the more invisible but vitally important 'back door sentencing' decisions (see Padfield and Maruna, 2005).

(iv) MENTAL HEALTH REVIEW TRIBUNALS

Mentally disordered offenders should, wherever possible, receive care and treatment from health and social services rather than from the criminal justice system. But as the number of hospital beds has decreased, community provision has not necessarily expanded: and we continue to see too many people with serious mental health problems in prison. Violent or dangerous mentally disordered offenders may find themselves in one of the three 'special hospitals'—Ashworth, Broadmoor, and Rampton—which are high security hospitals managed until 1995 by the Special Hospitals Service Authority. Since then there have been various management changes in this area as well, integrating prison mental health services into the wider National Health Service. In 2002, these three hospitals all became part of a local NHS trust. Regional health authorities also provide regional secure units, but these are normally reserved for those who are judged likely to improve and be discharged within two years. There are few long-term medium-security hospital provisions. The law itself may have little influence on practical decision making in a system very short of resources.

The Mental Health Act 1983 (as amended by the Mental Health Act 2007) **[10:17]** lays down the ground rules for the detention of mentally disordered people. Police powers under sections 135 and 136 of the Act were mentioned in Chapter 2. As Grounds (1992) says, 'the police are often a frontline agency, and may in effect act as a community psychiatric resource' (at page 287). Section 37 authorizes the courts to order hospital admission or guardianship, and they may do this even without convicting the accused (see section 37(3)). In any case where it makes a hospital order under section 37, a court may also make a restriction order under section 41 (see Street (1999)). The effect of a restriction order is that the patient may not be discharged (except by a Mental Health Review Tribunal), granted leave of absence or transferred to another hospital, without the consent of the Home Secretary. Section 47 allows the transfer of sentenced prisoners who require psychiatric hospital treatment. The Crime (Sentences) Act 1997 inserted into the 1983 Act 'hospital and limitation directions', which allow the court to order that if the offender does not respond to treatment, they be transferred to prison and not simply discharged from hospital. Public (or media?) concern about the need to protect the public from the risks presented by the mentally unstable led to the Home Office's *Managing Dangerous People with Severe Personality Disorder: Proposals for Policy Development* (1999). With its focus on reducing the risks to the public, the document considers the introduction of a 'dangerous severely personality disordered' order, which could be imposed by a civil court (i.e. without the safeguard of the criminal burden of proof, and merely on a balance of probabilities). Controversies continued with the Department of Health's consultation of a draft Mental Health Bill 2002 (see the Department of Health's website: <http://www.doh.gov.uk>), and more limited changes were eventually introduced in the Mental Health Act 2007. Perhaps the legal structure of the Mental Health Act 1983 needs less reform than the attitudes of those who provide the resources and facilities for them.

Under the European Convention on Human Rights, Article 5(4) **[1:12]**, everyone is entitled to take proceedings 'by which the lawfulness of his detention shall be decided speedily by a court'. In *X v United Kingdom* (1981) 4 EHRR 188 the European Court of Human Rights decided that all people held because they were of unsound mind were entitled to a periodic judicial consideration of the merits of their continued detention. As a result, the role of the Mental Health Review Tribunals (MHRTs)—composed of lawyers, doctors, and lay members—was strengthened by the Mental Health Act 1983. The role of MHRTs is to decide who can safely be released from hospital. They will usually meet in the hospital where the patient is detained. It is particularly difficult for a person who is or has been mentally disordered to prove to the satisfaction of the tribunal that their detention is not justified 'with a view to the protection of other persons' (see the Mental Health Act 1983, section 72(1)(a) **[10:17]**). Legal aid is available, which is rare in a tribunal: the legal aid provisions were expanded to cover MHRTs largely as a result of a high-profile campaign by the pressure group MIND. MHRTs have the advantages, over formal courts, of flexibility and informality, but as a result their performance is all the more difficult to assess. Peay (1989) conducted an important and thorough study. She is concerned by the covert dependence on the 'good sense' of tribunals: should legal criteria be taken more seriously or is the 'welfarist' approach more appropriate? Baker (1993) stressed the risks in using dangerousness as a criterion in decision making. Predictions of dangerousness, inevitably inaccurate, tend to lead to over-prediction. For this reason, if no other, it is particularly important to evolve clear legal criteria for the detention of those deemed 'dangerous'. Holloway and Grounds **[10:18]** researched the process more recently, and their conclusions include a discussion of the role of the medical member of the MHRT. The shortcomings of the system continue to be revealed by litigation: the House of Lords in *R (H) v Secretary of State for Health* [2006] 1 AC 441 confirmed once again that Article 5(4) required not only an initial right of access to a court or tribunal to decide whether the criteria for detention were met but also the availability of subsequent review at reasonable intervals, and the European Court of Human Rights in *HL v United Kingdom* (2005) 40 EHRR 32 once again upheld a complaint that a patient's Article 5(1) and (4) rights had been infringed. This case involved an autistic man who was kept at Bournewood Hospital by doctors against the wishes of his carers, and does not concern the criminal justice process, but it shows that there is no room for complacency! Amendments to the Mental Capacity Act 2005 have been made by the Mental Health Act 2007. It is not the purpose of this section to deal in detail with the role of the MHRT, but readers are encouraged to compare and contrast the different rules concerning the Parole Board with those of the MHRT. More offenders with severe mental health problems should be diverted away from prison and into more appropriate facilities: but it may be as difficult to get released from a mental hospital as it is to be released from prison. Peay (2007) also cautions that mentally disordered offenders are not, and should not be, treated as an isolated category. Treatment needs to be available in prisons, hospitals, and in the community.

An underlying concern highlighted in this book has been the need for procedural fairness and political accountability. Offenders need real procedural safeguards from the time of their arrest onwards. Such protections remain vital in a process which allows bodies such as the Parole Board or MHRTs to predict who is fit for release from prison or who is a danger to the public. However, as Lacey (1986) pointed out, the actual and perhaps inevitable powerlessness of the offender at the post-conviction stage may often render effective use of court-like procedures an impossibility. She suggested that it makes more sense, if we are concerned principally with substantive fairness, to concentrate on ensuring fair procedures involving participation and accountability at the policy-making stage. Procedural justice is important, but real, substantive, justice even more so. This book has highlighted some of the tensions evident in the criminal justice process, but it is important to look also at fundamental principles. A system which is under constant pressure to save money is likely to take shortcuts: it is unlikely to value procedural fairness adequately, and even less likely to tackle the underlying causes of crime. The time has now come to invite the student to go back to first principles, to consider the proper functions of the criminal law, and to analyse the meaning of criminal justice. Return to Chapter 1, and begin a further evaluation of the criminal justice process!

FURTHER READING

Annual Reports of HM Chief Inspector of Prisons for England and Wales, of the Probation Service, the Prison Service, the Parole Board etc

Baker, E, 'Dangerousness, Rights and Criminal Justice' (1993) 56 MLR 528

Bottoms, A, Gelsthorpe, L, and Rex, S, *Community Penalties: change and challenges* (2001) Willan

Carlen, P, *Sledgehammer: Women's Imprisonment at the Millennium* (1998) Macmillan

Corston Report, *A review of women with particular vulnerabilities in the criminal justice system* (2007)

Council of Europe Reports to the United Kingdom Government on Visits to the UK carried out by the European Committee for the Prevention of Torture and Inhuman and Degrading Treatment (<http://www.cpt.coe.int>)

Coyle, A, *Understanding Prisons: Key Issues in Policy and Practice* (2005) Open UP

Eastman, N and Peay, J, *Law without enforcement: integrating mental health with justice* (1999) Hart

Eaton, M, *Women After Prison* (1993) Open UP

Gelsthorpe, L and Morgan, R (eds), *Handbook of Probation* (2007) Willan

Gelsthorpe, L and Padfield, N (eds), *Exercising Discretion: Decision-making in the criminal justice system and beyond* (2003) Willan

Genders, E and Player, E, 'The commercial context of criminal justice: prison privatisation and the perversion of purpose' [2007] Crim LR 513

Grounds, A, 'Mental Health Problems' in Stockdale, E and Casale, S (eds), *Criminal Justice under Stress* (1992) Blackstone

Gunn, J et al, *Mentally Disordered Prisoners* (1991) Home Office

HM Chief Inspector of Prisons for England and Wales, *Women in Prison—a thematic review* (1997) Home Office

Hood, R and Shute, S, *Parole Decision-Making: Weighing the Risk to the Public* (2000) HO Research Findings No 114

Lacey, N, 'Discretion and Due Process at the Post-Conviction Stage' in Dennis, I H (ed), *Criminal Law and Justice* (1986) Sweet & Maxwell

Leibling, A, *Prisons and their Moral Performance* (2004) Oxford UP

Logan, C H, *Private Prisons, Pros and Cons* (1990) Oxford UP

Loughlin, M, 'The underside of the law: judicial review and the prison disciplinary system' (1993) 46 Current Legal Problems 23

Mair, G, Cross, N, and Taylor, S, *The use and impact of the community order and the suspended sentence order* (2007) CCJS

Morgan, R and Liebling, A, 'Imprisonment: An expanding scene' in Maguire, M, Morgan, R, and Reiner, R (eds), *The Oxford Handbook of Criminology* (4th edition, 2007) Oxford UP

Nash, M, *Police, Probation and Protecting the Public* (1999) Blackstone

Owen, T, Macdonald A, and Livingstone, S, *Prison Law* (4th edition, 2008) Oxford UP

Padfield, N, 'A Critical Perspective on Private Prisons in England and Wales' in Capus, N, et al (eds), *Public-Prive: vers un nouveau partage du controle de la criminalite?* (2005) Verlag Rüegger

Padfield, N, *Beyond the Tariff: Human Rights and the Life Sentence Prisoner* (2002) Willan

Padfield, N, 'The Parole Board in Transition' [2006] Crim LR 3

Padfield, N, (ed), *Who to release? Parole, fairness and criminal justice* (2007) Willan

Padfield, N and Liebling, A, with Arnold, H, *An Exploration of Decision-Making at DLPs* (2000) HO Research Findings No 132

Padfield, N and Maruna, S, 'The Revolving Door at the Prison Gate: Exploring the dramatic increase in recalls to prison' (2006) 6 Criminology and Criminal Justice 329

Peay, J, *Tribunals on Trial: A Study of Decision Making Under the Mental Health Act 1983* (1989) Clarendon Press

Peay, J, *Decisions and dilemmas: Working with mental health law* (2003) Hart

Peay J, 'Mentally disordered offenders, mental health and crime' in Maguire, M, Morgan, R, and Reiner, R (eds), *The Oxford Handbook of Criminology* (4th edition, 2007) Oxford UP

Polvi, N and Pease, K, 'Parole and its problems: a Canadian–English comparison' (1991) Howard Journal 218

Prison Reform Trust (2000) 'Justice For Women: The Need For Reform', The Report of the Committee on Women's Imprisonment, chaired by Professor Dorothy Wedderburn

Stern, V, *Creating Criminals: Prisions and People in a Market Society* (2006) Zed Books

Street, R, *The restricted hospital order: from court to community* (1999) Home Office Research Study No 186

Vagg, J, *Prison Systems: A Comparative Study of Accountability in England, France, Germany and the Netherlands* (1994) Clarendon Press

Valier, C, 'Litigation as a strategy in penal reform' (2004) 43 Howard Journal 15

DOCUMENTS

[10:1] Lord Carter, *Managing Offenders, Reducing Crime: A New Approach*
(2003) Summary (at pages 3–5)

Context of the review

Far greater use is being made of prison and probation, despite the number of people being arrested and sentenced remaining broadly constant.

- The use of prison and probation has increased by a quarter since 1996, whilst the use of fines has fallen by a similar amount. Sentencing practice has become more severe.
- One in four first-time domestic burglars were sent to prison in 1995/96.

By 2000, this had increased to one in two.
Tougher sentences have had some limited impact on crime.

- The increased use of prison is estimated to have reduced crime by around 5 per cent, compared to an overall fall of 30 per cent since 1997. Public confidence in sentencing has improved but remains fragile.
- The proportion of people believing sentencing to be "much too lenient" has fallen from one in two to one in three.

Additional investment in prison and probation since 1998 has improved delivery.

- The Prison Service has dramatically reduced the number of escapes, improved decency and increased the number of offenders achieving basic skills.
- The creation of the National Probation Service has given greater focus to performance management and seen the introduction of a range of new services. The objective now is to ensure that this additional investment is being used to best effect to reduce crime and maintain public confidence.

Current position

Sentences are poorly targeted and do not bear down sufficiently on serious, dangerous and highly persistent offenders.

- The increased use of prison and probation since 1997 has been concentrated on first time offenders, leading to poor use of additional investment. The variation in sentencing practice between areas remains too large.
- In Merseyside, Magistrates' Courts send one in four burglars to prison, compared to one in two in Staffordshire (despite the areas having the same burglary rates).

Judges and magistrates do not have sufficient information to make the most effective use of prison and probation and to take into account their capacity to deliver.

- This leads to increased overcrowding, reduced time spent by probation staff with offenders and poor transparency in sentencing with increased use of Home Detention Curfew.

The system remains dominated by the need to manage the two services, rather than focusing on the offender and reducing re-offending.

- There remain gaps in the system, with, for example, interventions in prison often not being followed up in the community.

The benefits of competition—from the private and voluntary sector—could be extended further, across both prison and probation.

- The introduction of competition in prisons has provided a strong incentive for improvements in public sector prisons.

Vision

A new approach is needed for managing offenders, to reduce crime and maintain public confidence.

Targeted and rigorous sentences

The Criminal Justice Act provides a platform for major reform and the more effective management of offenders in order to reduce crime and maintain public confidence.

- Judges and magistrates continue to need to have a full range of tough, credible and effective sentences that are enforced.
- Sentences need to reflect the seriousness of the offence and the risk of re- offending—with better targeting of serious, dangerous and persistent offenders.

This means:

- Diverting very low risk offenders out of the court system and punishing them in the community.
- Income-related fines for low risk offenders.
- More demanding community sentences for medium risk offenders.
- Greater control and surveillance (including satellite tracking) of persistent offenders, combined with help to reduce re-offending.
- Custody reserved for serious, dangerous and highly persistent offenders.

New role for the judiciary

Roles and responsibilities need to be clarified for the judiciary.

- Judges and magistrates need to continue to be able to make entirely independent sentencing decisions in individual cases.
- The judiciary needs to ensure the consistent and cost-effective use of prison and probation capacity and to ensure a clear understanding of the link between sentence given and sentence served.

The new Sentencing Guidelines Council provides an immediate opportunity to improve the effectiveness of sentencing.

- Each year the Council should discuss the priorities for sentencing practice with the Home Office. It should then issue guidelines that ensure offences are treated proportionately to their severity, are informed by evidence on what reduces offending and makes cost-effective use of existing capacity.
- The Sentencing Advisory Panel (which works to the Council) should be given responsibility for independently projecting future demand and should produce evidence on the effectiveness of different sentencing options in reducing crime and maintaining public confidence.

If there were new and convincing evidence on interventions that reduce crime then additional resources would need to be found (e.g. if greater use of custody was found to significantly reduce crime, more prisons would need to be built).

A new approach to managing offenders

Building on the significant improvements in delivery over the last seven years, a new approach is needed to focus on the management of offenders.

- Prison and probation need to be focused on the management of offenders throughout the whole of their sentence, driven by information on what works to reduce re-offending.
- Effectiveness and value for money can be further improved through greater use of competition from private and voluntary providers.

This means:

- The establishment of a National Offender Management Service—restructuring the Prison and Probation Services—with a single Chief Executive accountable to Ministers for punishing offenders and reducing re-offending.

- Within the new Service there should be one person—the National Offender Manager—who is responsible for reducing re-offending—supported by Regional Offender Managers. They would supervise offenders and commission custody places, fine collection and interventions—whether in the public, private or voluntary sector.

The Regional Offender Managers would break down the current silos of prison and probation and work across the two services. They would fund the delivery of specified contracts—based on evidence of what reduces re-offending—rather than leaving the services themselves to decide what to deliver.

[10:2] *Woolf Report—Prison Disturbances April 1990*
(1991) HMSO (at page 19)

1.167 Our programme is based on 12 central recommendations. These are that there should be:

 (i) closer co-operation between the different parts of the Criminal Justice System. For this purpose a national forum and local committees should be established;

 (ii) more visible leadership of the Prison Service by a Director General who is and is seen to be the operational head and in day to day charge of the Service. To achieve this there should be a published 'compact' or 'contract' given by Ministers to the Director General of the Prison Service, who should be responsible for the performance of the 'contract' and publicly answerable for the day to day operations of the Prison Service;

 (iii) increased delegation of responsibility to Governors of establishments;

 (iv) an enhanced role for prison officers;

 (v) a 'compact' or 'contract' for each prisoner setting out the prisoner's expectations and responsibilities in the prison in which he or she is held;

 (vi) a national system of Accredited Standards, with which, in time, each prison establishment would be required to comply;

 (vii) a new Prison Rule that no establishment should hold more prisoners than is provided for in its certified normal level of accommodation, with provisions for Parliament to be informed if exceptionally there is to be a material departure from that rule;

 (viii) a public commitment from Ministers setting a timetable to provide access to sanitation for all inmates at the earliest practicable date not later than February 1996;

 (ix) better prospects for prisoners to maintain their links with families and the community through more visits and home leaves and through being located in community prisons as near to their homes as possible;

 (x) a division of prison establishments into small and more manageable and secure units;

 (xi) a separate statement of purpose, separate conditions and generally a lower security categorisation for remand prisoners;

 (xii) improved standards of justice within prisons involving the giving of reasons to a prison for any decision which materially and adversely affects him; a grievance procedure and disciplinary proceedings which ensure that the Governor deals with most matters under his present powers; relieving Boards of Visitors of their adjudicatory role; and providing for final access to an independent Complaints Adjudicator.

1.168 In the following paragraphs and in the remainder of the Report we describe these recommendations more fully. They are central to resolving the problems which have been identified from the April disturbances. They are also a package. They need to be considered together and moved forward together if the necessary balance in our prison system is to be achieved.

[10:3] 'The Squeezed Capacity to Achieve the "Long Haul"'

Edited version of the Foreword by Andrew Bridges, HM Chief Inspector of Probation, to his Annual Report 2006/07 (July 2007)

For the fourth time now I find myself both proud and privileged to be presenting an annual report on behalf of HM Inspectorate of Probation. One of our key aims as an independent Inspectorate is to advise Ministers and the public what it is reasonable to expect probation and youth offending work to achieve, as well as advising how often that achievement is occurring. At a time when organisational change is becoming virtually a constant, I therefore now offer here our perspective on developments in the inspection world, and more importantly in the world of the work we inspect. With management of adult offenders, an area where we have previously said that a "Long Haul of gradual incremental improvement" is required, we see the capacity to achieve this being increasingly squeezed....

I turn now to the management of adult sentenced offenders. Here we have from the beginning warmly welcomed the principle of start-to-end management of each case, and the four purposes of punish, help, change and control, and we have been open-minded but cautious about the potential benefits of contestability. We have also argued that the way to bring about sustainable improvement in service will be through what we have called the "Long Haul of gradual incremental improvement" in performance, year on year, in each of the four purposes.

While it is possible for innovations, including further structural changes, to make a beneficial contribution, this can only be effective if applied with great care and patience. Meanwhile the really sustainable improvements are made by assiduous application to the "Long Haul" year on year. We still hold to this view, and our inspection findings over the last 12 months show some evidence of this process of sustainable incremental improvement starting to take place. However, we also see a major strategic threat to this progress in the form of an ever increasing squeeze on the capacity of the NOMS system to continue to deliver this. By capacity we mean not only resources in terms of money and people in relation to increasing demands, but also the other tools with which to do the job such as the IT infrastructure.

The 'business case'—or hypothesis—for NOMS was a sound one in principle, when it started in 2004: the prison population was steadily increasing, but most people agreed that although the more dangerous offenders should be locked up (and if necessary for longer), there were many other people currently in prison who could be managed more effectively in the community. The idea was that the use of prison sentences was to achieve an overall levelling off, and potentially a decline, and this would enable money to be spent on making management of offenders in the community both more widespread and more effective.

But this honourable intention has not been achieved in practice: the prison population has continued to increase (even though the overall level of crime is decreasing), and NOMS is having to accommodate this increased 'demand' from finite resources. NOMS has to build 8,000 new prison places now, and will almost certainly have to build several thousand more before too long, at a time when public expenditure has been fixed in real terms for the medium term future. Prison building is expensive of course, and it is almost inevitable that there will now be less money available to spend on offender management.

This is happening at a time when implicit public expectations of what offender management might be able to achieve in practice is continuing to rise to very unrealistic levels. There appears to be a growing assumption that an offender committing a further offence always constitutes a public service failure.

...

The combination over several years of increasing numbers of cases per officer, and increasing expectations about what is required to be achieved with each case, has made increasing demands a genuine part of the syndrome of squeezed capacity...it is clear to us that when the costs of new work, new requirements and new infrastructure have been taken into account, resources have in practice still not kept pace with the increasing demands.

Over the past ten years the increasing demands have included new Orders or requirements for drug treatment and testing, for accredited programmes and for managing prolific offenders, extended periods of post-release supervision, increased public protection expectations, enhanced standards of quality for unpaid work and other supervision requirements. Case numbers have also increased by taking in less serious offenders, due in part to pressures to meet national quantitative targets and in part due to the general increasing severity of Court sentencing—a decade earlier many such offenders would have been fined. In addition, a pay deal in 2006 for a layer of managers (excluding Chief Officers) that was agreed nationally must largely be funded locally.

Now the prospect of Offender Management, a principle almost everyone supports as a principle, risks being proven undeliverable in practice due to the additional increasing demands it will introduce. The Government was right to postpone the introduction of 'Custody plus' (statutory supervision after release of those serving shorter sentences) because of the capacity problem, but even so demands are continuing to increase faster than resources. This exacerbates the problem of public expectations rising faster than the capacity to satisfy them. The final point on this theme is infrastructure. There are at least two areas of significant increased expenditure in recent years: information technology (IT) and on NOMS HQ itself. Paying for both is necessary to make it possible to achieve a system of joined up management of offenders across England and Wales—but whether the amount being paid is proportionate to the benefit is open to question while the benefits are not yet being fully realised....

Our overall point here is not a proposal to pour extra resources unthinkingly into the problem but to highlight the contrast, which has developed slowly over a long period of time, between rising expectations and a squeezed capacity to meet them—the squeeze is a 'Long Squeeze'. As an organisation with a track record of taking a hard line on the issue of improving quality within existing resources or less, this Inspectorate is able to recognise when efficiency savings year-on-year reach their reasonable limits when demands are still increasing.

[10:4] *National Standards of Probation Service*
(2005 edition) Home Office

The following extracts give only an idea of their content.

Assessment of offenders before sentence

GS2 Where a court requests a report from the National Probation Service prior to sentencing, an appropriate assessment will be made of the offender's risk of harm and the likelihood of re-offending, in order to inform the court of a clear and realistic proposal for sentence or remand.

Bail Information

SS2.1 Bail information reports will:

- be written, objective, factual and impartial;
- if made orally when a written report cannot be prepared in time, be written up as soon as possible thereafter;
- satisfy the content, style and quality requirements defined in guidance by the National Probation Directorate;
- be targeted in accordance with the National Probation Directorate guidance.

SS2.2 In cases where risk of serious harm to the public is apparent, bail information reports will be copied to the police, social services or health authority as appropriate.

SS2.3 In cases where the defendant is subsequently remanded in custody, bail information reports will be copied, together with any other supporting documentation to the receiving prison.

SS2.4 Where a pre-sentence report is ordered following conviction or at the point of committal or allocation to Crown Court, a copy of the bail information report, if available, should be passed to the offender manager charged with preparing the report.

Pre-sentence reports

SS2.5 Offenders will be offered at least one face-to-face interview (which can be made via a video link where this is available and appropriate) in order to inform the report.

SS2.6 In all cases in which a report is requested, the National Probation Service will, as a minimum:

- obtain an OGRS score, giving a calculation of likelihood of reconviction;
- complete the OASys Risk of Harm screening tool;

SS2.7 Unless the court directs otherwise, a full OASys assessment does notneed to be completed if bothof the following conditions are met:

- the risk of harm screening shows that a full risk of harm analysis is not required and
- the OGRS score is less than 41

SS2.8 Unless the court directs otherwise, a full OASys assessment willbe completed if one or moreof the following conditions are met:

- the risk of harm screening shows that a full risk of harm analysis is required;
- the OGRS score is 41 or over;
- the court has adjourned for a full report because of the seriousness of the offence;
- the offender is a locally defined prolific or other priority offender.

SS2.9 Written reports to inform sentencing will:

- be based on the appropriate risk/needs assessment in accordance with SS2.6 to SS2.8;
- be objective, impartial, free from discriminatory language and stereotype, balanced, verified and factually accurate;
- only include information from the victim where it is drawn from the CPS papers or from a victim personal statement;
- satisfy the content, style and quality requirements defined in guidance by the National Probation Directorate;
- be completed using nationally approved report formats;
- be copied to the court, the defence, the defendant and (where required by section 159 of the Criminal Justice Act 2003) the prosecution.

SS2.10 Reports will make a clear proposal for sentence (including custody) taking into account the seriousness of the offence, and the purpose of sentencing.

SS2.11 Reports will make clear, in an outline sentence plan, what requirements are envisaged, including outline timescales, and how the sentence is likely to be implemented, including any plans for sequencing interventions.

SS2.12 Reports will be prepared within the timescale set by the commissioning court.

SS2.13 Where it has not been possible to complete a report for the court, for whatever reason, including non-attendance by the offender at interview, the report writer will notify the court at the earliest opportunity that a report will not be available for the hearing and submit in writing the reasons why the report has not been completed.

...

Enforcing the sentence

GS9 Where the offender fails to comply with the sentence, the offender manager will take steps to promptly enforce the requirements of the sentence.

Actions required following a failure to comply

SS9.1 For all offenders any failure to attend an appointment or any other failure to comply with any other requirement of a sentence should be deemed unacceptable unless the offender provides an acceptable explanation. A failure to comply will be considered as an unacceptable failure to comply only once in respect of any one day, regardless of the number of contacts arranged for that day, and an unacceptable failure to comply in relation to any requirement will count as one failure to comply with the whole sentence.

SS9.2 Where no explanation is provided within two working days of the apparent failure, the offender manager will send a letter to the offender warning that if no acceptable explanation is received within a further five working days of the date of the letter the failure will be deemed unacceptable and any further failure could lead to breach action.

SS9.3 If the offender provides an acceptable explanation within the above timescale, the offender manager will rescind the warning and ensure that the fact that the warning has been withdrawn is properly recorded on the offender's record.

SS9.4 If the explanation is unacceptable the offender manager will send a further letter drawing the attention of the offender to the warning already issued.

SS9.5 The offender manager will fully record every apparent failure within seven working days of the failure, including whether or not any explanation was given by the offender, and if so what that explanation was and whether or not it was acceptable.

SS9.6 If the explanation is not considered acceptable or no explanation is given within seven working days of the failure, the offender manager will record the incident as an unacceptable failure to comply.

SS9.7 The offender manager will place copies of any written warning on the offender's case record along with a note of the offender's comment on the warning.

Taking breach action

SS9.8 For all offenders, breach action may be taken after one unacceptable failure to comply, where appropriate.

SS9.9 For offenders on community sentences, the offender manager will give only one warning in any 12 month period of a sentence before commencing breach action.

SS9.10 For offenders released on licence, where breach action is not taken after one unacceptable failure to comply, the offender manager will give the offender a formal written warning of the consequences of further failure.

SS9.11 For offenders released on licence, where it is proposed not to take breach/recall action after a second unacceptable failure to comply, an officer of at least Assistant Chief Officer level, or equivalent grade, will confirm this course of action and give the offender a formal written warning.

SS9.12 For offenders released on licence, no more than two written warnings will be given within the total sentence period before commencing breach action.

SS9.13 For offenders released on licence, the offender manager will commence breach/recall action no later than the third unacceptable failure to comply. The offender manager is required to provide a Breach Notification Report, including a Risk Assessment, for the Early Release and Recall Section (ERRS) at the time of recall. The Risk Management Plan should be finalised and sent to ERRS within 15 days of the offender's return to custody.

SS9.14 Where breach proceedings are required, the offender manager will instigate these proceedings within 10 working days of the relevant failure to comply, or sooner if the offender poses a risk of harm to the public.

SS9.15 The offender manager will normally arrange further contacts in relation to the sentence requirements pending breach unless it is clear that the offender is completely uncooperative or disruptive, has a warrant outstanding, or that for other similar reasons arranging further appointments or work would serve no useful purpose and such a decision has been recorded and endorsed by the designated line manager.

SS9.16 The offender manager will ensure that the documentation to prove the breach and advise on sentencing is made available to the court dealing with the breach. Probation Areas should work in partnership with the courts to ensure that offenders appear in court and their cases are "resolved" within 25 working days of the second unacceptable failure (third for licences) unless there is a not guilty plea.

SS9.17 When an offender is charged with a serious offence this must be reported to the National Probation Directorate in the manner prescribed.

. . .

Working with victims

GS11 Victims, or their families, in cases involving a serious sexual or violent offence, which leads to a custodial sentence of 12 months or more, will be offered contact with the National Probation Service3.

Contact arrangements

SS11.1 A written offer of face-to-face contact between the victim (or victim's family) and local probation area/victim contact unit, or its agent, will be made within 40 working days of sentence.

SS11.2 Information will be provided to victims (or their families) about the criminal justice process.

Offender release arrangements

SS11.3 The offender manager will offer victims (or their families) the opportunity to give their views on proposed conditions surrounding the offender's release.

SS11.4 The offender manager will offer victims (or their families) the opportunity to see any part of the parole report which represents their views.

SS11.5 The offender manager will inform victims (or their families) of any conditions of release which relate to contact with the victim.

Information management

SS11.6 Information relating to victims (or their families) will be kept securely and separately from the offender's case record.

Note

3 In accordance with Section 69, Criminal Justice & Court Services Act 2000 and PC62/2001

[10:5] Worrall, A, *Punishment in the Community: Managing Offenders and Making Choices*

(2005) Willan (at page 205)

The final chapter of this book focuses on the future of punishment in the community (seen through the lens of 2004/05, of course), arguing that it is custody that should be seen as the alternative, and that probation officers 'must continue to engage with the social worlds that offenders inhabit' (at page 211).

Globalization of (community) punishment talk

The English-speaking world of probation and community corrections has been pre-occupied with a model of focused, accountable, standardized intervention in the lives of offenders, based on the actuarial concept of risk assessment, the science of cognitive behavioural psychology, the morality of individual responsibility and the politics of restorative justice. At the same time, that world has seen a dramatic rise in the prison population and a blurring of the boundary between freedom and custody. Offenders increasingly receive sentencing packages that involve time spent under supervision both inside and outside prison, and technology now makes it possible for many of the restrictions of imprisonment to be visited on offenders in their own homes and communities. In addition, practitioners are often overloaded with the bureaucratic demands of 'programme integrity' and evaluation, finding themselves with less and less time to consider the underlying values and philosophy of their work and thus making themselves vulnerable to the vagaries of crisis-driven law and order policy. The globalization of punishment talk has provided comforting prêt a manger solutions in the form of an international trade in penal ideas, of which 'What Works' is but one—the fast food of punishment in the community. Little account, it seems, need be taken of regional, let alone local differences of demography, culture or economy. So how do we make sense of these developments in the context of the globalization of crime and punishment discourses? How do we take advantage of the insights offered by global knowledge while at the same time taking account of national, regional and local differences? How can we learn from each other without being forced into adopting a bland and simplistic language which we *think* we all recognize but which may, in reality, mean very little to any of us? If the 'What Works' agenda is to be more than just a 'phase' in the treatment of offenders, then it needs to demonstrate that it has within it the seeds of its own development and adaptation to changing social, political and economic circumstances.

The question of *practice wisdom* involves national and international comparative research, in order to learn about approaches and programmes that are successful with particular types of offenders, in particular locations at particular times. Some will be cognitive-behavioural programmes that lend themselves to conventional forms of evaluation. But many more will have grown out of locally identified needs and resources, not the least of which will be enthusiastic and skilful individual workers. Not all will immediately reduce recidivism in any measurable way, but all will be aiming to influence offenders' attitudes, behaviour and circumstances, making them 'stop and think' before offending next time and thus offering the greatest hope of long- term protection for the public. In this search for practice wisdom, there is also a need to explore what *doesn't* work. It is part of the received wisdom of 'What Works' that intervention which focuses only on insight-giving or the therapeutic relationship and which does not include a problem-solving dimension is not successful with offenders. But what is less well publicised is that there is plenty of research on other things that don't work (Trotter 1999). These include approaches which focus on blame and punishment, those where the goals are set only by the worker rather than collaboratively, lack of clarity on the part of the worker about his or her role and authority, pessimism and a negative attitude by the worker and, finally, failing to see the offender in their family and social context.

The question of *political awareness* involves asking why the simple phrase 'What Works' has become so invested with meaning. Or is it precisely because it lacks meaning that it has become so ubiquitous? There are at least four interest groups whose purposes might be served by the 'What Works' agenda and whether those interests are to be viewed positively or negatively will depend entirely on one's standpoint:

- The interests of *governance* are served to the extent that the 'What Works' agenda demonstrates to a sceptical public that community sentences can be tough, demanding and based on scientific premises which can be tested and evaluated.

- The interests of *management* are served to the extent that the agenda demonstrates accountability—showing that resources are being used efficiently, effectively and, above all, economically—and giving managers confidence that they know exactly what their workers are doing and why.

- The interests of *professionalism* are served to the extent that the agenda reassures individual workers that they are doing something worthwhile with the minimum of risk to their own status—that the areas in which they have to exercise their own judgement are limited and consequently so is the potential for error, thus reducing the otherwise stressful nature of the job.

- Finally, the interests of *restorative justice* are served to the extent that the offender, victim and, possibly, the wider community believe that the agenda delivers on its promises. Whatever the content of any particular intervention, it can be argued that 'What Works' aims to instil in the offender a sense of responsibility towards the community in general and empathy for the victim in particular. But in return, the offender has the right to expect to be *reintegrated* into that community and unless that right is respected, 'What Works' becomes little more than a sophisticated form of the stocks—as indeed it is for many sex offenders who, no matter what programmes they have co-operated with, remain irredeemable and non-reintegratable in the eyes of the community.

[10:6] Martin, C, 'The voluntary sector and New Labour: how civil is the partnership?'
By Clive Martin, Director of Clinks, the organization which supports voluntary organizations working within the criminal justice system in England and Wales (in *Ten Years On... Criminal Justice Matters* (2007))

...a very basic but significant issue that won't go away—namely, that the voluntary sector is being pushed into becoming the cheap and equally mundane alternative to statutory provision. This has never been the sector's mission and we are right to be suspicious.

But is there any good reason for the sector's suspicion, especially for the offender-related voluntary and community sector (VCS)?

The first good reason to be suspicious is that our mission for social inclusion is being systematically undermined by the government's insistence on talking up crime and demonising people at risk.

There has been a consistent message from the voluntary sector and other stakeholders that the way the government is choosing to go about things is not an effective means of dealing with many offenders, especially those drawn into the criminal justice system because of the lack of resources elsewhere. The centuries of VCS experience of working with people in trouble with the law, and our role in public education, have at best been ignored, and at worst, treated with contempt.

Secondly, very basic VCS concerns have not been addressed. There has been no consistent investment in those crucially important sub-sectors that could make a substantial difference to the promotion of safe and inclusive communities. The black and minority ethnic sector that works specifically with offenders is shockingly under-funded with a recent grant of £250,000 representing almost all of the investment over the past five years. Is this because the work is not valued? Is it because the black and minority ethnic sector has little chance of playing a big role in the commissioning environment and is therefore of little relevance? The VCS that works with offenders' families is in a similar situation. It receives little investment despite the role that it plays in reducing inter-generational offending and supporting the parents and siblings of offenders—who are frequently also the innocent victims of crime.

So, while government ministers have been prepared to listen to views about different models of service delivery and the ways in which they might be commissioned, there has been no serious engagement with the sector about how to address the rise in the prison population and the criminalisation of so many people. Effective VCS initiatives that protect the public and work positively with offenders, such as 'Circles of Support and Accountability' and 'Smart Justice', barely get an audience, let alone funding.

As far as the VCS is concerned, it looks as if the government trusts the tabloid solutions to crime more than the world-class experiences and skills of the sector. This has left the sector feeling short-changed, and distrustful about the nature of the partnership with New Labour.

But this is not all that has disengaged the sector. We are being drawn into a battle that is not of our making. The sector's dynamic creativity has always ensured that we will make the most of opportunities when they are presented to us. We are not slow to take on new roles and relationships when they are presented. However, the government and Probation Service (and previously the Prison Service) have been at loggerheads for many years. They urgently need to sort out their differences so that the public can be served by a decent criminal justice system. The voluntary sector might well be part of the solution but we should not be part of the war. It is not our battle, nor do we have the remit or resources to fight it. We need to stay focused on the best interests of our service users and not get distracted by this statutory civil war.

So what are the possibilities for the future if the VCS are to believe that New Labour is a worthy partner? How is this for starters?

1. The VCS needs evidence that our mission, as well as our ability to deliver services, is respected, taken seriously, and will be acted upon.

2. It is imperative that the VCS is understood and supported as being the means by which services are transformed, and not as the repository of already-failing and discredited solutions.

3. The VCS has a fundamental role to play in promoting diversity and social inclusion and this needs investment—especially by those who are most affected by crime, for example BME communities and families.

4. Community education and public awareness about the reality of offending, social exclusion, and positive community solutions to crime remain at the heart of VCS activity—and should be supported by government actions and funding.

5. It needs to be understood that the role of the government is not to instruct the VCS or local communities about what to do, but to trust and facilitate the process by which local solutions can resolve the most pressing community problems.

[10:7] *The supervision of community orders in England and Wales*
(2008) National Audit Office (Value for Money Report: Executive Summary)

Summary

1 The Criminal Justice Act 2003 introduced a new style of community sentence, known as a community order. For offences committed after 1 April 2005, magistrates and judges have been able to tailor community sentences to the severity of the offence and, at the same time, address offending behaviour. This is done by creating an order with one or more of twelve possible requirements, such as unpaid work or drug rehabilitation, to be completed over a defined period. During 2006, the courts gave 121,690 community orders. The most common order contained a single requirement obliging the offender to complete a specified number of unpaid work hours (32 per cent of all orders).

2 The National Probation Service supervises all offenders subject to a community order, [Note 1] plus those released from prison on licence or given other sentences to be served in the community. During 2006–07, the 42 Probation Areas in England and Wales with direct responsibility for supervising offenders in the community spent £807 million. [Note 2] The Probation Service's total annual offender caseload has increased 32 per cent between 2001 and 2006, while staff increased by 35 per cent over the same period. [Note 3] The Offender Management Act 2007 allows providers outside the public sector to deliver probation services which will be commissioned on national, regional or local levels.

3 This report examines how well community orders are managed by the National Probation Service, in particular how well they have been implemented and whether they are meeting sentencing objectives.

Overall conclusion

4 In addition to punishment, community orders offer benefits to the community and offenders. Community orders enable offenders to stay with their families and in their jobs while they serve their

sentence and avoid additional pressure on the prison system (although this is not one of their primary purposes). A comparison between the actual reconviction rate and a predicted rate shows community sentences can reduce reconvictions proportionally more than a custodial sentence, although more evidence is required on the effectiveness of individual requirements (for example supervision).

5 Ninety four per cent of the orders we sampled were completed, breached or revoked by the court. [Note 4] One or more requirements within the remaining six per cent of orders had not been completed when the order expired, due to process and delivery reasons within Probation. No national data on non-completions is available. Some requirements, such as NHS-funded alcohol and mental health treatment, are not available in all Probation Areas, which could limit the effectiveness of an order if offending behaviour cannot be addressed.

6 Given the nature of demands placed on probation and a funding structure which imperfectly matches demand, the Probation Areas we visited are facing increasing challenges to provide probation services to the standard expected by both the courts and the public, which emphasises the importance of improving value for money.

7 The National Probation Service could improve efficiency by increasing the consistency with which community orders are implemented within and between local Probation Areas. Better data on capacity, costs and the number of orders completed as sentenced would help the Service demonstrate value for money in the management of community orders, and will be essential if the move to full commissioning and contestability of probation services, enabled by the 2007 Act is to be successful.

8 To build on the positive impact of community orders to date, our key findings are:
On the components of community orders:

- Some indicators show that community orders achieve positive outcomes such as improvements in offender attitude and behaviour. Recent Ministry of Justice research shows that participation in a group programme has positive effects on reconviction. [Note 5] However, more research and evaluation is required to determine the effectiveness of requirements, for example the supervision requirement, in achieving the desired sentencing outcomes.

- Some community order requirements, for example alcohol treatment which is largely funded by the National Health Service and delivered in partnership with other agencies, are not available or rarely used in some of the 42 Probation Areas (this is despite strong links between alcohol and offending behaviour). This means orders may not be addressing the underlying causes of offending behaviour as fully as they could.

On how community orders are implemented:

- Excluding cases where an offender is returned to court for failing to comply with their order, some requirements of an order remain uncompleted when the order expires. The National Offender Management Service's (NOMS) own data showed that in 2006–07 2.5 per cent of offenders did not complete their group programme before their order expired. Six per cent of the offenders in our case file review were unable to complete an order requirement before their order ended. Areas need to address the process and delivery issues within Probation which lead to non-completion of sentences given by courts. The chaotic lifestyles of offenders also contribute to the failure to complete requirements.

- There are long waiting lists for some order requirements, in particular group programmes on domestic violence, which increases the risk that requirements remain unfinished when the order ends.

- Neither local Areas nor NOMS can say whether sentences have been fulfilled because data on the completion of order requirements is not routinely reported.

- Estimates generated for this study of the costs of implementing community orders vary within and between Areas because of variations in the staff grades responsible for certain tasks and local procedures. For example, the Probation staff cost of managing a drug rehabilitation requirement ranges from £1,000 to £2,900 across the five Areas we visited.

On how community orders are resourced, monitored and reported:

- The Probation Service does not know with any certainty how many community orders it has the potential capacity to deliver within its resources, nor has it determined the full cost of delivering community orders. Since the potential capacity of the Service and local Areas is undetermined, the impact of any future changes in, for example, policy or sentencing trends is difficult to estimate and therefore manage.
- Funding of Probation Areas is imperfectly aligned with court demands in terms of the number and type of community orders given.

The Probation Service's performance targets do not focus sufficiently on outcomes, and in some instances targets can have the potential for unintended consequences. Central demands for data are perceived to be burdensome especially by smaller Probation Areas, and the information returned by the centre lacks sufficient analysis and detail for it to be as useful locally as it could be.

Recommendations: To demonstrate and improve effectiveness, the Ministry of Justice should in the near future:

1. Require Probation Areas to report the percentage of community orders which end before sentence requirements have been completed and the reasons for non-completion, such as breach, revocation by the court or lack of Probation capacity to deliver the requirements, in order to demonstrate effective service provision to sentencers and the local community.

2. Work with bodies such as the Department of Health and voluntary organisations to increase the provision of alcohol and mental health treatment across all Probation Areas to address the causes of offending behaviour.

3. As far as possible, rebalance the range of Probation performance targets to show how well offenders are being managed and the extent to which outcomes of community orders are achieved.

And in the longer term:

4. As far as possible, identify the degree to which the twelve community order requirements reduce reconvictions and achieve other sentencing outcomes for different types of offender to enable sentence planning to be better targeted, for instance through a longitudinal study assessing similar groups of offenders given different sentences. [Note 6]

To improve efficiency, the Ministry of Justice should in the near future:

5. Build on existing work to identify efficient operational practice, disseminate this across the Service and help local Areas implement changes to promote greater consistency in delivery between and within Areas.

6. Rationalise data demands on Areas.

To prepare for the introduction of full commissioning and contestability and enable value for money comparisons to be made, the Ministry of Justice should:

7. Determine the full cost range of implementing different types and volumes of community orders nationally, and assist individual Probation Areas to determine local costs.

8. Identify the capacity in terms of the number and mix of community orders the Service can manage nationally and assist local Probation Areas in identifying their capacity, for example by ascertaining the staff time available at each grade, time needed to manage all offenders under Probation supervision and the costs of services provided by other bodies.

9. Lengthen the funding cycle to three years and increase the flexibility of funding arrangements between Areas so resources can be redirected as necessary to better match courts' demands.

Scope and methodology

9 This report considers the delivery of community orders introduced by the Criminal Justice Act 2003 in England and Wales. To limit the study scope, the report does not consider suspended sentence orders [Note 7] or offenders under licence following release from custody who are supervised by the Probation Service. The number of offenders on licence, which are a priority for the Probation Service as they represent a large proportion of the high risk of serious harm offenders, rose by over 100 per cent between 1995 and 2006.

10 This report does not compare the effectiveness of community orders with the effectiveness of fines or custodial sentences because, in general, the types of offences for which those sentences are appropriate are different from those for which a community order is suitable. Our main sources of evidence are detailed in Appendix 2.

Notes

1. With the exception of those offenders subject to a stand-alone curfew monitored by an electronic tag or an attendance centre requirement.

2. Of the £807 million it is not possible to isolate how much is spent on community orders.

3. Research Development Statistics NOMS, Offender Manager Caseload Statistics 2006. The total offender caseload increased from 177,600 at the end of 2001 to 235,000 at the end of 2006.

4. Source: National Audit Office review of 302 offender case files. National data relating to the accredited programme requirement showed 97.5 per cent of programmes were completed, breached or revoked by the court in 2006–07 (see paragraph 3.4). Completion indicates all the order requirements given by the court were successfully completed before the period of the order expired. Breach occurs when an offender fails to comply with the terms of their order and is therefore returned to court. Probation staff can apply to the court for an order to be revoked if it is no longer considered appropriate to the offender's needs.

5. Research Development Statistics NOMS, Reconviction Analysis of Interim Accredited Programmes Software, September 2007. Group programmes, also known as 'accredited programmes', involve group sessions run by local Probation Areas to encourage offenders to behave differently. They cover topics such as drink driving and substance misuse.

6. Any comparison would have to control for the differences in predicted rates of re-offending and other characteristics for different offender cohorts.

7. If the offence committed breaches the custody threshold but the sentencer does not feel prison is appropriate they can sentence the offender to a suspended sentence order to be served in the community. The offender would be immediately sent to prison if they breached this order.

[10:8] Corston Report, *A review of women with particular vulnerabilities in the criminal justice system*
(2007) Home Office

1. This has been a short and economic review, not an in-depth lengthy resource intensive commission. In nine months I have held five consultation events, visited six women's prisons, three women's

community centres and one medium secure women's hospital. I have had over 40 meetings with individuals and groups and over 250 people have contributed in some way to my review. There is much more that could be done but I am confident that I have seen and heard enough to enable me to draw conclusions and make recommendations. I have interpreted my terms of reference liberally and sought to include all those women whom I regard as either inappropriately located in prison and all those outside who are at risk of offending. I consider these women in terms of their "vulnerabilities", which fall into three categories. First, domestic circumstances and problems such as domestic violence, child-care issues, being a single-parent; second, personal circumstances such as mental illness, low self-esteem, eating disorders, substance misuse; and third, socio-economic factors such as poverty, isolation and unemployment. When women are experiencing a combination of factors from each of these three types of vulnerabilities, it is likely to lead to a crisis point that ultimately results in prison. It is these underlying issues that must be addressed by helping women develop resilience, life skills and emotional literacy.

2. There are three important and very positive points that I want to make at the outset. First the number of self-inflicted deaths of women in prison custody has fallen. No one wishes to be complacent about this and every single death is one too many. Nevertheless, it is encouraging that the numbers have fallen from 14 in 2003 and 13 in 2004 to four in 2005 and three in 2006. I have no doubt that this reduction is in part due to the determined efforts of many staff and greatly improved drug treatment services in all women's prisons. The dark days of Waite Wing are, I hope, gone forever. Second, the provision of all types of health services within women's prisons has improved in recent years with prison health having been absorbed into the NHS and this is welcome. Third, I pay tribute to the many dedicated, caring staff working throughout all of the criminal justice agencies, who strive every day to provide a decent environment and improve the well-being of the women in their care. I have been very impressed by much of what I have seen.

3. I have, however, concluded that it is timely to bring about a radical change in the way we treat women throughout the whole of the criminal justice system and this must include not just those who offend but also those at risk of offending. This will require a radical new approach, treating women both holistically and individually—a woman-centred approach. I have concluded that there needs to be a fundamental re-thinking about the way in which services for this group of vulnerable women, particularly for mental health and substance misuse in the community are provided and accessed; there needs to be an extension of the network of women's community centres to support women who offend or are at risk of offending and to direct young women out of pathways that lead into crime.

4. Women have been marginalised within a system largely designed by men for men for far too long and there is a need for a "champion" to ensure that their needs are properly recognised and met. There is also a need for an integrated approach across government demonstrated by the creation of an Inter-Departmental Ministerial Group for women who offend or are at risk of offending supported by a Commission for this group of women as a visible, strategic lead. I have also concluded that there needs to be a re-design of women's custody introduced in parallel with other gender specific workable disposals and sanctions. I summarise below the main conclusions of my review. I also set out chapter-by-chapter all of my recommendations, which build into my Blueprint which can be found in Chapter 8 of my report.

Chapter 2. Men and women; equal outcomes require different Approaches—the need for a distinct approach

5. My first recommendation concerns the treatment of men and women within the criminal justice system. From April 2007 the government will have a statutory duty to take positive action to eliminate gender discrimination and promote equality under the Equality Act. I have seen little evidence that much preparatory work is in hand in respect of the imminent statutory duty or of any real understanding that treating men and women the same results in inequality of outcome. Equality does not mean treating everyone the same. The new gender equality duty means that men and women should be treated with equivalent respect, according to need. Equality must embrace not just fairness but also

inclusivity. This will result in some different services and policies for men and women. There are fundamental differences between male and female offenders and those at risk of offending that indicate a
different and distinct approach is needed for women. For example:

- Most women do not commit crime;
- Women with histories of violence and abuse are over represented in the criminal justice system and
  can be described as victims as well as offenders;
- The biological difference between men and women has different social and personal
  consequences;
- Proportionately more women than men are remanded in custody;
- Women commit a different range of offences from men. They commit more acquisitive crime and
  have a lower involvement in serious violence, criminal damage and professional crime;
- Relationship problems feature strongly in women's pathways into crime;
- Coercion by men can form a route into criminal activity for some women;
- Drug addiction plays a huge part in all offending and is disproportionately the case with women;
- Mental health problems are far more prevalent among women in prison than in the male prison
  population or in the general population;
- Outside prison men are more likely to commit suicide than women but the position is reversed
  inside prison;
- Self-harm in prison is a huge problem and more prevalent in the women's estate;
- Women prisoners are far more likely than men to be primary carers of young children and this
  factor makes the prison experience significantly different for women than men;
- Because of the small number of women's prisons and their geographical location, women tend to
  be located further from their homes than male prisoners, to the detriment of maintaining family
  ties, receiving visits and resettlement back into the community;
- Prison is disproportionably harsher for women because prisons and the practices within them have
  for the most part been designed for men;
- Levels of security in prison were put in place to stop men escaping;
- The women's prison population suffers disproportionately because of the rapidly increasing male
  prison population and the pressure to find places for men, leading to re-roling of female prisons;
- 30% of women in prison lose their accommodation while in prison; and Women and men are
  different.
- Equal treatment of men and women does not result in equal outcomes.

Recommendation

Every agency within the criminal justice system must prioritise and accelerate preparations to implement the gender equality duty and radically transform the way they deliver services for women.

Chapter 3. Life and death. How women experience prison—the need for a *radically different* approach

6. These were the women I saw in prisons:

- Most were mothers. Some had their children with them immediately prior to custody, others had
  handed them to relatives or their children had been taken into care or adopted.
- Some were pregnant. Some discovered they were pregnant when they had no idea that that could
  be a possibility.
- They were drug users. It was not uncommon to have £200 a day crack and heroin habits disclosed.

- They were alcoholics.
- They often looked very thin and unwell.
- They had been sexually, emotionally and physically abused.
- They were not in control of their lives.
- They did not have many choices.
- They were noisy and at first sight confident and brash but this belied their frailty and vulnerability and masked their lack of self-confidence and esteem.
- They self harmed.
- They had mental health problems.
- They were poor.
- They were not all the same, they were individuals.
- There were significant minority groups, including BME and foreign national women.

7. A soon-to-be published report of women in custody explains how women recounted the stress that came from newly encountering the prison environment, with crowding, noise and a threatening atmosphere. They were alarmed at sharing cells with women with mental health problems and who self-harmed; they were frightened and unprepared when confronted with women who were suffering severe drug withdrawal or seizures. They complained that the prison environment was dirty with unhygienic sharing of facilities. Five women in a dormitory could be sharing one in-cell sink, which was being used for personal washing as well as cleaning eating utensils. There was a lack of fresh air and ventilation. Some women reported that vermin were present in the areas where they ate, slept and stored their personal food items. Prison facilities hindered them from maintaining self-care, including limited access to personal hygiene products and restricted access to bathing. Shower facilities were often dirty. I too was dismayed to find that in some of the prisons I visited there were toilets, often without lids, in cells and dormitories, sometimes screened by just a curtain, sometimes not screened at all. It is humiliating for women to have to use these facilities in the presence of others, most particularly during menstruation.

8. The following describes a typical ten-day period in a women's local prison:

- A woman had to be operated on as she had pushed a cross-stitch needle deep into a self-inflicted wound.
- A woman in the segregation unit with mental health problems had embarked on a dirty protest.
- A pregnant woman was taken to hospital to have early induced labour over concerns about her addicted unborn child. She went into labour knowing that the Social Services would take the baby away shortly after birth.
- A young woman with a long history of self-harm continued to open old wounds to the extent that she lost dangerous amounts of blood. She refused to engage with staff.
- A woman was remanded into custody for strangling her six-year old child. She was in a state of shock.
- A woman set fire to herself and her bedding.
- The in-reach team concluded that there was a woman who was extremely dangerous in her psychosis and had to be placed in the segregation unit for the safety of the other women until alternative arrangements could be made.
- A crack cocaine addict who displayed disturbing and paranoid behaviour (but who had not been diagnosed with any illness) was released. She refused all offers of help to be put in touch with community workers.

9. We must find better ways to keep out of prison those women who pose no threat to society and to improve the prison experience for those who do. One example is the regular, repetitive, unnecessary overuse of strip-searching in women's prisons which is humiliating, degrading and undignified and a dreadful invasion of privacy. For women who have suffered past abuse, particularly sexual abuse, it is an appalling introduction to prison life and an unwelcome reminder of previous victimisation. It is also clear that prison is not the right place for many women. They need help and caring, therapeutic environments to assist them rebuild their lives. This is not an easy option; it is demanding a great deal of women to delve into issues they prefer to block out. For those with drug addictions clinical detoxification does not stop the habit. Those women for whom prison is necessary would clearly benefit from being in smaller units closer to home or more easily accessible for visitors, such as in city centres. The existing system of women's prisons should be dismantled and replaced by smaller secure units for the minority of women from whom the public requires protection.

Recommendations

The government should announce within six months a clear strategy to replace existing women's prisons with suitable, geographically dispersed, small, multi-functional custodial centres within 10 years.

Meanwhile, where women are imprisoned, the conditions available to them must be clean and hygienic with improvements to sanitation arrangements addressed as a matter of urgency.

Strip-searching in women's prisons should be reduced to the absolute minimum compatible with security; and the Prison Service should pilot ion scan machines in women's prisons as a replacement for strip-searching women for drugs. The work underway in respect of foreign national offenders should take account of the views expressed in my report. The strategy being developed should include measures designed to prevent prison becoming a serious option.

Deaths in custody and bereaved families

10. In Chapter 3 of my report I describe the circumstances of some recent self-inflicted deaths of women in prison and the grief these tragedies cause to their families. Most depressing was the familiarity of these events, which followed the same patterns time and again with little indication that lessons were being learned to prevent further deaths. I make a recommendation concerning families' access to public funding for legal representation at inquests. The state has unlimited access to legal funding and will always have legal representation and Counsel at inquests that engage Article 2 of the European Convention on Human Rights, the right to life. It is inequitable that families whose close relatives have died whilst being cared for by the state should undergo means testing when applying for legal funding to represent their interests.

Recommendation

Public funding must be provided for bereaved families for proper legal representation at timely inquests relating to deaths in state custody that engage the state's obligations under Article 2 of the European Convention on Human Rights. Funding should not be means tested and any financial eligibility test should be removed whenever Article 2 is engaged. Funding should also cover reasonable travel, accommodation and subsistence costs of families' attendance at inquests.

Chapter 4. Who's in charge? The need for visible leadership and a strategic approach

. . .

Seven pathways to resettlement

13. I considered work in hand in connection with the seven resettlement pathways which I fear are leading to fragmentation of services and funding streams. Many of the small voluntary agencies working with women do not fit exclusively into a sole pathway and these artificial divisions risk putting an intolerable administrative burden on these small bodies. I looked closely at the pathway on accommodation because that is women's greatest resettlement concern on release and it seems to me to be the pathway most in need of speedy, fundamental gender specific reform. I also spent some time during my review considering education, learning, training and skills because this is a subject in which I have a particular interest and which seemed to me during my visits and meetings very sadly lacking in the concept of emotional literacy, the base from which all learning must start. Respect for one another, forming and maintaining relationships, developing self-confidence, simply being able to get along with people without conflict must come before numeracy and literacy skills. Life skills, for example, how to live as a family or group, how to contribute to the greater good, how to cook a healthy meal, are missing from the experiences of many of the women in modern society who come in contact with the criminal justice system. The chaotic lifestyles and backgrounds of many women result in their having very little employment experience or grasp of some very basic life skills. Two additional pathways for women have been developed to the credit of the Prison Service Women and Young People's Group and I recommend that they should be mandatory in every regional resettlement plan for women, namely:

- Pathway 8: support for women who have been abused, raped or who have experienced domestic violence.
- Pathway 9: support for women who have been involved in prostitution.
- …

And finally

28. An additional 8,000 places for men are planned and a reported £1.5 billion is being sought to fund them. Unless the current sentencing trend can be reversed, more must follow. A much smaller level of funding would provide an opportunity for government to do something innovative for women. I do not pretend that my proposals will free up hundreds of prison places overnight. It will take time and determination and persistence but I do believe that, if my package of recommendations is implemented, over time the women's prison population will decrease. Another factor that makes this the right time to take action is that new commissioning arrangements are currently being worked up by the National Offender Management Service. The time is right to adopt a new approach to women in the criminal justice system, with central drive and direction at the highest level of a long-term strategy, coupled with a sound structure for commissioning services.

[10:9] Prison Act 1952 (as amended)

Sections 1; 47

1 General control over prisons

All powers and jurisdiction in relation to prisons and prisoners which before the commencement of the Prison Act 1877 were exercisable by any other authority shall, subject to the provisions of this Act, be exercisable by the Secretary of State.

47 Rules for the management of prisons, remand centres and young offender institutions

(1) The Secretary of State may make rules for the regulation and management of prisons, remand centres, young offender institutions or secure training centres respectively, and for the classification, treatment, employment, discipline and control of persons required to be detained therein.

(2) Rules made under this section shall make provision for ensuring that a person who is charged with any offence under the rules shall be given a proper opportunity of presenting his case.

(3) Rules made under this section may provide for the training of particular classes of persons and their allocation for that purpose to any prison or other institution in which they may lawfully be detained.

(4) Rules made under this section shall provide for the special treatment of the following persons whilst required to be detained in a prison, that is to say—

    (d) any...person detained in a prison, not being a person serving a sentence or a person imprisoned in default of payment of a sum adjudged to be paid by him on his conviction or a person committed to custody on his conviction.

(4A) Rules made under this section shall provide for the inspection of secure training centres and the appointment of independent persons to visit secure training centres and to whom representations may be made by offenders detained in secure training centres.

(5) Rules made under this section may provide for the temporary release of persons detained in a prison, remand centre, young offender institution or secure training centre not being persons committed in custody for trial before the Crown Court or committed to be sentenced or otherwise dealt with by the Crown Court or remanded in custody by any court.

[10:10] *Hague v Deputy Governor of Parkhurst Prison*
[1991] 3 All ER 733

Hague was deemed to be a trouble-maker, and was transferred to another prison, where he was removed from association under rule 43 of the Prison Rules. The Court of Appeal had granted a declaration that, because of errors of procedure, the removal had been unlawful, but refused *certiorari* and damages. Weldon alleged that he had been forcibly dragged downstairs and detained without clothes overnight in a strip cell. The (differently constituted) Court of Appeal had refused to strike out that part of the statement of claim which was based on false imprisonment. The House of Lords in both cases was concerned not with judicial review, but only with civil actions for breach of statutory duty and false imprisonment.

Lord Bridge (at page 737):

My Lords, there are two appeals before the House. I shall refer to them as Hague's case and Weldon's case respectively. They raise important questions with respect to the rights of convicted prisoners.

Introduction

The decisions of the Court of Appeal in *R v Hull Prison Board of Visitors, ex p St Germain* [1979] 1 All ER 701, [1979] QB 425 and of this House in *Leech v Deputy Governor of Parkhurst Prison* [1988] 1 All ER 485, [1988] AC 533 established that the courts have jurisdiction to entertain applications for judicial review of disciplinary awards made by boards of visitors and by prison governors respectively under the Prison Rules 1964, SI 1964/388. In both cases it had been contended, in effect on behalf of the Home Office, that jurisdiction should be declined on the ground that any interference by the courts in the management of prisons would be subversive of prison discipline. In *Leech's* case [1988] 1 All ER 485 at 499, [1988] AC 533 at 566, as I record, Mr Laws had urged that, if jurisdiction were accepted in relation to awards by prison governors, this would 'make it impossible to resist an invasion by what he called 'the tentacles of the law' of many other departments of prison administration'. In deciding the appeal your Lordships faced that prospect without undue alarm and I believe that the circumstances of *Hague's* case now before the House show that it was right to do so. In *Hague's* case both courts below held that they had jurisdiction to entertain an application for judicial review which questioned the legality of Hague's segregation under r 43 of the Prison Rules and the Court of Appeal declared that the procedure followed pursuant to the terms of a Home Office circular issued in 1974 (Circular Instruction 10/1974) was not warranted by the terms of the rule and was accordingly unlawful. In your

Lordships' House the Secretary of State, acting by Mr Laws, has chosen, very sensibly if I may say so, not to pursue any challenge either to the assumption of jurisdiction or to its exercise by the declarations granted. Instead the Home Office have issued a new circular prescribing a new procedure to be followed in future in the relevant circumstances which conforms to the requirements of r 43 as construed by the Court of Appeal. I believe this confirms the view that the availability of judicial review as a means of questioning the legality of action purportedly taken in pursuance of the Prison Rules is a beneficial and necessary jurisdiction which cannot properly be circumscribed by considerations of policy or expediency in relation to prison administration. Those considerations only come into play when the court has to consider, as a matter of discretion, how the jurisdiction should be exercised. But the issues which it is necessary to resolve in the present appeals relate neither to the scope of the courts' public law jurisdiction in judicial review nor to the exercise of discretion in that jurisdiction. The appeals raise the wholly different question whether a convicted prisoner who, in the course of serving his sentence, has been treated in a way which the rules do not permit has in any and what circumstances a cause of action in private law sounding in damages against the prison governor or the Home Office on the ground either of a breach of statutory duty or of the tort of false imprisonment.

(At page 739:)

Breach of statutory duty

It was not open to counsel for Hague in any court below your Lordships' House to advance a claim to damages for breach of statutory duty because of the decision of the Court of Appeal in Becker v Home Office [1972] 2 All ER 676, [1972] 2 QB 407, where one of the grounds on which it was held that the plaintiff failed was that a breach of the Prison Rules does not, per se, give rise to a cause of action. But Mr Sedley has now put the claim for damages in Hague's case on this alternative basis in the forefront of his argument and I think it logical to consider it first.

In *Becker v Home Office* [1972] 2 All ER 676, [1972] 2 QB 407 both Lord Denning MR and Edmund Davies LJ expressed their conclusion that a breach of the Prison Rules 1964 creates no civil liability in equally general terms. Mr Sedley submits that such a general approach is erroneous and that each provision in the rules must be considered separately. Whilst I do not accept this criticism of the earlier authorities, I do accept that we may properly be invited in asking the question whether the breach of a particular provision of the rules gives rise to a cause of action to examine that provision in its context. Adopting that course, I can find nothing in r 43 or in any context that is relevant to the construction of r 43 which would support the conclusion that it was intended to confer a right of action on an individual prisoner. The purpose of the rule, apart from the case of prisoners who need to be segregated in their own interests, is to give an obviously necessary power to segregate prisoners who are liable for any reason to disturb the orderly conduct of the prison generally. The rule is a purely preventive measure. The power is to be exercised only in accordance with the procedure prescribed by sub-r (2). But where the power has been exercised in good faith, albeit that the procedure followed in authorising its exercise was not in conformity with r 43(2), it is inconceivable that the legislature intended to confirm because of action on the segregated prisoner.

(At page 742:)

False imprisonment

The Court of Appeal in *Weldon's* case approached the question whether a prisoner serving his sentence can ever sustain a claim for false imprisonment, as they were invited to do so by Mr Laws, as a single question which must admit of the same answer irrespective of the identity of the defendant. Ralph Gibson LJ, delivering the leading judgment, with which both Fox and Parker LJ agreed, said ([1990] 3 All ER 672 at 681, [1990] 3 WLR 465 at 474): 'There is no reason, apparent to me, why the nature of the tort, evolved by the common law for the protection of personal liberty, should be held to be such as to deny its availability to a convicted prisoner whose residual liberty should, in my judgment, be protected so far as the law can properly achieve unless statute requires otherwise. If, however, as [Mr Laws] submits, the tort of false imprisonment is not available to a convicted prisoner against a prison officer, I accept his submission that it could not, for the same reasons, be available to a convicted prisoner against a fellow prisoner.'

Ralph Gibson LJ had also delivered the judgment of the Divisional Court in *Hague's* case in which he expressed the view that the segregation of a prisoner would not constitute the tort of false imprisonment if the order for segregation, although not lawfully authorised under r 43, was given in good faith. Giving the judgment in *Weldon's* case he found it unnecessary to express a final conclusion on this point since, if want of good faith were a necessary ingredient of the tort, he held that it was sufficiently alleged in the pleading against the officers concerned. The pleading, he held, also alleged circumstances capable of amounting to 'intolerable conditions of detention' such as would sustain a claim of false imprisonment on the authority of the decision of the Court of Appeal in *Middleweek v Chief Constable of the Merseyside Police* [1990] 3 All ER 662, [1990] 3 WLR 481. It was on these grounds that the Court of Appeal declined to strike out the pleading of false imprisonment in *Weldon's* case. Parker LJ, in adding his own reasons to his agreement with those given by Ralph Gibson LJ, was clearly much concerned with the problem of the rights of prisoners as against fellow prisoners or prison officers acting in bad faith. He said ([1990] 3 All ER 672 at 686, [1990] 3 WLR 465 at 480):

'Although the plaintiff may, in the end, fail to establish the facts, we must proceed for the moment on the basis that he was kept locked up naked overnight in a cell known as a strip cell. It is said that as he was lawfully detained in the prison this cannot amount to false imprisonment. If this be right it must I think follow that he could have had no claim for false imprisonment if his detention naked in that cell had continued for weeks. It would also seem to me to follow that if he had been locked up in a similar condition, not by prison officers, but by fellow inmates, he would have no such claim. It would follow, too, that, if a convicted criminal were confined in a prison which he and his fellows were permitted, within the confines of a perimeter fence enclosing some acres of ground, to lead normal lives he would have no such claim if he were locked up, with or without clothes, in a shed in some remote part of the grounds, whether by fellow inmates or prison officers. To hold that such treatment could not amount to false imprisonment offends in my judgment against common sense.'

In so far as the Court of Appeal's reasoning in these judgments proceeds from the premises urged upon them by Mr Laws that a prisoner's 'right to liberty' is either totally abrogated or partially retained in the form of a 'residual liberty', I think, with all respect, that it is erroneous. To ask at the outset whether a convicted prisoner enjoys in law a 'residual liberty', as if the extent of any citizen's right to liberty were a species of right in rem or a matter of status, is to ask the wrong question. An action for false imprisonment is an action in personam. The tort of false imprisonment has two ingredients: the fact of imprisonment and the absence of lawful authority to justify it. In *Meering v Grahame-White Aviation Co Ltd* (1919) 122 LT 44 at 54 Atkin LJ said that 'any restraint within defined bounds which is a restraint in fact may be an imprisonment'. Thus if A imposes on B a restraint within defined bounds and is sued by B for false imprisonment, the action will succeed or fail according to whether or not A can justify the restraint imposed on B as lawful. A child may be lawfully restrained within defined bounds by his parents or by the schoolmaster to whom the parents have delegated their authority. But if precisely the same restraint is imposed by a stranger without authority, it will be unlawful and will constitute the tort of false imprisonment.

I shall leave aside initially questions arising from the situation where a convicted prisoner serving a sentence is restrained by a member of the prison staff acting in bad faith, by a fellow prisoner or any other third party, or in circumstances where it can be said that the conditions of his detention are intolerable. I shall address first what I believe to be the primary and fundamental issue, viz whether any restraint within defined bounds imposed upon a convicted prisoner whilst serving his sentence by the þrison governor or by officers acting with the authority of the prison governor and in good faith, but in circumstances where the particular form of restraint is not sanctioned by the Prison Rules, amounts for that reason to the tort of false imprisonment. The starting point is s 12(1) of the Prison Act 1952 which provides: 'A prisoner, whether sentenced to imprisonment or committed to prison on remand pending trial or otherwise, may be lawfully confined to any prison.'

This provides lawful authority for the restraint of the prisoner within the defined bounds of the prison by the governor of the prison, who has the legal custody of the prisoner under section 13, or by any prison officer acting with the governor's authority. Can the prisoner then complain that his legal rights are infringed by a restraint which confined him at any particular time within a particular part of the prison? It seems to me that the reality of prison life demands an alternative answer to this question. Certainly in the ordinary closed prison the ordinary prisoner will at any time of day or night be in a particular part of the prison, not because that is where he chooses to be, but because that is where the prison regime required him to be. He will be in his cell, in the part of the prison where he is required to work, in the exercise yard, eating meals, attending education classes or enjoying whatever recreation is permitted, all in the appointed place and at the appointed time and all in accordance with a more or less rigid regime to which he must conform. Thus the concept of the prisoner's 'residual liberty' as a species of freedom of movement within the prison enjoyed as a legal right which the prison authorities cannot lawfully restrain seems to be quite illusory. The prisoner is at all times lawfully restrained within closely defined bounds and if he is kept in a segregated cell, at a time when, if the rules has not been misapplied, he would be in the company of other prisoners in the workshop, at the dinner table or elsewhere, this is not the deprivation of his liberty of movement, which is the essence of the tort of false imprisonment, it is the substitution of one form of restraint for another.

Mr Harris seeks to surmount these difficulties by submitting that whenever there is a breach of the rules which is sufficiently 'fundamental' this converts an otherwise lawful imprisonment into an unlawful imprisonment. This, as I understand it, is quite a different concept from that of an infringement of residual liberty. The submission is that any breach of the rules which is sufficiently far reaching in its effect on the prisoner, for example the failure to supply him with clothing 'adequate for warmth and health' pursuant to r 20(2), undermines the legality of his imprisonment. Logically this would lead to the conclusion that the prisoner who has not been supplied with proper clothing would be entitled to walk out of the prison, but Mr Harris understandably disclaims any such extravagant proposition. It follows that the authority given by s 12(1) for lawful confinement of the prisoner cannot possibly be read as subject to any implied term with respect to compliance with the Prison Rules and this is fatal to any submission which seeks to make the lawfulness of the imprisonment depend in any sense on such compliance.

In my opinion, to hold a prisoner entitled to damages for false imprisonment on the ground that he has been subject to a restraint upon his movement which was not in accordance with the Prison Rules would be, in effect, to confer on him under a different legal label a cause of action for breach of statutory duty under the rules. Having reached the conclusion that it was not the intention of the rules to confer such a right, I am satisfied that the right cannot properly be asserted in the alternative guise of a claim to damages for false imprisonment.

(At page 745:)

There remains the question whether an otherwise lawful imprisonment may be rendered unlawful by reasons only of the conditions of detention. In *R v Metropolitan Police Comr, ex p Nahar* (1983) Times, 28 May, two applicants for habeas corpus who had been remanded in custody were held pursuant to the provisions of s 6 of the Imprisonment (Temporary Provisions) Act 1980 in cells below the Camberwell Green Magistrates' Court which were designed only to enable persons to be held in custody for a few hours at a time and which were obviously deficient in many respects for the purpose of accommodating prisoners for longer periods. They sought their release on the ground that the conditions of their detention rendered it unlawful. The applications were rejected, but Stephen Brown J said in the course of his judgment: 'There must be some minimum standard to render detention lawful...' McCullough J said: 'Despite the temporary nature of the detention there contemplated, there must be implied into s 6 of the 1980 Act some term which relates to the conditions under which a prisoner may lawfully be detained. I say so because it is possible to conceive of hypothetical circumstances in which the conditions of detention were such as would make that detention unlawful. I do not propose to offer any formulation of that term. Were it broken in any particular case I would reject emphatically the suggestion that the matter would not be one for the exercise of the court's jurisdiction to grant the writ of habeas corpus.'

These observations were considered by the Court of Appeal in *Middleweek v Chief Constable of the Merseyside Police* [1990] 3 All ER 662, [1990] 3 WLR 481. The plaintiff has been awarded damages for false imprisonment by the jury on the basis that his otherwise lawful detention at a police station has been rendered unlawful because it was unreasonable in the circumstances to keep him in a police cell. The defendant successfully appealed, but Ackner LJ, delivering the judgment of the court, said ([1990] 3 All ER 662 at 668, [1990] 3 WLR 481 at 487):

> 'We agree with the views expressed by the Divisional Court that it must be possible to conceive of hypothetical cases in which the conditions of detention are so intolerable as to render the detention unlawful and thereby provide a remedy to the prisoner in damages for false imprisonment. A person lawfully detained in a prison cell would, in our judgment, cease to be so lawfully detained if the conditions in that cell were such as to be seriously prejudicial to his health if he continued to occupy it, eg because it became and remained seriously flooded, or contained a fractured gas pipe allowing gas to escape into the cell. We do not therefore accept as an absolute proposition that, if detention is initially lawful, it can never become unlawful by reasons of changes in the conditions of imprisonment.'

I sympathise entirely with the view that the person lawfully held in custody who is subjected to intolerable conditions ought not be to left without a remedy against his custodian, but the proposition that the conditions of detention may render the detention itself unlawful raises formidable difficulties. If the proposition be sound, the corollary must be that when the conditions of detention deteriorate to the point of intolerability, the detainee is entitled immediately to go free. It is impossible, I think, to define with any precision what would amount to intolerable conditions for this purpose. McCollough J understandably and perhaps wisely abstained from any attempt of definition in *Ex p Nahar*. The examples given by Ackner LJ of a flooded or gas-filled cell are so extreme that they do not, with respect, offer much guidance as to where the line should be drawn. The law is certainly left in a very unsatisfactory state if the legality or otherwise of detaining a person who in law is and remains liable to detention depends on such an imprecise criterion and may vary from time to time as the conditions of his detention change.

The logical solution to the problem, I believe, is that if the conditions of an otherwise lawful detention are truly intolerable, the law ought to be capable of providing a remedy directly related to those conditions without characterising the fact of the detention itself as unlawful. I see no real difficulty in saying that the law can provide such a remedy. Whenever one person is lawfully in the custody of another, the custodian owes a duty of care to the detainee. If the custodian negligently allows, or a fortiori, if he deliberately causes, the detainee to suffer in any way in his health he will be in breach of that duty. But short of anything that could properly be described as a physical injury or an impairment of health, if a person lawfully detained is kept in conditions which cause him for the time being physical pain or a degree of discomfort which can properly be described as intolerable, I believe that could and should be treated as a breach of the custodian's duty of care for which the law should award damages. For this purpose it is quite unnecessary to attempt any definition of the criterion of intolerability. It would be a question of fact and degree in any case which came before the court to determine whether the conditions to which a detainee had been subjected were such as to warrant an award of damages for the discomfort he had suffered. In principle I believe it is acceptable for the law to provide a remedy on this basis, but that the remedy suggested in the *Nahar* and *Middleweek* cases is not. In practice the problem is perhaps not very likely to arise.

Conclusion

For the reasons I have given I conclude that a claim for damages either for breach of statutory duty or for false imprisonment is not sustainable in either of the cases before the House.

[10:11] Hood, R and Shute, S, *Parole in Transition: Evaluating the Impact and Effects of Changes in the Parole System: Phase Two*
(1994) Oxford Centre for Criminological Research No 16 (at page 46)

1 Summary

(i) The new criteria

§96 From the summer of 1992 onwards, several changes in decision-making procedures were introduced which affected the consideration of prisoners sentenced under the 'old system'. The most important of these was the Home Secretary's announcement that the new criteria, laid down under section 32(6) of the 1991 Act to govern release under the DCR system, would, from 1 October 1992, also apply to old system cases. According to these criteria, before recommending parole, the Parole Board must be satisfied that:

'(a) the longer period of supervision that parole would provide is likely to reduce the risk of further imprisonable offences being committed. In assessing the risk to the community, a small risk of violent offending is to be treated as more serious than a larger risk of non-violent offending;

(b) the offender has shown by his attitude and behaviour in custody that he is willing to address his offending and has made positive efforts and progress in doing so;

(c) the resettlement plan will help secure the offender's rehabilitation.'

These are referred to in this report as Criteria RO, OB and RP respectively.

§97 Other changes were also introduced which affected old system cases. First, the number of Board members who sit on 'panels' which review parole applications was reduced from four to three. Second, six salaried full-time members were appointed in August 1993. Third, early in March 1994, the Board began to formulate detailed reasons in writing relating to the established criteria so that, should there be a judicial review of the decision, the reasons would be available for scrutiny. It was not intended that these reasons, which were required both for granting and for refusing parole, should yet be communicated to prisoners sentenced under the old system. But they were intended to encourage panels to frame their reasons in the form that would be necessary when, later in 1994, they were to be conveyed to all prisoners.

...

§99 From August 1993 to May 1994, we observed 24 panels at which 545 prisoners serving sentences of four years and more who had been sentenced under the old system were considered for parole. Eighteen of the panels were held before the Board began to record full reasons for its decisions in writing: these panels considered 423 long-term old system cases. Once full reasons were recorded, we attended a further six panels which dealt with 122 old system cases. In general, we have compared the base-line sample of 383 observed cases with the total 545 cases observed in phase two. However, where necessary, we have analysed the two samples separately.

§100 We received the parole dossiers in advance (as we had in the base-line study) and were privileged to have been able to take full notes—as far as possible verbatim—of all that was discussed. We were also sent copies of the 'panel result sheets', which record the decisions made and any reasons given.

§101 As in all evaluative studies which attempt to chart the outcome of change by comparing samples taken before and after that change has occurred, a fundamental question is the extent to which the samples are similar in respect of other factors which might influence the results. We were able to identify sufficient points of objective similarity between the two samples to feel confident in making comparisons between them. Using the data available we found that three variables were strongly associated with the probability of release. They were: the Local Review Committee (LRC) recommendation as 'suitable' or 'unsuitable'; our classification of a case as 'high risk' or not; and whether the case was at first or last review. We have, where appropriate, used these variables as a 'control' when comparing the decisions made by the Board in the base-line and phase two samples.

(ii) The board at work

§102 In the report of the base-line study, we remarked on the fact that panels rarely had an even distribution of members representing the various statutory categories: judges, psychiatrists, probation officers, criminologists and independents. An obvious consequence of reducing the size of panels from four persons to three has been to dilute the contribution that could be made by the 'expert' members. Thus, whereas in the base-line period independents outnumbered 'experts' on seven of the 16 panels (44%), in phase two they did so on 16 of the 24 panels (67%). Indeed, there were three panels in phase two on which only independent members sat. However, the greater preponderance of independents did not mean that any group sharing a similar background and experience (for example, former prison officials) predominated. It was noticeable that panels less often had an input from a probation officer: they were present on only a quarter of panels in phase two compared with over half of the panels in the base-line study. No criminologist member was present at any of the panels in phase two: indeed, there were only two of them on the Board.

. . .

2 Conclusions

§145 Reducing the size of panels—from five or six members in the early years of the scheme, to four members, and finally to three members in 1993—has radically altered the Board as originally conceived. It was envisaged that every case would be considered by persons drawn from each of the five categories set down in the statute. That no longer happens. The Carlisle Committee's warning—when it considered (and rejected) the possibility of a reduction in panel size from four to three—that 'the inter-disciplinary nature of panels would be impaired' has come to pass. This raises the important question of how best the Board can function effectively as a multi-disciplinary body.

§146 During the period covered by our field work, serious delays no longer appeared to be a major problem, although at first review they still occurred and in a few cases seriously disadvantaged the parole applicant. This is a matter which needs to be kept constantly under review.

§147 The requirement to give full written reasons means that the Board now takes considerably longer to reach and formulate its decisions. This may have implications for the workload of panels, especially if reasons have to be even fuller than those now given.

§148 The replacement of the former criteria for *refusal* (A–F) by criteria for *release* has inevitably shifted the focus of decision-making from considerations which could be either positive or negative to a presumption that parole will not be granted unless all three criteria are met.

§149 The pattern of parole decisions has changed. In some respects the Board is more liberal than it was prior to the introduction of the new criteria; in other respects it appears to be as restrictive on release as it was under the 'restricted policy'. The White Paper *Crime, Justice and Protecting the Public* (Cm 965, 1990) stated that the proposed new criteria 'are sufficiently stringent to replace the present restricted policy on parole'. This assessment has proved to be correct.

§150 Prisoners reviewed before they would be eligible under the DCR scheme were more likely to be released under the new criteria because of the ban on what is known as 'resentencing' (ie, insisting that those whose offences are regarded with distaste serve a longer proportion of their sentence in custody).

§151 Prisoners not released early in their sentence are less likely than formerly to be released at subsequent reviews, especially if the Board considers that they pose a high risk of committing a serious offence. This was so, even though they would not receive any supervision on release. We therefore predict that the reduction in the rate of release of 'high-risk' prisoners which has been due to the application of the new criteria will be even greater for such cases considered under the new DCR system.

§152 Nothing can be done (apart from shorter sentences being imposed) to alter the impact on the prison population of the change in the law which no longer allows DCR prisoners to be released before half their sentence has been served. We estimated, from the average number of days spent on parole licence prior to the halfway point of the sentence, by what percentage the length of prison sentences would have to be cut in order to ensure that prisoners who had earned parole before halfway under the old system would not have served longer in prison had they been sentenced under the DCR scheme and released at halfway. Our conclusion was that the sentences of such prisoners would have to be cut, on average, by 21 per cent.

§153 In relation to 'high-risk' prisoners, the way in which the Board reacts to the availability in the DCR scheme of supervision after two-thirds of the sentence may not remain constant. Everything depends on whether Board members believe that the statutory supervision provided between two-thirds and three-quarters of the sentence is sufficient to ensure that the public are protected and on how often they believe that 'the longer period of supervision that parole would provide is likely to *reduce* the risk of further imprisonable offences being committed' (Criterion RO; emphasis added). However, we know from this phase of our research that the new criteria have already had the effect of markedly reducing the proportion granted parole, even without the availability of statutory supervision after release at EDR. The Carlisle Report, on which much of the DCR scheme was based, certainly did not envisage that the extension of supervision for a period after EDR would mean that 'high-risk' cases would almost always fail to get 'parole' (ie, discretionary early release).

§154 The dossiers of prisoners considered under the DCR scheme should all contain newly calculated reconviction prediction scores, which show the probability of reconviction at monthly intervals over a two-year period separately for 'any offending' and for 'serious offending (resulting in a custodial sentence)'. In the final phase of this research it will be possible to see whether these scores are more often referred to and used as a basis for decision-making. We should also be able to gauge whether there is more consensus among Board members on how the score should be interpreted and the weight that ought to be placed on it.

§155 Prisoners' own 'reps' were not very influential in decisions whether or not to release. Nor was much attention paid to what the prisoner had told the LRC member. It remains to be seen whether the interview reports made by Parole Board members on DCR cases will prove to be more influential.

§156 When we interview prisoners and staff again in the final phase of this project, it will be interesting to see how they have responded to the rehabilitative challenge which has been introduced by the new criteria, particularly as reasons will have to be communicated to prisoners in writing.

§157 Although the reasons given for refusing parole were more detailed than they used to be, they were still rather brief. The next phase of this research should be able to show whether, in the light of judicial review, they will become more substantial and, if so, in what ways.

§158 Some interesting questions are raised by the finding that, in the majority of cases recommended for release, Board members failed specifically to record that they were satisfied that each of the three criteria had been met. This suggests that at least some prisoners are released who do not meet all three criteria and that the Board has exercised its discretion in their favour by weighing one criterion against others. In any event, Board members appear to favour an approach to reason giving which takes these criteria 'into account' rather than being bound by them. In this context, it is worth recalling that section 32(6) of the Criminal Justice Act 1991 gives the Home Secretary power to 'give to the Board directions as to the matters to be taken into account'. Some may argue that this is different from giving the Secretary of State power to *mandate* that a combination of specific criteria *must* be met before release can be recommended.

§159 The centrality of the problem of dealing with 'high-risk' prisoners under the new criteria raises the question of how accurate the Board is in predicting the likelihood of such prisoners committing very serious offences, both while on licence and in the period before the expiry of their sentence. In the base-line and in phase two of this study, 463 prisoners were having their last review, of which 148 were considered by Board members to pose a serious risk to the public. It would be valuable to follow-up the criminal records of all these prisoners, whether released on parole or not, in order to record the patterns of reconviction both for cases the Board identified as 'high risks' and those regarded as lesser risks. This would make it possible to assess to what extent the Board had correctly identified those who posed the greatest threat of committing a grave offence on release from prison. It might also be possible to assess if a period on parole lowered the risk of a 'high-risk' prisoner committing such a crime.

[10:12] Hood, R and Shute, S, *Parole Decision-making: Weighing the Risk to the Public*

(2000) HO Research Findings No 114 (at pages 2–4)

The research aimed to assess the effectiveness and efficiency of the parole system. It examined:

- how the Parole Board assessed applications
- whether interviews conducted by Parole Board members made a difference to the decisions reached
- the relationship between parole decisions and actuarially-based risk assessment scores
- reasons given for refusing or granting parole
- how probation officers' recommendations influenced parole decisions.

There are various stages in parole decision-making. In addition to the information in a prisoner's dossier (which includes details of the offence, previous convictions and reports from prison and probation officers), Parole Board Interviewing Members (PBIMs) visit prisons to interview prisoners about their parole application. Their reports are added to prisoners' dossiers and forwarded to the Parole Board. Three-member panels of the Board meet in London and on each occasion consider the dossiers of 24 parole applicants. Dossiers are read in advance and at the meeting members take it in turns to 'lead' the discussion, having prepared reasons for their decision which may be amended after discussion.

Research Methods

The research was carried out in two linked phases:

- 151 PBIM interviews were observed in 14 prisons and the prisoners and PBIMs concerned were interviewed
- interviews with 63 seconded probation officers, 112 prison officers and 103 prisoners who had recently been refused parole
- questionnaires were sent to the prisoners' home probation officers.

In addition, 20 Parole Board panel meetings were observed where the applications of the 151 prisoners were discussed along with others. Information was gathered on decisions made about 437 prisoners. Panel members were asked about the value of the PBIM report. They were also asked to make an assessment of the risk of reconviction posed by each prisoner.

Decision-Making

Members of panels rarely disagreed. The lead member's opinion was confirmed in 82% of cases. In a further 10%, the lead member's opinion was confirmed after some dissent and discussion. The final decision differed from that initially expressed by the lead member in only 8% of the cases observed. A prediction model of parole decision-making was calculated on the basis of data extracted from the prisoners' dossiers but not including the PBIM report. The model correctly predicted both Yes and No decisions in 85% of cases:

- 49% of the prisoners had a very low probability of release (between 0%–20%); only 4% of them were released

- at the other end of the scale, 17% had a very high probability of parole (80% and above); 89% were paroled

- taking these together, Parole Board decisions for 65% of prisoners were predicted by the statistical model with 94% accuracy.

With so many decisions correctly predicted from other information in the dossier, there was little room for the PBIM report to have a substantial impact on the decisions made. Indeed, those who drafted the reasons for the panel's decision said that their decision had been changed by something contained in the PBIM report in only 8% of cases.

The Parole Rate

Power to release on parole is now called Discretionary Conditional Release (DCR) and applies to those prisoners sentenced to four years or longer. The only valid comparison that can be made between the parole rate before and after the introduction of DCR is the proportion of prisoners in both periods who received parole at some time prior to having served two-thirds of their sentence. Of those serving four years or more who were reviewed between June 1992 and May 1995, under the old system, 69.7% were released on parole. By comparison, the latest Report of the Parole Board for 1998–99 shows that 47.7% of prisoners dealt with under the DCR system from its inception in October 1992 until March 1999 were granted parole. Thus, 22% fewer prisoners are now paroled during their sentence—equivalent to a 32% decline in the use of parole.

Reasons that might explain this decline are:

- the introduction of the Directions, which gave priority to risk, and the way that Board members have interpreted these Directions

- that under the new DCR system all prisoners are supervised after release whether paroled or not, whereas formerly prisoners only received supervision if granted parole

- that most prisoners now only get one parole review, whereas under the old system they had at least two.

Granting or Refusing Parole

As required by the Directions, panels, in their written reasons, placed great emphasis on risk factors and on whether or not prisoners had 'satisfactorily addressed their offending behaviour'—by completing an offending behaviour treatment course, for example.

When the panel refused parole, specific indicators of risk were mentioned in 84% of cases. These were mostly based on the prisoner's past history—factors such as the seriousness of the offence, previous history of sexual or violent offending, previous failure to respond to supervision and breaches of bail.

Progress, or lack of progress, made by the prisoner in addressing offending behaviour was the reason mentioned in 96% of refusals and 98% of cases where parole was granted. In a third of the cases refused, the panel stressed that 'more work' should be done, or should be 'consolidated' in prison, rather than while under parole supervision in the community.

Panels mentioned in their reasons that 73% of prisoners granted parole had 'satisfactory release plans'. However, in only one-third of cases where parole was granted did the panel state in their reasons that risk would be further reduced by a period on parole supervision. This perhaps suggests that members of the Board do not have a great deal of confidence in the effectiveness of parole supervision as a method of containing or reducing risk.

More than 80% of the refused prisoners who were interviewed said that the reasons they had been given were 'unfair'. Three-quarters said that the reasons given had not made them change their behaviour, and nearly all the rest said they had responded negatively to the 'knock back'.

Licence Conditions

The average period of parole licence granted to the paroled prisoners was 330 days. Before the introduction of DCR, 44% of prisoners were paroled with further conditions attached to their licence (see Hood and Shute, 1994 and 1995). In this study, 87% had conditions attached. For example, of those paroled, 52% had a residence condition in comparison with 15% under the old system. 82% were released on condition they continued to deal with their offending behaviour (including drugs, alcohol, anger and sexual behaviour) in comparison with 32%. Furthermore, 44% of those paroled had three or more conditions attached. All prisoners are now supervised on release from prison whether paroled or not. 60% of those not paroled (who formerly had no conditions at all) had at least three conditions attached on release from prison. Thus, the degree of control over prisoners after release has increased and widened.

Parole Related to Reconviction Risk

The risk of a prisoner committing further offences if released on parole licence is the main consideration of the Board. Parole decisions can be compared with actuarial, objectively determined risk of reconviction data. A risk of reconviction score (ROR) has been calculated by Copas et al., 1996, on the basis of a follow-up study of a large number of prisoners. Parole decisions in this study were analysed, separately for non-sex and sex offenders, in relation to the ROR for a serious offence (one likely to lead to imprisonment) during the period available for parole. The findings for non-sex offenders are shown in Table 1.

TABLE 1 Relationship between ROR for a serious offence on parole licence and parole decision (for non-sex offenders)

Actuarial risk of reconviction	No. of cases observed	Cases paroled (No.)	Cases paroled (%)	Percentage of cases in each risk group
0%–2%	52	43	83	15%
3%–7%	115	58	50	33%
Total (to 7%)	167	101	61	48%
8–16%	100	22	22	29%
17%	78	6	8	23%
Total (8%+)	178	28	16	52%

As can be seen in Table 1, there was a strong and statistically significant correlation between actuarial ROR and the parole decision so far as non-sex offenders were concerned. Although half of the sex offenders had a ROR of 7% or less (average 3.7%), 40% of them were denied parole, demonstrating the Board's considerable caution.

The Board was even more cautious in relation to sex offenders. Only 22% of those with a risk of reconviction rate of 7% or less (average 3.2%) were paroled. As the ROR was not a major factor explaining which sex offenders did and did not get parole, a different prediction score was calculated drawing on the formula devised by Dr David Thornton of HM Prison Service. This categorises prisoners into three risk levels and takes into account whether or not the prisoner has completed a Sex Offender Treatment Programme. The findings showed that the statistical risk of reconviction according to the Thornton scale was a less strong predictor of parole than whether the prisoner had successfully completed a Sex Offender Treatment Programme. Amongst those who had done so, the parole rate was virtually the same whatever their risk category.

'Clinical' assessments of risk compared with 'actuarial' risk

Panel members have to rely on their own 'clinical' assessment as the actuarially-based ROR score for each prisoner is not available to them. Their assessment of risk was compared with the actuarial risks calculated by Copas et al. The findings showed that panel members were making decisions on the basis of unduly pessimistic 'clinical' estimations of risk when compared with the actuarial risk calculation:

- 85% of prisoners had a statistical rate of reconviction of a serious offence during parole period in the 'low' category (0–19%). Half of them had a ROR of 7% or less. Yet, Board members estimated risk of reconviction to be 20% or higher for more than half the prisoners they assessed

- 73% of the sex offender cases fell into the lower Levels I and II of the Thornton sex offender predictor. Yet, Board members assessed the risk to be equivalent to Level III in more than half the cases.

Probation Officers' Reports

There was a strong correlation between parole decisions and the recommendations made by both seconded probation officers in the prison and home probation officers (see Table 2). If probation reports were negative the chances of getting parole were close to zero. However, over 40% of prisoners recommended by both probation officers were refused parole. This may partly explain why half of the prisoners interviewed said they found the reasons they had been given 'hard to take'.

TABLE 2 The relationship between probation officers' (seconded probation officers in prison and the prisoner's home probation officer) recommendations and parole decisions

Recommendation	Paroled		Total	
	No.	%	No.	%
Both recommended parole	133	54	247	56
Only one recommended parole	11	18	60	14
Neither recommended parole	3	2	131	30

Low-Risk Offenders and Parole

The study assessed what the consequences would be if the parole rate for low risk offenders was increased. Estimates were made of what the effect would have been if the Parole Board had released on parole all prisoners who had both a low actuarial risk of reconviction (ROR of 7% or less) for a serious offence while on parole licence and a recommendation from both probation officers.

The average risk of these prisoners being reconvicted of an offence while on parole for which they would be likely to receive a further prison sentence was less than four in a 100. Because they have such a low risk of reconviction, their inclusion amongst all parolees would actually reduce the average rate of reconviction from 6.2% to 5.7%.

If this group of prisoners had been released, the parole rate in the sample would have risen from 33.6% to 43.2%, which is equivalent to an increase of 29%. Translating this into a national estimate, this would mean that approximately 550 more prisoners would be released on parole annually. Of these, about 500 could be expected to complete parole without a conviction of any kind. Given the expense of imprisonment compared with supervision in the community, the cost of not granting parole to these low risk offenders is considerable.

Policy Implications

Procedural implications

- Both the degree of unanimity in decision-making and the ease of predicting parole decisions on the basis of recorded information raise the question of whether a formal meeting of three Board members in London is necessary for every case and, if not, how best the resources available might be used.

- The time and expense involved in the use of Parole Board Interviewing Members could be reassessed in view of the marginal role played by their reports in decision-making. Perhaps the prisoner's case could be communicated to the Board in a different way.

- There appears to be a strong argument for including an updated ROR score in parole dossiers. In a system that gives priority to risk, it is essential that risk should be assessed as accurately as possible, both to protect the public and to ensure that the liberty of low-risk prisoners is not unnecessarily restricted.

Wider implications

The 1988 Parole Review Committee (Carlisle Committee), whose recommendations led to the reform of the system by the 1991 Act, expected that, by moving the eligibility date forward from one-third to a half a sentence, and by providing supervision for all prisoners whether paroled or not, a higher, not a lower, proportion of prisoners would be granted parole. This has not happened. While the findings of this research show that parole decisions are in line with the Home Secretary's Directions, these Directions, together with the Board's interpretation of them, have undoubtedly created a more risk-averse approach than originally expected by the Carlisle Committee.

It will always be necessary to strike a balance between the risk to the public and the liberty that might be accorded the individual prisoner. These findings question whether the right balance has been found.

References

Copas, J.B., Marshall, P. and Tarling, R. (1996) *Predicting reoffending for Discretionary Conditional Release*. Home Office Research Study No. 150. London: Home Office.

Hood, R.G. and Shute, S.C (1994, 1995) *Evaluating the impact and effects of changes in the Parole System*. University of Oxford, Centre for Criminological Research. Occasional Papers Nos. 13 and 16. Oxford: University of Oxford.

[10:13] *Thynne, Wilson and Gunnell v United Kingdom*
(1991) 13 EHRR 666

The three applicants had been separately convicted of serious offences and sentenced to discretionary life sentences. All three applicants complained about the lack of regular judicial scrutiny of the lawfulness of their detention and, in the cases of the second and third applicants, re-detention. The court held, by a majority of 18 to 1, that there had been a violation of Article 5(4) of the European Convention on Human Rights, and in the case of the third applicant, also a violation of Article 5(5).

(At page 693:)

73 As regards the nature and purpose of the discretionary life sentence under English law, the Government's main submission was that it is impossible to disentangle the punitive and 'security' components of such sentences. The court is not persuaded by this argument: the discretionary life sentence has clearly developed in English law as a measure to deal with mentally unstable and dangerous offenders; numerous judicial statements have recognised the protective purpose of this form of life sentence. Although the dividing line may be difficult to draw in particular cases, it seems clear that the principles underlying such sentences, unlike mandatory life sentences, have developed in the sense that they are composed of a punitive element and subsequently of a security element designed to confer on the Secretary of State the responsibility for determining when the public interest permits the prisoner's release. This view is confirmed by the judicial description of the 'tariff' as denoting the period of detention considered necessary to meet the requirements of retribution and deterrence.

74 The court accepts the Government's submissions that the 'tariff' is also communicated to the Secretary of State in cases of mandatory life imprisonment; that the Secretary of State in considering release may not be bound by the intimation of the 'tariff'; and that in the assessment of the risk factor in deciding on release the Secretary of State will also have regard to the gravity of the offences committed.

However, in the court's view this does not alter the fact that the objectives of the discretionary life sentence as seen above are distinct from the punitive purposes of the mandatory life sentence and have been so described by the courts in the relevant cases.

75 It is clear from the judgments of the sentencing courts that in their view the three applicants, unlike Mr Weeks, had committed offences of the utmost gravity meriting lengthy terms of imprisonment. Nevertheless, the court is satisfied that in each case the punitive period of the discretionary life sentence has expired.

In the case of Mr Thynne, it was accepted that by the end of 1984 risk was the sole remaining consideration in his continued detention.

In addition to the life sentence imposed on him for the offence of buggery, Mr Wilson was sentenced in 1972 to seven years' imprisonment for each of the nine other counts to be served concurrently. In the circumstances of his case it would seem reasonable to draw the conclusion that the punitive period of his life sentence has expired when he was released in 1982 and that thereafter his re-detention pursuant to that sentence depended solely on the risk factor.

In Mr Gunnell's case, too, it may be taken that, notwithstanding the gravity of his offences on which the courts laid particular emphasis, the applicant had served the punitive period of his sentence by March 1982, the date fixed for his provisional release.

76 Having regard to the foregoing, the court finds that the detention of the applicants after the expiry of the punitive periods of their sentences is comparable to that at issue in the *Van Droogenbroeck* and *Weeks* cases—the factors of mental instability and dangerousness are susceptible to change over the passage of time and new issues of lawfulness may this arise in the course of detention. It follows that at this phase in the execution of their sentences, the applicants are entitled under Article 5(4) to take proceedings to have the lawfulness of their continued detention decided by a court at reasonable intervals and to have the lawfulness of any re-detention determined by a court.

(At page 695:)

79 Article 5(4) does not guarantee a right to judicial control of such scope as to empower the 'court' on all aspects of the case, including questions of expediency, to substitute its own discretion for that of the decision-making authority; the review should, nevertheless, be wide enough to hear on those conditions which, according to the Convention, are essential for the lawful detention of a person subject to the special type of deprivation of liberty ordered against these three applicants.

80 The court sees no reason to depart from its finding in the *Weeks* judgment that neither the Parole Board nor judicial review proceedings—no other remedy of a judicial character being available to the three applicants—satisfy the requirements of Article 5(4). Indeed, this was not disputed by the Government.

C Recapitulation

81 In conclusion, there has been a violation of Article 5(4) in respect of all three applicants.

[10:14] *Doody v Secretary of State for the Home Department*
[1993] 3 All ER 92

The four applicants were separately convicted of murder and received mandatory sentences of life imprisonment. Under the procedure adopted by the Secretary of State for the exercise of his discretionary power under section 61(1) of the Criminal Justice Act 1967 to decide the date on which a person serving a mandatory life sentence for murder could be released on licence, the trial judge and the Lord Chief Justice were invited to express their views on the period which the prisoners should serve for the purpose of retribution and deterrence (the 'tariff' period). The four applicants had each been told the date of the first review of their cases by the Parole Board, and considered that the Secretary of State had increased the tariff periods recommended by the judiciary. They sought declarations that:

 (i) the Secretary of State was required to adopt the judicial view of the penal element of the sentence;

 (ii) the prisoner was entitled to make representations before the Secretary of State set the date for the first review and, for that purpose, the right to be told of any information on which the Secretary of State would make his decision; and

(iii) the prisoner was entitled to be told the judicial view of the penal element of his sentence, the reasons for the recommendations of the judiciary and for any departure by the Secretary of State from that recommendation.

The House of Lords held that, whilst it was the Secretary of State, not the judges, who was entrusted with the task of deciding on prisoners' release, and that he was entitled to depart from the judge's advice, prisoners were entitled to be treated fairly.

Lord Mustill (at page 105):

Once it is concluded that the judicial opinion is not conclusive, and that it is the decision of the Home Secretary that matters, the opinion of the judges becomes no more than a component of the entire body of material in the light of which that decision is made.

Thus, although it is tempting to approach the question of disclosure and reasons as if it were the judges' opinions to which the applications for judicial review are directed this is mistaken. It is the decision of the Home Secretary which vitally affects the future of the prisoner, and it is the openness of this decision which is essentially in dispute. Although the shape of the arguments presented in the courts below led those courts to begin the inquiry with the judges' opinions, and hence to progress to the reasons for those opinions, and finally to a consideration of whether the reasons of the Home Secretary for departing from the judges' opinions should be disclosed, I prefer to go directly to the opposite end of the process to consider the prisoner's rights in relation to the decision by the Home Secretary. I emphasise once again that the court is not being asked to review and could not with any hope of success be asked to review this scheme in its entirety, the more so since the judges have themselves being playing an important part in it for the past ten years. Nor of course is it the task of the court to say how it would choose to operate the scheme if given a free hand. The only issue is whether the way in which the scheme is administered falls below the minimum standard of fairness.

What does fairness require in the present case? My Lords, I think it unnecessary to refer by name or to quote from, any of the often-cited authorities in which the courts have explained what is essentially an intuitive judgment. They are far too well known. From them, I derive the following. (1) Where an Act of Parliament confers an administrative power there is a presumption that it will be exercised in a manner which is fair in all the circumstances. (2) The standards of fairness are not immutable. They may change with the passage of time, both in the general and in their application to decisions of a particular type. (3) The principles of fairness are not to be applied by rote identically in every situation. What fairness demands is dependent on the context of the decision, and this is to be taken into account in all its aspects. (4) An essential feature of the context is the statute which creates the discretion, as regards both its language and the shape of the legal and administrative system within which the decision is taken. (5) Fairness will very often require that a person who may be adversely affected by the decision will have an opportunity to make representations on his own behalf either before the decision is taken with a view to producing a favourable result, or after it is taken, with a view to procuring its modification, or both. (6) Since the person affected usually cannot make worthwhile representations without knowing what factors may weigh against his interests fairness will very often require that he is informed of the gist of the case which he has to answer.

(At page 111:)

Before leaving this question, I wish to make it absolutely clear that if your Lordships are in agreement with this conclusion this will not be a signal for a flood of successful applications for judicial review. I repeat for the last time that Parliament has left the discretion on release with the Home Secretary, and that he has done nothing to yield it up. So long as this remains the case, prisoners should not deceive themselves into believing that they can obtain leave to move for judicial review simply by pointing to a difference between the opinion of the judges and the decision of the Home Secretary. Only if it can be shown that the decision may have been arrived at through a faulty process, in one of the ways now so familiar to practitioners of judicial review, will they have any serious prospect of persuading the court to grant relief.

This will result in an order in the following form:

> 'It is declared that: (1) The Secretary of State is required to afford to a prisoner serving a mandatory life sentence the opportunity to submit in writing representations as to the period he should serve for the purpose of retribution and deterrence before the Secretary of State sets the date of the first review of the prisoner's sentence. (2) Before giving the prisoner the opportunity to make such representations, the Secretary of State is required to inform him of the period recommended by the judiciary as the period he should serve for the purposes of retribution and deterrence, and of any other opinion expressed by the judiciary which is relevant to the Secretary of State's decision as to the appropriate period to be served for these purposes. (3) Secretary of State is obliged to give reasons for departing from the period recommended by the judiciary as the period which he should serve for the purpose of retribution and deterrence.'

[10:15] *Stafford v United Kingdom*
(2002) 35 EHRR 1121

This case concerned the power of the Home Secretary not to accept a recommendation of the Parole Board to release on licence an offender subject to a mandatory life sentence whose previous licence had been revoked. The court accepted that all life sentences are made up of two parts: the first, the punishment element of the sentence, is a sentencing exercise, not the administrative implementation of the sentence of the court. The second part, imposed for the protection of the public because of the offender's dangerousness, should be reviewed regularly by a body with a power to release, and under a procedure with the necessary judicial safeguards, including, for example, the possibility of an oral hearing. The court held unanimously that there had been a violation of both Article 5(1) and Article 5(4) of the European Convention on Human Rights in the case before it. The Home Secretary should not have the power to detain post-tariff lifers against the recommendation of the Parole Board. The court acknowledged that the Convention is a dynamic tool.

58 The applicant disputed that the true objective of the mandatory life sentence was life-long punishment. He remained the only mandatory life prisoner who had been detained post-tariff on the basis that the Secretary believed that he might commit a non-violent offence if released. Different considerations might apply where a risk of drug trafficking was concerned as such activity was clearly capable of causing physical or psychological harm to others. To justify indefinite imprisonment by reference to a belief that he might on release commit a non-violent crime involving no conceivable physical harm to others, was arbitrary, encompassing matters wholly unrelated in nature and seriousness to the reasons for the prisoner being within the power of the State in the first place.

2. The Government

59 The Government submitted that the imposition of a mandatory life sentence for murder satisfied Article 5(1) of the Convention. In its view, this continued to provide a lawful basis for his detention after the expiry of the six-year sentence for fraud offences as his life licence had been revoked. It rejected the applicant's argument that this detention, on the basis of a concern that he might commit serious non-violent offences of dishonesty bore no proper relationship to the object of the original mandatory life sentence. It argued that the original sentence was imposed because of the gravity of the offence of murder. A mandatory life sentence for murder fell within a distinct category, different from the discretionary life sentence, as it was imposed as punishment for the seriousness of the offence. It was not governed by characteristics specific to a particular offender which might change over time, factors such as dangerousness, mental instability or youth. A trial judge was required by Parliament to impose a life sentence for murder whether or not the offender was considered dangerous.

60 The object and purpose of the punishment was to confer power on the Secretary of State to decide when, if at all, it was in the public interest to allow the applicant to return to society on life licence and to empower the Secretary of State to decide, subject to the applicable statutory procedures, whether it was in the public interest to recall the applicant to prison at any time until his death. Whether or not the concern was about risk of further offences of violence or further non-violent offences, a refusal to release on life licence, or a decision to revoke the life licence, was closely related to the original mandatory life sentence by reason of the gravity of the offence and to ensure that the prisoner could only be released when the public interest made it appropriate to do so. The sentence also provided flexibility since it allowed reconsideration of the tariff if such had been set in ignorance of relevant factors, a possibility not available to a judge.

61 The Government submitted that, in deciding whether it was in the public interest to release the applicant, the Secretary of State was therefore entitled to have regard to the risk of serious non-violent offending. It would not be logical or rational if he was unable to refuse to order the release of a prisoner where there was an unacceptable risk of his committing serious non-violent offences such as burglary or trafficking in heroin, which attracted far longer prison sentences than some offences of a violent nature and which caused far more harm to the public interest. The Government referred to the previous case law of the Court which found that continued detention of life prisoners was justified by their original trial and appeal proceedings. The fact that the applicant had been released on life licence and had been living for some time at liberty had no relevance to the lawful basis of his detention after revocation of that licence. Nor had there been any relevant developments in either domestic or Convention

case law which altered the statutory basis of the mandatory life sentence or its proper meaning and effect.

B. The Court's assessment

1. Preliminary considerations

62 The question to be determined is whether, after the expiry on 1 July 1997 of the fixed term sentence imposed on the applicant for fraud, the continued detention of the applicant under the original mandatory life sentence imposed on him for murder in 1967 complied with the requirements of Article 5(1) of the Convention.

63 Where the 'lawfulness' of detention is in issue, the Convention refers essentially to national law and lays down the obligation to conform to the substantive and procedural rules of national law. This primarily requires any arrest or detention to have a legal basis in domestic law but also relates to the quality of the law, requiring it to be compatible with the rule of law, a concept inherent in all the Articles of the Convention. In addition, any deprivation of liberty should be in keeping with the purpose of Article 5, namely to protect the individual from arbitrariness.

64 It is not contested that the applicant's detention from 1 July 1997 was in accordance with a procedure prescribed by English law and otherwise lawful under English law. This was established in the judicial review proceedings, where the Court of Appeal and House of Lords found that the Secretary of State's decision to detain the applicant fell within his discretion as conferred by section 35(1) of the 1991 Act. This is not however conclusive of the matter. The Court's case law indicates that it may be necessary to look beyond the appearances and the language used and concentrate on the realities of the situation.[5] In the case of Weeks v. United Kingdom, which concerned the recall to prison by the Secretary of State of an applicant who had been released from a discretionary life sentence for robbery, the Court interpreted the requirements of Article 5 as applying to the situation as follows: The lawfulness required by the Convention presupposes not only conformity with domestic law but also, as confirmed by Article 18, conformity with the purposes of the deprivation of liberty permitted by the sub-paragraph (a) of Article 5(1) (see as the most recent authority the Bozano judgment of 18 December 1986, Series A No. 111, p. 23 (54)). Furthermore, the word 'after' in sub-paragraph (a) does not simply mean that the detention must follow the 'conviction' in point of time: in addition, the 'detention' must result from, 'follow and depend upon' or occur 'by virtue' of the 'conviction' (ibid., pp. 22–23, (3), and the Van Droogenbroeck judgment…p. 19, (35)). In short, there must be a sufficient causal connection between the conviction and the deprivation of liberty at issue (see the abovementioned Van Droogenbroeck judgment, p. 21 (39)).

65 The Court recalls that in the Weeks case it was found that the discretionary life sentence imposed on the applicant was an indeterminate sentence expressly based on considerations of his dangerousness to society, factors which were susceptible by their very nature to change with the passage of time. On that basis, his recall, in light of concerns about is unstable, disturbed and aggressive behaviour, could not be regarded as arbitrary or unreasonable in terms of the objectives of the sentence imposed on him and there was sufficient connection for the purposes of Article 5(1)(a) between his conviction in 1966 and recall to prison in 1977.

66 Much of the argument from the parties has focused on the nature and purpose of the mandatory life sentence as compared with other forms of life sentence and whether the detention after 1 July 1997 continued to conform with the objectives of that sentence. And since the procedures applying to the varying types of life sentences have generated considerable case law, both on the domestic level and before the Convention organs, there has been extensive reference to the judicial dicta produced as supporting the arguments on both sides.

67 Of particular importance in this regard is the Wynne case decided in 1994, in which this Court found that no violation arose under Article 5(4) in relation to the continued detention after release and recall to prison of a mandatory life prisoner convicted of an intervening offence of manslaughter, the tariff element of which had expired. This provides strong support for the Government's case while the

applicant sought to argue that this decision did not succeed in identifying the reality of the situation for mandatory life prisoners which subsequent developments have clarified still further. The Court in Wynne was well aware that there were similarities between the discretionary life and mandatory life sentences, in particular that both contained a punitive and a preventive element and that mandatory life prisoners did not actually spend the rest of their lives in prison. The key passage states: However the fact remains that the mandatory life sentence belongs to a different category from the discretionary life sentence in the sense that it is imposed automatically as the punishment for the offence of murder irrespective of considerations pertaining to the dangerousness of the offender. (p. 14, (35))

68 While the Court is not formally bound to follow any of its previous judgments, it is in the interests of legal certainty, foreseeability and equality before the law that it should not depart, without cogent reason, from precedents laid down in previous cases. Since the Convention is first and foremost a system for the protection of human rights, the Court must however have regard to the changing conditions in Contracting States and respond, for example, to any emerging consensus as to the standards to be achieved. It is of crucial importance that the Convention is interpreted and applied in a manner which renders its rights practical and effective, not theoretical and illusory. A failure by the Court to maintain a dynamic and evolutive approach would risk rendering it a bar to reform or improvement.

69 Similar considerations apply as regards the changing conditions and any emerging consensus discernible within the domestic legal order of the respondent Contracting State. Although there is no material distinction on the facts between this and the Wynne case, having regard to the significant developments in the domestic sphere, the Court proposes to re-assess 'in the light of present-day conditions' what is now the appropriate interpretation and application of the Convention.

2. Legal developments

70 The mandatory life sentence is imposed pursuant to statute in all cases of murder. This position has not changed, though there has been increasing criticism of the inflexibility of the statutory regime, which does not reflect the differing types of killing covered by the offence from so-called mercy killing to brutal psychopathic serial attacks.

71 The inflexibility of this regime was, from a very early stage, mitigated by the approach of the Secretary of State, who in all types of life sentences—mandatory, discretionary and Her Majesty's pleasure detention adopted a practice of setting a specific term known as the 'tariff' to represent the element of deterrence and retribution. This was generally the minimum period of detention which would be served before an offender could hope to be released. It was never anticipated that prisoners serving mandatory life sentences would in fact stay in prison for life, save in exceptional cases. Similarly, the decision as to the release of all life prisoners also lay generally with the Secretary of State. The tariff-fixing and release procedures applicable to life sentences have however been modified considerably over the past 20 years, to a large extent due to the case law of this Court. It is also significant that the domestic courts were frequently called upon to rule on lawfulness issues arising out of the Secretary of State's role in fixing the tariff and in deciding the appropriate moment for release, the courts requiring the establishment of proper and fair procedures in his exercise of those functions. Between Strasbourg and the domestic courts, a steady erosion on the scope of the Secretary of State's decision-making power in this field may be identified.

72 The first examination of the Court in this area focused on the situation of discretionary life prisoners. In the cases of Weeks and Thynne, Gunnell and Wilson, the Court analysed the purpose and effect of the discretionary life sentence, imposable for very serious offences such as manslaughter and rape. It was held that since the grounds relied upon in sentencing to a discretionary life term concerned risk and dangerousness, factors susceptible to change over time, new issues of lawfulness could arise after the expiry of the tariff which, in the context of Article 5(4), necessitated proper review by a judicial body. As a result, the Criminal Justice Act 1991 provided that the question of release, after expiry of tariff of a discretionary life prisoner, was to be decided not by the Secretary of State but by the Parole Board in a procedure with judicial safeguards. The same Act also gave statutory force to the Secretary of State's policy of accepting the judicial view of the tariff in discretionary life cases. The judges then took on the

role, in open court, of setting the punishment element of the sentence. Though no significant changes were made by statute to the regime of mandatory life sentences, the procedure whereby the tariff was fixed was shortly afterwards modified following the House of Lords decision in the Doody case, where it was found that procedural fairness required that mandatory life prisoners be informed of the judicial view of the tariff in order that they could make written representations to the Secretary of State before he reached his decision. This reflected a growing perception that the tariff-setting function was closely analogous to a sentencing function.

73 It was at this stage that the Court directly addressed the position of mandatory life prisoners in the Wynne case and took the view that the mandatory life sentence was different in character from the discretionary life sentence. In reaching that decision, it concentrated on the automatic imposition of the mandatory life sentence, which was perceived as pursuing a punitive purpose.

74 Not long afterwards, the situation of post-tariff juvenile murderers (Her Majesty's pleasure detainees) was the subject of applications under the Convention. Though this type of sentence, as with the adult mandatory life sentence, was imposed automatically for the offence of murder, the Court was not persuaded that it could be regarded as a true sentence of punishment to detention for life. Such a term applied to children would have conflicted with United Nations instruments and raised serious problems under Article 3 of the Convention. Considering that it must be regarded in practice as an indeterminate sentence which could only be justified by considerations based on the need to protect the public and therefore linked to assessments of the offender's mental development and maturity, it therefore held that a review by a court of the continued existence of grounds of detention was required for the purposes of Article 5(4).

75 The issues arising from the sentencing process for juvenile murderers at the tariff-fixing stage were then examined both in the domestic courts and in Strasbourg. In Ex parte T and V the House of Lords made very strong comment on the judicial nature of the tariff-fixing exercise and quashed a tariff fixed by the Home Secretary which, inter alia, took into account 'public clamour' whipped up by the press against the offenders in the case. This Court found that Article 6(1) applied to the fixing of the tariff, which represented the requirements of retribution and deterrence and was thus a sentencing exercise. The fact that it was decided by the Secretary of State, a member of the executive and therefore not independent, was found to violate this provision.

76 By this stage therefore, there were further statutory changes, which assimilated the position of juvenile murderers to that of discretionary life prisoners in giving the courts the role of fixing the tariff and providing the Parole Board with decision-making powers and appropriate procedures when dealing with questions of release.

77 While mandatory life prisoners alone remained under the old regime, the coming into force on 2 October 2000 of the Human Rights Act 1998 provided the opportunity for the first direct challenges to the mandatory life regime under the provisions of the Convention in the domestic courts. In the case of Lichniak and Pyrah the prisoners' arguments that the mandatory life sentence was arbitrary due to its inflexibility were rejected. It may be observed, as pointed out by the applicant, that the Government in that case contended that the mandatory life sentence was an indeterminate sentence by which an individualised tariff was set and that after the expiry of the tariff the prisoner could expect to be released once it was safe to do so. They expressly departed from the position that the mandatory life sentence represented a punishment whereby a prisoner forfeited his liberty for life. On that basis, the Court of Appeal found that there were no problems of arbitrariness or disproportionality in imposing mandatory life sentences. Then in the case of Anderson and Taylor, which concerned a challenge under Article 6(1) to the role of the Secretary of State in fixing the tariffs for two mandatory life prisoners, the Court of Appeal was unanimous in finding that this was a sentencing exercise which should attract the guarantees of that Article, following on from clear statements made by the House of Lords in the cases of Ex parte T and V and Ex parte Pierson.

78 The above developments demonstrate an evolving analysis, in terms of the right to liberty and its underlying values, of the role of the Secretary of State concerning life sentences. The abolition of the death penalty in 1965 and the conferring on the Secretary of State of the power to release convicted

murderers represented, at that time, a major and progressive reform. However, with the wider recognition of the need to develop and apply, in relation to mandatory life prisoners, judicial procedures reflecting standards of independence, fairness and openness, the continuing role of the Secretary of State in fixing the tariff and in deciding on a prisoner's release following its expiry, has become increasingly difficult to reconcile with the notion of separation of powers between the executive and the judiciary, a notion which has assumed growing importance in the case law of the Court.

79 The Court considers that it may now be regarded as established in domestic law that there is no distinction between mandatory life prisoners, discretionary life prisoners and juvenile murderers as regards the nature of tariff-fixing. It is a sentencing exercise. The mandatory life sentence does not impose imprisonment for life as a punishment. The tariff, which reflects the individual circumstances of the offence and the offender, represents the element of punishment. The Court concludes that the finding in Wynne that the mandatory life sentence constituted punishment for life can no longer be regarded as reflecting the real position in the domestic criminal justice system of the mandatory life prisoner. This conclusion is reinforced by the fact that a whole life tariff may, in exceptional cases, be imposed where justified by the gravity of the particular offence. It is correct that the Court in its more recent judgments in T and V, citing the Wynne judgment as authority, reiterated that an adult mandatory life sentence constituted punishment for life. In doing so it had, however, merely sought to draw attention to the difference between such a life sentence and a sentence to detention during Her Majesty's pleasure, which was the category of sentence under review in the cases concerned. The purpose of the statement had therefore been to distinguish previous case law rather than to confirm an analysis deriving from that case law.

[10:16] Padfield, N, '"Back door sentencing": is recall to prison a penal process?'

(2005) Camb LJ 276

While much effort has gone into training judges and advocates in the intricacies of the new sentencing regime introduced in the Criminal Justice Act 2003, and implemented in large measure in April 2005, it is refreshing to see the House of Lords turn its attention to what might be considered an area of equal importance: executive recall to prison, or 'back door sentencing'. The Parole Board's Annual Reports reveal the huge increase in recall cases in recent years: from 2,457 in 2000–01, to 9,031 in 2003–4, for example. The prison population is thus increasingly shaped by those who enter by the 'back door'.

The facts of the two cases before the House of Lords in *R v Parole Board, ex parte Smith; R v Parole Board, ex parte West* [2005] UKHL 1; [2005] 1 WLR 350; [2005] 1 All ER 755 were not untypical. Justin West was released at the halfway stage of his three-year sentence for affray on 6 August 2001, subject to the standard licence conditions. Ten days after his release, he had allegedly assaulted his former partner in a hostel, but the victim would not confirm the incident. He then failed to keep an appointment with his supervising officer, and on 22 August the Home Secretary revoked his license, under s. 39(2) of the Criminal Justice Act 1991. He was arrested on 24 August and returned to prison. The Home Secretary referred the case to the Parole Board under s. 39(4)(b) and his solicitors made written representations urging an urgent oral hearing to be attended by witnesses whose evidence should be heard on oath. The Parole Board rejected these representations in a letter of 2 October and Mr West remained in prison until 9 May 2002.

The Parole Board's decision was unsuccessfully challenged in the High Court and the Court of Appeal. The majority of the Court of Appeal concluded that Article 6 (the right to a fair trial) had no application because of 'the critical fact that when a parole licence is revoked and its revocation is subsequently confirmed this is solely with a view to the prevention of risk and the protection of the public and not at all by way of punishment' (Simon Brown LJ). Only Hale LJ recognised, in her dissenting judgement, that 'to the person concerned it is experienced as punishment, whatever the authorities may say'. However, the House of Lords (Lords Bingham, Slynn, Hope, Walker and Carswell) decided unanimously that he should have been allowed an oral hearing:

> In his representations against revocation the appellant West offered the Board explanations, which he said he could substantiate, of his failure to keep an appointment with his probation officer and of the incident at his ex-partner's hostel. The Board could not properly reject these explanations on the materials before it without hearing him. He admitted spending one night away from his approved address, staying (he said) with a cousin. While this was a breach of his licence conditions, it is not clear what risk was thereby posed to the public which called for eight months' detention. His challenge could not be fairly resolved without an oral hearing and he was not treated with that degree of fairness which his challenge required (per Lord Bingham).

The other case was that of Trevor Smith, who was released on license from a $6\frac{1}{2}$ year extended sentence for rape on 7 November 2001, which was his 'non-parole date', the date on which he was entitled to be released. Having tested positive for cocaine whilst living in a probation hostel, he was moved at his request to another hostel, but again tested positive to cocaine, and three days later to cocaine and opiates. His probation officer referred the case to the Parole Board under s. 39(1) of the Act of 1991. The Board supported the recommendation that he should be recalled, which he was, on 4 February 2002. Smith made written representations under s. 39(3), but these were rejected in a letter which explained that his drug use presented too great a risk to public safety. His original application for judicial review was turned down. At an oral renewal of the application, he was granted permission to seek judicial review, but only in relation to Article 6 and the common law. The case was listed before a third judge who refused to allow him to rely also on Article 5 (right to liberty). He appealed against that refusal, and the Court of Appeal (led by Lord Woolf CJ) ordered that he be permitted to rely on Article 5, as well as Article 6 and common law. The Court also ordered that the case be heard in the Court of Appeal, where the case was heard by Kennedy, Brooke LJJ, Holman J, who held that Mr Smith had no right to an oral hearing, and that there was no objective need for an oral hearing, as there was no dispute on the primary facts. Smith was eventually released on 3 December 2003, having served 22 months during the period of recall.

The House of Lords also unanimously allowed this appeal:

> The resort to class A drugs by the appellant Smith clearly raised serious questions, and it may well be that his challenge would have been rejected whatever procedure had been followed. But it may also be that the hostels in which he was required to live were a very bad environment for a man seeking to avoid addiction. It may be that the Board would have been assisted by evidence from his psychiatrist. The Board might have concluded that the community would be better protected by encouraging his self-motivated endeavours to conquer addiction, if satisfied these were genuine, than by returning him to prison for 2 years with the prospect that, at the end of that time, he would be released without the benefit of any supervision. Whatever the outcome, he was in my opinion entitled to put these points at an oral hearing. Procedural fairness called for more than consideration of his representations, on paper, as one of some 24 such applications routinely considered by a panel at a morning session (per Lord Bingham).

Much of the analysis in the House concerns the relationship between the appellants' common law and their Convention rights. They agreed that the common law demanded, in these cases, an oral hearing: 'the prisoner should have the benefit of a procedure which fairly reflects... the importance of what is at stake for him, as for society' (per Lord Bingham). Lord Hope explicitly identifies the breach of Article 5(4). Controversially they appear to conclude that recall is not a punishment, and that therefore the criminal due process rights of Article 6 are not engaged (though Lord Bingham thought it unnecessary to resolve this question). Lord Hope adds that Article 6 civil rights are not infringed by proceedings of this kind so long as the individual has access to the domestic courts to assert his right to liberty. Doubtless these conclusions will be challenged, but there are more fundamental points to question: is the Parole Board really 'an independent and impartial tribunal'? Who should bear the burden of proof before the Parole Board? (And is the Parole Board adequately resourced for the inevitable flood of applications?)

The statutory provisions and subordinate rules governing the release, licensing and recall of prisoners have, as Lord Bingham points out, been the subject of 'ceaseless change' over the past 10–15 years. Under ss. 254 and 255 of the Criminal Justice Act 2003, in force for all prisoners subject to license conditions on or after 4 April 2005 irrespective of the date of their offence, recall becomes more obviously an executive decision. This removes the previous anomaly whereby the Parole Board both advised on recalls and acted as an appeal body against those same recalls. It is time that lawyers, both academic and practising, paid much closer attention to the fairness (or otherwise) of these 'back door sentencing' decisions.

[10:17] Mental Health Act 1983 (as amended)
Sections 37; 41; 42; 47–49; 70–74; 118

37 Powers of courts to order hospital admission or guardianship

(1) Where a person is convicted before the Crown Court of an offence punishable with imprisonment other than an offence the sentence for which is fixed by law or falls to be imposed under section 109(2) of the Powers of Criminal Courts (Sentencing) Act 2000, or is convicted by a magistrates' court of an offence punishable on summary conviction with imprisonment, and the conditions mentioned in subsection (2) below are satisfied, the court may by order authorise his admission to and detention in such hospital as may be specified in the order or, as the case may be, place him under the guardianship of a local social services authority or of such other person approved by a local social services authority as may be so specified.

(1A) In the case of an offence the sentence for which would otherwise fall to be imposed—

    (a) under section 51A(2) of the Firearms Act 1968,

    (b) under section 110(2) or 111(2) of the Powers of Criminal Courts (Sentencing) Act 2000,

    (c) under any of sections 225 to 228 of the Criminal Justice Act 2003,[or]1

    (d) under section 29(4) or (6) of the Violent Crime Reduction Act 2006 (minimum sentences in certain cases of using someone to mind a weapon).

(1B) For the purposes of subsections (1) and (1A) above, a sentence fails to be imposed under section 109(2), 110(2) or 111(2) of the Powers of Criminal Courts (Sentencing) Act 2000 if it is required by that provision and the court is not of the opinion there mentioned.

(2) The conditions referred to in subsection (1) above are that—

    (a) the court is satisfied, on the written or oral evidence of two registered medical practitioners, that the offender is suffering from mental illness, psychopathic disorder, severe mental impairment or mental impairment and that either—

       (i) the mental disorder from which the offender is suffering is of a nature or degree which makes it appropriate for him to be detained in a hospital for medical treatment and, in the case of psychopathic disorder or mental impairment, that such treatment is likely to alleviate or prevent a deterioration of his condition; or

       (ii) in the case of an offender who has attained the age of 16 years, the mental disorder is of a nature or degree which warrants his reception into guardianship under this Act; and

    (b) the court is of the opinion, having regard to all the circumstances including the nature of the offence and the character and antecedents of the offender, and to the other available methods of dealing with him, that the most suitable method of disposing of the case is by means of an order under this section.

(3) Where a person is charged before a magistrates' court with any act or omission as an offence and the court would have power, on convicting him of that offence, to make an order under subsection (1) above in his case as being a person suffering from mental illness or severe mental impairment, then, if the court is satisfied that the accused did the act or made the omission charged, the court may, if it thinks fit, make such an order without convicting him.

(4) An order for the admission of an offender to a hospital (in this Act referred to as "a hospital order") shall not be made under this section unless the court is satisfied on the written or oral evidence of the registered medical practitioner who would be in charge of his treatment or of some other person representing the managers of the hospital that arrangements have been made for his admission to that hospital..., and for his admission to it within the period of 28 days beginning with the date of the making of such an order; and the court may, pending his admission within that period, give such directions as it thinks fit for his conveyance to and detention in a place of safety.

(5) If within the said period of 28 days it appears to the Secretary of State that by reason of an emergency or other special circumstances it is not practicable for the patient to be received into the hospital specified in the order, he may give directions for the admission of the patient to such other hospital as appears to be appropriate instead of the hospital so specified; and where such directions are given—

(a) the Secretary of State shall cause the person having the custody of the patient to be informed, and

(b) the hospital order shall have effect as if the hospital specified in the directions were substituted for the hospital specified in the order.

(6) An order placing an offender under the guardianship of a local social services authority or of any other person (in this Act referred to as "a guardianship order") shall not be made under this section unless the court is satisfied that that authority or person is willing to receive the offender into guardianship.

(7) A hospital order or guardianship order shall specify the form or forms of mental disorder referred to in subsection (2)(a) above from which, upon the evidence taken into account under that subsection, the offender is found by the court to be suffering; and no such order shall be made unless the offender is described by each of the practitioners whose evidence is taken into account under that subsection as suffering from the same one of those forms of mental disorder, whether or not he is also described by either of them as suffering from another of them.

(8) Where an order is made under this section, the court shall not—

(a) pass sentence of imprisonment or impose a fine or make a community order (within the meaning of Part 12 of the Criminal Justice Act 2003) in respect of the offence,

(b) if the order under this section is a hospital order, make a referral order (within the meaning of the Powers of Criminal Courts (Sentencing) Act 2000) in respect of the offence, or

(c) make in respect of the offender a supervision order (within the meaning of that Act) or an order under section 150 of that Act (binding over of parent or guardian),

but the court may make any other order which it has power to make apart from this section; and for the purposes of this subsection "sentence of imprisonment" includes any sentence or order for detention.

41 Power of higher courts to restrict discharge from hospital

(1) Where a hospital order is made in respect of an offender by the Crown Court, and it appears to the court, having regard to the nature of the offence, the antecedents of the offender and the risk of his committing further offences if set at large, that it is necessary for the protection of the public from serious harm so to do, the court may, subject to the provisions of this section, further

order that the offender shall be subject to the special restrictions set out in this section; and an order under this section shall be known as "a restriction order".

(2) A restriction order shall not be made in the case of any person unless at least one of the registered medical practitioners whose evidence is taken into account by the court under section 37(2)(a) above has given evidence orally before the court.

(3) The special restrictions applicable to a patient in respect of whom a restriction order is in force are as follows—

    (a) none of the provisions of Part II of this Act relating to the duration, renewal and expiration of authority for the detention of patients shall apply, and the patient shall continue to be liable to be detained by virtue of the relevant hospital order until he is duly discharged under the said Part II or absolutely discharged under section 42, 73, 74 or 75 below;

    (aa) none of the provisions of Part II of this Act relating to after-care under supervision shall apply;

    (b) no application shall be made to a Mental Health Review Tribunal in respect of a patient under section 66 or 69(1) below;

    (c) the following powers shall be exercisable only with the consent of the Secretary of State, namely—

       (i) power to grant leave of absence to the patient under section 17 above;

       (ii) power to transfer the patient in pursuance of regulations under section 19 above or in pursuance of subsection (3) of that section; and

       (iii) power to order the discharge of the patient under section 23 above;

       and if leave of absence is granted under the said section 17 power to recall the patient under that section shall vest in the Secretary of State as well as the responsible medical officer; and

    (d) the power of the Secretary of State to recall the patient under the said section 17 and power to take the patient into custody and return him under section 18 above may be exercised at any time;

and in relation to any such patient section 40(4) above shall have effect as if it referred to Part II of Schedule 1 to this Act instead of Part I of that Schedule.

(4) A hospital order shall not cease to have effect under section 40(5) above if a restriction order in respect of the patient is in force at the material time.

(5) Where a restriction order in respect of a patient ceases to have effect while the relevant hospital order continues in force, the provisions of section 40 above and Part I of Schedule 1 to this Act shall apply to the patient as if he had been admitted to the hospital in pursuance of a hospital order (without a restriction order) made on the date on which the restriction order ceased to have effect.

(6) While a person is subject to a restriction order the responsible medical officer shall at such intervals (not exceeding one year) as the Secretary of State may direct examine and report to the Secretary of State on that person; and every report shall contain such particulars as the Secretary of State may require.

42 Powers of Secretary of State in respect of patients subject to restriction orders

(1) If the Secretary of State is satisfied that in the case of any patient a restriction order is no longer required for the protection of the public from serious harm, he may direct that the patient cease to be subject to the special restrictions set out in section 41(3) above; and where the Secretary of State so directs, the restriction order shall cease to have effect, and section 41(5) above shall apply accordingly.

(2) At any time while a restriction order is in force in respect of a patient, the Secretary of State may, if he thinks fit, by warrant discharge the patient from hospital, either absolutely or subject to conditions; and where a person is absolutely discharged under this subsection, he shall thereupon cease to be liable to be detained by virtue of the relevant hospital order, and the restriction order shall cease to have effect accordingly.

(3) The Secretary of State may at any time during the continuance in force of a restriction order in respect of a patient who has been conditionally discharged under subsection (2) above by warrant recall the patient to such hospital as may be specified in the warrant.

(4) Where a patient is recalled as mentioned in subsection (3) above—

(a) if the hospital specified in the warrant is not the hospital from which the patient was conditionally discharged, the hospital order and the restriction order shall have effect as if the hospital specified in the warrant were substituted for the hospital specified in the hospital order;

(b) in any case, the patient shall be treated for the purposes of section 18 above as if he had absented himself without leave from the hospital specified in the warrant.

(5) If a restriction order in respect of a patient ceases to have effect after the patient has been conditionally discharged under this section, the patient shall, unless previously recalled under subsection (3) above, be deemed to be absolutely discharged on the date when the order ceases to have effect, and shall cease to be liable to be detained by virtue of the relevant hospital order accordingly.

(6) The Secretary of State may, if satisfied that the attendance at any place in Great Britain of a patient who is subject to a restriction order is desirable in the interests of justice or for the purposes of any public inquiry, direct him to be taken to that place; and where a patient is directed under this subsection to be taken to any place he shall, unless the Secretary of State otherwise directs, be kept in custody while being so taken, while at that place and while being taken back to the hospital in which he is liable to be detained.

47 Removal to hospital of persons serving sentences of imprisonment, etc

(1) If in the case of a person serving a sentence of imprisonment the Secretary of State is satisfied, by reports from at least two registered medical practitioners—

(a) that the said person is suffering from mental illness, psychopathic disorder, severe mental impairment or mental impairment; and

(b) that the mental disorder from which that person is suffering is of a nature or degree which makes it appropriate for him to be detained in a hospital for medical treatment and, in the case of psychopathic disorder or mental impairment, that such treatment is likely to alleviate or prevent a deterioration of his condition;

the Secretary of State may, if he is of the opinion having regard to the public interest and all the circumstances that it is expedient so to do, by warrant direct that that person be removed to and detained in such hospital...as may be specified in the direction; and a direction under this section shall be known as "a transfer direction".

(2) A transfer direction shall cease to have effect at the expiration of the period of 14 days beginning with the date on which it is given unless within that period the person with respect to whom it was given has been received into the hospital specified in the direction.

(3) A transfer direction with respect to any person shall have the same effect as a hospital order made in his case.

(4) A transfer direction shall specify the form or forms of mental disorder referred to in paragraph (a) of subsection (1) above from which, upon the reports taken into account under that subsection,

the patient is found by the Secretary of State to be suffering; and no such direction shall be given unless the patient is described in each of those reports as suffering from the same form of disorder, whether or not he is also described in either of them as suffering from another form.

(5) References in this Part of this Act to a person serving a sentence of imprisonment include references—

    (a) to a person detained in pursuance of any sentence or order for detention made by a court in criminal proceedings (other than an order made in consequence of a finding of insanity or unfitness to attend trial);

    (b) to a person committed to custody under section 115(3) of the Magistrates' Courts Act 1980 (which relates to persons who fail to comply with an order to enter into recognisances to keep the peace or be of good behaviour); and

    (c) to a person committed by a court to a prison or other institution to which the Prison Act 1952 applies in default of payment of any sum adjudged to be paid on his conviction.

48 Removal to hospital of other prisoners

(1) If in the case of a person to whom this section applies the Secretary of State is satisfied by the same reports as are required for the purposes of section 47 above that that person is suffering from mental illness or severe mental impairment of a nature or degree which makes it appropriate for him to be detained in a hospital for medical treatment and that he is in urgent need of such treatment, the Secretary of State shall have the same power of giving a transfer direction in respect of him under that section as if he were serving a sentence of imprisonment.

(2) This section applies to the following persons, that is to say—

    (a) persons detained in a prison or remand centre, not being persons serving a sentence of imprisonment or persons falling within the following paragraphs of this subsection;

    (b) persons remanded in custody by a magistrates' court;

    (c) civil prisoners, that is to say, persons committed by a court to prison for a limited term (including persons committed to prison in pursuance of a writ of attachment), who are not persons falling to be dealt with under section 47 above;

    (d) persons detained under the Immigration Act 1971 or under section 62 of the Nationality, Immigration and Asylum Act 2002 (detention by Secretary of State).

(3) Subsections (2) to (4) of section 47 above shall apply for the purposes of this section and of any transfer direction given by virtue of this section as they apply for the purposes of that section and of any transfer direction under that section.

49 Restriction on discharge of prisoners removed to hospital

(1) Where a transfer direction is given in respect of any person, the Secretary of State, if he thinks fit, may by warrant further direct that that person shall be subject to the special restrictions set out in section 41 above; and where the Secretary of State gives a transfer direction in respect of any such person as is described in paragraph (a) or (b) of section 48(2) above, he shall also give a direction under this section applying those restrictions to him.

(2) A direction under this section shall have the same effect as a restriction order made under section 41 above and shall be known as "a restriction direction".

(3) While a person is subject to a restriction direction the responsible medical officer shall at such intervals (not exceeding one year) as the Secretary of State may direct examine and report to the Secretary of State on that person; and every report shall contain such particulars as the Secretary of State may require.

70 Applications to tribunals concerning restricted patients

A patient who is a restricted patient within the meaning of section 79 below and is detained in a hospital may apply to a Mental Health Review Tribunal—

(a) in the period between the expiration of six months and the expiration of 12 months beginning with the date of the relevant hospital order, hospital direction or transfer direction; and

(b) in any subsequent period of 12 months.

71 References by Secretary of State concerning restricted patients

(1) The Secretary of State may at any time refer the case of a restricted patient to a Mental Health Review Tribunal.

(2) The Secretary of State shall refer to a Mental Health Review Tribunal the case of any restricted patient detained in a hospital whose case has not been considered by such a tribunal, whether on his own application or otherwise, within the last three years.

(3) The Secretary of State may by order vary the length of the period mentioned in subsection (2) above.

(4) Any reference under subsection (1) above in respect of a patient who has been conditionally discharged and not recalled to hospital shall be made to the tribunal for the area in which the patient resides.

Discharge of patients

72 Powers of tribunals

(1) Where application is made to a Mental Health Review Tribunal by or in respect of a patient who is liable to be detained under this Act, the tribunal may in any case direct that the patient be discharged, and—

(a) the tribunal shall direct the discharge of a patient liable to be detained under section 2 above if they are not satisfied—

(i) that he is then suffering from mental disorder or from mental disorder of a nature or degree which warrants his detention in a hospital for assessment (or for assessment followed by medical treatment) for at least a limited period; or

(ii) that his detention as aforesaid is justified in the interests of his own health or safety or with a view to the protection of other persons;

(b) the tribunal shall direct the discharge of a patient liable to be detained otherwise than under section 2 above if they are not satisfied—

(i) that he is then suffering from mental illness, psychopathic disorder, severe mental impairment or mental impairment or from any of those forms of disorder of a nature or degree which makes it appropriate for him to be liable to be detained in a hospital for medical treatment; or

(ii) that it is necessary for the health of safety of the patient or for the protection of other persons that he should receive such treatment; or

(iii) in the case of an application by virtue of paragraph (g) of section 66(1) above, that the patient, if released, would be likely to act in a manner dangerous to other persons or to himself.

(2) In determining whether to direct the discharge of a patient detained otherwise than under section 2 above in a case not falling within paragraph (b) of subsection (1) above, the tribunal shall have regard—

(a) to the likelihood of medical treatment alleviating or preventing a deterioration of the patient's condition; and

(b) in the case of a patient suffering from mental illness or severe mental impairment, to the likelihood of the patient, if discharged, being able to care for himself, to obtain the care he needs or to guard himself against serious exploitation.

(3) A tribunal may under subsection (1) above direct the discharge of a patient on a future date specified in the direction; and where a tribunal do not direct the discharge of a patient under that subsection the tribunal may—

(a) with a view to facilitating his discharge on a future date, recommend that he be granted leave of absence or transferred to another hospital or into guardianship; and

(b) further consider his case in the event of any such recommendation not being complied with.

(3A) Where, in the case of an application to a tribunal by or in respect of a patient who is liable to be detained in pursuance of an application for admission for treatment or by virtue of an order or direction for his admission or removal to hospital under Part III of this Act, the tribunal do not direct the discharge of the patient under subsection (1) above, the tribunal may—

(a) recommend that the responsible medical officer consider whether to make a supervision application in respect of the patient; and

(b) further consider his case in the event of no such application being made.

(4) Where application is made to a Mental Health Review Tribunal by or in respect of a patient who is subject to guardianship under this Act, the tribunal may in any case direct that the patient be discharged, and shall so direct if they are satisfied—

(a) that he is not then suffering from mental illness, psychopathic disorder, severe mental impairment or mental impairment; or

(b) that it is not necessary in the interests of the welfare of the patient, or for the protection of other persons, that the patient should remain under such guardianship.

(4A) Where application is made to a Mental Health Review Tribunal by or in respect of a patient who is subject to after-care under supervision (or, if he has not yet left hospital, is to be so subject after he leaves hospital), the tribunal may in any case direct that the patient shall cease to be so subject (or not become so subject), and shall so direct if they are satisfied—

(a) in a case where the patient has not yet left hospital, that the conditions set out in section 25A(4) above are not complied with; or

(b) in any other case, that the conditions set out in section 25G(4) above are not complied with.

(5) Where application is made to a Mental Health Review Tribunal under any provision of this Act by or in respect of a patient and the tribunal do not direct that the patient be discharged or, if he is (or is to be) subject to after-care under supervision, that he cease to be so subject (or not become so subject), the tribunal may, if satisfied that the patient is suffering from a form of mental disorder other than the form specified in the application, order or direction relating to him, direct that that application, order or direction be amended by substituting for the form of mental disorder specified in it such other form of mental disorder as appears to the tribunal to be appropriate.

(6) Subsections (1) to (5) above apply in relation to references to a Mental Health Review Tribunal as they apply in relation to applications made to such a tribunal by or in respect of a patient.

(7) Subsection (1) above shall not apply in the case of a restricted patient except as provided in sections 73 and 74 below.

73 Power to discharge restricted patients

(1) Where an application to a Mental Health Review Tribunal is made by a restricted patient who is subject to a restriction order, or where the case of such a patient is referred to such a tribunal, the tribunal shall direct the absolute discharge of the patient if—

    (a) the tribunal are not satisfied as to the matters mentioned in paragraph (b)(i) or (ii) of section 72(1) above; and

    (b) the tribunal are satisfied that it is not appropriate for the patient to remain liable to be recalled to hospital for further treatment.

(2) Where in the case of any such patient as is mentioned in subsection (1) above—

    (a) paragraph (a) of that subsection applies; but

    (b) paragraph (b) of that subsection does not apply,

    the tribunal shall direct the conditional discharge of the patient.

(3) Where a patient is absolutely discharged under this section he shall thereupon cease to be liable to be detained by virtue of the relevant hospital order, and the restriction order shall cease to have effect accordingly.

(4) Where a patient is conditionally discharged under this section—

    (a) he may be recalled by the Secretary of State under subsection (3) of section 42 above as if he had been conditionally discharged under subsection (2) of that section; and

    (b) the patient shall comply with such conditions (if any) as may be imposed at the time of discharge by the tribunal or at any subsequent time by the Secretary of State.

(5) The Secretary of State may from time to time vary any condition imposed (whether by the tribunal or by him) under subsection (4) above.

(6) Where a restriction order in respect of a patient ceases to have effect after he has been conditionally discharged under this section the patient shall, unless previously recalled, be deemed to be absolutely discharged on the date when the order ceases to have effect and shall cease to be liable to be detained by virtue of the relevant hospital order.

(7) A tribunal may defer a direction for the conditional discharge of a patient until such arrangements as appear to the tribunal to be necessary for that purpose have been made to their satisfaction; and where by virtue of any such deferment no direction has been given on an application or reference before the time when the patient's case comes before the tribunal on a subsequent application or reference, the previous application or reference shall be treated as one on which no direction under this section can be given.

(8) This section is without prejudice to section 42 above.

74 Restricted patients subject to restriction directions

(1) Where an application to a Mental Health Review Tribunal is made by a restricted patient who is subject to a limitation direction or restriction direction, or where the case of such a patient is referred to such a tribunal the tribunal—

    (a) shall notify the Secretary of State whether, in their opinion, the patient would, if subject to a restriction order, be entitled to be absolutely or conditionally discharged under section 73 above; and

    (b) if they notify him that the patient would be entitled to be conditionally discharged, may recommend that in the event of his not being discharged under this section he should continue to be detained in hospital.

(2) If in the case of a patient not falling within subsection (4) below—

    (a) the tribunal notify the Secretary of State that the patient would be entitled to be absolutely or conditionally discharged; and

(b) within the period of 90 days beginning with the date of that notification the Secretary of State gives notice to the tribunal that the patient may be so discharged,

the tribunal shall direct the absolute or, as the case may be, the conditional discharge of the patient.

(3) Where a patient continues to be liable to be detained in a hospital at the end of the period referred to in subsection (2)(b) above because the Secretary of State has not given the notice there mentioned, the managers of the hospital shall, unless the tribunal have made a recommendation under subsection (1)(b) above, transfer the patient to a prison or other institution in which he might have been detained if he had not been removed to hospital, there to be dealt with as if he had not been so removed.

(4) If, in the case of a patient who is subject to a transfer direction under section 48 above, the tribunal notify the Secretary of State that the patient would be entitled to be absolutely or conditionally discharged, the Secretary of State shall, unless the tribunal have made a recommendation under subsection (1)(b) above, by warrant direct that the patient be remitted to a prison or other institution in which he might have been detained if he had not been removed to hospital, there to be dealt with as if he had not been so removed.

(5) Where a patient is transferred or remitted under subsection (3) or (4) above the relevant hospital direction and the limitation direction or, as the case may be, the relevant transfer direction and the restriction direction shall cease to have effect on his arrival in the prison or other institution.

(5A) Where the tribunal have made a recommendation under subsection (1)(b) above in the case of a patient who is subject to a restriction direction or a limitation direction—

(a) the fact that the restriction direction or limitation direction remains in force does not prevent the making of any application or reference to the Parole Board by or in respect of him or the exercise by him of any power to require the Secretary of State to refer his case to the Parole Board, and

(b) if the Parole Board make a direction or recommendation by virtue of which the patient would become entitled to be released (whether unconditionally or on licence) from any prison or other institution in which he might have been detained if he had not been removed to hospital, the restriction direction or limitation direction shall cease to have effect at the time when he would become entitled to be so released.

(6) Subsections (3) to (8) of section 73 above shall have effect in relation to this section as they have effect in relation to that section, taking references to the relevant hospital order and the restriction order as references to the hospital direction and the limitation direction or, as the case may be, to the transfer direction and the restriction direction.

(7) This section is without prejudice to sections 50 to 53 above in their application to patients who are not discharged under this section.

Functions of the Secretary of State

118 Code of practice

(1) The Secretary of State shall prepare, and from time to time revise, a code of practice—

(a) for the guidance of registered medical practitioners, managers and staff of hospitals, independent hospitals and care homes and approved social workers in relation to the admission of patients to hospitals and registered establishments under this Act and to guardianship and after-care under supervision under this Act; and

(b) for the guidance of registered medical practitioners and members of other professions in relation to the medical treatment of patients suffering from mental disorder.

(2) The code shall, in particular, specify forms of medical treatment in addition to any specified by regulations made for the purposes of section 57 above which in the opinion of the Secretary of State give rise to special concern and which should accordingly not be given by a registered

medical practitioner unless the patient has consented to the treatment (or to a plan of treatment including that treatment) and a certificate in writing as to the matters mentioned in subsection (2)(a) and (b) of that section has been given by another registered medical practitioner, being a practitioner appointed for the purposes of this section by the Secretary of State.

(3) Before preparing the code or making any alteration in it the Secretary of State shall consult such bodies as appear to him to be concerned.

(4) The Secretary of State shall lay copies of the code and of any alteration in the code before Parliament; and if either House of Parliament passes a resolution requiring the code or any alteration in it to be withdrawn the Secretary of State shall withdraw the code or alteration and, where he withdraws the code, shall prepare a code in substitution for the one which is withdrawn.

(5) No resolution shall be passed by either House of Parliament under subsection (4) above in respect of a code or alteration after the expiration of the period of 40 days beginning with the day on which a copy of the code or alteration was laid before that House; but for the purposes of this subsection no account shall be taken of any time during which Parliament is dissolved or prorogued or during which both Houses are adjourned for more than four days.

(6) The Secretary of State shall publish the code as for the time being in force.

[10:18] Holloway, K and Grounds, A, 'Discretion and the Release of Mentally Disordered Offenders'

In Gelsthorpe, L and Padfield, N (eds), *Exercising Discretion: Decision-making in the criminal justice system and beyond* (2003) Willan (at page 158)

Conclusions and proposals for reform

The results of this research raise questions about the quality of Mental Health Review Tribunal decision-making in restricted cases and suggest that Tribunals are failing in their fundamental duty to safeguard some patients from unjustified detention in hospital. This failure, however, is not solely a response to the current climate of heightened concern for public safety. The majority of problems were observed in the decision-making *process*, but problems were also noted with the Tribunals' powers, the rules governing the Tribunal process, and the evidence upon which their decisions were to be based.

Although many doubtful practices were evident, the broad approach to decision-making was generally highly conscientious. Tribunal panels could spend hours ensuring that reasons were accurately and appropriately phrased. Medical members were heard persuading patients to try new courses of treatment in an effort to help them make progress. Annoyance and frustration were observed because of Tribunals' inability to transfer patients out of maximum security and efforts were regularly made to help improve the patient's situation. It was notable that the Tribunal members experienced real pleasure when granting discharges. Successful patients were usually invited back to the hearing room to be told the good news in person and to be congratulated on their success. In cases where no discharge was authorized the Tribunals endeavoured to emphasise progress that had been made rather than highlighting problems and failures. The members were anxious not to damage a patient's future chances of discharge or transfer.

In September 1998 the government appointed an Expert Committee to conduct a review of the Mental Health Act 1983. The Committee, chaired by Professor Genevra Richardson, was commissioned to inquire into 'how much mental health legislation should be shaped to reflect contemporary patterns of care within a framework which balances the need to protect the rights of individual patients and the need to ensure public safety' (Department of Health 1999a). In response to the Expert Committee's report a Green Paper was issued outlining the government's initial proposals for reform of the Mental Health Act (Department of Health 1999b). Following a consultation period the government published a White Paper in December 2000 (Department of Health 2000). These proposals have important and far-reaching implications, particularly for the Mental Health Review Tribunal system.

One of the main recommendations is to establish a new Tribunal system. This would extend the Tribunal's function to include the task of confirming an initial compulsory treatment order[1] and for renewing that order at regular intervals.[2] Patients would also be entitled to apply to the new Tribunals for a review of their case once during the currency of each order. The new system would, therefore, require Tribunals to review the need for a compulsory order that in some cases they themselves had confirmed.

As noted above, the White Paper does not remedy the lack of Tribunal powers to effect hospital transfers in restricted cases. It also appears possible that the influence of Tribunals will be further restricted by limitations in their ability to order deferred conditional discharges. Whilst a Tribunal would be able to order discharge from hospital that is conditional on co-operation with a community care plan, such an order could only be made if the necessary forms of care are available.

In addition to the change in the Tribunals' fundamental role, proposals are also made for an alteration in the composition of the Tribunal panel. The medical member's role as both an expert adviser and a decision-maker is viewed as incompatible and contrary to natural justice. Recommendations have therefore been made to separate these roles, so that the patient is assessed by a medical member of an independently appointed expert panel. The White Paper does not make clear, however, whether the patient would have access to this assessment. The Tribunal would have a clinical member (not necessarily medical). The loss of medical members from the Tribunal panels may have serious consequences for the quality of Tribunal decision-making. The observational research demonstrated that the medical members were crucial in the deliberations of Tribunals: they guided the members through the medical evidence, they explained key concepts and terms, and helped in the formulation of reasons that accurately described patients' conditions. It is likely, therefore, that the absence of a medical member would result in even greater reliance on the views of the patient's consultant or clinical supervisor, thereby compromising the 'independence' of the Tribunal system still further.

Notes

1 Offender patients would be subject to compulsory care and treatment on the decision of the court rather than the new Tribunal.

2 The new Tribunals would be required to renew orders after six months, after a second six months and thereafter annually.

INDEX